ENCYCLOPEDIA OF THE

ENLIGHTENMENT

Editorial Board

ENCYCLOPEDIA
OF THE
Enlightenment

ALAN CHARLES KORS

Editor in Chief

VOLUME 4

Sade–Zoology

OXFORD
UNIVERSITY PRESS
2003

OXFORD

UNIVERSITY PRESS

Oxford   New York

Auckland   Bangkok   Buenos Aires   Cape Town   Chennai
Dar es Salaam   Delhi   Hong Kong   Istanbul   Karachi   Kolkata
Kuala Lumpur   Madrid   Melbourne   Mexico City   Mumbai   Nairobi
São Paulo   Shanghai   Singapore   Taipei   Tokyo   Toronto

Copyright © 2003 by Oxford University Press, Inc.

Published by Oxford University Press, Inc.
198 Madison Avenue, New York, New York 10016
www.oup.com

Oxford is a registered trademark of Oxford University Press

Library of Congress Cataloging-in-Publication Data

Encyclopedia of the Enlightenment / Alan Charles Kors, editor in chief.
v. cm.
Includes bibliographical references and index.
Contents: v. 1. Abbadie–Enlightenment Studies—v. 2. Enthusiasm–Lyceums and Museums
—v. 3. Mably–Ruysch—v. 4. Sade–Zoology. Index.
ISBN 0-19-510430-7 (set: alk. paper)
ISBN 0-19-510431-5 (v. 1: alk. paper)
ISBN 0-19-510432-3 (v. 2: alk. paper)
ISBN 0-19-510433-1 (v. 3: alk. paper)
ISBN 0-19-510434-X (v. 4: alk. paper)
1. Enlightenment—Encyclopedias. 2. Enlightenment—United
States—Encyclopedias. 3. Philosophy—Encyclopedias. 4.
Europe—Intellectual life—18th century. 5. United States—Intellectual
life—18th century. I. Kors, Alan Charles.
B802. E53 2003
940.2′5—dc21
2002003766

1 3 5 7 9 8 6 4 2
Printed in the United States of America
on acid-free paper

Common Abbreviations Used in This Work

AD	*anno Domini*, in the year of the Lord
A.M.	*artium magister*, Master of Arts
b.	born
BC	before Christ
BCE	before the common era (= BC)
c.	*circa*, about, approximately
CE	common era (= AD)
cf.	*confer*, compare
d.	died
diss.	dissertation
ed.	editor (pl., eds), edition
f.	and following (pl., ff.)
fl.	*floruit*, flourished
l.	line (pl., ll.)
n.	note
n.d.	no date
no.	number
n.p.	no place
n.s.	new series
p.	page (pl., pp.)
pt.	part
r.	reigned
rev.	revised
ser.	series
supp.	supplement
vol.	volume (pl., vols.)

ENCYCLOPEDIA OF THE
ENLIGHTENMENT

S

SADE, DONATIEN-ALPHONSE-FRANÇOIS DE
(better known as marquis de Sade; 1740–1814), French aristocrat and man of letters.

Descended from ancient Provençal nobility on his father's side and allied to the Condé branch of the royal family through his mother, the young marquis de Sade grew up and was educated in a world that reinforced his sense of rank and privilege. Although little is known with precision of his early life, he appears to have been closer to his father, a minor diplomat whose sexual intrigues enjoyed greater success than his political maneuvers, than to his mother, who, estranged from her husband, ultimately took up residence in a convent. His father's younger brother, Jacques-François-Paul-Aldonse, abbé de Sade, played a significant role in his upbringing; the young marquis spent several years in his care at his residence in the south of France. The abbé, a friend and correspondent of Voltaire and Emilie du Châtelet, was a man of the world and a scholar, author of the three-volume *Mémoires pour la vie de François Pétrarque* (1764–1767), a study of the poet's life and works. The *Mémoires* offered evidence that Petrarch's beloved Laura was the wife of Hugues de Sade and thus a direct ancestress of the Sade family's principal male line. The image of Laura, as well as the attraction of the languages and literary traditions of Provence and Italy, would echo in the marquis's later writings.

Life. Sade was educated at the Jesuit Collège de Louis-le-Grand and the elite military academy of the Chevau-Légers; he served briefly as a cavalry officer during the Seven Years' War (1756–1763). By his early twenties, he had already established a reputation for sexual misconduct. His marriage in 1763 to Renée-Pélagie de Montreuil, daughter of a highly placed magistrate, would not prevent him from engaging in a series of liaisons with actresses—expensive and embarrassing to his wife's family, but not unusual for a man of his class—and an increasingly disturbing pattern of public scandals involving violent sexual assaults on indigent women, minors, and prostitutes. Sade was imprisoned several times on police charges as well as on *lettres de cachet* obtained by his mother-in-law, the influential Marie-Madeleine Masson de Plissay, présidente de Montreuil, who was evidently losing hope that her daughter's husband

would ever be anything but a liability to the family name. After an extended period of exiles, imprisonments, and escapes (twice to Italy), Sade was arrested under a new *lettre de cachet* and committed to the royal prison of Vincennes in 1778. Transferred to the Bastille in 1784 and to Charenton in 1789, he was freed in 1790, when the revolutionary government abolished the *lettres de cachet*.

During the Revolution, Sade participated in the activities of the radical municipal government in the Section des Piques, narrowly avoided execution during the Terror (1794), and tried to make a living as a playwright and novelist. His authorship of the pornographic novel *La nouvelle Justine* led in 1801 to his reimprisonment and ultimate confinement—in moderately comfortable circumstances—at the Charenton asylum, where he remained until his death.

The events of Sade's life continue to be subject to debate and reinterpretation by biographers, as witnessed by the large number of modern biographies and the increased availability of relevant archival material and correspondence. Biographers disagree on issues such as the true reasons for Sade's long confinement in the years preceding the Revolution, or the meaning of his participation in revolutionary politics, and they disagree fundamentally in their assessments of Sade the man, which range from praise for his "tragic knowledge" (Lely) to denunciation of his sexual abuse of women and children (Bongie). There exists something of a rift between the archivally oriented biographers, constantly searching for the new letter or police file that might bring us closer to the historical marquis, and the extended body of literary scholarship dedicated to his work, which to certain biographers appears to suffer "from the crippling notion that there is no person behind the text" (Bongie, 299).

A comprehensive survey of commentary on Sade's work, from Guillaume Apollinaire through Georges Bataille, Simone de Beauvoir, and Roland Barthes to the present, would certainly make the point that the marquis became a major author for twentieth-century critics, but to what extent should we consider him a man of the Enlightenment? To answer that, we must look to his writings.

Letters and Literary Works. Sade was clearly contemplating a literary vocation by the late 1760s. In addition to composing short plays and organizing amateur theatricals at his family chateau, La Coste near Avignon, he tried his hand at travel writing: a short *Voyage de Hollande* (1769), and later a more ambitious *Voyage d'Italie* (1776), neither published in his lifetime. He may have been involved in clandestine pornographic publication in Holland at this time, but it was only after the onset of his extended incarceration in 1778 that he began to develop into the writer we know.

Biographers and literary critics concur that Sade's prison letters contain some of his finest prose. Pleading to know the date of his release, expressing outrage at his detention, hurling abuse at his mother-in-law, launching vicious and unsubstantiated accusations regarding his wife's infidelity, or requesting books, food, or reactions to his manuscripts, Sade's letters vary in tone from learned disquisition to nostalgic evocation, hyperbolic outrage, irony, and lyricism. Significant in the early years in Vincennes is a series of letters written while Sade suffered from the delusion that his correspondents were secretly coding their letters with hidden numerical messages, such as the date of his release. This obsession with "ciphers" dissipated as Sade began undertaking more formal literary projects, but the work of ciphering and deciphering and the breakdown of meaning seem clearly to have left their mark on his thinking and writing.

While in Vincennes, Sade turned again to the writing of plays, and here his efforts went well beyond the small-scale productions for the actors at La Coste. Inspired by the domestic dramas of Diderot and others, the plots of Sade's plays *Le misanthrope par amour, Henriette et St-Clair, Le suborneur,* and others hinge on familiar themes such as narrowly avoided incest, deception, and hypocrisy. Although all the plays end with virtue's triumph, something frequently seems awry: social norms appear contingent, virtue more fragile, and depictions of character less coherent than in the earlier models. Only one of his plays, *Oxtiern ou les malheurs du libertinage,* was produced (1791) and printed (1798), despite Sade's constant efforts after his liberation to interest theaters in his projects.

While in prison, Sade kept a careful inventory of his numerous manuscripts and planned future projects. Published by Lely as an appendix to his 1962 biography, this document (known as the *Catalogue raisonné* of 1788) reveals that eighteen months prior to his release, Sade estimated that his complete works would fill fifteen volumes. His portfolio included his travel writing and theater; the *Historiettes, contes et fabliaux* (short fictions) inspired by Boccaccio; various reflections and essays; his epistolary novel *Aline et Valcour*; and a short novel or "philosophical tale" of the genre adopted by Voltaire and others, *Les infortunes de la vertu,* whose narrator, Sophie,

constantly endures punishments seemingly meted out by providence in response to her steadfast adherence to moral principle. The ceaseless activity of counting, classifying, and cataloging, as well as the practice of sketching new works to complete the overall system's lacunae, bespeak important features of Sade's literary production: first, the taxonomic urge that would structure the regimented, carceral worlds of *La nouvelle Justine* and *Les cent-vingt journées*; and second, the self-conscious projection of a literary career. The catalog contains no reference to pornographic works, underscoring the importance for Sade of "legitimate" participation in the Republic of Letters.

The manuscript of *Les cent-vingt journées de Sodome* (The 120 Days of Sodom), written in the Bastille in 1785 on a roll of pasted scraps of paper twelve centimeters wide and over twelve meters long, disappeared during the pillaging of the prison in July 1789. Sade had been transferred to Charenton a few days earlier, but his effects had not yet been sent after him. The manuscript surfaced a century later in the hands of a private collector, and Maurice Heine oversaw the first reliable edition in 1931. Sade wrote that he wept "tears of blood" at the loss of this major work, whose power derives to a great degree from the contrast between the excruciating violence of the narrative with the cold logic of its form and, in the final sections, the brutal concision of its cataloged "passions." Little could seem less "enlightened" than this cruel, enclosed world, in which various categories of victims live in sexual bondage to four representatives of the ancien régime power structure (an aristocrat, a churchman, a magistrate, and a financier); these men, in turn, are restrained from enacting any crime that has not been recounted by one of the four *historiennes*, or appointed storytellers, whose recitals of "passions" are carefully cataloged and scaled from "simple" to "murderous." Nevertheless, here as in later works, Sade showed himself a man of his age: steeped in its literary traditions as well as in the materialist philosophers d'Holbach, Helvétius, La Mettrie, and Diderot, whom Sade particularly admired. As in his approach to dramatic writing, Sade both extended and perverted the philosophical tradition. Much contemporary commentary has examined the "encyclopedic" ambitions evident here and epitomized by the heroine of *L'histoire de Juliette* (1797), whose declaration "Philosophy must tell all" ("La philosophie doit tout dire") simultaneously expresses completion and excess...and, as one critic puts it, results in "the saturation of the classical order of representation and in its actual violation" (Dalia Judovitz, " 'Sex,' or, the Misfortunes of Literature," in Allison et al., p. 172).

The marquis spent his years of liberty in the 1790s attempting to fulfill his literary ambitions, both mainstream and clandestine. An expanded version of *Les infortunes de la vertu* published as *Justine ou les malheurs de la vertu* (1791) belonged to the former category, as did *Aline et Valcour, ou le roman philosophique* (1795). Both works portray cruel worlds in which the innocent are terrorized and frequently overwhelmed by the wicked, and in which the justification of vice is more eloquent than the praise of virtue. The language, however, remains classical and controlled, without the flamboyant obscenity of the pornographic works. Chief among the latter are *La philosophie dans le boudoir* (Philosophy in the Bedroom, 1795), a set of dialogues depicting the sexual initiation of a young girl, whose libertine progress leads her to oversee the rape and torture of her own mother; and the last rewriting of the Justine story, *La nouvelle Justine, ou les malheurs de la vertu, suivie de l'histoire de Juliette, ou les prospérités du vice* (1797). The extraordinary length (some 2,000 pages) and range of this text, the recurring appearance of closed, carefully regimented societies—like the monastery of Sainte-Marie-des-Bois in *Justine* and the Society of the Friends of Crime in *Juliette*—reveal the same carceral, encyclopedic, transgressive sensibility that shaped the *Cent-vingt journées*. Other published works—these in Sade's "legitimate" mode—include a collection of short stories, *Les crimes de l'amour* (1800), accompanied by a critical essay on the history and aesthetics of the novel; "Idée sur les romans"; and later, from Charenton, the historical fiction *La marquise de Ganges* (1813). At his death, Sade left many unpublished manuscripts, among them his plays, personal notebooks, two more historical novels, and reportedly a massive, highly structured pornographic work, *Les journées de Florbelle*, apparently another attempt to recapture the lost *Cent-vingt journées*. This work was burned by order of Sade's surviving son.

The verbal and imaginative excesses of Sade's clandestine works, their juxtapositions of order and transgression, elegance and crudity of expression, have occasioned much critical commentary, especially in the wake of Roland Barthes's epigrammatic declaration, "Once written, shit does not smell." The violence of Sadian representation ultimately causes critics to cast a critical eye on the nature of representation itself, to reflect on its limits, and to call it into question. Sade's critical project, with all its corrosive skepticism, is thus a recognizable work of the Enlightenment.

[*See also* Literary Genres; Materialism; *and* Pornography.]

BIBLIOGRAPHY

WORKS BY SADE

Bibliothèque Sade. Edited by Maurice Lever. 7 vols. to date. Paris, 1993–. Contains extensive correspondence, as well as a new edition of the *Voyage d'Italie* based on new manuscript sources, greatly expanded from the Lely edition.

Correspondances du marquis de Sade et de ses proches, enrichies de documents, notes et commentaires. Edited by Alice M. Laborde. 27 vols. to date. Paris and Geneva, 1991–. Laborde has also published a number of biographical essays on Sade.

Oeuvres. Edited by Michel Delon. 3 vols. Paris, 1990. A scholarly edition of the major works; though no longer in print, the series of complete works edited by Gilbert Lely (Paris, 1961–1967) is still referred to by many scholars; for a more readily available complete edition, see *Oeuvres complètes*, edited by J.-J. Pauvert and Annie Le Brun (15 vols., Paris, 1986–1991).

The 120 Days of Sodom and Other Writings. Compiled and translated by Austryn Wainhouse and Richard Seaver. New York, 1966. A convenient anthology including selections from *The Crimes of Love*, *Oxtiern*, and essays by Simone de Beauvoir and Pierre Klossowski; there is no complete edition of Sade's works in English, but Austryn Wainhouse translated a number of individual works for Grove Press in the 1960s.

BIOGRAPHIES

Bongie, Laurence L. *Sade: A Biographical Essay*. Chicago, 1998.

Gray, Francine du Plessix. *At Home with the Marquis de Sade: A Life*. New York, 1998. Includes a good general bibliography.

Lely, Gilbert. *The Marquis de Sade*. Translated by Alec Brown. New York, 1961. English translation of *Vie du marquis de Sade*, published as vols. 1–2 of Sade, *Oeuvres complètes*, edited by Lely (Paris, 1961).

Lever, Maurice. *Sade: A Biography*. Translated by Arthur Goldhammer. New York, 1993. English translation of *Sade* (1991).

Pauvert, Jean-Jacques. *Sade vivant*. 3 vols. Paris, 1986–1989.

CRITICAL WORKS

Allison, David B., Mark S. Roberts, and Allen S. Weiss, eds. *Sade and the Narrative of Transgression*. Cambridge, 1995. Reprints several older essays (Bataille, Klossowski, et al.) in addition to work by contemporary critics.

Barthes, Roland. *Sade, Fourier, Loyola*. Paris, 1971.

Cryle, Peter. *Geometry in the Boudoir: Configurations of French Erotic Narrative*. Ithaca, N.Y., 1994.

DeJean, Joan. *Literary Fortifications: Rousseau, Laclos, Sade*. Princeton, N.J., 1984.

Frappier-Mazur, Lucienne. *Writing the Orgy: Power and Parody in Sade*. Translated by Gillian C. Gill. Philadelphia, 1996. Translation of *Sade et l'écriture de l'orgie* (1991).

Gallop, Jane. *Intersections: A Reading of Sade with Bataille, Blanchot, and Klossowski*. Lincoln, Neb., 1981.

Hénaff, Marcel. *The Invention of the Libertine Body*. Translated by Xavier Callahan. Minneapolis, 1999. Translation of *L'Invention du corps libertin* (1978).

Le Brun, Annie. *Sade: A Sudden Abyss*. Translated by Camille Naish. San Francisco, 1990. Translation of *Soudain un bloc d'abîme: Sade* (1986).

Michael, Colette Verger. *The Marquis de Sade: The Man, His Works, and His Critics: An Annotated Bibliography*. New York, 1986.

JULIE CANDLER HAYES

SAINT-HYACINTHE, THEMISEUL DE (1684–1746), cosmopolitan French man of letters.

Saint-Hyacinthe has remained a shadowy figure in the history of Enlightenment thought. His dislike of absolute monarchy influenced Montesquieu, and he had connections to radical philosophical circles in The Hague, surfacing there in about 1710. In that city Saint-Hyacinthe associated with Prosper Marchand and Willem Jacob 'sGravesande, all three being part of a coterie that edited *Journal littéraire* (Literary Journal). The records of the "society" that edited the journal indicate that it was prone to secrecy, addressed one another as "brothers" and spoke of their "order" (according to the information contained in the Marchand manuscripts at the University Library in Leiden). Given Prosper Marchand's close links to Jean Rousset de Missy, the leader of Amsterdam freemasonry up to 1747, Saint-Hyacinthe has also been linked to that movement.

Saint-Hyacinthe began life as a French Catholic and a soldier in Louis XIV's army, and in that capacity he was captured and imprisoned in The Netherlands in 1704, where he underwent a religious crisis. Although he was allowed to return to his native city of Troyes, Saint-Hyacinthe had ironically found freedom in the Dutch Republic and he returned to it frequently, often allowing himself to be identified as a French Protestant. In the Republic he appears to have fathered an illegitimate child who was placed in the Walloon orphanage. Saint-Hyacinthe became close to Albert-Henri de Sallengre, a Dutch citizen of French Protestant background, who in turn had close English ties, both to the deists and to the Royal Society.

In the second decade of the eighteenth century, when Saint-Hyacinthe was active in Holland, new clandestine manuscripts surfaced in the Dutch Republic. One of them, *Le militaire philosophe*, published by Marc-Michel Rey in 1768, has long been linked to the name of Saint-Hyacinthe. Only hearsay, however, some of it initiated by Voltaire, exists to "prove" that he wrote it. Far more tangible evidence does identify Saint-Hyacinthe as the author of a wickedly funny satire on academic learning, *Le chef d'oeuvre d'un inconnu* (1714); the copy in the Bibliothèque Nationale in Paris (Res.Z.2071) contemporaneously identifies him as the author. Perhaps inevitably—given his interest in science and his deistic leanings—Saint-Hyacinthe made his way to England in the 1720s, where we can find him associated with the Newtonian freemason Jean Desaguliers and with the international literary go-between and editor, the Huguenot Pierre Desmaizeaux. They socialized at the Rainbow Coffee House, where Montesquieu also could be found during his time in London. Sallengre also had ties to John Toland and Anthony Collins, and we may reasonably suppose that Saint-Hyacinthe knew these famous English freethinkers. In his writings, Saint-Hyacinthe consistently returned to the theme of friendship as solace in the face of the uncertainty inherent in human destiny. He may also have dabbled in the international traffic in clandestine manuscripts, and a letter in the state papers in London suggests that he was certainly suspect (PRO S.P. Dom, George II, 146, f. 226).

Saint-Hyacinthe also expressed republican and even democratic sentiments in his writings, again suggesting that he learned important lessons from the English freethinkers. His political leanings made him critical of Voltaire, whom he came to see as far too cozy with the courts of Europe. Saint-Hyacinthe appears to have settled in London and to have died there, as mysterious in his death as he was in his life.

[*See also* Coffeehouses and Cafes; Deism; Freemasonry; Gravesande, Willem Jacob 's-; Journals, Newspapers, and Gazettes, *subentry on* The Netherlands; Marchand, Prosper; Netherlands; Rey, Marc-Michel; Toland, John; *and* Voltaire.]

BIBLIOGRAPHY
Carayol, Elisabeth. *Themiseul de Saint-Hyacinthe, 1684–1746.* Oxford, 1984.
Jacob, Margaret C. *The Radical Enlightenment: Pantheists, Freemasons, and Republicans.* London, 1981.
Petzel, Anic. *Themiseul de Saint-Hyacinthe (1684–1746): Studien zum Werk eines Frühaufklärers.* Frankfurt-am-Main and New York, 1994.

MARGARET C. JACOB

SAINT-MARTIN, LOUIS-CLAUDE DE (1743–1803), French writer and mystic.

Saint-Martin, who modestly called himself "the unknown philosopher," was born in Amboise, in the Loire Valley. After studying law in Paris and an introduction to music (which would play an important role in his philosophical system), he served as an officer in the royal army from 1765 to 1771. While stationed at the port of Bordeaux, he was received into a fringe Masonic lodge, the Order of the Elected Cohen (Elected Priests). This secret society presented itself as a system of high chivalric degrees founded on magic rituals that claimed to reestablish man in his divine status. Fascinated by its founder, Martínez Pasqualis (1727–1774), Saint-Martin left the army in order to write his *Traité de la réintegration des êtres* (Treatise on the Reintegration of Beings, 1770–1772), a Judeo-Christian esoteric text dealing with the origins of the cosmos. (Martínez seems to have been of Judeo-Portuguese origin; he came from the Antilles). He quickly turned away from the ceremonial practices of the initiatory societies, however, in order to follow his own path, practicing magnetic therapeutics as formulated by Franz Anton Mesmer (1734–1815), and discovering, above all, German theosophy through the writings of the visionary and mystic Jakob Böhme (1575–1624) in Strasbourg in 1788.

Saint-Martin's theosophy is closely integrated with the preoccupations of the Enlightenment philosophers, both in the philosophical form of its exposition and in its openness to all "men of desire"—*Hommes de désir* (1790) was the title of one of his works—who are capable of developing their interior spiritual capacities. In *Des erreurs et de la vérité* (Of Errors and Truth, 1775), he compared music with the harmony of the celestial spheres as a way of reenvisioning man in his state of nature—that is, his divine state. In his *Tableau naturel des rapports qui existent entre Dieu et l'homme et l'univers* (Natural Tableau of the Relationships of God, Man, and the Universe, 1782), he extended the field of his reflection to include ancient mythologies, Egypt, primitive peoples, and the sciences of the physical-universe, lending the Bible only relative importance.

The historical dimension of his thought appeared in *Le ministère de l'homme-esprit* (The Ministry of Man and Spirit, 1802), integrating the tragic dimension of the French Revolution, which he approved as a necessary condition for the interior regeneration of man through knowledge in a world tested by suffering. There is no redemption without a Fall, nor can there be personal salvation that ignores the physical world and the fate of other men. Knowledge is inseparable from action and leads to God.

The similarity of the names Martínez and Saint-Martin generated confusion about Saint-Martin's involvement in a secret society that a certain Martínez was alleged to have founded and that French occultists claimed was revived under the name of the Martinist Order in the 1880s. However, Saint-Martin's historical role was purely intellectual. His thought exercised its influence—and continues to do so today from the United States to Russia—borne along by Romanticism. The best-known German theosophists corresponded with Saint-Martin, and the theoretician of the Counter-Revolution in France, Joseph de Maistre (1753–1821), made use of his thought, as did major novelists, such as Honoré de Balzac (1799–1850).

[*See also* Mysticism.]

BIBLIOGRAPHY

Benz, Ernst. *The Mystical Sources of German Romantic Philosophy.* Translated by Blair Reynolds and Eunice M. Paul. Allison Park, Pa., 1983. Originally published as *Les sources mystiques de la philosophie romantique allemande.* Paris, 1968.
Faivre, Antoine. *L'ésotérisme en France et en Allemagne au XVIIIe siècle.* Paris, 1973.
Godwin, Joscelyn. *L'ésotérisme musical en France, 1750–1950.* Paris, 1991.
Jacques-Chaquin, Nicole. "Martinisme." In *Dictionnaire critique de l'ésotérisme.* Paris, 1998.
Waite, Arthur-Edward. *Saint-Martin, the French Mystic, and the Story of Modern Martinism.* London, 1922. Includes bibliographical footnotes.

JEAN-PIERRE LAURANT
Translated from French by Susan and Eugene Romanosky

SAINT PETERSBURG ACADEMY. The Saint Petersburg Academy, the first Russian example of the learned societies that played so important a role in the Enlightenment, was the brainchild of Tsar Peter I, although he did not live to see its formal opening on 27 December 1725. For almost three decades, Peter had entertained ideas of creating a center of higher learning. He had long corresponded with Gottfied Wilhelm von Leibniz, a prime mover in the founding of the Berlin Academy, he had visited the Royal Society of London and the French Académie Royale des Sciences during his travels in 1698 and 1717, and he had been elected an honorary member of the latter. On 28 January 1724, the Russian Senate issued a decree establishing the Academy, according to a plan approved by Peter that had been submitted to him by his personal physician, Lavrentii Blumentrost, and the librarian Johann Schumaker, who were to become the Academy's first president and secretary, respectively. The provisions of this plan, which was never published, were to guide the Academy through its first two decades and only in 1747 was its first real statute approved.

Distinguished Members. Reflecting both Russian realities and Russian needs, the Academy was no mere imitation of its European counterparts. From the outset, research was linked with teaching and service to the state by the simultaneous creation of a university and a gymnasium. It was never an autonomous society of scholars, but a state-funded and state-directed institution. Foreign input, however, was crucial, enduring, and inevitably controversial. By the end of 1725, the first fifteen "academicians" (of whom Jacob Hermann, the professor of mathematics, was first in seniority) and two adjuncts had been appointed to the Saint Petersburg Academy, representing the sciences, the humanities, and, above all, mathematics. In the field of mathematics, Leonhard Euler brought international renown to the Academy. Euler arrived as a nineteen-year-old adjunct in physiology in 1726 and was made an academician in 1731. The naturalist Johann Gmelin was even younger; indeed, over one-third of the seventy academicians appointed during the eighteenth century were under the age of thirty. An even higher percentage were foreigners; it was not until 1733 that the first Russian, V. E. Adodurov, was appointed adjunct, and not until 1745 that the famous polymath M. V. Lomonosov and the philologist V. K. Trediakovskii became the first full-fledged Russian academicians.

The official head of the Academy was the president, appointed by the monarch. Five men occupied the post during the eighteenth century, and only the first, Blumentrost, was distinguished as a savant. The last, who was nominally president for fifty years, was Count Kiril Razumovskii, brother of the Empress Elizabeth's favorite, appointed as an eighteen-year-old in 1748. The true power, both before and certainly after the statute of 1747, lay with the chancellery, headed for forty years by Johann Schumaker, whose bureaucratic ways led to constant clashes

Saint Petersburg Academy. New Palace at Anitschki Gate, seat of the academy. (Bibliothèque Nationale de France, Paris.)

with the academicians. Not until 1766, when Catherine II was on the throne, was the chancellery replaced by a commission, chaired by a director, with members from among the academicians. The most notable and energetic director was Princess Ekaterina Dashkova, who presided from 1783 to 1793.

Research. Dashkova was simultaneously president of the newly created Russian Academy, which, along with the Academy of Arts (established in 1757), left the Saint Petersburg Academy to pursue its research specifically in the sciences. Indeed, it was in research rather than in teaching that the academicians made their contribution. By the end of the century, both the university and the gymnasium were closed because of a lack of students and a reluctance on the part of the professors to lecture. Moscow University, founded in 1755, became the center of education for Russian-speaking students. The return of Euler with his three sons in 1766, after an absence of twenty-five years, ushered in another high-profile period in the Academy's history. After his death in 1783, the Academy, despite Dashkova's efforts, saw yet another decline in its international standing.

Composed in its initial stages entirely of foreign—mainly German—scholars, the Academy brought European learning to the heart of the new Russian capital. By 1728, it occupied a series of new buildings on the embankment of Vasil'evskii Island, which included an excellent library, the famous Kunstkamera, an anatomical theater, and a well-equipped observatory. The Academy disseminated the results of its research throughout Europe. It had acquired its own press in 1727, and the following year it published the first issue of the *Commentarii Academiae*

scientiarum imperialis petropolitanae, which immediately commanded the attention of the scholarly world by the distinction of its articles. Euler alone published almost one hundred papers during his first sojourn in Russia, and many more after his return. His *Mechanica* (1736) was an outstanding example of the numerous monographs the press also produced. In addition to its publications in Latin, the Academy also served its slowly widening Russian audience by providing translations of foreign works, by publishing the *St. Petersburg News*—for many years the country's only newspaper—and by the production of journals, including the first literary-scientific journal, *Monthly Compositions*, edited from 1755 on by the great historian Gerhard Friedrich Müller, whose association with the Academy lasted over fifty years.

Among the most celebrated of the Academy's activities, serving both the state and the wider scientific community, were the great expeditions it sponsored to remote regions of the Russian empire to map unknown areas and gather vital empirical data for the natural sciences. The Great Northern Expedition of 1733–1743 generated Johann Georg Gmelin's *Flora sibirica* (1747–1769) and *Travels in Siberia*, Georg Steller's *De bestis marinis* (1751), and Stepan Krasheninnikov's *Description of the Land of Kamchatka* (1754); the last brought its author's elevation to academician and was translated into several European languages, including English. The Siberian expeditions of 1768–1774 produced even greater results, most notably in the works of the naturalist Peter Pallas, whose *Reise durch verschiedene Provinzen des russichen Reichs* (Travels through Various Provinces of the Russian Empire) was acclaimed throughout Europe.

From its earliest days, the Saint Petersburg Academy maintained lively contacts with its European counterparts, exchanging publications, sending representatives to visit other societies and academies, and electing leading scholars as honorary and foreign members. Despite periods of internal strife, organizational difficulties, and occasional loss of direction, the Saint Petersburg Academy came to occupy its rightful place among the leading European centers of scholarly excellence.

[*See also* Academies, *subentry on* Russia; Euler, Leonard; Explorations and Contact; Mathematics; *and* Natural History.]

BIBLIOGRAPHY

Boss, Valentin. *Newton and Russia: The Early Influence, 1698–1796.* Cambridge, Mass., 1972. Part 2 (chaps. 8–20) specifically on "Newton and the St. Petersburg Academy of Sciences."

Black, J. L. *G.-F. Müller and the Imperial Russian Academy.* Kingston and Montreal, 1986. A wide-ranging study of one of the most important members of the Academy, historiographer, journalist and archivist, from 1725 to 1765.

Filippov, M. S., ed. *Istoriia biblioteki Akademii nauk, 1714–1964.* Moscow and Leningrad, 1964. pp. 9–161 cover the formation of the great Academy library in the eighteenth century.

Kopelevich, I. K. *Vozniknovenie nauchnykh akademii: Seredina XVII–seredina XVIIIv.* Leningrad, 1974. Covers the first forty years of the Academy in the overall context of the founding of similar institutions in other European states.

Kopelevich, I. K. *Osnovanie Peterburgskoi Akademii nauk.* Leningrad, 1977. The basic study of the early years of the Academy up to the granting of its first statute in 1747.

Kopelevich, I. K. "The Creation of the Petersburg Academy of Sciences as a New Type of Scientific and State Institution." In *Great Britain and Russia in the Eighteenth Century: Contacts and Comparisons,* edited by A. G. Cross, pp. 204–211. Newtonville, Mass., 1979. On the distinctiveness of Peter the Great's Academy.

Ostrovitianov, K. V., ed. *Istoriia Akademii nauk SSSR.* 2 vols. Moscow and Leningrad, 1958. Vol. 1 of this official Soviet history covers the eighteenth century.

Pekarskii, P. P. *Istoriia Imperatorskoi Akademii nauk.* 2 vols. St. Petersburg, 1870–1873. The classic account of the Academy.

Schulze, Ludmilla. "The Russification of St. Petersburg Academy of Science and Arts in the Eighteenth Century." *British Journal for the History of Science* 18 (1985), 305–335.

Vucinich, Alexander. *Science in Russian Culture: A History to 1860.* London, 1965. pp. 3–183 cover the eighteenth century and the evolution of scientific thinking in Russia against a wide cultural background.

ANTHONY CROSS

SALONS. [*This entry contains four subentries, on salons in* France, England, Germany, *and* Italy.]

France

During the Enlightenment, the salon in France was primarily, but not exclusively, the domain of women—mature, intelligent, competent women—who clearly understood the importance of their rôle as salon hostesses. In small gatherings of men and women, the conversations at French salons were central in determining the course of the Enlightenment and in diffusing its effects throughout Europe.

The term *salon*, in the sense of a conversation salon, was first used in 1807 by Madame de Staël in her novel *Corinne.* The habitués of the salons preferred to use the term *bureau d'esprit,* derived from *bel esprit,* which designated a cultivated person who excelled in the art of conversation in a space open to and in the service of others. The *salon,* as we today understand the word, was begun in the early to mid-seventeenth century, in the Parisian townhouse of Catherine de Vivonne, marquise de Rambouillet—where she went to escape from the boisterous atmosphere of Louis XIII's royal court. In her own blue room, the famous *chambre bleue,* she received her guests, many of them writers. Together, during the 1630s, they developed conversation into an art—thus began the salon's golden age.

During the Enlightenment, the salon evolved through three stages that reflected the primary focus of the participants: the literary salon began in the 1730s; the philosophical salon in the 1760s; the political salon in the 1780s. In the literary discussions of the later salons, the first glimmerings of the Romantic tradition emerged, but political and philosophical problems dominated, in an atmosphere of unfettered critical inquiry. Although the composition and the subject of conversation varied continually, one element remained virtually constant: the gatherings were hosted by gifted, intelligent women, neither young nor particularly rich, whose faces we know from the oils and especially the pastel portraits by Jean-Baptiste Perroneau (1715–1783) and Maurice-Quentin de Latour (1704–1788). There were exceptions, such as the salons of M. de la Poplinière, Helvétius, and the baron d'Holbach, whose guests were male (with Mme. d'Holbach remaining discreetly in the background).

The Purpose of the Salon. Why were women the primary players, the ones who invited the guests and proposed the subjects to be discussed in their salons? Perhaps it was because these women were the models of good manners and might act as intermediaries between guests with opposing ideas; they also had tact and discretion and saw to bringing out the best in their circle, while encouraging others to shine, rather than attracting attention to themselves. They were arbiters of taste and frequently controlled the tone or the content of the conversation, demonstrating their disapproval when the language became coarse or the discussion heated. Surrounded by philosophes, the hostess's role was to encourage and mediate the discussion, to ensure that no one guest monopolized the conversation. She was also to ensure that in the search for truth, the language was clear, that no specialized jargon was used, so that all present, whether artists, musicians, scientists, philosophers, novelists, or journalists, could follow the entire discussion without difficulty. To this end, any Latin used in scientific exposés was eliminated in favor of French, which eased communication between specialists in many fields. All subjects were discussed in common: private conversations rarely took place. The importance of the salon of the Enlightenment was therefore as a facilitator of intellectual exchanges that took place in an atmosphere of politeness and respect for others. The frequency of the encounters resulted in the diffusion of the ideas of the Enlightenment: the salon, along with the literary café, was the principal means by which opinion on current affairs was circulated. The salon also provided a means of escape from two alternatives: the rigidity of royal court protocol, and the ubiquitous gambling and card-playing fashions that swept through eighteenth-century society, causing bankruptcies on a vast scale.

Many of the philosophes who frequented the salons in the 1760s and 1770s were contributors to Diderot's and d'Alembert's *Encyclopédie* (28 vols., 1751–1772), the aim of which was to overcome ignorance and superstition, and to help advance humankind through education. The salons facilitated meetings and discussions between the *encyclopédistes*, and the ideas contained in the *Encyclopédie* were debated by those philosophes who attended salons two, three, even four evenings a week. The topics discussed ranged from science, philosophy, current affairs, and economics to literature, art, and music—and these discussions were directly linked to the written output of the Enlightenment. Underlying the philosophes' interest in these subjects was also a desire to make changes in society, to challenge the authority of both the church and the king, and to reform the government.

The salons were an intermediary space between the philosophes and the public, providing the opportunity for them to read their latest manuscripts and thus be noticed by publishers. Plays were performed in the private salon theaters far from the troublesome eye of the censor and before receptive audiences ready to offer constructive criticism. All aspects of the theater and its aesthetics—comedy, tragedy, even the type of delivery expected of the actors—were discussed. Musical and operatic recitals offered other forms of entertainment, as in the salon of the portraitist Élisabeth Vigée-Lebrun, where debates on the musical superiority of Christoph Willibald Gluck or Niccolò Piccinni, Jean-Baptiste Lully or Jean-Philippe Rameau, often took place. The salon of M. de La Poplinière contributed much to the awareness of music and opera, both Italian and German, and he generously supported composers. Artists were also welcomed to the salons. To her Monday salon, Mme. Geoffrin invited such painters as Carle Van Loo, François Boucher, Maurice-Quentin de Latour, and Hubert Robert; she did much to advance their careers, including buying their works.

The salons were cosmopolitan in nature, and Paris became known as the "café de l'Europe" because it was its intellectual center, attracting thinkers from all parts of the Continent and the British Isles. From England came writers such as Horace Walpole and Lord Chesterfield, from Scotland the philosopher David Hume, from Italy the witty economist abbé Galiani, from Germany the philosopher Friedrich Melchior Grimm; and from America the irrepressible polymath Benjamin Franklin. The presence of these men in the salons, their correspondence, and their subsequent return to their countries promoted the spread of the Enlightenment throughout the Western world. Grimm's newsletter *La Correspondance littéraire* was particularly useful in informing European nobility and royalty of the intellectual and cultural events discussed in the Parisian salons. Mme. Geoffrin corresponded with King Stanislas of Poland, the Empress Maria Theresa of Austria, and Catherine II of Russia.

The French salon was not an exclusively Parisian phenomenon. Very active salons also existed in Bordeaux, Lyons, Autun, Toulouse, and Dijon, whose hostesses owned copies of the *Encyclopédie* and invited intellectuals such as Montesquieu and Voltaire. Yet the majority of the salons were in Paris, and eight main salons there were run by women. The older *salonnières* provided models for the younger ones: Mme. du Deffand learned from the duchesse du Maine; Julie de Lespinasse lived with Mme. du Deffand until opening her own salon; Mme. Geoffrin was inspired by Mme. de Tencin; and Mme. Necker modeled her salon on that of Mme. Geoffrin.

The Salon Hostesses. Mme. de Lambert was one of the senior salon hostesses. In 1710, at the age of sixty-three, she set up her salon in the Hôtel de Nevers, thus forming a transition between the seventeenth-century *style précieux* of Mme. de Rambouillet's salon and the philosophical style of the eighteenth century. Until her death in 1733, Mme. de Lambert received guests two days a week: intellectuals, artists, and writers on Tuesdays; society people on Wednesdays. It was considered a haven from the excesses of the Regency. Although Mme. de Lambert's rules were strict and decorum was essential, she welcomed serious discussion of literature, science, and philosophy and included many women among her guests. Her influence was very strong, and she helped many, including the philosopher Montesquieu, to be elected to the Académie Française.

Mme. Du Deffand belonged to the *noblesse d'épée*. Following the death of the duchesse du Maine, from whom she had learned the etiquette of the *salonnière*, Mme. du Deffand moved to the Saint Joseph convent in Paris, where she founded her salon, famous for its witty intelligent conversation and for what Horace Walpole called the "prodigious quickness" of its hostess. Her social and intellectual superiority made her very exacting in her choice of guests. Although admitting that she was opposed to the philosophes' ideas, she nevertheless welcomed them to her salon, thereby contributing to the diffusion of the Enlightenment.

Julie de Lespinasse was the niece of Mme. Du Deffand. She accompanied her aunt to Paris, where her intelligence and charm soon attracted a circle of admirers at the Saint Joseph convent, in particular the philosopher and mathematician Jean Le Rond d'Alembert, who introduced to her the group of *encyclopédistes*. This brought about a disagreement with Mme. Du Deffand, whose scepticism and acuity contrasted sharply with the warmth and sensitivity of her niece. Mlle. de Lespinasse, who was neither rich nor beautiful, provided a comfortable and unpretentious salon where she shared her passion for music, especially that of Gluck, with the leading thinkers of the 1760s and 1770s. The freedom of discussion and the wide range of topics were welcome changes, and her

tact and ability to reveal the brilliance of the minds of her guests were much admired by her loyal following.

Another salon that welcomed the *encyclopédistes* was that of Mme. Geoffrin on the rue Saint-Honoré. A bourgeoise who had married a rich manufacturer, she had no intellectual pretensions, yet she became the hostess of the brightest intellectuals of the time. Known for her common sense, her discipline, and her strong will, she was nonetheless dearly loved and admired by her guests, among whom were many artists and men of letters, including Edward Gibbon and John Wilkes from England, and David Hume from Scotland. Her guests were selected with great care, and she compiled a list of subjects that would not be tolerated in her salon. Intellectually stimulated by her guests, she freely admitted that it was from the serious discussions in her salon that she received her entire education. Her celebrated generosity prompted her to give financial help not only to artists but also to the *encyclopédistes*. In several cases, financial aid from salon hostesses helped to establish young writers, though not always directly, since it was sometimes in the form of bequests. More frequently

In the Salon. Reading of Voltaire's *L'orphelin de Chine* at the salon of Mme. Geoffrin. Painting (c. 1814) by Gabriel Lemonnier (1743–1825). (Château de Malmaison, France/Lauros-Giraudon/Art Resource, NY.)

they gave moral support: Julie de Lespinasse in particular did much to encourage the *encyclopédistes*.

Mme. Necker, wife of Jacques Necker, who would become Louis XVI's finance minister, had received a good education in her native Switzerland and was respected for her knowledge of literature, classical languages, and science. As an immigrant, the wife of a financier, and a Protestant, she used her salon to break down social barriers, to help her husband's career, and to meet the leading writers and philosophers of the time. Her ambition was that her salon rival those of Mme. Geoffrin and d'Holbach. Each Friday, she brought together political and economic theorists, philosophers, and many foreigners. The philosophes' observations on religion occasionally shocked her, yet she welcomed them and listened to them: it was in her salon that Diderot and Grimm tried out some of their more audacious theories, while abbé Galiani amused everyone with his witty repartee.

The salon in Enlightenment France was not a meeting place for people to exchange frivolous gossip. It was a serious working space, where new ideas were generated and profound changes in society were proposed by guests who believed in equality and whose intellectual abilities were unquestioned. It provided a framework for civilized deliberation in an atmosphere free from most constraints, where the subtleties of conversation could be explored, and where curiosity about the latest inventions—musical, scientific, or literary—was encouraged. These are the characteristics that explain the salon's extraordinary appeal to visitors from all over Europe.

[*See also* Clubs and Societies, Encyclopédie; Learned Societies; Men and Women of Letters; Music; Opera; Painting; *and* Paris.]

BIBLIOGRAPHY

Clergue, Helen. *The Salon: A Study of French Society and Personalities in the Eighteenth Century*. New York, 1971. First published in 1907, and despite its age, this book is still useful. Following a general introduction on the salon and its evolution, there are studies of four of the most important salons: those of Mme. du Deffand, Mme. d'Épinay, Julie de Lespinasse, and Mme. Geoffrin.

Glotz, Marguerite, and Madeleine Maire. *Salons du XVIIIème siècle*. Paris, 1949. An introduction to society life in the eighteenth century, followed by studies of eight groups of friends and salons, including those of Mme. du Deffand and Mme. Necker.

Goodman, Dena. "Seriousness of Purpose: *Salonnières*, Philosophes, and the Shaping of the Eighteenth-Century Salon." *Proceedings of the Annual Meeting of the Western Society for French History* 15 (1988), 111–118. Brief but important attempt to restore the idea that serious work was carried out in the salons, despite Rousseau's repudiation of this idea.

Goodman, Dena. "Julie de Lespinasse: A Mirror for the Enlightenment." In *Eighteenth-Century Women and the Arts*, edited by F. Keener and S. Lorsch, pp. 3–10. New York, 1988.

Goodman, Dena. *The Republic of Letters: A Cultural History of the French Enlightenment*. Ithaca, N.Y., 1994. Chapter 2, "Philosophes and Salonnieres," and Chapter 3, "Governing the Republic of

Letters: Salonnieres and the Rule(s) of Polite Conversation," are particularly noteworthy; interesting for detailed study of the salon.

Kors, Alan Charles. *D'Holbach's Coterie: An Enlightenment in Paris*. Princeton, N.J., 1976. A very thorough, well-researched book on the salon of Baron d'Holbach and its members.

Landes, Joan B. *Women and the Public Sphere in the Age of the French Revolution*. Ithaca, N.Y., 1988. Chapters 2 and 3 examine the role and the importance in the literary world of the women who ran the salons.

Rogers, Katharine M. "The View from England." In *French Women and the Age of Enlightenment*, edited by Samia Spencer, pp. 357–368. Bloomington, Ind., 1984. The French salons and their hostesses as viewed by English visitors; comparing France and England, most observers concluded that French society was superior.

Tornius, Valerian. *The Salon: Its Rise and Fall: Pictures of Society though Five Centuries*. Translated by Agnes Platt. New York, 1971. First published in 1929, two chapters are of special interest in this rather fanciful book: "The Kingdom of the rue St. Honoré" (Mme. Geoffrin) and "The Muse of the Encyclopedia" (Julie de Lespinasse).

ROSENA DAVISON

England

A French word, *salon* did not describe even in France of the eighteenth century the social gatherings that are referred to now by that term: the definition is, inevitably, somewhat arbitrary. *Conversation parties* was a useful English term that Hannah More, a frequent guest, used in her descriptions of the events hosted by the two most famous English *salonnières*, Elizabeth Vesey (1715?–1791) and Elizabeth Montagu (1720–1800). Salons were cousin to academies, clubs, and informal literary circles—with which they sometimes overlapped—yet it is worthwhile to distinguish among them. Academies and clubs had rules and the election of members; they were also typically male only. Salons were informal. They met in private houses, sometimes at regular intervals (as Vesey's, for example, every other Tuesday); they attempted to promote sociability between men and women and between upper-class people and others of "merit" and talent; and they were typically presided over by a woman or by a woman and a man together. Academies were devoted to the production and advancement of knowledge by learned men; salons, while sometimes concerned to advance knowledge by means of nonexpert conversational exploration, were sometimes interested in the production of belles lettres and almost always interested in criticism and in the dissemination of knowledge and culture to an audience of amateurs.

Most salons were presided over by women of wealth and high social position. Such women functioned as patrons of talented people of lesser wealth and lesser social position, whom they admitted to their splendid houses. Other English *salonnières* included Ann Dillingham Ord; Margaret Cavendish Bentinck, duchess of Portland; and Margaret Smith Bingham, baroness Lucan. As in all patronage relations, both patrons and patronized expected to gain from the relationship. The English *salonnières* expected entertainment and instruction from their humbler guests, and they enjoyed the social cachet of being known to host celebrities. In turn, they offered many benefits, including access to entertainments that the humbler guests might not otherwise have experienced; important introductions that had professional and intellectual value; effective solicitation of subscriptions to books and cultural events; presents of game, books, money, and tickets or box space at theaters; and a quasi-public recognition of merit and talent.

Montagu, "the female Maecenas of Hill Street," was especially important as a patron of women writers, including Elizabeth Carter, the learned translator of Epictetus. In fact, Montagu had a gift for reinventing what was, by the social standards of the day, a very unequal relationship between a great lady and a clergyman's daughter. She transformed it into a reciprocal relationship of equals: Montagu introduced Carter to learned men in London and gave her presents of books, but in exchange she gratefully accepted Carter's knowledge about Greek drama and philosophy, knowledge that the press of her social obligations as a great lady deprived her of the time to acquire by herself.

The quintessential activity of the salons was talking, although exactly what kind of talking there should be was disputed. Generally, hostesses aimed at promoting civil, polite, rational conversation, free of insult and quarreling. To achieve this end by banning talk about controversial matters, such as religion and politics, however, compromised the Enlightenment goal of the free exploration of all subjects. The English salons of Vesey and Montagu were constructed both in imitation of the French salons and in opposition to their supposed fostering of infidelity, immorality, and sexually suggestive language. The principal English *salonnières* of the second half of the eighteenth century self-consciously attempted to advance not only knowledge and culture but also religion and morality. They banned card playing and ribaldry, and they invited significant numbers of pious bishops and other learned clergymen. Hannah More wittily celebrated their ideals in her mock-heroic panegyric "The Bas Bleu; or, Conversation. Addressed to Mrs. Vesey" (written in 1784; published in 1786):

> Here sober duchesses are seen,
> Chaste wits, and critics void of spleen,
> Physicians, fraught with real science,
> And whigs and tories in alliance;
> Poets, fulfilling Christian duties,
> Just lawyers, reasonable beauties...

Because the salons were also importantly spaces in which literary and intellectual reputations were enhanced or impaired, one man's witty derogation easily enough produced another man's injured feelings. Witty guests were entertaining, and their witticisms repeated outside the salon, enhanced its reputation; yet witty or even well-informed prolix guests threatened to turn talking into a narcissistic performance art and compromised the supposed ideals of equal exchange and mutual exploration. Elizabeth Vesey's tactic of organizing her parties into small groups of three to five worked against the celebrity talker trying to attract a complete audience for himself. Hester Thrale Piozzi's *Anecdotes of the Late Samuel Johnson* (1786) explored the problematics of entertaining Johnson, a brilliant talker and the ornament of her salon, but a man who could also be insulting to other guests.

Catharine Macaulay (1731–1791), author of a *History of England* (1763–1783) is not usually considered as having presided over a salon; she was not a woman of wealth or elevated social position, yet she had regular gatherings at her London house in the 1760s and 1770s. Conversation there was focused on history and politics rather than on literature. She brought together English and American radicals, both in person and through the network of correspondence that typically emanated from salons.

Direct and lively observation of the salons comes from the letters, journals, or memoirs of many notable participants: Frances Burney, Edmund Burke, Elizabeth Carter, David Garrick, Elizabeth Montagu, Hannah More, Catherine Talbot, Horace Walpole, and Nathaniel Wraxall. Male participants, except Garrick, were apt to demonstrate condescension and, occasionally, resentment toward these new pretensions of women. The women participants, while sometimes critical of their hostesses' skills, generally expressed enthusiasm about the intellectual and cultural opportunities that the salons provided. Salons inevitably backslid, on occasion, into less edifying gossip or petty personal rivalries; they could even produce trivial verse, like that of the *Poetical Amusements* (1775–1781) written by Lady Anna Miller and the guests at her villa outside Bath. Nonetheless, they created in their time both an important cultural space for women's intellectual and cultural progress and models for less sexualized relationships between men and women.

[*See also* Clubs and Societies; Patronage; *and* Politeness.]

BIBLIOGRAPHY

Bodek, Evelyn Gordon. "Salonieries and Bluestockings: Educated Obsolescence and Germinating Feminism." *Feminist Studies* 3 (3/4 1976), 185–199. Considers the salons and bluestocking circles an "informal university" for women, stresses the difference between French and English salons, and suggests a continuity between late eighteenth-century bluestockings and nineteenth-century feminist reformers.

Doran, John. *A Lady of the Last Century (Mrs. Elizabeth Montagu): Illustrated in Her Unpublished Letters.* New York, 1973. First published in 1873; quotes copiously from her letters. One of several older biographies of Montagu; there is no recent biography.

Heller, Deborah. "Bluestocking Salons and the Public Sphere." *Eighteenth-Century Life* n.s. 22 (May 1998), 50–82. Perhaps overestimates the power of the *salonnières*, but rightly emphasizes their concern with reason and education; argues that the salons represent women's full and active participation in the public sphere, and that both French and English salons were developments of early 1700s ideas first expressed by Joseph Addison, Richard Steele, and the earl of Shaftesbury.

Hill, Bridget. *The Republican Virago: The Life and Times of Catharine Macaulay, Historian*. Oxford, 1992. Chapter 9 describes the connections between English and American radicals that Macaulay promoted, including her correspondence with John and Abigail Adams and Mercy Otis Warren.

Meyers, Sylvia Harcstark. *The Bluestocking Circle: Women, Friendship, and the Life of the Mind in Eighteenth-Century England*. Oxford, 1990. Offers rich biographical detail about Vesey and Montagu based on published and unpublished sources, as well as about several of the women whose work they patronized.

Shields, David S. "British American Belles Lettres." In *The Cambridge History of American Literature*, vol. 1: 1590–1820, edited by Sacvan Bercovitch and Cyrus R. K. Patell, pp. 307–344. Cambridge, 1994. A fine account of American provincial imitation of metropolitan polite literature, including consideration of Elizabeth Graeme Fergusson (1737?–1801), who presided over a salon in a country house outside of Philadelphia.

Stone, George Winchester, and George M. Kahrl. *David Garrick: A Critical Biography*. Carbondale and Edwardsville, Ill., 1979. Chapter 13 on "Garrick's Friendships with Women of Distinction" nicely explores the relationship between the actor and Elizabeth Montagu: Garrick was one of the most affable, forthcoming, and grateful ornaments of the English salon, and better than most men of his era at heterosocial intercourse.

Tinker, Chauncy Brewster. *The Salon and English Letters: Chapters on the Interrelations of Literature and Society in the Age of Johnson*. New York, 1915. Still worthy for its effort to construct an ideal type of the salon; its suggestive if impressionistic history that traces the salon from the Italian Renaissance court; and its exploration of the relation between the salon and literary forms. That Tinker preferred the selfless hostess to the ambitious woman writer will now seem quaint.

SUSAN STAVES

Germany

On 17 October 1733, the poet Christiana Mariana von Ziegler was crowned with a laurel wreath and proclaimed to be the official poet of the University of Wittenberg. She was the first female writer in German history to be honored in this way. A decade before, Ziegler had established Germany's first salon in Leipzig, which was an important cultural center, home to a university, many publishers, an annual book fair, and a theater. In 1724, Johann Christoph Gottsched moved to Leipzig; he was the German Enlightenment's most ardent enthusiast of women's learning. When she began hosting her salon, Christiana von Ziegler was twenty-eight, but she was already twice widowed, and her children from the two marriages had all died. She had returned to live in her parents' home, where she began to host musical and literary gatherings.

The salon was not Ziegler's only public intellectual activity. She was the first female member of the Deutsche Gesellschaft (Germanic Society), an important Enlightenment forum organized by Gottsched. She published enough poems, song lyrics, and essays to fill three large volumes of collected works. Although her name vanished from the canon after her death, Ziegler was well known and highly regarded in her day. Her widowed status seems to have been connected with her public profile and productivity; after 1741, when she remarried and moved away from Leipzig, she withdrew completely from the public intellectual scene.

After Ziegler's retirement, few other German women hosted salons in the following decades. During the years when the Enlightenment was a dominant intellectual movement, between 1720 and 1780, a vibrant and influential salon subculture did not really emerge in the Germanies. The few exceptions were led by noblewomen, and several met at courts. This pattern reflects the wide gulf between the German nobility and the higher bourgeoisie. Within each class, many intellectuals articulated enlightened ideas, but the men who spoke for each group disagreed strongly about what elements of gender roles should be imitated from the French models.

Enlightened male intellectuals not born into the nobility tended to be outraged by the sexually risqué atmosphere at the German courts, which they attributed to excessive enthusiasm for all things French. One of their chief aims was to convince their own female friends, wives, and daughters not to waste their time, their virtue, and their fathers' money by imitating the aristocratic lifestyle. They wanted no erotically charged conversational settings in which their daughters might fall in love with charming noble cads. Noblewomen found social support if they wished to become patrons and salon hostesses; wives of commoner intellectuals, in contrast, were encouraged to publish and to learn, but not to host salons. Johann Gottsched's wife, Luise, was an accomplished translator and playwright, but she declined to join his Deutsche Gesellschaft and seems never to have hosted her own salon.

Witty and learned conversation was possible among people from different classes only if they all spoke the same language, but even this could not be assumed. Nobles at court followed French intellectual fashions and laced their conversations with French phrases, even if they did not really master the language. In addition, the Germanies were a chaos of towns, city-states, and states; the absence of a single capital city meant that there was no obvious destination for intellectuals who sought to leave their families, class, region, or religion behind and mingle with like-minded strangers.

Scholars usually define a salon as a regular intellectual gathering led by a woman (which, unfortunately, excludes the "literary tea tables," "aesthetic Teas" and "literary societies" that may have been more common in the Germanies of the eighteenth century). There are traces, however, of four additional salons in the Germanies in the years after Ziegler's activity in the 1720s. Three took place at courts, and all were led by women who were either born or married into the nobility. Queen Sophia Dorothea von Hohenzollern (1687–1757), the wife of King Frederick William I, hosted regular artistic discussions in her small private castle, Monbijou. The king, however, forwent her gatherings and spent his evenings in a convivial all-male circle.

A second court salon was led by countess Caroline von Hessen-Darmstadt (1721–1774) at her palace in Darmstadt from the 1760s until her death in 1774. It was attended mainly by women, almost all noble, and their enthusiasms in literature and lifestyle were early Romantic rather than enlightened. One of her guests was the philosopher Johann Herder, who met his wife at the countess's salon.

Herder later moved to Weimar, home to another court salon, led by duchess Anna Amalia of Sachsen-Weimar (1739–1807). She maintained a traditional courtly social life, limited severely by rank and title, but she also hosted Wednesday dinner parties where most of the guests were commoner intellectuals, including the novelist and poet Johann von Goethe, whom she raised to the nobility in 1782. Herder and Goethe, as well as their friend Christoph Martin Wieland, were admirers of the successful novelist Sophie la Roche, who hosted a salon in Mainz while she was married to a court official there. After her husband's death, la Roche supported herself from her publications and also edited a journal for women called *Pomona*.

Perhaps the best-known circle of salons in eighteenth-century Germany opened their doors in 1780, when Henriette Herz and her husband, Dr. Markus Herz, began hosting their "double salon" in Berlin. During the next quarter-century in Berlin, a handful of Jewish *salonières* hosted gatherings famous for their avant-garde mix of nobles and commoners. By the time the social hierarchy of Berlin had become fluid enough to allow such radical social and religious mixing, however, the distinctive features of Enlightenment sociability were already waning across the Germanies. Perhaps if class relations had not been so rigid in eighteenth-century Germany, both salons and the enlightened thinking they promoted would have been more frequent.

[*See also* Aufklärung; Germany; *and* Men and Women of Letters.]

BIBLIOGRAPHY

Bovenschen, Silvia. *Die imaginierte Weiblichkeit: Exemplarische Untersuchungen zu kulturgeschichtlichen und literarischen Praesentationsformen des Weiblichen*. Frankfurt am Main, 1979.

Bruford, W. H. *Culture and Society in Classical Weimar, 1775–1806*. Cambridge, 1962.

Dollinger, Petra. *Frauenzimmer—Gespraechsspiele: Salonkultur zwischen Literatur und Gesellschaftsspiel*. Munich, 1996.

Hertz, Deborah. *Jewish High Society in Old Regime Berlin*. New Haven, Conn., and London, 1988.

Heyden-Rynsch, Verena, von der. *Europaeische Salons: Höhepunkte einer versunken weiblichen Kultur*. Munich, 1992.

Joeres, Ruth-Ellen B. "'That girl is an entirely different character!' 'Yes, but is she a feminist?' Observations on Sophie von la Roche's *Geschichte des Fraeuleins von Sternheim*." In *German Women in the Eighteenth and Nineteenth Centuries: A Social and Literary History*, edited by Ruth-Ellen B. Joeres and Mary Jo Maynes, pp. 137–156. Bloomington, Ind., 1986.

Seibert, Peter. *Der literarische Salon*. Stuttgart and Weimar, 1993.

DEBORAH HERTZ

Italy

This classic type of informal sociability, described before the name existed by Baldassarre Castiglione in the sixteenth century, played an important part in Italian urban culture in the age of the Enlightenment (*Illuminismo*). There was no sharp distinction between this and other more formal private cultural organizations. At times, salons became academies bearing the names of their founders, as did the Accademia di Medinacoeli in Naples, which originated as a discussion group at the home of the duke of Medinacoeli, and included the heirs of the tradition of the Accademia degli Investiganti and representatives of the Neapolitan pre-Enlightenment. Alternatively, private schools of eminent educators might function like salons. This was certainly the case at the palace in Castelfranco belonging to the Ricatti family, where the quality of discussions, particularly on philosophical matters, impressed visitors such as Leibniz. Although the discussion group of the dominican friar Tommaso Pio Maffei at San Giovanni e Paolo in Venice, which inspired Venetian disciples of Isaac Newton including Antonio Conti and Giovanni Poleni, might more properly be called a school, certainly the name salon belongs to the group led by the Franciscan friar Carlo Lodoli at San Francesco della Vigna, which met to discuss the application of Enlightenment principles to architecture and city planning. After all, Lodoli himself had benefited from discussions carried on in the palace of the Venetian nobleman Girolamo Ascanio Giustiniani, whose brilliant salon in the 1730s hosted the reformer Pietro Giannone, in flight from Naples.

University towns were particularly rich centers for cultural conviviality of all sorts. Alberto Fortis recalled having been powerfully influenced in his choice of a career promoting the application of science to problems of public policy in Venice and Naples by the group of eminent professors at the University of Padua—Marco Carburi, Pietro Arduino, Simone Stratico, Marcantonio Leopoldo Caldani—who gathered around his mother, Francesca Maria Bragnis, in Palazzo Capodilista. Similarly in Bologna, the private gatherings in the home of Laura Bassi, a professor of philosophy and correspondent of Voltaire, are known to have inspired her cousin, Lazzaro Spallanzani.

No one salon could be called the midwife to the Milanese Enlightenment, but among those that made notable contributions were that of Duchess Maria Vittoria Serbelloni-Ottoboni, frequented by Pietro Verri and Giuseppe Parini, and the receptions held at Palazzo Melzi by Carlo Firmian, the minister of the Austrian government, which must have aided their host in his task of implementing many of the reforms suggested by the Milanese philosophes Pietro and Alessandro Verri, Cesare Beccaria, and others. The young Mozart gave a concert here. Neapolitan salons in the mid-eighteenth century include the informal gatherings held by Raimondo di Sangro, prince of San Severino, alchemist, naturalist, and collector. Perhaps Raimondo's Masonic connections are no more certain indications of his Enlightenment sympathies than his publication of an antiecclesiastical tract later placed on the Index. Much better documented are the sympathies of Bartolomeo Intieri, the Tuscan economist whose villa became a gathering place for Neapolitan intellectuals. We know much less about the salon belonging to the De Gennaro family in Posillipo, where the Neapolitan cultural luminaries included a future Jacobin, Francesco Maria Pagano.

Renowned more for its brilliant company than for any contributions to the Enlightenment was the salon of Maria Pizzelli in Rome in the last decades of the century; the same went for the fashionable circles of the Niccolini and Corsini families in Florence. Even Madame de Staël is reported to have admired the conversations that went on in the home of Luisa d'Albany in Palazzo San Clemente in Florence from the 1770s. The attachment formed by Luisa with the Piedmontese poet Vittorio Alfieri during such meetings determined her eventual transfer to Paris. On her return to Florence in 1792, the salon met every Saturday, reinvigorated by a common animus against the French Revolution, with the hostess occasionally masquerading as Marie Antoinette, and always parading the scandalous ménage à trois among herself, Alfieri, and Xavier Fabre. With Alphonse Lamartine among the distinguished guests, the group's interests at this point had already begun to foreshadow the aesthetic of romanticism.

[*See also* Milan *and* Naples.]

BIBLIOGRAPHY

Brusatin, Manlio. *Venezia nel Settecento: stato, architettura, territorio*. Turin, 1980. Discusses the activities of Lodoli and Smith and their contemporaries in Venice.

Cortese, Nino. *Cultura e politica a Napoli dal Cinque al Settecento*. Naples, 1965. Discusses cultural organizations in Naples.

De Brosses, Charles. *Lettres familieres d'Italie: Lettres écrites d'Italie en 1739 et 1740*. Edited by Hubert Juin. Brussels, 1995. Contains important information concerning early-eighteenth-century salons in Milan.

Dooley, Brendan. *Science and the Marketplace in Early Modern Italy*. New York, 2001. Chapters 5 and 7 outline various forms of scientific sociability.

Heyden-Ruysch, Verena von der. *Europäische Salons: Hohepunkte einer versunkenen weiblichen Kultur*. Munich, 1992. Views salons in the context of feminist emancipation.

Levi Pisetsky, Rosita. "La vita e le vesti dei Milanesi." In *Storia di Milano*. 17 vols. Milan, 1953–1962. Vol. 12, pp. 837–902. Places Milanese salon life in its Enlightenment setting.

Pellegrini, Carlo. *La contessa d'Albany e il salotto del Lungarno*. Naples, 1951. The standard study of Luisa d'Albany's Florentine salon.

BRENDAN DOOLEY

SALVIUS, LARS (1706–1773), Swedish printer and publisher.

Salvius, the son of a vicar, concentrated on the humanities during his studies at Uppsala University. He came to Stockholm, where he served on the court of appeals and, in 1738, obtained a position on the board of commerce. By then he had also started a career as a writer in the field of political economy. His weekly, *Tanckar öfwer den swenska oeconomien igenom samtal yttrade* (Thoughts on the Swedish Economy, Displayed in Discussion) championed a mainly mercantilistic point of view; Salvius was, however, not doctrinaire and argued at the same time for a less regulated trade.

Salvius's most ambitious undertaking as a writer was a multi-volume work on topography that presented a comprehensive view of Sweden; however, a competing work forced him to give up this project in 1741 after the printing of a volume covering Uppland. Instead, Salvius made his mark as a printer, publisher, and bookseller. The first printer in Sweden with academic training, he was energetic and inventive, and modernized prevailing modes of producing and distributing books. His bookstore became Sweden's best, encompassing a wide spectrum of genres, and in the late 1750s he added a circulating library; in this he was a pioneer. Furthermore, he fought successfully against regulations and guild restrictions, although he did not live to see free trade in books become a reality in 1787. He also was the first to pay a fair price to his authors, which encouraged many of the best Swedish writers of the day to publish with him. He published an especially impressive array of scientific and scholarly books; even the famous Carolus Linnaeus, who had longstanding ties with Wishof in Leiden, chose to have a majority of his works published by Salvius.

For Salvius, the printing of the books of this great naturalist, and of other scientists, was of great value; they made it possible for him, as the first Swedish publisher, to balance import orders with export profits from sales in Paris, Amsterdam, and Leipzig. He was also commercially successful in his attempts to popularize science. In 1745 he launched a journal, *Lärda Tidningar* (Journal of Learning), which reported on new books and related news from the seats of learning and the Royal Academy of Sciences. Salvius would continue editing this highly successful journal until his death.

Salvius combined a keen eye for profit with idealism and a genuine interest in science and learning. He was an early member of the Royal Swedish Academy of Sciences, where he was a staunch proponent of the use of roman type in the Academy's *Proceedings*, and, as a good patriot, he fought for giving the Swedish language priority. His book *Undersökning om de följder hvarmed inhemskt språks förakt verkar på folkets seder* (1770) was an argument against the increasing use of French among the educated classes.

[*See also* Print Culture; Publishing; *and* Scandinavia.]

BIBLIOGRAPHY

Björkman, Margareta. *Läsarnas nöje: Kommersiella lånbibliotek i Stockholm 1783–1809.* Uppsala, Sweden, 1992. A history of the circulating libraries that also contains information on Salvius's activities in this field.

Lindberg, Sten G. "The Scandinavian Book Trade in the Eighteenth Century." In *Buch und Buchhandel in Europa im achtzehnten Jahrhundert,* edited by Giles Barber and Bernhard Fabian, pp. 225–248. Hamburg, 1981. Brief account of the Scandinavian book trade and the role played by Salvius. Contains a valuable bibliography.

Schück, Henrik. *Lars Salvius.* Stockholm, 1929. The only general biography to date.

JAKOB CHRISTENSSON

SAN MARTÍN, JOSÉ DE (1778–1850), soldier, statesman, national hero, and liberator of Argentina, Chile, and Peru.

Son of a Spanish official stationed in the United Provinces of the River Plate (present-day Argentina), San Martín, with a liberal education and a profound affection for his native land, returned from Spain to the South American continent in 1812 and became involved in the colonial revolution. With clear objectives and an iron will to achieve them, he spared no personal sacrifice to liberate Latin America.

Enlightenment Influence. San Martín is of singular importance to the history of South America, as much for his independence project—continental in scale—as for his political ideas in the context of the Spanish and Ibero-American Enlightenment. He participated in this movement in Spain, where he was introduced to liberalism and new forms of political sociability. Together with a group of officers, university students and professors, lower-level

clergy, artisans, members of the middle class, and liberal aristocrats, he formed a part of this cultural elite and its various clubs and societies. Its leaders read Mably and Rousseau. In Cádiz and Madrid, its predominant centers, Chileans, Venezuelans, Peruvians, Paraguayans, and Argentines gathered: Bernardo O'Higgins, Simón Bolívar, José Moldes, Juan Martín de Pueyrredón, and Carlos M. de Alvear. At the Olavide House in Madrid, a *junta* of Delegates of the Communities and Provinces of South America met, including Francisco de Miranda, Antonio José de Sucre, and Antonio Nariño, who already had been involved in the emancipation process since 1794.

Among these societies, masonic lodges were prominent. San Martín's indubitable Masonic affiliation allows us to understand his republicanism and his constitutionalist objectives. Initiated as a Freemason in Cádiz, he continued these activities in London, and in 1812, in the River Plate region, he founded the Lautaro Lodge, whose objectives were "independence" and "constitution." The Enlightenment, the North American (U.S.) and French revolutions, and the lodges prepared the way to South American independence.

Beginning in 1810 with the May Revolution, war and revolution were intertwined until independence. During this period, San Martín was in Spain and fought against the Napoleonic forces. Because of events in the River Plate region, he returned on 9 March 1812, coming from London with other American-born Spaniards associated with Freemasonry and eager to liberate South America. San Martín understood that the only way of doing that was to form an army, achieve political unity, and obtain the support of Great Britain. Around 1812, the Lautaro Lodge went into action; the failures of the First Triumvirate gave rise to a coup d'état that constituted the Second Triumvirate, whose purpose was to bring about the Lodge's objectives of organizing the country constitutionally as a republic and attaining independence. A constituent body called the Assembly of 1813 was convened; it did not accomplish these objectives, but its constituent labor in favor of a liberal democratic process was substantial. For San Martín, however, the declaration of independence was fundamental in the war against Spain.

Chile and Peru. The period 1814–1816 was critical. A break with Alvear, an ambitious man who favored the creation of a strong government, displaced San Martín from the Lodge. The situation in the north was aggravated by the royalist advance. Simultaneously, the international situation worsened: with Napoleon's defeat and the beginning of the absolutist restoration, Ferdinand VII returned to the throne, poised to send a fleet to America. Republican spirit waned in the River Plate region, where—through fear and opportunism—a monarchical government was organized.

After realizing the impossibility of defeating the royalists in Upper Peru (present-day Bolivia), San Martín reaffirmed his plans to organize to liberate Chile and attack Peru, for which he relied on the support of Juan Martín de Pueyrredón, director of the United Provinces. In precarious health and with a disciplined but modest army, San Martín crossed the Andean Cordillera (a truly epic feat for the period) and penetrated Chile. After two decisive battles—Chacabuco (17 February 1817) and Maipú (5 April 1818)—he delegated political power to O'Higgins, the Chilean officer and collaborator in his campaigns. Previously he had requested the dispatch of a Chilean representative to the Constituent Congress that had met in Tucumán (a province in northwestern Argentina) since 1816. He entered Chile to unite both countries, and consequently created a branch of the Lautaro Lodge and established a republic.

Disillusioned by events in the River Plate area, San Martín's enlightened ideas faded before a country "without industry, without political, social, and economic development." Between 1816 and 1820, the Congress of 1816 failed, the constitution was rejected by the country, and the disintegration of political power resulted in the "anarchy of 1820." Shaken, he reflected on the viability of a federal republican system like that of the United States, but he opted for a confederate monarchical system of government. This apparent abandonment of his principles, strongly criticized, must be analyzed in light of the prevailing situation, the struggle against Peru (the center of viceregal power), and peninsular threats to dispatch a powerful fleet.

Supported by his officers and the Chilean people, San Martín, joined at sea by Admiral Lord Cochrane, arrived in Peru on 13 September 1820. The favorable strategic situation compensated for the numerical inferiority of his forces. The loss of Chile had important psychological and military consequences for the royalists, now on the defensive. Internationally, Rafael de Riego y Núñez (a liberal officer in command of the Spanish fleet that was to go to America) rose up against Ferdinand VII, thereby diminishing this threat. On 28 July 1821, occupying Lima, the capital of Peru, San Martín proclaimed independence. Faced with the absence of a local patriot to lead the government, however, the Liberator accepted the office of Protector of Peru until the war ended.

In Peru, San Martín put his political thought into action. In various documents, he expressed his position as an enlightened man. Surpassing this exceptional situation, he convened a sovereign congress and returned to his condition as citizen. He insisted on securing Peru's freedom and its legislative autonomy. Essentially democratic, he recognized the congress as sovereign and demonstrated his respect for public opinion as an important republican resource.

Retirement. San Martín's political thought, centered on the Statute of 1821, included the separation of powers in the organization of the state and recognized the rights of its inhabitants. The Statute recognized liberty, security, property, life, and freedom of expression. In the social realm, it suppressed servitude and slavery, depriving the proprietary classes of the right to treat others as chattel.

In 1822, San Martín resigned from military and public life, leaving Bolívar in command. Later that year, he left Peru with an organized but unstable state. When taking his leave, he pointed out: "My promise . . . is fulfilled, to bring about independence . . . The presence of a successful soldier, no matter how altruistic he may be, is threatening to States."

San Martín returned to Europe, where he worked diplomatically to obtain recognition of South American independence. He returned to Latin America in 1829; from his ship, he painfully observed a civil war and the absence of constitutional government, supplanted by a despot. San Martín decided to stay away permanently.

In this period, his political thought turned pragmatic and leaned "toward a vigorous military government." His letters reveal hostility toward the masses, the lower class, and demagogues. Fearing anarchy, he justified any means to pacify the country. He delivered his saber to the despot, Juan Manuel de Rosas, an inexplicable act for a liberal republican. He also placed himself at Rosas's service during the Anglo-French blockade of the River Plate (1838), putting sovereignty before personal conflicts.

San Martín was a man of great affections and bitter enemies, with the uncertainties of every human being concerning health and money; however, he was an exceptional man who renounced the luxury of power and refused to participate in civil wars; and he was a visionary with respect to the integration of South America. As an enlightened statesman, he contributed to making public law for liberated peoples and international law that rejected conquest and colonialism. His objective was for peoples "to be lifted up from colonial depression to the dignity of free nations."

[*See also* Latin America; *and* Republicanism, *subentry on* Latin America.]

BIBLIOGRAPHY

Acevedo, Edberto Oscar. "San Martín y el sistema político de Cuyo (1815–1817)." *Revista de Academia Nacional de la Historia. Investigaciones y Ensayos* (Buenos Aires) 31 (1981), 115–155.

Acevedo, Edberto Oscar. "San Martín y su ideario hacia 1810." *Revista de Academia Nacional de la Historia. Investigaciones y Ensayos* (Buenos Aires) 41 (1991), 89–105.

Assadourian, Carlos Sempat, Guillermo Beato, and José Carlos Chiaramonte. *Argentina: De la Conquista a la Independencia.*

Buenos Aires, 1987. Contains an important chapter written by José Carlos Chiaramonte concerning the enlightened phase, 1750–1806, particularly the sections dedicated to economics, society, culture, and ideology. The author's interpretation of the Ibero-American Enlightenment is especially interesting.

Bethell, Leslie, ed. *The Cambridge History of Latin America*, vol. 3, *From Independence to c. 1870*. Cambridge, 1985. Spanish edition: *Historia de América Latina*, vol. 5, *La Independencia*. Barcelona, 1991. Outstanding for its objectivity and presentation of multiple perspectives, especially chapters 1, 3, and 5.

Corbiére, Emilio J. *La masonería política y sociedades secretas en la Argentina*. Buenos Aires, 1998. Comprehensive, up-to-date study on freemasonry in the River Plate region; scientifically investigates historical sources as well as myths concerning the Fraternity.

Floria, Carlos Alberto, and César A. García Belsunce. *Historia de los argentinos*, vol. 1. Buenos Aires, 1975. General text recommended for those unacquainted with the topic.

Halperín Donghi, Tulio. *Revolución y guerra: Formación de una élite dirigente en la Argentina criolla*. 3d ed. Buenos Aires, 1994. English edition: *Politics Economics and Society in Argentina in the Revolutionary Period*. Translated by Richard Southern. Cambridge, Mass., 1975. Important book by one of the best historians of Argentine history. Chapters 1, 2, 3, 4, and 7 are recommended.

Halperín Donghi, Tulio. *Tradición política española e ideología revolucionaria de Mayo*. Buenos Aires, 1985. Chapters 4, on the disintegration of the Spanish monarchy's political tradition, and 5, on the emergence of the Spanish monarchy's crisis, are necessary reading.

López Rosas, José Rafael. "San Martín y sus ideas políticas." *Revista Universidad* (Santa Fe, Argentina) 90 (1978), 93–143.

Mitre, Bartolomé. *Historia de San Martín y de la emancipación sudamericana*. Buenos Aires, 1940. Well-documented, classic, traditional history by a nineteenth-century historian.

Romero, José Luis, and Romero Luis Alberto. *Pensamiento político de la emancipación*. Caracas, 1977. Fundamental book given the stature of these historians as well as their treatment of the topic in the preface.

Romero, José Luis. *La experiencia argentina y otros ensayos*. Mexico City, 1989. First-rate Argentine historian; chapters 2, on culture, and 3, on ideas—especially the section concerning the encyclopedia and liberal ideas—are outstanding.

Rouquié, Alain, and Jean Touchard. *L'Argentine*. Paris, 1984. The first chapter on Argentine space is particularly recommended.

Guillermo Ignacio Salvatierra
Judith Casali de Babot
Translated from Spanish by Scott Sessions

SANTA CRUZ Y ESPEJO, FRANCISCO JAVIER EUGENIO DE. *See* Espejo, Eugenio de.

SATIRE. Satire is militant irony, and irony honed the Enlightenment. Satire was also a risky business. Satirists were hounded, imprisoned, occasionally executed; they saw their works banned and burned. Today, such masterpieces as Jonathan Swift's *Gulliver's Travels* (1726), Voltaire's *Candide* (1759), or Lord Byron's *Don Juan* (1819–1824)—fantastic travelogues in which mock heroes are used to indict the status quo back home—still command an appreciative audience among those unfamiliar

with the vicissitudes of their authors. Denis Diderot diverted himself, anonymously but remuneratively, with *Les bijoux in discrets* (1748), a libertine tale whose exotic settings barely conceal his innuendoes about the French monarchy or his lampoons on contemporary scholars. From Pierre Bayle's *Dictionnaire* (1697) to Edward Gibbon's *History of the Decline and Fall of the Roman Empire* (1776–1788), great works of nonfiction also bristle with ironical barbs. Some practitioners of Enlightenment satire, however, are now scarcely remembered as being such. Benjamin Franklin (1706–1790) enriched his career as a philanthropist, scientist, and statesman with myriad bagatelles, ranging from a paean to "Old Mistresses" to a scientific spoof on how to perfume farts. Franklin also lobbed revolutionary squibs, which, like those of satirists everywhere, upset the old world order; not one of these prose works, however, met the strict definitions of satire in the era's reference books.

In *A Dictionary of the English Language* (1755), Samuel Johnson (1709–1784) defined *satire* as "A poem in which wickedness or folly is censured. Proper *satire* is distinguished by the generality of the reflections, from a *lampoon* which is aimed against a particular person; but they are too frequently confounded." In Diderot's *Encyclopédie*, Louis de Jaucourt (1704–1779) defined *satyre* as a "poem in which one directly attacks vice, or some reprehensible absurdity." Such "trivial" varieties of satire as "burlesque," "parody," and "travesty" were relegated by the editors to shorter entries, where they were glossed as *belles lettres* rather than as *poesie* proper. During the Enlightenment, proper satire demanded thumping sentiments delivered by long poems in heroic couplets (rhymed iambic pentameter). The preferred models were provided by the Latin poets Horace (65–8 BCE) and Juvenal (c. 60–c. 130 CE), to whom Jaucourt devoted much of his six-page entry on *satyre*. The acidulous verse epigrams of Juvenal's friend Martial (c. 38–c. 104 CE) did not meet such strict definitions, although the influence of Martial's brevity sharpened the antithesis and poise of the heroic couplet.

Poets like John Dryden (1631–1700) did not find such definitions cramped or dogmatic, for they had cut their literary teeth while translating Latin poetry at school. In *A Discourse Concerning the Original and Progress of Satire* (1693)—prefixed to a series of vigorous translations from Juvenal—Dryden agreed that the poet must "give his reader some one precept of moral virtue, and caution him against some one particular vice or folly." Yet for *Absalom and Achitophel* (1681), his satirical triumph, Dryden used lampoons to slice up adversaries of England's Charles II. "There is," Dryden rationalized in his *Discourse*, "a vast difference betwixt the slovenly butchering of a man, and the fineness of a stroke, that separates the head from the body and leaves it standing in its place." Thus did Dryden reconcile lampoon with satire proper; thus did he wield the radicals' weapons with a conservative edge.

Identifying the "original" of satire fascinated poets and scholars alike. Two etymologies still vied, as they had in Rome and during the Renaissance. Was the word *satire* (Latin, *satira* or *satura*) derived from *satyrus*, Greek for the semidivine goat-man—phallic and feral, but quick-witted and smart-mouthed—who roamed a mythical country-side? (Europe's proto-satirists, scholars now suggest, were bards who pronounced curses against rival tribes or engaged in other forms of magical wordplay, such as "rhyming rats to death.") Or did *satire* derive from *satura lanx*, Latin for a large "mixed dish"? This was originally a cold collation of the year's first fruits and vegetables, which rustic worshippers in Italy offered to Ceres and Bacchus. These festivities attracted bawdy, scoffing ver-sifiers whose descendants migrated to Rome, and satire became an urban genre. Scholars today support the second etymology—already endorsed by Dryden, Johnson, and Jaucourt—and complement it with *satura* as "sausage" or "stuffing." As the Romans knew, formal poetic satire could be served hot and meaty as well as cold and vegetarian. It was heterogeneous in content; its intensity and plots varied; but it was long and metrically rigorous. Horace boasted that satire "was poetry untouched by the Greeks"; indeed, he has been credited with defining its genre for Rome. The etymology from *satyrus*, however, has been an irresistible pun for cocky, cursing satirists.

Feelings of belatedness about the Greeks and Romans during the Enlightenment might be assuaged by dedica-tion to a genre that had been new even in later antiquity. It was, moreover, Rome rather than Athens that resembled Amsterdam or Paris or London. "Imitations" of Horace and Juvenal—imaginative reworkings rather than literal translations—proliferated across Europe as neoclassicists diagnosed, sometimes formulaically, the ills of their own societies. Samuel Johnson eschewed lampoon in his gruff poem "The Vanity of Human Wishes" (1749, 1755) and subtitled it "The Tenth Satire of Juvenal Imitated." Today, most readers ignore this signpost and savor Johnson's generality of reflection not as literary imitation but as pro-found personal wisdom memorably expressed. It is both.

Nicholas Boileau (1636–1711) pioneered the Enlight-enment art of urbane imitation, reconciling Horace's affable reproofs with Juvenal's bitter diatribes. In peren-nial comparisons, Horace rather than Juvenal usually took the laurel because he offered the Enlightenment a model—conversational, polite, and reasonable—for cri-tiques of society, and Jaucourt celebrated Boileau as the modern Horace. Like Horace, Boileau presented his "Art of Poetry" as an elegant poem (1674). Boileau also pio-neered the mock epic or "heroi-comic poem," in which

audience laughter is provoked by incongruities between a parochial squabble and the Homeric and Virgilian grandeur used to depict it. In *Le lutrin* (1674, 1683), Boileau employed heroic and mythical descriptions to chronicle a tiff between priests over the placement of a lectern (*lutrin*). Boileau's imitations, literary criticism, and mock epic were praised everywhere, from London to St. Petersburg.

Alexander Pope (1688–1744) was the greatest formal verse satirist of the Enlightenment. Working within a literary milieu like Boileau's, Pope achieved fame with his precocious *Essay on Criticism* (1711) and with *The Rape of the Lock* (1712, 1714), a glittering mock epic about a spat between empty-headed beaux and belles. Late in his career, Pope polished his *Imitations of Horace* (1733–1738), but he had come to distrust the Roman satirist: "His sly, polite insinuating style / Could please at court and make Augustus smile." Pope was not alone when he descried behind Horace's own smiles a *faux*-satirist toadying to a Roman tyrant. Voltaire and Diderot found themselves in comparable quandaries, whether chatting with Louis XV or enjoying the hospitality of "enlightened despots" in Prussia and Russia. Urbanity revealed its ethi-cal limitations. What modern folly and knavery demanded, many readers agreed, was not Horatian raillery but the snarl of Juvenal's unaccommodated goat-man. Juvenal's fangs impressed many readers as genuinely satyric, even when they were coated with Johnson's generality of Chris-tian reflection.

Pope worked for many years on *The Dunciad* (c. 1719–1743), a satire centered on literary warfare in Lon-don; finally he twisted his many lampoons on hacks and politicians into the stunning form of an apocalyptic mock epic (1743). Its last line—"And Universal Darkness buries all"—distills Pope's skepticism about Enlighten-ment rationality, theodicy, and belief in perfectibility (in all of which he had once dabbled). Ultimately, Pope embraced the Christian pessimism of his friend Jonathan Swift (1667–1745). An Irish parson and oddball conser-vative who proclaimed that "Fair Liberty was all his cry," Swift commemorated, in his self-penned epitaph, the Juve-nalian "savage indignation" that had fueled both his prose and poetry.

Yet Swift also reveled in the rough-and-tumble of popular culture: fairground barkers, freaks, puppets, astrologers, hack writers, sex workers, peddlers, quack doctors, revivalist preachers. This motley crew barely impinged on formal verse satire, but its members were spotlighted by Lucian (c. 115–c. 180 CE) in the dis-dainful prose of *Alexander, or The Sham Prophet*. Lucian was a "Menippean" satirist who indelibly influenced not only Renaissance satirists like Erasmus (1466–1536), Rabelais (c. 1494–c. 1553), and Cervantes (1547–1616) but also their many Enlightenment disciples. The works of Menippus (c. 300–c. 250 BCE)—which influenced Lucian—are now lost, but they confirm that, when broadly construed, Greek satire antedated Roman claims to primacy in the genre. Satire, indeed, is a universal impulse. Lucian's *Dialogues*, his picaresque romance *The Ass*, and the phantasmagoric voyage of his *True Story* offer "Menippean" gallimaufries of carnivalesque fun, learned parody, lampoon, and poetical gobbets.

Crucial to the rise of Enlightenment satire are the Menippean genres of travesty and burlesque. In *Virgile travesti* (Virgil Travestied, 1649–1659), Paul Scarron (1610–1660) chose a form of "imitation" different from that of Boileau's mock-epic. Instead, Scarron reduced Virgil's grandeur to knockabout farce, delivered in jogtrot octosyllabic couplets. In *Hudibras* (1663, 1664, 1678), Samuel Butler (1613–1680) used the same meter for a sprawling mock romance in which he simultaneously satirized England's Puritan Revolution (1640–1660) and the absurdities of romance as a genre. Despite the continuing popularity of travesty and burlesque during the Enlightenment, high-minded poets and critics soon rejected such works as embarrassingly "low." As satiric medicine approved for vice and folly, the heroic couplet of formal satire replaced the vaudevillean styles of Scarron and Butler.

In the kaleidoscopic *oeuvre* of Swift—which encompassed penny lampoons, a mock-statistical exhortation to cannibalism, irreligious tracts, and hudibrastic imitations of Horace—Menippean fun collided with Juvenalian savagery to beget one of the world's greatest satirists. The mendacious narrator of Lucian's *True History* and the long-suffering Lucius of *The Ass* provided Swift and Voltaire with cues for their guileless protagonists in *Gulliver's Travels* and *Candide*. The Enlightenment vogue for homespun travelers who voyage to far-fetched places was complemented by the introduction to Europe of foreign visitors—like those in Montesquieu's *Lettres persanes* (Persian Letters, 1721), anonymously published in Amsterdam—who record their bafflement at the customs, politics, and religion they find there.

Enlightenment satirists often wrote pseudonymously, and Swift took such indirection to new heights, most famously in the asinine voice of Gulliver, who goes insane. In *A Tale of a Tub* (1704, 1710) Swift mimicked a meretricious literary critic with no name: starving, syphilitic, deranged by his failure to save the world, logorrheic but descanting upon "nothing." Whatever Swift's personal respect for the ancients, he ventriloquized his disorderly volume as the mad diary of a modern nobody who reduces all politics, philosophy, religion, and literature to yesterday's mountebankery, or to a Bedlamite vaporing that rises from groin and anus. Instantly notorious, the *Tale*

Candide at Supper. "Candide's Supper with Abbé Perigourdin and the Marquise de Parolignac," engraving by Charles Monnet from Voltaire's *Candide* (Paris, 1778). (Pierpont Morgan Library/Art Resource, NY.)

was soon translated into French, German, and Dutch; its bizarrerie has inspired James Joyce, Samuel Beckett, and Vladimir Nabokov.

Swift's zest for culinary (and, thus, excretory) metaphors is integral to satire, but his scatology was hyperbolic. Many Enlightenment satirists may seem "anti-Enlightenment" in emphasizing how bodily functions trump progress and rationality. Byron exploited sexual congress thus in *Don Juan*. Food and sex (and their consequences) were repeatedly used by the period's engravers when caricaturing the rich and powerful. The path toward the guillotine for Louis XVI and Marie Antoinette was littered with rank cartoons.

Because verbal satire does not have an intrinsic plot or denouement—unlike epic, tragedy, comedy, or the novel—parody proved especially important. Satire insinuated itself parasitically into other narratives or genres, even when its authors followed recipes for formal verse satire: in search of plots, even Boileau and Pope turned to mock epic. Swift's *Tale* includes a mock epic in prose, *The Battle of the Books*, but it primarily leeches off catch-penny and prolix volumes by hacks and quacks. In *Die Freuden des jungen Werthers* (1775)—an Enlightenment salvo against the new vogue for sentimentalism—Christoph Friedrich Nicolai (1733–1811) recalled the standards of Boileau when he parodied *Die Leiden des jungen Werthers* (1774), a proto-Romantic novel with which Goethe (1749–1832) had made Europeans weep. *Gulliver's Travels*, *Les bijoux indiscrets*, *Candide*, and *Don Juan* all required readers to hark back to travel books, romances, and Oriental tales. Invoking "Ye shades of Pope and Dryden," Byron propelled Don Juan through a rambling plot enlivened by goofy hudibrastic rhymes; Byron was a political radical but a literary conservative.

Franklin's bagatelles also depend on parody. His "Old Mistresses Apologue" (1745) masquerades, bawdily, as the familiar letter of moral advice to a younger man. His Swiftian treatise on perfuming farts, "To the Royal Academy of*****" (c. 1781) mimics the scientific treatises "of this enlightened age." *Poor Richard's Almanack* (1733–1758) is, however, unique. Riffing on Swift's counterfeit role as Isaac Bickerstaff (1708–1709)—a pasticheur of astrological almanacs—the pseudonymous Franklin converted the mock genre back into best-selling real calendars, rendered unique by his wholesale infusion of old proverbs drolly stropped to a new edge. Unlike Swift's Bickerstaff or the almanac-makers of the French Revolution, "Poor Richard" avoided political satire.

In his almanac, Franklin dispensed miniature exercises in Horatian raillery that are now better known than the razor-sharp maxims of La Rochefoucauld (1613–1680), a French aristocrat, or the blunter aphorisms of Georg Christoph Lichtenberg (1742–1799), a German scientist and art critic. Whether modeled on folk traditions or on Martial's epigrams, the adage or *bon mot* represents a satiric genre that was well whetted during the Enlightenment. However defined, satire flourished throughout the long eighteenth century.

[*See also* Franklin, Benjamin; Literary Genres; Pope, Alexander; Swift, Jonathan; *and* Voltaire.]

BIBLIOGRAPHY

Bourguinat, Élisabeth. *Le siècle de persiflage.* Paris, 1998. Provocative analysis of the social contexts of satire and mockery in eighteenth-century France.

Carretta, Vincent. *The Snarling Muse: Verbal and Visual Satire from Pope to Churchill.* Philadelphia, 1983. A detailed, well-illustrated study that sets English literary satire within the context of contemporary satirical engravings.

Carretta, Vincent. *George III and the Satirists from Hogarth to Byron.* Athens, Ga., 1990. Another meticulous study that shows how George III became the butt of verbal and visual satirists.

Coffey, Michael. *Roman Satire.* 2d ed. London, 1989. An authoritative and readable introduction that establishes the origins and practice of ancient satire as those were understood (and sometimes misunderstood) during the Enlightenment.

Darnton, Robert, and Daniel E. Roche, eds. *Revolution in Print: The Press in France 1775–1800.* Berkeley and Los Angeles, 1989. Contributors explore how satire in all its forms contributed to the flood of print that helped sweep away the ancien régime.

Elliott, Robert C. *The Power of Satire: Magic, Ritual, Art.* Princeton, N.J., 1960. Anthropological perspectives on the origins of satire that brilliantly illuminate its practice during the Enlightenment.

Frye, Northrop. *Anatomy of Criticism: Four Essays.* Princeton, N.J., 1957; repr. with an introduction by Harold Bloom, Princeton, N.J., 2000. Classic and influential commentary from a master critic, developing his conception of satire as "militant irony."

Hunt, Lynn, ed. *The Invention of Pornography: Obscenity and the Origins of Modernity, 1500–1800.* New York, 1993. Contributors explore the impact of pornography on revolutionary satire throughout Enlightenment Europe.

Lord, George DeForest, et al., eds. *Poems on Affairs of State: Augustan Satirical Verse, 1660–1714.* 7 vols. New Haven, Conn., 1963–1975. Comprehensive, well-annotated collection of formal and informal satires on a turbulent period in English politics.

Pocock, Gordon. *Boileau and the Nature of Neo-Classicism.* Cambridge, 1980. A valuable introduction to a poet not much read today.

Rawson, Claude. *Satire and Sentiment, 1660–1830.* Cambridge, 1994. Lively essays on "patrician culture in decline" include commentary on individual satirists from the earl of Rochester (1647–1680) to Jane Austen (1775–1817).

Real, Hermann J. "A Dish Plentifully Stor'd': Jonathan Swift and the Evaluation of Satire." In *Jonathan Swift: Selected Essays,* edited by Hermann J. Real, pp. 43–64. Dublin, 2001. A fecund survey by the editor of *Swift Studies,* invaluable for its German bibliography.

Relihan, Joel C. *Ancient Menippean Satire.* Baltimore, 1993. A comprehensive survey of nonformal satire (the particulars of which are still debated) in the classical world from Menippus to Boethius (c. 480–524 CE).

Rogers, Pat. *Grub Street: Studies in a Subculture.* London, 1972. A classic and readable study of the disreputable world of London's literary hacks, mocked by Swift and Pope, but a world from which great writers like Samuel Johnson also emerged.

Stallybrass, Peter, and Allon White. *The Politics and Poetics of Transgression.* Ithaca, N.Y., 1986. A dazzling socio-historical study of popular culture and satire in Europe, 1550–1900, that employs innovative theories of the "carnivalesque" from the Russian theorist Mikhail Bakhtin (1895–1975).

Weinbrot, Howard D. *The Formal Strain: Studies in Augustan Imitation and Satire.* Chicago, 1969. The authoritative study of formal verse satire in England that also discusses its classical and European contexts.

Weinbrot, Howard D. *Eighteenth-Century Satire: Essays on Text and Context from Dryden to Peter Pindar.* Cambridge, 1988. A wide-ranging collection of scholarly essays that explore both satiric theory and individual authors.

H. J. ORMSBY-LENNON

SCANDINAVIA. The eighteenth-century courses of the Scandinavian archrivals, Sweden (then including Finland) and the dual kingdoms of Denmark and Norway showed many similarities. Exhausted after the great Nordic war of 1700–1721, they concentrated on peaceful relations and on internal matters; the period from 1720 to 1800 in Denmark was aptly called *den lange fred* ("the long peace"). Sweden, though less inclined to give up its ambitions as a great power, mainly lived in peace with its neighbors, except for a misfired attack on Russia in 1740, a negligible participation on the French side in the Seven Years' War, and Gustav III's fruitless campaign against Russia (1788–1790).

Economy. For both countries, the century was a time for charting natural resources, for industrial experiments, and mercantilist privileges, monopolies, and tariffs. From the 1760s on, agricultural development also stirred enthusiasm among both government officials and country squires, partly in response to the French Physiocrats, but more influenced by the English example. Two agrarian reformers with an English orientation were the Dane Gregers Begtrup (1769–1841), a prolific writer on husbandry, and Baron Rutger Maclean, the driving force behind a far-reaching Swedish enclosure act in 1803. This was also a time for examining the human capital, then scarce in the north: by midcentury, the two monarchies harbored only about four million inhabitants in an immense area stretching from northern Germany to the North Cape, and from Iceland to Finland's Karelian frontier. Especially in the far northern regions, vast areas were nearly unpeopled. Cities were few and mostly small, seldom with more than a few thousand inhabitants: as late as 1800, the largest community of Iceland, Reykjavík, had about 300 inhabitants; the largest town in Finland, Åbo, numbered 11,000. The main exceptions were the Danish capital, Copenhagen, with around 100,000 inhabitants, and its Swedish counterpart, Stockholm, with around 75,000. Communications were often hindered by the harsh climate; the Swedish capital often was cut off from Finland during winter, when ice and storms made it impossible to cross the Baltic Sea. News from Copenhagen was usually a week old by the time it reached Stockholm; from Paris and London, it normally took at least three or four weeks to reach the Swedish capital.

Intellectual Life. Nevertheless, Scandinavia, was not merely a distant and impassive spectator of intellectual currents on the Continent. The educated classes were cosmopolitan, often fluent in at least French and German. Both Denmark and Sweden possessed German territories which to some extent functioned as bridgeheads for new ideas. Denmark, making use of its policy of neutrality, was a leading shipping nation, with wealthy companies trading all over the world; Sweden lagged not far behind, and from 1731 on, it had a successful East Indian Company. Young noblemen routinely went on the Grand Tour to Paris, London, the Netherlands, and Italy. Accompanied by tutors, many of them also visited university towns such as Leiden, Leipzig, Halle, Jena, and Göttingen. A cautious estimate of the number of Swedish scholars and scientists studying or teaching at Georg August University in Göttingen after 1737 exceeds one hundred. Swedish scientists made expeditions to America, Arabia, Sierra Leone, South Africa, China, and Japan. Naturalists trained by Carolus Linnaeus gained especially high reputations; Joseph Banks, on his and James Cook's exploratory circumnavigation in 1768–1771, engaged the Linnaean natural scientist Daniel Solander. Many Danes distinguished themselves in the humanities, including the erudite Hans Gram, Jacob Langebek, P. J. Suhm, and Rasmus Nyerup.

In Scandinavia, science and learning—particularly with an unabashedly utilitarian stance—were favored by government, aristocracy, and plutocracy alike. Learned societies and academies were established in both countries, meeting a long-felt need for utilitarian and applied science that the more conservative universities could not satisfy. The Royal Swedish Academy of Sciences, the bastion of the early Swedish Enlightenment, was founded for this purpose in 1739. In Denmark, the Royal Academy of Sciences and Letters started its sessions in 1742. In Norway, the Royal Society of Science and Letters was founded (1760) in Trondheim on the initiative of Bishop Johan Ernst Gunnerus. The Scandinavian clergy played an important role in eighteenth-century science, promoting inoculation against smallpox, making astronomical and botanical observations, and providing examples of scientific farming to their parishioners, as well as collecting statistical data for the authorities. In Denmark, the learned Pietist bishop Erik Pontoppidan (1698–1764) played a key role, editing the important journal *Danmarks og Norges oekonomiske Magazin* (1757–1764). In Sweden, Anders Chydenius (1729–1803), a vicar, wrote profusely on economic subjects from a liberal point of view; he also fought for freedom of the press, religious tolerance, and social justice.

Sweden and Denmark were quite receptive to French and German culture. News from Paris concerning arts and letters was always in great demand. Bayle was a favorite author of the poets Ludvig Holberg and Hedvig Charlotta Nordenflycht. Montesquieu's theory of the influence of climate on political and social conditions, which evoked a Scandinavian past of strong, brave and uncorrupted inhabitants, made a deep impact on Scandinavian historiography, which it reached through the Swiss historian Paul-Henry Mallet, who during the 1750s worked in Copenhagen at the invitation of the cosmopolitan, noble Bernstorff family. Voltaire was widely read, and many of his works were either reprinted or translated in Scandinavia—some seventy editions from the 1730s to 1800. The Encyclopédises and Rousseau also found an eager, if not always admiring, public. There is evidence that Helvétius's

De l'esprit was debated even in the provincial press in the 1770s.

Religion and Philosophy. German influences were even more important. Denmark and Sweden were both rigidly Lutheran, but the Pietist and Moravian movements also made their marks. In the late 1720s, the radical Pietist Johann Conrad Dippel visited Copenhagen and Stockholm and gained numerous disciples, and when Ludwig von Zinzendorf first arrived in Denmark, he was received kindly at court, making it possible for him to launch missionary expeditions to Greenland and the Danish West Indies. The second half of the eighteenth century saw a vogue for more rationalist theologians and biblical scholars, such as Johann David Michaelis and Johann Loren Mosheim in Göttingen, and Johann Saloma Semler in Halle. Georg Joachim Zollikofer and Johann Joachim Spalding, who stressed the more moral and practical aspects of Christianity, won support among reform-minded pastors.

Philosophy was long dominated by Christian Wolff's Leibnizian view; his books, subtly harmonizing revelation and reason, were for decades obligatory reading at the universities. At Uppsala University, their influence declined to an appreciable extent only in the 1770s and 1780s, owing in part to the increasing popularity of British empiricists like John Locke, David Hume, Adam Smith, and Francis Hutcheson. In the 1790s, Kant's writings—under somewhat tumultuous intellectual and political circumstances—regained German supremacy in philosophy in Sweden. Philosophy at the academies of Denmark was constantly German in spirit, the sole exception being Johannes Boye, whose *Statens ven* (A Friend of Polity, 1792–1814) offered an empiricist and eudaimonic philosophy.

Influence of the Enlightenment. From around 1750, the Enlightenment became less controversial in Scandinavia and was increasingly embraced by officials, clergy, physicians, and other intellectuals. Enlightenment ideas were transmitted by an emerging press and were discussed in clubs, salons, and coffeehouses. The universities, though frequently mocked by wits and poets, were open to new ideas; the greatest author of the period, Ludvig Holberg, who enjoying great popularity in Sweden as well in his native Denmark, was a professor at the university in Copenhagen. The success of the Scandinavian Enlightenment was undoubtedly due to the relative caution displayed by the majority of its adherents. They promoted progress, lampooned prejudices, worked on utilitarian projects, tried to raise civic spirit and morale, hailed freedom of the press, asserted the rights of the individual, and increasingly harbored democratic ideas. But at the same time, they were content to work within a hierarchical society; thus, experiments in the 1770s in Denmark and in Sweden to govern in accordance to the doctrines of enlightened despotism were initially quite popular.

Scandinavian proponents of Enlightenment ideals were similarly wary in matters of theology. They might castigate Roman Catholicism as superstitious and denounce the deeds of the Inquisition, and they might also cherish tolerance, but at the same time they might attack freethinkers and materialists. Protestant faith represented man's liberation and furthermore was compatible with reason. By the end of the eighteenth century, enlightened Scandinavians generally believed that Luther had secured enlightenment for their fortunate part of the world. When the Swedes, in 1793, commemorated the bicentennial of the rescue of the true faith, it generated a host of orations that more or less overtly equated enlightenment with Lutheranism.

In the last decades of the eighteenth century, popular instruction too was increasingly equated with enlightenment. The immediate inspiration came from Germany and writers such as Christian Gotthilf Salzmann, Rudolf Zacharias Becker, and Joachim Heinrich Campe, though domestic efforts to spread knowledge were by no means insignificant. Denmark and Sweden boasted a high level of literacy; it is estimated that as much as 80 percent of the Swedish population could read by the end of the century. The Swedish Royal Academy of Sciences, having received monopoly on the distribution of almanacs in 1747, championed popular education by inserting instructive essays on medicine, farming, and other practical subjects in every new edition. By the end of the century, this popularizing tendency had gained momentum. A growing number of books and journals emphatically dedicated to "universal enlightenment" were published. An important figure in this context was the Danish chaplain to the king and energetic spokesman of rational theology, Christian Bastholm, who wrote *Philosophie for Ulaerde* (Philosophy for Unschooled People, 1787), soon reprinted and translated into Swedish and German.

Sweden. There were, of course, important differences between the two archrivals, Sweden and Denmark. Particularly conspicuous were their different constitutional bases. While eighteenth-century Denmark always remained absolutist in principle, Sweden (including Finland in a unitary kingdom) in the wake of the Great Nordic War embarked on a political experiment that gave ultimate power to the Riksdag (parliament), composed of four estates—nobility, clergy, burghers, and peasants. This system—dominated by two parties, the Francophile Hats and the Russophile Caps—functioned more or less successfully until Gustav III's coup d'état in 1772.

Parliamentary in character, the whole era preceding Gustavus III's intervention is called the Age of Liberty. It has proved difficult to assess. Some scholars have dismissed it as oligarchic; others have hailed it as a precursor to later democracies. Initially, the high nobility had a dominant position, but burghers and non-noble persons of standing, as well as peasants, gained ground. (For a nuanced account, see the work of Michael Roberts.) The Swedish experiment earned recognition by the philosophes: Mably called Sweden's constitution a "masterpiece of modern legislation"; for Rousseau, it was "an example of perfection"; and Voltaire declared Sweden to be "the freest country in the world"—even though he would later welcome Gustav's seizure of power. Modeling himself as an enlightened despot, Gustav embarked on an ambitious program of reforms, reorganized the civil administration, encouraged free trade in grain, suppressed guild restrictions, abolished torture, and made the penal laws more humane. In 1781, he proclaimed limited toleration for non-Lutheran Christians. Freedom of the press was a lower priority for him: a liberal press law passed in 1766 was narrowed step by step during his reign.

Although opinion is divided on the party politics of the Age of Liberty, the cultural achievements of this era are unanimously praised. Scientists made important discoveries and corrected misunderstandings in a way that attracted international attention. Their unrivaled leader was Carolus Linnaeus, whose taxonomic system proved indispensable to generations of naturalists, but many other scientists earned recognition abroad. The astronomer Anders Celsius (1701–1744) helped Maupertuis prove the Newtonian view of the universe and wrote popular science in the vein of Fontenelle. His younger colleague Pehr Wilhelm Wargentin (1749–1783), secretary of the Royal Academy of Sciences, used his computational skills from the 1750s on to make a pioneering contribution to population statistics. The physicist Johan Carl Wilcke (1732–1796) became a leading authority on electricity, siding with Benjamin Franklin against Jean-Antoine Nollet. His tutor, Samuel Klingenstierna, was one of the most skilled mathematicians of his time. Also mathematically gifted were the ingenious technician and inventor Christopher Polhem (1661–1751) and Emanuel Swedenborg, the great mystic who devoted much effort to reconciling faith and science. On the whole, though, the fields of knowledge where Swedish scientists most distinguished themselves belonged to natural history: botany, zoology, geology, and chemistry. The two latter disciplines, of great importance to Sweden's mining industry, attracted such competent men as Torbern Bergman and Carl Wilhelm Scheele. In botany and zoology, Carolus Linnaeus and his disciples dominated the scene; after his death in 1778, his intellectual heritage was carried on primarily by Carl Peter Thunberg (1743–1828).

The Age of Liberty also brought a breakthrough for arts and letters. The work of Count Gustaf Fredrik Gyllenborg bore traces of Montesquieu and Rousseau. Two publishers and journalists contributing to the diffusion of Enlightenment ideas were Lars Salvius and Carl Christopher Gjörwell, whose *Swenska Mercurius* was the best-informed and most reliable magazine of the epoch. A pivotal role was played by Olof von Dalin, a wit who won a public by writing for and editing a weekly, *Then Swenska Argus* (1732–1734), in the manner of Addison and Steele. Later, Dalin shone as a historian; like contemporary academic historians, he stereotyped the Middle Ages as "dark," but he made use of natural science in order to repudiate chauvinist historians who identified Sweden with the legendary Atlantis. Dalin's main rival as a poet was Hedvig Charlotta Nordenflycht, an early feminist writer and a central figure in the literary society Tankebyggarorden.

With the ascendancy of Gustav III, belles-lettres received new impetus, manifest in the foundation of the Swedish Academy in 1786. Its leading members included Johan Henrik Kellgren, poet laureate and a passionate admirer of Voltaire; Nils Rosén von Rosenstein (1752–1824), civil servant and philosopher; and Carl Gustaf Leopold (1756–1829). All Francophiles and men who emphatically allied themselves with Enlightenment ideals, they tried to defend these as well as they could in the wake of the French Revolution and the murder of Gustav III in 1792. Kellgren campaigned in his paper, *Stockholmsposten*, against all tendencies toward superstition and mysticism; in 1789, Rosenstein gave a substantial address on the subject of the Enlightenment to the Royal Swedish Academy of Sciences, published in 1793; and Leopold, after Kellgren's death and the temporary suspension of the Swedish Academy in 1795, managed to preserve some of the force and reputation of the Swedish Enlightenment well into the nineteenth century. These men, it should be stressed, were far from radical; on the contrary, they used every means available to attack "enthusiasm" and Jacobinism. When the otherwise irreverent Kellgren, in the name of the imaginary society Pro Sensu Communi, denounced the Swedenborgians, he ended as an ally of Lutheran orthodoxy.

Denmark and Norway. In the 1780s and 1790s, Swedenborgian heretics as well as the Swedish regicides and other radicals, including the prodigious Thomas Thorild, found refuge in Copenhagen. In these years, the Danish capital was something of a melting pot. In 1770, four years after the same move in Sweden, censorship had been lifted in Denmark as part of Count Struensee's strenuous reform efforts. Freedom of the press here would prove more lasting than its Swedish counterpart, although the upstart Struensee, the physician of the insane King Christian VII, was soon forced out of power and was executed in 1772. He was an easy target, being the queen's lover and of German origin.

The great influence of German culture on Danish life provoked a nationalist movement in Denmark. If the Swedes, despite being called the "Frenchmen of the North," actually were profoundly influenced by German culture, the Danes were even more so. The Danish state, a conglomerate including Norway, Iceland, and Greenland, also controlled the densely populated duchies of Schleswig and Holstein. These German possessions—where the cities of Altona, with its colony of writers, and Kiel, with its university, were bridgeheads for the diffusion of new ideas—gave a German character to eighteenth-century Danish culture that was underlined by the engagement of competent Germans in government service and related occupations. In particular, the noble Bernstorff family, who dominated Danish political life for decades, encouraged writers, artists, scholars, and officials from abroad to settle in Denmark. Among the Germans they supported were the poet Friedrich Klopstock; Georg Christian Oeder, economist, botanist, and author of *Flora Danica*; and Johan Anders Cramer, editor of the weekly *Der Nordische Aufseher* (1758–1761), an instrument of moral education and mouthpiece for the Bernstorff government. The philanthropic pedagogue Johan Bernhard Basedow, professor at Sorö in the 1750s, also enjoyed official support.

This trend provoked a reaction, and the Danish nationalist movement gained strength from midcentury onward. Tyge Rothe, philosopher and tutor to the hereditary prince, published a patriotic treatise, *Tanker om Kiaerlighed til Faedernelandet*, as early as 1759. In 1767, Eiler Hagerup intensified the discussion with his *Brev om Kiaerlighed til Faedernelandet*, in which he maintained that a citizen could only be the product of and loyal to his native land, and attacked the Bernstorffs' protection of Klopstock and other German poets. More quietly, Basedow's colleague at Sorö, Jens Schelderup Sneedorff (1724–1764), cultivated the Danish language in his writings and the weekly *Den Patriotiske Tillskuer*. With Struensee's political ascendancy, nationalist feelings were further roused, ultimately leading to his downfall.

Ove Høegh Guldberg, who succeeded Struensee as Denmark's most forceful political personality, was an eager proponent of these feelings of Danskhed ("Danishness"). His rule, ending in 1784, was characterized by conservative wariness, and many of Struensee's humanitarian reforms were either abolished or suspended. The following years, however, saw a return to reform. In 1788, the peasantry was released from serfdom, and in 1792, slavery was prohibited. Radical writers such as Malte Conrad Bruun and P. A. Heiberg made use of Denmark's liberal press law to denounce inherited nobility and to preach the gospel of political liberty. Religion was under debate; Bruun derided it, and the Norwegian baron Fritz Wedel-Jarlsberg attacked the legitimacy of clergymen. In 1799,

however, these activities came to an end when censorship was tightened and the most radical authors exiled.

Post-Napoleonic Scandinavia. In the dawn of the nineteenth century, the two Scandinavian countries were dragged into the maelstrom of the Napoleonic Wars. Sweden lost Finland to Russia, but under the command of the French Marshall Bernadotte it obtained Norway from Denmark in exchange for its German possessions. The intellectual elites in Norway and Finland, increasingly nationalistic, quickly adapted to the situation and won considerable autonomy for their countries under their new masters.

To the Danes and Swedes, the new situation was less palatable. Revived animosity and mistrust on each side of the Skagerrak and Kattegat would for decades hamper an emerging Pan-Scandinavian cultural life. The Scandinavian Enlightenment, which to many minds perfectly reconciled Lutheran faith and reason, fared better. A generation of Romantic writers debunked the rationalism and freethinking of the eighteenth century, but this did not prevent the continuing influence of Enlightenment civic activism and ideals. That influence is apparent in Sweden's constitution of 1809–1810—in many ways an attempt to apply Montesquieu's theory of balancing powers—and, less theoretically, in the establishment of elementary schools in Denmark in 1814, in economic reforms, and in an increasingly scientific agricultural sector in both countries.

[*See also* Gustav III.]

BIBLIOGRAPHY

Baack, Lawrence J. *Agrarian Reform in Eighteenth-Century Denmark.* Lincoln, Neb., 1977.

Barton, H. Arnold. *Scandinavia in the Revolutionary Era, 1760–1815.* Minneapolis, Minn., 1986. Superficial when depicting the intellectual climate, but valuable for its detailed account of political changes.

Bohnen, Klaus, and Sven Aage Jörgensen, eds. *Der dänishe Gesamtstaat: Kopenhagen, Kiel, Altona.* Tübingen, Germany, 1992. The contributions on Denmark's German duchies are of great interest.

Christensson, Jakob. *Lyckoriket: Studier i svensk upplysning.* Stockholm, 1996. The only synthesis to date on the Enlightenment in Sweden; emphasizes how religion and enlightenment in eighteenth-century Sweden went harmoniously hand in hand; summary in English.

Feldbaek, Ove. "Clash of Cultures in a Conglomerate State: Danes and Germans in 18th Century Denmark." In *Clashes of Cultures: Essays in Honour of Niels Steensgaard*, edited by Jens Christian V. Johansen et al., pp. 80–93. Odense, Denmark, 1992. Good summary of the perspectives in *Dansk identitetshistorie*.

Feldbaek, Ove, ed. *Dansk identitetshistorie.* 4 vols. Copenhagen, 1991–1992. Important collection of texts on the complicated rise of Danish nationalism in opposition to primarily German influences; vols. 1–2 cover the eighteenth century.

Horstbøll, Henrik, and Uffe Østergaard. "Reform and Revolution: The French Revolution and the Case of Denmark." *Scandinavian Journal of History* 15 (1990), 155–179. Brief account of the radicalization of the Danish Enlightenment in the wake of the French Revolution.

Jarrick, Arne. *Back to Modern Reason*. Liverpool, 1998. Translation of *Mot det moderna förnuftet: Johan Hjerpe och andra småborgare i Upplysningstidens Stockholm* (Stockholm, 1992), a history of thought and a bold, though inconclusive, attempt to situate Enlightenment ideas in a bourgeois context.

Lindhardt, Poul Georg. *Skandinavische Kirchengeschichte seit dem 16. Jahrhundert*, vol. 3 of *Die Kirche in ihrer geschichte*, edited by Bernd Moeller. Göttingen, Germany, 1982.

Lindroth, Sten. *Les chemins du savoir en Suède: De la fondation de l'Université d'Upsal à Jacob Berzelius*. Dordrecht, 1988. A collection of essays by Sweden's premier historian of science and ideas; pp. 101–207 give a supreme guide to Swedish science and scholarship in the eighteenth century.

Olsen, Albert. *Danmark-Norge i det 18. arhundrede*. Copenhagen, 1936. Still a useful account of Danish-Norwegian relations.

Roberts, Michael. *The Age of Liberty: Sweden 1719–1772*. Cambridge, 1986.

Sigurdsson, Ingi, ed. *Upplýsingin á Íslandi*. Reykjavik, Iceland, 1990. Contains a brief summary in English.

JAKOB CHRISTENSSON

SCHILLER, FRIEDRICH (1759–1805), German writer.

Johann Christoph Friedrich Schiller was born the son of a low-ranking army officer in Marbach in the state of Württemberg in southwest Germany. At the age of fourteen, he was obliged to become a pupil at the military academy established by Duke Karl Eugen of Württemberg in Stuttgart, from which he emerged as a military doctor. After the extraordinary success on the Mannheim stage of his first play, *Die Räuber* (*The Robbers*, 1781), and forbidden by Karl Eugen to pursue his literary aspirations, Schiller fled in 1782 to Mannheim in the Palatinate, where he was eventually engaged for a year (1783–1784) at the Mannheim National Theater as resident playwright. His next two plays, *Die Verschwörung des Fiesco zu Genua* (The Conspiracy of Fiesco at Genoa, 1783) and *Kabale und Liebe* (Intrigue and Love, 1784) were performed there. After the lapse of his contract he was rescued by the generosity of four admirers from Leipzig, one of whom, Christian Gottfried Körner, became his patron until, in 1787, Schiller moved to Weimar. In the course of completing a fourth drama, *Don Carlos* (1787), he turned to historiography and it was on the strength of his *Geschichte des Abfalls der vereinigten Niederlande von der spanischen Regierung* (History of the Revolt of the United Netherlands against Spanish Rule, 1788) that he was appointed to a chair of history at the University of Jena in 1789. A severe illness in 1791 left his health permanently damaged, but a three-year pension from Danish patrons allowed him to recover sufficiently to complete his *Geschichte des Dreissigjährigen Krieges* (History of the Thirty Years' War, 1790–1793) and to devote himself to the study of Kant, whose moral and aesthetic theories profoundly influenced him (see

Friedrich Schiller. (Prints and Photographs Division, Library of Congress.)

in particular *Über Anmut und Würde* [On Grace and Dignity, 1793] and *Briefe über die ästhetische Erziehung des Menschen* [On the Aesthetic Education of Man, 1794]). His last great critical work, *Über naive und sentamentalische Dichtung* (On Naïve and Sentimental Poetry, 1795–1796), was prompted in part by his close friendship and literary alliance from 1794 onward with Johann Wolfgang von Goethe with whom he created the corpus of critical and creative works known collectively as Weimar Classicism. With the three-part drama *Wallenstein* (1799) Schiller returned to writing plays. In 1799, he moved from Jena to Weimar and completed *Maria Stuart* (1800), *Die Jungfrau von Orleans* (The Maid of Orleans, 1801), *Die Braut von Messina* (The Bride of Messina, 1803), and *Wilhelm Tell* (1804) before his death on 9 May 1805. Schiller was also a highly accomplished poet, spanning the more popular with, for example, his ode "An die Freude" ("To Joy"), "Das Lied von der Glocke" ("Song of the Bell"), and his ballads, and the profoundly philosophical in poems such as "Das Ideal und des Leben" ("The Ideal and Life") and "Der Spaziergang" ("The Walk").

Schiller's medical training introduced him to a wide range of philosophical and scientific theories of the later Enlightenment. Medicine at the military academy was held to be inseparable from philosophy; the "philosophical doctor" devoted himself to the study of the whole human being in the interaction of mind and body. This empirical turn in medicine coincided with a growing fascination with psychology evident in the works of, for example, the philosophers Moses Mendelssohn and Christian Gottfried Garve, which indicates the move in the later German Enlightenment away from Wolffian rationalism to a more empirically based spirit of enquiry drawn from the British and French Enlightenment. Schiller's successful doctoral dissertation *Über den Zusammenhang der Tierischen Natur des Menschen mit seiner geistigen* (On the Connection between the Animal and Spiritual Natures of Man, 1780) explores the reciprocal relations between mind and body and sheds considerable light on Schiller's first play, *The Robbers*, in which he explores in Karl and Franz Moor the mental and physical disequilibrium of two opposed philosophical and psychological types.

His first three dramas, *The Robbers, Fiesco*, and *Intrigue and Love*, all express Schiller's belief in the dignity of human beings and his perception of manifest injustices in the world, but also his skepticism about the ability of imperfect human beings to effect change. In style they are marked by an exuberant disregard for classical convention, reminiscent of the *Sturm und Drang* (Storm and Stress) movement of the 1770s, and by an often extreme language. In *The Robbers*, which reworks the archetypal theme of fraternal enmity, Karl Moor denounces his age in the name of Nature, conceived in Rousseauian terms, though his rebellion against family and society only reinforces his despair, while the nobleman Ferdinand of *Intrigue and Love*, a domestic tragedy, rejects social convention and divisions in favor of the claims of the heart but then destroys the object of his love. In both plays there is overt criticism of aristocratic abuse of power, in particular in the latter play's portrayal of the mores of the court of an absolutist German state. In *Fiesco*, Schiller explores a charismatic leader who succumbs to the temptations of power. In all three early plays, he shows himself fascinated by the contradictions within the idealist figure, who rides roughshod over the lives of others. Less complex in its perspective is his short story *Der Verbrecher aus velorener Ehre* (The Criminal from Lost Honor, 1785), which reflects the contemporary debate on criminal reform. Schiller's narrative presents not the trial and execution of the criminal, as was usual in such stories, but the early psychological impact on him of unduly harsh penalties that lead to the loss of his honor and thus of his stake in society.

His work of the second half of the 1780s identifies Schiller most strongly with some of the great public themes of the Enlightenment. While writing his fourth drama, *Don Carlos*, about the ill-fated son of Philip II of Spain, he devoted himself to historical study. The resulting play is an uneasy combination of love, intrigue, and political drama but also a work of great passion and eloquence. The old repressive order, represented by the cynical Philip and the Inquisition, is challenged by the freethinking marquis of Posa, who attempts to save the hapless Carlos from the scheming of his enemies at court and protect the Spanish Netherlands from further brutal suppression of religious freedom. Protestantism, with its emphasis on individual conscience, is unequivocally presented in the play as the vehicle of liberalism. When Posa pleads with Philip to grant his people freedom of thought, to restore their dignity, and to cease ruling by fear, we hear echoes of Rousseau and Montesquieu. The play's imagery of sowing and blossoming reinforces the underlying assumption that progression toward liberal government is in tune with nature and thus inevitable. The representatives of the new order perish but their vision endures.

As a result of his source work on *Don Carlos*, Schiller began *History of the Revolt of the United Netherlands against Spanish Rule*, the confident introduction to which claims the account will show what people can do by united effort in a just cause. The implication is again one of the inevitability of progress toward civil liberties and freedom of conscience. This idealized view of the Protestant fades as history progresses and factionalism of both sides emerges. The work remained unfinished. The same optimism that informs it permeates Schiller's inaugural lecture as professor of history at the University of Jena, *Was heisst und zu welchem Ende studiert man Universalgeschichte?* (What Is Universal History and to What Purpose Is It Studied?, 1789). His second substantial historiographical work, *History of the Thirty Years' War*, is much less overt in its Protestant bias and after initial idealization gives a more sober appraisal of the Swedish king Gustavus Adolphus. The distrust of the political power of the Catholic Church that underlies these works is evident again in his novel, *Der Geisterseher* (The Ghostseer, 1787–1789), in which a Protestant prince is manipulated psychologically by a mysterious Armenian to the point where he converts to Catholicism. Though unfinished, the novel signals that the same Catholic forces will by criminal means secure his succession as ruler of the state.

In the first half of the 1790s, Schiller devoted himself to two tasks in aesthetics: a theory of tragedy and a theory of beauty. For both of these he drew on his study of Kant, whose dualism of nature and reason is fundamental to them. His theory of tragedy is indebted to Kant's notion of the sublime, according to which (*Kritik der Urtheilskraft* [Critique of Judgment], paragraph 28) the aesthetic effect of the sublime occurs when we contemplate from a position of safety an object of overwhelming natural force and yet know that as denizens of the realm of reason we share in an infinity that dwarfs any natural phenomenon. In Schiller's theory of tragedy (see in particular *Über das Pathetische* [On Tragic Pity, 1793]), the play must evoke an awareness of the power of the moral will to rise above physical destruction, thus producing the exhilaration associated with the sublime. Like Kant, Schiller is careful to locate the sublime in the observer, not in the object. His own later dramatic practice stands, however, in a complex relationship to this theory and does not necessarily exemplify it. In developing a theory of beauty (see especially *On Grace and Dignity* and *On the Aesthetic Education of Man*) Schiller's aim is to link beauty to the moral sphere and yet to free it from didactic ends. Kant's *Critique of Judgment* suggested to him (§59) that beauty could be regarded as the symbol of morality, for the harmony of imagination and the understanding that underlies the perception of beauty provides an analogue to the harmony of the subject with the universal moral law that is the ground of moral action. All Schiller's accounts of beauty rest on the idea that the marriage of form and matter that we perceive in the beautiful offers us the hope of reconciling sense and spirit within ourselves and thus of regaining our wholeness as individuals.

The course taken by the French Revolution was a decisive influence on Schiller's intellectual development. His ambivalence toward Enlightenment rationalism was already evident in his poem "Die Götter Griechenlands" (The Gods of Greece, 1788), an eloquent lament for the loss of unity of sense and spirit expressed as a longing for ancient Greece. Disappointment at the Terror in France and at what he saw as the failure of Enlightenment rationalism led him in *On the Aesthetic Education of Man* to expound a theory of the ability of aesthetic experience to restore human wholeness and thus create the conditions necessary for moral, social, and political regeneration. The belief that the whole person must be cultivated can be related back to his early medical training but is also characteristic of German humanists of the middle and later eighteenth century, for example the influential art historian Johann Joachim Winckelmann, the theologian and philosopher of history Johann Gottfried Herder, and Goethe. Schiller's last critical work of this period, *On Naïve and Sentimental Poetry* reasserts his belief in the mission of art to restore wholeness, while also being a seminal statement of the problem of the modern ("sentimental") poet's divided consciousness.

After the mid-1790s, Schiller returned to poetry and drama, his best poems expressing his belief in the value of aesthetic experience. In a series of verse dramas influenced by the classical and Shakespearian traditions and showing great stylistic and thematic range, he gives imaginative shape to some of the political and moral questions of the revolutionary age. In *Wallenstein*, he explores political legitimacy and usurpation, individual conscience versus authority, change versus tradition. In *Maria Stuart* he examines not only Mary's guilt and final transcendence

but also the challenge facing Elizabeth to adhere to the principle of law that she has given herself for the sake of the stability of her rule. In *The Maid of Orleans* and *Wilhelm Tell*, he presents the phenomenon of the folk hero and the political forces to which he or she is subject but often oblivious. His only later play not based on historical sources is *The Bride of Messina*, an experiment in reviving the classical chorus that uses the theme of fraternal enmity to explore the possibility of moral choice.

In the nineteenth century, Schiller's works were frequently plundered as a source of political slogans by German liberals oblivious to his ambivalence toward the pursuit of political goals. His notion of aesthetic education profoundly influenced the philosopher and statesman Wilhelm von Humboldt and through Humboldt's education reforms the German tradition of humanist education in the nineteenth and early twentieth centuries.

[*See also* Aesthetics; Humboldt, Wilhelm von; Poetry; Sturm und Drang; *and* Theater.]

BIBLIOGRAPHY

Abrams, M. H. *Natural Supernaturalism: Tradition and Revolution in Romantic Literature.* New York, 1971. Looks at Schiller's notion of universal history and aesthetic education in the light of late-eighteenth-century reworkings of myths of progress.

Dewhurst, K., and N. Reeves. *Friedrich Schiller: Medicine, Psychology and Literature.* Oxford, 1979. The only English translation of Schiller's medical writings with full commentary, a detailed account of Schiller's education, and valuable discussion of the impact of his early psychophysiological ideas on his creative work.

Koopmann, Helmut, ed. *Schiller Handbuch.* Stuttgart, 1998. A compact, scholarly, and yet accessible analysis of Schiller's creative work and intellectual world with extensive bibliographies of secondary literature.

Lahnstein, Peter. *Schillers Leben.* Munich, 1981. A readable, comprehensive biography, particularly strong on Schiller's early life and career.

Lamport, F. J. *German Classical Drama.* Cambridge, 1990. Sets Schiller's dramas in the context of contemporary German literature and theater.

Nisbet, H. B. *German Aesthetic and Literary Criticism,* vol. 3: *Winckelmann, Lessing, Hamann, Herder, Schiller, Goethe,* edited by H. B. Nisbet. Cambridge, 1985. Contains an English translation of *On Naïve and Sentimental Poetry* with a helpful introduction and commentary.

Pugh, David. *Dialectic of Love: Platonism in Schiller's Aesthetics.* Toronto, 1996. The book argues that the logical impasses in Schiller's writings stem from the Platonic legacy and in so doing brings out well the dynamics of his thought.

Reed, T. J. *Schiller.* Oxford, 1991. A concise and penetrating introduction.

Sharpe, Lesley. *Friedrich Schiller: Drama, Thought and Politics.* Cambridge, 1991. A study with extended discussions of all Schiller's major works.

Wellek, René. *A History of Modern Criticism,* vol. 1: *The Later Eighteenth Century.* New Haven, Conn., 1955. Contains chapters on late-eighteenth-century German critics, with a chapter on Kant and Schiller that includes a lucid account of *On Naïve and Sentimental Poetry.*

Wilkinson, E. M., and L. A. Willoughby, eds. *Friedrich Schiller: On the Aesthetic Education of Man in a Series of Letters.* Oxford, 1967. The

German text is given with an English translation on facing pages. The edition comprises a lengthy introduction, notes, glossary, and bibliography.

LESLEY SHARPE

SCHLÖZER, AUGUST LUDWIG (1735–1809), German historian and statistician.

Born in Gaggstedt in the county of Hohenlohe-Kirchberg, Schlözer studied theology and Oriental languages at the universities of Wittenberg and Göttingen. He went as a tutor to Sweden in 1755, returning to Göttingen in 1759 to study medicine. He held academic posts in Russia from 1761 to 1767, after which he returned to the university of Göttingen, where he was professor of statistics from 1769. He published scholarly works on a variety of subjects, notably a study of northern European history and a translation of the Russian chronicler Nestor. He was most widely known, however, for his editing of the two journals *Briefwechsel* and *Staatsanzeigen*, the aim of which was to raise the German public's awareness of politics and economics.

Schlözer was a pioneer in the academic study of statistics, in particular as it related to the political, economic, and social circumstances of the population. Although he wrote in the language of historical studies, his outlook and methods resemble those of modern mathematical statistics.

Schlözer was inspired by William Petty's *Political Arithmetic* (1690), which treats the problem of how a small country can optimize its resources and institutions in order to compete against a larger country. Schlözer highlighted the practical difficulties involved in explaining the behavior over time of systems with a large number of variables. In contrast, probabilistic theorists of Schlözer's own time, such as Thomas Bayes, attempted to find ways of predicting the behavior over time of systems with only a few variables. Schlözer, however, conjectured that with systems of a large number of variables, such as human societies, the variables could be more easily determined if time was eliminated from the sets of equations. Accordingly, he developed his synchronous method, which involves studying the state of societies at a given instant in time. He argued that one could either treat a continuum at an instant in time, or one could treat discrete parts of it over time; there was, however, no theoretical basis for predicting the behavior of a continuum over time.

Schlözer's synchronous method contrasts with *Historismus*. *Historismus* addressed the development of discrete parts of political systems over time, concentrating on the rise of Prussia and its role in the creation of modern Germany. In the end, however, the *Historismus* method of selecting variables for analysis proved to be too limited to explain Germany's development in the wider context of European history.

Schlözer conjectured that the wealth of a society is related to the proportion of its members who are engaged in its administration, and he directed the academic study of statistics to discover whose interests are served by a given political system. However, many of the contributors to his statistical periodical *Briefwechsel* wrote that many political institutions in Germany served sectional interests. Schlözer, who believed that a free press and statistics were mutually complementary indicators of the political health of a society, had his own journalistic activities curtailed in 1794 as a result of the general censorship imposed in response to the perceived threat of disruption arising from the revolutionary upheavel in France.

[*See also* Germany *and* Mathematics.]

BIBLIOGRAPHY
Bayes, Thomas. "An Essay towards Solving a Problem in the Doctrine of Chances" (1763). Reprinted in *Biometrika* 45 (1958), 293–295.
Schlözer, August Ludwig. *Stats-Gelartheit nach ihren haupt Theilen*: part 1, *Allgemeines Stats Recht und Stats Verfassung*; part 2, *Theorie der Statistik nebst Ideen ber das Studium der Politik überhaupt*. Göttingen, Germany, 1793, 1804.
Schlözer, August Ludwig, ed. *Briefwechsel: Meist statistischen Inhalts, 1774–1775; Meist historischen und politischen Inhalts, 1776–1782.* 16 vols. Göttingen, Germany, 1774–1782.
Sweet, Geoffrey. "*Historismus* and Experimental Philosophy." *Modern Language Review* 90 (1995), 944–953. *Historismus* is defined and discussed in the context of scientific outlook and methods.

GEOFFREY SWEET

SCHOLARLY ASSOCIATIONS AND PUBLICATIONS.
The principal scholarly associations devoted to the study of the Enlightenment are the International Society for Eighteenth Century Studies (ISECS), founded in 1968, and the various national and regional societies affiliated with it. These include the Société Française d'Étude du XVIIIe Siècle (founded 1964), the American Society for Eighteenth-Century Studies (ASECS, founded 1969), the British Society for Eighteenth-Century Studies (BSECS, founded 1971), the Deutsche Gesellschaft für die Erforschung des 18. Jahrhunderts (founded 1975), and societies in Argentina, Australia, Austria, Brazil, Bulgaria, Canada, China, the Czech Republic, Denmark, Greece, Hungary, Iceland, Ireland, Italy, Japan, Korea, the Netherlands, Norway, Poland, Portugal, Romania, Russia, Serbia, Spain, Sweden, Switzerland, Tunisia, and the Ukraine.

The ISECS is interdisciplinary in orientation, and its goal is "to promote the growth, development and coordination of studies and research relating to the eighteenth century in all aspects of its cultural heritage (historical, philosophical, ideological, religious, linguistic, literary, scientific, artistic, juridical) in all countries, without exception." The organization was founded in the wake of two successful International Congresses on the Enlightenment organized by the Voltaire scholar Theodore Besterman. The ISECS has held subsequent quadrennial congresses—which bring together scholars working in the areas of literature, history, philosophy, religious studies, and other disciplines in the humanities. Its various national and regional associations typically hold annual meetings.

Since 1971, the activities of the ISECS have been supported by the Voltaire Foundation, a center for eighteenth-century research and publication at Oxford University. The origins of the Foundation can be traced to the Institut et Musée Voltaire, established by Besterman in 1951 at Les Délices, Voltaire's residence in Geneva. The Foundation is responsible for the publication of *Studies on Voltaire and the Eighteenth Century*, a series begun by Besterman in 1955 which, in addition to publishing the proceedings of the International Congresses, publishes monographs and edited volumes on a wide range of eighteenth-century topics. The various national and regional societies affiliated with ISECS also publish journals concerned with eighteenth-century matters. These include *Dix-huitième Siècle* (the journal of the Société Française d'Étude du XVIIIe Siècle), *Eighteenth-Century Studies* and *Studies in Eighteenth-Century Culture* (both of which are associated with the American Society for Eighteenth-Century Studies), *The British Journal for Eighteenth-Century Studies* (the journal of the British Society for Eighteenth-Century Studies), *Lumen* (the journal of the Canadian Society for Eighteenth-Century Studies, which until 1993 published under the title *Man and Nature*), *Die Achtzehnten Jahrhundert, Studien zum 18. Jahrhundert*, and *Aufklärung* (all of which are associated with the Deutsche Gesellschaft für die Erforschung des 18. Jahrhunderts).

Other societies (and the journals associated with them) whose work has influenced studies of the Enlightenment include: the Société Jean-Jacques Rousseau (*Annales de la Société Jean-Jacques Rousseau*), the Société Diderot (*Recherches sur Diderot et sur l'Encyclopédie*), the Société Montesquieu (*Revue Montesquieu*), the Lessing Society (*Lessing Yearbook*), the International Herder Society (*Herder Yearbook*), and the Gottfried-Wilhelm-Leibniz-Gesellleschaft (*Studia leibnitiana*).

In addition to the Voltaire Foundation (whose ongoing publication projects include complete editions of the works of both Voltaire and Montesquieu), a number of other research centers devoted to eighteenth-century studies also maintain active publishing programs. These include the Yale Johnson and Boswell editions at Yale University, the Center for Seventeenth- and Eighteenth-Century Studies at the Clark Library at the University of California, Los Angeles (*The Center & Clark Newsletter*

and separately published volumes of conference papers), the Groupe d'Étude du XVIIIe Siècle at the Université Libre de Bruxelles (*Études sur le XVIIIe Siècle*), the Bibliothèque d'Études Rousseauistes (*Études Jean-Jacques Rousseau*), the Herzog August Bibliothek at Wolfenbüttel (*Wolfenbütteler Studien zur Aufklärung*), and the Kant-Archiv in Marburg (*Kant-Forschungen*).

A few other journals, not directly affiliated with the organizations mentioned thus far, whose concerns include the period of the Enlightenment include: *The Eighteenth Century: Theory and Interpretation* (published prior to 1978 as *Studies in Burke and His Time* and prior to 1967 as *The Burke Newsletter*), *The Eighteenth Century: A Current Bibliography* (established in 1978 under the aegis of the American Society for Eighteenth-Century Studies to continue *English Literature 1660–1800*, the bibliography begun by Ronald S. Crane in 1926), *Eighteenth-Century Life* (established in 1974 and at one time associated with the East-Central Conference of the American Society for Eighteenth-Century Studies), *Enlightenment and Dissent* (a journal with a focus on relations among religion, politics, and society in eighteenth-century Britain), *The Scriblerian and the Kit-Kats* (begun as a newsletter devoted to "Pope, Swift, and their Circle" but enlarged to include other early eighteenth-century writers), the *Johnsonian News Letter* (begun by James Clifford in 1940 as "an informal medium for exchange of ideas among eighteenth-century research scholars"), and *1650–1850: Ideas, Aesthetics, and Inquiries in the Early Modern Era*. Finally, a survey of journals dealing with the Enlightenment must not overlook the short-lived journal *Enlightenment Essays*, published between 1970 and 1972, which has been, to date, the only English-language journal explicitly devoted to the Enlightenment.

The Development of Associations for Eighteenth-Century Studies. During the discussions that led to the establishment of the ISECS, Theodore Besterman's preference was that the organization be named the Society for the Study of the Enlightenment. In the face of objections from American and British scholars that many aspects of the eighteenth century were not encompassed by the Enlightenment, a compromise was reached in which the new society would be called the International Society for Eighteenth-Century Studies while its conferences would continue as International Congresses on the Enlightenment. The compromise drives home what is perhaps the single most important characteristic of those scholarly associations that have had the greatest influence on studies of the Enlightenment: They have also been concerned with many things besides the Enlightenment. Taking the long eighteenth century as its domain, the field of eighteenth-century studies encompasses a number of writers and intellectual movements indifferent to, if not sometimes hostile toward, the Enlightenment. The place of the Enlightenment within the eighteenth century—indeed, the identity of the Enlightenment itself as a particular movement within the eighteenth century—has thus remained a question within the field of eighteenth-century studies that has, on occasion, been explicitly addressed, but for the most part, has been passed over in favor of more immediate concerns.

Obstacles to the development of societies for eighteenth-century studies. The establishment of the ISECS was part of an upsurge of interest in the eighteenth century dating from the third quarter of the twentieth century. Despite the classic contributions published in the 1930s by Ernst Cassirer (*Die Philosophie der Aufklärung* [1932, translated 1952]) and Paul Hazard (*La crise de la conscience européenne* [1935, translated 1953]) the development of a widespread and organized scholarly interest in the eighteenth century in general, and the Enlightenment in particular, did not commence until after World War II. This may be attributed to three factors: 1) the less than positive reputation of the eighteenth century in general and of the Enlightenment in particular; 2) the lack of adequate resources for serious scholarly work; and 3) the ambiguous status of the Enlightenment as an object of inquiry.

As Lawrence Lipking (1992) has observed, "eighteenth-century studies were born defensive." For much of the nineteenth and early twentieth centuries, the intellectual and cultural achievements of the eighteenth century were not widely appreciated. In Great Britain and the United States, there was a pervasive sense of the "triviality" or "superficiality" of eighteenth-century literature and philosophy, especially when contrasted with the literary achievements of the Romantic period. The Enlightenment suffered a similar fate among German scholars, and those eighteenth-century German thinkers whose stature could not be denied (for example, Goethe, Schiller, Kant, Herder) were typically treated as having "overcome" or "transcended" the limitations of their age. While such attitudes were less pronounced in France, even here scholarship on the eighteenth century tended to be subordinate to and colored by changing evaluations of the French Revolution. Prior to the middle of the twentieth century, the only French journal devoted to the study of eighteenth-century French literature was the *Revue du Dix-huitième Siècle*, published between 1913 and 1918.

One consequence of this general neglect exacerbated the problem: the absence of adequate resources for serious scholarly work. Except for the works of the major figures, many eighteenth-century texts had not been republished and were difficult to obtain. Critical editions were lacking, even for some of the most important figures (including Voltaire), and comprehensive bibliographies were either nonexistent or incomplete. It is thus hardly surprising that much of the initial impetus for the founding of scholarly associations devoted to the study of the Enlightenment came from scholars engaged in bibliographical and editorial work such as Theodore Besterman, Ronald S. Crane, and James Clifford.

Beyond the problems of reputation and resources, a further impediment to the formation of scholarly associations concerned with the Enlightenment lay in the ambiguous status of the object of inquiry itself: As a movement that spanned the areas of literature, philosophy, politics, economics, religion, and history, the Enlightenment did not fit easily into established divisions between scholarly disciplines. Groups of literary scholars interested in eighteenth-century English literature gathered regularly during meetings of the Modern Language Association throughout the 1940s (and their meetings were announced and recorded in issues of Clifford's *Johnsonian News Letter*), but scholars with an interest in works that would come to be seen as part of the canon of texts comprising the Enlightenment found it difficult to enter into contact with scholars with similar interests in other disciplines. Thus, those working in English departments explored something called the Augustan Age or the Age of Johnson, while art historians spoke of neoclassicism and scholars in the history of ideas examined arguments associated with the Age of Reason. A concerted investigation of the Enlightenment had to await the formation of organizations that crossed disciplinary boundaries.

Bibliographers, editors, and early publications. The origins of such organizations can largely be traced to the efforts of a few scholars who, devoted to the work of particular eighteenth-century authors, inaugurated projects aimed at addressing the shortage of bibliographies and editions. Among the earliest Anglo-American efforts was Ronald S. Crane's annual bibliography of "English Literature of the Restoration and Eighteenth Century," begun in 1926 and initially published in the *Philological Quarterly*. Although the focus of the bibliography was literary, Crane's approach to literature emphasized the importance of its historical context. From the beginning, the bibliography included discussions of publications outside the area of literature as well as of non-English authors. As Donald Greene (1976) notes, however, Crane was suspicious of the "reckless generalization" of such global terms as *preromanticism* or *neoclassicism*. As a result, a consideration of how the works reviewed might contribute to an understanding of the broader movement known as the Enlightenment was alien to the venture. The same may be said for the *Johnsonian News Letter*. Although the newsletter did survey publications concerned with topics outside of Samuel Johnson and his circle, the primary focus remained on English literature. That the newsletter found Peter Gay's

Voltaire's Politics an important enough work to review, but began its brief discussion of the book by stating that its concerns fell "for the most part outside our specific field" (*Johnsonian News Letter* 21, September 1961, p. 7) testifies to the newsletter's somewhat ambivalent relation to other parts of the eighteenth century.

The efforts of Theodore Besterman had a considerably greater impact on subsequent studies of the Enlightenment. A professional bibliographer with a wide range of interests, Besterman amassed a collection of manuscripts and other materials related to the study of Voltaire and the Enlightenment that he offered to the city of Geneva in 1951 in return for a pledge to renovate and maintain Voltaire's Genevan residence, Les Délices, as a museum and institute devoted to Voltaire's work. From this venue, Besterman began the publication of Voltaire's notebooks, his correspondence, the ambitious monograph series *Studies on Voltaire and the Eighteenth Century*, and various other bibliographic and textual resources relevant to the study of Voltaire and the Enlightenment in France. Disagreements with authorities in Geneva prompted Besterman to move his various ventures to Oxford University in 1965, where they have continued, after his death, under the direction of the Voltaire Foundation.

Publication series, journals, conferences. Besterman's dedication to the cataloging and editing of Voltaire's works—combined, as Robert Wokler (1997) has noted, with his considerable skills as an academic entrepreneur—led to an extensive publications program that has had a considerable impact on the direction of scholarship on the Enlightenment.

Inaugurated in 1955, *Studies on Voltaire and the Eighteenth Century* has published, to date, close to four hundred volumes. Most have been monographs devoted to a single subject, although other volumes in the series consist of collections of shorter essays on unrelated topics. The series also publishes the multivolume proceedings of the International Congresses on the Enlightenment. From the start, the series maintained a strong interest in writers other than Voltaire: Early volumes were devoted to d'Alembert, Condorcet, Diderot, La Mettrie, Maupertuis, Montesquieu, Prévost, and Rousseau, along with a number of less familiar figures. The series has concentrated on the French Enlightenment: Prior to 1989, 89 percent of the monograph volumes were devoted to French writers or topics (studies on Voltaire accounted for about 30 percent of the total number of monographs, with Diderot accounting for a little under 12 percent). In recent years, the focus of the series has shifted somewhat, with studies of Diderot and Rousseau outnumbering those on Voltaire. Beginning in 2000, the connection with Voltaire was deemphasized with the adoption of the acronym *SVEC* as the title of the series. More recent publishing initiatives of the Voltaire Society include a new series, *International Studies on the Eighteenth Century*, devoted to examining differing approaches to the study of the eighteenth century, and an electronic publishing series that includes Besterman's edition of Voltaire's correspondence, a CD-ROM edition of the important eighteenth-century newspaper *Gazette d'Amsterdam*, and an on-line edition of the correspondence between Brissot de Warville and his publisher, the Société Typographique de Neuchâtel.

While the Yale Johnson and Boswell have had a significant impact on the study of eighteenth-century English literature, the British Enlightenment has, as Roy Porter (2000) argues, been largely overlooked. There is no single publication series dealing with the Enlightenment in England that could be compared to the publications of the Voltaire Foundation. The publications associated with ASECS and BSECS have tended to focus broadly on English literature in the eighteenth century, while at the same time publishing articles dealing with the canonical figures in the French Enlightenment. Papers from the national and regional meetings of ASECS appear in the yearly collection *Eighteenth-Century Culture*, while *Eighteenth-Century Studies* offers both articles and, increasingly, lengthy review symposia on various topics in eighteenth-century studies. In both, studies by scholars working in the area of either English or French literature are the norm, although *Eighteenth-Century Studies* has published a number of issues focusing on topics (for example, recent interpretations of the French Revolution) where research is done by historians. It also regularly provides coverage of a broad range of disciplines concerned with the eighteenth century in its review section.

German associations concerned with the eighteenth century have pursued a somewhat different course in their research and publishing programs. Perhaps because the dominant figures in eighteenth-century German literature have long been the focus of work by German literary scholars, much of the more recent German work within the area of eighteenth-century studies has been done by historians and—in response to the influential studies of Reinhard Koselleck (*Kritik und Krise* [1959, translated 1988]) and Jürgen Habermas (*Strukturwandel der Öffentlichkeit* [1962, translated 1989])—has focused on the sociological and political dimensions of the Enlightenment. The work of Werner Krauss, an East German scholar working within Marxian traditions of literary history, has also had an impact on the development of sociological approaches to the study of literature. Finally, perhaps because of an awareness of the differing forms taken by the Enlightenment in England, France, and Germany, German scholars have devoted more attention than their counterparts in France, England, and North America to the question of what, precisely, defines the Enlightenment.

Prior to the founding of the Deutsche Gesellschaft für die Erforschung des 18. Jahrhunderts in 1975, German research in the area of eighteenth-century studies was typically carried on in conjunction with editorial projects and research programs devoted to particular thinkers (for example, Wolff, Thomasius, Pufendorf, Leibniz). That no one figure could occupy the place held by Voltaire within French studies of the eighteenth century may be attributed, in part, to the tendency of older German scholarship to view the dominant figures of eighteenth-century German literature and philosophy (for example, Kant, Goethe, Schiller, and Herder) in isolation from the broader context of European thought in the eighteenth century.

To a certain extent, Lessing is an exception to this rule, and two organizations devoted to the study of his work have had a significant role in supporting scholarship exploring the Enlightenment in Germany. The Lessing Society (an international society founded at the University of Cincinnati in 1966) has, since 1969, published the *Lessing Yearbook*, which has served as a venue for articles exploring differing aspects of eighteenth-century German thought, including supplemental volumes on the relationship of Lessing and Mendelssohn (1979), Lessing and toleration (1986), and the "dialectic of enlightenment" in German thought (1993).

An ambitious research and publication program has grown up at the Herzog August Bibliothek at Wolfenbüttel, where Lessing served as librarian at the end of his life. In the years after World War II, the library was revived as an international research center and, under the directorship of Paul Raabe, began to pursue research and publication programs in the area of eighteenth-century studies. The Lessing-Akademie was established there in 1971, with the mission of undertaking research on the German Enlightenment and, in 1974, the first volume of the *Wolfenbütteler Studien zur Aufklärung* appeared. Volumes in this series have explored a number of issues in the social history of eighteenth-century literature and philosophy, including volumes on Judaism in the age of Enlightenment, the role of secret societies, and a four-volume series of studies on different centers of Enlightenment including Königsberg, Riga, Leipzig, and Denmark. The series also has published volumes devoted to individual writers including Spinoza, Mendelssohn, Daniel Chodowiecki, and a 1996 volume on Voltaire in Germany, which marks the sole point where the publication programs of the Voltaire Foundation and the *Wolfenbütteler Studien* have intersected.

The Deutsche Gesellschaft für die Erforschung des 18. Jahrhunderts was established at Wolfenbüttel in 1976 and both its journal, *Die Achtzehnte Jahrhundert*, and its publication series, *Studien zum achtzehnten Jahrhundert*,

are now based there. Like the *Wolfenbütteler Studien*, both have favored sociological and historical studies of the Enlightenment, including volumes on the work of Wolff, Thomasius, Winckelmann, and Herder, the relation of ethics and anthropology in the English Enlightenment from Shaftesbury to Hume, natural law and revolution, and a number of historical and sociological explorations of the Enlightenment in a European context. Perhaps the most important of the Wolfenbüttel journals for scholars working on the Enlightenment is the interdisciplinary journal *Aufklärung*, established in 1986. Published twice a year, each issue features essays focused on a single theme (topics have included the struggle between Enlightenment and enthusiasm and the impact of natural rights theories on legal reform). Issues include short biographies of Enlightenment figures (usually related to the main topic). The journal is interdisciplinary in intent (although work by historians tends to dominate) and European in scope (although the focus tends to fall on Germany).

The Place of the Enlightenment in Eighteenth-Century Studies. While the area of eighteenth-century studies has blossomed, the prospect for research on the Enlightenment within scholarly associations devoted to eighteenth-century studies faces challenges on at least three fronts: 1) while strenuous efforts have been made by organizations for eighteenth-century studies to pursue an interdisciplinary program of research, this intention remains to a certain extent unfulfilled; 2) while such organizations have been quite successful in cultivating an internationalization of eighteenth-century studies, much still remains to be done in encouraging comparative studies of the Enlightenment in its various national contexts; and 3) the identity of the Enlightenment remains somewhat problematic.

Despite their avowedly interdisciplinary orientation, the membership of societies for eighteenth-century studies, at least in England and North America, remains heavily weighted toward the study of literature. Because a good many of the first generation of scholars of the eighteenth century eschewed formalist approaches to literature in favor of more historical approaches, possibilities have long existed for fruitful collaboration with scholars working in the other areas of the history of ideas. Yet, at the same time, criticisms of the theoretical conservatism of the field and its attendant failure to incorporate approaches from disciplines outside the areas of literary history and biography have been voiced at regular intervals. Under Besterman's guidance, *Studies on Voltaire and the Eighteenth Century* remained fairly traditional in the theoretical approaches it embraced, with the exception of an early and steadily growing interest in the history of the book and in studies of readership. A recent statement of editorial policy perhaps signals a greater openness to other approaches, expressing the intention "to promote publication in the broad field of cultural studies." Scholars influenced by approaches associated with the work of Jacques Derrida, Michel Foucault, and Pierre Bourdieu have been especially critical of the resistance to theory that they allege is reflected in much literary scholarship dealing with the eighteenth century (see, for example, the essays collected in Nussbaum and Brown [1987]). Since 1978, *The Eighteenth Century: Theory and Interpretation* has provided a venue for more theoretically inclined literary scholars to develop such approaches. A heightened concern with the role of theory in eighteenth-century studies does little, however, to alter the predominantly literary orientation of the major Anglo-American organizations concerned with eighteenth-century studies. Currently, approximately 45 percent of the membership of ASECS works in the area of English literature, 17 percent in other modern foreign languages, classics, or comparative literature, and only 8 percent in history or economics. It is, to say the least, difficult to fulfill the interdisciplinary program of research required for an understanding of the Enlightenment within organizations where a number of disciplines in the humanities and the social sciences are underrepresented.

The ISECS was intended not only to be interdisciplinary in orientation but also to investigate the eighteenth century "in all countries, without exception." The proliferation of national and regional societies is ample evidence of the internationalization of eighteenth-century studies. Yet, Anglo-American studies of the Enlightenment tend to remain largely Francocentric. The neglect of the so-called British Enlightenment may in part be attributed to the failure of either British or North American societies for eighteenth-century studies to find a figure who could play the same role that scholarship on Voltaire played in the development of scholarship on the French Enlightenment. The contrast with recent German scholarship is suggestive in this regard. German associations devoted a fair amount of attention to exploring the particular characteristics of the German Enlightenment and the journal *Aufklärung* has devoted issues to explorations of the German Enlightenment by French and Italian scholars.

Finally, in a period when scholars working in the area of eighteenth-century studies are skeptical of generalizations, the status of the Enlightenment as an object of research has become increasingly unclear. The issue of the identity of the Enlightenment returns, from time to time, as a topic of discussion at International Congresses on the Enlightenment but, as reviewers of these congresses have noted, increased attention to the particularities of eighteenth-century life tends to dissolve whatever identity the Enlightenment might once have possessed and, in recent years, even to displace efforts at considering the implications of the loss of this identity. In the early 1970s,

Enlightenment Essays carried a statement on its title page informing prospective contributors that "Essays presenting a theory of the Enlightenment, or basic definitions, are encouraged," but nothing along these lines ever appeared in the journal and, after three volumes, the journal ceased publication. Perhaps, with the upsurge in interest in the eighteenth century over the last thirty years, another attempt along these lines would not be out of place.

[*See also* Enlightenment Studies.]

BIBLIOGRAPHY

Danneberg, Lutz, Michel Schlott, Jörg Schönert, and Friedrich Vollhardt. "Richtungen und Tendenzen in der deutschen Aufklärungsforschung." *Die Achtzehnte Jahrhundert* 19 (1995), 163–192. Exhaustive discussion of the main tendencies in recent German research on the Enlightenment. An abbreviated French translation of this essay may be found in Delon and Schlobach.

Delon, Michel, and Jochen Schlobach, eds. *Eighteenth-Century Research: Objects, Methods, and Institutions (1945–1995).* Paris, 1998. A collection of essays on the development of eighteenth-century studies since the end of World War II.

Epstein, William. "Professing the Eighteenth Century." *ADE Bulletin* 81 (Fall 1985), 20–25. Brief sketch of the professionalization of eighteenth-century studies between 1925 and 1975.

Greene, Donald. "'More than a Necessary Chore': The Eighteenth-Century Current Bibliography in Retrospect and Prospect." *Eighteenth-Century Studies* 10 (Autumn 1976), 94–110.

Greene, Donald. "The ASECS's Early Years: A Personal Memoir." In *The Past as Prologue: Essays to Celebrate the Twenty-Fifth Anniversary of ASECS*, edited by Carla H. Hay with Syndy M. Conger, pp. 3–17. New York, 1995.

Lipking, Lawrence. "Inventing the Eighteenth Century: A Long View." In *The Profession of Eighteenth-Century Literature: Reflections on an Institution*, edited by Leo Damrosch, pp. 7–25. Madison, Wis., 1992.

Nussbaum, Felicity, and Laura Brown, eds. *The New Eighteenth Century: Theory, Politics, English Literature.* New York, 1987. Collection of essays advocating and illustrating a more theoretically informed approach to eighteenth-century literature.

Porter, Roy. *The Creation of the Modern World: The Untold Story of the British Enlightenment.* New York, 2000.

Saine, Thomas P. "Scholarship on the German Enlightenment as Cultural History: An Essay." *Lessing Yearbook* VI (1974), 139–161. Excellent, if now somewhat dated, survey.

Wieczorrek, Michael, Cerstin Bauer-Funke, and Sandra Pott. "Nach der Aufklärungsforschung ist immer vor der Aufklärungsforschung. Eindrücke vom Zehnten Internationalen Aufklärungskongress in Dublin vom 25. bis 31. Juli 1999." *Die Achtzehnte Jahrhundert* 23:2 (1999), 136–141. Critical review of the Tenth Congress on the Enlightenment.

Williams, David. "Theodore Besterman and the Resurrection of Voltaire." *Studies in Burke and His Time* 17 (1976), 44–70. Account of Besterman's career and its impact on eighteenth-century studies.

Wokler, Robert. "Dr. Besterman, I Presume." In *Voltaire et ses combats*, edited by Ulla Kölving and Christiane Mervaud, pp. 21–36. Oxford, 1997. Account of Besterman's career and its impact on eighteenth-century studies.

Zelle, Carsten. "Fragmentation des Lumières. Zum Siebten Internationalen Aufklärungskongress in Budapest vom 26. Juli bis 2. August 1987." *Die Achtzehnte Jahrhundert* 11 (1987), 74–78. Critical review of the Seventh Congress on the Enlightenment.

JAMES SCHMIDT

SCHOLARSHIP AND RESEARCH. The eighteenth century was a period of theoretical reorientation for the scholarly disciplines, which also gained increasing practical significance. These changes were the result of both internal developments and external pressures. Thus, the eighteenth century saw not so much the emergence of new disciplines as the increasing differentiation and reorganization of existing ones, as well as many changes in subject matter. The disciplines saw an expansion of scope and change and development with respect to methods; in this process, by no means uniform or linear, the natural sciences came to be an important model. Though the Enlightenment's objectives did not yet include the ever increasing specialization of scientific fields and the development of professional experts, learning and scholarship became "scientific"—that is, critical toward authorities and written records, and argumentative, explorative, and experimental. Scholarship's main task was no longer merely the transmission of expert opinions claiming authoritative validity but rather the systematic increase of knowledge as well as its critical examination and improvement.

Though the modern era saw physics and, later, metaphysics put on a new scientific basis, the old idea of a learned discipline as essentially a fund of orderly and solid knowledge was still the prevailing one in the eighteenth century. Gradually, this notion was superseded by the idea of science as exact knowledge founded on irreducible principles. The German term *Wissenschaft* referred to a system of knowledge and truths; the term designated a scholarly discipline, and this meaning eventually replaced the older sense of the sciences as collections of "news, tidings, art, skill." At the same time, this changed concept of scholarly research included a claim to objectivity, which made learning more than the subjective communication or individual possession of knowledge. At the end of the eighteenth century a narrower concept of science as knowledge depending on hypotheses and their experimental verification became generally accepted.

The decisive turning point in the development outlined above occurred around 1800. Prior to that, the Latin *scientia* had always meant *cognitio ex principiis*, never *cognito principiorum*, an interpretation that Immanuel Kant continued to confirm in his work. The changes in the natural sciences during the seventeenth and eighteenth centuries decisively shaped the Enlightenment's concept of disciplinary knowledge. However, initially the term *sciences* was used only occasionally to describe natural scientific inquiry; the more frequent term was *natural philosophy*. As a rational and secularized concept of science developed, it was necessary to differentiate science from magic and mysticism; that is, from what has been called pseudoscience since the Enlightenment.

As early as the end of the seventeenth century, cognition became a problem in its own right. As the theoretical investigation of existence continued, the subjective dimension of knowledge and cognition increasingly became a matter of interest. Symptomatic of eighteenth-century epistemology was the distinction between two kinds of knowledge: the truths of reason (*vérités de raison*, or relations of ideas) and factual truths (*vérités des faits*, or matters of fact). While the former could be known through intuition or demonstration, in knowing the latter, sensory perception and experience played a central role. The essential differences between the two kinds of knowledge emerged most clearly in the question of the empirical foundation of knowledge. This issue was problematic not only regarding truths of reason but especially so in relation to knowledge of facts or "historical" truths. Initially, the European scientific tradition left no room for empirical knowledge, and as a consequence the different ways of knowing facts were defined primarily in relation to the knowledge of reason—which alone was understood to be "science"—and were gathered under the imprecise heading of "history." This history consisted of knowledge of facts or of individual facts and contented itself with describing or ordering these facts. Francis Bacon defined history as the "foundation of science" and as irreplaceable in that function. Though he still did not include history among the sciences proper, his position became the traditional assessment of the function of history in relation to the sciences.

The structure of the various meanings in which the term *experience* had been used since the time of Aristotle also changed fundamentally during the eighteenth century. The traditional philosophical concept of experience still referred to knowledge of special instances and was therefore included under the general heading of "historical knowledge." However, in the actual pursuit of knowledge, the process of attaining new insights, through observation and experiment in the natural sciences and through textual criticism in the historical disciplines, came to the fore. In the age of Enlightenment intellectual and cultural life opened itself to empirism and even shifted to where empirical knowledge could be found. Empirical knowledge has a constructive dimension: observations are made on the basis of the theoretical formulation of a question and with the use of technical equipment. As a result, the Enlightenment could no longer accept as valid a concept of science that excluded empirical methods and knowledge.

The duality of knowledge of reason and knowledge of facts was replaced by juxtapositions formulated within the disciplines themselves, such as empirical experience and theory, empirical knowledge and knowledge of laws, and the Kantian distinction between historical (empirical) knowledge and the knowledge of reason. The value of mere knowledge of facts and traditional scholarship was thus reduced, and at the same time the concept of disciplinary knowledge was made more abstract so that it could encompass even the classical subject areas of scholarly learning—for example, the ones later called "humanities." These subject areas then had to prove themselves genuine forms of philosophical knowledge (knowledge of causes). At the same time it was claimed that each discipline had a philosophy of its own.

As the concept of a scholarly discipline changed, its distinction from the fine arts became more pronounced. The fine arts comprised belletristic literature, the plastic arts, and music; only occasionally were theoretical treatises included under this heading. The sciences separated themselves from the arts, and the five fine arts formed a system of their own. The relationship between the sciences and the arts, which underwent many changes throughout history, shaped the historical and systematic structure of disciplinary knowledge in the modern era. As part of this process aesthetics became a separate, independent discipline, although in the English and French context this applies only with qualifications. The unity of the concept of art could not be preserved, and the "free arts"—meaning a system of rules that one knows—were separated from the "mechanical arts"—meaning a system of rules and instruments or tools that one masters; that is, moral and technical disciplines essentially became independent of each other. Nevertheless, the encyclopedists, for example, did not want to grant the fine arts a privileged position among the disciplines. The older dichotomy between *arts et sciences* (arts and sciences) gave rise to the *lettres* (humanities) as a kind of knowledge different from that of the methodical sciences and the applied disciplines. Literary education occupied the middle position between pure scholarship and the systematic mastering of knowledge. While literature and scholarship were held to be different, the Enlightenment saw literary education and disciplinary knowledge as interpenetrating. Making the humanities (*lettres*) more scientific was the beginning of a reorganization of the system of the sciences. The scientific disciplines of mathematics and the natural sciences were joined by the disciplines of the humanities (*humanités*).

In the traditional hierarchy of faculties passed down from the medieval universities, the philosophical or "arts" faculties had only a propaedeutic or preparatory function and were therefore subordinated to the so-called "faculty disciplines" of medicine, law, and theology, in that order. Originally also serving as a classification of the disciplines, this hierarchy, though already discredited in eighteenth-century scientific theory, was firmly established in the institutions and therefore persisted. The Enlightenment's numerous attempts to reclassify the disciplines were still based on the notion of an ordered, static mass of knowledge, not critical of its own status. The boundaries between fields of knowledge were conceived as unchanging and fixed, separating historically unvarying fields of knowledge from each other. Knowledge was considered to be ordered in a "tableau"; that is, in a synchronous way, as a taxonomy. However, at least in theory, the hierarchy of knowledge of reason and of facts, of history and of philosophy, which reconstructed the hierarchical criteria solely from within the disciplines, superseded the classical hierarchy of faculties. From this it was only a small step to the conclusion that the higher faculties basically were only capable of an empirical knowledge of their subject matter, while philosophy alone made it possible to elevate this knowledge to the level of ultimate truths. This is the first indication of an emerging concept of learning that saw the faculty of philosophy as the institutional embodiment of true knowledge. The term *philosophy* had two meanings: it referred to a theory of the disciplines and also designated a group of disciplines based on "reason." At the same time, the college of philosophy gained significance because the differentiation among the scholarly disciplines belonging to the modern canon took place there. More and more the philosopher played the key role in understanding the most important arts and sciences from a superior standpoint. Thus, the *encyclopédistes* (encyclopedists) could attempt to present the totality of human knowledge only because seeing it from the philosopher's privileged vantage point guaranteed that all knowledge was interconnected. This also made the alphabetic arrangement of that knowledge possible.

Since the Enlightenment joined the problem of epistemology to that of nature, research in the natural sciences intensified. Around 1750, Jean Le Rond d'Alembert had divided the natural sciences into two great branches: mathematics and physics. The Enlightenment's classification of individual disciplines as belonging to one or the other of those branches differs widely from the present-day classification. Astronomy and cosmology were among the growing scientific disciplines; widespread interest in these persisted into the second half of the century. The interest in cosmology, in particular, was directly connected with observations regarding the natural history of the Earth. Projects included the measuring of the equator and the precise determination of the Earth's shape. The discovery of fossils over the course of the century gave rise to countless observations, reflections, and classification systems. This burgeoning interest in fossils and archaeological remains joined with a growing critical examination of religious dogma and research into the origins of life. In addition, the questions of inheritance and the origin and future of life were the focus of debates among professional scholars and the educated. The science of life (biology) received its name at this time and became a separate discipline with its own subject matter and methods. Together with other disciplines it emerged when the natural sciences were separated from philosophy and natural history and became autonomous. Most of the endeavors in the natural sciences were strongly influenced by a natural theology aimed at connecting science and religion in various ways.

The natural sciences in general shaped the Enlightenment's understanding of the disciplines. They also influenced its concept of the human being and its ambitious attempt to conceptualize a "science of man" that would place humankind as defined by the Enlightenment at the center of scientific inquiry. The disciplines developed a new understanding of the human being; they added new knowledge about the human physical constitution and psychological predispositions, the human capacity for knowledge and motivation for action, human malleability and (ability to act in) accordance with moral categories, and also about human weaknesses and shortcomings. This new scientific view of the human being exerted an influence on society as a whole, which in its turn began to expect more from science than before, expectations that the sciences in large part had generated themselves. This new "science of man" did not yet have the formal and conceptual structures of modern academic disciplines.

The Enlightenment concept of science retained the connotation of scholarly research and that of systematically arranged knowledge as well as the criterion of practical usefulness. Usefulness was not determined based solely on the principle of social relevance, which deduced future value exclusively from contemporary functionality and accepted only general technical and applied research. D'Alembert had unequivocally rejected such a short-sighted, reductive notion of science, which would have led to a ban on philology, for example, because its research and inquiries lacked practical application. Rather, proper knowledge was considered a precondition for right action. After all, it was generally accepted that human beings are able and destined—as a result of the reason with which they have been endowed—to learn about the laws of nature and to shape and improve their moral and social world according to the principles of reason. The disciplines and the education based on them were to enable people to arrive at a clearer, rationally grounded understanding of the world and to take practical actions guided by rational and moral principles of usefulness. In employing the term *useful* with respect to the disciplines, the philosophers of the Enlightenment often conveyed the expectation that such learning would be useful to society. Even jurisprudence turned increasingly to problems of the contemporary legal system and its improvement. Independent disciplines formed that dealt with the problems of politics, economy, and finance.

The sciences, especially in regard to the natural laws of the physical world, also became increasingly mathematical; that is, relations were more and more expressed in mathematical formulas after development of the theories of calculus and probability calculus. These theories enabled scientists to express movement in mathematical formulas and to introduce a certain predictability into natural processes. At the same time, probability calculus served as a strong impetus for the emerging "social sciences," especially for demographics. These sciences endeavored to apply the model of the natural sciences to the exploration of human behavior. The impetus for increasing mathematization was directly connected with tendencies to replace qualitative description with quantitative methods.

In addition, during the eighteenth century the disciplines saw their subject matter and questions increasingly historicized. Whether for the purpose of criticism or legitimation, questions about how existing institutions and ideas claiming validity had developed historically and what the conditions of such a development were became ever more important. Consequently, the return to original sources and their critical textual and factual examination as well as the process of their transmission to the present gained fundamental importance. The philosophers of the Enlightenment were no longer primarily motivated by an all-encompassing historical interest, but rather increasingly by the desire to arrive at reliable historical information, the chronological and factual interconnections of which could explain the actual process of history. Although the principles of explanation have since changed, the historical method continued to develop and later came to dominate the humanities.

In Germany and Scotland, more so than in the rest of western Europe, the universities were the centers of scholarly endeavor. This was despite the fact that the Enlightenment's concept of disciplinary knowledge—especially its emphasis on usefulness—rejected the institution of the university because of its outdated traditions, its general ineffectiveness, its status consciousness, and its internal restrictions that resembled those of the guilds. Nevertheless, no other institution could replace the universities in their training function. The Enlightenment intellectuals' interest and inquisitiveness regarding the arts and sciences was cultivated above all in the academies; these were not educational institutions but reflected the beginnings of the modern concept of scholarship that followed the development of disciplines in the faculty of philosophy. What Wilhelm von Humboldt's definition of a university later joined together, namely, teaching and research, was still separated in various seventeenth- and eighteenth-century notions of the academy. The academies began to give the Enlightenment's understanding of scholarly knowledge its characteristic institutional form. The functional separation of university and academy, which ultimately led to research being moved outside of the university, was not as strictly implemented in the German-speaking countries as in France and England.

As the disciplines became institutionalized, they also developed into a social system with social norms, with guarantees for maintaining those norms and for assuring the legitimation of goals and methods of activity, and with a type of activity unique to them. Through most of the eighteenth century, mobility between faculties and the hierarchic ordering of faculties to a large extent still served to institutionally stabilize intellectual and cultural homogeneity. It was not until the late eighteenth and early nineteenth centuries that this scholarly culture, which was based on shared theoretical traditions, began to be superseded by the gradual differentiation of disciplines and professions.

With the new understanding of science as an open system of knowledge, the "scholar" as the representative of traditional science was replaced by the "scientist," a term that was coined in the 1830s. The emphasis had shifted from existing knowledge to the capacity for gaining new knowledge, for asking the right questions that would make the unknown known. The older type of scholar, who wrote learned texts to be read by other scholars, was gradually replaced by a new type: that of the researching and teaching scientist. This led to a corresponding change in the material being published. The philosophes, that is, the philosophers and intellectuals, were superseded by the scientists. The audience for scientific publications also changed accordingly. Specialized scientists replaced a general educated reading public as the intended audience for scientific publications. This transition to recruitment from within the discipline made the "amateur" into what is nowadays meant by that term; the amateur's relationship to the sciences was defined by the fact that he was not a professional scientists. Increasingly, amateurs were pushed out of the sciences and excluded; however, in some scientific disciplines and in some countries, especially in England, amateur science continued well into the nineteenth century.

Much of the writing published during the eighteenth century was scholarly in nature, but the bulk of it was not actually innovative. Typically, scholars wrote textbooks and compendiums. In German university towns, the local subculture of dissertations and programs offered scholars an additional possibility for publishing their work. In fact, these publications played an important role in German scholarship. The interest in encyclopedic scientific publications that had gained ground in the seventeenth century persisted but took on a new character with the new

objective of examining knowledge critically and applying it in practice. The *Dictionnaire* (Dictionary) by Pierre Bayle is symptomatic of this trend, as is the *Encyclopédie* and Johann Heinrich Zedler's *Universallexikon* (General Encyclopedia). In addition to the compendiums and textbooks, there was also a growing number of treatises, essays, reports, and long reviews, in other words, a literature that allowed far-reaching and fairly rapid communication. The first scholarly journals focused on reproducing the contents of books, either in detailed reports or excerpts, thus resembling books in many ways. They were usually not an alternative to books, but more a reflection of the increase in the number of books published. From 1770 onward the specialized journal emerged out of journals that had been highly popular with the reading public but were considered dubious by scholars. These new types of journals soon became the prevailing media for publication of scholarly material, and to some extent they either superseded the two other main alternatives—the academy journal and the book—or relegated them to complementary roles in systematic and scholarly communication.

Although this development of the sciences was also accompanied by a mere gathering of facts for its own sake, and with a certain empty reasoning, it nevertheless undeniably popularized science. The natural sciences had become to an unprecedented extent—which was never again equaled—part of the general cultivation and the cultural life of educated people. By midcentury the number of popular scientific books and journals devoted to the natural sciences had increased considerably and continued to grow. Judging by the print runs of various publications, the demand for them must have been great. And the enthusiasm for the natural sciences did not end there; people wanted not only to learn about scientific advances from books, but to observe them directly for themselves. Those who could afford them bought laboratory sets for experiments and research in physics. Owning such equipment carried roughly the same prestige as owning a good private library. Larger cities offered public lectures on physics, and these were usually well attended. Itinerant electrifiers traveled from town to town with their machines; thus "doing science" became a public spectacle.

The disciplines were not yet a matter of national interest, however. The scholarly community on the whole was European; its members were in lively communication with one another—individually and institutionally—through corresponding memberships in organizations, personal correspondence, translations, and reviews, all of which led to mutual stimulation of and receptivity for individual practitioners' work.

It is often said that as disciplinary knowledge in the age of Enlightenment developed into a method of attaining and communicating established knowledge, a systematic path to knowledge, and a theory to guide practical action, it became increasingly important in determining the nature of reality—a significance it had neither claimed nor achieved previously. However, this statement must be qualified. The expansion and differentiation of the disciplines, their theoretical and methodological development, ran its course with many delays and stops along the way; there was certainly no general and rapid "modernization." Instead, received opinions persisted for a long time. The notion of a "Copernican revolution" does not apply to the development of the sciences in the eighteenth century, neither to any individual discipline nor to the sciences as a whole. Typically, change does not happen in a radical way. This said, it is nonetheless true that the individual scholarly disciplines and the whole system of scholarship at the end of the century differed considerably from what they had been at its beginning.

The social and institutional organization of present-day scholarship into disciplines is a relatively late outcome of the development of modern scholarship. It was not until the early nineteenth century that the first individual disciplines were separated out from the natural sciences as a whole: first chemistry and then physics. At about the same time, in the area later called humanities, the first disciplines formed in classical studies and history. Only in the twentieth century did a third area of disciplines emerge when the synthesis of methodological approaches in the humanities and the natural sciences led to the formation of the behavioral and social sciences. Since the early nineteenth century this internal differentiation of the disciplines has given rise to a system of scholarly disciplines. The historical significance of this process in the development of the modern sciences has not yet been fully grasped. Presumably this development correlates with structural changes in society, and it is directly connected to the reorganization of the universities, which started in early nineteenth-century Germany.

[*See also* Astronomy; Epistemology; Human Nature; Life Sciences; Natural Philosophy and Science; Philosophy; Print Culture; *and* Universities.]

BIBLIOGRAPHY

Bödeker, Hans Erich, Peter H. Reill, and Jürgen Schlumbohm, eds. *Wissenschaft als kulturelle Praxis, 1750–1900.* Göttingen, 1999.

Fox, Christopher, Roy Porter, and Robert Wokler, eds. *Inventing Human Science: Eighteenth-Century Domains.* Berkeley, Calif., 1995.

Hankins, Thomas L. *Science and the Enlightenment.* Cambridge, 1985.

Mocek, Reinhard, ed. *Die Wissenschaftskultur der Aufklärung.* Halle an der Saale, Germany, 1990.

Rousseau, G. S., and Roy Porter, eds. *The Ferment of Knowledge: Studies in the Historiography of Eighteenth-Century Science.* Cambridge, 1980.

Vierhaus, Rudolf, ed. *Wissenschaften im Zeitalter der Aufklärung.* Göttingen, 1985.

HANS ERICH BÖDEKER

SCIENCE. *See* Natural Philosophy and Science.

SCIENTIFIC EXPEDITIONS. An essential part of the Enlightenment's rationalization of the world was to show that the whole globe could be understood and studied in scientific terms. Where ancient mapmakers put pictures of fantastic creatures in unknown regions, the Enlightenment's impulse was to ensure that the sun of scientific scrutiny shone on such dark corners.

Expeditions to far regions cost large sums and generally required the support of governments who wished to be paid back in currency other than the mere advancement of learning. The Enlightenment's attempt to bring the globe under the sovereignty of science therefore meant an alliance with the imperial designs of the European states, and scientific exploration brought both an increase in knowledge and an increase in European control over much of the globe. Justification for expansion was given a new ideological edge as the colonial religious rationale (employed particularly by the Spanish in the sixteenth century) gave way to one based on the advance of science and rational civilization. Enlightenment science merged with the spread of empires claiming to provide both better modes of utilizing the world and its products and a better ordering of its societies.

Lapland and Peru. The pattern of eighteenth-century scientific exploration reflected the pace of European expansion more generally. The first major scientific expedition, the Académie des Sciences' joint expeditions to Lapland under Pierre Maupertuis and to Peru under Charles-Marie de La Condamine, extended to areas of the globe already known, though still poorly explored by Europeans. The voyage to Lapland lasted from 1736 to 1737; the Peruvian venture proved more complex, departing in 1735 but not completed until 1743. La Condamine did not return to Paris until 1745, using the extra time to study the natural history, ethnology, and science of unfamiliar areas of South America.

The aim of both expeditions was to provide empirical information that would settle the long-running dispute within French intellectual circles between the followers of Descartes and those of Newton. If one followed Descartes's vortex model of the workings of nature, then Earth should be flattened at the equator and elongated at the poles. The Newtonian conception of gravitation dictated the opposite: since the gravitational attraction of the Sun would be weaker at the poles than at the Equator, where the mass of Earth is greatest, the Equator should bulge while the poles should be flattened. The pendulum experiments conducted by Jean Richer at Cayenne in 1672 seemed to favor Newton, whereas the astronomical calculations of Jacques Cassini in 1718 seemed to reassure the Cartesians. Plainly, then, the issue had to be resolved by measurement on the ground—and so the Académie sponsored the expeditions to Lapland and Peru, the nearest approaches then practical to the North Pole and the Equator. The arduous and lengthy observations of the differing curvature of Earth by these two missions decisively settled the issue in favor of the Newtonians.

Although these voyages were prompted primarily by the physical sciences, they also provided opportunities for the collection of many natural history specimens, objects that were increasingly being accommodated within that characteristically Enlightenment project, an orderly system of classification. Owing to the system of Carolus Linnaeus and, subsequently, Antoine Laurent de Jussieu, nature no longer appeared to be a chaos of confused and multifarious plants and animals, but rather to conform to a rational order. This ability to order nature provided incentive and purpose for further expeditions to expand the range of specimens.

The Pacific. Once the major conflicts of the Seven Years' War were settled in 1763, this desire to map the geography and describe the flora and fauna of unexplored areas of the globe increasingly led the major European powers into the

Natural History Specimen. *The Rhinoceros*, painting (1751) by Pietro Longhi (1702–1785). (Museo Ca' Rezzonico, Venice/Archivo Cameraphoto Venezia/Art Resource, NY.)

new world of the Pacific. The voyage (1766–1769) of Louis Antoine de Bougainville, which helped to create the myth of the Edenic world of Tahiti inhabited by noble savages, not only added more islands to the map but also augmented the range of the classification of nature. Thanks to the work of Bougainville and his accompanying botanist, Philibert Commersen, large numbers of specimens were brought back to the Parisian Jardin du Roi to be studied at leisure by a culture increasingly confidant of its ability to bring the whole world under the sway of an impartial and universalizing science.

The promotion of both the physical and the natural sciences was even more apparent in James Cook's great *Endeavour* voyage (1768–1771). It was originally prompted by a great exercise in scientific cosmopolitanism, the observation of the transit of Venus, which required the cooperation of most of the major European powers to observe the passage of Venus across the disc of the Sun in 1769 from as many different vantage points across Earth as possible. The aim was to establish the astronomical unit, the mean distance of Earth from the Sun, which could then be used to establish the real size of our planetary system as it was then known. Tahiti, first encountered by Europeans in the person of John Wallis in 1767, was a convenient astronomical observatory in the Southern Hemisphere; in addition, it and Cook's other Pacific stopping points, such as New Zealand and Australia, gave Cook's traveling companion, the self-funded gentleman-botanist Joseph Banks, and his party an opportunity to add greatly to the store of known and described flora and fauna.

Cook and Banks set a standard for scientific exploration that was emulated on Cook's two subsequent Pacific voyages (1772–1775, 1776–1780) and on the voyages of Britain's rivals in the Pacific. When the Spanish belatedly (and vainly) sought to reassert their claims to the Pacific, they sponsored a fully equipped scientific voyage under Alessandro Malaspina from 1789 to 1794. Having lost the new world of North America to the British, the French were anxious to prevent too easy a domination of the new world of the Pacific by their traditional rivals. Therefore, they laid some claim to this area through the promotion of science with the ill-fated voyage of Jean-François de Galaup, comte de Lapérouse, from 1785 to 1788, and with two French Pacific expeditions of the Revolutionary period, commanded by Antoine-Raymond-Joseph de Bruni d'Entrecasteaux (1791–1793) and Nicholas-Thomas Baudin (1800–1804).

In Pacific exploration or in the systematic exploitation of the conquests of Napoleon, the ideals of the French Revolution meshed well with the advancement of science. Both the Revolution and science were, in Enlightenment fashion, perceived to be about the elimination of the "mind-forg'd manacles" of the past: superstition, priestcraft, and the dead hand of tradition. Just as European explorers used science to take possession of the Pacific, the Revolution strengthened its claims over conquered territories by linking them to the advancement of learning. The less an area had been exposed to the gaze of science, the greater the need for the Revolution to effect this; this accounts for the particular attention devoted to Egypt, the object of European curiosity since classical times.

Egypt. At Napoleon's instigation, the conquering French armies brought in their wake scientists and historians sufficiently numerous to prompt the establishment in 1798 of the Institut d'Égypte under the presidency of the mathematician Gaspard Monge (1746–1818), ably assisted by the chemist Claude Berthollet (1748–1822). Other scientists seconded for the task of taking stock of Egypt were Marie Savigny and Geoffrey Saint-Hilaire, who divided the zoology of the region between them (the former studying invertebrates and the latter vertebrates), the botanist Alire Delile, the geologists Dieudonné de Gratet de Dolomieu and Pierre Cordier, the chemist Hippolyte-Victor Collet-Descatils, and the polymath Michel Lancret—archaeologist, engineer, mathematician, and entomologist. Lancret returned from Egypt in 1801 to oversee the publication of the vast *Description de l'Égypte*, which presented in systematic form the French intellectual conquest of that ancient land.

Private Ventures. The Egyptian venture was of such a scale that it could be conducted only with the support of the state, but scientific expeditions could take more modest forms less overtly linked with the goals of government. The great German geographer Alexander von Humboldt on his own initiative conducted a research tour through the Spanish colonies in South America from 1799 to 1804, returning with a wealth of data covering most fields of science. His voyage was prompted in part by his admiration for Cook's voyages, in particular for the work done by Johann George Forster, who (along with his father, Johann Reinhold Forster) accompanied Cook on his second voyage as a naturalist, and who came to know Humboldt while he was studying at Göttingen. For these Germans, citizens of a disunited territory without imperial designs, scientific exploration held few rewards other than intellectual. Many of the data that Humboldt collected provided the intellectual foundation for his great *Kosmos* (1845–1862), which attempted a synthesis of the sciences around a geographical framework. Though by the time it appeared, the impulses of the Enlightenment had merged into the more specialized scientific disciplines that developed during the nineteenth century, it continued the Enlightenment quest to make the globe better known and accessible by bringing order and system to the study of nature.

[*See also* Academies; Astronomy; Banks, Joseph; Botany; Cartesianism; Cook, James; Humboldt, Wilhelm von; Natural History; Natural Philosophy and Science; Newton, Isaac; *and* Taxonomy.]

BIBLIOGRAPHY

Dunmore, John. *French Explorers in the Pacific*. 2 vols. Oxford, 1965–1969. The first volume deals chiefly with the eighteenth century, the second with the nineteenth.

Frost, A. "European Explorations of the Pacific Ocean." In *Nature in its Greatest Extent: Western Science in the Pacific*, edited by Roy MacLeod and Philip Rehbock, pp. 27–44. Honolulu, 1988.

Gascoigne, John. "Motives for European Exploration of the Pacific in the Age of the Enlightenment." *Pacific Science* 54 (2000), 227–237.

Hankins, Thomas. *Science and the Enlightenment*. Cambridge, 1985. Provides a succinct account of the La Condamine–Maupertuis expeditions.

Jardine, Nicholas, James Secord, and Emma Spary, eds. *Cultures of Natural History*. Cambridge, 1996. The articles by Dettelbach, Browne, Beer, and Bravo are of particular relevance.

Lincoln, Margarette, ed. *Science and Exploration in the Pacific: European Voyages to the Southern Oceans in the 18th Century*. Woodbridge, U.K., 1998.

Miller, David, and Peter Reill, eds. *Visions of Empire: Voyages, Botany, and Representations of Nature*. Cambridge, 1996. Part One focuses on Joseph Banks, the remaining three parts on more general themes.

Smith, Bernard. *European Vision and the South Pacific*. New Haven, Conn., 1985. Brings to bear insights from both the history of ideas and the history of art.

Thomas, Nicholas. "Exploration." In *An Oxford Companion to the Romantic Age: British Culture 1776–1832*, edited by Iain McCalman, pp. 345–353. Oxford, 1999.

Woolf, H. *The Transits of Venus: A Study in the Organization and Practice of Eighteenth-Century Science*. Princeton, N.J., 1959.

JOHN GASCOIGNE

SCIENTIFIC INSTRUMENTS. The Royal Society of London was founded in 1660, the Académie Royale des Sciences in 1666, and other national academies of science during the eighteenth century. These academies had experiments demonstrated before members and visitors. Their activities depended on scientific instruments, made sometimes by members of the academy, and increasingly over time, by professional instrument makers. The air pump used by Robert Boyle (1627–1691), and the microscopes made by Robert Hooke (1635–1703), curator of experiments to the Royal Society of London from 1662, are two early examples. Francis Hauksbee (c. 1666–1713) invented the first glass frictional electrical machine, was elected a fellow of the Royal Society in 1705, and sold instruments including air pumps and barometers. Hauksbee combined academic science and commercial practice, both based upon instruments.

Academic science was just one area where scientific instruments were developed and deployed. Following the prescription of Francis Bacon (1561–1626), natural philosophers sought to apply science to practical ends. Water pumps operated by steam engines contributed to mining and to the provision of drinking water to towns. The steam engine, culminating in the improved version invented by James Watt (1736–1819) and manufactured by him in partnership with Matthew Boulton (1728–1809), symbolized the Industrial Revolution. Industrialists sought to harness science to production, as for example when Josiah Wedgwood invented his pyrometer for measuring the temperature in pottery ovens. Trade benefited also from improved navigation. The scientific revolution was accompanied by, and drew on, the growth of merchant and royal navies. Their voyages required the best available navigational instruments, and contributed to geomagnetism, a necessary adjunct to the use of the magnetic compass. Sailors were supported by the work of astronomical observatories, for example in Paris and at Greenwich. There, accurate timepieces, powerful telescopes, transit instruments, and precisely divided observing instruments, such as sextants and quadrants, contributed to the measurement of time, the mapping of the stars, and the navigation of the earth.

The instrument makers who supplied these varied needs constituted an increasingly organized industry. By the last quarter of the century, leading practitioners oversaw large-scale production and coordinated specialized work on different components, for example, in the construction of chronometers. Some of the finest work was still carried out by a small number of master craftsmen, of whom Jesse Ramsden (1735–1800) was arguably the finest. His instruments achieved a very high degree of precision, based on the excellence of his dividing engines, instruments used to mark the circular and linear scales of measuring instruments. Improved dividing engines had been encouraged by the enormous prizes offered for determining longitude at sea, which required extraordinarily accurate timepieces. Such were the marine chronometers invented by John Harrison (1693–1776), culminating in his fourth model in 1759. Chronometers were important in the voyages of Captain James Cook, but the merchant navy first made regular use of them.

Instruments were not only of theoretical and practical importance, but were also increasingly a part of popular and fashionable culture. Monarchs, noblemen, and bourgeois patrons collected instruments, and took pride in their cabinets of natural philosophy. George III of England owned one of the finest collections, which is

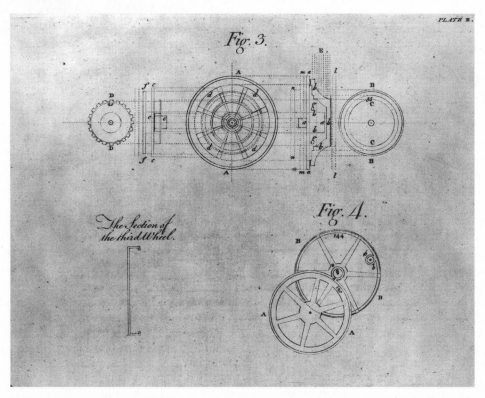

Marine Chronometer. Chronometers were used to determine longitude. Drawings of part of the inner workings by the inventor, John Harrison. From *The Principles of Mr. Harrison's Time-Keeper* (1767). (Prints and Photographs Division, Library of Congress.)

now in the Science Museum, London; some of the pieces were supplied by George Adams Sr. (c. 1704–1773), who also provided more workaday instruments for Captain James Cook. Adam Wilhelm Hauch (1755–1838), courtier, soldier, and natural philosopher, built a collection that he subsequently gave to the king of Denmark, who in turn gave it to the Sorø Academy, where it can still be seen. In the Netherlands, Martinus van Marum (1750–1837) assembled a fine collection that he used for research and for public lectures and demonstrations. His collection survives in Teyler's Museum, Haarlem, a time capsule of the turn of the eighteenth and nineteenth centuries. Universities also built cabinets of natural philosophy at this time, for teaching and for research, and several such cabinets have been preserved. Georges Parrot (1767–1852) created one at the new University of Tartu in Estonia in the first decade of the nineteenth century. The Playfair collection at the University of Edinburgh and the remarkable cabinet at Coimbra University in Portugal are also noteworthy.

The core of any eighteenth-century cabinet of natural philosophy was generally devoted to Newtonian mechanics. The implications of Newton's *Principia* (1687) could be demonstrated using instruments, and the French-born English scientist John Desaguliers (1683–1744) was one of the first to popularize Newton through demonstrations and experiments. His work was taken up and developed first by Willem Jacob 'sGravesande (1688–1742) and then by Petrus van Musschenbroek (1692–1761). Their devices illustrated centrifugal force, impact, uniform acceleration under gravity, and other parts of the Newtonian canon. From Holland, experimental Newtonianism spread to France, where Abbé Jean-Antoine Nollet (1700–1770) was the most influential of the next generation of public and fashionable lecturers. Further mechanical apparatus included a fall machine, to illustrate the behavior of bodies acted on by constant forces. It was designed in the 1770s by Cambridge mathematician George Atwood (1740–1807), and constructed by George Adams Jr. (1750–1795), one of the leading London instrument makers.

Musschenbroek also built electrical apparatus, including a device for storing (static) electricity, which Nollet later named the "Leiden jar." Electrostatic or frictional electric generators were descended from an invention in about 1680 by Otto von Guericke (1602–1686). This was a sulfur ball that was rotated and rubbed by hand. Isaac Newton showed that glass was also a good "electric," and this was the principle of Francis Hauksbee's machine. In the 1750s, a plate machine was developed, in which glass disks replaced globes or cylinders, and leather cushions provided the friction. The largest such machine was made in 1783 by John Cuthbertson (1745–1851) for Marum; it produced up to half a million volts. Cylinder machines, for example, those made by Edward Nairne

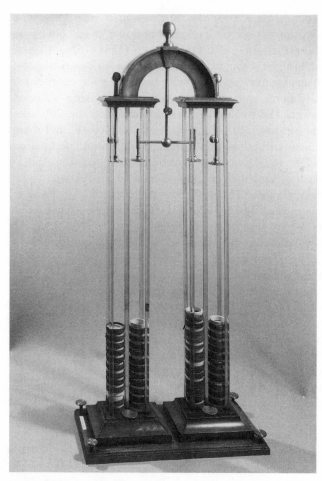

Voltaic Battery. Model constructed in 1800, Paris. (Giraudon/Art Resource, NY.)

(1726–1806), continued alongside disk ones. In 1800, Alessandro Volta (1745–1827) invented the voltaic pile, a source of a continuous current, and chemists and natural philosophers throughout Europe, including Humphry Davy (1778–1829) in England and Jöns Jakob Berzelius (1779–1848) in Sweden, rushed to make bigger and better batteries for electrochemical and other researches.

The principal optical instruments were telescopes and microscopes. Once Newton had explained the problems of chromatic aberration produced by the refraction and dispersion of light within lenses, and of spherical aberration, almost all telescopes until the mid-eighteenth century were reflectors, using mirrors rather than lenses. Then John Dollond (1706–1761) found that by using a combination of flint and crown glass, he could produce an objective lens with almost no chromatic aberration. He and his son Peter (1730–1820) put such achromatic lenses on the market from 1758. James Short (1710–1768), born in Edinburgh and with a business in London, continued to make excellent reflecting telescopes, and took out a patent for a reflector with more than two mirrors. At the end of the century, the astronomer William Herschel (1738–1822) built some of the largest and finest reflectors, including a forty-foot instrument.

The earliest microscopes were simple, that is, they had a single lens, and so were less liable to chromatic aberration than were the early compound microscopes. Dollond's invention of achromatic lenses was applied to the very small lenses of the microscope by the Amsterdam instrument maker Harmanus van Deijl (1738–1809) in the late eighteenth century. During the late seventeenth century, and throughout the eighteenth, the main improvements were to the microscope stand, increasing stability, and making possible finer adjustment and better illumination. Robert Hooke's *Micrographia* (1665) made the compound microscope instantly popular; it was improved further by John Cuff (ca. 1708–1772), Benjamin Martin (1714–1782), and George Adams, father and son.

Chemistry saw important developments in several areas, including: instrumentation for measuring heat; in the beginnings of calorimetry and in handling gases, from the pneumatic trough of Stephen Hales (1677–1761) to the gasometers of Antoine-Laurent Lavoisier (1743–1794); in the development of precision balances, from the midcentury balance used by Joseph Black (1728–1799) that could weigh to one part in two hundred, to the great balance made by Jean Nicolas Fortin (1750–1831) for Lavoisier in the 1780s, weighing to one part in 400,000; in electrochemistry, using the voltaic pile; and in the use of the blowpipe for qualitative analysis, first by German chemists, including Georg Ernst Stahl (1660–1734) and then by Swedish chemists Torbern Bergman (1735–1784), Axel Cronstedt (1722–1765), and Johann Gahn (1745–1818).

Medical instruments in this period were either the largely traditional tools for dissection, trepanning, and so forth, or drew upon the inventions of chemistry and physics. Thus, physicians explored the effects of electricity on the body, and of breathing different kinds of air—James Watt and Thomas Beddoes (1760–1808) collaborated in the invention and manufacture of a device to be used for breathing factitious airs. Watt and Beddoes were both pneumatic chemists and political radicals. It is worth remembering that radical chemist and theologian Joseph Priestley (1733–1804) wrote that the English hierarchy, if there was anything unsound in its constitution, had reason to tremble at an air pump or an electrical machine.

BIBLIOGRAPHY

Anderson, R. G. W. A. *The Playfair Collection and the Teaching of Chemistry at the University of Edinburgh, 1713–1858*. Edinburgh, 1978.

Bud, Robert, and Deborah Jean Warner. *Instruments of Science: An Historical Encyclopedia*. New York and London, 1998.

Clifton, Gloria. *Directory of British Scientific Instrument Makers, 1550–1851*. London, 1995.

Daumas, Maurice. *Scientific Instruments of the Seventeenth and Eighteenth Centuries*. Translated and edited by Mary Holbrook. New York and Washington, D.C., 1972. The best survey of the instrument-making industry in the Enlightenment.

Hackmann, W. D. *Electricity from Glass: the History of the Frictional Electrical Machine, 1600–1850*. Alphen aan den Rijn, Netherlands, 1978.

Holbrook, Mary, R. G. W. Anderson, and D. J. Bryden, eds. *Science Preserved: A Directory of Scientific Instruments in Collections in the United Kingdom and Eire*. London, 1992.

Holmes, Frederic L., and Trevor H. Levere. *Instruments and Experimentation in the History of Chemistry*. Cambridge, Mass., 1999. Concentrates the long eighteenth century.

King, Henry C. *The History of the Telescope*. London, 1955.

Millburn, John R. *Adams of Fleet Street: Instrument Makers to King George III*. Aldershot, U.K., 2000.

Stewart, Larry. *The Rise of Public Science: Rhetoric, Technology, and Natural Philosophy in Newtonian Britain, 1660–1750*. Cambridge and New York, 1992. An excellent treatment of the links between the scientific revolution of the seventeenth century and the later Industrial Revolution.

Taylor, E. G. R. *The Mathematical Practitioners of Tudor and Stuart England*. Cambridge, 1954.

Taylor, E. G. R. *The Mathematical Practitioners of Hanoverian England, 1714–1840*. Cambridge, 1966.

Turner, Gerard L'E., ed. *Storia delle scienze: Gli strumenti*. Turin, 1991. The best one-volume history of scientific instruments.

Turner, G. L'E. *Essays on the History of the Microscope*. Oxford, 1980.

Turner, G. L'E., and T. H. Levere. *Martinus van Marum: Life and Work*. Edited by E. Lefebvre and J. G. de Bruijn. Volume 4: *Van Marum's Scientific Instruments in Teyler's Museum*. Leiden, 1973. The history of a museum and cabinet, and a model catalog of the instruments.

TREVOR H. LEVERE

SCIENTIFIC JOURNALS. The appearance in 1665 of both the Paris-based *Journal des sçavans* and the *Philosophical Transactions* of the Royal Society of London marked the advent of the scientific journal and the beginning of a new era in the history of the scientific press. The periodical form proved more effective as a communications medium than the book or informal and formal correspondence networks, such as those that had arisen around Marin Mersenne (1588–1648), Théophraste Renaudot (1586–1653), or Henry Oldenburg (1617?–1677) before he launched the *Philosophical Transactions*. In the long run, especially by creating the new genre of the scientific paper and experimental report, the periodical press superseded the monograph as the primary means for scientific communications.

The model of the learned journal spread quickly in the seventeenth century, as evidenced by the *Acta eruditorum* (Leipzig, 1682–1782), the *Nouvelles de la République des Lettres* (Amsterdam, 1684–1718, edited in its early years by Pierre Bayle), the *Miscellanea curiosa medicophysica* (from 1670, published by the Academia Naturae

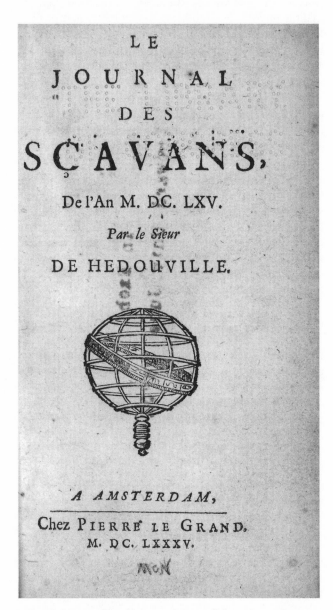

Curiosorum), and the *Giornale de' letterati d'Italia* (Rome, 1668–1681, followed by several other periodicals with the same name). As much as the form was established in the seventeenth century, an exponential growth of such journals occurred in the eighteenth century. In Kronick's 1976 survey of the scientific and technical press, for example, he counted more than one thousand serials extant from 1700 to 1790, as compared to only thirty-five before 1700. The scientific importance of those journals varied considerably; Gascoigne (1985) counted only sixty-three scientific and technical periodicals as having significant scientific impact before 1793. Geographically, the periodical press spread throughout Europe and its colonies, but the Germanic lands proved to be the center, with 62 percent of titles originating there. This somewhat surprising distribution occurred because most German periodicals were very short-lived and because of the decentralized political character of the German states, many of which were university centers, each with its own press or presses.

The scientific periodical press of the eighteenth century included several different sorts of publications. The general learned journal that contained scientific and technical material must be distinguished from scientific periodicals per se. Then, independent journals were notably different from those carrying institutional sponsorship. Another distinction concerns the so-called substantive journal (the locus of original publication of science) versus derivative publications that reprinted or excerpted materials from other published sources. Experts also differentiate the collection, the review journal, and the abstract journal as other entities. While this taxonomy of the scientific press is helpful, it should not be applied rigidly. For example, few imprints were exclusively concerned with the natural sciences; conversely, general journals regularly reported from the world of science. Derivative publications occasionally published original scientific material, as was the case of the weekly *L'avantcoureur* (Paris, 1759–1773), which reported on some of Antoine-Laurent Lavoisier's early work in chemistry. Similarly, dividing periodicals from anthologies or from abridgments issued at regular intervals is not always possible. Further, there was the diffusion of science reporting into the popular press; for example, certain English almanacs had circulations numbering in the tens and hundreds of thousands, compared to the fifteen hundred or fewer copies of the ordinary journal.

The General Learned Journal. The scientific journals played various roles. They provided outlets for establishing priority, as eighteenth-century scientists and inventors increasingly turned to periodical publication instead of monographs (which took longer and cost more to produce). Journals afforded a generally inexpensive means of communication, and they encouraged scientific exchanges and debate. They brought scientific news from the polyglot international domain into local vernacular languages, and they served archival functions in the preservation of the record of scientific accomplishment.

Among general learned journals of the 1700s, the *Journal des sçavans*, the *Acta eruditorum*, and the Jesuit-sponsored *Journal de Trévoux* (officially, the *Mémoires pour servir à l'histoire des sciences et des beaux arts*, Trévoux, then Paris: 1701–1767, with related titles to 1782) were mainstays of literate culture. They primarily reviewed books, and, although their scientific importance declined with the century, they regularly devoted about a quarter to a half

Scientific Journal. Title page of *Journal des sçavans* for 1665, printed at Amsterdam in 1685. (Prints and Photographs Division, Library of Congress.)

of their pages to reviews and reports from the world of science. For the most part, however, independent journals were ephemeral: slightly more than 25 percent failed in their first year; less than 33 percent lasted longer than five years. A single editor most often provided the motive force, but sometimes a board of editors, some of whom specialized in science managed a journal; Bernard de Fontenelle and, later, Alexis Clairaut, for example, handled mathematical articles in the *Journal des scavans*; Father Cotte superintended meteorology. Reprint or pirated editions of the better known journals were often available during the eighteenth century; for example, Protestant counterfeit editions of the *Journal des sçavans* and the *Journal de Trévoux* appeared in Amsterdam from 1665 to 1782.

While constituting only one quarter of the total number of journals, publications of learned societies represented the dominant segment of the scientific periodical press in the eighteenth century. The century has been labeled the "Age of Academies." The most important scientific academies and societies received government patronage, and they provided an essential institutional base for contemporary science and scientific publications. Learned societies then became responsible for the bulk of original publication in the sciences, and because of their institutional sponsorship, proceedings of the societies carried greater authority and lasted longer than the typical independent journal. Of the top forty-one scientific journals of the 1700s identified by Gascoigne (1985), only ten lacked institutional affiliation. The *Philosophical Transactions* of the Royal Society of London and the *Histoire et mémoires* series of the Parisian Académie Royale des Sciences were the two most important scientific periodicals of the period, and some four dozen other *Acta, Abhandlungen, Commentarii, Handlingar, Mémoires, Memoirs, Miscellanea, Saggi, Samling, Transactions, Verhandelingen*, and like serials appeared with institutional sponsorship through the 1790s. These publications can be roughly divided into types modeled either after the *Philosophical Transactions* of the Royal Society (published by quarter or by trimester) or after the *Histoire et mémoires* of the Parisian Académie des Sciences (in nominally annual tomes). Scientists published their original research in those journals and looked to them first and foremost to learn what others were producing.

Challenges. As central as society proceedings were to the contemporary scientific press, they did face some challenges. They were expensive and were printed in limited editions, difficult to obtain by nonmembers or those without access to the distribution system established by the societies. The problem of sometimes lengthy delays between a paper's presentation before the membership and its appearance in print was further undermining.

These delays might range from a year or two to a decade or more. The average lag time for the *Mémoires* of the Paris Académie Royale des Sciences was three years, but at the extreme, the Paris volume for 1761 was not available until 1768. At one point, the Imperial Russian Academy of Sciences in Saint Petersburg took five years to produce a volume of its *Commentarii*. The first volume of *Commentarii* of the Bolognese Accademia took eight years to publish, and the second took fourteen years. Even the more regular *Philosophical Transactions* of the Royal Society of London appeared only semiannually after 1763 and had a backlog of fifteen to eighteen months. Such delays raise the question of whether society publications were intended to foster the dissemination of knowledge or to serve more archival functions.

Language barriers compounded the difficulties; that is, most eighteenth-century journals were published in local vernaculars. In the cases of the lesser languages, like English or Swedish, the vernacular proved an obstacle to the ready dissemination of science through the Republic of Letters. The Swedish *Handlingar* were translated into Latin, German, English, Danish, Dutch, and French. The *Philosophical Transactions* were rendered into Latin, German, Dutch, Italian, and French. The emergence of the first review and abstract journal devoted to the natural sciences was in Latin, *Commentarii de rebus in scientia naturali et medicina gestis* (Leipzig, 1752–1798), and was an early indicator of the problem. Even more striking, from 1755 to 1779, the thirteen-volume foreign series of the *Collection Académique* republished, using the presumed, universal language of French, parts of the *Philosophical Transactions*, the *Mémoires* of the Berlin Academy, the *Commentarii* of the Bolognese Academy, the *Handlingar* of the Swedish Academy, and the *Mélanges* of Turin's Société Royale des Sciences, among other sources.

In this connection, the periodical edited by abbé François Rozier, *Observations sur la physique, sur l'histoire naturelle et sur les arts* (Paris, 1771; 1773–1826)—or Rozier's Journal, as it is commonly called—deserves particular attention. Rozier's was the first independent periodical to be concerned exclusively with science and the latest news from the world of science. Rozier personally edited the journal through 1780 and was committed to publishing original articles for use by active scientific researchers. That Rozier published monthly, with little or no delay between submission and publication, distinguished his journal from all others and made it the premier vehicle for scientific publication in the last decades of the 1700s. As Kronick (1976) has remarked, "Such promptness of publication would be considered exemplary even today." Rather than competing with the publications of the scientific societies, however, Rozier's Journal complemented their proceedings. The Parisian Académie Royale des Sciences elected Rozier a correspondent in 1783, and the institution and its members used his journal as a quick outlet for publication. Furthermore, as a mechanism to distribute his journal, Rozier tapped the international system of exchanges previously established between and among scientific societies. Rozier's Journal indicates the seriousness of the problem of communications that affected the eighteenth-century scientific press and efforts to ameliorate that problem.

Specialized Journals. Earlier than once thought, some specialized scientific journals had originated in this period. Medical journals were the first specialized periodicals: the seventeenth-century *Acta medica et philosophica Hafniensia* (Copenhagen, 1673–1680) and the *Nouvelles découvertes sur toutes les parties de la médecine* (Paris, 1679–1682); their eighteenth-century successors included the publications of the Académie Royale de Chirurgie (founded Paris, 1731; 5 volumes of *Mémoires*, 1743–1774) and the Société Royale de Médecine (founded Paris, 1776; 10 volumes of *Mémoires*, 1776–1789). Journals devoted to agriculture and technology also should be noted in this connection. With subject matter limited to the *sciences physiques* (as opposed to the *sciences mathématiques*), Rozier's Journal represents a step in the direction of scientific specialization. With their exclusive concern with natural history, *Der Naturforscher* (Halle, 1774–1804) and the *Beschäftigungen* of the Gesellschaft naturforschender Freunde (Berlin, from 1775) likewise exemplify this trend. Journals specializing in a single scientific discipline also arose in the eighteenth century. The French *Connaissance des temps*, for example, started as an annual almanac in 1679, but under Jérôme de Lalande it became a true journal of astronomy, publishing astronomy papers from 1766. The *Nautical Almanac* published by the Board of Longitude (London, 1767) and the *Astronomisches Jahrbuck* published by the Berlin academy (Berlin, 1776) also evidence this step toward specialization in astronomy. The Meteorological Society of Mannheim (the Societas Meteorologicae Palatinae) was a specialized scientific society that produced twelve volumes of meteorological *Ephemerides* from 1781 to 1792. Such specialization increased in the 1780s, decreasing the importance of general journals and society publications. New specialized journals soon included Lorenz Crell's *Chemische Journal* (Lemgo, then Leipzig, from 1778); the *Magazin für die* (later *Annalen der*) *Botanik* (Zurich, 1787); *The Botanical Magazine* (later *Curtis's Botanical Magazine*, London, 1787); the *Bergmännisches Journal* (Freiburg, 1788); the *Annales de Chimie* (Paris, 1789); the *Journal der Physik* (Halle and Leipzig from 1790, followed by the *Annalen der Physik* from 1799); and the *Archiv der reinen und angewandten Mathematik* (Leipzig, 1794, with antecedents to 1781).

Some of the above-mentioned titles were independent journals; some had institutional affiliations. With the Linnean Society and its *Transactions* (London, 1788), a growing number of specialized societies soon produced many specialized scientific serials. That development was particularly pronounced in the early 1800s in Great Britain, with the foundation of the Geological Society of London and its *Transactions* (from 1807), the Royal Astronomical Society (founded 1820; *Memoirs* from 1821), the Zoological Society of London (1826; *Proceedings* from 1830), the Royal Entomological Society (founded 1833; *Transactions* from 1834), and the Chemical Society of London (1841, *Memoirs* from 1841). The creation of professional societies like the British Association for the Advancement of Science (1831; its annual *Report* from 1831) also changed the landscape of the periodical press in the nineteenth century and set another pattern taken up by other scientific nations. The general scientific society and its periodical publication that predominated in the 1700s thus in the 1800s became supplanted by a proliferation of disciplinary and professional societies and journals. In response, in 1835, a revived French Académie des Sciences launched its weekly *Comptes rendus hebdomadaire*, which proved the most important scientific periodical of the nineteenth century. Such a weekly, however, was far removed from the staid volumes of the institution's eighteenth-century predecessor, and it testifies to the changed conditions for scientific journals and patterns of scientific publication after 1800.

[*See also* Academies; Correspondence and Correspondents; Learned Societies; *and* Natural Philosophy and Science.]

BIBLIOGRAPHY

Bazerman, Charles. *The Genre and Activity of the Experimental Article in Science.* Madison, Wis., 1988. A suggestive, postmodern analysis of the development of the scientific paper and the rhetorical strategies involved. Part Two: "The Emergence of Literary and Social Forms in Early Modern Science" focuses on the *Philosophical Transactions* in the eighteenth century, on article publishing, and on the effect on scientific communities of the new form of the scientific paper.

Capp, Bernard. *English Almanacs, 1500–1800: Astrology and the Popular Press.* Ithaca, N.Y., 1979. An overlooked study that traces the diffusion of science to popular culture.

Dooley, Brendan. *Science, Politics and Society in Eighteenth-Century Italy: The* Giornale de' letterati d'Italia *and Its World.* New York and London, 1991. A close-up study of the most successful literary and scientific journal in contemporary Italy, the *Giornale de' letterati d'Italia*, published in Venice from 1710 to 1740. Offers details of high generality and is unique in delving into the entrepreneurial and sociocultural context of early journal publishing. Chapter 2 concerns "Periodical Publishing in Eighteenth-Century Italy"; chapter 5 concerns "Journalism and Science."

Gascoigne, Robert Mortimer. *A Historical Catalogue of Scientific Periodicals, 1665–1900: With a Survey of Their Development.* New York and London, 1985. An important source; catalogs journals with greatest scientific effect and includes statistics. Chapter 3.1 has an overview of the scientific periodical literature.

Houghton, Bernard. *Scientific Periodicals: Their Historical Development, Characteristics, and Control.* Hamden, Conn., 1975. Somewhat dated, and Thornton and Tully (1978) criticize this work as limited and selective, but chapters 1 and 2 present an accessible, short introduction to the origins and history of the scientific periodical through the eighteenth century.

Hunter, Andrew, ed. *Thornton and Tully's Scientific Books, Libraries, and Collectors: A Study of Bibliography and the Book Trade in Relation to the History of Science.* "4th ed, considerably revised and rewritten." Aldershot, U.K., 2000. This strangely mistitled volume is not a fourth edition of Thornton and Tully's classic work, but it is a useful and informed collection of twelve articles dealing with scientific books and journals, notably including "Eighteenth-Century Scientific Publishing" by Brian J. Ford.

Kronick, David A. *A History of Scientific and Technical Periodicals: The Origins and Development of the Scientific and Technical Press, 1665–1790.* 2d ed. Metuchen, N.J., 1976. A pioneering work that provides the still standard account, but criticized by Gascoigne (1985) as "written from a librarian's viewpoint."

Kronick, David. *Scientific and Technical Periodicals of the Seventeenth and Eighteenth Centuries: A Guide.* Metuchen, N.J., 1991. The most comprehensive list of the era's scientific and technical periodicals; 1,858 entries in all, including continuations, each with full bibliographic details. An essential reference.

McClellan, James E., III. "The Scientific Press in Transition: Rozier's Journal and the Scientific Societies." *Annals of Science* 36 (1979), 425–449. A study of that key journal with references to the antecedent literature.

McClellan, James E., III. *Science Reorganized: Scientific Societies in the Eighteenth Century.* New York, 1985. A survey of learned societies and their publications. Chapter 6 examines the distribution system effected by learned societies, the problem of communications, and complementary publication outlets developed toward the end of the 1700s.

Meadows, A. J., ed. *Development of Science Publishing in Europe.* Amsterdam, 1980. Includes chapter by A. A. Manten, "Development of European Scientific Journal Publishing before 1850," with an appendix listing pioneer specialized journals.

Sgard, Jean, ed. *Dictionnaire des journaux, 1600–1789.* 2 vols. Paris, 1991. A magisterial historical and bibliographic inventory of some one thousand French-language journals, produced collectively by a team of leading scholars. Provides detailed information concerning journal titles, dates, and places of publication, format, editor(s), content, references, and present-day library holdings, in addition to often substantial historical discussions. Covers all the French-language journals mentioned in this article.

Sgard, Jean, ed. *Dictionnaire des journalistes, 1600–1789.* Oxford, 1999. A biblio-biographical dictionary of French-language journalists that complements Sgard (1991).

Thornton, John Leonard, and R. I. J. Tully. *Scientific Books, Libraries, and Collectors: A Study of Bibliography and the Book Trade in Relation to Science,* 3d ed. London, 1971. *Supplement 1969–1975* (London, 1978). A standard source that includes chapters on the scientific societies and their journals and on the growth of periodical literature.

Vittu, Jean-Pierre. "Périodiques" In *La science classique, XVIe–XVIIIe siècle: Dictionnaire critique,* edited by Michel Blay and Robert Halleux, pp. 140–148. Paris, 1998. A sophisticated, up-to-date overview.

JAMES E. MCCLELLAN III

SCOTLAND. Scotland shared the problems of most other European countries in the eighteenth century, but it had those problems to an exaggerated degree. It was a poor country, with not much more than 10 percent of the land suitable for crops. Another 20 percent was usable for pasturage, but much of that was of extremely poor quality. The remaining wastes lacked both easily worked timber stands and usable mineral resources. The distribution of resources had divided the country into three regions: the mountainous Highlands, which lacked roads and towns; the Lowlands, comprising the Border area contiguous with England in the south; and a narrow central region of fairly good land stretching from the northeast to the southwest, which included most of the towns. The Highlands possessed about 40 percent of the people. They were mostly Gaelic-speaking and possessed a distinct culture that was regarded by their Lowland cousins as barbarous and needing to be changed. The Lowlanders wanted the Highlands to be made Presbyterian, weaned from loyalties to clans and chiefs, and brought into the law-governed modern world of the money economy and rational thought. Essential to all that were economic development, education, and the extension of law and order to unruly areas. Much of that agenda had existed for Lowlanders since the sixteenth century, but by 1700 it seemed realizable, and imperative to realize because the stability of the state depended on it.

Scotland's poverty had long meant that it had been an exporter of people from every area. Many had gone abroad as mercenaries, serving in the armies of most European powers. Poverty had also meant that Scots had been unable to train in their own universities the professional men the country required. For education in law, medicine, and even divinity, Scots had gone to Europe, especially to France and Holland. All this ensured that Scots in the eighteenth century would try to make the country more prosperous, more orderly, culturally united, better educated, and more modern—more like Holland, France, and England.

Economy and People. Scots were a fairly cosmopolitan people whose orientation before 1740 was more to Europe than to England, partly because the English had tried for centuries to conquer and to absorb their smaller neighbor. Scots were as proud of their long-maintained independence as of their rather distinguished intellectual history in the late Middle Ages and the Renaissance. Hard times had come to them in the 1600s, partly as a result of climatic change, but largely because of their relationship to the English, with whom they had shared a common king since 1603. Their state had withered once it was ruled principally from London, and their economy had been weakened by the departure of the court from Edinburgh and by the consequences of English wars, both civil and foreign. Oliver Cromwell had incorporated Scotland into England and governed it as an English province. All those things would force eighteenth-century Scots to think about the nature of societies, politics, and the ends and means they should pursue to preserve their character and self-respect.

By the 1680s, those concerns merged with others in the minds of Scottish virtuosi affected by the new learning and the scientism of the age. Those trends are best seen in the careers of Sir Robert Sibbald, M.D. (1641–1722) and those associated with him in many enterprises. These men worked in Edinburgh, but they had their counterparts in other cities and in the countryside of Scotland. They enjoyed the support of royalist politicians, just as most of the enlightened later would be supported by influential men such as Archibald Campbell, third duke of Argyll. The generation to which Sibbald belonged set the agenda for much of the eighteenth century and helped to determine the practical outlook of enlightened Scots.

Sibbald set out to improve Scotland in every way he could. He launched a survey of the country designed to inventory its resources, establish its physical features, and collect its rarities and history. This project was to be completed only in the 1790s, with the appearance of *The Statistical Account of Scotland* edited by Sir John Sinclair. Both Sibbald and Sinclair hoped their work would stimulate economic development. To further that project, around 1702 Sibbald proposed, but failed to obtain, a charter for a Royal Society of Scotland, which was to serve as a research institute for the country and give dignity to its members, both at home and abroad. In the famine years of the 1690s, he and his friends proposed more schemes for the development of the fisheries, agriculture, mining, and other industries. They were equally keen on educational reforms, including the introduction of medical and legal education for professional men. All that had come by 1726. Sibbald and his friends also kept alive for many years antiquarian clubs designed to defend the historical reputation of Scots as learned men and as warriors whose valor had kept them independent of the English. Their projects led to the accumulation of data that would make possible the writing of a narrative history of the country based on critically examined sources, finally accomplished by writers of the mid-eighteenth century. The history that the virtuosi did produce was also driven by religious passions and by their desire to resist the union with England in 1707, when England and Scotland were incorporated in the United Kingdom. Their works thus contributed to the great debate about politics, economics, society, independence, and civic virtue, best seen in the works of Andrew Fletcher of Saltoun. Finally, Sibbald and his friends joined in clubs and societies and urged their creation as venues

in which improvement, learning, and politeness might flourish. They thus sought to change the manners of their countrymen as well as their ways of thinking. The models Sibbald cited for this were the Italian and French academies.

Learning and Ideas. During the late seventeenth century, there was a convergence of learning and ideas throughout Europe, and in that Scots joined. Because they could not educate their own professional men or print their own books until well into the eighteenth century, they kept up with the latest European ideas. When medical and legal education did come to Scotland, it was modern; when arts curricula were changed, they too were up to date. Indeed, since Scots often had to go abroad to find careers, they had to be prepared to compete. This also meant that when they thought about their shameful backwardness and its remedies, they aimed at the improved Dutch and English standards in agriculture, or banking, or other fields, and not at those typical in Europe generally. This accelerated the pace of change in Scotland, as did the very small size of its social and political elite. If one could persuade the political core of perhaps three thousand landowners and other elites of the desirability of a change, it was likely to come fairly quickly. This had an important bearing on the rate at which Scots modernized their practices and ideas.

After the Revolution of 1688, Scots also had to pay more attention to the English in virtually every way. Those who wanted political careers could not fail to be loyal to politically Whiggish ideas, because those had triumphed in the Revolution that replaced James II with William III. This was not a great problem for many Scots; Calvinists had generally favored the ideas that kings could be deposed and that quasi-republican and limited governments were good. Those same notions, however, were rejected by Jacobite Scottish Episcopalians and became rallying points for those opposed to union with England, or to Presbyterianism, which union also sanctioned. Eighteenth-century Scots were long divided by these issues, with most of the enlightened siding with the Whigs. William III and his Anglican English supporters also had qualms about the intolerance of the Scots in 1690. By 1712, Scottish intolerance of Episcopalians had so rankled the English that a measure of toleration was forced on the Scots; another act gave control of church patronage to the gentry, from whom it had been taken in 1690. The long-term effect of these changes was to end a great deal of the religious harassment in the country and to make the Kirk (the Church of Scotland) reflective of the outlook of the gentry. It was then able to support much of the program of the enlightened, once the generation of intransigent Calvinists had died off by about 1730. Their replacements were men like William Wishart Jr., Robert

Wallace, William Robertson, Hugh Blair, John Home, and others in the so-called Moderate Party of the Kirk. English influence on enlightened Scots was also to be seen in other important areas of intellectual life. Scots who made careers in medicine in England often had close ties to the Royal Society of London and to the scientific community. After about 1690, they included many—like Archibald Pitcairne, M.D.—who were early proponents of Newtonianism and who saw to its introduction in the Scottish universities long before it was generally taught in England.

This scientific movement was accompanied by an increased Scottish interest in the English language. In part, this was rooted in the need for those in the United Kingdom to have a common language; in part, it reflected the need of Scots to be (or appear) more polished and refined. By this time, refinement was less likely to be marked by good French than by good English, and by knowing and being able to talk about what the journalists Addison and Steele were making the fashionable topics of tea-table conversation. With more interest in English as a language came the works of philosophers like John Locke, Samuel Clarke, Joseph Butler, Bishop Berkeley, and Lord Shaftesbury, all of whom were being read in the universities before the end of the 1720s.

Enlightenment Cities. The Scottish Enlightenment flourished principally in three cities—none of which had Grub Streets to furnish educated but alienated and vocal critics of their time and place. Aberdeen's intelligentsia came from its two universities and from its few enlightened clergymen, medical men, and landowners. At Glasgow the comparable circle embraced also some lawyers, merchants, and learned printers. To all these Edinburgh added, as any capital would, military men, jurists, genteel holders of state offices, and members of the nobility whose social center was the city. As a result, the development of themes and ideas varied among these diverse settings, but everywhere it also took a professional and academic tone. Edinburgh is discussed in its own entry, so here we focus on the other cities.

Aberdeen. Aberdeen at the beginning of the eighteenth century was a port town of about 12,000 people; by midcentury, it had grown to 22,000 and would rise to 27,000 by 1800. Aberdeen lacked Glasgow's Presbyterian intolerance and had closer relations with both London and France. Until midcentury, it had many citizens who were sympathetic to Jacobitism and members of the Scottish Episcopal Church; such people looked back to the time of episcopacy with fondness. Men like the philosopher George Campbell had attended college with boys who were to become Roman Catholic bishops, as did his friend George Hay. Aberdeen's rather tolerant enlightenment was rooted, like Edinburgh's, in the work

of virtuosi interested in everything. It took a decisive turn with the appearance at Marischal College of three young teachers, Colin Maclaurin, George Turnbull, and Thomas Blackwell Jr. Maclaurin arrived in 1717 and reinforced the Newtonian ideas that had been brought to the city ten years earlier by Thomas Bower. Maclaurin, like Turnbull, also came with an interest in Shaftesbury and modern philosophy. Turnbull had been a member of Edinburgh's Rankenian Club and had corresponded with the deist John Toland and his protector, Robert, Lord Molesworth. Turnbull believed that all knowledge and standards of taste and morality were based on experience, and he later tried to show this in works on natural law and ancient art and education. Blackwell became the Marischal College professor of Greek and wrote important works on Homer, Greek myth, and Roman history. Like his colleagues, he was impressed by Shaftesbury. Their most distinguished student was Thomas Reid, who, along with James Beattie and George Campbell, would articulate Scottish Common Sense philosophy, partly in reaction to the immaterialism of George Berkeley and to the more skeptical philosophy of David Hume, which these men sought to refute in the interests of common sense and Christianity.

Their philosophy was to become the distinctive Scottish Empiricism, taken by Reid to Glasgow, where he taught after 1764, and polished in Edinburgh by his protégés James Gregory and Dugald Stewart. By the 1750s, papers read to the Aberdeen Wise Club (1758–1773), which was mostly attended by the professors of the King's and Marischal Colleges and by a few local ministers and physicians, had sketched this view in some detail. These papers centered on the epistemic and moral topics made pressing by the skeptical writings of Hume, but they also showed the members' awareness of and engagement with the works of many British and continental European thinkers. David Skene, their best naturalist, supplied specimens to Linnaeus; others learnedly debated the views of Georges-Louis de Buffon, organized an observation of the transit of Venus in 1761, and discussed mathematical topics. They were equally wide-ranging when it came to discussions of genius, style, language, and the characteristics of human nature or of evidence. All these topics surfaced in the works they published.

Later in the century, others—including James Dunbar and Robert Hamilton—would make substantial contributions to the study of society and political economy. Hamilton, a mathematician, and Patrick Copland, a professor of natural philosophy, would be useful to Aberdeen's manufacturers and businessmen, Hamilton by doing the actuarial mathematics for the first of the city's insurance companies, and Copland as a consultant to manufacturers and the teacher of classes for artisans. These men were no less concerned to be useful improvers than were their counterparts elsewhere. That is also shown by the work of the Gordon's Mill Farming Club (1758–c. 1770), to which several of them belonged; this group listened to papers on agricultural experiments and discussed such things as leases, plows, roads, and markets. Like the enlightened elsewhere, the Aberdeen men protested slavery—Beattie lectured against it from 1760 on—and some of them even favored both the American and French revolutions. They also supported the Aberdeen Musical Society (founded 1748), which after 1753 gave concerts in the town and could boast a notable library of scores by Handel, Corelli, Gluck, Rameau, and other composers from across Europe. Aberdeen may have been small, but its enlightenment made lasting contributions in the philosophy of Thomas Reid and in the Rev. George Campbell's widely used rhetoric book, and ecclesiastical history.

Glasgow. Glasgow's Enlightenment was different because of the character of the town. In 1700, it may have had 12,000 inhabitants, a figure that had burgeoned to 80,000 by the end of the century. That growth was attributable to the increase of Glasgow's trade with North America and to the industrial developments that took place as shippers tried to find cargoes to send out in the ships that would bring back American sugar, tobacco, cotton, and other goods. This was a merchants' town, but the merchants were not much interested in enlightened ideas or in politeness. Glasgow had to wait until 1799 for a permanent musical society, and its mobs several times burned or tried to burn the city theater—theaters were thought to be immoral and ungodly. Still, in 1700 Glasgow too had its virtuosi, who were in contact with those in Edinburgh and thinking about the same sorts of things. Several were present in the university, including Robert Wodrow, who became a parish minister and a notable historian, somewhat in the manner of Cotton Mather, with whom he corresponded. In time, Wodrow came to distrust the enlightened because they were not sufficiently Christian and evangelical. To understand his views, we need only look at the city's most notable professor in the first half of the century: the Irish Presbyterian Francis Hutcheson.

Hutcheson came to Glasgow in 1729 to be professor of moral philosophy, bringing with him a Dissenter's Whiggism and interest in religious freedom, including the freedom not to subscribe to creeds. In Glasgow, he succeeded Professor Gershom Carmichael, who had taught a version of Samuel Pufendorf's system of natural law in which morality was ultimately grounded on the commands of God known to us through reason, revelation, and conscience. Hutcheson, who had been much impressed by Locke, Shaftesbury, Berkeley, and Bernard Mandeville, rooted moral distinctions in a secular manner in sense or feeling, and in utility, a move in which he would be followed, more or less, by Hume and by Adam Smith, who succeeded him in this chair. As a moralist, Hutcheson extended his considerations of contracts in his moral philosophy lectures to include elementary economics and the basis of politics, which for him lay in an agreement or contract that led more easily to republicanism than to monarchy. On Sundays, he lectured on Grotius's *Truth of the Christian Religion*, which the orthodox regarded as an Arminian work little better than deism. They had no reason to be better pleased with Adam Smith, his successor, since he objected to opening classes with prayers and lectured even more on political economy, as well as on literary criticism and rhetoric.

Like others on the faculty, Hutcheson was much interested in the classics and praised the Stoic *Meditations* of Marcus Aurelius, which he translated with a biography of the Roman emperor, published in Glasgow in 1742 by Robert and Andrew Foulis, the university's printers. Other professors supplied the Foulis brothers with texts and original works on the ancients, notably Robert Simson, who wrote on ancient mathematics, and James Moor, who was interested in the Greek language. All of them helped the Foulis brothers in their efforts to set up an art school within the precincts of the university in 1754. It ran until 1775 and served as the model for the Board of Trustees' Academy established in Edinburgh in 1786. Both schools trained students in the fine arts and in what might be called industrial design; both aimed to raise the standards of taste in Scotland.

The University of Glasgow had had, from the beginning of the century, a strong interest in science of a practical sort. Its professors of mathematics had practical interests and skills. The holder of that chair in 1712 was certainly teaching Newtonian physics. By about 1730, the professor of natural philosophy added practical and experimental classes for the city's artisans to his regular teaching. Attempts at professional education had led to the founding of chairs in botany and anatomy, medicine, and law. Other local medical men taught at the town's hospital. By 1760, much more had been done for the sciences. The university had added a chair of astronomy, hired a first-class teacher of science in the person of John Anderson, and begun serious medical education with classes by William Cullen, who had earlier taught chemistry and agriculture. Cullen was the first of a long line of chemists that included Joseph Black, John Robison, William Irvine, and T. C. Hope, all of whom also acted as consultants to local manufacturers, in whose works they sometimes had a financial interest. Associated with them was James Watt, who had a shop on the university grounds and joined in their activities; some of them were later to assist him in his.

The enlightenment of these men is best seen in the work of the Glasgow Literary Society (1752–c. 1803), who listened to many papers in which the scientific ideas of foreigners such as Maupertuis, Buffon, Linnaeus, and d'Alembert were discussed. They also heard Black's papers on latent heat, Hope's on the discovery of strontium, Anderson's essays on firearms and how to improve them, and much more of an innovative nature. There were, of course, papers and debates on criticism, language, the faculties of the mind, politics, history, education, and much else. Most of the work of Thomas Reid published after 1764 was first heard here, as were works by John Millar, some of Adam Smith's essays, and the materials that formed the books of many other members. The society listened to a good deal of literary criticism and heard poems by William Richardson. As in Aberdeen and Edinburgh, the works of Rousseau, Condillac, Voltaire, Beccaria, and other philosophes occasioned papers and discussions from members who had sometimes met these men.

There also developed in Glasgow by the 1760s an evangelical enlightenment led by local clerics and eventually supported by Anderson and some of his mercantile and medical friends. These Calvinists were, like Locke, willing to tolerate all sorts of Christians save Roman Catholics, whose political allegiance they thought uncertain because their oaths might be dispensed by the pope. They supported the American Revolution and, initially, the French Revolution, and they hoped for more freedom and cheaper, better government in Britain. They tended to think freer trade was a good thing as long as their own was not hurt. They were interested in science and improvements and believed that good letters and sound learning would always support true religion. In this respect, their views were close to those of some in the American colonies, such as John Witherspoon, who had emigrated from the region to become president of what is now Princeton University.

Other centers. Outside the larger towns, there were few other signs of enlightenment. At St. Andrews, the university could boast men like the historian Robert Watson or the liberal theologian George Hill. In Perth, by the 1780s there was a club that included a local printer, some ministers, and schoolmasters. A few worked on their estates, but in Scotland, as elsewhere, the Enlightenment was an urban movement associated with towns and the conviviality of club life, with libraries and salons. Here it was also a movement dominated by men. Women shone only in drawing rooms, at the keyboards, and as the writers of poems and songs; only one was a philosopher—Lady Mary Shepherd (1777–1847). Still, Scots were exceptional in contributing much to the thought of the age, and much that has lasted. Every discipline of the social sciences owes something to eighteenth-century Scottish thinkers, just as many places still treasure the cultural heritage that Scots took with them to the British Empire or to America.

There was no wholly typical enlightened Scot, but Hume embodied much of what the Scottish Enlightenment was about. None of Hume's compatriots thought him correct in his philosophical ideas, but his preoccupations with knowledge, morals, and taste were widely shared. His interest in society, economics, and politics was also typical of his time and place and was expressed in essays of unequaled brilliance and concision. Less brilliant but equally typical were his concerns with aesthetics and criticism. His *History of England*, as an analytical narrative history, was bettered in the century only by Gibbon's *Decline and Fall of the Roman Empire* (1776), a work that recognized Hume's earlier achievement. Hume was also the century's most profound critic of natural and revealed religion, but there he was not a typical Scot. Most of the enlightened in Britain were sincerely Christian and found it virtually unthinkable that there might be no God requiring duties of us. Hume, on the other hand, was driven by a hatred and suspicion of religious beliefs that informs most of what he wrote. Profoundly different in outlook from Samuel Johnson, he was his equal as an eminent man of letters, and by far more respected and read on the European continent. Hume's views today are very much alive—as are Reid's refutations of them. For a nation of no more than 1.5 million people, the Scots had a wonderful eighteenth century.

[*See also* Campbell, Archibald; Clerk, John; Clubs and Societies; Economic Thought; Edinburgh; Education; Home, Henry; Hume, David; Medicine; Moral Philosophy; National Churches; Reformed Churches, *subentry on* Presbyterianism; Smith, Adam; Stewart, Dugald; *and* Universities.]

BIBLIOGRAPHY

Berry, Christopher. *Social Theory of the Scottish Enlightenment.* Edinburgh, 1997. A fine study of the social theory of the better known Scottish thinkers.

Broadie, Alexander, ed. *The Cambridge Companion to the Scottish Enlightenment.* Cambridge, 2002. Seventeen essays on most aspects of eighteenth-century Scotland.

Campbell, R. H., and Andrew Skinner, eds. *The Origins and Nature of the Scottish Enlightenment.* Edinburgh, 1982. A collection that looks more to origins than to nature.

Cairns, Craig, ed. *The History of Scottish Literature*, 4 vols. Aberdeen, 1989. Vol. 2 is edited by Andrew Hook and deals with the period 1660–1800. The best introduction to the literature of the period.

Carter, Jennifer J., and Joan H. Pittock. *Aberdeen and the Enlightenment.* Aberdeen, 1987. Essays on many aspects of Aberdonian culture in the period.

Craig, David. *Scottish Literature and the Scottish People, 1680–1830.* London, 1961. An eccentric account of the damage done to vernacular culture by the enlightened.

Daiches, David, and Jean and Peter Jones, eds. *A Hotbed of Genius: The Scottish Enlightenment, 1730–1790.* Edinburgh, 1986. Essays on Scotland, America, David Hume, Joseph Black, and James Hutton.

Devine, T. M., and Rosalind Mitchison. *People and Society in Scotland*, vol. 1, *1760–1830*. Edinburgh, 1988. Surveys by various authors of the social and economic history of the period.

Devine, T. M., and J. R. Young, eds. *Eighteenth-Century Scotland: New Perspectives*. East Linton, Scotland, 1999. Social and economic in orientation.

Hook, Andrew, and Richard B. Sher, eds. *The Glasgow Enlightenment*. East Linton, Scotland, 1995. Essays on numerous aspects of the enlightenment in Glasgow.

Hont, Istvan, and Michael Ignatieff, eds. *Wealth and Virtue: The Shaping of Political Economy in the Scottish Enlightenment*. Cambridge, 1983. Valuable essays on many of the thinkers of the period.

Macmillan, Duncan. *Painting in Scotland: The Golden Age*. Oxford, 1986. Useful and well illustrated.

McIntosh, John R. *Church and Theology in Enlightenment Scotland: The Popular Party, 1740–1800*. East Linton, Scotland, 1998. A needed complement to R. B. Sher's study of the Moderate Party in the Kirk.

Markus, Thomas A., ed. *Order in Space and Society: Architectural Form and its Context in the Scottish Enlightenment*. Edinburgh, 1982. A work studying form, structure, and social relations in Scotland c. 1730–1830.

Robert Adam. Architectural Heritage IV. Oxford, 1993. A special issue of the serial devoted to Scotland's greatest architect.

Robertson, John, ed. *A Union for Empire: Political Thought and the British Union of 1707*. Cambridge, 1995. This contains the best discussion of late seventeenth- and early eighteenth-century Scottish perplexities and how they might be resolved.

Shaw, John Stuart. *The Political History of Eighteenth-Century Scotland*. London and New York, 1999. The only survey for the period.

Sher, R. B. *Church and University in the Scottish Enlightenment: The Moderate Literati of Edinburgh*. Princeton, N.J., 1985. The best book on the moderate *literati* of Edinburgh.

Tait, A. A. *The Landscape Garden in Scotland, 1735–1835*. Edinburgh, 1980. Deals with one of the great forms of eighteenth-century art.

Wither, Charles W. J., and Paul B. Wood. *Science and Medicine in the Eighteenth Century*. East Linton, Scotland, 2002. A fine collection of essays on these topics.

Wood, Paul B., ed. *The Scottish Enlightenment: Essays in Reinterpretation*. Rochester and Woodbridge, 2000. Essays on many aspects of the Scottish enlightenment with new insights into the life and work of David Hume.

ROGER L. EMERSON

SCOTT, WALTER (1771–1832), Scottish historical novelist and poet.

Literary history identifies Scott with the Romantic movement, and there is no denying his immense contribution to the creation, diffusion, and popularization of romanticism. Scott's own values and beliefs have little or nothing to do with the ideologies of romanticism, however. Like Jane Austen, Scott regarded the romantic sensibility as a much less reliable guide to action than rationality, common sense, and balanced judgment. Given his background, such an attitude is not surprising.

Scott grew up in Edinburgh in the heyday of the Scottish Enlightenment. His father was a lawyer, his mother the daughter of a medical professor at the University of Edinburgh. He was a pupil at the High School of Edinburgh, under the influential rector Dr. Alexander Adam. Subsequently he undertook two periods of study at the University of Edinburgh. In the years 1783–1785, he studied Latin under Professor John Hill, Greek under the distinguished Professor Andrew Dalzel, and logic and metaphysics under Professor John Bruce. With a law career in mind, he returned to the university in 1789–1792. In the session 1789–1790, he took two courses that would influence his future as a writer: Dugald Stewart's class on moral philosophy and Alexander Fraser Tytler's universal history class. Thereafter Scott studied civil law and Scots law (for which his teacher was Professor David Hume, nephew of the philosopher). Stewart's course, while centering on the commonsense school of Scottish philosophy, ranged widely across the arts and humanities, while that of Tytler, also a man of wide literary interests, did much to reawaken student interest in history as a subject at Edinburgh.

Scott's exposure to Scottish Enlightenment thinking was not limited to his attendance at university courses. Through an enduring friendship with his son, he came to know and admire the philosopher and historian Adam Ferguson; when Ferguson died in 1816, Scott said that he had looked up to him for more than thirty years. Additionally, Scott was an active member of several of the debating societies that were a feature of the Enlightenment in Edinburgh: At both the Literary Society and the Speculative Society, he took part in discussions on a range of moral, philosophical, and historical issues.

Scott's historical fiction does reflect his Scottish Enlightenment background and training. The theme of man in society was a particular focus of the Scottish luminaries and just such a theme is at the heart of the Waverley Novels. Scott's characters are always a product of the society in which they live, and of the stage of civilization it has attained. Scott was able to create the new genre of the historical novel because he had learned from Scottish historians and analysts of society that history was essentially a dynamic, ongoing process, inevitably involving change and conflict. Hence, Scott's accounts of Scottish history, of the Scottish Highlands and Lowlands, of the histories of England and the countries of Europe—however romantically exciting—are ultimately shaped by the analysis of society, past and present, undertaken by the thinkers of the Scottish Enlightenment.

[*See also* Edinburgh; Literary Genres; Revolution; Romanticism; Scotland; *and* Tradition.]

BIBLIOGRAPHY

WORKS BY SCOTT

The Journal of Sir Walter Scott. Edited by W. E. K. Anderson. Oxford, 1972. Best source for information for the closing years of Scott's life.

The Letters of Sir Walter Scott. Edited by H. J. C. Grierson. 12 vols. London, 1932–1937. To this may be added *Notes and Index to Sir*

Herbert Grierson's Edition of The Letters of Sir Walter Scott, edited
by James C. Corson. Oxford, 1979. A complete edition of Scott's
letters is still not available.
Sir Walter Scott: Selected Poems. Edited by Thomas Crawford. Oxford,
1972.

WORKS ABOUT SCOTT

Forbes, Duncan. "The Rationalism of Sir Walter Scott." *Cambridge
Journal* 7 (1953), 20–35. Reprinted in *Critical Essays on Sir Walter
Scott: The Waverly Novels*, edited by Harry E. Shaw, pp. 83–97. New
York, 1996. Addresses Scott's relationship to the Enlightenment in
this article.
Hewitt, David. "Walter Scott." In *The History of Scottish Literature*, vol. 3, *The Nineteenth Century*, edited by Douglas Gifford,
pp. 65–85. Aberdeen, Scotland, 1988. Author of this chapter is the
general editor of the New Edinburough Edition of the Waverley
Novels.
Johnson, Edgar. *Sir Walter Scott: The Great Unknown*. 2 vols. London,
1970. Best modern biography.
Lockhart, J. G. *Memoirs of the Life of Sir Walter Scott, Bart*. 2d ed.
10 vols. Edinburgh, 1839. Official biography produced by Scott's
son-in-law.

ANDREW HOOK

SCOTTISH COMMON SENSE PHILOSOPHY.

The Scottish school of common sense philosophy had
many members and lasted for about a century from the
1740s, but its main contributions came from the pen
of Thomas Reid (1710–1796), regent at King's College,
Aberdeen, and later professor of moral philosophy at the
University of Glasgow. He published three major works:
*An Inquiry into the Human Mind on the Principles of
Common Sense* (1764), *Essays on the Intellectual Powers*
(1785), and *Essays on the Active Powers* (1788). George
Campbell (1719–1796), whose two major works were *A
Dissertation on Miracles* (1762) and *The Philosophy of
Rhetoric* (1776), was also a member of the school, as
were Henry Home, Lord Kames (1696–1782), *Essays on
the Principles of Morality and Natural Religion* (1751);
James Beattie (1753–1803), *An Essay on the Nature and
Immutability Truth* (1770); James Oswald (1711–1793), *An
Appeal to Common Sense in Behalf of Religion* (1766–1772);
Dugald Stewart (1753–1828), *Philosophy of the Human
Mind* (1792); and Sir William Hamilton (1788–1856),
Lectures on Metaphysics and Logic (1869).

A Reaction to Hume. Scottish common sense philosophy, in the technical sense of the phrase, is a detailed
response in the name of realism to Hume's skepticism
about science, morality, and religion. His skepticism was
seen by the common sense school as the culmination of
Western philosophy in that (according to Reid and his followers) it was in Hume's *Treatise of Human Nature* (1739,
1740) that the full skeptical implications of the theory
of ideas—a theory accepted by practically all previous
philosophers—finally surfaced. The central tenet of this
theory is that what we know of the world is known by
means of our ideas, so that either our ideas come between
ourselves and the world, or, as was held by Hume, they are
the very material out of which we construct the world by an
act of imagination. Common sense philosophy interpreted
Hume as saying that, although we believe we perceive an
external world, we are really trapped in our minds; not
only can we not get out, but we have no good reason to
believe that there is an outside. Furthermore, since the
natural sciences are about the external world if they are
about anything, it seemed to the common sense school that
Hume was therefore also denying a role for the natural
sciences. Morality too had become a matter of sensations,
feelings, and ideas and had lost its objective qualities, as
did both natural religion and Christianity.

Reid's response to the theory of ideas was to deny the
existence of ideas, if by ideas are meant objects of thinking
that we have to grasp if we are to come by a knowledge
of anything in the external world. Reid does not deny that
we have ideas, but in his system ideas are held to be acts
of thought rather than objects of such acts. Thus, to have
an idea of X is to think about X.

Reid replaced the theory of ideas with a distinct theory
of perception according to which the act of perception
has three elements: first, a sensation that, as a mental
act, in no way resembles the external object or quality;
next, a conception suggested by that sensation, where
the conception is of an external object or quality; and
finally, a firm belief in the existence of the external object
and the quality. That our sensations suggest conceptions
and prompt beliefs is due to the "original constitution
of our nature," a favorite phrase of the common sense
philosophers. We do not reason our way to the external
world, but by our nature we know how to read our
sensations. Sensations are thus natural signs of external
things. This move is one part of Reid's lengthy and detailed
theory of semiotics. It is plain from these points that,
contrary to a common account of the common sense
school, its philosophy is not merely a destructive attack
on Humean skepticism but presents a positive philosophy.

Contribution to Philosophical Thought. Part of the
positive philosophy is a theory of common sense principles—beliefs that all human beings have by the original
constitution of our nature, which concern, for example,
the reliability of our natural faculties. If, for example, I am
conscious of a sensation, then that sensation truly exists.
Our actions and our language demonstrate our acceptance
of these principles. Common sense philosophers attended
closely to language, especially grammar, in defense of
their philosophy.

They also made a positive contribution to the philosophy
of action. Here again the starting point was Hume,
who was interpreted as having rejected the doctrine of
freedom of the will in favor of a doctrine of determinism

according to which we are determined by motives—be they sentiments or beliefs (also for Hume a kind of sentiment)—about what is the best thing to do. Common sense philosophy took seriously the notion that the agent, not what motivates the agent, is the cause of acts. We no doubt always act in the light of various motives, but we never are determined to act by them. We are always open to opposites; we are able to act on a motive and also able to reject it, however strong it may be as a passion or as a well-thought-out plan. Motives thus have the character of recommendations or pieces of advice. If we think they are good, we will, as reasonable people, probably act on them, but we are not compelled to.

The school also made a significant contribution to the philosophy of religion, again partly in reaction to Hume's arguments. For example, George Campbell's *Dissertation on Miracles* was a powerfully argued attack, from the direction of common sense, on Hume's essay on miracles.

Legacy. Scottish common sense philosophy was widely influential beyond Scotland in the early nineteenth century. In France, Théodore Jouffroy, P. P. Royer-Collard, Victor Cousin, and Maine de Biran were heavily influenced by it and contributed to its dissemination. In Spain, its influence was strong; for example, Ramon Marti d'Eixala taught the Scottish philosophy at the University of Barcelona, as did Francesc Llorens i Barba, who paid especial attention to the writings of William Hamilton. This was also the case in America, where common sense philosophy was widely taught until after the Civil War.

[*See also* Campbell, George; Clubs and Societies; Empiricism; Epistemology; Home, Henry; Hume, David; Hutcheson, Francis; Natural Law; Natural Religion; *and* Stewart, Dugald.]

BIBLIOGRAPHY

Holcolm, Kathleen. "A Dance in the Mind: The Provincial Scottish Philosophical Societies." *Studies in Eighteenth Century Culture* 21 (1991), 89–100. Includes material on Reid's work in the Glasgow Philosophical Society.

Lehrer, Keith. *Thomas Reid*. London, 1989.

Reid, Thomas. *Practical Ethics*. Edited by Knud Haakonssen. Princeton, N.J., 1990. The best source for Reid's moral philosophy and its background. This and the following are the initial volumes of a planned series, the New Edinburgh Edition of Thomas Reid, intended to contain many unpublished essays and lecture notes as well as critical editions of published works.

Reid, Thomas. *On the Animate Creation*. Edited by Paul B. Wood. Edinburgh, 1995. Much new material on Reid's scientific interests.

Ulman, H. Lewis, ed. *The Minutes of the Aberdeen Philosophical Society 1758–1773*. Aberdeen, 1990. Contains much on the society that nurtured Reid's work to 1764.

ALEXANDER BROADIE

SCULPTURE. With the new understanding and appreciation of Greek antiquity in the eighteenth century, cultural theorists such as Johann Joachim Winckelmann and Johann Gottfried Herder privileged sculpture in the hierarchy of the arts, favoring it as a paradigm of the aesthetic object and emphasizing its ideal corporeal qualities. The more scholarly awareness of antique art also profoundly influenced sculptural style from around 1770, stimulating a movement away from Baroque and Rococo forms. Antique works of statuary available for viewing in Rome (in Greco-Roman copies), such as the Laocöon group, the Farnese Hercules, the Belvedere Torso, and the Belvedere Apollo, gained particular prestige as the gauge of excellence in artistic achievement.

Home to a network of prominent collectors, antiquarians, art historians, and artists, Rome in the second half of the eighteenth century also became the center of an international community of sculptors working in the neoclassical idiom. Among the most significant of them were Antoine Houdon (1741–1828), Thomas Banks (1735–1805), Johan Tobias Sergel (1740–1814), Alexander Trippel (1744–1793), John Flaxman (1755–1826), Antonio Canova (1757–1822), and Bertel Thorvaldsen (1768–1844). The Italian Canova engaged with the theoretical considerations of Winckelmann most influentially for his own and subsequent generations, as the creator of what Hugh Honour has called a grand neoclassical style "revolutionary in its severity and uncompromising in its idealistic purity." (Among his most celebrated works are *Cupid and Psyche*, 1787–1793; *Hercules and Lichas*, 1795–1815; *Pauline Borghese*, 1804–1808; and public monuments to popes Clement XIII and Clement XIV.) Dubbed by Stendhal as one of the three greatest men of his time—along with Napoleon and Byron—Canova also gave the medium of sculpture new prominence through his appointment as inspector general of Roman antiquities. Thorvaldsen, who arrived in Rome from Denmark in 1797, can be seen as both heir and rival to Canova's neoclassicism. Favoring a more sober sculptural expressiveness than Canova, Thorvaldsen insisted on greater archaeological precision—in particular, after the public exhibition of the Elgin Marbles in 1816, a cultural sensation that forced a reevaluation of the status of antique works known only through copies, such as the Belvedere Apollo. Central to aesthetic concerns throughout the eighteenth century, antique sculpture also acquired more general cultural currency, as the marketability and prevalence of plaster copies, carved cameos, and porcelain miniatures indicates. So thoroughly did sculpture permeate the European imagination in the latter part of the century that a new theatrical trend of "attitudes" or "mimoplastic art" came into being, which involved the representation of famous classical statues by living bodies.

"Noble simplicity and calm grandeur" (*edle Einfalt und stille Größe*) were central to Winckelmann's enormously influential interpretations of ancient art, which reacted

Antonio Canova, *Pauline Borghese as Venus.* (Galleria Borghese, Rome/Alinari/Art Resource, NY.)

against what he perceived as the exaggerated plasticity and gesture of Baroque sculpture. Winckelmann, from 1758 the curator of Cardinal Albani's Roman collection of antique sculpture, saw his writings rapidly disseminated throughout Europe in translation (*Gedanken über die Nachahmung der greichischen Werke in der Malerei und Bildhauerkunst*, 1755; *Geschichte der Kunst des Altertums*, 1764). Inaugurating the centrality of sculpture in a pan-European neoclassical revival, Winckelmann's works presented the beautiful Greek body (implicitly, the male nude) as an ideal mirror into which moderns were to project themselves: "For us the only way to become great and, if possible, inimitable, is by imitation of the ancients."

One of the central problems for eighteenth-century sculptors, then, was the question of copying (generally perceived as a negative, derivative aesthetic response) versus imitation (for Winckelmann, Canova, and others, a regenerative and productive relationship with an antique model). Winckelmann's rapturous descriptions of classical statues such as the Belvedere Apollo also ushered in a new kind of writing on art, with a pronounced tendency toward animation. Theorists tended to emphasize a process of mutual animation: not only do the viewer's gaze, touch, and descriptive powers bring the statue to life, but the sculpture itself is said to vivify those faculties in the viewer. In the 1780s, it became a modish activity to visit the Italian sculpture galleries at night, by torchlight, in order to experience the pleasurable illusion that the statues were moving. It is no coincidence that the story of Pygmalion gained special resonance during this period, inspiring works such as Rousseau's popular monodrama of that title and Herder's writings in the 1770s on sculpture, published under the title *Plastik*.

Gotthold Ephraim Lessing, whose well-known Laocöon essay (1766) marked a crucial point in the aesthetic discussion of sculpture, engaged in a polemic that favorably contrasted literature with sculpture, the dominant medium of his day. Departing from notions of commensurable or kindred "sister arts," Lessing cautioned that the riches of one artistic medium are the poverty of another, with verbal representation the domain of temporal movement and the visual arts the domain of the frozen moment. In this systematic attempt to delineate the limits and limitations of representational media, it is the arbitrary linguistic sign that, for Lessing, provides the greater stimulus to the imagination and offers access to intellectual abstraction.

The anthropological approach to sculpture taken by Herder, however, emphatically sought to rehabilitate sensuality in art: Herder's Concern was the experiential effect on a spectator, rather than the semiotic system that was focal to Lessing. Sculpture, because of its corporeal appeal to the sense of touch, gains aesthetic primacy, in particular as a spectator apprehends it haptically (with

Relief. Plaster frieze by John Flaxman (1755–1826). (©The Board of Trustees of the Victoria & Albert Museum, London/Art Resource, NY.)

the sense of touch, as opposed to optically). In essays that inveigh against the two-dimensionality he saw as a prevalent tendency of the age, Herder granted sculpture the advantage over painting in that it does not deaden the body by flattening it out. Herder's work, obviously indebted to Winckelmann, implicitly presents the idealized, immaculate sculptural form as protection against the fragmentation and disintegration of the spectator's body: a corrective to human mortality.

The compensatory cultural function of sculpture at the close of the eighteenth century is confirmed anecdotally by Goethe's account of meeting a sickly and melancholic young poet and prescribing the youth his colossal Juno bust as an antidote to fragmentation. Sculpture serves here as a means of recollecting the aesthetically and psychologically dissipated self. Schiller's *Briefe über die ästhetische Erziehung des Menschen* (On the Aesthetic Education of Man, 1795) similarly places the viewing experience of the Juno Ludovisi at the center of an aesthetic program. Positing the modern sensibility as fragmented and dissociated, that work nevertheless describes the harmonizing of antagonistic drives, and the integration of the spectator, through the aesthetic experience of sculpture.

[*See also* Aesthetics; Herder, Johann Gottfried; Lessing, Gotthold Ephraim; Neoclassicism; *and* Winckelmann, Johann Joachim.]

BIBLIOGRAPHY

Haskell, Francis, and Nicholas Penny. *Taste and the Antique: The Lure of Classical Sculpture 1500–1900.* New Haven, Conn., 1981. Standard work on antique sculptures and their significance for artists, collectors, scholars, and archaeologists of the eighteenth century; especially useful for its informative catalog entries and discussions of the works' critical reception.

Honour, Hugh. *Neo-Classicism.* Harmondsworth, U.K., 1968. Excellent general introduction to neoclassicism in painting, sculpture, and architecture.

Potts, Alex. *Flesh and the Ideal: Winckelmann and the Origins of Art History.* New Haven, Conn., 1994.

West, Alison. *From Pigalle to Préault: Neoclassicism and the Sublime in French Sculpture, 1760–1840.* Cambridge, 1998. Although its focus is primarily on eighteenth-century French sculpture and theory,

West's study contains much helpful information on Rome as a center of artistic activity.

CATRIONA MacLEOD

SECKENDORFF, VEIT LUDWIG VON (1626–1692), German politician and political writer.

Seckendorff was among those pragmatic politicians responsible for shaping the reconstruction of the Holy Roman Empire and its many small territories after the Thirty Years' War. Formed by the experience of this war and following several other positions, Seckendorff found employment at the court of Duke Ernst von Sachsen-Gotha. Here, he soon became one of the most important advisers to the sovereign prince, nicknamed "Bet-Ernst" ("Praying Ernst"), who developed his humble territory into a model country. The rise of a modern intellectual landscape from the war's devastation—a vital element in the rise of early German Enlightenment—would enable Germany to overcome spiritual and economic degeneration.

For this purpose, the duke commissioned Seckendorff to draft a political syllabus to guide his statesmen and leaders. The first edition of *Fürsten-Stat* (Sovereign's State, 1656) was an immediate success. Several other editions followed in quick succession, twelve altogether. Although this work may not have displayed any originality and may not have had any relevance in a wider European context, it was still considered important and was a frequently used instructional work for the contemporary empire and its territories after the Peace of Westphalia (1648).

Seckendorff, having further advanced in services to his sovereign, wrote other works, such as *Christen-Stat* (State of Christians) in 1685, a history of Lutheranism, as well as other more sporadic writings and poems. He was, like many German Protestants of the period, influenced by Dutch Protestantism. He valued Justus Lipsius's ideas, yet he remained a moderate absolutist. Seckendorff, also a member of the Fruchtbringende Gesellschaft (Fruitbearing Society), strove to reconcile the differing interests of the Holy Roman Empire and its territories. The common good *(bonum commune)* was to him the highest priority, and he proposed new methods, based on empirical knowledge and what might today be considered a statistical survey, to mend as quickly as possible the devastation caused by the war. According to Seckendorff's ideas, the sovereign prince was to be granted executive power; he should have the last word in questions of religion, finances, and jurisdiction, yet should be restricted to acting in the sole interest of his territory. Much like the Dutch role model, free trade should prevail and the land was to be repopulated under unified jurisdiction. The secular government should take precedence over the religious—without contradicting religious values, of course—and should improve the quality of life on all levels from health care to education.

Seckendorff's political program was applicable to most German territories; this program made available a set of guidelines that illustrated how a well-organized government (representing politics initially understood as secular, yet retaining their essentially Lutheran-Christian characteristics) could effect reconstruction. It was natural for Seckendorff—and in this respect he can be only partly understood as an initiator of the Enlightenment—to believe that the emperor was bound to God, and that as he put it, "the main purpose of all of this is the salutary conservation of the state administration (*policey*) and the entire rule in his [the Emperor's] honor, power and majesty, where the ultimate goal is the honor of God" (*Fürsten-Stat*, 207).

[*See also* Aufklärung; Cameralism; Political Philosophy; *and* War and Military Theory.]

BIBLIOGRAPHY

Hammerstein, Notker. *Staatslehre in der Frühen Neuzeit*. Bibliothek der Geschichte und Politik, Deutscher Klassikerverlag. Frankfurt, 1995. This work contains sections of *Fürsten-Stat* on pp. 237–482.
Seckendorff, Veit Ludwig von. *Teutscher Fürsten-Stat*. Frankfurt-Leipzig, 1656; repr. of the 7th edition of 1737, Aalen, 1972.
Small, A. W. *The Cameralists: Pioneers of German Social Polity*. Chicago, 1909, pp. 60–106.
Stolleis, Michael. "Veit Ludwig von Seckendorff." In *Staatsdenker in der Frühen Neuzeit*. 3d ed., pp. 148–171. Munich, 1995.

NOTKER HAMMERSTEIN

Translated from German by Andreas Quintus

SELF. *See* Human Nature *and* Moral Philosophy.

SEMLER, JOHANN SALOMO (1725–1791), German theologian.

Semler, the most important Protestant theology professor of the later German Enlightenment, was active at the Prussian University of Halle from 1753 on. He was noted especially for work on biblical interpretation, on the formation and significance of the canon of scriptural books, and on the contemporary application of Christian faith in historical context. (The main points are masterfully treated by Gottfried Hornig, on which I rely, as do almost all commentators on Semler.) Linked to this were his affirmation of the "perfectibility," or forward development, of a faith not normatively tied to any one epoch or region, and his minting of the concept of a theology "liberal" in its investigative freedom from ecclesiastical constraint.

All major scholars have sought to reconcile Semler's apparently radical historicizing and relativizing of Scripture and doctrine in the context of emergent religious individualism with his repeated support for holding clergy in the established church to some kind of publicly valid norm or standard. This tendency toward a certain conservatism came decisively to the fore in 1779, with Semler's answer to the so-called Wolfenbüttel Fragments of Reimarus, as published by Lessing under the title *Beantwortung der Fragmente eines Ungenannten* (Reply to the Fragments of an Anonymous Author).

Specialists in historical theology have increasingly sought an explanation that integrates the strains of Semler's thought. Early in the twentieth century, Leopold Zscharnack argued for an essential consistency in Semler's career, seeing it as marked by opposition to both Pietist emotionalism and rigid orthodoxy. For Emanuel Hirsch, close study of Semler's roughly two hundred publications suggested that he is best understood not as a simple rationalist and moralist suffering from the anxiety of old age, but instead as a complex and far-sighted guardian and transformer of tradition who, in key ways, anticipated the creative moves made by F. D. E. Schleiermacher in his post-Kantian refounding of theology a decade or more after Semler's death.

Recent detailed work has, on the whole, borne out the intuitions of Zscharnack and Hirsch. Summaries of his work by Dirk Kemper and Kurt Nowak stress the breadth and originality in his legacy: from the *Untersuchung Theologischer Streitigkeiten* (Examination of Theological Controversies, 1762–1764) through the *Abhandlung von freier Untersuchung des Canon* (Treatise on Examination of the Canon, 1771–1775) and on to the *Institutio ad Doctrinam Christianam Liberaliter Discendam* (Introduction to Christian Doctrine, 1774), Semler made repeated moves of future theological interest. Indeed, at the time he was an equal-opportunity offender, provoking opposition from the remnants of Protestant orthodoxy, from the nonorthodox Pietists, and from the radically rationalist or pro-absolutist wing.

Great interest and debate attended Semler's works. This is not surprising, since Semler advocated studying Scripture and dogma from the point of view of this-worldly historical criticism, separating the "word of God" from the text of a Scripture that he held to be extremely uneven and diverse in its character—see his *Vorbereitung zur theologischen Hermeneutik* (Preparation for Theological Hermeneutics, 1760–1769). He developed further both the Old Protestant notion of divine teaching in transitory cultural forms (the theory of "accommodation") and J. A. Bengel's hypothesis of families of scriptural text types. At the same time, he abandoned the "high" view of scriptural inspiration characteristic of earlier Protestant orthodoxy, and with it any conventional view of the "unity" of Scripture. His work on historiography explicitly reflects the selective and criteria-based agency of the historian, and it implicitly acknowledges the issue of perspective, or relativism (see Meinhold).

The religious and cultural implementation of Semler's approach showed itself in strategies designed to reassert the abiding significance of his religious heritage (see Hirsch). The paradoxically non-Pietistical emphasis on both inner religious experience (see Nowak) and critical evaluation of the sources of private or personal faith by individual believers and researching scholars was for Semler a strength, not a weakness—at least, so long as it was socio-culturally stabilized. This explains Semler's recurrent interest in enforcing some kind of public norm for the activity of ministers in the established church. Semler repeatedly expressed a need to offset the unending debate over the pursuit of unattainable finality in religious truth with institutionally anchored concessions to public responsibility on the part of religious leaders. Certainly Semler recognized a necessity to hold ministers of religion to basic adherence to the historic standards of the legally recognized varieties of Christianity in order to protect what toleration had been achieved during the Enlightenment, and to avoid slipping back into religious war.

Given the realities of Europe between 1648 and Napoleon, Semler's concessions to traditional standards for the public exercise of religion hardly imply narrow-mindedness. It is equally impossible, however, to sustain an indictment of intent to betray the Protestant heritage, even in the face of Semler's shaping the distinctive conceptual and terminological framework for the later liberal Protestant notion of a "private" religion or religiosity. Here Semler himself (like the Pietists before him) believed that he was continuing the work of Martin Luther—and, in a sense, he was. Indeed, a lifetime of detailed investigation by Hornig has established Semler as the German Enlightenment's most explicit and committed reformulator of Luther's dialectic of Law and Gospel, taken as fundamental to any profound appreciation of the tradition of Augustinian Protestantism. Semler both parted company with the moralism characteristic of the later rationalist theologians and simultaneously anticipated deep and controversial currents of Reformation reappropriation in

the nineteenth and twentieth centuries. In view of these considerations, Hornig correctly termed Semler the pioneer, or anticipator, of Neoprotestantism.

Nonetheless, it must be emphasized that however much this pillar of early Protestant liberalism may have been influenced by "perspectivalist" or "relativistic" tendencies in historical study, Semler saw even private faith as subject to restraints that would keep it from merging into an ocean of relativism. The struggle within Semler here has been highlighted by Peter Hanns Reill as well as by Hornig. For Semler, both God and Christianity are "infinite," but Christian faith even in its private form remains bound not only to conscience but also to the nonparticularistic revelation of the love of a triune God dealing graciously with all of humanity by means of Jesus Christ and the Holy Spirit.

[*See also* Aufklärung; Bible; Germany; *and* Revealed Religion.]

BIBLIOGRAPHY

PRIMARY SOURCES

Hornig, Gottfried. *Johann Salomo Semler: Studien zu Leben und Werk des Hallenser Aufklärungstheologen.* (Hallesche Beiträge zur Europäischen Aufklärung, 2.) Tübingen, 1996. Contains a full bibliography of primary sources.

Semler, Johann Salomo. *Christologie und Soteriologie.* Edited by Gottfried Hornig and Hartmut H. R. Schulz. Würzburg, 1990.

SECONDARY WORKS

Hirsch, Emanuel. *Geschichte der neuern evangelischen Theologie im Zusammenhang mit den allgemeinen Bewegungen des europäischen Denkens.* 5 vols. Gütersloh, Germany, 1949–1954.

Hornig, Gottfried. *Die Anfänge der historisch-kritischen Theologie: Johann Salomo Semlers Schriftverständnis und seine Stellung zu Luther.* (Forschungen zur systematischen Theologie und Religionsphilosophie, 8.) Göttingen, 1961. Pioneering.

Hornig, Gottfried. "Der Perfektibilitätsgedanke bei J. S. Semler." *Zeitschrift für Theologie und Kirche* 72 (1975), 381–397. Essential study.

Hornig, Gottfried. "Semlers Dogmengeschichtsschreibung und Traditionskritik—zur Analyse der Argumente und Kriterien." In *Denkender Glaube: Festschrift Carl Heinz Ratschow*, pp. 101–113. Berlin, 1976.

Hornig, Gottfried. "Johann Salomo Semler." In *Gestalten der Kirchengeschichte*, edited by Martin Greschat, vol. 8, pp. 267–280. Stuttgart, 1983.

Hornig, Gottfried. "Schleiermacher und Semler." In *Schleiermacher-Archiv*, edited by Hermann Fischer et al., pp. 875–897. (Internationaler Schleiermacher-Kongress Berlin 1984, vol. 1, part 2.) Berlin, 1985.

Hornig, Gottfried. "Hermeneutik und Bibelkritik bei Johann Salomo Semler." In *Historische Kritik und biblischer Kanon in der deutschen Aufklärung*, edited by Henning Graf Reventlow et al., pp. 219–236. (Wolfenbütteler Forschungen, 41.) Wiesbaden, 1988.

Hornig, Gottfried. "Semler, Johann Salomo." In *Theologische Realenzyklopädie*, edited by Gerhard Müller, vol. 31, pp. 142–148. Berlin, 2000. Important overview.

Kemper, Dirk. "Semler, Johann Salomo." In *Literatur Lexikon*, edited by Walther Killy, vol. 11. Gütersloh, Germany, 1991.

Lüder, Andreas. *Historie und Dogmatik: Ein Beitrag zur Genese und Entfaltung von Johann Salomo Semlers Verständnis des Alten*

Testaments. Special issue of *Zeitschrift für die alttestamentliche Wissenschaft* 233.

Meinhold, Peter. *Geschichte der kirchlichen Historiographie.* (Orbis Academicus III/5, vol. 2.) Freiburg im Breisgau, 1967.

Nowak, Kurt. "Semler, Johann Salomo." In *Deutsche Biographische Enzyklopädie*, edited by Walther Killy and Rudolf Vierhaus, pp. 282–283. Munich, 1998.

Reill, Peter Hanns. *The German Enlightenment and the Rise of Historicism.* Berkeley, Calif., 1975.

Zscharnack, Leopold. *Lessing und Semler.* Giessen, Germany, 1905.

JOHN STROUP

SENSIBILITY. The concept of sensibility figures in three areas of Enlightenment culture: literature, medical science, and social and moral theory. The reasons for the versatility of the concept, and the nature of the links between these areas that the common presence of the concept suggests, will be analyzed later in this article. Sensibility is probably best known as a literary movement, exemplified in such authors as Laurence Sterne, Samuel Richardson, and Jean-Jacques Rousseau, and having to do with the celebration of emotion and the public shedding of tears. This article begins, however, with a discussion of the concept in the physiology and medical science of the period.

Physiological Concepts. Sensibility attained prominence in Enlightenment physiology and medicine as a result of a shift away from the mechanistic Cartesian philosophy that characterized the theories of scientists such as William Harvey and Herman Boerhaave. Such theories viewed the body as a complex hydraulic machine strictly separated from the soul, which was the seat of sensation and will. This separation is referred to as dualism. One feature of the mechanistic philosophy is that, since the body is imagined as a structure, structures have to be imagined in order to explain a particular bodily function, even if these structures rest on no observable data whatsoever.

Sensibility emerged as a key preoccupation as the emphasis in physiology and medicine began to shift toward vitalism, which can be understood (following Jacques Roger, 1980) as a tendency to recognize the originality of living beings and to approach the study of them in a more phenomenological and less rigid fashion. A key figure in this process was the Swiss physiologist Albrecht von Haller (1708–1777), whose experimental observations, based on dissection, exerted influence throughout Europe. Haller distinguished irritability, an involuntary and unconscious reaction in which a stimulus produces movement in an organ, and sensibility, which is carried by the nerves and leads to perceived sensation. It can be argued that Haller's distinction was a remnant of dualism, a compromise between empirical physiology and dualistic metaphysics, and he certainly was not a vitalist, but other forces were at work. Among these were the French naturalist George-Louis de Buffon, who introduced the notion of "living matter"; Pierre-Louis de Maupertuis, who used Leibniz's notion of the monad to conceptualize living organisms as being made up of living atoms endowed with psychic qualities; and Charles Bonnet, whose *Essai analytique sur les facultés de l'âme* (1759) tried to build a bridge between Haller and the conjectural sensationalism of Etienne Bonnot de Condillac. Bonnet blurred Haller's irritability-sensibility distinction and contributed to a generalizing, monistic vision of vital reactivity that was becoming dominant in the 1750s.

We can gain more insight into the way in which the concept of sensibility contributed to new currents of thinking by looking at two centers: Edinburgh and Montpellier. In the early years of the eighteenth century, teaching at the Edinburgh Medical School had been dominated by the influence of the mechanist Boerhaave, professor of medicine at Leiden, but by midcentury the nervous system had come to occupy a central role in the school's research. This was due in large measure to the work of Robert Whytt, who saw in the "active sentient principle" the source of the body's purposeful behavior. According to this theory, sympathy between the different organs and parts of the body accounts for the integration of the body's different functions. This sympathy is generally unconscious, but it can become conscious—for instance, when certain sights or stories cause fainting in "delicate people." (Here we see where the physiological and the psychological and moral began to merge.) Whytt postulated a more centralized model of sensibility than did Haller, for whom the irritability of muscle was autonomous, or Bordeu.

The Montpellier school, led by Théophile Bordeu (who appears in Denis Diderot's fictional conversation, *Le Rêve de d'Alembert*), exerted considerable influence in France. It, too, challenged Haller's separation between irritability and sensibility, and it shared with the Edinburgh school the notion that the different parts of the body interact sympathetically. The image of a swarm of bees was commonly used to evoke the way in which the different parts of the body, operating independently, nevertheless coalesce to form a being greater than the sum of the parts. Sensibility operates at all levels in the human being. Thus, life is spontaneous activity, not simply a mechanism; but it does not require the intervention of a spiritual principle. The revolutionary and materialist implications of this thinking were not lost on Diderot, who took considerable interest in medical and physiological research on sensibility. Diderot developed a physiological theory of the human as a being that emerges from the combination of organic parts. The antispiritual potential of a decentralized model of sensibility is clear in Diderot's case: his theory has no place for the "unintelligible little harpist" (the soul): *L'organisation et la vie, voilà l'âme* ("Organization and life—there is the soul").

Diderot's *Encyclopédie* published a long article on the medical and physiological aspects of sensibility by Henri Fouquet, one of the Montpellier school, followed by a much shorter one on moral sensibility. The opening definition of the entry on physiological sensibility strikes a lyrical and adulatory note: "The faculty of feeling, the sentient principle, or the feeling of all the parts, the basis and preserver of life, animality *par excellence*, the most beautiful and the most singular phenomenon of nature." Fouquet disagreed with the view of the German doctor Georg Stahl (1660–1734) that the spiritual soul must intervene, providing judgments to guide the reactions of sensibility. No, said Fouquet, the rational soul can remain an onlooker, separate from physical or material manifestations of bodily life. Pleasure and pain are the "scale" on which all other sensations are built; and though the rational soul can complement physical reactions with moral judgments, it is important to see that this dimension is not part of the physical basis humans share with other animals, since the soul is described as "that beneficent distinction which it has pleased the Creator to establish in favor of man." Fouquet described the development of a human fetus into a fully developed child. New impressions stimulate an extension of sensibility. "Everything comes to life, everything enters into motion in this new man, and as *sensibility* comes to enjoy almost all its rights, it opens the circle of the phenomena of life." There are strong echoes here of Condillac's image of the statue that progressively comes to life through the impact of sense impressions. Among the "particular effects of sensibility," Fouquet listed the phenomenon of past trauma leading to repeated physical symptoms, as well as the aesthetic effect of beauty or music on particularly sensitive individuals. We also find the notion that the greater sensibility of women is attributable to the importance of the uterus as a site of sensibility. This idea played an important role in the strengthening of sexual distinctions from the early nineteenth century on. Finally, two elements of broader context are referred to by Fouquet: sensibility, he says, is most developed in humans, and this accounts for their ability to learn, as their organs "bend" or conform to habit of instruction or example. Second, sensibility introduces an environmental element into our understanding of human beings, since it is the vehicle by which the air, the stars, or the climate can exert an influence. Montesquieu, in *L'esprit des lois* (1748), had already written extensively about the impact of ecology on human society, as Fouquet acknowledged.

Historians broadly agree that at least part of the versatility of the notion of sensibility in the Enlightenment derived from characteristics embedded in it as an area of scientific research. The best way to approach this question is through the notion of *reaction*, which, at the most general level, is inseparable from the huge and often unspoken debt that Enlightenment thinking owed to the empiricism of John Locke. Locke imagined the human mind as a *tabula rasa* that registers, reacts to, and is molded by its encounters with the external world. To think of human beings in terms of sensibility is to think of a shared disposition to respond in various ways to external stimuli. Reactivity is in itself a form of bridging: a reaction moves us from one domain into another. So we can say that empiricism generally offers a model of interconnectedness that helps to explain the versatility of sensibility as a concept.

Within that framework, medical science made specific contributions to the creative potential of the concept. First, one of the most important bridging functions of sensibility in the period was between the physical and the moral; this confirms the antidualist and potentially materialist implications of the phenomenon. Second, the idea of sympathy between different organs of the body (an idea which can, as Lawrence has argued, become a metaphor for the social body) led to the concept of a medical semiotics. If different organs react to changes within the body, then it becomes possible to interpret visible signs as the symptom of something less visible: external signs of inner states are one consequence of a reactive model. W. F. Bynum tells us that it was at this time that medical practice shifted toward observation, consultation, and the interpretation of symptoms by the doctor, whereas previously it had been quite common for doctors to diagnose and prescribe by letter, on the basis of the patient's own account. Third, the notion of reactivity linked medicine with Enlightenment thinking about the power of environment to influence human behavior. If the social body is an aggregate of individuals, and if both react to environmental factors, then the analogy between medicine and a project of education, social reform, and even social engineering becomes powerful. Vila and Kramnick, among others, have argued that, for exactly these reasons, medicine saw itself as the key discipline within the Enlightenment enterprise of the reform and management of the social body.

Moral and Literary Concepts. The model of reactivity was extended into the area of moral thought and literary representation. The long *Encyclopédie* article on physiological sensibility is followed by a much shorter one on moral sensibility, defined as a "tender and delicate disposition of the soul, which makes it easily moved, touched." The author recognized that "sensitive souls" may, by virtue of their very sensibility, fall into errors that a more rational temperament might avoid; but he argued that the benefits of such sensibility far outweigh the disadvantages.

"Sensitive souls have more existence than others: good things and bad are multiplied in them. Reflection may make the man of probity; but *sensibility* makes the man of virtue. *Sensibility* is the mother of humanity, of generosity; it serves merit, succors the mind, and brings persuasion in its train."

Sensibility lies at the heart of much Enlightenment thinking about society, sociability, and solidarity among individuals. British (and particularly Scottish) thinkers were at the forefront of this movement. So-called moral sense theorists like Francis Hutcheson developed notions of a natural moral sense, a kind of intuitive empathy felt by one human subject for the sufferings of another. Work on moral theory was then carried forward by David Hume and Adam Smith. Particularly in his early *Treatise of Human Nature* (1739–1740), Hume presented sympathy as the fundamental mechanism whereby the passions of each individual are communicated to others. Passions and sentiment are the very stuff of sociability, and it is sympathy that generalizes them, overcoming differences between individuals. Sympathy is thus an underlying principle or mechanism, and it should not be confused with the specific sentiments of compassion, pity, or benevolence, which are the products of sympathy. John Mullan argues that Hume's *Enquiry Concerning the Principles of Morals* (1751) adopts a less radical position, with sympathy losing its general, systemic role and shifting much closer in sense to the moral virtues of benevolence, compassion, and pity—a shift in the direction of Adam Smith's *Theory of Moral Sentiments* (1759). Here, the individual who reacts with compassion to the sufferings of another does so not in a spontaneous or intuitive way. Smith took for granted the assumptions of empiricist sensationalism and believed that moral ideas, rather than being in some sense innate, spontaneous, and inexplicable, are constructed from the basic building blocks of sensory perception. The imagination is thus crucial: we do not feel the sufferings of others in our own bodies, but through the imagination, we project ourselves into the position of the other, and we do this as external spectators. Our sympathy is an imaginative extrapolation from our own experience. In this sense, Smith took seriously the empiricist premises that also govern scientific work on sensibility in the period. Our sympathy must be explained, not marveled at.

To claim that sensibility became an element of popular culture in the second half of the eighteenth century would be excessive; as a literary phenomenon, however, sensibility certainly entered the public domain and affected modes of behavior and ways of writing. Sentimental drama and the sentimental novel were the major sites for the exploration and celebration of sensibility. In Britain, the phenomenon began before midcentury with the novels of Samuel Richardson (*Pamela*, 1740–1741;

Clarissa, 1747–1748); it continued in Laurence Sterne's *Tristram Shandy* (1760–1767) and *Sentimental Journey* (1768), and in novels by Henry Mackenzie (*The Man of Feeling*, 1771). It was still an issue when Jane Austen wrote *Sense and Sensibility* (begun 1797, published 1811). In France, the abbé Prévost's *Manon Lescaut* (1731) was an early landmark and Rousseau's *La nouvelle Héloïse* (1761) a high point, but imitations of Sterne's *Sentimental Journey* were still appearing in the 1780s and 1790s. The most famous Russian sentimental text is Nikolay Mikhaylovich Karamzin's *Bednaya Liza* (Poor Lisa, 1792), the influence of which can be seen in Dostoevsky; Karamzin traveled widely in western Europe around the time of the French Revolution and published *Pisma russkogo puteshestvennika* (Letters of a Russian Traveler) in 1791–1792. The German situation is particular. The Sturm und Drang ("storm and stress") movement of the 1770s certainly exalted emotion and childhood at the expense of cold rationality, but it was also strongly marked by cultural nationalism and a concern for Promethean genius. The work of the northern group of Sturm und Drang poets, the Göttinger Hain, was aptly characterized by the title of an essay by Friedrich Stolberg, *Fülle des Herzens* (Overflow of Hearts, 1777). The main figures of the more famous southern group based around Strasbourg and Frankfurt were Johann Gottfried Herder and Johann Wolfgang von Goethe. Folk poetry and folk song were part of their cultural-nationalist manifesto. Goethe's novel *Die Leiden des jungen Werthers* (Sorrows of Young Werther, 1774) enjoyed European renown. Finally, it should be noted that Enlightenment in Germany had all along included an element of Christian Pietist sentimentality and introspection, which are relatively foreign in the French context.

It makes sense to distinguish two thematic strands within the literature of sensibility: the representation of romantic love, and narratives of misfortune. Love in the literature of sensibility is an involuntary passion, that overtakes the individual without his or her volition. The greater an individual's sensibility, the more strongly will he or she be affected by this passion. Indeed, the characters Saint-Preux and Julie in Rousseau's *La nouvelle Héloïse* reflect on the fact that such sensibility may be a mixed blessing, since it exposes the individual to suffering as well as to joy. In Rousseau's novel, there is no happy ending: Julie sacrifices romantic passion to filial duty by marrying the husband of her father's choice, and proceeds to die. The paradox of much sentimental writing in this vein is that, even where the story line seems to subvert any optimistic equation between sensibility and happiness, sensibility remains the central value, celebrated through the mode of melancholy even when it is denied in narrative practice. Julie's sensibility—her capacity both for love and for its virtuous sacrifice—continues to resonate from beyond the grave in what appears to be a secular form of transcendence.

Some of the significance of this idea of transcendence is captured in the invitation issued by Diderot to his reader in the *Éloge de Richardson*: *Venez, nous pleurerons ensemble sur les personnages malheureux de ses fictions* ("Come, let us weep together over the unfortunate characters of his fiction"). Sensibility is not only what is exhibited by the character represented in the text; it is also the faculty that enables the reader to react appropriately to what is read. In other words, the model of reactivity central to eighteenth-century notions of sensibility can be extended to the relationship between text and reader. In Diderot's phrase, we see one possible role for the text, as a site of communication between readers: the text as a social space. The text-reader relationship can also be envisaged in a more private mode, through the notion of self-exploration. In this view, the enormous popularity of the sentimental novel would have to do with an emerging taste or need on the part of readers for a kind of reading that allowed for processes of projection and identification. Represented sensibility resonated within the private space of the individual, providing models of self-understanding, expectation, and behavior. This seems to be a way of understanding the relationship between the literature of sensibility on the one hand,

and on the other, broader social and ideological changes such as the growth of individualism. Sentimental love was endlessly represented in the eighteenth century in opposition to parental choice and dynastic strategy, so it often crosses divisions of class and hierarchy. At one level, love can be said to have chosen the lovers rather than their choosing it, but it nonetheless stands for individual choice over arranged marriage (in militant vocabulary, the "law of nature" against the "tyranny of convention"), and this fits into the broader individualist thrust of much Enlightenment thinking. Writing in 1793, Pierre-Louis Roederer argued that the Revolution's legislative reforms in the area of marriage and divorce were based on the ideological groundwork of the sentimental novel.

Narratives of misfortune represent a second strand within the literature of sensibility. Beggars, the victims of financial ruin, and disinherited sons join persecuted lovers in the pantheon of victimhood. Such victims may weep over their own misfortune, but more tears are shed by those who observe their misfortune. We are thus brought back to eighteenth-century moral theory, in which the relationship of observation between victim and spectator plays a central role. Such spectators may be explicitly represented: the sentimental travelers inspired by Sterne's *Sentimental Journey* take their sensibility with them and react to the spectacles of misfortune and the hard-luck

Curse. *La Malédiction Paternelle*, painting (1777) by J.-B. Greuze (1725–1805). (Musée du Louvre, Paris/Giraudon/Art Resource, NY.)

Punishment. *Le Fils Puni*, painting (1778) by Greuze. (Musée du Louvre, Paris/Lauros-Giraudon/Art Resource, NY.)

stories they encounter. Such phrases such as *au spectacle de* and *au récit de* ("at the sight of, at the account of") emphasize the *reactive* character of this celebration of sensibility: what is constantly repeated is the sequence of stimulus and response. Spectators are not always explicitly represented, however. The presence of an observer can be implied, and this is done aesthetically by the use of tableau. In tableau, various techniques such as immobilization, the description of the spatial relations between characters, gesture, and facial expression suggest that the scene is being visualized, and in this way the reader becomes the observer. Once again, the text becomes a site in which the reader experiences, experiments with, and maybe even learns certain kinds of social relations. This invokes a parallel with painting. Diderot more than any other writer was conscious of this parallel, and one of the painters most praised by him, Jean-Baptiste Greuze (1725–1805), provided a wonderful visual counterpoint to the literary representation of sensibility, especially in paintings such as a *La Malédiction Paternelle* and *Le Fils Puni* (The Father's Curse, The Punished Son).

Sentimentalism's concern with gesture and expression went beyond tableau. Together with tears and inarticulate cries, nonlinguistic forms of expression come into their own under the pressure of emotion. Indeed, they were

in a sense considered more reliable pointers to the internal life than mere words, in that they reach deeper and more directly into sense experience. Here is one of the closest links between the aesthetic of sensibility and the empiricism and sensationalism that dominated psychological theory in the Enlightenment. If, as the eighteenth century learned from Locke, language and rational thought are constructed on the basis of sense experience, it is logical that the prelinguistic should come to the fore in moments of psychological crisis. The sentimental text thus operated as what Peter Szondi, speaking of Diderot's theater, has called a "psychograph," charting via an observing eye the signs of the inner life of observed subjects—just as the Montpellier school taught doctors to diagnose illness through the interpretation of the external signs of the hidden workings of the body.

Janet Todd has shown the strength of the reaction that arose at the end of the century against the excesses of the literary fashion of sensibility. In Britain and France, sensibility was perceived as linked to the excesses of the Revolution. James Gillray's famous cartoon "New Morality" shows the figure of Sensibility weeping over a dead bird, with the works of Rousseau in her hand, while her foot rests on the head of Louis XVI. From a more left-wing perspective, the sentimental representation of victimhood and suffering was accused of combining voyeurism with self-indulgence: suffering is aestheticized to provide an excuse for tears, and these tears can then replace political action, assuaging the conscience of the class that sheds them. Mary Wollstonecraft's attack on sentimentalism is in these terms. Tears are only eloquent, she wrote, "when they flow down fair cheeks": sentimentalization and political exclusion go hand in hand. This was linked to the critique of novel-reading as at best a trivializing and at worst an immoral influence on young women; thus, Marianne Dashwood in Jane Austen's *Sense and Sensibility* views the world through a sentimental prism. Overall, the feminization of sensibility—in the sense that women were both represented in and consumed sentimental texts—certainly contributed to a growing split at the end of the eighteenth century between two worlds, one male, public, and political, and the other female, intimate, and domestic. This divide is widely regarded as having set back women's rights in the opening phase of modernity. John Mullan's interpretation of the failures of sentimentalism should be mentioned here: the sensibility widely celebrated in literary texts belonged not to everyone, but to a privileged minority of souls so sensitive that they verged on the pathological. "There is no social space for sensibility. Illness is its appropriate metaphor" (p. 240).

Conclusion. These criticisms are powerful, but I want to argue that the set of ideas, relations, and modes of representation that gravitated around the concept of sensibility in the late eighteenth century were extremely productive then and retain some relevance today. This potential is fundamentally to do with creating links between interiority and the public space. Politics in a post-conventional world must be defined as seeking ways of coordinating individuals on the basis of their given, creaturely nature. Sensibility, defined in the broad way adopted in this article, had and has a contribution to make to that project. Today, when we are bombarded by competing discourses, sensibility suggests a way of thinking about justice that connects with our bodily nature. Sentimentalism's concern with gesture and the prelinguistic is important for that reason, and it also reminds us that animals, as "sentient beings" (the phrase comes from late twentieth century legislation), also have rights. Another way to approach the question is through emotion. However much they are fetishized, the inner states that figure in sentimental texts do not exist in isolation. They are always generated by narrative and are always situational, and in that sense, one can speak of the rationality of emotion. By the same move, emotion enters into history: the sufferings of individuals can generate change. Sensibility is at the heart of the Enlightenment concern for justice, and it is no coincidence that the language of sentiment is omnipresent in the discourse of the French Revolution. The view that the Enlightenment was a rationalist movement hostile to sensibility and emotion—a view that reduced sensibility to an anachronistic "pre-Romantic" phenomenon, is unsustainable. Sensibility as I have described it has reverberated beyond the Enlightenment. In Dickens, Dostoevsky, and Hugo, we find noble representations of victimhood inherited from the eighteenth century. In late nineteenth and early twentieth century France, writers as diverse as Émile Durkheim, Daniel Mornet, and Julien Benda pointed to a living Enlightenment heritage in which sensibility went hand in hand with an agenda of social reform. Today, the place of sentimentality in debates about justice and humanitarianism is once again on the agenda.

[*See also* Aesthetics; Diderot, Denis; Human Nature; Imagination; Natural Sentiment; Novel; Optimism, Philosophical; Reason; *and* Virtue.]

BIBLIOGRAPHY

Boltanski, Luc. *La souffrance à distance: Morale humanitaire, médias et politique*. Paris, 1993. Excellent on the nineteenth- and twentieth-century transformations of Adam Smith's spectator model of moral sentiment.

Brooks, Peter. *The Melodramatic Imagination*. New Haven, Conn., and London, 1976. An outstanding analysis of the aesthetic of melodrama, which shares many features with sentimentalism.

Bynum, W. F. "Health, Disease and Medical Care." In *The Ferment of Knowledge: Studies in the Historiography of Eighteenth-Century Science*, edited by G. S. Rousseau and Roy Porter, pp. 211–253. Cambridge, 1980. Of interest for the idea of semiotics in changing forms of medical diagnosis.

Denby, David J. *Sentimental Narrative and the Social Order in France, 1760–1820*. Cambridge, 1994. Chapter 2 offers a model of sentimental narrative; chapters also on the French Revolution, the Ideologues, and Madame de Staël.

Denby, David J. "La modernité du sentimentalisme." *Eighteenth-Century Fiction* 7 (1995), 373–392. On the relevance of sentimentalism to contemporary moral and political debate.

Denby, David J. "Amour sentimental, démocratie et universalisme." In *Sexualité, mariage et famille au XVIIIᵉ siècle*, edited by Olga B. Cragg and Rosena Davison. Quebec, 1998. On the connection between sentimental representations of love and the politics of the French Revolution; see Roederer.

Duchesneau, François. "Diderot et la physiologie de la sensibilité." *Dix-huitième siècle* 31 (1999), 195–216. Shows how Diderot synthesized a wide range of scientific work on sensibility.

Kohlschmidt, Werner. "Sturm und Drang." In *German Literature: A Critical Survey*, edited by Bruno Boesch. London, 1971.

Kramnick, Isaac. "Eighteenth-Century Science and Radical Social Theory: The Case of Joseph Priestley's Scientific Liberalism." *Journal of British Studies* 25 (1986), 1–30. On medical discourse as a model of social reform.

Lawrence, Christopher. "The Nervous System and Society in the Scottish Enlightenment." In *Natural Order: Historical Studies of Scientific Culture*, edited by Barry Barnes and Steven Shapin, pp. 19–40. London, 1979. On sensibility in the work of the Edinburgh Medical School.

Mullan, John. *Sentiment and Sociability: The Language of Feeling in the Eighteenth Century*. Oxford, 1988. Very good on the relation between moral theory (Hume and Smith) and literature (Sterne and Richardson); takes a less optimistic view than Denby.

Ridgway, R. S. *Voltaire and Sensibility*. Montreal and London, 1973. Shows clearly the importance of sensibility in Voltaire's concept of justice.

Roederer, P. L. *Cours d'organisation sociale*. In his *Oeuvres*, edited by A. M. Roederer, vol. 8. Paris, 1953–1959. See especially pp. 129–305. Lectures delivered at the Paris Lycée in 1793, fascinating on the relation between models of sensibility and political practice in the French Revolution.

Roger, Jacques. *Les sciences de la vie dans la pensée française du XVIIIᵉ siècle*. Paris, 1963. See especially pp. 600–668.

Roger, Jacques. "The living world." In *The Ferment of Knowledge: Studies in the Historiography of Eighteenth-Century Science*, edited by G. S. Rousseau and Roy Porter, pp. 255–283. Cambridge, 1980. An excellent synthesis on the significance of vitalism in relation to dualism.

Rorty, Richard. "Human Rights, Rationality and Sentimentality." In *On Human Rights: The Oxford Amnesty Lectures 1993*, edited by Stephen Shute and Susan Hurley, pp. 111–134. New York, 1993. Argues from a pragmatic and relativist perspective that sentimentality plays a particularly important role in the discourse of justice.

Staum, Martin. *Cabanis: Enlightenment and Medical Philosophy in the French Revolution*. Princeton, N.J., 1980. On the social and political applications of medicine among the Ideologues.

Szondi, Peter. "Tableau and coup de théâtre: On the Social Psychology of Diderot's Bourgeois Drama." *New Literary History* 11 (1980), 323–343. The idea of text as "psychograph," representing the inner life.

Todd, Janet. *Sensibility: An Introduction*. London and New York, 1986. An excellent introduction to sensibility in English Literature; chapter 8, "The Attack on Sensibility," is particularly useful.

Vila, Anne C. *Enlightenment and Pathology: Sensibility in the Literature and Medicine of Eighteenth-Century France*. Baltimore and London, 1998. Excellent on the scientific background in France, and its relation to literature.

DAVID J. DENBY

SENTIMENT. *See* Sociability.

SERMONS. [*This entry contains three subentries, on Protestant sermons, Roman Catholic sermons, and Evangelical sermons.*]

Protestant Sermons

In an age when European politics and warfare were divided along denominational lines and the pulpit was a mass medium of communication, it is interesting to note the development of a northern European model of the Protestant sermon characterized by the decline of orthodox Calvinism and influenced by the philosophy of the English Enlightenment. The prevailing trend among Anglican preachers in England may be defined as latitudinarian, in the broad sense of the term. The underlying philosophy was clearly enlightened and Lockean, with emphasis on plain style and moderation and diffidence toward "enthusiasm," or emotional religiosity.

The Anglican pulpit typically emphasized the supremacy of infallible reason, which could be complemented by faith. This underlined the continuity between the "natural religion" that could prove the existence of a supreme clockmaker, creator of heaven and earth, and the specific tenets of revealed religion.

The corpus of English eighteenth-century printed sermons may be almost equally divided into three major categories: "practical"—that is, ethical—political, and doctrinal. Preachers were wont to stress that humans are social animals, and that the public good prevails over individual wellbeing—hence the need to practice benevolence, as summarized by Bishop Butler's first sermon, on human nature: "We were made for society and to do good to our fellow creatures" (*Fifteen Sermons*, 1726). Because the English Glorious Revolution was felt to have implemented such a contractual view of the body politic, many preachers were prepared to campaign for the regime. This led to consensus on the fight against "superstition," synonymous with Catholic obscurantism and against French absolutism, and on the defense of unrestricted trade and constitutional monarchy.

Recurrent providentialism characterized natural disasters and military defeats as divine acts that should spur a sinful people into moral reform in order to avert the wrath of God. This may seem less enlightened. Far from being specifically Anglican—or Protestant, for that matter—it originated from a much older Christian tradition that could coexist easily with an emphasis on ethical concerns.

The insistence on moral applications, evident in the "charity sermons" preached for institutions set up to provide medical or educational assistance to the poor, gradually shifted away from the staunch solifidianism of the Thirty-nine Articles (the Protestant emphasis on justification by faith alone that had been laid as a doctrinal standard in the Church of England since the adoption of the Thirty-nine Articles in 1571) and unconsciously grew closer to the idea that works might secure salvation. That was one reason why the Methodist revival originally attempted to bring the established church back to the fold of Protestant purity. Logically enough, the first sermon in the collection of sermons published in John Wesley's lifetime as an epitome of Methodist doctrine is entitled "Salvation by Faith" (first preached in 1738). However, the wide range of other European religious and mystical traditions from which Methodism drew its inspiration should not be overlooked.

Among these trends was a Puritan tradition that still survived among the minority groups of the "Old Dissent," whose sermons actually differed little from those of their Anglican counterparts. They insisted even more than the latter on ethical issues, but they laid greater emphasis on doctrinal matters; this, along with numerous and funeral orations, probably contributed to giving nonconformists a sense of their identity.

The pattern of Anglican preaching became fashionable overseas. In Ireland—where, unlike anywhere else in Europe, a religious minority held most of the political and socio-economic power—the undeniable influence of Locke, latitudinarians, and reasonable Christianity was conspicuous in the Anglican pulpit. Thomas Sprat had noted as early as 1665 the plagiarism of English sermons by Dutch preachers. Demand for a latitudinarian model of preaching was so high in Germany that a textbook about the English homiletic method was published in German.

The demise of the funeral sermon in eighteenth-century Germany, probably in response to the introduction of a clinical approach to death, may provide evidence of the dialectical tension inherent in the philosophy of the Enlightenment, since rational improvement is necessarily cut short by the Grim Reaper. Accordingly, the *Aufklärung* may have contributed to the demotion of bereavement to the private sphere of life.

As for French Protestant preachers, they had experienced persecution since the 1685 repeal of the Edict of Nantes, though historians generally agree that after 1760 there were interludes of semitoleration. In the heroic times of persecution, French Protestant sermons were unquestionably Calvinistic. Such leading figures as Antoine Court (1695–1760) preached on the sinner's trials and tribulations on the way to heaven and called for repentance. They also supported nonviolent resistance to the civilian authorities who kept trying to break up Huguenot meetings.

Later generations of French Protestant preachers had been trained abroad, particularly in Switzerland, where the influence of the Enlightenment prevailed. Their sermons therefore became increasingly less Calvinistic and more latitudinarian, emphasizing a rational approach to ethical issues. Like their English counterparts, to whose philosophy exiled Huguenots had been exposed, such influential preachers as Antoine Court's son, Court de Gébelin (1724?–1784), and the best-known pastor in the Languedoc, Rabaut Saint-Etienne (1743–1793), advocated natural religion, supplemented by revealed religion. Even their rhetoric was akin to the plain style practiced in the English pulpit. With few exceptions, they were more familiar with Lockean ideas than with the works of the French philosophes. Among the latter, they were mostly acquainted with, and grateful for, the fight against intolerance, as evidenced by the Calas affair of 1761–1762, and Rousseau's attempt to reconcile Christianity and philosophy. Whether such an alliance between the reformed tradition and the Enlightenment, which paved the way for those pastors' eager contribution to the early stages of the French Revolution, may be deemed "unnatural,"

as John Woodbridge, borrowing the phrase from David Bien's work on the Calas affair, has argued, is disputable. After all, French Protestant thinkers and pastors had also long been subject to the drift toward rationalism and moralism that characterized their co-religionists in other European countries.

[*See also* Aufklärung; Calvinism; Latitudinarianism; Reformed Churches; Revealed Religion; *and* Wesley, John.]

BIBLIOGRAPHY

Bien, David D. *The Calas Affair: Persecution, Toleration, and Heresy in Eighteenth-century Toulouse*. Princeton, N.J., 1960.

Boulaire, Francis. "Le Sermon anglican en Irlande à l'époque de la reine Anne." Ph.D. diss., Université de Paris III, 1987. 5 typescript vols. The standard reference work on Anglican sermons in early eighteenth-century Ireland.

Deconinck-Brossard, Françoise. "Eighteenth-Century Sermons and the Age." In *Crown and Mitre: Religion and Society in Northern Europe since the Reformation*, edited by W. M. Jacob and Nigel Yates, pp. 105–121. Woodbridge, U.K., 1993. A survey of English eighteenth-century sermons.

Kowalik, Jill Anne. "The Demise of the Funeral Sermon in Eighteenth-Century Germany: Disturbed Mourning and the Enlightenment's Flight from the Body." In *Impure Reason: Dialectic of Enlightenment in Germany*, edited by Daniel Wilson and Robert C. Holub, pp. 407–424. Detroit, 1993.

Ligou, Daniel, and Philippe Joutard. "Les Déserts (1685–1800)." In *Histoire des Protestants en France*, edited by Robert Mandrou et al., pp. 189–262. Toulouse, 1977. A good view of the plight of French Protestants after the repeal of the Edict of Nantes.

Ward, R. G. "The Eighteenth-Century Church: A European View." In *The Church of England c. 1689–c. 1833: From Toleration to Tractarianism*, edited by John Walsh et al., pp. 285–298. Cambridge, 1993. Emphasizes the emergence of a common Protestant mind in eighteenth-century Europe.

Woodbridge, John Dunning. "An 'Unnatural Alliance' for Religious Toleration: The Philosophes and the Outlawed Pastors of the 'Church of the Desert.'" *Church History* 42 (1973), 505–523. Summarizes the influence of Enlightenment philosophy on French pastors in the Languedoc in the latter half of the century.

FRANÇOISE DECONINCK-BROSSARD

Roman Catholic Sermons

Within the framework of the Roman Catholic Church, preaching followed rules established by the Council of Trent (1545–1563). Confronting Protestant attacks that accused the Roman Catholic clergy of an inability to preach the word of God correctly, the council had given this problem special attention, and the set of decisions that it made during its various sessions were still valid and observed in the eighteenth century. In each diocese the duty of preaching fell to the bishop, who was supposed to ensure that the curé or his representative in each parish strictly performed the complementary and equally essential duty of providing catechism for the children.

The Council of Trent also took great pains to define both the themes and the manner of preaching, recommending in particular the use of comprehensible and appropriate vocabulary. Nevertheless, the instruction of Christians by preaching presupposed that each diocese was provided with clergy who were intellectually and spiritually well prepared for such a task by their education in a seminary. There were, however, depending on the country, important differences in when this indispensable Catholic reform was undertaken: it began during the second half of the sixteenth century in the Italian states and on the Iberian Peninsula; in France, however, it was not until the end of the seventeenth century or even the beginning of the eighteenth that such seminaries were numerous enough that future curés trained in them left fully prepared for their role as preachers of the Word of God.

In the eighteenth century, three main types of preaching can be identified: the ordinary instruction or exhortation given in the Sunday sermon or on feast days; extraordinary preaching, particularly the stations for the observance of Advent and Lent; and the sermons preached over a period of several days during missions. The ordinary sermon was a break in the celebration of the Sunday high mass after the gospel reading. Usually the break included first the recitation of prayers for the dead, the pope, the king or the local lord, then the Our Father, the Hail Mary, the Creed, and the commandments of God and the church. Then came the instruction proper. It was supposed to be short (usually fifteen minutes to half an hour) and given not in Latin but in the language spoken by the faithful, which was, if need be, a regional language and not the official language of the state. The subjects of this instruction comprised the entire Christian doctrine, Sunday after Sunday throughout the liturgical year, usually as support of and commentary upon the gospel reading for the day. Some curés took advantage of the many printed collections of sermons to aid them in their task, particularly those of Charles Borromeo, archbishop of Milan from 1564 to 1584.

Extraordinary preaching was "extraordinary" for several reasons. First, it was done only for certain occasions during the liturgical year: eulogies of patron saints on their feast days; sermons for the great celebrations such as All Saints, Pentecost, Corpus Christi, or the Assumption (at least in France); the stations during Advent and Lent, when there were two sermons a week, and during Holy Week, when there was a daily sermon; and funeral orations. Urban parishes and royal or princely courts were almost exclusively affected by this sort of sermon. They were delivered by specialized preachers who were generally members of the episcopate or of the regular clergy. Among the latter, the presence of many Jesuits

(before the Society was dissolved by the pope in 1773) as highly visible sacred orators certainly played a substantial role, along with the influence of their schools, in the homogenization of Roman Catholic Europe. These great orators conformed to rules of sacred eloquence developed in France in the seventeenth century by Jacques-Bénigne Bossuet (1627–1704), Louis Bourdaloue (1632–1704), and Jean-Baptiste Massillon (1663–1742). These rules had been defined in numerous works at the end of the seventeenth century, then constantly republished in the eighteenth in works such as the *Art de prêcher la parole de Dieu* (Art of Preaching the Word of God, 1687) by the Jesuit Foix.

Evangelical sermons made up the third category. These were parish or "internal" missions, as opposed to the "external" missions intended to convert pagans. A formula perfected in Italy in the sixteenth century by Filippo Neri in Rome and Charles Borromeo in Milan (both later canonized) was applied in most Catholic countries. It consisted of a series of sermons and exercises of piety performed in an urban or rural parish over several consecutive days by one or several specialized preachers, often Capuchins, Oratorians, or Jesuits. In the eighteenth century, the aim was—according to Louis-Marie Grignion de Montfort, the founder in France of an order dedicated to this sort of evangelism—"to renew the spirit of Christianity in Christians." Instructions, conferences leading to discussions with the participants, and actual sermons followed a carefully scheduled sequence. A grand procession, during which a cross was erected, usually marked the close of the mission. The missionaries used simple language in their sermons, adapting them to their audience, whether urban or rural, and sprinkled them liberally with familiar images. Some did not hesitate to question the faithful directly in order to arouse their active participation; they even used spectacular effects such as holding up a skull while speaking of death. Missions were special times in the life of the parish and the faithful and justified the use of special preaching methods.

Though there were different forms of sermons for different occasions, the same teachings were given to all the faithful of Roman Catholic Europe in the eighteenth century, despite varying nuances from one country to the next. The instruction remained the same as in the previous century, and it left its mark even longer: throughout the entire post-Tridentine period of the Roman church, ending only with the Second Vatican Council. The discourse was remarkably coherent, based on a fundamental pessimism leading to a religion of suffering and fear. The great driving force behind Christian life was less God's love freely given than the fear of sin and hell. The gospel, in the mouths of most of the preachers, seemed to come down to strict moralism and a systematic denial of wordly things, which were presented as incompatible with salvation. Though it can claim ties with Saint Paul and Saint Augustin, this austere and demanding religion seems to have been created more for the clergy and the monks than for the committed men and women in the world. In any case, a discourse of this sort made it all the more difficult for the religious to engage in dialogue with the philosophy of an Enlightenment that was based on values almost diametrically opposed to it.

[*See also* Counter-Enlightenment *and* Roman Catholicism.]

BIBLIOGRAPHY

Darricau, Raymond. "Prédication, pt. 3, La prédication à l'époque moderne." In *Catholicisme hier, aujourd'hui, demain*, vol. 11, col. 791–798. Paris, 1985.

Histoire du christianisme, vol. 9, *L'âge de raison (1620–1750)*, edited by Jean-Marie Mayeur, et al. Vol. 10, *Les défis de la modernité (1750–1840)*, edited by Bernard Plongeron. Paris, 1997.

Lebrun, François "La predication au XVIIIᵉ siècle." In *Histoire vécue du peuple chrétien*, edited by Jean Delumeau, vol. 2, pp. 43–66. Toulouse, 1979.

FRANÇOIS LEBRUN

Translated from French by Betsy Wing

Evangelical Sermons

The relationship between evangelical preaching and the Enlightenment is ambiguous. "The Enlightenment" implies an optimistic and rational understanding of human nature and supports scientific analysis. Many evangelicals agreed with these premises. However, Enlightenment ideas were challenged by the evangelicals in their insistence that revelation took precedence over reason. Ironically, in insisting upon an individual decision for or experience of conversion, evangelical preaching paralleled and reinforced Enlightenment thinking, although the rationale was different.

Evangelical preaching traces its roots to the missionary preaching of the early church, but more immediate influences were the continental Pietists, particularly Philipp Jacob Spener and Franke, and the English nonconformists. Evangelical preaching arises periodically as a reaction to rationalistic preaching. Eighteenth-century Latitudinarians offered a moderate message that appealed to all, but the effect was that the lower classes were ignored. Evangelicals both within established churches and in nonconformist groups reacted by emphasizing God's sovereignty, a spiritual encounter as preaching's objective, and new ways to reach the poor.

Preaching was the chief evangelical tool for exposing people to the Gospel and transforming them into committed Christians. While most clergy within state-established churches explained the reasonableness of the faith, evangelicals read the Bible as divine truth and insisted upon an experience of the grace of God. Preaching was undergirded by assumptions of its power and authority, and preachers argued that sin would lead to damnation unless the sinner experienced rebirth.

Innovations in preaching methodology included the sharing of pulpits, itinerancy, open-air meetings, and an extemporaneous style and the use of colloquial speech. Anglican clergy were annoyed by Methodist evangelicals, who preached in fields, factories, and mines. Innovations in sermon content included the centrality of conversion, the nature of the New Birth, and the need for spiritual guidance and accountability. An appeal to human hearts and the religious affections characterized the message. Music was also a significant means of reaching the unlearned. Hymns by Isaac Watts and Charles Wesley captured interest with lively tunes, even tavern tunes set to evangelical texts. John Wesley's sermons focused on God's love, offering hope to despairing workers. George Whitefield preached the New Birth with dramatic flair, and in America was notable for "Christianizing" slaves. Similar themes were preached in Scotland at Kilsyth and Cambuslang, where in the 1740s large revivals resulted, and in the American colonies, where at about the same time the Great Awakening swept the nation.

The enlargement of women's roles to include preaching extended from the Quaker precedent of women's public speaking. John Wesley encouraged women's leadership in small class meetings; when participation in these meetings grew, women leaders were effectually preaching. Similar situations occurred in America during and immediately following the Great Awakening with the practice of lay women's exhortation. In 1771 John Wesley reluctantly affirmed Mary Bosanquet's call to preaching. A decade later, women were participating in open-air preaching in England, and in 1787 a woman was formally authorized to preach. However, tendencies on both sides of the Atlantic toward egalitarianism in ministry diminished with institutionalization.

Regardless of occasion, evangelical preaching was revivalist in nature, particularly in its dependence on Scripture as the primary source of truth, emphasis on religious experience, and urgency. Evangelical sermons may be divided into categories as occasional and doctrinal sermons and those for the purpose of social and moral reform. Even occasional sermons (for funerals, ordinations, political occasions, and fast days) commonly had a revivalist tone. Funerals often celebrated the attainment of eternal life by one presumed righteous, whose example the hearers were exhorted to follow. Alternatively, a funeral sermon might lament the fate of one presumed damned, with admonishments to take heed lest the hearers fall into the same pit. Ordination sermons encouraged clergy to model lives of righteousness for their congregations and to preach for the conversion of souls. Jeremiads, sermons lamenting the sinful state of the nation and urging spiritual awakening, were often preached on political occasions and appointed fast days. All occasions were opportunities for preaching the need for conversion and opportunity for grace. Likewise, all sermons challenged assumptions that reason alone could satisfy the soul.

Doctrinal sermons focused primarily on the sovereignty of God, the dependence of human beings, and conversion or New Birth. Methodist sermons also focused on the doctrine of Christian perfection, as well as perfect love and holiness of heart and life. These subjects focused on God and hence both extended and challenged Enlightenment assertions of human possibility.

Sermons directed at issues of moral reform addressed such topics as purity, profanity, abstention from alcohol, modesty, charity, public confession, and good works. Other sermons promoted social reform, advocating better labor practices and support of foreign missions. Sermons for social reform encouraged action, women's action in particular. A shift in the portrayal of women, from creatures of sin to people of moral and religious superiority, created more opportunity for women's action in philanthropic and educational endeavors. While patriarchy and subordination of women continued to govern the official church rhetoric, new possibilities for women's leadership were opened through preaching about reform and through Wesley's affirmation of women's spiritual gifts for teaching and preaching.

Evangelicals were a diverse group. Divisions occurred between Calvinists and Arminians, and over the charge of "enthusiasm." Evangelicals were found among almost every denomination, including Presbyterians; General Baptists; Methodist/Anglicans; Anglicans; German, Dutch, and Swiss Reformed; Congregationalists; and Lutherans and Moravians. Evangelicals in England included the Methodists John and Charles Wesley and Whitefield, as well as the Anglicans William Wilberforce, Samuel Walker, and John Newton and dissenter Richard Davis; in Wales, Howel Harris, Daniel Rowland, and Griffith Jones; the Erskines (Ebenezer, Ralph, and John) and Robert Colman in Scotland; and Jonathan Edwards, Theodorus Freylinghuysen, and Gilbert and William Tennent in the American colonies.

The evangelicals represented a subtle blend of interest in and resistance to the authority of reason. Jonathan Edwards blended Enlightenment reason with orthodox Christianity. Edwards utilized Lockean philosophy and Newtonian physics in his reformulation of Calvinism and defense of revival. John Wesley, another Lockean, included reason as a source of truth, balancing it with Scripture, tradition, and experience.

Commitments to religious revival united evangelicals. Their preaching challenged the idea that reason could fully satisfy the human soul, insisted on divine mystery, and addressed the pervasiveness of evil. Their affective preaching style was a major factor in the spread of evangelical religion, and a means of God's "work of redemption."

[*See also* Enthusiasm; Great Awakening; Pietism; Revealed Religion; Rhetoric; Sermons; *and* Wesley, John.]

BIBLIOGRAPHY

Campbell, Ted A. *The Religion of the Heart: A Study of European Religious Life in the Seventeenth and Eighteenth Centuries*. Eugene, Ore., 2000. Provides an overview of movements across the globe with concern for religion of the heart. Chapter 4 on Pietism and chap. 5 on the evangelical revival in Britain are especially helpful.

Cowing, Cedric. *The Saving Remnant: Religion and the Settling of New England*. Urbana and Chicago, 1995. Cowing describes the differences between rationalists and evangelicals in the British Isles and traces their immigration to the American colonies with emphasis on patterns of revival.

Crawford, Michael J. *Seasons of Grace: Colonial New England's Revival Tradition in Its British Context*. New York and Oxford, 1991. The idea of revival is traced in its development, with attention to affective preaching, hymnody, and the resulting revivals on both sides of the Atlantic. Chapter 11 describes the connections among the evangelicals on both sides of the Atlantic. Connections Scottish, English, and American revivals are especially well drawn.

Downey, James. *The Eighteenth Century Pulpit: A Study of the Sermons of Butler, Berkeley, Secker, Sterne, Whitefield and Wesley*. Oxford, 1969. An interesting look at eighteenth-century preachers in Great Britain, comparing their characteristics and significance.

Gill, Sean. *Women and the Church of England: From the Eighteenth Century to the Present*. London, 1994. A helpful historical tracing of the roles of women in the Anglican Church.

Juster, Susan. *Disorderly Women: Sexual Politics and Evangelicalism in Revolutionary New England*. Ithaca, N.Y., and London, 1994. The best detailing of the rise in involvement of women in the revivals of New England and their subsequent decline in leadership with institutionalization.

Ward, W. R. *The Protestant Evangelical Awakening*. Cambridge, 1992. A comprehensive overview of the revivals in Europe, with a brief look at revivals in the American colonies.

Willimon, William H., and Richard Lischer, eds. *Concise Encyclopedia of Preaching*. Louisville, Ky., 1995. A helpful source for information on many topics related to preaching. The brief history of preaching provides an excellent broad sweep.

KATHERINE THOMAS PAISLEY

SEXUALITY. Sexuality existed in the age of Enlightenment as a web of practices, acts, cultural and scientific beliefs, laws and juridical findings, and religious codes. It was influenced by contemporary understanding of physiology and health and shaped by the community's need to ensure its survival by balancing the number of people with the necessities of life that land and labor could produce. Artists and writers also helped to structure sexuality by depicting an array of characters in situations that spoke of sexual mores and strictures. Thus, although sexuality may be linked to physiology, it is also a part of history, and never more so than in the years of rapid change between 1650 and 1800. Historians attribute change in sexual practices and ideology over the course of the Enlightenment to urbanization, secularization, the democratization of politics (to include more men in the body politic), and the growth of manufacturing. The development of a middle class promoted a code of sexual fidelity while the drastic political turmoil of the late eighteenth century helped produce a wave of sexual panic and what is often called the "invention" of pornography.

Religious, Scientific, and Popular Views of Sexuality. Informed understanding of sexuality rested on the creeds of various religions and the findings of the scientific establishment—two authorities whose ideas were often intertwined. Judeo-Christian society generally valued heterosexuality because it reproduced the population. To this end, sexual relations were expected to occur within marriage, and non-consummation was grounds for separation or annulment. As science became caught up in sexual differences, the sexual fantasies abounded, leading the Swedish botanist Carolus Linnaeus to describe the multiplication of plants in terms of heterosexual passion and the processes of heterosexual intercourse.

The Roman Catholic Church valued sexual chastity and therefore decreed celibacy for religious leaders and those who chose a religious vocation. Although there was an equal value accorded to both male and female chastity, the church emphasized women's greater sexual sinfulness, which it associated with Eve's seduction of Adam. Protestantism assigned greater worth to the married state and active heterosexuality than to chastity, though it did nothing to alleviate the onerous sexual stigma of Eve. Western religions generally saw sexuality as important, but only because it produced pregnancy. Sexual chastity before marriage was highly valued, even demanded by the church, which emphasized the virginity of Mary and celebrated women who preferred death to loss of their "honor." In the context of Enlightenment rationality and middle-class insurgency, a literature of seducers, loose women, and faked virginity existed, publicizing the threat of sexual fraud on women's part.

Late in the seventeenth century a number of important sex manuals appeared in western Europe, and were soon translated into several European languages. Nicholas Venette, a doctor in La Rochelle, published *Tableau de l'amour conjugal* (Conjugal Love, or, The Pleasures of the Marriage Bed), which was translated into Spanish, Dutch, German and also English, and which remained the best-selling sex manual until 1900. The manual was important for the range of medical, popular, and moral soundings it gave readers. The best of manuals provided physiological information on genitalia, and how they worked or failed

to work, and also discussed the psychological aspects of sexuality. Presented in Enlightenment terms, sexuality was seen as part of nature and as an essential component of health, and for the sick and ill-disposed, sexual intercourse could prove healing. One manual put the matter bluntly: "There is no surer or safer means to preserve health and avoid a sudden death than now and then to take a frisk with a woman." The manuals uniformly saw sexual pleasure in terms of procreation, leading their authors to describe the most efficacious sexual positions for ensuring conception.

A second genre of manual covered the sins of masturbation and, like the *Tableau de l'amour conjugal*, laid the groundwork for the modern compulsion to talk about sex. These were written by eminent physicians such as S.-A.-A. Tissot (*L'Onanisme*, 1760) and by anonymous authors, all of whom condemned the practice. Commentators found the young, unmarried state to be the cause of the "sin" of masturbation, and one title in particular sums up their views: *Onania, Or the Heinous Sin of Self-Pollution, And all its frightful Consequences, in both Sexes, Consider'd with Spiritual and Physical Advice to those, who have already injur'd themselves by this abominable practice. And seasonable Admonition to the Youth of the Nation, (of both Sexes) and those whose Tuition they are under, whether Parents, Guardians, Masters, or Mistresses.* The authors of these manuals fell into the paradox first expressed by French theorist Michel Foucault: that most found it difficult to talk directly about masturbation, expressing their desire not to deal explicitly with so evil a subject because of the dangers to the young. However, in order to discuss the matter indirectly, they filled more and more pages with equivocation, illusion, and imprecations not to discuss what they were discussing. The argument goes that increased oversight of sexuality (though not necessarily official oversight), produced talk, and the talk itself became a form of oversight, including self-regulation.

The Impact of Enlightenment Thought. Developments in Enlightenment philosophy influenced ideas of sexuality. Examining René Descartes's proposition that humans are thinking things (*res cogitans*), with priority given to the mind, the philosopher Julien Offray de La Mettrie disagreed. He pointed to the body's complexity and the attendant failure of scientists and philosophers to sort out physiological matters. This puzzling complexity led philosophers to yield priority to the soul or mind simply because it was easier. La Mettrie meant to bring them back into alignment by supporting the man-machine complexity and wholeness. For some, sexuality was part of the machine's economy—a matter of mechanical sensations and operations, such as ejaculation—and thus a logical consequence of La Mettrie's materialist understanding of the human nature. Mechanistic views of the body influenced a range of fields, leading to mechanistic scenes of sex in some literary works.

The progress of physiological science and experimentation did little to change the view of women as highly sexed creatures, except that their sexuality became more threatening and less rational. For the Enlightenment doctor Pierre Rousel, whose accounts of sexuality subtracted the agency from women's reproductive organs and saw semen as the sole determinant of fertility, men's sexuality was purposive whereas women's was totally sensuous. "The exterior parts of men carry a character of sensible utility; those of women seem to be nothing other than simple organs of pleasure," he noted. Other physicians were even more materialistic in assigning a sole goal of seduction to female physiology, maintaining an alliance with most church teachings. Physicians wrote that the female uterus was sexually "furious," with tendencies to spin out of control in its appetites. A certain congruence remained between the sexual nature of the female body and its moral stature, although, increasingly, some physicians insisted that women's natural modesty kept seduction in check. Such scientific beliefs spilled over into the culture at large.

Physiological discussions of sexuality merged with Enlightenment politics and theories. The regulatory, autocratic state was newly subjected to rational criticism, and human reason was valorized, leading to reformulations of the nature of appropriate sexuality. As a result, the autocratic state slowly began withdrawing its hand from overt sexual regulation, allowing civil society—in the form of the press, civic institutions, and the churches—to step into the breach if they so desired. Simultaneously, increasing responsibility for self-governance slowly gave birth to the concept of the self-governing citizen. Although sexuality remained an important part of human behavior, especially for reproduction of the species and the consequent empowerment of the kingdom, depletion of semen was much feared. In fact, the man of reason realized that, in accord with older ideas of internal flows of blood (from which semen developed) that nourished the entire being, as much semen as possible needed to be retained to promote bodily health. Sexuality remained vivifying, but the individual's body now competed with the destiny of the human race for each man's semen. The successfully self-regulating man of reason would balance those needs. He would thus be alert to sexual excess, sexual fraud, and sexually transmitted disease. At the same time, there developed a cult of sensibility, which aimed to transform men's sexual appetite into a regard for the feelings of others.

Women's sexuality became intertwined with reform thought because of concerns for fertility as a sign of national strength. Populations in China, the Ottoman empire, and even such newly appreciated places as Tahiti were lauded as places where women's natural sexuality was responsible for a strong and numerous people. Diderot's *Supplément au voyage de Bougainville* (1772) champions the social concern for population that is at the heart of Tahitian, and other societies', sexuality. Restricted by concerns for propriety and property, Europe produced "flirtatious," not fertile women, some thinkers believed. These critics contested both the sexual and non-sexual influence of women like the king's mistresses, and the proprietary sexual mores of the rising middle classes in which prudence and calculation of family well-being entered into family mores. Other reformers, however, fought back on contiguous terrain. Presenting himself as a man of sensibility, Jean-Jacques Rousseau advanced the appeal of female chastity and sexuality exercised exclusively within marriage as part of his attack on the political and cultural power wielded by highly placed women through their sexuality. Only within the confines of the patriarchal family could female sexuality be controlled as a social force, neutralized in politics, and deployed for optimal reproduction.

There were models in Enlightenment literature of the male sexual predator or libertine, who seemed to represent the hypersexed nobleman of the declining aristocracy. The notorious seducer Valmont of *Les liaisons dangereuses*, a novel by Choderlos de Laclos, sets out to destroy women's virtue, and he does so with the connivance of Mme. de Merteuil, a wealthy woman of so few scruples that she lures young unmarried women of the best families into Valmont's snare. Packed with scenes of Valmont's conquests and of the descent of women into decadent sexual license, *Les liaisons dangereuses* (1782) is said to reflect the wanton sexuality of the aristocracy in the eighteenth century. By other accounts, however, the many libertine novels of the century reflect an attitude toward women's sexuality that is extremely instrumental: Mme. de Merteuil and Valmont enter into a wager over seduction of other women, and Valmont defeats enemies and trumps other members of society through seduction. Simultaneously, men are brought together politically, as they bond around their shifting but enduring sexual access to women—an access that has signaled for some historians the political unification of men preliminary to contesting the exclusive prerogatives of the king. Libertines existed in real life, for example, in the person of Giovanni Giacomo Casanova, a figure of Enlightenment erudition, who wrote and had extraordinary success seducing women, even by eighteenth century standards. However, historians now believe that Casanova invented many if not all of his conquests, making his memoirs another example of libertine fiction.

Sexuality changed in the eighteenth century in that a more restrictive standard came to apply to same-sex relationships. Throughout most of European history, men had had relationships with other men as well as with women. In the male-male relationship, younger men played the passive partner, and then as they grew older, adopted the more active role. Likewise experiencing no change in social status, women could have relationships with other women, although it is believed statistically that more men than women engaged widely in same-sex sexual acts. By the beginning of eighteenth century, however, this situation was beginning to change, with the attribution of a stigmatizing name "sodomite" applied to men who engaged in same-sex acts and relationships. Nonetheless, homosocial and homoerotic relationships among men continued to be valorized by many writers, some even seeing these relationships as an important bulwark to Enlightenment society. The coming to power of a collective male citizenry that displaced the king in the French Revolution and in the spread of male representative government amounted to a band of brothers displacing the father. Some historians see the unity of these men as embedded in a "sexual contract" that allowed men sexual governance over women. Other historians, however, emphasize the homosocial and homoerotic nature of the ties and use classical art as evidence. This art, which became increasingly popular after the middle of the eighteenth century, depicted heroic groups of muscular Roman and Greek men and celebrated their virile, civic, and military unity. Important theorists like Johann Joachim Winckelmann, publicizing the male nude in his revival of an appreciation for classical art, strengthened aspirations for an uplifting, even aestheticized, and essentially virtuous experience rooted in same-sex love.

By the end of the Enlightenment a full-scale attack on the dimorphism in sexuality took place in Mary Wollstonecraft's *Vindication of the Rights of Woman* (1792) and in *Maria, or the Wrongs of Woman* (1797). Having borne a child out of wedlock and been abandoned by the child's father, Wollstonecraft had complaints against the legal system, the educational status of women, and the inequity in sexual beliefs and practices. To her mind, failure to educate women led to their general ineptitude and to their inequality in marriage. Without the full development of their rational faculties, women could only rely on their sexuality to hold on to their men, making them simultaneously vulnerable and tyrannical. Moreover, the legal system, as indicted in Wollstonecraft's *Maria, or the Wrongs of Woman*, allowed men to prey on women's sexuality and then abandon them. Within marriage it allowed them the right to rape their wives and virtually to keep them incarcerated in the house as sexual prey.

Sexuality in Practice. During this period sexual practices varied, depending on the area of Europe, financial status or class, and gender. Among the peasantry,

sexual activity had to be coordinated with the ability to produce enough to feed the population. The community controlled sexuality and regulated it according to community resources, generally leading to a high age at marriage. Community control of sexuality among youth was exercised by parents, the community as a whole, or peers. Families chose children's marital, and thus sexual, partners, whereas in areas like Scandinavia, young people monitored the behavior of their peers and developed customs such as bundling. In bundling and other similar customs, control of sexuality revolved around "practice" nights that couples spent together without sexual intercourse during their celibate adolescent and early adult years. The idea behind bundling and other physical activity was that young people should get to know one another physically, short of engaging in intercourse. Groups of youth would charivari couples who might be breaking taboos against sexual intercourse, and they might similarly charivari inappropriate sexual alliances—an older woman and a youth, for example. Communities would also censure adultery with charivaris, as well as other shaming activities. In eastern Europe, where agricultural workers were bound to large landowners as serfs and thus restricted in freedom, the landowners enforced a low age at marriage in order to increase the amount of labor they were owned. Sexual activity in Russia and several other eastern European areas where serfdom still existed began at a low age and led to a high birth rate (and a high death rate).

Because reproduction was the central goal, so long as people reproduced, their extramarital, same-sex relationships did not meet social or political resistance. Men had sexual relationships with one another as did women. In Amsterdam in the middle of the eighteenth century, a neighbor complained of two older women "living together as if they were man and wife...feeling and touching one another under their skirts and at their bosoms. This complaint, however, led to no trial. Mistresses and their maids and married women who enjoyed one another sexually were also part of the sexual landscape, as were single women who openly lived together—the well-known "Ladies of Llangollen" Scotland are one example from affluent society. From the mid-eighteenth century on, this sexuality became more questionable, with trials of men for sodomy and for women for "tribadism," but often only if there were severe crimes involved. In urban areas men had usually developed a rich culture around their sexuality, consisting of special words or slang, initiations and rituals, and special meeting places.

In this overwhelmingly landed society based on agricultural wealth, the upper-classes and royal families had more expansive sexual customs. Parents found mates for their children based on economic and political considerations set within networks of patronage and clientage. They often sent their children to religious institutions until they reached a marriageable age in the late teens. Alternatively they were supervised by tutors, nurses, and other chaperones. Legitimate sexuality within marriage occurred to reproduce and, it was hoped, enrich the matrix of influence in which the marriage took place. However, because aristocracy entailed privileges of many sorts, aristocratic spouses often engaged in a extramarital sexual relationships as part of their privilege. Women of the aristocracy saw sexual pleasure as one of their prerogatives. The talented and well-connected French aristocrat Stéphanie-Félicité de Genlis was the lover of the duc d'Orléans, in addition to being a wife and mother. The Swedish countess Hopken unabashedly posed nude in public for a statue called "Venus of the Beautiful Backside." Some aristocratic women were famed mistresses to the king.

Monarchs in Europe married other royalty for reasons of diplomacy and depended on alliances with both large and small states. Yet, as the person whose prerogatives encompassed all others, the monarch usually had publicly acknowledged mistresses and favorites, who held official positions at the court. In contrast to common prostitutes, mistresses were married women either of the upper-middle class or aristocracy. There were exceptions: Madame du Barry, last mistress of Louis XV of France, was the sexy, fun-loving, and illegitimate daughter of a monk and seamstress; she started off with a casual one-night fling with the king, only to become a permanent fixture in the royal household. Women monarchs, like Catherine the Great of Russia, also took lovers from the upper classes. Sexual relations often led to political and cultural power: Madame de Pompadour, the favorite of Louis XV, was a patron of Enlightenment thinkers and an ad-hoc political adviser. Catherine chose some of her lovers from the ministerial ranks and military, giving these lovers cultural influence as well.

What one might call freer sexual expression among the ranks of royalty did not prevent the appearance of sexual dysfunction, as the letters from Marie-Antoinette, queen of France, to her mother Maria Theresa, empress of Austria, show. Married at the age of fourteen to the fifteen-year-old heir to the throne of France she had received instruction in the sexual conduct of a married woman from her mother. For the first several years of her marriage, the French queen did not become pregnant, mainly because her husband did not have the same sexual knowledge and because he needed to be circumcized to cure his phymosis, which prevented him from having sex. From 1770 until 1777, the correspondence between mother and daughter concerned the non-consummation of the marriage, the necessity for the couple to share a bed in any case, and finally news of the circumcision of the new king. On 30 August 1777 Marie-Antoinette wrote: "It is a thrilling

occasion for me. I am in the most essential happiness of my entire life. It has already been more than eight days since my marriage was entirely consummated; the proof has been repeated and yesterday even more completely than the first time." From then until Maria Theresa's death in 1780, their letters continued to discuss the couple's intimacy, Marie-Antoinette's menstrual periods, and her pregnancy, in 1778.

The Enlightenment was a period of rapid population growth and urbanization, especially in western Europe, leading to a situation in which many young people in cities were released from parental and community control. Domestic service also gradually shifted from being a male occupation to a female one. These developments are associated with rising rates of urban illegitimacy, as the young lost the regulatory institutions—either familial or peer—for their sexuality. Foundling homes increased in importance, and novels about the seduction of young women new to the city abounded. By some reports, in times of heavy rains infanticides spewed forth from flooded city sewers. In certain areas of the countryside, where agricultural improvements and the introduction of industry produced the need for workers, extra marital sex had less regulation because day laborers were at work.

Thus, a range of sexual regimes, determined by the extent of urbanization, manufacturing, and agricultural modernization, existed in this transitional period. Among the growing middle class, whose prosperity was tied to these economic changes, a supposedly new sexual morality was taking shape, based on sexual fidelity as a positive for emotional reasons. Distinguishing itself from the aristocracy by its capacity for thrift and hard work, the middle class also set itself off because of its more developed sense of sentiment and its worthier values. Whereas the aristocracy flaunted its instrumentalist sexuality, the middle class, in the name of its distinctive sentiment, promoted finer feelings rather than gross physical ones. Whereas the aristocracy was sexually wanton, the middle-class was sexually restrained and self-governing. For a while in the eighteenth century, some writers feared that the result of the middle-class cult of sensibility would feminize men emotionally, and eventually sexually. Critics, however, saw that the expression of middle-class sensibility could also be a way to seduce unsuspecting women. Characters like Tom Jones and Lovelace invented a variety of schemes—such as displaying sensitive manners or showing their knowledge of novels of sensibility—to triumph over a heroine's sexual defenses.

As Europeans went to other parts of the world as traders, plantation owners, officials, settlers, and soldiers, different patterns of sexuality emerged Most men had sexual relationships with women outside of Europe. Eighteenth-century officials in India had mistresses, some of them long-term partners, and reported home on the very erotic and loving nature of Asian women. The governor-general in India (1793–1798), though a founder of the Foreign Bible Society, had one of these lengthy relationships; others kept a dozen or more women. Ordinary soldiers easily lived in concubinage as wives seldom settled outside of Europe, and in India alone, some 50 percent of soldiers had wives or concubines. Some men used the sexual services of prostitutes, who, unlike the prostitutes in Europe, were often learned and very highly mannered. Some officials even underwent circumcision and other genital modifications to please Muslim women and those in cultures with different sexual expectations. By contrast, in the eighteenth century African women were described by some travelers as being monstrous and asexual, and were sold into slavery or brought to Europe (in particular, southern Europe) as prostitutes. Those women sold into slavery to the colonies were subject to rape. As the chastity and asexual sensibility of European women became more highly valued in the later years of the eighteenth century, women of color were often equated with excessive sexuality, creating a link of race and sex that remains to this day.

Wide-ranging sexual encounters, along with rapid urbanization, meant that venereal disease plagued many Europeans in the eighteenth century. (Effective cures were not developed until the twentieth century.) James Boswell, writer and biographer of Samuel Johnson, was always searching for a sexual partner who would not infect him. Encountering a London actress who looked healthy and untouched, he had sex with her, leading to inflammation that "too plain was Signor Gonorrhea." About the same time, Jacques Ménétra, the Parisian glazier who had many sexual encounters, listed in his autobiographies those women with whom sex resulted in venereal disease. Boswell, like others, resorted to condoms when he visited brothels, but sometimes, according to his version of the story, an amorous partner would convince him not to use it as it spoiled the sexual pleasure.

Sexuality in Politics and the Politics of Pornography. By the end of the Enlightenment sexuality was used as a political weapon that was especially powerful when it depicted women in sexual acts. Fraught with danger, women's sexuality served the cause of counter-revolutionary and revolutionary political satirists after 1789. Revolutionaries depicted aristocratic women and nuns as sexually perverse, or at least excessive in their appetites. Their favorite target was Marie-Antoinette, portrayed in a variety of sexual scenes with women and men or both simultaneously. Sexuality shaped the trial against the queen, as seen in charges that she had molested her own son, the heir to the French throne. Counter-revolutionaries were not immune to the lure of pornographic portrayals

of market women and members of republican clubs. Their sexuality was frightening in its actual monstrosity rather than perverse. Deploying female sexuality almost exclusively, satirists nonetheless focused on masculine sexuality to suggest an effeminate inability to rule, especially symbolized in cuckoldry—one of the taunts used to delegitimize Louis XVI. In the American colonies, the case of Lord Cornbury also exemplified this trend. Amidst growing resistance to the British crown, colonists, and later commentators, tagged Lord Cornbury as a notorious cross-dresser and effeminate pervert, even though no direct evidence existed of his cross-dressing or of any "perverse" acts. Even the New York Historical Society displays a portrait of a woman and identifies it as Lord Cornbury, though no evidence exists that it was the Tory colonial administrator.

By the 1790s a sexual panic associated with the Revolution, its spread to other countries, and the series of revolutionary wars swept Europe. This panic was fueled by news reports that revolutionaries or counter-revolutionaries were raping women in the civil war in the Vendée region of France and that revolutionary or counter-revolutionary armies were doing the same. There was a great fear for women's chastity, and writers like Mary Wollstonecraft were suddenly exemplary of the sexual dangers menacing society. Using the trump card of sexuality, which had shown its efficacy against Marie-Antoinette and other women in the French Revolution, English papers held Wollstonecraft's sexuality, not her ideas, up to scrutiny. For some, she was just one of the oversexed women who "breathe their loose desires," while others claimed Wollstonecraft's real problem was that she was frigid and sexually inept, losing her mates to other, more feminine women. In England accusations of adultery and divorce petitions mushroomed, and in the German states the marital musical chairs among the romantic elite caused alarm. The change was that abundant sexuality was no longer accepted as an aristocratic privilege and, in many cases, a social good but rather as something to be feared by the public. In fact, sexuality was said to endanger not only individuals but the public as a whole, even national strength: "Female chastity is the true foundation of national honor," one British commentator wrote in 1800. In the early years of Napoleon's reign, new regulations allowed for the monitoring of women for sexual disease. Although the decree was directed at prostitutes who might have congress with the armed forces, so great was the danger to national security that police were given such latitude that they could arrest any woman on the streets.

The complex trajectory from less regulated to more regulated sexuality, much of it focused on questions of female virginity and on the growing stigmatization of same-sex relationships, contributed to the burgeoning, even the invention, of pornography. To avoid censorship for their political critique, many Enlightenment books and tracts had been disguised as erotic works. The theme of "philosophy in the boudoir," used to advance political reform, marked one step on the road to the invention of pornography. The sharp delineation of the private from the public world over the course of the eighteenth century added to this development, and the suspense evoked by public man's efforts to conquer the private or domesticated woman sexually was a hallmark of pornography. The use of explicit sexual satire in politics was still another stage on the road to pornography. Once women had been explicitly removed from the public sphere and politics, in sagas of ongoing sexual domination pornography provided an array of situations and sexual details that spoke implicitly of a founding political event—the domination of women and the private sphere by men—that worked itself out in a panoply of sexual practices.

The writings of the marquis de Sade (1740–1814) are exemplary of the development of pornography. An aristocrat, Sade spent some three decades of his life incarcerated for crimes and mental illness. Although his behavior was notorious, his writings have been enduringly so, condemned for their sexual cruelty and debasement. Others, however, see Sade's writing from a literary and historical point of view as depicting, and in many senses critiquing, Enlightenment values. For instance, *Les 120 Jours de Sodome* (The 120 Days of Sodom) and other of his writings involve numeracy, exactitude, a mechanized body, and precise description of complicated bodily functioning. Both a violent turn-on and highly politicized, his writing addresses "citizens" and preaches a raw form of individualism, even for women. Sade seems to promote a rational rather than moralizing attitude toward sexuality, making moralizers the victims, and calculating thinkers acting out of self-interest the victors. Although rational, Sade's protagonists find women's bodies utterly disgusting except when violent domination sexualizes and eroticizes them. Thus Sade's writing marks an important turn, showing pornography as political because it focuses on subjugating women, and as erotic because that subjugation is the source of arousal and sexual performance.

BIBLIOGRAPHY

Bernier, Olivier. *Secrets of Marie Antoinette: A Collection of Letters*. New York, 1986.

Binhammer, Katherine. "The Sex Panic of the 1790s." *Journal of the History of Sexuality* 6 (1996).

Boucé, Paul-Gabriel. *Sexuality in Eighteenth-Century Britain*. Totowa, N.J., 1982.

Higgs, David. *Queer Sites: Gay Urban Histories since 1600*. London, 1999.

Hull, Isabel V. *Sexuality, State, and Civil Society in Germany, 1700–1815*. Ithaca, N.Y., 1996.

Hunt, Lynn, ed. *Eroticism and the Body Politic*. Baltimore, 1991.

Hunt, Lynn. *The Family Romance of the French Revolution*. Berkeley, Calif., 1992.

Fout, John, ed. *Journal of the History of Sexuality*. Chicago, 1992.

Laqueur, Thomas. *Making Sex: Body and Gender from the Greeks to Freud*. Cambridge, Mass., 1990.

Merrick, Jeffrey, and Bryant T. Ragan, Jr. *Homosexuality in Early Modern France: A Documentary Collection*. New York, 2001.

Nicholas, Venette. *Conjugal Love; Or, The Pleasures of The Marriage Bed Considered. In Several Lectures On Human Generation*. London, 1750.

Porter, Roy, and Mikuláš Teich, eds. *Sexual Knowledge, Sexual Science: The History of Attitudes to Sexuality*. Cambridge, Mass., 1994.

Schiebinger, Londa. *Nature's Body: Gender in the Making of Modern Science*. Boston, 1993.

Stone, Lawrence. *The Family, Sex, and Marriage in England, 1500–1800*. New York, 1977, p. 577.

Trumbach, Randolph. *Sex and the Gender Revolution: Heterosexuality and the Third Gender in Enlightenment London*. Chicago, 1998.

Van der Meer, Theo. "Tribades on Trial: Female Sex Offenders in Late Eighteenth-Century Amsterdam." In *Forbidden History: The State, Society, and the Regulations of Sexuality in Modern Europe*, edited by John Fout, p. 192. New York, 1992.

Venette, Nicholas. "Conjugal Love, or, The Pleasures of the Marriage Bed Considered." In *Several Lectures on Human Generation*. London, 1750.

Wellman, Kathleen. "Physicians and Philosophes: Physiology and Sexual Morality in the French Enlightenment." *Eighteenth Century Studies* 35 (Winter 2002), 267–277.

BONNIE SMITH

SHAFTESBURY, ANTHONY ASHLEY COOPER,
third earl of (1671–1713), British politician and philosopher.

Lord Shaftesbury was one of the shaping influences on the intellectual currents of the early and mid-eighteenth century both in Britain and abroad. His *Characteristicks of Men, Manners, Opinions, Times* (1711), a collection of writings, proved extraordinarily influential in literary and artistic circles as well as the world of philosophy and, to a lesser extent, religion. Reprinted as one part of *Characteristicks* was Shaftesbury's *Inquiry Concerning Virtue or Merit*, which John Toland had published, allegedly without Shaftesbury's permission, in 1699. If this work on the relationship of virtue and human nature provoked the ire of Bernard Mandeville in his *Fable of the Bees* (1723, 2d ed.), not least for its remorseless optimism with regard to the nature of man, it also stimulated Joseph Butler, Francis Hutcheson, and David Hume to reflect on and offer differing accounts of human nature and its relationship to virtue.

Shaftesbury, following Thomas Hobbes, accepts that we are motivated by our passions, but he denies that these are wholly self-regarding. This in turn enables him to ground a claim that we can be motivated by a desire for the well-being or interests of others. With motives grounded in man's other-regarding or benevolent passions, benevolence becomes, as a part of our nature, a force in its own right and not merely, as both Hobbes and Mandeville would have it, the product of the operation of self-interest in us.

For Shaftesbury, human nature is a system, the parts of which must be brought into harmony if we are to be virtuous; virtue consists in just this harmony, balance, or right proportion of parts. In particular, our "self-affections" must be in balance with our equally "natural" or other-regarding affections. Importantly, while he envisages the possibility that the other-regarding affections may be more powerful than the self-regarding affections, just the reverse, he thinks, is the chief imbalance in most men's natures. He is emphatic that this preponderance of the self-affections leads to misery, something which Mandeville disputes. To avoid misery, then, we must bring our self-affections and natural affections into some right proportion. Fortunately, we are equipped with something akin to a moral sense—almost aesthetic, in its sensitivity and perception of balance and harmony—that tells us when our affections are in or have achieved that proportion. (We also have unnatural affections, which are drives toward or desires for what is wrong, spiteful, or evil, and these must be controlled and, if possible, eliminated from our nature.)

Accordingly, the virtuous man is one who has brought his self-affections and natural affections into a balance or harmony that his moral sense approves. He remains motivated by his passions, but now by his harmonized passions. This implies that his self-affections are not too strong or his natural affections too weak, that, in a word, he has tempered the strength of his self-affections by allowing himself to feel in full measure his natural other-regarding affections. In this way, the specific balance in his passions that his moral sense approves always reflects his possession of other-regarding affections. Thus, we are not the creatures of the self-affections and self-interest that Hobbes and Mandeville would have us believe. In the eighteenth-century battle between egoism and benevolence as motives within human nature, Shaftesbury originates one kind of solution to the problem of their relationship.

But why should we allow ourselves to feel in full measure our natural affections? While Shaftesbury could claim, as does Hutcheson, that we must come to love virtue for its own sake and that this love of virtue could lead to increased strength in our natural affections, he does not do so. Rather, he claims that allowing ourselves to feel our natural affections full and strong is the chief means to happiness. If to have a preponderance in the self-affections is to be miserable but to feel the natural affections full and strong is to have the chief means to happiness, then we have an excellent motive for harmonizing our affections. Of course, a desire for our own happiness

neither precludes nor impedes our desiring virtue for its own sake. Yet, even if we never come to desire this, we have a self-regarding motive for bringing our affections into some right proportion, which we cannot do without allowing ourselves fully to feel our natural affections, and so for pursuing virtue. Thus, even if we never come to desire virtue for its own sake, we can know that it is in our interest to be virtuous. This theme reappears prominently in the ethics of Butler and Hume and thus becomes one of the distinctive themes of eighteenth-century British moral philosophy.

Shaftesbury may be said to have, in effect, secularized moral thought. Yet his deistical impulses led him to think that we live on lives in a world, ordered by a deistical God, that we can enjoy through our senses and the experience of beauty, which is obtained through a sense analogous to the moral sense. This ordered world appears best reflected in human lives if they are ordered politically in a somewhat republican manner.

[*See also* Aesthetics; Butler, Joseph; Deism; Friendship; Human Nature; Hume, David; Hutcheson, Francis; Imagination; Mandeville, Bernard; Moral Philosophy; Natural Religion; Natural Sentiment; Stoicism; *and* Toland, John.]

BIBLIOGRAPHY

Cooper, Anthony Ashley (Lord Shaftesbury). *Characteristics of Men, Manners, Opinions, Times*. Cambridge, 2000.

Darwall, Stephen. *The British Moralists and the Internal 'Ought': 1640–1740*. Cambridge, 1995.

Rivers, Isabel. *Reason, Grace, and Sentiment: A Study of the Language of Religion and Ethics in England*. Cambridge, 2000.

Voitle, Robert. *The Third Earl of Shaftesbury, 1671–1713*. Baton Rouge, La., 1984.

R. G. FREY

SHERIDAN, THOMAS (1719–1788), Irish actor, elocutionist, theater manager, playwright, educational theorist, and lexicographer.

Sheridan was born in Dublin, the son of a noted schoolmaster, poet, wit, and friend of Jonathan Swift. He himself was Swift's godson; in his later years, he wrote a useful early biography of Swift, and he was much influenced by Swift's theories on elocution and education.

Sheridan was educated at his father's classical academy in Capel Street, at Westminster School in London, and at Trinity College, Dublin, where he received his B.A. in 1739 and his M.A. sometime before March 1743. Accounted one of the ablest scholars of his time, he nevertheless quickly deserted academe for the theater. He began as a writer, adapting for the Smock Alley Theater in Dublin his father's translation of Battista Guarini's *The Faithful Shepherd* (1740). The theater also produced his popular broad farce *The Brave Irishman* (1744), very loosely adapted from Moliere's *Monsieur de Porceaugnac*.

Sheridan soon made his mark as a leading actor and was at one time the chief rival of David Garrick, who was considered the more natural actor. Sheridan had neither the figure, the face, nor the voice to dominate the stage; he was a formal and declamatory actor, at his best in tragic or stately roles such as Joseph Addison's *Cato*. Many of Sheridan's defects were roundly flayed by the young Trinity College student and would-be playwright Edmund Burke in his paper, *The Reformer* (1745). Toward the end of his stage career, Sheridan was increasingly seen as mannered and pompous, but his coaching inspired John Philip Kemble and his sister, the majestic Sarah Siddons, who called him "the father of my career."

As manager of Smock Alley, Sheridan instituted significant reforms. When he took over the theater, he described it as part bear-garden and part brothel: "It was no uncommon Thing to see more than an hundred People upon the Stage, who mixed with the Actors in such a Manner as scarce to be distinguished from them." He removed the bucks and beaux from the stage and from behind the scenes, generally quieted the house, and made the play the focus of attention. He paid the actors promptly, conducted regular and disciplined rehearsals, invested heavily in costumes and new scenery, and instituted seasons of Shakespeare and of William Congreve. He also hired the best players available, among them David Garrick, Spranger Barry, George Anne Bellamy, and Peg Woffington.

Sheridan's tenure as manager was, however, turbulent and marked by pamphlet wars over his policies and by two devastating riots. The Kelly riots of January 1747 were instigated by a young man who assaulted the actresses in the Green Room and, being ordered out of the house by Sheridan, entered the pit and pelted Sheridan with oranges. During the next night's disruption, Sheridan announced from the stage that he was as much a gentleman as Kelly, and this caused further uproar. Even worse was the riot of 2 March 1754, when the actor West Digges informed the audience that Sheridan had advised him not to encore a speech in *Mahomet the Imposter*, which had been taken politically. Sheridan then left the theater, after which the audience remained until two in the morning and tore up the benches, destroyed the auditorium, and nearly set fire to the house. Deeply in debt and thoroughly disillusioned, Sheridan continued to act and occasionally to manage, but his main interest was no longer the stage.

In December 1755, Sheridan published *British Education; Or, The Source of the Disorders of Great Britain*, a volume of more than 500 pages which developed a grand plan of education founded in a thorough grounding in English and in oratory. Despite earlier pleas by Milton and Locke for an emphasis on English, in eighteenth-century England the schooling of the young was still dominated by a formalistic approach to Latin and Greek.

Sheridan's well-taken criticism was weakened by his fanatical belief that training in oratory would weed out vernacular "corruptions" and standardize the language. He proselytized for his view in a series of hugely popular lectures in London, Oxford, Cambridge, and Edinburgh, and both Oxford and Cambridge awarded him honorary M.A. degrees. A lecture in Dublin (6 December 1757) proposed the establishment of a Hibernian Academy, a scheme that initially received much support.

Sheridan's notion that the language could be purified and standardized did not take into account the way living language works; it was based on a narrow idea of correctness derived from the age of Queen Anne and embodied particularly in the pronunciation of such figures as the duke of Dorset, the earl of Chesterfield, and Jonathan Swift. Nevertheless, his obsession bore valuable fruit in his *Complete Dictionary of the English Language* (1780). Sheridan's dictionary was based solidly on Samuel Johnson's great dictionary of 1755, following Johnson's spelling and utilizing, although often abridging, his definitions. It omitted Johnson's etymologies and the quotations indicating how previous writers had used words, but where Johnson indicated pronunciation merely by marking the stressed syllable with an accent, Sheridan utilized phonetic spelling and an exact notation of sounds. His judgment about some pronunciations was criticized, but, as William Benzie remarked, "English lexicography had been raised to a new level.... Sheridan's work was without doubt the first regular pronouncing dictionary on a large scale, and provided a pronouncing system that was to persist relatively unmodified up to the present day."

Another major fault of Sheridan's grand educational design was that it did not study written English. The Rhetorical Grammar prefacing his Dictionary is neither a rhetoric nor a grammar, but a manual on pronunciation and delivery. Unlike his father, his godfather, his novelist wife Frances, or his eminent playwright son Richard Brinsley Sheridan, he did not write very well.

Sheridan also had the bad luck to have his acting overshadowed by Garrick's, his innovative dictionary by Johnson's, and his general reputation by the glitter of his son's achievements. Nevertheless, he was the one innovative thinker in ten generations of remarkable Sheridans.

[*See also* Burke, Edmund; Dictionaries; Education, *subentry on* Reform and Experiments; *and* Ireland.]

BIBLIOGRAPHY

WORKS BY SHERIDAN

The Brave Irishman. In *Ten English Farces*, edited by Leo Hughes and A. H. Scouten. Austin, Tex., 1948.

British Education: or, the source of the disorders of Great Britain .... London, 1756.

A Course of Lectures on Elocution .... London, 1762.

A General Dictionary of the English Language .... London, 1780.

The Life of the Rev. Dr. Jonathan Swift, Dean of St. Patrick's, Dublin. London, 1784.

WORKS ABOUT SHERIDAN

Benzie, William. *The Dublin Orator: Thomas Sheridan's Influence on Eighteenth-Century Rhetoric and Belles Lettres.* Leeds, 1972. A sound and excellent account.

Brown, Wallace A. "The Elocutionary Career of Thomas Sheridan (1719–1788)." *Speech Monographs* 30. 1 (March 1964).

Howell, W. S. *Eighteenth-Century British Logic and Rhetoric.* Princeton, N.J., 1971.

Sheldon, Esther K. *Thomas Sheridan of Smock-Alley.* Princeton, N.J., 1967. A detailed discussion of Sheridan as theater manager and actor.

ROBERT G. HOGAN

SKEPTICISM. Traditionally considered to be the golden age of *raison*, the Enlightenment was nevertheless marked by a profound awareness of the limits of human knowledge. Although this awareness is not in itself an indicator of skepticism, it was interwoven with motifs from the classical Pyrrhonist and Academic traditions, giving rise to original combinations. At the same time, replies to the skeptical challenge were elaborated that assigned it a positive function in moderating the claims of knowledge. Thus the history of skepticism in the age of the Enlightenment is also a history of interpretations and syntheses that may not have adhered with philological exactness to the ancient sources, but that were highly effective in delineating new perspectives.

Pyrrhonism, Fideism, and "Moderate" Skepsis in Pierre Bayle. This breadth of phenomena was the case in the first episode: the revival of Pyrrhonist themes by Pierre Bayle, the erudite savant and philosopher who lived in exile in Rotterdam. His stance had seminal importance for all the discussions that followed, despite the fact that it was characterized by an intrinsic ambiguity. At first glance the *Dictionnaire historique et critique* (Historical and Critical dictionary, 1st edition 1697, definitive edition, 1702) offered a very successful mixture of extreme skepticism and an equally radical form of fideism, setting Pyrrhonist ideas against the kind of theological debates that typified modern Christianity in the period since the Reformation. This would be, of course, a context very different from the serene classical atmosphere of the original texts of Aenesidemus, Sextus Empiricus, or Cicero. The dogmatists whom Bayle had to confront were principally René Descartes and the Cartesians, whose criterion of intellectual distinctness as a means of access to indubitable truths he contested. In addition, he also took aim at the Christian theologians as a group, for Bayle placed dogmas accepted by all, including the Protestants (such as the Holy Trinity), and dogmas peculiar to Catholicism (such as the Eucharist) on the same plane of incomprehensibility. He emphasized, furthermore, how the new Newtonian science—as long as it was understood as the knowledge of phenomena—could easily coexist with an antimetaphysical and antitheological skeptical stance. This followed a line of thought running from Sextus Empiricus (third century) to Gassendi (1592–1655), for among the principles of Pyrrhonist philosophy was one that "the absolute and internal nature of objects remains hidden from us, and all we can be sure of is how, in certain respects, objects appear to us" (Bayle, *Dictionnaire,* article "Pyrrhon," main text). Both physics and politics thus remained immune from the assault of the skeptics: natural philosophers (scientists) were seen by Bayle as Academics or Pyrrhonists because they were convinced of the limitations of the human mind and were satisfied merely to "search out probable hypotheses and collect experimental data." Also, ethics and civil life did not require absolute certainty, basing themselves on rules of conformity to established custom, or simply on probable reasons. Only religion has anything to fear from Pyrrhonism, Bayle concluded, adding that its beliefs demand certainty and firm conviction. If Arcesilaus returned to life he would undoubtedly be "a thousand times more terrible toward our theologians than he was with the dogmatic philosophers of ancient Greece" (Bayle, *Dictionnaire,* "Pyrrhon," note B).

The truth is, though, that Bayle's *Dictionnaire* supplied different versions of skepticism and of its relation to fideism that did not coincide with one another. In more orthodox texts like the *Eclaircissement sur les pyrrhoniens* (Clarification concerning the Pyrrhonists), an addendum written to respond to criticism from Calvinist circles, he underlined the orthodox, preparatory function of skepticism: to renounces reason) in order to accept faith from the viewpoint of the most rigid biblical fundamentalism, based on the mere fact that "God spake thus," a faith that was stark, incomprehensible, and undemonstrable. In other passages, however, the appraisals of the philosopher of Rotterdam seem to be more finely shaded and complex.

Note C to the article "Pyrrhon" is an emblematic case in point. Here, Bayle effectively lumps together the apologetics of John Calvin, the antilibertine arguments of Blaise Pascal, and the Christian skepsis of the libertine par excellence, François de La Mothe Le Vayer, showing precisely how the self-destruction of reason at the moment of *epokhé* (the technical term for the skeptical suspension of judgment) could be seen as a useful preamble to the leap toward faith. A little further along in the same text, other passages from La Mothe Le Vayer are cited to support the claim that "there is nothing more opposed to religion than Pyrrhonism."

In articles touching on the problem of evil, Bayle did not merely assert the irreconcilability of faith and reason, biblical narrative, and philosophical argumentation. In the celebrated entries on "Manichéens," "Pauliciens," and "Origène," the doubts of the skeptic gave way to a much more aggressive and determined critique of faith, which he demonstrated positively and categorically to be in direct contradiction to religion. As he puts it in one of his most telling passages, in the case of religious doctrines like those of sin, predestination, and reward and punishment, the problem arises not from the fact that we lack the illumination necessary to understand them (because of the limitations of reason), but precisely from our having reasons that go squarely against them. In these influential articles the problem arises from the univocal significance that reason assumes in both philosophical and theological questions. In other articles that focus on exponents of the Protestant tradition (such as "Luther" and "Hoffman"), Bayle insists again on the strong opposition between faith and reason, virtually to the point of maintaining the position of "double truth" (a single dogma is at the same time both false and true—false in philosophy and true in theology), while in articles like "Simonide" he brings to bear all the resources of negative theology, blending it with the antitheological skepticism of Pierre Charron's *De la sagesse* (On Wisdom, 1601).

This dramatic account of skepsis, in which it is seen as the high point of the destructive and self-destructive potentialities of human reason, is accompanied, however, in Bayle's *Dictionnaire* by a more nuanced portrayal of the *epokhé*. With respect to the self-refutation that the notion of "total doubt" predictably generates (an argument that the article "Pyrrhon" had also employed), other entries, like the ones dedicated to the Academic skeptics "Arcesilas" and "Carnéade," emphasize instead the importance that needs to be given to skepticism as a critical instrument aimed at liberation from all forms of dogma. "Opting neither for nor against," the skeptic escapes "the embarrassing difficulties," "the grave and serious objections, the reprisals, the arguments ad hominem" that are "generally the inevitable rocky shoals of the dogmatists." Thus, skeptics can claim victory when they constrain their adversaries to abandon the appeal to distinctness and to withdraw to the more limited field of simple probability. Bayle also answered the accusation of apraxia (meaning "inaction" or "quietism") to which the skeptic was supposedly vulnerable (according to the widespread topos of the unlivability of skepticism) by producing the arguments of Academic probabilism, according to which the conduct of life can be based on appearances, without waiting for the "speculative judgments that we pronounce on the nature of things" (Bayle, *Dictionnaire*, "Carnéade," note B). The relation between doubt and credence could not, therefore, be seen in terms of reciprocal exclusion: skeptical doubt took the concrete form of an attitude that accompanies

credence, assigning it a merely probable and provisional degree of certainty that can always be revised. Simply put, the value of truth or reality that the skeptics attribute to things of which they are persuaded is not identical to what dogmatists call truth; it does not derive from an infallible criterion such as (Cartesian) distinctness, but from a subjective and instinctive necessity: "Inside ourselves we can never deny that which appears to us to be true, nor affirm internally that which appears to us to be a lie" (Bayle, *Réponse aux questions d'un provincial*, II. XC).

In the theological field, too, alongside the extreme fideism of certain articles in the *Dictionnaire*, there subsists a more moderate form of skepsis (exemplified in the articles "Mélancthon" or "Synergistes"), which attributes to religious beliefs the status of hypothetical opinions with the power to save or account for both natural and civil phenomena. The more or less explicit consequence is that all systems appear equally possible if compared to the infinite wisdom that has infinite means of revealing itself, all of them worthy of it, with the sole exception of those hypotheses that Bayle himself viewed as being in conflict with the concept that he had formed of God. This attitude is a revival, in skeptical dress, of the entire humanistic heritage, with its attendant ideal of a moral and tolerant religiosity, its animosity toward theological hair-splitting, and its hostility to the dogmatism of the opposing sects. Skepticism remains adverse to categorical declarations, but it shows itself to be compatible with a moderate form of belief, one aware of its own limits and primarily dedicated to the task of moral and civil edification.

The Antireligious Skepticism of the Clandestine Philosophical Manuscripts. Bayle's position, like an unstable amalgam, contained most of the elements that would, through successive disintegrations and reintegrations, give rise to the diverse molecular compounds of skepticism in the eighteenth century. The first bond to snap was the one between skepsis and fideism, and a series of clandestine philosophical manuscripts made an important contribution to this rift. In the manuscript known as *Doutes des pyrrhoniens* (Doubts of the Pyrrhonists, datable to 1696–1711 and held in the Royal Library of Brussels), through a distinction between the "raging Pyrrhonists," who deny the existence of God, and the "moderate Pyrrhonists," a deistic conception is advanced. In it, the divinity is reduced to the role of first cause, indifferent to the government of the universe, extraneous to the concepts of providence and theodicy, yet upon which all events necessarily depend, even the most frightful ones, "in the order that it has established." The contents of the work are arranged into eight "doubts" through which the anonymous author mounts an escalating polemic against all the positive religions, which are reduced to the status of "human inventions to make men better through fear of the punishments God may inflict upon them." Laws, institutions (like private property), norms, and beliefs are the work of wise human legislators who have adopted this means to put an end to the right of all to all typical of the state of nature. If a preference can be expressed among the motley universe of the positive religions, it would go, if anything, to the Chinese religion, the doctrine of which is described as a sort of "atheism or deism," and the contents of which are preponderantly ethical and political. In the eyes of the "moderate Pyrrhonist," the ancient Confucian religion of the learned mandarins seems to embody Bayle's viable "republic of atheists," and thus, notwithstanding the distinction made at the outset, the role of skepticism inclines decidedly in the direction of a civil religion, formally deistic but effectively just a veiled atheism.

In the case of another clandestine manuscript, the *Symbolum sapientiae* (Symbol of Wisdom, a Latin work of German provenance from the period 1696–1720), the union of skepticism and a brand of Spinozism deriving from Spinoza's *Tractatus theologico-politicus* (rather than from the *Ethics*) is advanced in even more specific form. The anonymous author develops a form of wisdom radically contrary to religion, excludes the possibility of miracles, and offers an interpretation of the figure of Christ in philosophical terms: Jesus intended to teach not a religion (a *lex*, or law) but a moral philosophy aimed at the inner perfection of man. God is thus not a "legislator" nor does he prescribe any external or ceremonial cult. Christ was certainly not an atheist, the author specifies, but his precepts were purely philosophical since their goal was "to live in tranquillity and happiness according to moral philosophy in this life and not in the future one." It is principally in the section "De Deo" (On God), however, that the *Symbolum* makes the case once again for the application of skepticism, in a critical sense, against every type of dogmatism (even the negative type represented by atheism). The contrast between the positions of the *deicola* or *entheus* (believer in God) and those of the *atheus* (atheist) is set out in a way that privileges skeptical caution, following a principle of parsimony that does not amount to actual denial, but that leaves the burden of proof on the one who affirms. The author for his part prefers to maintain a kind of skeptical equilibrium, adopting the classical posture of *epokhé*, or suspension of judgment: "If we want to reason carefully, we ought neither to deny nor believe in God; it is best to assign this topic to the class of unknown doctrines, about which our judgment should be suspended." The appeal to reason in the *Symbolum* is thus bolstered by empirical and moderately skeptical ideas, with an insistence on the motif of the limits that hedge in human knowledge, limits that

dogmatism, in its metaphysical and theological shapes, only manages to surpass in an empty and illusory fashion.

If the *Doutes* links skepticism and Deism (formally at least), while the *Symbolum* holds to a position of critical agnosticism, another manuscript text that circulated clandestinely takes its inspiration from a radical, and not at all moderate, version of doubt: It is the *Art de ne rien croire* (The Art of Believing in Nothing), written probably in the first decade of the eighteenth century. This work presents itself as a forceful antidote to the fideistic versions of skepticism found in Bayle, and before that in Pascal. Though he makes a show of taking up a position midway between the extreme (and symmetrical) positions of the believers and the atheists, the author of the *Art* applies his whole critique to the idea of God, the inevitably anthropomorphic content of which he highlights.

The traditional relation of dependence between reason and God is thus reversed: "It is not reason that is an offshoot of divinity, it is rather divinity that is a swollen outgrowth of reason." The only attributes that withstand demystification are those of infinitude and omnipotence, though from the shadow of these notions there is already emerging a representation of divinity identifiable only as something indeterminate, as the complex of nature spread out through infinite space in an endless process of mutation ("general movement," "continual change," without beginning or end). Even with regard to the concept of order, skeptical doubt counsels us not to overleap these narrow boundaries of reason, and therefore not to attribute order to things themselves, but rather to the representation of them formed in the human imagination. The outcome of this critique is a sort of ontological indifference: "God, soul, instinct, reason, spirit" are all equally valid names for the principle of movement, since what they designate surpasses human capacity. In conclusion, the author of the *Art* does not limit himself to recommending the advantages of skeptical suspension ("doubt, ignore, know nothing"), but goes so far as to claim ethical and rational superiority for doubt over and against the argument of Pascal's wager.

Skepsis and Newtonianism: Voltaire. However paradoxical it may seem, the alliance of skepticism (more or less materialistic) and Spinozism had its own logic. The "distant gaze" that *Deus sive natura* (God or nature) directed upon the universe entailed radical doubt concerning such beliefs as the providential ordering of the world, its assumed purposefulness, and the axiological hierarchy of values. As an alternative to this Spinozistic vision, in which the naturalistic heritage of the erudite libertines lived on, the Newtonian conception of the universe lent itself to an alliance with a different kind of skepticism, more modest and gentler. Thus the writings of

Voltaire outline a sort of convergence between the Lockean theme of the "limits of the human mind" (which is unable to arrive at the "first principles" of matter or spirit, and thus cannot even resolve the traditional problems of metaphysics), on one hand, and, on the other, the vision of the great architect who purposefully orders the world in accord with will and intelligence.

Although Voltaire had notable sympathy for Bayle, whom he saw as the prototype of the philosophe, and although the sage of Ferney assumed the pose of the "ignorant philosopher" (*Le philosophe ignorant* is the title of a work of 1766 in which he insists on the "strait limits" of human knowledge), he was drawn much more to empiricism than he was to skepticism or Pyrrhonism. Beginning with the *Traité de métaphysique* (1734), the philosophe set out the requirement that reason be contained within the bounds of experience, and that we not "overstep the limits of our nature." Precisely for that reason he attacked with equal vigor the "skeptics who go to extremes," the Pyrrhonists who—by throwing doubt on the external existence of bodies, exaggerating the fallaciousness of the senses, and bringing back the Cartesian argument that sleep and waking are indistinguishable—transcend the certainties of experience in a direction clearly opposite, but in the final analysis symmetrical to the "romances" excogitated by metaphysical dogmatism. The *Lettres philosophiques* (1734) already made it clear that recognition of one's own ignorance went hand in hand with the affirmation of the potency of the creator, and Voltaire, in a coherent development of both these perspectives, used the topos of the limits of human knowledge as the basis on which to propose heterodox solutions to the classic problems of Enlightenment metaphysics, such as, among others, of the nature of the relations between the "grand Tout et son Seigneur" (the great Whole and its master), a question of whether matter is capable of thought, the issue of whether the "first principle" is infinite in actuality, and the problem of whether human liberty is anything other than the effect of a chain of necessary causes.

The principle of Deism provided a reassuring frame, yet within it, there still persisted the most disquieting doubts to which the most radical skepsis, with its almost Heraclitean vision, had given rise. "Since I am an imperceptible part of the *grand Tout*." wrote Voltaire in one of his last works, *Il faut prendre un parti ou du Principe d'action* (One Must Choose or On the Principle of Action, 1772), "being a point situated between two eternities, it will be impossible for me to understand that great Whole and its Master, which engulf me on every side."

Skepsis and Materialism: The Case of Diderot. In Diderot's case, the use of skepticism was different again. He deployed it to force the limits of Newtonian Deism and to break through to an atheistic and materialistic outlook in which matter is self-organizing into an order that is not the result of any intelligent purpose—an outlook at the antipodes of Voltaire's intent. Through Diderot's work we can also perceive how skeptical themes acted directly to help form the great philosophe, and how Pyrrhonist ideas were handled differently by the same author in the works he wrote for public consumption as opposed to his clandestine works that were circulated privately.

"What is a skeptic? A philosopher who has subjected all he believes in to doubt, and who believes in that which a legitimate use of his own reason and his own senses shows him to be true." With these words from the *Pensées philosophiques* (Philosophical Thoughts), published in 1746 and immediately condemned to be burned by the parlement of Paris, Diderot dispatched centuries-old accusations aimed at skepticism and endowed it with a signification that was both positive and compatible with the new certainties of scientific knowledge. "Force the Pyrrhonist to be sincere and you will have the skeptic." With this distinction the philosophe reacted against both the hyperbole of Cartesian doubt (imbued as it was with the "subtleties of ontology") and the fideistic temptation of "semiskepticism" typical of the weak spirits who claim to safeguard privileged notions by shielding them from the test of doubt. The philosophe thus presented himself as "the skeptic alone against all," especially on the terrain of religion. The *Pensées philosophiques* contains radical doubt about the reality and significance of miracles, the authority of pretended revelations, the divinity of the Scriptures and the canon of the Bible, and it goes so far as to insinuate the superiority of natural religion. Even if it is the truth of Deism rather than the negation of the skeptical atheists that emerges from Diderot's first application of "universal doubt" to the historical religions (for skepticism, if it is to constitute the first step toward truth, has to be general), nonetheless the *Pensées philosophiques* suggests more radical hypotheses, such as movement as intrinsic to matter and the order of the universe as the outcome of infinite chance combinations in the course of an equally infinite duration.

This evolution from skepticism to materialism was to take much more explicit form in a clandestine work left in manuscript form by Diderot, the *Promenade du sceptique* (also known as the *Promenade de Cléobule*, from the name of the principal interlocutor). In the prologue the author in vain describes the marvelous harmony that reigns among the philosophes who have come together in the garden of Cléobule, where "I have seen the Pyrrhonist embrace the skeptic, the skeptic take pleasure in the successes of the atheist, the atheist open his purse to the deist, and the deist offer his services to the Spinozist." Nevertheless, in the account itself of the discourses held under the alley of chestnut trees, it is conflict among the atheists, the deists, and the Spinozists that looms largest. Diderot sketches here the traits of the more radical philosophy that he will develop in *Le rêve de d'Alembert* (D'Alembert's Dream) or in the *Lettre sur les aveugles* (Letter on the Blind), and that will mark paid to the teleological and theological conception of the design of the universe. The only role assigned to the Pyrrhonists and the skeptics is that of critical provocation, strongly colored by paradoxical sallies, whereas if any speaker can be said to propound a doctrine, it is the Spinozist Oribaze.

The Paradoxes of Skepticism and the Immaterialistic Solution: Berkeley. Bayle had already alluded to the need to escape the paradoxes of skepticism by incorporating them into an idealistic perspective, and George Berkeley, an author certainly not unknown to Diderot, took up the task. The descriptions offered in the *Promenade du sceptique* of the Pyrrhonists (for whom "there does not exist either an alley, or trees, or voyagers"), and even more of the skeptics (who "admit the existence of a sole being," the thinking being that is themselves) are drawn as much from the dialogues of Berkeley as they are from the articles in Bayle's *Dictionnaire*. Diderot's description of the order of the universe as "a tissue of ideas that do not lead to anything" amounts, however, to a radical simplification of certain idealistic and immaterialistic themes that had been addressed with a very different intent by the bishop of Cloyne.

The very thesis that matter exists absolutely, outside the mind, constituted for Berkeley the root of the skeptical attitude. He took this thesis to be the inevitable consequence of Lockean realism and its causalist and representative conception of knowing. It was, above all, against the doctrine of truth as the correspondence between the idea and the external object that Berkeley directed his blows, inasmuch as when qualities or ideas are understood as "notes or images, referred to *things* or *archetypes* existing without the mind, then are we all involved in *scepticism*." In sum, "All this skepticism follows from our supposing a difference between *things* and *ideas*, and that the former have a subsistence without the mind, or unperceived" (*The Principles of Human Knowledge* 1.87). Immaterialism, thus, was seen by Berkeley as at once the result and the overcoming of skeptical doubts. On one hand, it brought to completion the process of the phenomenalistic dissolution of qualities, which Bayle had already pointed to as one of the marks of modern skepticism. Persuaded that extension, form, and movement were inconceivable when they were abstracted from the other sensible qualities, Berkeley did not hesitate to take their ontological primacy away from even these primary qualities and place them among the list of sensible qualities that "have no existence in matter, or without the mind" (*Principles* 1.14). On the other hand, immaterialism offered itself as "a firm system of sound and

real knowledge, which may be proof against the assaults of *scepticism*" (*Principles* 1.89) and which might bring philosophy back within the limits of common sense, and of the perceptual phenomenalism that undergirds common sense.

Berkeley's battle against skepticism had a strong religious and apologetic component, and was a defense of orthodox concepts against the temptations of materialism valiantly woven into skepticism, a fact that comes out clearly in all the arguments contained in Berkeley's work. He held that skepsis, atheism, and freethinking flowed from the same source, the conviction that things and matter existed absolutely outside the mind, or the "doctrine of matter or corporeal substance" as he called it (*Principles* 1.92). Along with the paradoxes advanced by the skeptic, the immaterialist wished above all to liquidate the audacity of the freethinkers and "minute philosophers" against whom he aimed his dialogue *Alciphron*. Against the radicalism of the new skeptics, one of the protagonists of the dialogue, Crito, opposed "the diffidence, the modesty, or the timidity" typical of the skeptical fideist, for whom "the more doubt, the more room there is for faith" (*Alciphron* 7.24). Nonetheless, the active and energetic doubt practiced by the freethinkers against religious belief, against prejudice, and against conventional morality demonstrated that a return to skeptical fideism by Berkeley's time was no longer a realistic possibility.

The Enlightened Skepticism of David Hume. When he composed *A Treatise of Human Nature* between 1734 and 1737 during a sojourn in France, David Hume undoubtedly had a wide and deep acquaintance with the debates that had flourished around the topic of skepticism during the preceding century. In the pages of the *Treatise* (1739–1740), the "Pyrrhonist crisis" invests both rational and perceptual knowledge, even though doubt is accompanied by the awareness that nature is always too strong to submit to the dictates of the reasoning process, no matter how subtle it may be. Tellingly, the fourth part, devoted to the discussion "Of the skeptical and other systems of philosophy," opens with an examination of the value of demonstrative inference that combines the trope of Sextus Empiricus—about the infinite regress in the search for apodictic foundations—with a notably psychological consideration of reason, which Hume portrays as "a kind of cause, of which truth is the natural effect," with all the consequent impediments to its efficacy "by the irruption of other causes, and by the inconstance of our mental powers."

The gap between Hume and the classic paradigms of neo-Pyrrhonism is seen, if anywhere, in the fact that the iteration of doubt seems fated to clash with the sensible nature of belief. For that reason, "these arguments above-explain'd produce not a total suspense of judgment." If his appeal to the cogency of the natural habits of assent and the ineluctable necessities of praxis call to mind well-known aspects of anti-Pyrrhonist apologetics, with their commitment to demonstrating the impracticability of the precepts of "that fantastic sect," it would nevertheless be an error to reduce Hume's arguments, which are much more subtle, to their level. He himself warns us: "I . . . cannot approve of that expeditious way, which some take with the sceptics, to reject at once all their arguments without enquiry or examination." From the viewpoint of the Scottish philosopher, the doubts of the skeptics preserve an indispensable theoretical function because they represent the mirror image and symmetrical opposite of the dogmatic paradigm, whose unsustainability they thus reveal. In describing the dialectic that opposes reason—"prescribing laws, and imposing maxims, with an absolute sway and authority"—to skepticism—founded on an array of rational arguments just as imposing—Hume observes that the doubt resulting from this procedure "gradually diminishes the force of that governing power, and its own at the same time; till at last they both vanish away into nothing, by a regular and just diminution" (*Treatise*, 1.4.1).

It is highly likely that in evoking the liberating function of the *epokhé* in this manner, Hume had in mind the celebrated medical metaphor, also used by Sextus Empiricus, of the cathartic, the drug that, in expelling the residue of the ailment, eliminates itself as well, so as to restore the body to health, and its natural condition—which is in turn an image of "life free of dogma." The result of the process was very different for Hume than it was for the strict Pyrrhonists, however. Instead of suspension of judgment and ataraxia ("imperturbable calm"), nature reestablishes the powers of the natural habits of assent. For Hume, "The skeptical and dogmatical reasons are of the same kind, tho contrary in their operation and tendency." They both reembody—one in a negative, the other in a positive sense—an identical model of rationality that hinges on the paradigm of demonstration and on the search for ultimate foundations. Each has its offspring: the subtle and unnatural inconclusiveness of the skeptic, on the one hand, and the aporias of metaphysical dogmatics, on the other.

Quite apart from the question of how faithful he was, in the philological sense, to the texts of ancient Pyrrhonism, the fact remains that even when he comes closest to the authentic spirit of the skeptical position, Hume gives it an interpretation that still constitutes an original and, in many respects, more radical reading, since it matures in the context of the modern evolution of the *epokhé*. Hume's treatment of the things to which humans give credence, prominent among them causal inference, is a case in point—indeed an exemplary case. He sings the praises

of "modest scepticism," and he appears to commend the value of a kind of knowing that takes the form of an internal, horizontal organization of phenomena. But the requirement to go "beyond the impressions of our senses" (to the point of obtaining information about "existences and objects, which we do not see or feel"), however, is detectable, according to Hume, not just in metaphysical elaborations, but even more in the common beliefs on which both ordinary life and science are based. An example is belief in the efficient power of causes, or in the uniform and regular course of nature, or the opinion that external objects exist. Hume thus even aims the bolts of his critique against two citadels that had until then remained nearly untouched: the idea of "necessary connexion" in the belief in the "power and efficacy of causes"; and "the supposition that the future resembles the past," which is the hypothesis that justifies our inductive inferences.

From Hume's point of view, the origin of the idea of causal connection is found not in things, but in the mind, in that complex of habits and imaginings that combine with sensory input to give rise to credence. Hume knew that by making these claims he was offering a thesis that would appear a "paradox" to his readers—"the most violent" of the many paradoxes generated by the skeptical challenge. The same was true of his "scepticism with regard to the senses," and again of his section on "modern philosophy." In these, Hume heaps up doubts concerning the status of the external existence of objects, something that was taken as a given not only in ingenuous realism but also in the more elaborate conceptions of philosophers. To these difficulties he added further ones deriving from the impossibility of distinguishing between the primary and secondary qualities on the basis of their epistemological worth, or the *aporias* connected to the idea of a fundamental substrate underpinning personal identity. The conclusions Hume reached in the *Treatise* about these matters were drastic, and brought back into prominence the concept of the 'invincibility' of theoretical skepticism, which had been the leitmotiv of the "Pyrrhonist crisis" of the age of Bayle. The portion of the work that probes the problem of skepticism concludes, in fact, by acknowledging this inescapable impasse. It is a malady to be treated and cured not by reason, which has been forced to confront its own impotence, but by nature. With this appeal to the therapeutic power of nature, however, Hume did not so much undo the knots of skepticism as simply slash through them.

Only as he progressed from the *Treatise of Human Nature* to the *Enquiry Concerning Human Understanding* (1748, revised 1758) did Hume lay the base from which to overcome the most destructive kind of doubt or, at any rate, to transform it into an approach compatible with the scientific method. His more selective orientation in the *Enquiry* is evident in the more precise distinctions introduced between two kinds of negative, or merely destructive, skepsis, and an acceptable, even propitious, form of doubt (the "*mitigated* skepticism or *academical* philosophy"). The first form of destructive skepticism, which he qualifies as "universal doubt" (or skepticism "*antecedent* to all study and philosophy") and attributes to Descartes, actually produces an unredeemable situation. The second, that "*consequent* to science and inquiry," is a restatement of the arguments that the *Treatise* had already developed in the section on "scepticism with regard to the senses."

"There is, indeed," Hume notes however, "a more *mitigated* skepticism or *academical* philosophy, which may be both durable and useful, and which may, in part, be the result of this Pyrrhonism, or *excessive* skepticism, when its first undistinguished doubts are, in some measure, corrected by common sense and reflection." With this definition Hume introduces what for him was a new configuration into the typology of skeptical attitudes. Its most prominent characteristics are the "limitation of our enquiries to such subjects as are best adapted to the narrow capacity of human understanding," and the attenuation of the asseverative character of judgments in favor of a more ductile and circumspect probabilistic approach that lay in the Academic tradition, both ancient and modern.

Within the framework of the *Enquiry*, recognition of how naturally and easily certain basic types of belief impose themselves leads neither to a sort of uncritical coercion to believe nor to an unredeemable dualism separating the moment of reflection from the moment of actually living. Whereas from the Pyrrhonist vantage point of the *Treatise*, the recovery of the natural outlook entailed the suspension or, at any rate, the interruption, of speculative activity, and vice versa, it is only in the *Enquiry* that Hume finds a way to relate the reflection of the philosopher to the mode of thinking inherent in daily living in a more useful and collaborative way. The adoption of this viewpoint implied neither the total restoration of the prejudices of common sense nor a tendency to relapse into uncritical acceptance of prephilosophical opinion. This is seen clearly from the fact that Hume still did nothing to conceal the "falsity" and lack of grounding of the largest part of our beliefs, while he recuperated from everyday experience only those aspects that link it to an immanent construction, regulated by internal criteria and free of any residue whatsoever of dogmatic objectivism, whether of the ingenuous or the philosophically refined sort. The "moderate doubt" of the Academics manifests itself as an attempt to make a measure of rational control (such as that which dictates the basic rules of induction, even after its logical *aporias* have become clear) coexist

with the recognition of the "natural and instinctual," but frequently also "fallacious and deceitful" character of the presuppositions on which our operations are grounded.

For Hume, it was clear that this approach did not resolve all doubts, whether those inherited from the tradition or those excogitated by the author himself. It was a solution (as he reminds us about the problem of induction) to the extent that any skeptical solution can be. Focused on exhibiting the problem, on throwing light on all the logical and psychological terms that constitute it, the ultimate purpose of skepticism is to "discover the difficulty ourselves before it is objected to us," and set it free from false solutions—even if that entails the frank recognition of "our very ignorance" in the end.

The "moderate skepticism" propounded in the *Enquiry* represents, from Hume's perspective, a remedy intended to occupy a permanent place in the therapeutic repertoire to which philosophical reflection resorts when it undertakes to free us of both the illusion that shackles the dogmatic philosophies and the stupidity that permeates vulgar modes of thought.

The Utility and Overcoming of Skepticism in Kant. "Hume is perhaps the most acute among all the skeptics, and incontestably the most important on account of the influence that the skeptical procedure can have in awakening a grounded examination of reason." With these words from the *Kritik der reinen Verkunft* Critique of Pure Reason. Immanuel Kant recognized the importance of skepticism, to which he attributed the role of a "preliminary exercise" in the "critique of the intellect," while giving a decidedly reductive interpretation of the Scottish thinker, though one with a tincture of sympathy. In Kant's ideal reconstruction of the path of pure reason, its first step, almost its childhood, is represented by dogmatism, while the second step is taken by the skeptic, who thus achieves actual progress. Kant describes in tones of evident interest the struggle and the conflict of the speculative claims advanced by the opposing dogmatisms (theism and atheism, determinism and liberty, and so on), and he deprecates the dogmatic supporters of orthodoxy for demanding that the conflict be halted with arguments that amount to an act of "blinding" and a source of prejudices. From this stance, the philosopher of Königsberg praised the attempt of Hume ("this man of such balanced judgment") to "tear down, with laboriously excogitated difficulties" even the most "consolatory and useful" convictions, such as that rational speculation is sufficient "to conceive and affirm in a precise way the existence of a Supreme Being."

It remains clear to Kant, however, that there cannot be a "skeptical satisfaction of reason in disaccord with itself," and that a third step therefore must be taken beyond dogmatism and skepticism in the critique of pure reason, passing from simple censure to a real critique. Where the censure characteristic of the "geographers of human reason" like Hume stops (for example, in the examination of causality) at identifying the empirical limits of our knowledge, and grounds them at most on the associative and psychological properties of habit, critique subjects not the workings of reason but reason itself in all its potency and capacity for a priori knowledge, to inspection, designating its precise confines in exactly the same way that, with the sphericity of the earth established, it becomes possible to calculate its diameter and surface area, though nothing may be known of the things to be found there.

In Kant's strategy, which takes as its point of departure the recognition of the Newtonian scientific fact considered as synthetic a priori knowledge, skepticism is not a negative element, but it does represent a provisional phase, to be overcome in the perspective of the transcendental critique: "It is a resting place for human reason, where it can reflect on its own dogmatic peregrinations and catch a glimpse of the country in which it finds itself," but it is in no way able to constitute "a habitable place adapted to a fixed residence." Certainly Kant reveals that he has learned from Bayle the lesson of antimetaphysical skepticism (though Bayle is not cited) when in the "transcendental Dialectic" he shows how from the claim of metaphysics to cross over the limits of all possible experience there arose dialectically antithetical positions, the conflict between which perfectly reproduces the conflict of the metaphysical and theological systems as it is described in celebrated articles in the *Dictionnaire*.

"These sophistical affirmations," Kant declares, constitute a "theater of struggle" very much like the "dialectical conflict" in which by turns "the upper hand is gained by the party that has the freedom to attack, while the one forced to hold a defensive position is doomed to succumb." These "bold knights" can only hope to win if they can execute "a final charge, without then having to withstand a new attack from the adversary," in the way that—as Bayle had written in the article "Zénon d'Elée"—each of the philosophical sects "triumphs, demolishes, and flattens when it is on the attack, but is flattened and wrecked in its turn when it goes on the defensive." This was the highest recognition that Kant could award to the skeptical tradition, inasmuch as the critical enterprise of the transcendental philosophy by now had the capacity to dispatch the "ambitious" metaphysical systems (as Condillac called them) without forgoing the advance in knowledge represented by the motto *aude sapere* ("dare to know") which for Kant encapsulated the substance of the *Aufklärung*—almost the exact reverse of Montaigne's "*Que sais-je?*" ("what do I know?") but with the additional modesty and sense of limits that

even the most systematic of the Newtonians had learned from the *aporias* of skepticism.

[*See also* Bayle, Pierre; Berkeley, George; Clandestine Literature; Empiricism; Hume, David; Kant, Immanuel; Newtonianism; Philosophy; Rationalism; *and* Reason.]

BIBLIOGRAPHY

Burnyeat, Miles, ed. *The Skeptical Tradition*. Berkeley, Calif., 1983. This volume contains three articles dealing with the eighteenth century: Richard H. Popkin, "Berkeley and Pyrrhonism," pp. 377–396; Robert J. Fogelin, "The Tendency of Hume's Skepticism," pp. 397–412; and Barry Stroud, "Kant and Skepticism," pp. 413–434."

Force, James E., and David S. Katz, eds. *Everything Connects: In Conference with Richard H. Popkin*. Leiden, Boston, and Cologne, 1999. The essay by José R. Maia Neto, "Bayle's Academic Skepticism," pp. 263–276, is of particular interest.

Fosl, Peter S. "The Bibliographical Bases of Hume's Understanding of Sextus Empiricus and Pyrrhonism." *Journal of the History of Philosophy* 36 (1998), 261–278.

Groarke, Leo, and Graham Solomon. "Some sources for Hume's account of causation." *Journal of the History of Ideas* 52 (1991), 645–663.

Kreimendahl, Lothar, ed. *Aufklärung und Skepsis: Studien zur Philosophie und Geistesgeschichte des 17. und 18. Jahrhunderts*. Stuttgart and Bad Cannstatt, Germany, 1995.

Laursen, John Christian. *The Politics of Skepticism in the Ancients, Montaigne, Hume, and Kant*. Leiden, Neth., New York, and Cologne, 1992. Chaps. 6 and 7 are on Hume, pp. 145–192; chaps. 8 and 9 are on Kant, pp. 193–232.

Livingston, Donald W. *Hume's Philosophy of Common Life*. Chicago and London, 1988. This work presents Hume's philosophy as post-Pyrrhonist.

Mulsow, Martin. "Eclecticism or Skepticism? A Problem of the Early Enlightenment." *Journal of the History of Ideas* 58 (1997), 465–477.

Norton, David Fate. *D. Hume: Commonsense Moralist, Sceptical Metaphysician*. Princeton, N.J., 1982. See especially chap. 5, "Hume's Skepticism Regarding Natural Beliefs," pp. 192–238 and chap. 6, "Traditional Scepticism and Hume's Scepticism," pp. 239–310, which highlight the "critical" significance of the Humean skepsis, well summarized on p. 235: "Hume adopted a mitigated naturalism as the complement of his mitigated skepticism."

Olaso, Ezequiel de. *Escepticismo y ilustracion: La crisis pirronica de Hume y Rousseau*. Valencia, Venezuela, 1981.

Olshewsky, Thomas M. "The Classical Roots of Hume's Skepticism." *Journal of the History of Ideas* 52 (1991), 269–287.

Paganini, Gianni. *Analisi della fede e critica della ragione nella filosofia di Pierre Bayle*. Florence, 1980. Chap. 2, "Scetticismo e fideismo nel *Dictionnaire*," pp. 75–134, and a large part of chap. 6, "Storia e dialettica dei problemi filosofici," pp. 274–374, are dedicated to problems of the interpretation of Bayle's skepsis. See especially pp. 275–281 on the skeptical method, and pp. 312–330 on the origins, character, and limits of skepticism in the philosophy of Bayle. The author highlights the different aspects revealed by Bayle's skepsis according to themes and contexts.

Paganini, Gianni. *Scepsi moderna: Interpretazioni dello scetticismo da Charron a Hume*. Cosenza, Italy, 1991. The volume contains an ample historical introduction, pp. 13–197, relevant parts of which include chap. 4, "Accademici e Pirroniani nel Seicento: da Foucher a Bayle," pp. 123–150, and chap. 5, "Scetticismo 'debellato' o 'invincibile'? Da Villemandy a Hume," pp. 151–197.

Paganini, Gianni. "Du bon usage du scepticisme: Les *Doutes des Pyrrhoniens*." In *La philosophie clandestine à l'age classique*, edited by Antony McKenna and Alain Mothu, pp. 291–306. Paris and Oxford, 1997.

Paganini, Gianni. "Haupttendenzen der clandestinen Philosophie." In *Grundriss der Geschichte der Philosophie: Die Philosophie des 17. Jahrhunderts*. Vol. 11, edited by Jean-Pierre Schobinger, pp. 121–195. Basel, 1998. With a complete bibliography on the topic of clandestine philosophical literature. Sections 9–10, pp. 167–184, are dedicated to skeptical themes in the clandestine philosophies.

Paganini, Gianni, Miguel Benitez, and James Dybikowski, eds. *Scepticisme, clandestinité et libre pensée / Scepticism, Clandestinity and Free-Thinking*. Proceedings of the Round Tables Organized during the Tenth International Congress on the Enlightenment. Paris, 2002.

Paganini, Gianni, ed. *The Return of Scepticism: From Descartes to Bayle*. Proceedings of the Vercelli International Conference. Forthcoming.

Pittion, J. P. "Hume's Reading of Bayle: An Inquiry into the Source and Role of the Memoranda." *Journal of the History of Philosophy* 15 (1977), 373–386.

Popkin, Richard H. *The High Road to Pyrrhonism*. San Diego, Calif., 1980. The volume collects many important studies dedicated to Bayle, Hume, Berkeley, and skeptical themes from the late seventeenth and eighteenth centuries.

Popkin, Richard H. Popkin, and Arjo Vanderjagt, eds. *Scepticism and Irreligion in the Seventeenth and Eighteenth Centuries*. Leiden, Neth., New York, and Cologne, 1993. A very useful collection of essays for framing the problem of the relations between skepsis and religious beliefs. For a general treatment of the question, see Alan Charles Kors, "Skepticism and the Problem of Atheism in Early Modern France," pp. 185–215. On the significance of Bayle's skepticism, see Ruth Whelan, "The Wisdom of Simonides: Bayle and La Mothe Le Vayer," pp. 230–253. On the clandestine texts see Olivier Bloch, "Scepticisme et religion dans la *Réponse à un théologien* du médecin Gaultier et sa postérité clandestine," pp. 306–323.

Popkin, Richard H., ed. *Scepticism in the History of Philosophy: A Pan-American Dialogue*. Dordrecht, Neth., Boston, and London, 1996. See in particular the essays of José A. Robles, "Berkeley: Scepticism, matter, and infinite divisibility," pp. 87–98; and Barry Stroud, "Hume's skepticism: Natural instincts and philosophical reflection," pp. 115–134.

Popkin, Richard H., Ezequiel de Olaso, and Giorgio Tonelli. *Scepticism in the Enlightenment*. Dordrecht, Neth., Boston, and London, 1997. The volume contains a series of articles by the three historians both on the general theme of skepticism in the Enlightenment and on specific authors (Berkeley, Rousseau, Changeux, Kant).

Popkin, Richard H., and Charles B. Schmitt. *Scepticism from the Renaissance to the Enlightenment*. Wiesbaden, Germany, 1987. The essay by Schmitt, "The Development of the Historiography of Skepticism: From the Renaissance to Brucker," pp. 185–200, is particularly useful.

Schröder, Winfried. *Ursprünge des Atheismus: Untersuchungen zur Metaphysik—und Religionskritik des 17. und 18. Jahrhunderts*. Stuttgart and Bad Cannstatt, Germany, 1998. On the relations between clandestine materialism, atheism, and Pyrrhonist themes, see in particular chap. 6, pp. 321–388.

Van der Zande, Johan, and Richard H. Popkin. *The Skeptical Tradition around 1800*. Dordrecht, Neth., Boston, and London, 1998. Parts 1 and 2 deal especially with the theme of skepticism in the French and German Enlightenment; with a useful annotated bibliography by José R. Maia Neto, pp. 387–454.

GIANNI PAGANINI

Translated from Italian by William McCuaig

SLAVERY. Chattel slavery is a grim and irrepressible theme governing the settlement of much of the western hemisphere. In the eighteenth century, Africans easily outnumbered Europeans as immigrants to the New World. Slavery was the cornerstone of a vast Atlantic labor market, and slaves were present everywhere—from the Saint Lawrence to the Río de la Plata. Much of the wealth of the eighteenth-century New World derived from slave-produced goods and products. In the world's first multinational system of production for a mass market, slaves in the Americas were principally responsible for production of the commodities, services, and capital that flowed through the early modern Atlantic world. Slaveholders dominated most New World colonies, shaping their politics, controlling their economies, defining their societies, and establishing their cultural norms. Possession of slaves was the clearest route to riches and status in the Americas: control over people was generally more important than land ownership, because labor was usually in short supply and land widely available. In classical and Judeo-Christian traditions, slavery was the central paradigm for understanding the nature of liberty. In large measure, conceptions of freedom were formed in opposition to the condition of slavery. Most people in the early modern world found servile labor neither embarrassing nor evil. As a result, the institution of New World slavery became deeply entrenched, fully legitimate, and highly profitable.

Slavery in the New World. Between 1500 and 1820, more than eight and a half million enslaved Africans made the Middle Passage to the Americas. This forced migration was the largest intercontinental migration then known to the world. The ratio of African to European immigrants to the New World was 1.7 to 1 between 1640 and 1700, 3.4 to 1 between 1700 and 1760, and 4.3 to 1 between 1760 and 1820. Before 1640, 90 percent of the roughly 800,000 Africans who left their homelands arrived in Portuguese ships. Thereafter, the British, who had been slow to transport slaves, emerged as the premier slave-trading nation. The reason for British preeminence lay in the efficiency of its shipping: British slavers carried more slaves per crew member and per ton, and their voyages were faster than those of other West European slave traders. The British carried over 40 percent of the Africans forced to leave for the New World between 1640 and 1820, which was twice the number of their nearest rival, the French. The number of Africans arriving in the Americas rose staggeringly—two and three quarter million between 1700 and 1760, over four million between 1760 and 1820. The transatlantic slave trade was predominantly an eighteenth- and early-nineteenth-century phenomenon, and Europe's sweet tooth was primarily responsible for this concentration. A dramatic expansion of sugar output in the eighteenth century fueled the need for more African slave laborers, the overwhelming majority of whom landed in a sugar colony.

Accordingly, slavery grew at different rates in different parts of the New World. No part of the Americas was more influenced by slavery than the Caribbean region, where sugar production was dominant. Spanish colonists brought the first black slaves to the region—to Hispaniola—in about 1501; in 1519 the first known vessel direct from Africa arrived in Puerto Rico; the "sugar revolution" of the mid–seventeenth century, first associated with Barbados and then expanding to the other islands of the Lesser Antilles, saw African slavery transform the region. In three and a half centuries, almost half—about five million—of the Africans transported to the New World arrived in the Caribbean, and by the late eighteenth century, slaves comprised 80 to 90 percent of the population of most Caribbean colonies. The region rivaling the Caribbean in having a long-standing and deep-rooted familiarity with slavery was Brazil. By the early sixteenth century the Portuguese were using enslaved Africans in parts of Brazil and by the middle of the century the direct slave trade with Africa had begun. It lasted until the 1850s, and introduced an estimated 4 million Africans. Of the Africans exported to the Americas, Brazil received about 40 percent. Within eighteenth-century Brazil, African slaves and their descendants formed about 40 percent of the population; in mining regions the percentage was double. African

slavery was never as intense or widespread in other parts of the New World as in Brazil and the Caribbean. Spanish America received about 7 percent of the Africans imported to the New World and North America a mere 5 percent.

Nevertheless, North America in particular developed significant slave societies, and by the early nineteenth century, more African Americans lived there than in either Brazil or the Caribbean. The reason is that the slave population in North America was unusual in growing by natural increase. By the early eighteenth century, births exceeded deaths among the slaves of the Chesapeake region, an unprecedented event for any New World slave population. The same process occurred in other North American slave societies somewhat later in the century. By midcentury North America's slave population was growing naturally at a faster rate than any European population. There were pockets—New England, for example—where slavery was not a major institution. Nevertheless, even leading New Englanders asserted their high status by owning slaves for personal use, and the region as a whole benefited indirectly from slavery in that nearly all its agricultural products were destined for the British West Indies.

Unease about Slavery. Few people questioned the morality of slavery before the late eighteenth century. The institution had existed since ancient times, and critics were few. Indeed, in the regions where slavery was integral, such as the Caribbean, Brazil, and the southern parts

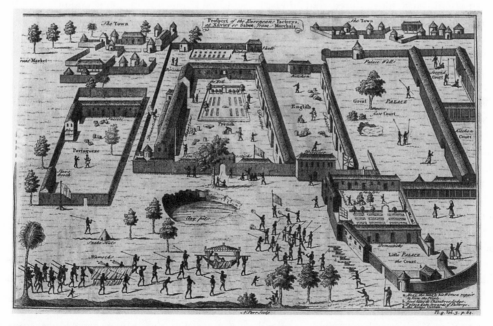

Slave Compound. Slave factory, or compound, maintained by traders from four nations—Portugal, France, England, and the Netherlands—on the Gulf of Guinea (present-day Nigeria). Engraving by N. Parr published in Thomas Astley, *A New and General Collection of Voyages* (London, 1746). (Rare Books and Special Collections Division, Library of Congress.)

of North America, little antislavery sentiment emerged. Similarly for most of its history, the slave trade was not considered morally reprehensible but was rather a routine, perfectly reputable business. The buying and selling of human beings raised no problems for most people. In a hierarchical world, where various degrees of restraint on liberties seemed natural, slavery aroused no special opprobrium, no particular abhorrence. Sustained opposition to slavery is a relatively recent occurrence in world history.

The question then becomes, Why did people begin to see slavery as an evil? "For some two thousand years," notes David Brion Davis, people "thought of sin as a kind of slavery. One day they would come to think of slavery as sin." After accepting slavery without question for so long, why did people begin to object to its presence?

Slavery had a long-standing pedigree and was everywhere simply taken for granted, but it also was a source of tension. The core contradiction of slavery—treating persons as things—guaranteed that the validity of slavery would always be troublesome. As slavery also became virtually extinct in Northwest Europe, it could be expected that some might question its utility, although for the most part the associations of slavery with sin, subordination, and the divine order held firm. Nevertheless, by the fifteenth century many Europeans thought enslavement inappropriate for Christians. In the late sixteenth century, Jean Bodin's *Les six livres de la République* (1576) marked the beginnings of a true antislavery philosophy. Good government, Bodin argued, required that nobody be excluded, no matter how degraded, and that everyone should be subjects of an absolute sovereign. Bodin defended absolute power and its use in abolishing slavery, but few political thinkers followed his lead. More influential was John Locke, whose philosophy of inalienable rights and a voluntary social contract challenged slavery, even as he himself invested in the Royal African Company and clearly thought black slavery justifiable.

The colonization of the New World heightened unease about slavery even as the institution took deep and extensive hold. From the first discoveries, Europeans saw America as a liberating and regenerating place, a land of promise, even if also an unlimited field for exploitation, cruelty, and vice. Those inspired by the utopian possibilities of America could be expected to question slavery, particularly the intensely exploitative form of slavery that developed in the New World, but at first, only a few isolated voices objected to the institution. In the early sixteenth century, for example, Bartolomé de las Casas became a crusader against Indian slavery and briefly acknowledged the unjustness of African-American bondage. Later in the century a small number of Catholic writers, no one more radically than Bartolomé de Albornozo, questioned the legitimacy of black slavery. In the 1580s a Jesuit in Brazil refused to hear confession from anyone involved in the injustice of slaveholding, and in the seventeenth century the Capuchins in Brazil petitioned against the African slave trade. The attempt to exclude slavery from Georgia, making it briefly the only nonslaveholding colony in the New World, derived largely from practical and utilitarian considerations but also in part from a belief that slavery was incompatible with the potentiality of America.

In the Anglo-American world, Quakers were in the vanguard of opposition to slavery. From the mid–seventeenth century onward individual Quakers preached against the ownership of and trade in slaves. Rejecting traditional religious authorities, they looked to their individual consciences for moral guidance. They were far more likely than orthodox churchmen to associate moral evil with institutions of the external world. In 1688 the Germantown Meeting in Pennsylvania issued a "Remonstrance against Slavery and the Slave Trade" and five years later George Keith published *An Exhortation and Caution to Friends Concerning Buying or Keeping of Negroes*. Other religious groups and movements converged with Quaker beliefs and actions. A few Puritans made the connection between sin and slavery, issuing ringing denunciations of the institution. Another group of British Protestants, known as latitudinarians, stressed man's capacity for moral improvement, contributed to a new ethic of benevolence, and helped arouse compassion for the slave. Evangelical religion was also notable for stimulating individual commitment and social action. By the 1760s these forces came together. Calvinist revivalists such as Samuel Hopkins and Jonathan Mayhew joined with Quaker evangelicals such as John Woolman and Anthony Benezet and Methodists such as Francis Asbury to condemn slavery as a transgression of God's will. Yet, despite the convergence of forces, Quakers were the first group to take action against those trading in slaves. In 1761 the Society of Friends in England approved a resolution disowning dealers in slaves, and two years later their Philadelphia counterparts followed suit. The first abolition society anywhere was formed in Philadelphia in 1775 and its members were almost all Quakers.

Enlightenment Criticism. Adding to the swelling chorus of religious dissent, spokesmen of the Enlightenment argued that slavery was both anachronistic and contrary to nature and thus universally wrong. Emphasizing secularism, rationality, and universal human rights, this libertarian and anticlerical intellectual movement did much to undermine traditional defenses of slavery. The most influential thinker was Montesquieu, who argued that individual liberty was a fundamental principle of natural law, that this eternal and rational system of law was transcendent over any local institution, and that wise government concerned about the public good could determine social utility from general laws. In addition to this new faith in the ability of wise legislators to shape institutions to fulfill the public good and in government to serve the public interest rather than the interests of the state, Enlightenment thinkers were skeptical of established institutions—none more so than Voltaire, who ridiculed the Roman Catholic Church's acceptance of slavery—and, in some cases, inclined to question the significance of racial differences based on a belief in human equality.

Another Enlightenment critique focused less on humanitarian than on economic grounds. Viewing slave labor as inefficient and expensive, this line of argument saw slavery as economically irrational. David Hume in Scotland, Benjamin Franklin in America, and Victor Riqueti in France all promoted this form of attack on slavery. Adam Smith made it famous when he emphasized the benefits of freedom of trade (and freedom of labor) and raised doubts about the wisdom of a highly protected imperial slave system. In his widely influential *The Wealth of Nations* (1776), Smith argued that free labor was more profitable than slave. For early political economists such as Smith, slavery prevented the free buying and selling of labor power and eliminated the possibility of self-improvement, which was seen as the main incentive to productive labor.

As with religious dissenters, Enlightenment thinkers were far from uniformly opposed to slavery. Montesquieu's emphasis on climate's influence on culture suggested the position that slavery might be appropriate in tropical countries. Environmentalism was a two-edged sword: it could be used to oppose slavery but it could also support it. Many philosophes believed that the degrading effects of slavery rendered slaves unfit for immediate freedom.

Economists were just as ambiguous as the humanitarians: they tended to be optimistic that self-interest would ultimately bring about the demise of slavery, and were respectful of private property. By elevating utility, they sometimes weakened the defense of liberty. Furthermore, the Enlightenment paved the way for racism based on scientific grounds, partly because it undermined Christian traditions of the unity of mankind, and partly because of the growth of biological science and its attempt to classify all living things. Even those who favored abolition believed that gradual change rather than radical transformation was in order. Erosion by "imperceptible degrees" was preferable to sudden cataclysms.

Nevertheless, despite the limitations of the Enlightenment's antislavery stance, the movement prepared the way for more direct abolitionist opposition. By destroying the traditional arguments that slavery was divinely ordained, and by questioning its efficiency, Enlightenment thinkers made slavery harder to defend. More generally, the Enlightenment's challenge to traditional authority and its criticism of authoritarian government, often using slavery as a metaphor, created a climate in which all forms of social organization could be scrutinized. No institution could hope to escape examination simply because it had remained unchallenged in the past. The increased circulation of print also enabled those distant from the institution of slavery to form opinions about its character.

Other Traditions. Although the Enlightenment was generally conducive to antislavery, other traditions were also influential. For example, well before the Enlightenment, dating back at least to the late sixteenth century, a libertarian juridical tradition—in essence a free-soil ideology—had taken root in northwest Europe. A famous English legal judgment of 1569 led to the manumission of a slave because "England was too pure an aire for slaves to breath in." As early as 1571, the parlement de Paris consistently ruled in favor of blacks seeking their freedom on the grounds that any slave who set foot on French soil became free. This "freedom principle," as Sue Peabody terms it, was also part of Dutch popular culture from the seventeenth century onward: masters knew when they brought slaves to the Netherlands that they implicitly manumitted them. In England, the principle became fully manifest in the landmark Somerset case of 1772 when Lord Chief Justice Mansfield ruled that English law could not countenance the deportation of James Somerset, a slave of a British custom official, back to the colonies. Although Mansfield attempted to confine his ruling to a particular slaveholder prerogative—forcing a slave to return to the colonies—and did not mean to remove the presumption that slaves brought to England should serve their masters, his action was a severe blow to slaveholding in England. Somerset's fellow blacks certainly interpreted the ruling as such.

Also in the 1770s, a few farsighted British individuals concerned with imperial administration, and particularly with the perceived need to enhance imperial power and central authority in the wake of the Seven Years' War, produced the first tentative emancipation plans. Men such as Maurice Morgann and the Reverend James Ramsay believed that the empire would be stronger with blacks as full British subjects, and imagined a new imperial community based on a wider inclusiveness. Admittedly, their ideas had little immediate influence, but they did represent a shift in antislavery thought, by offering practical alternatives, not just condemnation. They also reveal that colonial slaveholding, not the Atlantic slave trade, was the initial target of reform.

The role slaves themselves played in undercutting the institution of slavery should also not be underestimated. Some slaves petitioned colonial assemblies for their freedom. Many others took advantage of colonies' struggles for independence to flee to whichever army had advertised liberty for slaves, usually in exchange for military service. Some African Americans drew connections between revolutionary ideology and their own bondage, and argued that emancipation should flow from the Enlightenment belief that all humans possessed natural rights and the evangelical assumption that Christians must take their message of universal redemption to all creatures. The most dramatic actions by slaves occurred in the French Caribbean in the aftermath of the French Revolution. The St. Domingue revolution was the greatest and most successful example of slave resistance in history.

Revolution and Antislavery Sentiment. The American Revolutionary era inaugurated a deep questioning of slavery, even as it buttressed the institution. Its ideology challenged slavery's moral legitimacy, and American leaders often admitted that slavery was contrary to the principles for which they fought. As a result, in the northern colonies where slavery was not a major institution, it was put on the road to extinction. During the war thousands of blacks escaped from bondage while many others gained greater autonomy within slavery. The loss of the North American colonies not only helped to popularize libertarian ideas in Britain but, more important, removed a serious obstacle that would have made abolition much more difficult. At the same time, the American Revolution also strengthened slavery in the United States, by speeding slavery's growth westward, by freeing southern slaveholders from imperial restraints, and eventually by throwing the power of the federal government behind the institution.

After the Revolutionary War, antislavery sentiment focused on the slave trade. Regarded as the most barbaric aspect of slavery, its elimination seemed most readily achievable. Furthermore, ending the trade would, theoretically, improve the treatment of those already enslaved as their value would grow, while also supposedly killing the institution by cutting off its lifeline—the continued influx of newcomers. Focusing benevolent attention on a remote symbol of suffering and exploitation also had the benefit of confining to far-off places the attack on inequality and social rank and displacing fears and emotions that might have had serious social consequences domestically. Britain was the leader, with Thomas Clarkson an indefatigable worker in the countryside and William Wilberforce the political manager in Parliament. Helped by the proliferation of dissenting churches, the abolition movement became popular in plebeian communities, and attracted the support of middle-class women. Petitions, tracts, and public meetings sustained the campaign. This public agitation over slavery was the first large-scale attempt in modern times to mobilize national opinion in support of a humanitarian cause. A ban on the slave trade was passed in 1807. In the same year, the United States Trade Act prohibited the importation of slaves.

During and immediately after the American Revolution, abolition societies dedicated to the ending of slavery in particular states emerged throughout the northern United States, as well as in Virginia, Maryland, Delaware, and Kentucky. A few states—Vermont (1777), Massachusetts (1780), and New Hampshire (1784)—provided immediate freedom for all of the enslaved and their offspring. Other states, where slavery was of greater significance, adopted a gradualist approach. Between 1780 and 1808 the passage of emancipation statutes, freeing only those born after a specific date, subject to having the offspring work for the owner of the mother for a period of time generally ranging from eighteen to twenty-eight years, occurred in Pennsylvania (1780), Connecticut (1784), Rhode Island (1784), New York (1799), and New Jersey (1804).

Scholars fiercely debate the origins of the antislavery movement. Whether it owed more to evangelical Protestantism, the philosophical ideas associated with the Enlightenment, or a free-soil juridical tradition is still open to question. The precise role of the slaves in bringing about abolition—central for some historians, marginal for others—is contentious. Without a doubt, however, the key question that has concerned scholars is the link between capitalism and antislavery. Eric Williams (1944) set the terms of the debate when he argued that the profitability of "free trade" and its attendant free labor system encouraged capitalists to abandon slavery as outmoded and cumbersome. Since most historians now believe that slavery was economically viable, and near its peak when abolished, other causal connections between capitalist development and abolition have been sought. Some have detected in the abolitionists' commitment to a free labor ideology a willingness to legitimize a new domestic labor discipline that working people at home resisted. Denouncing an antithetical labor system, it is argued, was a way of validating the values and needs of the emerging capitalist order. Others suggest that capitalism stimulated antislavery even more indirectly through the impact of market activity, producing a new cognitive style. According to this view, humanitarianism arose from the interplay of market-fostered values.

In the final analysis, most notable are, first, that New World slavery during the era of the Enlightenment was a strong and vigorous institution, and second, that its demise occurred rather rapidly after thousands of years of almost unquestioning acceptance. By 1800 very few slaves had been freed. At that point, the Atlantic slave economy was dynamic, expanding, and profitable. The ending of the slave trade—first by the Danes in 1803 and then England and the United States in 1808, followed by the Netherlands and France in 1814 and 1815, and other countries decades later—was then followed by a fairly long period of at least a quarter of a century before slavery itself was ended. Even by the 1830s, after British abolition, only one-seventh of New World slaves were freed. And yet in the space of the next half-century or so, American slavery was ended. The abolition of chattel slavery is one of the most remarkable events of modern history and represents, as Seymour Drescher notes, "the first and, in a narrow sense, the most successful human rights movement."

[*See also* Colonialism; Natural Rights; North America; *and* Republicanism.]

BIBLIOGRAPHY

Anstey, Roger. *The Atlantic Slave Trade and British Abolition, 1760–1810*. London, 1975. An exploration of the intellectual and religious origins, the economic circumstances, and the politics of the first major abolition measure.

Bender, Thomas, ed. *The Antislavery Debate: Capitalism and Abolitionism as a Problem in Historical Interpretation*. Berkeley, Calif., 1992. A seminal collection of essays that attempts to explain the emergence of antislavery as an organized movement in Anglo-America, particularly by examining putative linkages between changes in capitalism and transformations in moral perceptions.

Blackburn, Robin. *The Overthrow of Colonial Slavery, 1776–1848*. London, 1988. A wide-ranging synthesis of antislavery movements throughout the Americas, notable for its attempt to connect metropolitan abolition and the struggles of slaves in plantation America.

Blackburn, Robin. *The Making of New World Slavery: From the Baroque to the Modern, 1492–1800*. London, 1997. An account of the making of colonial slavery in the Americas, paying particular attention to the institution's role in the formation of modernity.

Brown, Christopher. "Empire without Slaves: British Concepts of Emancipation in the Age of the American Revolution." *William and Mary Quarterly* 56 (1999), 273–306. An enlarged British empire after the Seven Years' War stimulated some farseeing minds to think the unthinkable: making blacks full British subjects.

Davis, David Brion. *The Problem of Slavery in Western Culture*. Ithaca, N.Y., 1966. Beginning with the Greeks, Romans, and early Christians, this panoramic survey examines the contradictory ideas and practices that led to the debates over slavery in the late eighteenth century.

Davis, David Brion. *The Problem of Slavery in the Age of Revolution, 1770–1823*. Ithaca, N.Y., 1974. The best study of the abolition of slavery in an international context.

Davis, David Brion. *Slavery and Human Progress*. New York, 1985. Tracing the shift from slavery to emancipation, from ancient times to the twentieth century, this work probes these developments from the perspective of changing conceptions of progress.

Drescher, Seymour. *Capitalism and Antislavery: British Mobilization in Comparative Perspective*. New York, 1987. Most notable for its investigation of popular pressure on national policy.

Drescher, Seymour. *From Slavery to Freedom: Comparative Studies in the Rise and Fall of Atlantic Slavery*. New York, 1999. A collection of essays that offers a comparative analysis of transatlantic abolition movements.

Eltis, David. *The Rise of African Slavery in the Americas*. Cambridge, 2000. A penetrating look at why those countries most committed to individual freedom created the most exploitative systems of slavery.

Oostindie, Gert, ed. *Fifty Years Later: Antislavery, Capitalism and Modernity in the Dutch Orbit*. Pittsburgh, 1996. Dutch emancipation came late in the abolitionist movement; these essays explain why.

Peabody, Sue. *"There Are No Slaves in France": The Political Culture of Race and Slavery in the Ancien Regime*. New York, 1996. An investigation of how and why political antislavery and institutional racism combined in France prior to the French Revolution.

Solow, Barbara L., and Stanley L. Engerman, eds. *British Capitalism and Caribbean Slavery: The Legacy of Eric Williams*. New York, 1987. Essays exploring the connection between slavery and capitalism.

Turley, David. *The Culture of English Antislavery, 1780–1860*. London, 1991. Antislavery is seen as a cultural response to change in English society and to change in the international economic and political order.

Williams, Eric. *Capitalism and Slavery*. Chapel Hill, N.C., 1944. A classic, arguing, among other things, that abolition was driven not by philanthropy or humanitarianism but by economic motives.

PHILIP MORGAN

SMITH, ADAM (1723–1790), Scottish political economist and moral philosopher.

Adam Smith was born in Kirkcaldy, on the east coast of Scotland, and baptized on 5 June 1723. He was the son of Adam Smith, clerk to the court martial and comptroller of customs in the town (who died before his son was born) and of Margaret Douglas of Strathendry.

Adam Smith. Engraving by Mackenzie after a portrait by Tassie. [For an illustration of the title page of Smith's *Wealth of Nations*, see the article "Mercantilism."] (Prints and Photographs Division, Library of Congress.)

Smith attended the High School of Kirkcaldy and then proceeded to Glasgow University. He matriculated in 1737, at the age of fourteen. At this time the university, or more strictly the college, was small. It housed only twelve professors, who had in effect replaced the less specialized system of regents by 1727. Of the professoriate Smith was most influenced by the "never-to-be-forgotten" Francis Hutcheson (*Correspondence*, letter 274, dated 16 November 1787). Hutcheson had succeeded Gerschom Carmichael, the distinguished editor of Samuel Pufendorf's *De Officio Hominis et Civis*, as professor of moral philosophy.

Smith left Glasgow in 1740 as a Snell Exhibitioner to Balliol College, to begin a stay of six years. The atmosphere of the college at this time was Jacobite and, according to Smith, "anti-Scotch." Smith was also to complain: "In the university of Oxford, the greater part of the publick professors have, for these many years, given up altogether even the pretence of teaching" (*Wealth of Nations*, 5.i.f.8). There were benefits, however, most notably ease of access to excellent libraries, which in turn enabled Smith to acquire an extensive knowledge of English and French literature, which was to prove invaluable.

Smith left Oxford in 1746 and returned to Kirkcaldy without a fixed plan. In 1748, however, he was invited to give a series of public lectures in Edinburgh, with the support of three men—the lord advocate; Henry Home, Lord Kames; and a childhood friend, James Oswald of Dunnikier. The lectures, which are thought to have been primarily concerned with rhetoric and belles lettres, brought Smith £100 a year (*Correspondence*, letter 25, dated 8 June 1758). They also seem to have been wide-ranging.

Smith's reputation as a lecturer brought its reward. In 1751 he was elected to the chair of logic at Glasgow University, again with the support of Lord Kames. According to John Millar, Smith's most distinguished pupil, he devoted the bulk of his time to the delivery of a system of rhetoric and belles lettres, which was based on the conviction that "the best way of explaining and illustrating the various powers of the human mind, the most useful part of metaphysics, arises from an examination of the several ways of communicating our thoughts by speech, and from an attention to the principles of those literary compositions which contribute to persuasion or entertainment" (Stewart, 1.16).

Smith's teaching from the chair of moral philosophy to which he was elected in 1752, fell into four parts and in effect set the scene for the major published works that were to follow. Again on the authority of John Millar, it is known that Smith lectured on natural theology, ethics, jurisprudence, and "expendiency," or economics, in that order. The lectures on natural theology (a sensitive subject at the time) have not been found, but Millar made it clear

that the lectures on ethics form the basis for Smith's *Theory of Moral Sentiments* (1759) and that the subjects covered in the last part of the course were to be further developed in his *Inquiry into the Nature and Causes of the Wealth of Nations* (1776).

Smith's work on ethics was closely linked with the economic analysis that was to follow. For example, if Smith gave prominence to the role of self-interest in this context, auditors of his lecture course and readers of the *Theory of Moral Sentiments* would be aware that the basic drive to better our condition was subject to a process of moral scrutiny. It would also be appreciated that economic aspirations had a social reference in the sense that it is chiefly from a regard "to the sentiments of mankind, that we pursue riches and avoid poverty" (*Theory of Moral Sentiments*, 1.3.2.1). Later in the book the position was further clarified when Smith noted that we tend to approve the means as well as the ends of ambition: "Hence . . . that eminent esteem with which all men naturally regard a steady perseverance in the practice of frugality, industry, and application" (*Theory of Moral Sentiments*, 4.2.8).

The lectures on jurisprudence helped Smith to specify the nature of the system of positive law that might be expected in the stage of commerce, and also threw some light on the form of government that might conform to it, together with the political pressures to which it may be subject. The treatment of jurisprudence is also important in that it helps to explain Smith's understanding of the origins of the modern economy and the emergence of an institutional structure where all goods and services command a price and where "Every man . . . lives by exchanging, or becomes in some measure a merchant" (*Wealth of Nations*, 1.4.1).

The English politician Charles Townshend was among those to whom David Hume had sent a copy of Smith's treatise. Townshend had married the widowed countess of Dalkeith in 1755 and was sufficiently impressed by Smith's work to arrange for his appointment as tutor to her son, the young duke of Buccleuch. The position brought financial security (£300 sterling per annum for the rest of his life), and Smith duly accepted, formally resigning his chair early in 1764.

Smith and his party left almost immediately for France to begin a sojourn of some two years. At the outset, the visit was unsuccessful, causing Smith to write to Hume, with some humor, that "I have begun to write a book in order to pass away the time. You may believe I have very little to do" (*Correspondence*, letter 82, dated 5 July 1764, Toulouse). Matters improved, however, with Smith's increasing familiarity with the language and the success of a series of short tours. In 1765 Smith, the duke, and the duke's younger brother, Hew Scott, reached Geneva, giving Smith an opportunity to meet Voltaire, whom he genuinely admired as "the most universal genius perhaps which France has ever produced" (*Correspondence*, letter 17). The party arrived in Paris in mid-February 1766, where Smith's fame, together with the efforts of David Hume, secured him a ready entré to the leading salons and, in turn, introductions to philosophes such as Jean Le Rond d'Alembert, Paul-Henri Thiry d'Holbach, and Claude-Adrien Helvétius.

During this period Smith met François Quesnay, the founder, with Victor Riqueti, the marquis de Mirabeau, of the physiocratic school of economics. At the time, Quesnay's model of the economic system as embodied in his *Tableau économique* (1757) had already been through a number of editions. Quesnay was then working on the *Analyse*, while Anne-Robert-Jacques Turgot was engaged in writing his *Réflexions sur la formation et la distribution des richesses* (Reflections on the Formation and Distribution of Riches, 1766). Thus Smith, who already had developed an interest in political economy, had arrived in Paris at a time when the French school had reached the zenith of its influence and output. The contents of Smith's library amply confirm his interest in this work.

Smith's stay in Paris was enjoyable both socially and in academic terms. It was marred, however, by the developing quarrel between Hume and Jean-Jacques Rousseau and terminated by the death of one of his young charges, Hew Scott. Smith returned to London on 1 November 1766.

Smith spent the winter in London, where he was consulted by Townshend and engaged in corrections of the third edition of the *Theory of Moral Sentiments*. By the spring of 1767 (the year in which Sir James Steuart published his *Principles of Political Oeconomy*) Smith was back in Kirkcaldy to begin a study of some six years. It was during this period that he struggled with *The Wealth of Nations*. Correspondence of the time amply confirms the mental strain involved. But by 1773 Smith was ready to return to London, leaving his friends, notably Hume, under the impression that completion of the book was imminent. As matters turned out, it took Smith almost three more years to finish, a delay that may have been due in part to his increasing concern with the American Revolution and with the wider issue of the relationship between the colonies and the mother country. *The Wealth of Nations* was finally published by Strahan and Cadell on 9 March 1776. The book sold well, with subsequent editions in 1778, 1784, 1786, and 1789.

Economic Analysis. In *The Wealth of Nations* the theory of price and allocation was developed in terms of a model that made due allowance for distinct factors of production (land, labor, capital) and for the appropriate forms of return (rent, wages, profit). This point, now so obvious, was an important innovation and permitted Smith to develop an analysis of the allocative mechanism, which ran in terms of interrelated adjustments in both factor and commodity markets. The resulting version of general interdependence also allowed Smith to move from a discussion of micro- to that of macroeconomic issues, and to develop a model of the "circular flow," which relies heavily on the distinction between fixed and circulating capital.

These terms, however, which were applied to the activities of individual entrepreneurs, were transformed in their meaning by their application to society at large. Working in terms of period analysis, where all magnitudes are dated, Smith in effect represented the working of the economic process as a series of activities and transactions that linked the main socioeconomic groups (proprietors, capitalists, and wage labor) and productive sectors. In Smith's terms, current purchases in effect withdrew consumption and investment goods from the circulating capital of society. These goods were in turn replaced by virtue of productive activity in the same time period.

Policy. Smith's treatment of domestic policy shows evidence of his support for the creation of an environment that would best release individual effort and maximize both incentive and efficiency. For example, he recommended that the statutes of apprenticeship and the privileges of corporations be repealed on the ground that they adversely affect the working of the allocative mechanism. In the same chapter, Smith pointed to barriers to the movement of labor represented by the Poor Laws and Laws of Settlement (*Wealth of Nations*, 1.10.100; 4.2.42).

Smith's basic objection was to positions of privilege, such as monopoly powers, as being both unjust and impolitic; unjust in that a position of monopoly is a position of unfair advantage and impolitic in that the prices of goods so controlled are "upon any occasion the highest that can be got"—the problem being that of blocked entry (*Wealth of Nations*, 1.7.27).

At the same time, however, Smith advocated a series of interventionist policies—all cataloged by Jacob Viner (1927)—that range from government control of the coinage to regulation of mortgages and the legal enforcement of contracts. Four broad areas of intervention recommended by Smith are of particular interest, in the sense that they involve issues of general principle. First, he advised governments that, where they were faced with taxes imposed by their competitors in trade, retaliation could be in order, especially if such an action had the effect of ensuring the "repeal of the high duties or prohibitions complained of" (cf. Winch, 1983, 609). Second, Smith advocated the use of taxation, not simply as a means of raising revenue but as a way of controlling certain activities, and of compensating for what would now be known as a defective telescopic faculty—that is, a failure to perceive our long-run interest (cf. *Wealth of Nations*, 5.2.9.4; 5.2.k 50; 5.2.g.12), commonly now referred to as "short-termism."

Smith was also well aware that the modern version of the circular flow depended on paper money and on credit; in effect, a system of "dual circulation" involved a complex of transactions that would involve cash (at the level of the household) and credit (at the level of the firm). It is in this context that Smith advocated control over the rate of interest, set in such a way as to ensure that "sober people are universally preferred, as borrowers, to prodigals and projectors" (*Wealth of Nations*, 2.4.15). He was also willing to regulate the small-note issue in the interests of a stable banking system.

Although Smith's monetary analysis is not regarded as among the strongest of his contributions, it should be remembered that he witnessed the collapse of major banks in the 1770s and was acutely aware of the problems generated by a sophisticated credit structure. It was in this context that he articulated a very general principle, namely that "those exertions of the natural liberty of a few individuals which might endanger the security of the whole society, are, and ought to be, restrained by the laws of all governments' of the most free, as well as of the most despotical" (*Wealth of Nations*, 2.2.94).

Emphasis should be given, finally, to Smith's contention that a major responsibility of government must be the provision of certain public works and institutions for facilitating the commerce of the society, works that were "of such a nature, that the profit could never repay the expense to any individual or small number of individuals, and which it, therefore, cannot be expected that any individual or small number of individuals should erect or maintain" (*Wealth of Nations*, 5.1.100.1). In short he was concerned to point out that the state would have to organize services or public works that the profit motive alone could not guarantee.

The examples of public works that Smith provided include such items as roads, bridges, canals, and harbors—all thoroughly in keeping with the conditions of the time and with Smith's emphasis on the importance of transport as a contribution to the effective operation of the market and to the process of economic growth. The theme is continued in his treatment of another important service, namely education; a subject developed in the course of Smith's discussion of the social and psychological costs of economic growth (*Wealth of Nations*, 5.1.f).

The year 1776 was marred for Smith by the death of Hume, after a long illness, and by Smith's concern over the future of Hume's *Dialogues Concerning Natural Religion*. This work, together with Hume's account "My Own Life" had been left in the care of William Strahan, to whom Smith wrote expressing the hope that the *Dialogues*

should remain unpublished, although Hume himself had determined otherwise. When it became clear that the work would be published, Smith proposed to "add to his life a very well authenticated account" of Hume's formidable courage during his last illness (*Correspondence*, letter 172, dated 5 September 1776). The letter was published in 1777, and as Smith wrote later to Andreas Holt, "brought upon me ten times more abuse than the very violent attack I had made upon the whole commercial system of Great Britain" (*Correspondence*, letter 208, dated October 1780).

In 1778 Smith was appointed commissioner of customs and excise in Edinburgh. The office brought an income of £600, in addition to the pension of £300, which his former pupil the duke refused to discontinue. In Edinburgh, he was joined by his mother and a cousin, Janet Douglas.

During 1778 Alexander Wedderburn sought Smith's advice on the future conduct of affairs in America. Smith's "Thoughts on the State of the Contest with America" was written in the aftermath of the battle of Saratoga. The memorandum was first published by G. H. Guttridge in 1932/1933 in the *American Historical Review*. In this document, Smith returned to a number of arguments that he had stated in *The Wealth of Nations*. He advocated the extension of British taxes to Ireland and to America provided that representatives from both countries were admitted to Parliament at Westminster in conformity with accepted constitutional practice. Smith noted that "Without a union with Great Britain, the inhabitants of Ireland are not likely for many ages to consider themselves as one people" (*Wealth of Nations*, 5.3.89). With respect to America, he observed that its progress had been so rapid that "in the course of little more than a century, perhaps, the produce of American might exceed that of British taxation. The seat of the empire would then naturally remove itself to that part of the empire which contributed most to the general defense and support of the whole" (*Wealth of Nations*, 4.7.100.79).

Smith also repeated a point already made in *The Wealth of Nations*; namely, that the opportunity for union had been lost. He proceeded to review the bleak options that were open to the British Government. Military victory was increasingly unlikely, and military government, even in the event of victory, unworkable. Voluntary withdrawal from the conflict was a rational but politically impracticable course, given the probable impact on domestic and world opinion. The most likely outcome, in Smith's view, was the loss of the thirteen united colonies and the successful defense of Canada—the worst possible solution, since it was also the most expensive.

Smith's work as commissioner of customs, affected, on his own admission, his literary pursuits. He nevertheless completed in this period the third edition of *The Wealth of Nations* (1784), incorporating major developments that were separately published as "Additions and Corrections." The third edition also features an index and a long concluding chapter to book 4 titled "Conclusion of the Mercantile System."

After 1784 Smith must have devoted most of his attention to the revision of his *Theory of Moral Sentiments*. The sixth edition of 1790 features an entirely new part 6, which includes a further elaboration of the role of conscience, and the most complete statement that Smith offered as to the complex social psychology that lies behind man's broadly economic aspirations. In addition to an essay titled "Imitative Arts," which is mentioned in his letter to Andreas Holt (*Correspondence*, letter 208), Smith had "two other great works upon the anvil, the one is a sort of Philosophical History of all the different branches of Literature, of Philosophy, Poetry and Eloquence; the other is a sort of theory and History of Law and Government" (*Correspondence*, letter 248, dated 1 November 1785, addressed to the duc de la Rochefoucauld).

Smith's literary ambitions also feature in the advertisement to the 1770 edition of *Theory of Moral Sentiment*, where he drew attention to the concluding sentences of the first edition of 1759. In these passages Smith makes it clear that the *Theory of Moral Sentiments* and *The Wealth of Nations* are parts of a single plan which he hoped to complete with a published account of "the general principles of law and government, and of the different revolutions which they had undergone in the different ages and periods of society." Smith's "present occupations" and "very advanced age" prevented him from completing this great work, although the approach is illustrated in *Lectures on Jurisprudence* and by those passages in *The Wealth of Nations* that can now be recognized as being derived from them.

Smith died on 17 July 1790, having first instructed his executors, Joseph Black and James Hutton, to burn his papers, with the exception of those that were published in *Essays on Philosophical Subjects* (1795).

[*See also* Aesthetics; Economic Thought; Education, *subentry on* Reform and Experiments; Ferguson, Adam; Home, Henry; Human Nature; Hume, David; Hutcheson, Francis; Imagination; Moral Philosophy; Physiocracy; Scotland; *and* Sociability.]

BIBLIOGRAPHY

PRIMARY SOURCES

The Works and Correspondence of Adam Smith. Oxford, 1976–1983. The edition has been published in paperback by the Liberty Fund, Indianapolis, and is now available in CD-ROM through Oxford University Press in conjunction with Intelex. The various editions consist of the following primary works.

Bryce, J. C., ed. *Lectures on Rhetoric and Belles Lettres*. Indianapolis, 1983.

Cambell, R. H., A. S. Skinner, and W. S. Todd, eds. *The Wealth of Nations*, 1976.

Macfie, A. L., and D. D. Raphael, eds. *The Theory of Moral Sentiments*. Indianapolis, 1976.

Meek, R. L., D. D. Raphael, and P. G. Stein, eds. *Lectures on Jurisprudence*. Oxford, 1978.

Mossner, E. C., and I. S. Ross, eds. *Correspondence of Adam Smith*. Indianapolis, 1977.

Raphael, D. D., and A. S. Skinner, eds. *Essays on Philosophical Subjects*. 1980.

SECONDARY WORKS

Brown, V. *Adam Smith's Discourse*. London, 1994.

Johnson, E. A. G. *Predecessors of Adam Smith*. New York, 1937.

Mizuta, H. *Adam Smith's Library*. Oxford and New York, 2000.

Ross, L. *Life of Adam Smith*. Oxford, 1995.

Skinner, A. *A System of Social Science*. Oxford, 1996.

Stewart, D. *Account of the Writings of the Life and Writings of Adam Smith*. Edinburgh, 1793.

Viner, J. "Adam Smith and Laisser-Faire." *Journal of Political Economy* 35 (1928).

Vivenza, G. *Adam Smith and the Classics*. Oxford, 2001.

Winch, D. *Adam Smith's Politics*. Cambridge, 1978.

ANDREW S. SKINNER

SMOLLETT, TOBIAS (1721–1771), Scottish man of letters.

Smollett was born into a genteel Scottish Whig family that had produced many lawyers. He studied at Dumbarton Grammar School and then at Glasgow University. In 1736, he was apprenticed to a Glasgow surgeon. In 1739, he left for London, hoping to establish himself as a medical man and to have his tragedy, *The Regicide*, performed. He failed on both counts, but the War of the Austrian Succession made it possible for him to get a warrant as a naval surgeon's mate and to join the expedition that sailed to Cartagena on 26 October 1740. His experiences on this disastrous expedition provided details for his first novel, *Roderick Random* (1748), and led to a number of miscellaneous publications.

Smollett returned to England in 1741 to practice as a surgeon, but it was his literary career that really mattered. In 1746, he produced "The Tears of Scotland" and "Advice," and the following year "Reproof"—poems that took account of current events and brought him some popular success. Smollett was also doing some hack writing in these years, including translations of Alain-René Lesage's *Gil Blas* (1748) and *Le diable boiteux* (as *The Devil upon Crutches*, 1750). In 1752, he translated Voltaire's satire on science and the limitations of the human condition, *Micromegas*, and other short works. That was also the year he published his only medical work, *An Essay upon the External Use of Water*, which played to the popular interest in mineral spas and bathing; it was also Smollett's valedictory to medicine, since he thereafter earned his livelihood from writing. In 1755, he issued his translation of *Don Quixote*. He was also writing novels: *Roderick Random* was followed by *Peregrine Pickle* (1751) and

Ferdinand Count Fathom (1753). In March 1756, Smollett began the *Critical Review*, which he edited until 1763. He published essays and reviews on most topics of concern to the enlightened—agriculture, chemistry, economics, geography and travel, history, medicine, natural science, politics, and a good deal of literary criticism. His work helped to make known in England the work of Scottish Enlightenment figures.

In 1760, Smollett founded the *British Magazine*, to which he contributed poetry and prose; it is best remembered for the serial publication of his fourth novel, *Sir Launcelot Greaves* (1760–1761). Smollett was also a prolific, if not great, historical writer; he was accused in this role of being a Tory, Papist, and Jacobite, but his real fault was being a Scot. He wrote a complete four-volume *History of England ... to ... 1748* (1757–1758), to which he added a *Continuation* (1760–1765) dealing with years whose events he had witnessed. From the mid-1750s until the end of his life, he was also an editor and writer for the *Universal History* (44 vols. octavo; 16 vols. folio). He served a similar role for the *Present State of All Nations* (1768–1769). In the early 1760s, he contributed translations and notes to the thirty-five-volume edition of the *Works of Voltaire*. In 1762, Smollett defended the administration of the third earl of Bute, in thirty-eight issues of *The Briton*.

Worn out by work and depressed by the death of his only daughter, Smollett went abroad from June 1763 until July 1765. On his return, he published his somewhat jaundiced *Travels through France and Italy* (1766). That mood persisted in his satirical and score-settling *The History and Adventures of an Atom* (1769), which attacked political corruption in Britain. From 1768 until his death he lived abroad, mostly in Italy, where he wrote his greatest novel, *Humphry Clinker* (1771).

Smollett's more than seventy volumes show him to have been socially rather conservative but interested in improvement and in the promotion of civic virtue. He distrusted religious enthusiasm, looked to science as the source of progress, and hoped that good literature would foster good morals. This in part explains his interest in Voltaire and others whose works he helped to make available to English-speaking readers. In the end, he feared that his fellow Britons could not make a society shaped by the values of Enlightenment, and he proposed a return to the values of an earlier society in which life was simpler and social order more hierarchical and respected.

[*See also* Exhibitions; Journals, Newspapers, and Gazettes, *subentry on* Great Britain; Novel; Publishing; Translation; *and* Voltaire.]

BIBLIOGRAPHY

Basker, James G. *Tobias Smollett: Critic and Journalist*. Newark, Del., 1988. Identifies and evaluates the numerous contributions to the periodical press.

Beasley, Jerry C. *Tobias Smollett Novelist*. Athens, Ga., 1998. An excellent study of the complexities of his narratives.

Bouce, Paul-Gabriel. *The Novels of Tobias Smollett*. London, 1976. A comprehensive study of sources, literary devices, and thematic structures.

Knapp, Lewis M. *Tobias Smollett: Doctor of Men and Manners*. Princeton, N.J., 1949. Dated, but still the standard biography.

Knapp, Lewis M. *The Letters of Tobias Smollett*. Oxford, 1970.

Smollett, Tobias. *The Works of Tobias Smollett*. Athens, Ga., 1988–. Edited by Jerry C. Beasley, O. M. Brack, and Jim Springer Borck. Standard scholarly edition of all the major works and a selection of the more important minor ones.

O. M. BRACK

SOCIABILITY. One of the key concepts in Enlightenment thought, sociability refers to the capacity of human beings to live peacefully without the continuous intervention of a coercive power. It thus goes hand in hand with the belief that society creates and sustains itself. Sociability is one of the most enduring ideas of the Enlightenment. Western liberalism continues to rely on the principle that social harmony arises spontaneously, and that government exists not to make social order possible but only to enhance the benefits that society naturally produces.

Absolutism and Sociability. One major source of reflection on the nature of man as a sociable being was absolutist political thought. With their arguments attempting to prove systematically that humans are not naturally fit to live in society, defenders of absolute monarchy challenged the Aristotelian-humanist tradition of defining man as a communal being. In this way, absolutist thinkers triggered vigorous counter-assertions in favor of the associational structure of human life.

In *Leviathan* (1651), the English philosopher Thomas Hobbes wrote:

> It is true that certain living creatures, as bees and ants, live sociably one with another ... and yet have no other direction than their particular judgments and appetites .... And therefore some man may perhaps desire to know, why mankind can not do the same. To which I answer ...
>
> (225)

The answer Hobbes gave was a theory emphasizing the unsuitability of humans for collective living. Human beings are not content with obtaining comfort. Each takes pleasure in "comparing himself with other men" and "can relish nothing but what is eminent." In other words, each person seeks a position of relative superiority over others. This quest for distinction is not compatible with peace. The tendency toward social instability is aggravated further by humankind's special gifts of reason and speech. Other animals do not deliberate on their mode of social organization or try to change it—"whereas amongst men, there are many, that think themselves wiser, and abler to govern the public, better than the rest; and these strive to reform and innovate, one this way, another that way, and thereby bring it into destruction and civil war" (225–227). From these features of the human condition Hobbes deduced the necessity of subordinating the inhabitants of a community to the will of an absolute sovereign.

Jacques-Bénigne Bossuet, a French defender of absolute monarchy, made the same argument in a more theological framework. In *Politique tirée des propres paroles d l'Écriture sainte* (Politics Derived from the Words of Holy Scripture, published posthumously in 1709), he affirmed that "Human society has been destroyed and violated by the passions.... The first man separated himself from God, and as just punishment discord was put in his family, and Cain killed his brother Abel." Human nature, corrupted by original sin, is incompatible with society. Government is necessary as "a brake on the passions." A powerful ruler is required to overcome the confusion stemming from what Bossuet calls man's "unsociable" disposition (11–13).

Arguments such as these constituted a challenge to other political and social thinkers. The absolutist arguments were subversive, because they overturned the Aristotelian and humanist tradition of seeing man as naturally inclined to political life. According to absolutist thinkers, human beings are destined to be tax-paying and laboring subjects, not debating and legislating citizens. Many thinkers of the Enlightenment attempted to counteract this reduction of humanity to a passive role in the community. At the same time, most of these thinkers were accustomed to kingship and did not advocate the establishment of democratic courts and councils. The idea of sociability mediated between absolutism and democracy. In doing so, it took on an apolitical inflection. The point was not merely to affirm the possibility of human solidarity but to locate this solidarity outside of the governmental sphere. Sovereignty would remain in the hands of the king, but the citizens would cultivate sociability in those private spaces which Enlightenment thinkers configured into the ideal of "society" or "civil society."

Sociability and the Market. One way in which Enlightenment thinkers envisioned this civil society was in the form of a free market. The foundation for market theory was laid by natural-law theorists of sociability such as Samuel Pufendorf. In his *De jure naturae et gentium* (The Law of Nature and Nations, 1672), Pufendorf used a Latin word, *socialitas*, which became *sociabilité* when the original Latin was translated into French in the early eighteenth century. From there, the word passed into other languages, and in this way, "sociability" was born. Sociability meant the inability of humans to survive alone. Expressed in positive terms, it meant the human need for cooperation. Pufendorf fashioned his concept of *socialitas* as part of a refutation of Hobbes's position that the state

of nature (the condition of humans prior to the existence of government) is a state of war. According to Pufendorf, people in the state of nature avoid conflict. They see the convenience for themselves of maintaining peace with others, and they begin to make agreements with each other even before law is formally implemented by a state. It should be stressed that for Pufendorf this spontaneous movement toward social relations does not flow from gregariousness or benevolence. It is a purely self-interested strategy for avoiding the economic hardships of solitude. In this way, he held to Hobbes's premise that humans are self-absorbed, but he reached the anti-Hobbesian conclusion that associations emerge prior to the construction of sovereign power.

In *The Second Treatise Of Government* (1689), John Locke also attempted to demonstrate that society is prior to government. According to Locke, "The state of nature has a law of nature to govern it, which obliges everyone" (263). By this Locke meant that individuals in the state of nature opt to show respect for others even though there is no positive law requiring them to do so. Humans incline toward "communion and fellowship" in order to furnish themselves with the necessities of life. Locke vividly portrayed the economic rationality of individuals in the state of nature. Each person acquires property through his own labor; each person also deduces from his own self-interest that what another person has labored for belongs to that person alone and should not be appropriated. In this way Locke suggested that private property is prepolitically respected. He also suggested that the economy as a whole undergoes change in the state of nature. Of great importance in this context is his argument that money is instituted "by mutual consent" before government exists. Nothing could make it clearer that Locke's aim was to show that the market economy creates itself and contains the motor of its own progressive development.

On the foundation built by state-of-nature theorists such as Pufendorf and Locke, eighteenth-century thinkers created a science of the analysis of economic self-interest. When Adam Smith declared in *The Wealth of Nations* (1776), "It is not from the benevolence of the butcher, the brewer, or the baker, that we expect our dinner, but from their regard to their own interest" (1:18), he was not suggesting that all human action is based on selfishness. He was simply continuing a natural-law tradition according to which even human selfishness contains internal control mechanisms. He was also arguing that no contrivance of political policy could create an economy as productive as one that functioned on the basis of self-interest and free choice. This paradox, that selfishness is the best route to the general welfare, had a powerful effect on political debate and policy in the late eighteenth century, but few Enlightenment thinkers became complacent about the utilitarian defense of selfishness. Immanuel Kant expressed his reservations in an essay *Idee zu einer allgemeinen Geschichte im weltbürgerlicher Absicht* (Idea for Universal History with a Cosmopolitan Purpose, 1784). Kant amply acknowledged that the free pursuit of property and status brings out the individual's productive power and yields benefits for society as a whole. Yet Kant did not regard this "unsocial sociability" as sufficient. It produces "semblances of morality" and "glittering misery" but not intellectually and morally "mature" individuals. Even Adam Smith wrestled with the problem of how to promote noncommercial values in a society committed to reaching commercial prosperity through self-interest. In *The Wealth of Nations*, he noted that capitalist development entailed the decline of "virtues" and "the nobler parts of the human character" (302–304). He advocated state-sponsored education to correct these faults. Such reservations help to explain why Enlightenment thinkers were fascinated with forms of sociability besides the "unsocial sociability" of economic enterprise.

The Art of Conversation. Absolutism expressed itself not only in the Hobbesian theory of total sovereignty but also in quintessentially absolutist institutions. One of these was the royal court of which the supreme example was the court of Louis XIV. In the 1680s, Louis moved his permanent residence from Paris, the largest city in France, to Versailles, an undeveloped region about twenty miles outside of Paris. In doing so, he deliberately separated himself from a multidimensional metropolis and constructed a unitary theater in which he would be the sole source of favors, prestige, and wealth. Here he also developed a courtly social life designed to attract and domesticate the nobility. Nobles wishing to obtain pensions and titles, or simply wishing to be seen where *les grands* dwelled, now felt the compulsion to reside in the royal court at Versailles. This opened up a rift between court nobles, who were obliged to pay obsequious homage to the monarch, and other nobles who viewed courtly life as inconsistent with the dignity of their estate. The tension played itself out in competing conceptions of politeness.

Courtly manners were designed to reinforce a hierarchy that culminated in the monarch. Respect flowed upward but not downward in the hierarchy. Most of the rules found in the popular treatises on courtly etiquette, such as Antoine de Courtin's *Nouveau traité de la civilité* (The Rules of Civility, first published in 1671 and reprinted in many subsequent editions), instructed courtiers on how to show deference toward persons of superior rank. A courtier was supposed to keep to the left of a superior when walking outside; a courtier should never contradict a grandee; and so forth. In opposition to this hierarchical code, however, other nobles united with members of

the wealthy bourgeoisie to fashion an alternative code of politeness. Gathering in salons, this noncourtly elite prided itself in constituting an alternative community, which it called *le monde, le public*, or *la société*. Here it was not hierarchy but reciprocity that functioned as the basic norm. The salons were designed to sustain an atmosphere where the preoccupation with social distinction would not obstruct the free flow of conversation. Linguistic exchange was to be pursued as an end in itself. A kind of game in which the distinctions based on genealogy and titles were to be suspended, the "art of pleasing in conversation," as it was called in the Old Regime, acquired quasi-democratic characteristics. The twentieth-century sociologist Georg Simmel intelligently emphasized the intrinsically egalitarian and liminal character of such sociable play:

> The fact is that whatever the participants in the gathering may possess in terms of objective attributes—attributes that are centered outside the particular gathering in question—must not enter it. Wealth, social position, erudition, fame, exceptional capabilities and merits, may not play any part in sociability. At most they may play the role of mere nuances of that immaterial character with which reality alone, in general, is allowed to enter the social work of art called sociability.
>
> (45–46)

This highly articulate distinction between the artifice of sociability and normal social hierarchy is meaningful as retrospective sociological analysis, but similar distinctions were reiterated over and over again in contemporary sources, particularly in the numerous books instructing the elite in the art of polite conversation. It is thus clear that the discourse of politeness, far from having only decorative meaning, was an important instrument for rethinking the structure of social relations.

Excellent examples can be found in the writings of Jean-Baptiste Morvan de Bellegarde (1648–1734), the most prolific French author of guides to polite behavior in the last decades of the seventeenth century and first decades of the eighteenth. Bellegarde consistently made it clear that politeness was an achievement that had to be cultivated, not a distinction given by birth. "Personal merit should be preferred to rank. It is not with the greatest seigneurs that communication is the most agreeable. Their manners do not always correspond to their high birth" (1696, 247–248). Bellegarde also maintained that conversation should be organized so as to exclude social hierarchy. He dismissed the obsession with ceremonies and precedence that characterized the court:

> Everyone is permitted to say his sentiment, and we must suffer with good grace those who contradict us. It would be an insupportable tyranny to wish to fix the thought of others under one's own opinion. Kings, with all their authority,

have no jurisdiction over the sentiments of their peoples, and individuals should not claim to be more absolute than kings.

(1690, 183)

Passages such as these occur repeatedly not just in Bellegarde's writings but in the writings of other popular commentators on politeness, such as Madeleine de Scudéry (1607–1701) and François de Callières (1645–1717). The general force of their arguments can be reduced to three key claims. The first is that nobility of spirit is separate from and superior to nobility of birth. The second is that the sphere of polite conversation is sui generis—that is, beyond the control of outside powers such as the monarch. The third is that language, when exercised for the sake of intellectual and sociable pleasure, has a unique set of rules to govern it, and these rules must displace the hierarchical considerations that regulate the rest of society.

Literature on the art of conversation thus provided a way to think about the autonomy of sociable experience. Just as free-market theory portrayed the economy as a domain separate from the state, so the theory of the art of conversation constituted private conversation as a self-instituting republic. These two strands of thought, however, did not remain separate. What makes the Enlightenment particularly rich in conceptions of sociability is the creative fusion of the more utilitarian, economic notion of civil society with the more linguistic, urbane notion of civil society.

The Temporalization of Sociability. David Hume's essays are an important locus of this fusion. In the essay "Of Refinement in the Arts" (1752), he provided an outline of universal history in terms of the rise of sociability. According to Hume, the advancement of commerce and science inevitably leads to the growth of cities and the intensification of social interaction:

> The more these refined arts advance, the more sociable men become: nor is it possible, that, when enriched with science, and possessed of a fund of conversation, they should be contented to remain in solitude, or live with their fellow-citizens in that distant manner, which is peculiar to ignorant and barbarous nations. They flock into cities; love to receive and communicate knowledge; to show their wit or their breeding; their taste in conversation or living in clothes or furniture.
>
> (270–271)

And Hume added: "Particular clubs and societies are everywhere formed: Both sexes meet in an easy and sociable manner; and the tempers of men, as well as their behavior, refine apace" (271). In this way, Hume established a temporal framework, or what could also be called a historical sociology, in which conversational sociability symbolized much more than a hobby of the elite. Hume generalizes sociability so that it appears constitutive of the city as opposed to the country. He also regards it as characteristic of the contemporary world as opposed to "barbarous" times. In short, sociability appears

here as the linchpin of a theory of urban modernization and total social progress.

Hume was Scottish, but he had lived in France and had become intimately familiar with French courtesy literature. Moreover, Scotland had developed its own polite literature in the early eighteenth century. Scottish thinkers of the middle and late eighteenth century continued Hume's effort to conceptualize sociability in broadly historical terms. William Robertson is a key figure in this context. He was one of the most popular historians not only in Britain but in the American colonies and in the early American republic. Translated by Jean-Baptiste Suard, a man of letters regarded by Diderot and others as the most polite figure of the Parisian salons, Robertson's works had a substantial impact on France. In two works, "A View of the Progress of Society in Europe," which was the introduction to his *History of the Reign of the Emperor Charles V* (1769), and *The History of America* (1777), Robertson presented a scheme of evolution in which sociability was the emblem of "civilized" societies. In the first of these works, he contrasted European feudalism with Europe since the sixteenth century. Robertson used the term "feudal" to refer not to medieval law—this is how the term was generally used before him—but to refer to a stagnant and isolating mode of economic and social organization. The feudal system thus becomes the antithesis of sociability: "Europe was broken into many separate communities. The intercourse between these divided states ceased almost entirely during several centuries" (38). Even within a particular region, "communication was rare and difficult" (41). The revival of commerce in modern Europe intensified interaction across geographical boundaries. As a result, local prejudices dissolved. Animosity among states declined. The manners of men and women became "polished."

In *The History of America*, Robertson used the same categories to construct an anthropological account of the differences between the "refined" Europeans and the "savages" of the New World. Just as he described the feudal system as fragmented and uncommunicative, so he described the American continent as an assemblage of unsociable warriors. Robertson stated that the character of the Indian is marked by "that taciturnity which is so disgusting to man accustomed to the open intercourse of social conversation" (132):

> When they are not engaged in action, the Americans often sit whole days in one posture, without opening their lips. When they go forth to war, or to the chase, they usually march in a line at some distance from one another, and without exchanging a word. The same profound silence is observed when they row together in a [canoe].
>
> (192)

Robertson did not consider the European to be superior to the Indian in every respect. The Indian had an inimitable "consciousness of its own freedom" and could be observed to act at times "with astonishing force, and perseverance, and dignity" (193). Yet the procivilization thrust of Robertson's commentary is unmistakable. According to him, the absence of "liberal communication" deprived Native Americans of tender affections and intellectual refinement. Each was "indifferent about the manner in which his actions may affect other man" (192). While the savage individual displayed a discipline and physical strength that the polished European lacked, it was only the Europeans who had humane and egalitarian sentiments.

Robertson claimed that the Indians were particularly cruel toward women, and that improvement in the treatment of women occurs only with the progress of sociability. This was in fact a common theme in Enlightenment theories of the civilizing process. Women such as Marie-Thérèse Geoffrin and Germaine Necker de Staël played a leading role in the French salons. They were frequently the patrons of men of letters, and it has well been argued that they shaped the very terms of Enlightenment social thought. The philosophes considered the ability to shine in private conversation, as opposed to political oratory, to be well within the capacity of women. Both French and Scottish thinkers emphasized the softening effect that regular sociable contact with women had on male aggression. Thus, it was believed that while civilized society entailed improvement in the treatment of women, women in turn would further improve the quality of civilized life.

Historians who have carefully examined French and British ideas in their historical context have emphasized that the main intention of theorists of sociability was to give men and women living in these undemocratic regimes an outlet for moral and civic energy. In France, the absolutist state provided few institutions in which the upper classes could exercise the public spirit and the relish for debate acquired in humanistic schools that were still shaped by Ciceronian values. Scotland's subordination to England similarly deprived the Scottish elites of frequent opportunities for political expression. England itself had a vigorous political culture, but many British thinkers of the eighteenth century believed it would be dangerous to further extend the franchise or augment the power of Parliament over the crown. The ideal of sociability allowed the view that the private sphere was adequate for the self-realization of humans as speakers and actors. Many of the Enlightenment's greatest thinkers—Montesquieu, Voltaire, Hume, to name a few—were determined to prove that participating in the construction of a "civil society" was wiser and more productive than attempting to democratize the political constitution.

Sociability, Republicanism, and Revolution. The concept of sociability could not be strictly confined, however, to this undemocratic idiom. The belief that modern society had advanced decisively over previous societies could serve as a foundation for revolutionary manifestoes in favor of further change. Further, the idealization of civil society enabled radical thinkers to argue that the citizens were now mature enough to exercise sovereignty.

Thomas Paine is a case in point. Located somewhere between journalism and systematic theory, Paine's political writings repeatedly affirm the simple idea that society is good and government evil. In fact, his most original rhetorical maneuver was to apply to the governments of "civilized" European countries the appellations of "savagery" and "barbarism" that other Enlightenment thinkers reserved for feudal and primitive societies. By locating the antithesis of sociability in the present, specifically in the state, Paine powerfully recharged the concept of sociability. In *The Rights of Man* (part 2, 1792), he noted in Pufendorfian fashion: "No one man is capable, without the aid of society, of supplying his own wants; and those wants, acting upon every individual, impel the whole of them into society as naturally as gravitation acts to a center." Society is thus "prior to government, and would exist if the formality of government was abolished" (165). "When men...have habituated themselves to social and civilized life, there is always enough of its principles in practice to carry them through any changes they may find necessary or convenient to make in their government" (166). In this way, Paine argued that the overthrow of a government would not lead to violence and chaos. He claimed that this was particularly true in European societies, because "The more perfect civilization is, the less occasion has it for government, because the more does it regulate its own affairs, and govern itself" (167). From this he deduced that the primary source of suffering in European countries is the state. Even economic shortage is rooted in governmental despotism:

> By thus ingrafting the barbarism of government upon the internal civilization of a country, it draws from the latter, and more especially from the poor, a great portion of those earnings which should be applied to their own subsistence and comfort...it is a melancholy fact that more than one fourth of the labor of mankind is annually consumed by this barbarous system.
>
> (207)

Paine's thought, considered as a whole, contains some ambiguities, which reveal that the relationship between the idea of sociability and revolutionary thinking was an unstable one. In *The Rights of Man*, he described himself as "an advocate for commerce." "It is a pacific system, operating to unite mankind by rendering nations, as well as individuals, useful to each other" (208). In *Common Sense* (1776), however, he disparaged commercial nations:

> Commerce diminishes the spirit both of patriotism and military defense...the bravest achievements were always accomplished

in the nonage of a nation.... The more men have to lose, the less willing are they to venture. The rich are in general slaves to fear, and submit to courtly power with the trembling duplicity of a spaniel.

(34)

The difference can be explained contextually. *Common Sense* exhorted the American colonists to rebel against England. By equating rusticity and civic strength, Paine wished to reassure the Americans that they could triumph in a conflict with a European power. *The Rights of Man* was a defense of the French Revolution against its European critics, notably Edmund Burke. Here Paine's goal was to establish a stark contrast between maturity of French society and the injustices of the state.

Although the contradiction can be explained in this way, it still shows that the idea of sociability coexisted uneasily with the burgeoning defense of republicanism against monarchy. Paine's reference in *Common Sense* to the "slaves" of the "courtly power" provocatively suggested that there was no real separation between state and civil society in European countries. The royal court exerted its corrupting influence through the social order, while commercial riches made men value security more than they hated tyranny. Yet his defense of the French Revolution rested upon the state-society dichotomy. Where Paine was inconsistent, Jean-Jacques Rousseau was consistent. His social and political thought is a powerful critique of the Enlightenment's tendency to idealize civil society as distinct from the state. In his *Discours sur les sciences et les arts* (Discourse on the Sciences and the Arts, 1750), he portrayed politeness and intellectual refinement as "garlands of flowers," which decorate the chains of despotism, accustom men to slavery, and "fashion them into what is called civilized people" (6). In *Discours sur l'origine et les fondements de l'inégalité parmi les hommes* (Discourse on the Origin of Inequality, 1755), he inverted the values of the dominant anthropology by contrasting the freedom of the savage to the economic and psychological dependence of the modern individual: "The savage lives within himself; sociable man, always outside himself, is capable of living only in the opinion of others and, so to speak, derives the sentiment of his own existence solely from their judgment" (187). For Rousseau, the dense communication networks of modern society suffocate the moral conscience and impose a veil of false politeness over genuine sentiments.

The purpose of his *Du contrat social* (The Social Contract, 1762) is to explain how human autonomy and authenticity can be preserved without going back to the solitary life of the savage, that is, how they can be preserved inside a community. In a particularly revealing passage, Rousseau writes that the citizens convening in the legislature should have "no communication among themselves" prior to voting (60). Political decisions should register the opinion of each individual, not a public opinion created through interchange. Communication only encourages individuals to worry about how they are perceived by others; it also permits those who are verbally sophisticated but not honest to exercise power over more taciturn but virtuous citizens. Rousseau thus takes sociability out of the political sphere to preserve the possibility of forming a General Will. The political sphere for Rousseau is sui generis: it is designed to preserve the very things—autonomy, equality, and empathy—that civil society tends to obliterate. The institutions and procedures that Rousseau describes in *The Social Contract* are almost all designed to ensure that civil society does not undergo the process of commercialization that thinkers such as Locke and Hume idealized.

Rousseau's suspicion of sociability and commercial society was shared by many defenders of republican government in the late eighteenth century. It became common to contrast the virtue of the "citizen" with the frivolous sociability of the "cosmopolitan." (See the article on "Citizenship" for further discussion.) Paine's tendency to oscillate between the two poles of republicanism and sociability, however, is more paradigmatic of the late eighteenth century than the consistent views of a Rousseau. The ideologies of the American and French Revolutions drew upon the ideals of both republicanism and commercial sociability. It is true that the Jacobins in France owed much to Rousseau, and the Federalists in America to the Scots, but revolutionary thought in both countries tends to be schizophrenic. This could be ascribed to a lack of philosophical clarity, or to a utopian syncretism, a tendency to believe in the possibility of harmonizing opposing viewpoints. It is also likely, however, that the debates of the 1760s and 1770s had made the revolutionaries aware of the strengths and weaknesses of each position to such a degree that they found it impossible, when making concrete decisions, to hold fast to only one theory.

None of this is to imply that ideas were unimportant in the revolutions. Indeed, it is only through these ideas that one can understand the contradictions of revolutionary thought: the tendency in the French Revolution, for example, to idealize the "public opinion" produced by civil society combined with a tendency to adopt a repressive stance toward civil society. In the making of the American Constitution, a belief in the blessings of capitalist development coexisted with the cult of the rustic citizen-soldier. Hence, the right to bear arms granted in the Second Amendment, a provision that would never have materialized if theorists of sociability were the only ones influencing the framers of the Constitution. Hume, Smith, and other believers in the progress of civilization were in favor of standing armies. They saw the citizen militia as an outdated institution inconsistent with the sociable preoccupations of the modern citizen.

The intellectual history of sociability and of its republican antithesis illuminates what are still the fundamental tensions in Western political cultures. The Enlightenment as a whole is best understood as a set of debates that never reached a conclusion. The moral uncertainties that we continue to feel about many basic institutions of modern society are due to the competing visions inherited from the Enlightenment. It should be no surprise, then, that the most brilliant twentieth-century accounts of eighteenth-century sociability do not merely narrate the debates of the Enlightenment but replay them so that the Enlightenment seems to extend into the present.

Recent Interpretations. In the writings of Hannah Arendt and Jürgen Habermas one can find variations on the theme of republicanism. In *The Human Condition* (1958), Arendt, an admirer of the ancient Greeks and Romans, decried the "rise of society" in the seventeenth and eighteenth centuries. In her view, the Enlightenment's idealization of commerce was based on a shallow utilitarianism. Labor became all-important and the potential of humans as speakers and creative political actors was forgotten. Arendt argued that humans can thrive only in a public sphere where the individual's preoccupation with evanescent biological and material needs gives way to the expression of immortal ideas and the construction of enduring institutions. In *On Revolution* (1963), she was favorable to the American and French Revolutions to the extent that they rekindled political idealism. She was critical of them, however, to the extent that they directed political policy to "the social question," that is, the satisfaction of the economic needs of the poor. She regarded this populism as a corrupt form of sympathy that unwisely subordinated politics to socioeconomic ends.

Arendt may well be the most incisive and prophetic political thinker of the late twentieth century, but her historical understanding of the early modern era gives very short shrift to the ideals of the Enlightenment. As a result, she never acknowledged the complex ways in which the Enlightenment reimagined social space. Given her interest in speech, she ought to have noted that the terms "society," "civil society," and "civilization" in the Enlightenment signified spheres of sociable interaction, not merely labor for the enhancement of physical life. Instead of comparing Enlightenment ideas and her own idea of politics in terms of different conceptions of communication, she simply presumes that speech was of no importance in the Enlightenment. Hence she never really engages the liberal alternative to classical republicanism.

This is a mistake that Jürgen Habermas did not make in his *Structural Transformation of the Public Sphere* (1962). Sharing Arendt's basic ideals, Habermas nevertheless examined the emergence of civil society out of the absolutist state with much more care. The work has had a profound impact on the writing of eighteenth-century history because of its nuanced account of how forms of private sociability, such as the salon, dilated into a critical public sphere. According to Habermas, social equality first became possible behind closed doors, where it appeared to be unthreatening to the state. Nourished in privacy, those who cultivated this equality eventually found the daring to redefine society in terms of egalitarian exchange. Habermas shows much sympathy for the sociable ideals of the Enlightenment, yet he argues that the natural tendency of modern civil society is to undermine the worthy ideals that first legitimized it. Capitalism, for Habermas, produces a culture based on crude entertainment, not on refined intellectual dialogue. It also concentrates power in the mass media, undermining the possibility of universal and equal participation in political debate. To save society from itself, Habermas advocates governmental restrictions that will create an authentic public sphere out of unjust social materials. At this point it could be said that he joins Rousseau and Arendt, because his praise of the Enlightenment serves the same purpose as their condemnation of it: to undo the liberal idealization of the social realm and reassert the primacy of the political.

Rousseau did not live to witness the Jacobin Terror of 1793–1794. Neither Habermas nor Arendt paid much attention to it. It seems to be characteristic of republican and neorepublican thought to underestimate the dangers of affirming the superiority of political man over social man. In the early nineteenth century, Benjamin Constant brilliantly deconstructed the political thought of Rousseau and the Jacobins by arguing that they artificially attempted to revive ancient ideals of citizenship in modern civil society. Constant insisted that the growth of capitalism and sociability had fundamentally altered human consciousness. The modern individual had a more subtle psychology than the ancient individual. This was because the modern individual experienced more absorbing forms of privacy—luxury markets, conversation, letter writing, domestic and romantic dramas—that were unimaginable in the simpler cultures of antiquity. When the ancient Greek or Roman put aside private interests in order to play the role of a citizen, he was not, according to Constant, sacrificing very much. With the enrichment of private sociability, the modern individual had much more to lose. In fact, only coercion could make the modern individual abandon the social sphere for the supposed privilege of participating in the General Will on a regular basis. That is why the republicanism of Rousseau and the Jacobins was bound to lead to the Terror.

Ignored throughout much of the twentieth century, Constant's writings were rediscovered by French and American scholars in the 1970s. His analysis echoes in the work of the "Revisionist" historians of the French Revolution, such as Keith Baker, Marcel Gauchet, Mona Ozouf, and François Furet, who rejected the Marxist tradition of focusing on class conflict and emphasized instead the significance of sociability and dreams of political unity. The charismatic star of this movement was Furet, author of the exquisitely polemical book, *Interpreting the French Revolution* (1978). Close inspection, however, shows that Furet's work actually stakes out a position that is distinct from both the neorepublican and neoliberal positions. Instead of defending democracy against the social spirit, or the social spirit against democracy, Furet linked them together into a single causal process. Drawing on the ideas of Augustin Cochin, a Catholic conservative scholar of the early twentieth century, Furet emphasized the similarity between Enlightenment sociability, as found in salons and Masonic lodges, and the utopianism of the Revolution. The voluntary associations promoted in the Enlightenment transformed how the participants imagined the relationship between truth and social interaction. Truth, instead of being ontologically prior to social institutions, became a byproduct of sociability, the result of communication among free and equal individuals. Truth was what emerged as the consensus of intellectual exchange. Each individual had to submit to the judgment of this public opinion.

Furet and Cochin noted that this legitimation of group experience deprived the individual of rights against the group. For having pledged allegiance to the collective production of truth, the individual relinquished all possible grounds for opposing decisions that the group made—or that a leader might make in the name of the group. Furet and Cochin regarded Enlightenment sociability as a prototypical form of the Jacobin dictatorship. It should also be noted that Reinhart Koselleck's important work, *Kritik und Krise: Eine Studie zur Pathogenese der bürgerlichen Welt* (1959), follows a similar path of interpretation. What Cochin, Furet, and Koselleck have in common is an acutely epistemological perspective. They all believe that the Enlightenment, in both its liberal and republican expressions, mistakenly imagined politics to be the process of formulating and implementing truth. Politics, however, is inevitably about the clash of opposed interests that cannot be reconciled intellectually but only politically, which is to say through the exercise of will, not reason. Paradoxically, the Enlightenment effort to replace arbitrary authority with neutral truth resulted in a state that had more power over society than absolute monarchy ever had.

An interesting dimension to this historical debate is that the participants are difficult to classify on the usual political spectrum of "Left" and "Right." Those, such as Furet, who criticize the Enlightenment or the great revolutions are not against equality in all forms. Those who support the Enlightenment or Revolution, such as Habermas, are conscious of the problematic side of the eighteenth-century legacy. Thus, if it is true that all scholarship is political, it is also true that acute scholarship rises above conventional political divisions. What is really in question is an intractable problem: How to conceptualize the Enlightenment critically without turning one's back on the ideals of freedom and equality that the Enlightenment advanced. The perennial urgency and endless difficulty of this question is what stimulates Enlightenment scholarship at its best.

[*See also* Aristocracy, *subentry on* Cultural Contributions; Bourgeoisie; Citizenship; Civil Society; Commerce and Trade; Democracy; Economic Thought; Enlightenment Studies; Enthusiasm; Habermas, Jürgen; Human Nature; Koselleck, Reinhart; Moral Philosophy; Natural Sentiment; People, The; Politeness; Political Philosophy; Prejudice; Republicanism; *and* Revolution.]

BIBLIOGRAPHY

PRIMARY SOURCES QUOTED IN THE ARTICLE

Bellegarde, Jean-Baptiste Morvan de. *Réflexions sur ce qui peut plaire ou déplaire dans le commerce du monde.* Paris, 1690.

Bellegarde, Jean-Baptiste Morvan de. *Réflexions sur le ridicule.* Paris, 1696.

Bossuet, Jacques-Bénigne. *Politique tirée des propres paroles de l'Écriture sainte.* Geneva, 1967.

Hobbes, Thomas. *Leviathan.* Harmondsworth, U.K., 1968.

Hume, David. *Essays, Moral, Political, and Literary.* Indianapolis, Ind., 1987.

Kant, Immanuel. *Political Writings.* Cambridge, 1992.

Locke, John. *Political Writings of John Locke.* New York, 1993.

Paine, Thomas. *Political Writings.* Cambridge, 1997.

Robertson, William. *The History of America.* London, 1777.

Robertson, William. *The History of the Reign of the Emperor Charles V.* Boston, 1857.

Rousseau, Jean-Jacques. *The Discourses and Other Early Political Writings.* Edited by Victor Gourevitch. Cambridge, 1997.

Rousseau, Jean-Jacques. *The Social Contract and Other Later Political Writings.* Cambridge, 1997.

Smith, Adam. *The Wealth of Nations.* Chicago, 1976 (two volumes in one).

SECONDARY STUDIES

Arendt, Hannah. *The Human Condition.* Chicago, 1958.

Furet, François. *Interpreting the French Revolution.* Cambridge, 1981.

Goodman, Dena. *The Republic of Letters: A Cultural History of the French Enlightenment.* Ithaca, N.Y., 1994.

Gordon, Daniel. *Citizens without Sovereignty: Equality and Sociability In French Thought, 1670–1789.* Princeton, N.J., 1994.

Habermas, Jürgen. *The Structural Transformation of the Public Sphere.* Cambridge, 1989.

Hont, Istvan, and Michael Ignatieff, eds. *Wealth and Virtue: The Shaping of Political Economy in the Scottish Enlightenment.* Cambridge, 1983.

Koselleck, Reinhart. *Critique and Crisis: Enlightenment and the Patho-genesis of Modern Society.* New York, 1988.

La Vopa, Anthony J. "Conceiving a Public: Ideas and Society in Eighteenth-Century Europe." *Journal of Modern History* 64 (1992), 76–116.

Phillipson, Nicholas. "The Scottish Enlightenment." In *The Enlightenment in National Context,* edited by Roy Porter and Mikulas Teich, pp. 19–40. Cambridge, 1981.

Roche, Daniel. *France in the Enlightenment.* Cambridge, Mass., 1998.

Simmel, Georg. *The Sociology of Georg Simmel.* Glencoe, Ill., 1950.

DANIEL GORDON

SOCINIANISM. A form of Unitarian theology that depicts Jesus Christ as the recipient of an adoptive divinity inferior to that of God the Father. Socinianism derives its name from a family of Italian evangelical rationalists, notably Fausto Paolo Sozzini (1539–1604), who died in Poland. Especially influential were Sozzini's moralism and his biblical hermeneutics, which stressed right reason and philology over and against all ecclesiastical traditions. In 1660, after decades of intermittent harassment had turned into official persecution, the committed Socinian remnant was expelled from Poland. From the safety of Holland, some of them began in 1665 to republish the major works of their theological tradition in a uniform Latin edition. Those volumes were widely distributed, though anti-Trinitarianism was proscribed everywhere in Christian Europe except Transylvania.

As Unitarianism. The term *Socinianism* lost theological particularity. By the late seventeenth century, it was coming to be used as a synonym either for Unitarianism in general or for any theory of religious knowledge that treated the Bible as uniquely authoritative, essentially clear, and finally subject to the natural light of reason. At once an illegal doctrine and an unstable category, Socinianism became for many late early-modern theological polemicists a convenient, sometimes irresistible term of abuse, applicable to Arminians and Jansenists alike.

That capacity was perhaps most vividly exhibited in Britain at the end of the seventeenth century. King James II's decision in 1687 to suspend the enforcement of all ecclesiastical penal legislation persuaded Stephen Nye, a beneficed Anglican clergyman, to produce (anonymously) *A Brief History of the Unitarians, Called Also Socinians.* Because *Socinian* was a pejorative title, English anti-Trinitarians generally identified themselves as either Unitarians or Arians. Sponsored by Thomas Firmin, a wealthy and philanthropic Anglican, Nye's pamphlet inaugurated a ramifying controversy within the established church over the extent to which inherited Trinitarian formulas should limit its doctrinal comprehension. Nye, Firmin, and nearly all the other identifiable contributors to the three volumes of Unitarian tracts published by Firmin lived and died in communion with the Church of England. The Unitarians presented themselves both as defenders of Christianity against deists and other infidels and as sincere Protestants, duty-bound to exorcise enthusiasm by undertaking a free and impartial inquiry into traditional and corrupted notions of Christianity. The Unitarians also insisted that whatever is false according to reason—which for them meant common sense and natural knowledge—can never be true as revelation.

The Unitarian controversy set various dignitaries of the church both against Unitarian pamphleteers and, increasingly, against one another. The revolution of 1688 and church factionalism inflamed those battles. Into the early eighteenth century, divines warred among themselves over the meaning of Trinitarian orthodoxy, sometimes more truculently than they warred against those who called themselves Unitarians. High churchmen accused several latitudinarian prelates of that heresy. At the same time, the pressure of debate moved Unitarian pamphleteers to articulate more completely the rationalist implications of their biblical hermeneutics. By 1694, one of them insisted that God had given the human race an original revelation that was expressible in clear and distinct ideas. Others depicted Christ as having abrogated whatever in religion was mysterious, imprecise, or unintelligible. By 1696, John Toland's *Christianity Not Mysterious* was widely attacked as a deist book for espousing the same principles, as was John Locke's *The Reasonableness of Christianity* (1695), notwithstanding its difference in content and in tone.

Evolution from Establishment to Radical. Socinians were often lumped with deists, new laws against anti-Trinitarianism were enacted, and a few distinguished but outspoken Unitarians like the Cambridge mathematician William Whiston were penalized for their beliefs. Nonetheless, discreet Unitarians survived comfortably within the established church throughout the eighteenth century. Their movement, in its elitism, resembled that of the Genevan Socinians whom Voltaire encountered during the 1750s and who are alluded to in the article on Geneva that appeared in Denis Diderot's *Encyclopédie.* Whiston finally became a General Baptist, and his religious journey encapsulates the subsequent translation of the center of gravity of English Unitarian theology from establishment to dissent. Self-conscious, assertive, and often politically radical, Unitarians like Joseph Priestley came to see themselves by the 1790s as constituting a distinct church and came to be seen by others, from rioting crowds in Birmingham to High Church bishops, as a threat to the regime.

[*See also* Arminianism; Deism; Enthusiasm; Latitudinarianism; Locke, John; Natural Religion; Rationalism; *and* Skepticism.]

BIBLIOGRAPHY

Bradley, James E. *Religion, Revolution, and English Radicalism: Nonconformity in Eighteenth-Century Politics and Society.* Cambridge,

1990. Together with Ditchfield, explains the emergence of Unitarianism as an identifiable and politically radical movement of dissent.

Ditchfield, G. M. "Anti-Trinitarianism and Toleration in Late-Eighteenth-Century British Politics: The Unitarian Petition of 1792." *Journal of Ecclesiastical History* 42 (1991), 39–67.

Florida, R. E. *Voltaire and the Socinians.* Banbury, U.K., 1974. An accurate and accessible summary of the relationship between Socinianism and Continental deism.

Fock, Otto. *Der Socinianismus nach seiner Stellung in der Gesammentwickelung des christlichen Geistes.* 2 vols. Kiel, Germany, 1847. The classical doctrinal history of Socinianism; remains indispensable for its detail and analytic precision.

McLachlan, H. J. *The Story of a Nonconformist Library.* Manchester, U.K., 1923. The fullest account of the large seventeenth-century pamphlet literature.

McLachlan, H. J. *Socinianism in Seventeenth-Century England.* London, 1951. The only general history of English Unitarian thought in the period, limited by its teleological interpretation.

Szczucki, Lech, Zbigniew Ognowski, and Janusz Tazbir, eds. *Socinianism and Its Role in the Culture of the Sixteenth to Eighteenth Centuries.* Warsaw and Lodz, 1983. A wide-ranging but uneven collection of essays that demonstrates the ramifying implications of Socinianism.

Trowell, Stephen. "Unitarian and/or Anglican: The Relationship of Unitarianism to the Church from 1687 to 1698." *Bulletin of the John Rylands University Library of Manchester* 78 (1996), 77–101. A scrupulous and persuasive effort to locate late-seventeenth-century English Socinianism within its Anglican context.

Wilbur, Earl Morse. *A History of Unitarianism.* 2 vols. Boston, 1945. The standard history in English.

Williams, George H., ed. and trans. *The Polish Brethren: Documentation of the History and Thought of Unitarianism in the Polish-Lithuanian Commonwealth and in the Diaspora, 1601–1685.* 2 vols. Missoula, Mont., 1980. A collection of great learning that illustrates the unfolding of some of the radical philosophical and theological possibilities of Continental Socinianism.

ROBERT E. SULLIVAN

SOUL. In the eighteenth century, it was generally accepted that a human being is the union of a material body with an immortal, immaterial soul. By the late seventeenth century, soul was no longer conceived as the Aristotelian "form" of a potentially living body; largely as a consequence of Descartes's philosophy, it lost its connection with life functions and was conflated with the rational soul (mind) as pure thinking substance. Since thought, memory, and consciousness were properties of soul, the conceptual boundaries of "soul" and "self" were blurred by the Cartesian link between self (*moi*) and thought, and by the Lockean definition of personal identity as a continuity of memory and consciousness.

In his *Essay Concerning Human Understanding* (1690), John Locke explained that we form the idea of substance by combining simple ideas of the properties of things and by postulating some invisible, unknowable entity as support of those properties. From the perspective of the Enlightenment, Locke invalidated the doctrine of innate ideas, proved that ideas originate in the senses, and transformed metaphysics into an "experimental physics of the soul" (*Encyclopédie*, Preliminary Discourse). Empiricism and sensationalism became common to most empirical approaches to soul.

Hume's notion of self as a "bundle of perceptions" reinforced claims about the impossibility of knowing soul-as-substance. Christian thinkers replied that our feeling of self as an indivisible, stable unity proves the existence of the soul. Sensations, they argued, are the basis of self; if self were material, it would be divisible into distinct parts, each endowed with different sensations. They thus identified self with the soul's consciousness of its own existence.

Three positions framed discussions about soul-body union. According to the system of physical influence, the two substances affect each other materially. In Malebranche's occasionalism, God is the causal agent of their union: when the soul desires to move the body, God makes it move. Leibniz saw soul and body as regulated by preestablished harmony, like two perfectly synchronized clocks. A distinction was made between the postulate of soul-body union, and soul–body interaction as a topic of empirical enquiry. While union was accepted as a fact confirmed by faith, reason, and inner sense, yet in itself mysterious, *commercium* (interaction) could be elucidated by examining the phenomena of live organisms that seemed to manifest the mutual dependency of soul and body.

Soul was therefore studied within "animal economy." Some sought a location in the brain where soul would interact with body, believing that a single structure where nerves converge was more consistent with the unity of consciousness than were scattered localizations. Soul was basic to medicine and physiology. Both emphasized body-soul interaction and tended to reject mechanism and to reinstate the connection between soul and vital faculties. Nerves, as intermediaries between soul and body, played a key role in explaining many medical, mental, and cultural phenomena. Empirical psychology became a major late Enlightenment intellectual and disciplinary project, especially in Germany, that would provide principles for natural law, natural theology, ethics, and logic.

That a thinker as pious as Charles Bonnet was suspected of materialism illustrates how sensitive were all issues pertaining to soul. In Britain, Locke's suggestions that God could superadd the power of thinking to matter and that the soul's immortality did not necessitate its immateriality gave rise to debates that lasted the entire century. In "On the Immortality of the Soul" (1755, printed 1777), David Hume argued that the analogy of religion to nature indicated that soul and body meet "their common dissolution in death." It was in France, however, that the radical case for mechanical man developed.

The groundwork for this development was laid in clandestine works such as *L'âme matérielle* (1724–1737). Drawing eclectically on Descartes, Hobbes, and Locke, "Spinozism," Epicureanism, and the life sciences, free-thinkers and *libertins*, such works interpreted all human functions through the organization of matter. The "soul of brutes" was intensely discussed from Descartes to the mid-eighteenth century. The human soul, in turn, was materialized in two ways. One concept imagined soul as composed of imperceptible material particles; another, which evolved into La Mettrie's "machine man" (1748), reduced soul to a neurophysiological effect. The same assumptions were expounded by Helvétius, whose *De l'esprit* (1758) stressed the power of education; by d'Holbach, whose *Système de la nature* (1770) proclaimed the self-sufficiency of matter and motion; and by Diderot, whose masterpiece *Le rêve de d'Alembert* (1769) argued that thought results from *sensibilité*, a universal property of matter.

Protestant and Catholic antimaterialist responses dealt with moral, theological, and political factors. The "activity" of soul was opposed to the passivity of matter; its "simplicity" implied that it cannot disintegrate (therefore, die). The historical consensus of nations showed that such ideas cannot be false: Finally, it was asked, would God have implanted the desire of immortality in our hearts had he not intended to satisfy it? For Cartesians, the heterogeneity of *res extensa* and *res cogitans* implied that no modification of the former could provoke the annihilation of the latter, and this seemed confirmed by the "testimony of inner sense" about the unity of self.

Major changes in discourses on soul occurred in the century's final decades. In the *Kritik der reinen Vernunft* (Critique of Pure Reason, 1781), Kant argued that since no a priori knowledge can be obtained from the concept of a thinking being, "soul" designates the phenomena of the empirical self alone. Scottish universities instituted chairs in the "philosophy of the human mind." Since the 1770s, long before Cabanis's *Rapports* (1802), the use of *physique-moral* instead of *corps-âme* suggested a homogenous human "organization" in which the psychological derives causally from the physical. Nevertheless, the immaterial soul became essential in Romanticism, and psychology discussed it well into the nineteenth century.

Soul was profoundly implicated in the Enlightenment reconstruction of religion. The immaterialists saw their advocacy of soul as consistent with reason and experience. The historicizing of dogma, the critique of authority, the increased inwardness of worship, and the interpretation of the doctrine of original sin as contrary to reason and morality all helped to center religion on its ethical,

individual, and experiential dimensions. Soul remained the locus of experience. The movements deprecated as "enthusiasm" believed that God and humanity communicate through the "heart"—the soul's will and affections. Such works as Friedrich Christoph Oetinger's *Inquisitio in sensum communem et rationem* (1753) convey the richness of esoteric, Theosophical, and Christian-Cabalistic writings on soul, and their relation to philosophy, theology, and science.

The vicissitudes of "soul" in the eighteenth century reach beyond intellectual history. Apologists claimed that belief in its immortality and immateriality was a pillar of society and government. The materialization of soul required the renouncing of otherworldly beliefs, hopes, causes, and ends; it helped to dissolve principles that had fulfilled crucial spiritual and political functions, and that would have to be replaced. In the meantime, Kant's *Kritik der practischen Vernunft* (Critique of Practical Reason, 1788) maintained that the soul's immortality was a postulate necessary for fulfilling the moral law.

One of the final episodes of the century involved celebrating soul. In a speech given in 1794, the French revolutionary Robespierre promulgated a civic religion based on the "social and republican" ideas of a supreme being and the immortality of the soul. Three months after the new cult was elaborately celebrated, he perished at the guillotine—convinced, however, that "death is the beginning of immortality."

[*See also* Clandestine Literature; Epistemology; Kant, Immanuel; Materialism; Natural Philosophy and Science; Philosophy; *and* Romanticism.]

BIBLIOGRAPHY

Baertschi, Bernard. *Les rapports de l'âme et du corps: Descartes, Diderot et Maine de Biran*. Paris, 1992.

Hagner, Michael. *Homo cerebralis: Der Wandel vom Seelenorgan zum Gehirn*. Berlin, 1997. A history of the mind-brain relation from the seventeenth to the late nineteenth century.

Holzhey, Helmut. "Seele (§ 4. Neuzeit)." In *Historisches Worterbuch der Philosophie*, vol. 9, edited by Joachim Ritter and Karlfried Gründer. Darmstadt, Germany, 1995. A major encyclopedic article on soul, with rich primary and secondary literature.

Rey, Roselyne. "L'âme, le corps et le vivant." In *Histoire de la pensée médicale en Occident*, edited by Mirko D. Grmek with Bernardino Fantini, vol. 2, pp. 117–155, Paris, 1997. An excellent study about soul in eighteenth-century medical thought, with emphasis on the emergence of vitalism.

Risse, Wilhelm. *Bibliographia Philosophica Vetus*. Part 5, *De Anima*. Hildesheim, Germany, 1998. The most recent major bibliographic resource relevant to the topic.

Yolton, John. *Thinking Matter: Materialism in Eighteenth-Century Britain*. Minneapolis, 1983. Detailed examination of the debate launched by Locke's statement that God could superadd the power of thinking to matter.

FERNANDO VIDAL

SOUTH AMERICA. *See* Latin America.

SOUTH SEAS. The term *South Seas* entered eighteenth-century European consciousness when European navigators ventured west of the Strait of Magellan and began to explore the Pacific Islands, the continent of Australia, and the Southern Ocean. The entire Pacific as far north as the islands of Hawaii fell initially under this geographically immense and quasi-mythological rubric. Today, the term survives mainly in German ethnography (as *Südsee*) as a general term for the indigenous cultures and peoples of the South Pacific.

Explorations and Narratives. In the second half of the eighteenth century, facts, conjecture, and outright fiction readily mingled in the cultural mapping of lands and peoples remote from Europe. Narratives of the exploratory voyages of French and English explorers, such as Louis-Anne de Bougainville (1729–1811), George Anson (1697–1762), and James Cook (1728–1779), sought legitimation as scientific accounts, but they inevitably activated earlier associations of the South Seas with the fantasies of wealth conjured up by the South Sea Company between its formation in 1711 and its collapse in 1720, as well as dreams of the Golden Age or other mythical perfect societies. Diderot read Bougainville's account of sexual practices in Tahiti as a utopian critique of European sexual repression, but John Wesley not only dismissed Cook's stories of sexual license as "absolutely incredible," but also insisted it was "absolutely impossible" that a common language could be understood across the huge region now known as Polynesia.

These narratives of exploration also reminded readers of how Daniel Defoe's hero, Robinson Crusoe, gradually transformed his desert island into a colonizing project and set up a master–servant relationship with the indigene Friday. Dorinda Outram wrote that Defoe's novel can be read "as a parable, conscious or otherwise, of the relationship between the European Enlightenment and the rest of the world.... Colonialism, the exotic, and the exploitation of nature were inextricably linked in the eighteenth century, and provide verification of the contention that Enlightenment and the control of nature were parts of the same project" (1995, 63).

Colonization. European exploration of the South Seas in pursuit of trading opportunities was the first step, and colonization was the second. The city of Batavia (now Jakarta, capital of Indonesia) was founded at the beginning of the seventeenth century by the Dutch East India Company and was used as a base by the Dutch explorer Abel Tasman (1603?–1659). Tasman, employed by the Company, charted many lands in the North and South Pacific, including the Philippines, Taiwan, Tonga, and Australia. He discovered Van Diemen's Land (later renamed Tasmania) and the islands of Aotearoa, bestowing the Dutch name New Zealand on them in 1642.

Europeans made no further contacts with Pacific Islanders for the next century.

By the mid-eighteenth century, Dutch commercial power had waned, and the conclusion of the Seven Years' War in 1763 left Great Britain as the dominant colonial power; French overseas possessions were also much diminished. At this time, Europeans finally charted the whole of the Pacific, and the South Seas became the object of scientific collecting, taxonomic scrutiny, and eventual large-scale diffusion of European languages and systems of knowledge.

James Cook's three voyages to the Pacific between 1768 and 1779, when he was killed in Hawaii, had multiple goals—navigational, astronomical, zoological, botanical, ethnographic, and geopolitical. Following secret instructions from the British Admiralty, Cook not only liberally scattered the names of British monarchs and ministers upon the new lands but also claimed possession of so-called unoccupied lands for the British crown. Australia, for this purpose, was declared unoccupied, or *terra nullius* ("no one's land"), because definitions of what constituted occupation were based on European concepts of agricultural cultivation. The European settlement of Australia, Nicholas Thomas has written, was founded "less in Enlightenment science than in violent dispossession."

Through the Lens of Enlightened Thought. There is still much work to be done to understand the ways in which key terms and images of Enlightenment and Counter-Enlightenment thinking clashed or colluded in the late eighteenth and nineteenth century as Europeans planted communities and structures of knowledge around the Pacific. Three strands of Enlightenment thinking about social and cultural difference were particularly affected by French and British voyages to the South Seas: utopianism and sexual and gender politics; taxonomic debates about vertical or horizontal ways of classifying human cultural and physical variety, and the question of "race"; and debates on the efficacy of natural morality versus a morality based on religious revelation.

Cook's and other voyages to the Pacific carried scientists intent on collecting specimens of natural history and ethnography, so these debates were accompanied by a massive new accumulation of objects, loosely divided at the time into "natural curiosities"—botanical and zoological collections—and "artificial curiosities," a catch-all for almost everything used or manufactured by humans. In time, the latter were relabeled "ethnographic collections," and the Otaheiti Room at the British Museum became a repository for items from all over the South Pacific.

The three figures who were most instrumental in assembling and introducing material from Pacific natural and cultural history into European museums, academies, and libraries were the wealthy natural scientist Sir Joseph

Banks (1743–1820), who took an entourage of scientists and artists with him on Cook's first voyage, and the German naturalists Johann Reinhold Forster (1729–1798) and his son Georg (1754–1794), both of whom accompanied Cook on his second voyage and then wrote their own accounts of their travels.

Banks subsequently held the presidency of the Royal Society from 1778 until his death. Through his friendship with King George III, he helped to turn the Royal Botanic Gardens at Kew (founded in 1761) into a major scientific resource, and his vast library later passed to the British Museum. Banks saw science and colonization as related projects. In 1779, on the strength of his brief visit to the southeastern coast of Australia, he enthusiastically recommended New South Wales as the site of a British penal colony, arguing that such a colony could support itself inside a year. The prime minister, William Pitt the younger, was informed that Botany Bay would make a good base for British ships "should it be necessary to send any into the South Seas." In May 1787, the eleven ships of the First Fleet sailed out of Portsmouth with a cargo of 736 convicts, sentenced to transportation and bound for Botany Bay. Utopian dreams had been abruptly transformed into a new dystopia. Tahiti, by contrast, remained a privileged space for French utopian imagining into the nineteenth century, though from the 1790s onward, its indigenous culture was under attack from missionaries sent out by the London Missionary Society.

Georg Forster's thinking was anti-hierarchical and opposed to the assumption that European civilization was superior to the so-called primitivism of indigenous Pacific peoples. Although he shared Banks's enthusiasm for the South Pacific as a scientific space to be ordered according to Linnaean taxonomy, he was unwilling to introduce a single taxonomy to classify human variety, because he viewed humans as full of potentialities that could unfold differently in different conditions. With the authority of his Pacific travels behind him, he argued: "Everywhere man has become what it was possible for him to become in the face of local conditions. Climate, the situation of his settlements, the height of mountains and the direction of rivers, the character of the soil, the multiplicity and characteristics of the plants and animals have sometimes given him an advantage on the one side and limited him on the other.... Thus in no place has he become everything that was possible, although everywhere he has become something different" (quoted in Thomas P. Saine, *Georg Forster* [New York, 1972], p. 63).

Forster's influence in Germany after his move to Kassel in 1778 affected such diverse figures as the Göttingen physicist and aphorist Georg Christoph Lichtenberg (1742–1799) and Alexander von Humboldt (1769–1859),

who acknowledged Forster's impact on his own attempts in *Cosmos* to consider the interrelations of geography, climate, and culture on a global scale. When the young Charles Darwin sailed into the Pacific on the *Beagle* in the 1830s, his work on the adaptation of living beings to their changing environments was a continuation of patterns of thinking pursued by Forster.

Current Pacific historical scholarship is following the art historian Bernard Smith in actively exploring the content and the limits of cross-cultural exchanges, while also engaging in a more complex dialogue with contemporary indigenous perspectives and epistemologies. Museums globally are also reworking colonial displays and taxonomies that decontextualized indigenous Pacific cultures and displayed material artifacts and cultural treasures without reference to their spiritual and intellectual underpinnings.

[*See also* Colonialism; Cook, James; Diderot, Denis; Slavery; *and* Utopianism.]

BIBLIOGRAPHY
Banks, R. E. R., et al. *Sir Joseph Banks: A Global Perspective.* Kew, 1994.
Beaglehole, J. C., ed. *The "Endeavour" Journal of Joseph Banks.* Sydney, 1962.
Bougainville, Louis de. *A Voyage Round the World.* Translated by John Reinhold Forster, J. Nourse, and T. Davies. Amsterdam, 1967.
Bowen, Margarita. *Empiricism and Geographical Thought: From Francis Bacon to Alexander von Humboldt.* Cambridge, 1981. Particularly useful for the relations between Georg Forster and Humboldt.
Cook, James. *The Journals of Captain James Cook.* Edited by J. C. Beaglehole. 3 vols. Cambridge, 1955–1967.
Forster, George. *A Voyage round the World, in His Britannic Majesty's Sloop, Resolution ... during the Years 1772, 1773, 1774, and 1775.* London, 1777.
Forster, Johann Reinhold. *Observations Made during a Voyage round the World.* Edited by Nicholas Thomas, Harriet Guest, and Michael Dettelbach. Honolulu, 1996.
Hoare, Michael E. *The Tactless Philosopher: Johann Reinhold Forster (1729–1798).* Melbourne, 1976. Defends the scientific importance of Forster's contributions to botany and zoology.
Hoare, Michael E., ed. *The "Resolution" Journal of Johann Reinhold Forster, 1772–1775.* 4 vols. London, 1982.
Hughes, Robert. *The Fatal Shore: The Epic of Australia's Founding.* New York, 1986. An overview of the internal British political issues that led to the founding of the penal colony in Botany Bay.
Joppien, Rüdiger, and Bernard Smith. *The Art of Captain Cook's Voyages.* 4 vols. Melbourne, 1985–1987.
Larson, James J. *Interpreting Nature: The Science of Living Form from Linnaeus to Kant.* Baltimore, 1994.
MacLeod, Roy M., and Philip F. Rehbock, eds. *Darwin's Laboratory: Evolutionary Theory and Natural History in the Pacific.* Honolulu, 1994.
Obeyesekere, Gananath. *The Apotheosis of Captain Cook: European Mythmaking in the Pacific.* Princeton, N.J., 1992.
Outram, Dorinda. *The Enlightenment.* Cambridge, 1995. See especially chap. 5, "Europe's Mirror? The Enlightenment and the Exotic."
Smith, Bernard. *European Vision and the South Pacific, 1768–1860: A Study in the History of Art and Ideas.* Melbourne, 1992.

Smith, Bernard. *Imagining the Pacific: In the Wake of the Cook Voyages*. Melbourne, 1992.

The South Pacific in the Eighteenth Century: Narratives and Myths. Special issue of *Eighteenth-Century Life* 18:3 (1994), edited by Jonathan Lamb, Robert Maccubbin, and David Morrill.

Thomas, Nicholas, and Diane Losche, eds. *Double Vision: Art Histories and Colonial Histories in the Pacific*. Cambridge, 1999. See especially Jonathan Lamb, "Re-imagining Juan Fernandez: Probability, Possibility and Pretence in the South Seas," pp. 19–43.

Wagenitz, Gerhard. "Georg Forsters botanische Sammlungen und ihre Auswertung." In *Georg Forster in interdisziplinärer Perspektive: Beiträge des Internationalen Georg Forster-Symposions in Kassel, 1–4 April 1993*. Berlin, 1994. This volume contains a valuable Forster bibliography for 1970–1993, and a geographical register.

M. KAY FLAVELL

SPACE. *See* Natural Philosophy and Science *and* Physics.

SPAIN. Spain at the close of the seventeenth century was the center of an impressive worldwide empire that included not only Spain itself—Castile and the three territories comprising the kingdom of Aragon (Aragon proper, Valencia, and Catalonia)—but also much of Italy (Milan, Naples, Sicily, and Sardinia), the southern Netherlands, a great swath of North, Central, and South America, the Philippines, and outposts in North Africa. By this time, however, Spain was not the economic or political power it had been a century earlier. Spain's problems were exacerbated by the failure of its last Habsburg king, Charles II (r. 1665–1700), to generate heirs; the question of who would succeed him as king became one of the most important issues in contemporary international relations.

Bourbon Monarchs. Charles's death and the accession of Spain's first Bourbon ruler, Philip V (r. 1700–1746), grandson of Louis XIV, provoked the Wars of the Spanish Succession (1701–1713/14). Philip's rival, the Austrian Habsburg archduke who claimed the throne as Charles III, was backed by the "Grand Alliance" led by England and the Dutch, and Philip by Louis XIV. The conflict was, in many respects, a Spanish civil war, since—broadly speaking—Castile supported Philip, while Aragon, Valencia, and Catalonia effectively joined the Alliance. Bourbon victories at Almansa (1707) and Villaviciosa (1710), and Charles's succession as Holy Roman Emperor Charles

Market in Madrid. Plaza de la Cebada. Painting by Manuel de la Cruz, c. 1800. (Museo Municipal, Madrid/Laurie Platt Winfrey.)

VI (1711), helped to ensure that Philip kept the Spanish throne, although by this time he had lost Gibraltar and Spain's possessions in both Italy and the Low Countries. Spain largely retained its vast overseas American empire, although it was obliged by the Peace of Utrecht (1713) to allow the English South Sea Company trading privileges there.

More important, Philip was able to restore by conquest his authority in the kingdom of Aragon; he took the opportunity to reduce the de facto autonomy of its component territories, with his so-called *nueva planta* ("new establishment") of 1714. Henceforth, they would be governed from Madrid by the Council of Castile and would be represented in the Cortes of Castile, although the latter hardly met in the eighteenth century. Customs barriers between Castile and the kingdom of Aragon were abolished, and henceforth the latter was expected to bear much more than it formerly had of the fiscal burden of the monarchy. Other changes, too, were introduced by Philip V during and after the Wars of the Spanish Succession. Aided by a number of able ministers, Philip increased and improved the army and the navy, established new funds to finance them, and put them on a better administrative footing. The last included the first steps toward a network of intendants, modeled in part on those of France, as royal agents in the provinces. Philip also transformed the central government, replacing the conciliar system that he had inherited from the Habsburgs with one that revolved around a small number of secretariats of state, each headed by a minister reporting to the king. Finally, Philip reduced the hold on government of the great nobles, or grandees, whose power had reflected both the weakness of the monarchy and their own landed wealth and influence. Philip did not attack, however, the social and economic position of the nobility.

Following the end of the Wars of the Spanish Succession, Philip sought—with some success—to build on the domestic transformation under way in Spain to ensure its return to the ranks of the major powers, to overturn the Utrecht peace settlement, and to recover Spain's lost European territories; he also wished to find thrones for the two sons of his second marriage (1714), with Elizabeth Farnese of Parma. In 1717, a Spanish force conquered the island of Sardinia, although this had subsequently to be surrendered; in 1718, Spain launched an unsuccessful bid to recover Sicily. In 1724, Philip abdicated in favor of Luis I, his son by his first wife, Marie Adelaide of Savoy. However, Luis died within the year, and Philip resumed the throne. Success against his old rival, Charles VI, in the War of the Polish Succession (1733–1738) enabled Philip to secure for his younger son, the future Charles III, the kingdoms of Naples and Sicily. In 1739–1740, poor relations with England, dogged by the issues of

Gibraltar and of the privileged access to Spain's American colonies granted in 1713, provoked a colonial war. This was soon part of the larger War of the Austrian Succession (1740–1748).

Philip was succeeded by Ferdinand VI (reigned 1746–1758). Ferdinand brought the war to an end and preferred to pursue domestic reform, with the aid of his able chief minister, the marques de la Ensenada. Among the achievements of the reign were a new concordat with the papacy (1753), which—building on regalist policies already evident in Philip V's reign—extended the royal *patronato*, or control, over the church in Spain and its overseas empire. Other projects included an attempt at agrarian reform and plans to replace the rather complex tax system with a new, fairer, simpler, and more effective single tax, or *unica contribución*. Before these projects could come to fruition, however, Ferdinand died, to be succeeded by his half-brother, Charles III (1758–1788).

New Ideas. Spain's international weakness in the later seventeenth century was accompanied by a certain backwardness in the intellectual sphere, in part attributable to the progress there of the Counter-Reformation. The Roman Catholic Church had extended its wealth and influence, while the hold of traditional ideas was underpinned by the Inquisition. Nevertheless, new ideas were gaining ground, at least among a small elite. The latter included the Jewish doctor Diego Zapata, whose *Crisis medica* (1701) was a stout defense of the new scientific ideas. Many of those who were attracted by the new ideas met privately, forming unofficial academies, such as that hosted from 1697 by the Seville doctor Juan Muñoz y Peralta. In 1700, Charles II gave official sanction to that academy, which became the Royal Society of Medicine and Other Sciences; Philip V continued to establish official institutions, including the Royal Library (1712) and the Royal Academy of History (1735). The advent of the Bourbon dynasty brought in a court increasingly in touch with the ideas of Enlightenment thinkers in France and elsewhere in Europe. In 1745, Benito Hieronimo Feijoo, in many respects the leading figure of the early Spanish Enlightenment, could say "I speak as a Newtonian." A generation later, the poet and university teacher Juan Meléndez Valdés claimed that he owed his understanding of the process of reasoning to a reading of John Locke's *Essay Concerning Human Understanding*. However, Spain was not completely open. The *Encyclopédie* of Denis Diderot and Jean Le Rond d'Alembert was banned by the Inquisition in 1759, and no Spanish translations of Montesquieu's works were published before 1820. We should not ignore the influence of earlier native Spanish authors—of the so-called Golden Age of the sixteenth and seventeenth centuries—on Spanish enlightened thinkers in the eighteenth century.

Whatever the source of their ideas, at the end of the 1750s the small enlightened elite looked to the new king, Charles III, for progressive change, not least because of his record as a reformer in Naples since the 1730s. Among Charles's early reforms in Spain were improvements in the amenities and appearance of the capital, Madrid. Other measures included further "regalist" steps toward restricting the power and influence of the clergy and of Rome in favor of the crown, and toward limiting the power of the many confraternities, which—in the opinion of many enlightened Spaniards in tune with the views of both Muratori and Jansenist tendencies—contributed to the superstitious excesses of popular religion. More important, however, were the measures to stimulate the Spanish economy, associated with one of Charles's leading reform-minded ministers, Pedro Rodríguez Campomanes. Apart from measures to improve communications throughout Spain by the building of new roads, in 1765 the centuries-old restriction on the price of grain was lifted and wholesale trade in grain allowed. Steps were also taken at this time to end the longstanding monopoly of trade between Spain and its American colonies, which had been officially channelled through Cadiz since 1717, and to open this trade to other Spanish and American ports, but not to non-Spaniards.

Reform and Resistance. Unfortunately, these limited moves in the direction of free trade, particularly the reform of the system of grain supply and pricing, were deeply unpopular. This helped to provoke riots in Madrid, whose inhabitants were also offended by decrees outlawing their traditional dress, and in provincial towns throughout Spain. These were the most serious disturbances faced by any monarchy in western Europe in the generation before the French Revolution. Charles III recovered control, but he was obliged to concede the dismissal of his chief minister, the Italian Leopoldo de Gregorio, marquis of Esquilache. More important, his government had received a shock and now sought a scapegoat, finding it in the Jesuits, who were accused by a committee of inquiry headed by another reforming minister, the count of Aranda, of fomenting the riots. The Jesuits were expelled from Spain and its empire in 1767.

The work of reform then continued. In local administration, the election of representatives of the hitherto largely unrepresented mass of the population was introduced, breaching the monopoly of the local oligarchs, in order to prevent a return of the discontent and disorder of 1766. Educational reforms included an attack on the *colegios mayores*, a small group of postgraduate colleges whose members had long enjoyed privileged access to the top posts in church and state, as well as modernization of the university curriculum. Further efforts were made to reform the fiscal system and to solve the problems of rural poverty and landlessness, which were greatly exacerbated by a growing population and a stagnant land market, the latter partly caused by the extensive landholding of church and nobles. Campomanes continued to promote efforts to stimulate Spain's economy by further liberalizing trade between Spain and its overseas colonies. He also encouraged the creation of local improvement societies, the so-called economic societies, or Societies of Friends of the Country, in imitation of that founded (1765) on private initiative in Spain's Basque country. About seventy of these economic societies had been founded in Spain and its empire by 1820, their members drawn largely from the local elites. In 1782, the Banco de San Carlos was established, largely to ensure the success of the government's attempts to raise funds—by means of the *vales reales* (in effect, bank notes)—to pay for both an expensive foreign policy and important public works such as the Aragon canal. Measures were also taken to limit the privileges of the centuries-old corporation of sheepowners, the Mesta, which were thought harmful to Spanish agriculture. A concern with the improvement of popular culture found expression in, for example, an attack on bullfighting (1785). Spain's overseas empire was fully caught up in the reform process, which in some respects represented an attempt to reinforce royal authority in the Americas.

Many of the concerns of the reformers fused in the creation, in the late 1760s, of model settlements in what had hitherto been a wild, bandit-ridden part of Andalusia, the Sierra Morena. These settlements, named La Carolina and La Carlota in honor of Charles III, were largely the responsibility of Pablo de Olavide, who in extensive travels in France and Italy between 1757 and 1765 had come into contact with Voltaire and other leading lights of the European Enlightenment. As intendant of Seville, Olavide made that city a center of Enlightenment and reform. In the new communities of the Sierra Morena, which were soon thriving, monasteries and "idle" clergy were not to be allowed, nor were restrictions on the sale of land.

This was an extensive reform program, but the reforms were not always successful; the single tax project, for example, proved unworkable. In general, reform failed because conservative forces were still entrenched and powerful. This became clear in 1776–1778, when Olavide was arrested and condemned by the Inquisition (with the consent of the very orthodox Charles III) in connection with his reforming efforts in Seville and the new settlements. This episode no doubt contributed to the negative perception of Spain in many other parts of Enlightenment Europe. This perception surfaced in the French *Encyclopédie méthodique* (1783), provoking great anger in Spain and stimulating much latent hostility there to the Enlightenment. Already before the death of Charles III, the limited success of reform meant a growing gulf between the regime and those—often associated with the developing press in Madrid—who sought more radical change.

The accession of Charles III's son, Charles IV (reigned 1788–1808) and the outbreak of the French Revolution dealt further blows to the reform movement, prompting the dismissal of a number of reformers and a tightening of the laws on censorship and subversion. However, the enormous cost of war against Revolutionary France (1793–1795) and then, in alliance with France, against England (from 1796) obliged the government at last to introduce some of the more radical changes urged by reformers of the preceding generation, and to seek to raise funds by obliging ecclesiastical and other landowners to release their property for sale (1798–1799). The same reforming ministry looked set to introduce "Jansenist" reforms and to curtail the powers and role of the Inquisition, but a powerful conservative backlash promptly put an end to this. The overthrow of the Bourbon monarchy by Napoleon (1808) opened up the prospect of a fundamental overhaul of Spain's ancien régime, and with it the realization of the hopes of Spanish enthusiasts of the Enlightenment. In succeeding decades, enlightened values would contribute an important strand in liberal opposition to royal absolutism.

[*See also* Diplomacy; Feijoo, Benito Jeronimo; Portugal; *and* War and Military Theory.]

BIBLIOGRAPHY

Carr, Raymond. *Spain, 1808–1975.* Oxford, 1966. The opening chapters are very useful for the eighteenth-century background.
Defourneaux, Marcelin. *Pablo de Olavide.* Paris, 1959. An invaluable study of one reformer and his activity.
Herr, Richard. *The Eighteenth-Century Revolution in Spain.* Princeton, N.J., 1958. Now rather old, this remains the key English-language study of reform in Spain.
Herr, Richard. *Rural Change and Royal Finances in Spain at the End of the Old Regime.* Berkeley, Calif., and London, 1989. A massive, excellent, detailed study of the land reforms of the 1790s.
Kamen, Henry. *The War of Succession in Spain, 1700–15.* London, 1969. A useful account of this crucial first phase of eighteenth-century reform.
Kamen, Henry. *Spain in the Later Seventeenth Century.* London, 1983. Chapter 12, "Towards a Spirit of Criticism," identifies the late seventeenth-century antecedents of Enlightenment and reforming attitudes after 1700.
Lynch, John. *Bourbon Spain, 1700–1808.* London, 1989. A good general account.
Mestre Sanchis, Antonio. *La ilustración española.* Madrid, 1998. A good, brief, up-to-date survey by a master of the subject.
Noel, Charles. "Charles III of Spain." In *Enlightened Absolutism: Reform and Reformers in Later Eighteenth-Century Europe,* edited by Hamish Scott, pp. 119–143. London, 1990. An invaluable, concise, up-to-date survey.
Ringrose, David. *Transportation and Economic Stagnation in Spain, 1750–1850.* Durham, N.C., 1970. A good specific study, and broader than the title suggests.
Rodriguez, Laura. "The Spanish Riots of 1766." *Past and Present* 59 (1973), 117–146. A very good modern study of this crucial episode.
Sanchez-Blanco Parody, Francisco. *Europa y el pensamiento español del siglo XVIII.* Madrid, 1991.
Sarrailh, J. *L'Espagne éclairée de la seconde moitié du XVIIIe siècle.* Paris, 1954. A modern classic.
Shafer, Robert. *The Economic Societies in the Spanish World (1763–1821).* Syracuse, N.Y., 1958. A good study of one important aspect.
Spell, Jefferson Rea. *Rousseau in the Spanish World before 1833: A Study in Franco-Spanish Literary Relations.* New York, 1969. Interesting study of one aspect of Spanish relations with one key Enlightenment figure.

CHRISTOPHER STORRS

SPALDING, JOHANN JOACHIM (1714–1804), leading theologian of the Enlightenment in Germany.

The son of a Lutheran pastor of Scottish descent, Spalding completed his philosophical and theological studies in Rostock and Greifswald. Then having served as a private tutor, he became a pastor in Lassahn (1749) and a provost in Barth West Pomerania (1759). He became widely known through his *Betrachtungen über die Bestimmung des Menschen* (Reflections on the Destination of Man, 1748). This basic book on the philosophy of religion of the German Enlightenment was expanded several times and by 1793 had been published in at least thirteen editions. There were translations into several languages, including a French translation by no less a personage than the queen of Prussia. The work documents not only the end of confessional orthodoxy, but also a turning away from Christian Wolff's system on the one hand and from rigid pietism on the other. In their place appears an analysis of the self-experience of man and his emotions *(Empfindungen)* through the stages of sensuality, of mind, of virtue, of religion, and of immortality. Spalding thus contradicted French materialism, especially Julien Offroy de La Mettrie (*L'homme-machine*, 1748), and adopted, with a Leibnizian background, the anthropology of the English Enlightenment, for example, the doctrine on virtue of Shaftesbury and Francis Hutcheson.

Spalding's criticism of a formalistic pietism did not preclude him from cultivating the emotional aspects of the Christian faith, as is evidenced by numerous published sermons and by his *Gedanken über den Werth der Gefühle im Christentum* (Thoughts about the Value of Feelings in Christianity, 1761). Spalding effected far-reaching changes in church policy and liturgical practice after he became provost and member of the Prussian church board in Berlin in 1764. In his book *Über die Nutzbarkeit des Predigtamtes und deren Beförderung* (On the Utility of the Office of a Preacher and Ways to Improve It, 1772) he justified an up-to-date role for the public preacher as teacher of devotion and of morals. He was successful in popularizing Enlightenment theology, which was at first disapprovingly dubbed "Neology." Indeed, Spalding was rebuked for having religious deficits by Johann

Gottfried Herder and Gotthold Ephraim Lessing (the Voltairian spirits in Berlin were contemptuous of him); and the introduction of a new hymn book (1780–1783) evoked opposition in the parishes. But Johann Gleim, Moses Mendelssohn, Immanuel Kant, with whom he corresponded, and many others valued Spalding as a personification of the convergence of honest Christianity and thoughtful Enlightenment. This image was confirmed by his strength of character: Spalding responded to Wöllner's Religious Edict (1788) by resigning as provost. A summary of Spalding's "reasonable Christianity" can be found in *Religion, eine Angelegenheit des Menschen* (Religion, a Matter of Man, 1797).

[*See also* Aufklärung *and* Revealed Religion.]

BIBLIOGRAPHY

Bourel, Dominique. *La Vie de Johann Joachim Spalding: Problèmes de la théologie allemane au XVIIIᵉ siècle*. Paris, 1980. The best account written from the perspective of intellectual and theological history.

Hinske, Norbert, ed. *Die Bestimmung des Menschen*. Aufklärung 11.1. Hamburg, 1999. The tenth (?) edition (1768) of Spalding's work, along with a presentation of ways in which the philosophical and literary topic of the "destination of man" has been treated since Spalding (by Goethe, Fichte, etc.).

Schollmeier, Joseph. *Johann Joachim Spalding, Ein Beitrag zur Theologie der Aufklärung*. Gütersloh, Germany, 1967. Comprehensive biography with extensive bibliography.

WALTER SPARN

SPALLANZANI, LAZZARO (1729–1799), Italian biologist.

Spallanzani conducted research into a vast array of subjects—from chemistry to mineralogy, from vulcanology to physics—but concentrated his interest principally on biology. Neutral at first about the opposing theories of epigenesis and preformation, Spallanzani passed from a generic preference for the first to cautious support for the second. He confuted the thesis of Buffon and John Needham in his first work, *Saggio di osservazioni microscopiche* (Essay on Microscopic Observation, 1765). Also in 1765, he began to correspond with the naturalist Charles Bonnet, and shifted the focus of his own interest to phenomena of animal regeneration. After several years of experimentation, Spallanzani published *Prodromo di un opera da imprimersi sopra le riproduzioni animali* (Precursor of a Work to be Published Concerning Animal Reproduction). This little work enjoyed great success and earned Spallanzani an invitation in 1769 to take up the chair of natural history at the prestigious University of Pavia.

In the 1770s, Spallanzani published protocols on phenomena of circulation (1773), and with his *Opusculi di fisica animale e vegetabile* (Short Works on the Nature of Animals and Vegetables, 1776) he launched a definitive onslaught on the theory of spontaneous generation. His *Dissertazioni di fisica animale e vegetabile* (Dissertations on the Nature of Animals and Vegetables, 1780) contained the results of experiments on the important role of the gastric juices in digestion, on the generation of the higher animals, and on artificial insemination, which he was the first to attempt successfully.

In 1785, he undertook a voyage to Constantinople, during which he carried out geological and mineralogical research, studied marine fauna, and gathered precious specimens. He dedicated the last years of his life to the study of the nonvisual flight of bats, chemical research, experiments on respiration, and phenomena of gaseous exchange at the level of the parenchyma.

[*See also* Life Sciences *and* Natural Philosophy and Science.]

BIBLIOGRAPHY

Bernardi, Walter. *Le metafisiche dell'embrione: Scienze della vita e filosofia da Malpighi a Spallanzani (1672–1793)*. Florence, 1986. This work proposes a new reading of the history of embryological theory in light of two new interpretive categories, "strong visibility" and "weak visibility." Parts 5 and 6 deal with Spallanzani.

Bernardi, Walter, and Paola Manzini, eds. *Il cerchio della vita: Materiali di ricerca del Centro Studi Lazzaro Spallanzani di Scandiano sulla storia della scienza nel Settecento*. Florence, 1999.

Bernardi, Walter, and Marta Stefani, eds. *La sfida della modernità: Atti del convegno internazionale di studi nel bicentenario della morte di Lazzaro Spallanzani*. Florence, 2000.

Montalenti, Giuseppe, and Paolo Rossi, eds. *Lazzaro Spallanzani e la biologia del Settecento: Teorie, esperimenti, istituzioni scientifiche. Atti del convegno di studi. Reggio Emilia, Modena, Scandiano, Pavia, 23–27 marzo 1981*. Florence, 1982.

MARIA TERESA MONTI

Translated from Italian by William McCuaig

SPECTACLES.

One defining feature of the ancien régime was its reliance on spectacle as an organizing principle of public life. Spectacles were ubiquitous and all-purpose, especially in Catholic countries ruled by monarchs. They took myriad forms—processions, entries, fireworks, funerals, coronations, executions, and more—and they routinely filled the public spaces of cities and towns. Royal ceremony was not limited to the court, and religious rituals took place as much outdoors, in streets and plazas, as within the confines of churches and cloisters. Almost every institution, from religious orders and guilds to city governments and even some masonic lodges, had a ceremonial face which it regularly presented to the public. In the "society of orders," where honor and prestige counted heavily, it was largely through ceremony and spectacle that ruling bodies, corporations, institutions, and some prominent individuals promoted and affirmed their appropriate rank in the hierarchy of power.

View of Philosophes. As an integral part of the culture of the ancien régime, festive and ceremonial life attracted the critical attention of the philosophes. The

Encyclopédie, for example, contains twenty-three articles with *fête* in the entry title, and many others also deal with the subject. Most are critical of contemporary festive forms, especially when compared to their antique or rustic counterparts. The authors' critiques fall largely into three categories. Some contributors blamed excessive celebration for promoting economic languor and sanctioning idleness, a complaint echoed by Montesquieu in *L'esprit des lois* (Spirit of the Laws, 1748), or they condemned the profligacy and waste engendered by such extravagant displays as royal fireworks or general processions. Others ridiculed local or traditional rites for perpetuating superstition and creating disorder; this critique derived from the larger objection, raised repeatedly by other philosophes, that popular customs only contributed to the people's benighted enthrallment. Finally, a more profound critique found contemporary festive forms fundamentally lacking in the ability to edify the people. Unlike the public games in ancient Greece, contributors argued, the abounding present-day celebrations merely amused and distracted; they failed to instill in people a moral or civic sense and did not even strive to instruct in the virtues necessary for a healthy political and social order.

The last critique was voiced most strenuously by Jean-Jacques Rousseau, who perhaps more than any other philosophe took the subject of festive life as his particular concern. His disapproval of modern spectacles was only an instance of his more general disapproval of most aspects of modern life; but though his alternative vision was characteristically idyllic, it did convey an appreciation for the value of festive participation in fostering social solidarity. "Plant a stake crowned with flowers in the middle of a square; gather the people together, and you will have a festival," he wrote in a famous passage in the *Lettre à d'Alembert sur les spectacles* (Letter to Monsieur d'Alembert, 1758). "Do better yet: let the spectators become an entertainment to themselves; make them actors themselves; do it so that each sees and loves himself so that all will be better united." Rousseau's letter was provoked by d'Alembert's criticism of Geneva for refusing to host a theater. In taking up his native city's defense, however, he was not insisting on the legitimacy of the Calvinist prohibition against staged drama; Rousseau's point, rather, was to contrast what he viewed as the decadent and frivolous entertainments of the theater, which the Genevans were fortunate to be spared, with the virtuous simple pastimes they already enjoyed.

Despite Rousseau's great popularity in the decades before the Revolution, there is not much evidence that his views had any impact on festive life, except in one significant case: the *Rosières* movement began in the late 1760s. A *fête de la rose* had long been staged in the village of Salency, near Noyon in Picardy; it

was a Maytime festival in which a young, unmarried girl was designated as the *rosière*, or queen of virtue, and then feted by the villagers with a procession, a church service, and other rustic celebrations. In 1766, the festival was discovered and publicized by an aristocratic woman of letters, whose efforts subsequently spawned imitations throughout northern France. Although these were patronized mainly by aristocratic landlords, they also were clearly inspired by Rousseauist sentiments regarding the morally edifying properties of rustic festivals in celebration of simple virtues. A Norman village, Canon, attempted to improve on the *rosière* model with a "festival of the good people," which chose not only a "good girl," but also a "good mother," a "good old man," and a "good householder."

For the most part, however, festive life in the eighteenth century remained traditional, exhibiting little in the way of innovation, and certainly precious little inspired by the Enlightenment. It was generally not the character of the Enlightenment to manifest itself through spectacles on the public stage, except for one notable exception that celebrated the very personification of the Enlightenment. In March 1778, just months before his death, Voltaire was lavishly honored—first at the Académie Française and then at the Comédie Française—with demonstrations of affection that amounted to a public apotheosis of the great philosophe. These spectacles were unprecedented; no other individual outside the royal family had been accorded such ceremonial attention, let alone great encomiastic outbursts and popular acclaim. For Voltaire, who had once been publicly caned in the streets of Paris, twice imprisoned in the Bastille, and forced to flee his homeland, it was indeed a moment of personal triumph. It symbolized the triumph of the Enlightenment, as well.

There were other novel additions to the repertoire of spectacles in the eighteenth century that can be linked to the Enlightenment. One was the public displays mounted by many masonic lodges. The Freemasonry movement, despite its often bizarre rituals, cultivated a sensibility that was akin to the Enlightenment, and, despite its occult customs, it sometimes exhibited a public ceremonial presence. In Sweden, Britain, and France, for example, lodges in the second part of the eighteenth century regularly participated in celebrations for the monarchy. Although there was nothing "enlightened" about the nature of their ceremonial contributions—indeed, they were virtually indistinguishable from those of more traditional groups—the public was reminded of the existence and prominence of these new institutions that espoused the ideals of brotherhood and equality.

Another novel eighteenth-century spectacle also suggests a certain kinship with the Enlightenment: the hot-air balloon launchings by the Montgolfier brothers and their

Balloon. Balloon flight of Jacques Charles and Nicholas Robert, Paris, 1783. Anonymous watercolor.
(Prints and Photographs Division, Library of Congress.)

imitators in the 1780s. These great technical feats by their very occurrence celebrated the utilitarian and scientific spirit dear to many philosophes. Moreover, the festivities these spectacles occasioned represented a departure in the style and decorum of public gatherings. Simon Schama has written of the launching at Versailles in 1783:

The ascent . . . was itself a major beach of court protocol . . . No serious attempt was made to restrain numbers or to order them in the neat, ordained spaces generally required by old regime regulations. . . . Instead of being an object of privileged vision—the speciality of Versailles—the balloon was necessarily the visual property of everyone in the crowd. On the ground it was still, to some extent, an aristocratic spectacle; in the air it became democratic.

(Schama, 1989, 124.)

An Enlightened Spirit. This illustrates what was perhaps the most pervasive effect of the new sensibility on the nature of spectacle and ceremony in the eighteenth century. Although the Enlightenment may not have promoted specific forms of spectacle, an enlightened spirit seemed to alter people's tastes with regard to festive life. One might ascribe this change to Rousseau, insofar as it generally conformed to his preference for celebrations marked by simplicity, informality, spontaneity, and participation, but the shift was more widespread than even his considerable influence. In short, ceremonial rigidity and exclusion were giving way to a more relaxed and inclusive style of public entertainment and display. In some respects, this trend went so far as to foster a breakdown of the barriers between popular and elite cultural spheres: in Paris, for example, the upper and lower classes took to mingling in such venues as marketplace theaters, street fairs, the Waux Hall, and the carnivalesque milieu of the Palais Royal. For the most part, however, the new spirit manifested itself in more discreet gatherings of a mixed yet still generally upper-class public in entertainments and pastimes marked by civility and good taste rather than by an aristocratic concern for rank, privilege, and form. In English provincial towns like York and Bath, this development took the form of so-called assemblies, or assembly rooms—establishments that offered the gentry, both local and visiting, a space for congregating and socializing, dancing and dining. By 1770, more than seventy English towns and spas had assembly rooms.

These indoor venues had outdoor counterparts. Eighteenth-century cities underwent a major clearing out process which resulted in significantly expanded public spaces. Although these changes were prompted by a mix of interests—among them, economic development and a need to create an adequate stage for large-scale monarchical displays—they also were meant to provide suitable venues for polite gatherings of the cultivated upper classes. From Saint Petersburg to Washington, eighteenth-century cities and towns were newly graced with gardens, parades, circuses, malls, and squares intended to appeal not to the crowd but to people of refinement and civility. Thus, as Baudelaire and Walter Benjamin would later observe for the modern urban experience, the true spectacle of city life in the eighteenth century was not so much its still impressive political and religious displays: it was already the concourse of its people.

In all of this, there was an emphasis on taste and civility as hallmarks of public display, or at least as ideals. Thus, the circuses of Bath or the Champs-Élysées in Paris were known as venues where a standard of comportment prevailed that appealed particularly to people of fashion. The same sort of people seemed to be altering the style of their religious devotions as well. For example, certain aspects of so-called Baroque piety—a tendency toward ostentatious and emotive ritual characteristic of post-Tridentine Catholicism—were on the wane. One indication of this trend was evident in burial and mourning rites, in which some people were turning away from extravagant funerals and masses for the dead in favor of simpler and more private devotions. Another was a general decline in the popularity of religious processions.

This shift in sensibility reached even the realm of royal ceremony. Starting with Louis XV, the ceremony of the Royal Touch, in which French kings traditionally bestowed a curative touch for the disease of scrofula, was accompanied not with the customary phrase, "God heals thee" but rather "May God heal thee." What in previous times had been commanded by the king by virtue of his mystical properties was now merely requested. As for the ritual itself, it had been mocked by Montesquieu in *Lettres persanes* (The Persian Letters, 1721), and by Voltaire, who proclaimed: "The time will come when reason, which is already beginning to make some headway in France, will abolish this custom." These examples suggest nothing so radical as a waning of faith or a rise in secularism, but they evidence a more subtle move, in keeping with the spirit of the Enlightenment, toward simpler, less mystical, more "tasteful" styles of piety.

The Enlightenment was primarily a movement of thought, and it viewed spectacles—like other aspects of society and culture—critically, in need of reform. Considered in a wider sense, however, as a sensibility that merged with other acculturating trends, the Enlightenment also worked to detach people from some of their traditional festive ways, fostering more refined, less constrained patterns of public life.

[*See also* Freemasonry.]

BIBLIOGRAPHY

Bloch, Marc. *The Royal Touch: Monarchy and Miracles in France and England.* Translated by J. E. Anderson. New York, 1960. Translation of *Les rois thaumaturges: Étude sur le caractère attribué à la puissance royale particlièrement en France et en Angleterre* (1924), the indispensable source on the origins and history of this royal ritual.

Borsay, Peter. *The English Urban Renaissance: Culture and Society in the Provincial Town, 1660–1770.* Oxford, 1989. A good guide to the multiple transformations of English provincial towns, with special attention to the changing nature of entertainments and sociability.

Ehrard, Jean. "Les lumières et la Fête." In *Annales historiques de la révolution française* 87 (1975), 356–374.

Everdell, William. "The *Rosières* Movement, 1766–1789: A Clerical Precursor of the Revolutionary Cults." *French Historical Studies* 9 (1975), 23–36.

Isherwood, Robert. *Farce and Fantasy: Popular Entertainment in Eighteenth-Century Paris.* New York, 1986. An interesting interpretation of festive life, which challenges the thesis regarding a split between popular and elite cultures.

Leith, J. A. "Les trois apothéosis de Voltaire." *Annales historiques de la révolution française* 51 (April–June, 1979), 161–209.

Maza, Sarah. *Private Lives and Public Affairs: The Causes Célèbres of Prerevolutionary France.* Berkeley, 1993. An important work that contains a chapter on the *rosière* festival.

Ozouf, Mona. *Festivals and the French Revolution.* Translated by Alan Sheridan. Cambridge, Mass., 1988. Translation of *La fête révolutionnaire, 1789–1799* (1976), an analysis of the revolutionary festivals which sees them as attempting to replace the sacrality of the monarchy in the new political culture.

Rousseau, Jean-Jacques. *Politics and the Arts: Letter to M. d'Alembert on the Theatre.* Translated by Allan Bloom. Ithaca, N.Y., 1968. Translation of *Lettre à M. D'Alembert sur le théâtre* (1758).

Schama, Simon. *Citizens: A Chronicle of the French Revolution.* New York, 1989.

Schneider, Robert A. *The Ceremonial City: Toulouse Observed, 1738–1780.* Princeton, N.J., 1995. A look at the public and festive life of a provincial city through the eyes of a local diarist, with special emphasis on the competing ceremonial forms, religious and political, that marked the period.

Vovelle, Michel. *Piété baroque et déchristianisation en Provence au XVIIIe siècle.* Paris, 1974. A pioneering study in the field of *mentalités*, which suggests a decline in demonstrative expressions of piety in the latter part of the eighteenth century.

ROBERT A. SCHNEIDER

SPINOZA, BARUCH DE

SPINOZA, BARUCH DE (also Benedictus Spinoza or d'Espinosa; 1632–1677), Dutch philosopher.

Spinoza was born in Amsterdam. After being raised in the Jewish tradition, he was solemnly expelled from the synagogue in 1656. He then sold his share in the family firm and lived successively in Amsterdam, Rijnsburg (near Leiden), Voorburg (near The Hague), and The Hague. The only works published during his lifetime were a "geometrical" version of the first two books of René Descartes's *Principia* (1663)—with an appendix on metaphysical problems (*Cogitata metaphysica*)—and the *Tractatus theologico-politicus* (1670). His main work, *Ethica*, as well as the unfinished *Tractatus de intellectus emendatione* and *Tractatus politicus*, was published after his death along with his correspondence (*B. D. S. Opera posthuma*, 1677). Two manuscript copies of a Dutch translation of an early work, known as "Short Treatise on God, Man and Happiness" (*Korte verhandeling van God, de Mensch en deszelvs Welstand*), resurfaced in the nineteenth century. Until the end of the eighteenth century, Spinoza was generally seen as an atheist, but later this interpretation gave way to a "religious" one. In fact, he is best seen as an early representative of the Enlightenment.

Philosophy and Piety. According to its full title, the *Tractatus theologico-politicus* (*TTP*) contains "several dissertations" showing that, in a republic, the "freedom to

Baruch de Spinoza. Portrait by Ernst Hader. Carte de visite (Berlin, 1884). (Prints and Photographs Division, Library of Congress.)

philosophize" (*libertas philosophandi*) not only can be conceded without damage to peace or piety, but also that it cannot be prohibited without making those conditions impossible. This strongly indicates the way in which Spinoza believed knowledge of truth—his own philosophy—to be practically—that is, morally, politically, and religiously—relevant. As far as peace is concerned, rational discourse helps us to overcome emotional and political antagonisms; moreover, knowing the truth about human behavior makes clear what political institutions are necessary.

The connection with piety is less clear, if only because Spinoza's philosophy was generally seen as atheistic. However, in the seventeenth century *pietas* ("holiness") denoted habitual behavior based on the strict observance of God's revealed will, whereas atheism (or impiety) would be whatever implies or presupposes the denial of that will. Accordingly, Spinoza's point would be to show that, in spite of his denial of the existence of a divine legislative will, his philosophy is not "impious" but instead forms the basis of habitual moral behavior. This is a useful key to Spinoza's philosophy as a whole. In the *Ethics*, Spinoza defines "God" as an "absolutely infinite" and "infinitely perfect" being; however, the meanings of "reality," "being," and "perfection" are identical. To say that God is absolutely infinite or infinitely perfect is to say that God is absolute being; and this, according to Spinoza, implies that all being is part of God's reality: "Whatever is is in God; without God nothing can be or be conceived to be" (*Ethics*, i, pr. 15). This means that, in their own limited way, "things"—actually "modes" of God's being—are also "perfect"; that is, things have all the reality they can have. As a result, the religious idea that obedience to God could make a being more perfect is absurd. "God's will" is a causal and intelligible law that is universally necessary and also absolutely inescapable. The image of a God-Lawgiver whose will could be disobeyed is contrary to the idea that God is absolutely perfect. God's being coincides with the power by which he exists and "creates" whatever can be conceived. However, if God's being is power, the being of "things" is also power, albeit finite power, limited as it is either by their own internal constitution or by the power of other things. Accordingly, on the level of finite natural things (particularly human beings), there is always competition and strife.

This system has obvious consequences for ethics (the quest for happiness), morality (behavior toward others), and politics (the institutions we need to live peacefully together). The fundamental law of human behavior, deriving from the idea that all being is power, is that everyone necessarily does what he believes to be in his own interest. But since people may be mistaken about their interest, they may do what is actually against it. This is especially the case if they are governed by "passions"—that is, emotions ("affects") that involve passivity and dependence, such as sadness, hope, fear, and hatred. Such passions can be good only in relation to an end. Moreover, only insofar as people have passions can they be opposed to one another. By contrast, insofar as people live "under the guidance of reason"—either because they understand that their individual happiness depends on peace, or because they are governed by a rational system of laws—can they overcome the antagonisms of the state of nature.

God and Religion. Spinoza's political doctrine is based on the idea that, given the fact that God cannot be conceived as a lawgiver, all authority is of human origin. The only source of authority, therefore, and the only person or persons we can be obliged to obey, is the sovereign. However, authority is not a static property like physical power; it can be exercised only if others respect it. As a result, the will of a sovereign is never absolute, being by definition limited by the will of the people—except, of course, where the people constitute the sovereign, as in a democracy.

The role of revealed religion is crucial for two reasons. First, for many people it functions as an independent source of obligations, so there can be a conflict between the perceived will of God and the will of the sovereign. Second, it is based on a type of imagination (prophecy) that is incontestable, and so religious convictions are beliefs dogmatically held. As long as the alleged will of God agrees with the will of the sovereign, revealed religion is helpful in establishing peace. This is especially the case if religion is based on devotion, a form of love that—at least ideally—makes it possible to distinguish "true" religion from superstition based on hope and fear. True devotion would allow the people to behave as they should not because they fear the sovereign, but because they love God. If, however, there is even the smallest difference between God's alleged will and the will of the sovereign, revealed religion undermines the latter's authority, and therefore the peace.

The perfect solution would be to make God sovereign and so create a perfect identity between the law of a country and God's revealed will. From that point of view, the theocratic model of the old Testament, where the law was the will of God and God the king of Israel, was perfect. That model is also perfectly democratic because it subordinates everyone to the same impersonal law. The condition, however, is not only that all members of the nation firmly believe that God is king, but also that there is no disagreement about the interpretation of God's will. The law, therefore, must be simple, and God must be a national god. Moreover, the law must be good and just, contributing effectively to safety and peace: Moses was a political genius not only because he convinced his people that their law was divine (that their king was God), but also because his law was good and just. However, the theocratic model no longer works, for four reasons: in an open and commercial society, the belief that laws are divine cannot easily be maintained; the will of the Christian God does not have the form of a law; the Christian God is universal and not national; and insofar as the Christian religion is also a doctrine claimed to be true, it spawns different sects. Unlike Thomas Hobbes, who solved these problems by placing the sovereign at the head of a national Christian church, Spinoza did not believe that there was a political solution. All one can do is, first, to reduce the Christian religion to a single precept of neighborly love that, since it does not have the form of a law, requires a sovereign to become politically meaningful; and second, to show that theology (knowledge of God by means of an interpretation of scripture) is impossible.

Scripture. Even though Spinoza's presentation of this last point is complex, ambivalent, and highly rhetorical, it has earned him the reputation of being a forerunner of modern biblical scholarship (actually, he was preceded by Hobbes). First, using Baconian vocabulary, Spinoza claimed that any "interpretation" (identification of the meaning of a text) should be preceded by a "history" (review of all relevant facts concerning that text). From the history of scripture, he concluded that there can be no interpretation because it was written by many authors who disagreed on important issues, and that its texts are corrupt and its tradition unreliable. All we can say is that its texts seem to be directed to a common goal, virtue or piety, and in that sense scripture is clearly a "pious" text. Since, however, there is no coherent system of ideas about reality that could serve as the "doctrine" of scripture, there can be no other theology than the private thoughts of people reading the Bible piously, in a moral spirit.

This argument indicates that the notion of the authority of scripture is elusive. If authority serves as the counterpart of obedience, scripture has no authority in itself, but only insofar as its precepts are condoned by a sovereign. If "authority" is taken to mean "truth" and "certainty," its use in this connection is inappropriate, because the only way to become convinced of truth is by rational argument. Besides, beliefs cannot be acts of obedience, because, according to Spinoza, the will plays no role in judgment. Traditionally theology is not only interpretation but also, given the authority of its text, true knowledge. Spinoza's argument, however, implies first that knowledge and interpretation have nothing to do with each other; second, that interpretation is impossible; and third, that the notion of authority is inappropriate. As a result, theology is impossible unless we define it as individual moral motivation. In that case, however, its criterion is not truth but moral efficacy. It is in that sense that theology (moral motivation based on the imagination) and philosophy (knowledge of truth and, as a result, of virtue and happiness) are completely separate. This means, finally, that any authority based on the alleged authority of scripture collapses. Neither the church nor the theologians and priests can enjoy any authority other than that granted by the sovereign. In a modern society, however, the best way for a sovereign to keep his authority is not to meddle with the truth of any particular theology at all, but to place himself above all religious differences.

Responses to Spinoza. Spinoza's reputation as an atheist was established immediately. In the Netherlands in particular, his philosophy came under attack from two sides: Orthodox Calvinists, who saw Spinoza as an Antichrist, and Cartesian philosophers, who, afraid of being associated with Spinoza' atheism, argued that Descartes's method could not be applied to moral, political, and religious problems. From the start, however, Spinoza had been surrounded by a group of friends recruited, on the one hand, among liberal Christians and deists (like Jarig Jelles, who financed the printing of Spinoza's *Opera Posthuma*, or the "Collegiant" Jacob Ostens), and on the other, among radical freethinkers like Lodewijk Meyer and Adriaan Koerbagh. The first group were probably attracted by Spinoza's undogmatic view of faith and his rejection of ecclesiastical authority, whereas the second were interested in his rational view of the world. Moreover, before William III seized power in 1672, Spinoza may have found some friends among the political classes, although little is known on this point. It is clear, at any rate, that his view that the sovereign can keep his authority only by placing himself above religious and ideological differences was entirely in line with the republican ideas developed in the age of Jan de Wit.

Before long, however, the image of Spinoza as an atheist came to prevail in the Netherlands as well as abroad. This image was not based on a close reading of the *Ethics*, which in the eighteenth century was reprinted only in a German translation (Frankfurt and Leipzig, 1744, together with a refutation by Christian Wolff), but rather on two or three types of sources—clandestine manuscripts and related printed books, and real or supposed refutations of Spinoza. Among supporters and adversaries there was broad consensus on the contents of Spinoza's system. Julien Offray de La Mettrie, for example, whose views were close to the clandestine tradition, gave the following summary: no substance can be produced by another substance; nothing comes from nothing; there is one substance, which, although eternal and indivisible, is subject to perpetual change without changing as a whole. Moreover, thinking is caused by the movements of the body (not Spinoza's explicit view, in fact), which La Mettrie replaced by his own view that "thinking" is a modification of the sensitive principle (which, as he claimed elsewhere, is material). Finally, one of the implications of the Spinozist system would be that there is no natural moral law, and that our "natural principles are nothing but our habitual principles," or, in La Mettrie's words, that man is nothing but a machine, albeit a machine that can be taught.

This broad view of Spinoza made it possible to associate "Spinozism" with various other ideas; indeed, its vagueness on all things except human freedom turned it into a flexible carrier of all strains of naturalism. Two ideas are often associated with Spinozism: first, that the history of Spinozism is older than Spinoza himself; and second, that revealed religion is a politically motivated mystification. The first claim became influential in the version of Pierre Bayle, who, associating Spinoza with the doctrine of the world soul, saw forerunners in David of Dinant, Strato, Peter Abelard, the Stoics, certain Chinese sects, and so on. The idea was embraced with some enthusiasm by "Spinozists," if only because it provided them with an impressive ancestry. Thus, in his *Histoire critique de la philosophie* (Amsterdam, 1737), Andre-François Boureau-Deslandes managed to present Spinozism as the ordinary view of most philosophers of sound mind. The second claim found its most influential expression in the anonymous "Traité des trois imposteurs," earlier versions of which carried the name of Spinoza ("La vie et l'esprit de Spinoza"). In this text, Moses, Jesus, and Muhammad are pictured as popular leaders who used religion as a means to obtain authority and establish a system of positive laws.

By the end of the eighteenth century, the atheist interpretation of Spinoza gave way to a religious interpretation that relies heavily on part V of the *Ethics*. The notion developed in this part is that of the "intellectual love of God" as the fruit of "intuitive knowledge." In this way, Spinoza tried to solve the paradox that, on the one hand, an affect (passion, emotion) can be effaced only by another affect that is stronger, whereas, on the other hand, he believed that by developing reason we make more rational choices. On the basis of Spinoza's theory of action, the development of reason could have that effect only if it is allied with an emotion so active and strong that it can efface the evil passions. In the *Short Treatise*, Spinoza solved this problem by giving love precedence over knowledge of good and evil, which in itself is powerless as a motive for action. The problem created by the *Ethics* and the *TTP* is that an emotion has a particular object (known or imagined), whereas scientific knowledge is general and so does not seem suitable to be linked to love. By claiming that there is a form of true knowledge that is not only intuitive—that is, has a particular object—but is also based on scientific knowledge, Spinoza made it possible to speak of an "intellectual love" of God (that is, Nature), sufficient to overcome all evil. Although it is easy to confound those ideas with religious notions as they were developed in the context of German Idealism, especially by G. W. F. Hegel and F. E. D. Schleiermacher, this is probably an anachronistic projection.

[*See also* Bayle, Pierre; Bible; Cartesianism; La Mettrie, Julien Offray de; *and* Netherlands.]

BIBLIOGRAPHY

WORKS BY SPINOZA

Opera. Edited by Carl Gebhardt. 4 vols. Heidelberg, 1925; repr., 1972. Standard edition of the works.
The Collected Works of Spinoza. Translated by Edwin Curley. 2 vols. Princeton, N.J., 1988. Good English translation (with glossary and indices) of Spinoza's works.
The Political Works. Translated by A. G. Wernham. Oxford, 1958; repr., 1965.
Tractatus theologico-politicus/Traité théologico-politique. Edited by Pierre-François Moreau and Fokke Akkerman. Paris, 1999. Vol. 3 of a new edition of the works; other volumes forthcoming.
Korte verhandeling van God, de mensch en deszelvs welstand/Breve trattato su Dio, l'uomo e il suo bene. Edited by Filippo Mignini. Aquila, Italy, 1986. New edition of the Korte Verhandeling (Short

treatise), an early work of Spinoza, which survives only in a Dutch translation.

WORKS ABOUT SPINOZA

Bayle, Pierre. *Écrits sur Spinoza.* Edited by Françoise Charles-Daubert and Pierre-François Moreau. Paris, 1983. Collection of articles, short pieces, etc., of an influential eighteenth-century commentator.
Bell, David. *Spinoza in Germany from 1670 to the Age of Goethe.* London, 1984. On the German reception of Spinoza.
Berti, Silvia, Françoise Charles-Daubert, and Richard H. Popkin, eds. *Heterodoxy, Spinozism, and Free Thought in Early-Eighteenth-Century Europe: Studies on the Traité des trois imposteurs.* Dordrecht, Neth., 1996. Spinoza's influence on the clandestine manuscript tradition.
Bloch, Olivier R., ed. *Spinoza au XVIIIᵉ siècle.* Paris, 1990. Collection of articles on Spinoza's influence in the eighteenth century.
Curley, Edwin. *Spinoza's Metaphysics.* Cambridge, Mass., 1969. Good introduction to Spinoza's general philosophical position.
Ehrard, Jean. *L'idée de nature en France dans la première moitié du XVIIIᵉ siècle.* Paris, 1963; repr., 1981. Together with Vernière (see below) the best introduction to Spinoza reception in France.
Fix, Andrew. *Prophecy and Reason.* Princeton, N.J., 1991. On the Dutch context of Spinoza, concentrating on the "Collegiants" (a Protestant sect).
Gueroult, Martial. *Spinoza.* 2 vols. Hildesheim, 1969–1974. Thorough general commentary on the first two parts of the *Ethics*.
Israel, Jonathan I. *Radical Enlightenment.* Oxford, 2001. Good general description of Spinoza's ideas, interpreting him as a figure of the radical Enlightenment; much on Spinoza's influence in the early eighteenth century.
Kolakowski, Leszek. *Chrétiens sans Église.* Translated by Anna Posner. Paris, 1969; new ed., 1987. Detailed history of Protestant, nonconfessional, sects, providing some background to Spinoza's philosophy.
Matheron, Alexandre. *Individu et communauté chez Spinoza.* Paris, 1969; repr., 1988. Thorough commentary of Parts III–IV of the *Ethics* and of *The Political works*.
Meinsma, K. *Spinoza en zijn kring.* The Hague, 1896. On Spinoza's circle of friends (reprinted in 1980; German translation 1909; French translation 1983).
Verbeek, Theo. *Spinoza's Theologico-political Treatise: Exploring "The Will of God."* London, 2002. Commentary on the *TTP*, interpretation of Spinoza as an enlightened figure.
Vernière, Paul. *Spinoza et la pensée française avant la Révolution.* 2 vols. Paris, 1954; repr., 1982.

THEO VERBEEK

SPINOZISM. *See* Pantheism *and* Spinoza, Baruch de.

SPONTANEOUS GENERATION. Spontaneous generation is the belief that living organisms can form from nonliving matter. In the eighteenth century, the term used was *equivocal generation*, meaning that the process was accidental and random. Most naturalists rejected equivocal generation, believing instead that organisms originate in regular, nonaccidental ways. Most also believed that all generation proceeds from preexistent germs fashioned by God at the Creation and encased one within the other until their appointed times of development. The problem with equivocal generation was that it implied the generation of life by chance, which might mean that there was no need for God and that the Earth and all its inhabitants could have arisen from the random interactions of matter.

In the 1680s, spontaneous generation at the macroscopic level was challenged by the experiments of Francesco Redi and Jan Swammerdam. Redi showed that meat covered with a net does not become covered with maggots, as meat open to the air does. He concluded that the maggots came from eggs deposited by flies, rather than spontaneously generating from the decaying meat. Swammerdam showed that gall flies come from eggs inserted into a plant by an insect, not from plant matter itself. Swammerdam was also an early proponent of the preexistence of germs, and the promotion of spontaneous generation declined as support for preexistence grew.

Spontaneous generation reemerged in the late 1740s and the 1750s, with the work of Georges-Louis Leclerc de Buffon and John Turberville Needham. Each presented a theory of generation based on epigenetic, or gradual, development; each also incorporated spontaneous generation at the microscopic level, although in somewhat different ways. Buffon believed that all organisms are formed from "organic particles" (*molécules organiques*) that are organized into particular living forms by "internal molds" (*moules intérieurs*); his organic particles, being active, also formed spontaneously into microscopic organisms whenever they were freed from organized living beings, for example, in seminal fluid or in rotting organic matter.

Needham's theory was also based on a belief that matter's activity is observable at the microscopic level. He argued that the succession of microscopic organisms that appear in infusions of organic matter demonstrates the existence of a vegetative force in all organic matter. Needham objected whenever he was accused of supporting equivocal generation, arguing that the microorganisms he observed always appeared in the same lawful succession and not by chance.

Needham's experimental work and observations were challenged by Lazzaro Spallanzani, who claimed that his own observations showed all microscopic organisms to arise from eggs deposited from the air into infusions. Although modern scientists and some historians have hailed Spallanzani as disproving spontaneous generation, the issue had not been resolved in their day. Those who believed in the preexistence of germs thought that Spallanzani's work was convincing; those who believed in active matter and leaned toward materialism were convinced by Needham. Support for spontaneous generation continued into the late eighteenth century and the early

nineteenth. Jean-Baptiste Lamarck, after converting to evolution in the 1790s, made the spontaneous generation of simple organisms the foundation of his theory of transmutation. Belief in spontaneous generation also flourished in early nineteenth-century Germany, where *Naturphilosophie*, with its developmental view of the world's history, incorporated both spontaneous generation and epigenesis. Nonetheless, the issues that underlay eighteenth-century controversies over spontaneous generation—whether matter is active or passive, and whether the world was preordained by God or is the product of chance—were no longer those that preoccupied proponents and opponents in the nineteenth century.

[*See also* Buffon, Georges-Louis Leclerc de; Life Sciences; Materialism; Natural Philosophy and Science; Needham, John Turberville; *and* Spallanzani, Lazzaro.]

BIBLIOGRAPHY

Farley, John. *The Spontaneous Generation Controversy from Descartes to Oparin*. Baltimore, 1977. Comprehensive treatment from the seventeenth to the twentieth century.

Montalenti, G., and P. Rossi, eds. *Lazzaro Spallanzani e la Biologia del Settecento: Teorie, Esperimenti, Istituzioni*. Florence, 1982. See articles by Giuliano Pancaldi, Shirley A. Roe, and Richard Toellner.

Pancaldi, Giuliano. *La Generazione Spontaneo nelle prime Richerche dello Spallanzani*. Quaderni di Storia e Critica della Scienza, 1. Pisa, 1972.

Roe, Shirley A. "Buffon and Needham: Diverging Views on Life and Matter." In *Buffon 88*, edited by Jean Gayon, pp. 439–450. Paris, 1992.

Roger, Jacques. *Les sciences de la vie dans la pensée française du XVIIIᵉ siècle: La génération des animaux de Descartes à l'Encyclopédie*. Paris, 1963. Translated from French by Robert Ellrich (except for Diderot chapter) as *The Life Sciences in Eighteenth-Century French Thought*, edited by Keith R. Benson. Stamford, Conn., 1997. The standard source on generation during the eighteenth century.

SHIRLEY A. ROE

STAËL, GERMAINE NECKER DE (1766–1817), French intellectual and woman of letters.

Her father was Jacques Necker, a Genevan who became Director of Finances in France in 1777, and attempted to rescue the nation from bankruptcy; faced with royalist opposition, he resigned in 1788. Necker wrote extensively about politics, morals, religion; his daughter worshiped him. Her mother maintained the last great salon of the century, attended by Denis Diderot, Jean Le Rond d'Alembert, Claude-Adrien Helvétius, George-Louis Leclerc de Buffon, and preromantics such as Bernardin de Saint-Pierre. Madame Necker educated Germaine well, teaching her Latin and English, encouraging her to read Jean-Jacques Rousseau, Montesquieu, Voltaire, allowing her to participate in the salon. At age 11, she was already discussing important matters with major figures. Her relations with her mother were strained; she acquired from her an indulgence in emotional excesses. Both parents were deeply committed to religion, and she would always remain a liberal Calvinist, emphasizing the social role of religion.

Marriage posed problems. She had to marry a Protestant, and Protestantism was illegal in France. An international search first produced William Pitt, but she refused to move to England. In 1786 she married the Swede Baron Eric de Staël. It was not a happy marriage; in 1788 she fell in love with Narbonne, a liberal noble. Then came the Revolution. Mme. de Staël at first was enthusiastic. She quickly grasped that the role of literature had changed; it must instruct, contribute to progress. When the Terror began, she fled to England and Switzerland. Meanwhile, her love life also became tumultuous; in 1794 she met Benjamin Constant, who for years would remain her intellectual and amorous partner. Passion for her was always a source of torment, she lived in fear of being abandoned. She returned to Paris in 1795, and reopened her salon. In April 1796, an arrest warrant was issued against her; she had only returned to France in December.

If she at first admired Napoleon, shortly after the 18 Brumaire she and Constant joined the opposition; Napoleon sacrificed individual liberties, he reestablished

Mme de Staël. Portrait by Marie Éléonore Godefroid. (Châteaux de Versailles et de Trianon, Versailles, France/Réunion des Musées Nationaux/Art Resource, NY.)

Catholicism and declared himself emperor. In 1802, Bonaparte fired Constant from his legislative post, and Staël's support of Bonaparte's enemies became active. She became more and more cosmopolitan in her friendships and ideas. Around 1801, she began studying German philosophy; her years of exile would bring her into contact with Italian, German, and English thinkers and writers. She substituted Kantian transcendental ethics for the enlightened self-interest of the eighteenth century; faced with the tragedies of life, enlightened self-interest seemed insufficient. In 1803, Bonaparte exiled her from Paris, an exile that lasted ten years, and in December, with Constant, she left for Germany (Weimar, Berlin), meeting various German intellectuals, such as Goethe, Schiller, and Auguste-Wilhelm Schlegel, who became the major source of her knowledge of German thought. In April 1804, because of her father's death, she returned to Coppet. In December, she went to Italy.

From then until 1812 she lived mostly at Coppet. There she entertained many visitors, later known as the Coppet Group, an impressive assembly of noted minds, including Constant, Sismondi, Barante, Mackintosh, Byron, Mme. de Krüdener, the Schlegels. They lived together, at times slept together, put on plays, translated, above all talked about literature, philosophy, politics, religion. Coppet was a place of serious, seminal reflection.

In 1810, her book *De l'Allemagne* (On Germany) was confiscated by Napoleon's police; the Emperor decreed that it "was not French." In 1812 she fled Coppet, going via Vienna, Moscow, and Saint Petersburg to reach Stockholm and then London where she published *De l'Allemagne*. After Napoleon's abdication, she returned to Paris, where she worked hard to prevent the return of the Bourbons.

Staël began writing at an early age, and in 1785 published a number of short stories and plays. Many are marked by the theme of remorse and the problems of a man in love with two women, one superior, intelligent, a social outcast, and the other sweet, young, acceptable. In her *Lettres sur les écrits de Jean-Jacques Rousseau* (Letters about the Writings of Jean-Jacques Rousseau, 1788), whom she admired fervently, she refused Rousseau's opposition of good nature and evil society. She also practiced what was a constant of her criticism—judge the work, not according to any exterior criteria, but within its own framework.

Her career as literary theoretician began in 1795 with the *Essai sur les fictions* (An Essay on Fiction). The novel was the coming literary form; it should avoid fantasy and allegory and study human beings and their passions: love, ambition, pride, avarice, and so on. The novel combines philosophy and imagination, shows moral truths in action. *De l'influence des passions sur le bonheur des individus et des nations* (Concerning the Influence of the

Passions on the Happiness of Individuals and of Nations, 1796) is primarily an autobiographical meditation. Our dependency on others causes us to suffer; after youth, we lose our illusions, intellectual activity offers consolation. In 1800, she published *De la littérature considérée dans ses rapports avec les institutions* (On Literature, and its Relations with National Institutions). Her definition of literature includes almost everything except the sciences. Faithful to the Enlightenment, she reiterates Condorcet's theses on perfectibility and applies Montesquieu's theories to literature: each society, each period has its kind of literature. She thereby introduces the comparative study of literature and destroys the neoclassical esthetic; there is no one ideal beauty, no model of excellence.

Her most influential work was *De l'Allemagne*. Begun during her travels, it is as much a result of her conversations with eminent Germans as of her readings. Rather than a methodical manual, it shows how Germany enriched her thought about moral, political, esthetic problems; there are many digressions, though the book follows a logical order: society, literature, philosophy, religion. In literature, she wrote, the Germans prefer their own national heritage to the sterile imitation of classical antiquity. They prefer genius to good taste, reject artificial rules. She distinguishes between classical and romantic poetry; the latter must be inspired, mysterious, religious; the poet perceives the divine in nature, meditates on the meaning of life and death. Art does not imitate; it creates. She also demands a renewal of tragedy in France, using historical subjects, imitating Shakespeare and German models rather than the seventeenth century. She uses German philosophy to criticize the empirical tradition of Thomas Hobbes and Paul-Henri Thiry d'Holbach. The greatest German philosopher is Immanuel Kant; she offers résumés of his major works, finding there a justification for religion. Heroic good deeds are the product of virtue, not of reflection. Only religion can make sense of grief and of melancholy. In an important chapter, enthusiasm is defined as "God-in-us" and deemed necessary for poetry and heroism. Meditating on Goethe's *Faust* and on Jean-Paul Richter, she expresses her fear of nothingness, of the void. Napoleon tried to destroy all copies; luckily, four escaped.

Staël felt that literature has a social and moral function that serves as a vehicle of ideas. She innovated in attributing this function to the woman as writer. The author's life is an unhappy one of suffering for the good of humanity. She was fascinated by Tasso and Cassandra, symbols of the author's own fate. *Delphine* (1802), attacks Catholicism, argues for divorce and for English political liberty. Its epistolary form allowed for the psychological examination of the self that the Enlightenment had developed. More centrally, it studies the evil effects of calumny, of

the sufferings that result from a love rendered impossible by social prejudices. Society imposes a conformity that destroys the self. Delphine finally commits suicide; but a male character pursues political action toward progress. Woman remains subordinate. Staël's novels end tragically, whereas her political works end on an optimistic note.

The heroine of *Corinne ou l'Italie* (Corinne, or Italy, 1807) is an inspired poet, highly cultivated, who falls in love with an English lord, who typifies the sense of duty and of moral conduct, and who finally weds (as his father wished) a rather pale, subdued proper English lass. Again, passion is made impossible by social pressures. *Corinne* also portrays the north-south polarities elaborated in *De la littérature*. Much of the novel is spent describing Italy—its ruins, architecture, art, literature—and hoping that Italy will recover its past glory. Above all, the story shows how the woman of genius is destined to suffer.

Both novels, while they provoked a good deal of controversy, particularly because of their feminism, were quite successful. Her final work of fiction, *Sapho* (1811, published posthumously), proposes that suicide is the only solution for the woman of genius destroyed by deceptions in love. Yet *Réflexions sur le suicide* (Thoughts about Suicide, 1813) states that suicide is only justified if done for honor's sake; otherwise, one must go beyond suffering by turning to philosophy and religion, to a sense of duty.

Staël wrote extensively about the Revolution. She was well informed about political and economic matters. Though her view is somewhat influenced by her admiration for her father, the main cause of the revolution, she suggests, was the king's refusal of her father's reform of fiscal policy. She had little sympathy for the clergy (often incompetent) or the nobility (hardly deserving of their tax exemption), and preferred an aristocracy of merit. Her ideal remained that of an English-style constitutional monarchy. She was in favor of religious freedom, of the confiscation of clerical wealth, of judicial reforms. She identified with La Fayette and the liberal party and was opposed to the Terror. A revolution, she felt, might stop Enlightenment's progress, but only for a time.

In her *Réflexions sur le procès de la reine* (Thoughts about the Trial of the Queen, 1793), she denies the criticisms and calumnies directed against the queen, whom previously she had hardly admired. *Des circonstances actuelles qui peuvent terminer la révolution* (Present Circumstances Which May Lead to an End of the Revolution, 1798–1799, publ. 1906) attacks terrorism, despotism, arbitrary government, is quite prescient about the dangers of military despotism, and calls for political equality, popular sovereignty, the separation of powers, and above all universal public education, essential for any republican government. She believed in the necessity of a state religion, which in a republic must be Protestant.

After Napoleon's fall, she wrote two other political works, both published posthumously, *Dix années d'exil* (Ten Years of Exile) and *Considérations sur la révolution française* (Thoughts about the French Revolution). The former offers a striking portrait of the misery of a Europe suffering everywhere under tyranny. She was very struck by Russia, its immensity, its patriotism. The victory over Napoleon should bring liberty and enlightenment to all Europeans. The *Considérations* reflect a growing admiration for English institutions. She explains the Terror and revolutionary excesses by the sufferings the French knew under the ancien régime. Bonaparte remains the central object of criticism, for the cynical and immoral way in which he enslaved the French and perverted the Revolution, replacing the goal of liberty with that of war.

Germaine de Staël was the first woman intellectual; she wrote novels and plays as well as works on history, philosophy, and politics. She always proclaimed the woman's right to speak and be heard. Her constant and paramount concern was liberty, for which enlightenment was necessary, but which must also stem from a heartfelt commitment.

[*See also* French Revolution; Literary Genres; Novel; *and* Rousseau, Jean-Jacques.]

BIBLIOGRAPHY

ENGLISH TRANSLATIONS
Corinne. Translated by Avriel Goldberger. New Brunswick, N.J., 1987.
Delphine. Translated by Avriel Goldberger. De Kalb, Ill., 1995.
Ten Years of Exile. Translated by Avriel Goldberger. De Kalb, Ill., 2000.
An Extraordinary Woman: Selected Writings of Germaine de Staël. Translated and introduced by Vivian Folkenflik. New York, 1987.
Madame de Staël on politics, literature, and national character. Translated, edited, and introduced by Monroe Berger. Garden City, N.Y., 1964.

CRITICAL STUDIES
Balayé, Simone. *Madame de Staël: lumières et liberté*. Paris, 1979. An essential study by the dean of Staël scholars.
Gutwirth, Madelyn. *Madame de Staël, Novelist: The Emergence of the Artist as Woman*. Chicago, 1978. Shows how Mme. de Staël changed the image of the woman writer.
Herold, J. Christopher. *Mistress to an Age: A Life of Mme. de Staël*. Indianapolis and New York, 1958. The best biography in English, though it perhaps emphasizes too much her private life.
Isbell, John. *The Birth of European Romanticism: Truth and Propaganda in Staël's* De l'Allemagne. Cambridge, 1994. A learned study of the genesis of *De l'Allemagne* and its importance in the development of Romanticism.

FRANK PAUL BOWMAN

STAHL, GEORG ERNST

STAHL, GEORG ERNST (1659–1734), German physician and chemist.

Stahl was born 21 October 1659 in Ansbach, graduated in medicine in 1684 from Jena, and in 1687 was appointed court physician to the duke of Saxe-Weimar. From 1694 to 1715 he was professor of medicine at Halle, thereafter serving as court physician to the king of Prussia and as president of the Collegium Medicum in Berlin. He spent the most creative part of his life at the newly founded University of Halle, a center of the Enlightenment, as well as of religious pietism in Germany.

As a student, Stahl developed an intense interest in chemistry and it was part of his research and his teaching of medicine thereafter. At present, he is known mostly for his phlogiston theory of combustion, which claimed that burning (or "calcination") of a material is the result of the release of a lightweight substance, phlogiston. The theory was very influential in the eighteenth century, but attempts at consistently identifying phlogiston, or assigning a weight to it, failed. Eventually, Antoine Lavoisier discovered that oxygen is taken up upon combustion, implying that phlogiston does not exist. However, major discoveries by Stahl originally related to the phlogiston concept remained valid and fruitful. These include (as Lavoisier enthusiastically and gracefully acknowledged) that seemingly different reactions, burning (for example, of fat or sulfur) and calcination (of metals), are of the same basic type, and that they are reversible, suggesting conservation of constituents transferred in the reactions.

Of particular interest are Stahl's views on medicine and biology, explained in a large number of smaller works, and at length in his *Theoria Medica Vera* (Theory of True Medicine, 1708). He took exception to prevailing Cartesian notions about the separation of the mental and physical that allowed only for somewhat vague mind-body interactions, and about the predominantly mechanistic functioning of the body. Instead, he insisted that organisms are characterized by *anima* ("soul") sustaining the life of the organisms and integrating their emotional, behavioral, and mental processes and actions.

Stahl sympathized with pietism. At first sight, his thought might seem primarily motivated by resistance to the cold rationality of Cartesian-type enlightenment, turning instead to Aristotelian ideas of the *anima* and its hierarchy of capabilities; but such an evaluation would not do justice to his stimulating concepts. His main purpose was the improvement of medicine, which in his view suffered from radical, irresponsible methods based on unjustified intrusions of mechanistic "Cartesian subtleties and inventions" into his discipline. Rather than "fighting nature instead of disease," physicians should support nature by synergy (Stahl's term) with moderate modes of treatment.

Philosophical and medical questions raised by Stahl's ideas were subjects of a controversial correspondence with Leibniz, with a main focus on the relation of body and soul. Implying their preestablished harmony, Leibniz insisted that movements and changes of all matter occur according to exclusively mechanistic principles, in contrast to Stahl's notions on the distinction of mechanisms and organisms, and the role of the *anima* in the latter. Stahl's concept of *anima* appears as somewhat vague and dogmatic, and hence of little explanatory value. However, assignments of its functions led him to the specification of essential features of living systems, often neglected by mechanistic lines of thought: the generation and maintenance of spatial order, regulating the positioning and proportion of structures and substructures (textures) to be formed in a certain order and in certain sequences; the principle of homeostasis: the integration of components, which by themselves would undergo rapid decay, into a self-regulating and self-sustaining system capable of regeneration and the correction of distortions; the maintenance of the species by the generation of new individuals, "mediated by an originally implanted motive," implying the transfer of developmental programs from one generation to the next. Aside from organizing basic life processes, the *anima* directs behavior (a robot may go left or right, whereas it is up to the soul to give rise to the appropriate choice). His notions on voluntary movements, contradicting simple stimulus-response concepts and insisting instead on the introduction of purpose by central psychic states and processes, are of particular interest. He distinguished *ratiocinatio*—deliberate consequential thought—from most forms of organic function and behavior that are in accordance with *ratio* (=reasonable) without deliberate thought, memory, and fantasy, a distinction closely related to that between the conscious and the unconscious. Stahl called attention to strong physical expressions of emotional states. For actual behavior, emotions are often more dominating than conscious thoughts. "Without due consideration of psychic conditions and without an understanding of emotions, medicine would be doomed to failure."

Despite such remarkable concepts, Stahl's approach and even more his mode of expression were often dark and one-sided. His antimechanistic views led him to partially neglect important aspects of biology and medicine, such as anatomy and neurobiology. He underrated the potential of physics in relation to life sciences. Nevertheless, his role in the Enlightenment now appears as positive and fruitful: The mechanistic notions of his time were indeed insufficient for explaining life processes; the topics and the systems features of organic life he introduced and emphasized at this early stage were of crucial importance to the further development of medicine, biology, and psychology.

[*See also* Chemistry; Lavoisier, Antoine-Laurent; *and* Soul.]

BIBLIOGRAPHY

Stahl's main biomedical work is *Theoria Medica Vera* (Halle, 1708). An abridged translation into German was made by K. W. Ideler (Berlin, 1831).

ON HIS LIFE AND WORKS

Engelhardt, D. von, and A. Gierer, eds. "Georg Ernst Stahl in wissenschafts-historischer Sicht." *Acta Historica Leopoldina* 30. Halle, 2000.

Geyer-Kordesch, J. *Georg Ernst Stahl—Pietismus, Medizin und Aufklärung in Brandenburg-Preussen im 18. Jahrhundert.* Tübingen, Germany, 2000.

ON THE CHEMICAL ASPECTS IN THEIR COMPLEX HISTORICAL CONTEXT

Metzger, H. *Newton, Stahl, Boerhaave et la doctrine chimique.* Paris, 1930.

Partington, J. R. *A History of Chemistry.* Vol. 2, chapter 18, pp. 653–686. London, 1961–1970.

ON STAHL'S BIOLOGICAL, PHYSIOLOGICAL, PSYCHOLOGICAL, AND MEDICAL IDEAS

Geyer-Kordesch, J. "Georg Ernst Stahl's Radical Pietist Medicine and Its Influence on the German Enlightenment." In *The Medical Enlightenment of the Eighteenth Century,* edited by A. Cunningham and R. French, pp. 67–87. Cambridge, 1990.

Gierer, A. "Organisms-Mechanisms: Stahl, Wolff and the Case Against Reductionist Exclusion." *Science in Context* 9 (1996), 511–528.

Rather, L. J. "G. E. Stahl's Psychological Physiology." *Bulletin of the History of Medicine* 35 (1961), 37–49.

Rather, F. L. J., and J. B. Frerichs. "The Leibniz-Stahl Controversy." Parts I and II. *Clio Medica* 3 (1968), 21–40, and 5 (1970), 53–67.

ALFRED GIERER

STERNE, LAURENCE (1713–1768), English cleric and writer.

Sterne's relationship to the Enlightenment is encapsulated in a witty moment chronicled in his last work, *A Sentimental Journey through France and Italy* (1768), which, though fictional, has roots in Sterne's own sojourns in France during 1762–1764 and 1765–1766. The character Yorick, Sterne's alter ego, attends a salon where, he tells us, he had been "misrepresented to Madame de Q**** as an *esprit*." One indeed suspects that Sterne's reputation as "the English Rabelais," in Diderot's phrase, predetermined his own century—and ours—to see him as more freethinking than he actually was. Sterne seems to have been aware of this early misconception: in a second salon meeting, with Madame de V***—a coquette, Yorick tells us, but contemplating the second stage for every Frenchwoman, turning deist. Yorick discourages her, "There was not a more dangerous thing in the world than for a beauty to be a deist." He declares that only his belief in religion (his own and hers) has prevented him from trying to seduce her: "We are not adamant, said I, taking hold of her hand—and there is need of all restraints, till age in her own time steals in and lays them on us . . . ." Thus, Yorick declares, "I had the credit all over Paris of unperverting Madame de V***.—She affirmed to Mons. D[iderot] and the Abbe M[orellet] that

Sterne's *Tristram Shandy*. Illustration from *The Life and Opinions of Tristram Shandy, Gentleman* (London, 1781). (Rare Books and Special Collections Division, Library of Congress.)

in one half hour I had said more for revealed religion, than all their Encyclopedia had said against it."

Sterne's enduring reputation as an author rests on two works, *The Life and Opinions of Tristram Shandy, Gentleman* (1759–1767), which Diderot labeled "a universal satire," and *A Sentimental Journey* (1768), both written and published during the last nine years of his life. He was born in Clonmel, Ireland, but he resettled in Yorkshire when he was ten. He spent almost his entire adult life, after a clerical education at Cambridge, in a village outside York where he served as parish priest. From 1737 to 1759, Sterne ministered to his Anglican flock and lived the country life of a minor cleric with intermittent ties to the grander York establishment; had he died in 1759, he would not be known today.

In December 1758, however, Sterne wrote a Swiftian pamphlet belittling a church squabble in York. It was suppressed by higher authority, but the effort awakened his pen, and within the year he was offering to a London publisher the first two volumes of a work in the tradition of Rabelais, Cervantes, and Swift, yet amazingly new—at least in part because it depended on so much older, almost forgotten literary traditions. He was turned down, but he persisted, publishing the first two volumes in York; instant success followed, and within a few months, he was paid a princely sum for two more volumes of *Tristram Shandy* (published in 1761)—and for two volumes of sermons as well. Volumes 5 and 6 followed the year after, but ill health caused a three-year delay of volumes 7 and 8 (1765). In 1766, he published two additional volumes of sermons; in 1767, a single volume of *Tristram Shandy*; and a year later, in late February, *A Sentimental Journey*. He died a few weeks later, on 18 March 1768. Three additional volumes of his sermons were published posthumously in 1769.

Although this is not a large canon, Sterne was perhaps the most celebrated and most imitated of English authors on the Continent at the end of the eighteenth century and the beginning of the nineteenth. His reputation then suffered something of a setback as Victorian attitudes toward his bawdiness held sway, but he returned to eminence as a model for modernist and postmodernist fiction writers. Marcel Proust, Virginia Woolf, James Joyce, and Thomas Mann all spoke of his influence, and one need only read Milan Kundera, Juan Goytisolo, Salman Rushdie, and Carlos Fuentes to realize the international sweep of Sterne's continuing influence.

As with any major author, there has been a sea of commentary, typically divided. On one side, Sterne is seen as vatically celebrating individualism and freedom—the welcome breakdown of order, control, design, and authority that one might readily associate with the Enlightenment. On the other side, he is found to look back, in the ironic manner of his primary English model, Jonathan Swift, to a skeptical literary and philosophical tradition (Montaigne was another of his favorite authors) that scorned human pretensions to knowledge, advancement, progress—a skepticism not antireligious, but on the contrary an underpinning, as in Descartes, for resort to revealed religion.

Sterne's consistent play with human sexual appetite, typified in his encounter in the salon, suggests that this critical division has not been imposed on his work but is a predictable and consciously elicited response to it. Sterne's sexual dalliances were well known to his congregation, and given the persistent bawdy innuendo of *Tristram Shandy* (not even the bishop of Gloucester could get him to relinquish such play), he certainly carried to London and then to Paris the odor of a freethinking, freeliving, man-of-the-town. In many ways he embraced that reputation, "shandying it," as he said, from one dinner to the next, one salon after another.

In Paris, Diderot (who wrote the first major work derivative of Sterne, *Jacques le Fataliste*), d'Alembert, Buffon, Crébillon *fils*, and d'Holbach were all Sterne's companions, and he seems to have spent a good deal of time spreading the doctrine of sentimentalism among them. With the later help of Goethe's *Des Leiden des jungen Werthers* (The Sorrows of Young Werther) (Goethe called "Yorick-Sterne" the "most beautiful spirit that ever lived"), he achieved iconic status as the century drew to its close; in imitation of Yorick, young men throughout Europe exchanged snuffboxes and sought mad Marias under every tree. By "sentimentalism," Sterne seems to have meant the privileging of heart over head, and an instantaneous sympathy with one's fellow creatures. This is standard enough "moral sense" fare for any student of the century, but Sterne immensely complicated sentimentalism by locating the heart somewhere between the pulse and the groin, and by finding it a great deal easier to sympathize with a pretty woman than with any other fellow creature. At the same time, his sentimentalism seems to draw on a spiritual tradition as old as Scripture itself, an affective Christianity that posits Jesus as the original "man of feeling," a theology evident in his highly unoriginal sermons, most of which were copied from predecessors like John Tillotson. That tradition, in various revitalizing moments in European history such as English Methodism, generated changes in doctrine and practice based on a "moving" or "heartfelt" faith.

If Madame V*** represents for Sterne the Enlightenment itself, encountered at its peak in the salons of Paris in the 1760s, what then was his real attitude toward her? Was he indeed seduced by her, and saved, ironically, only by his own religion, if not by hers? Or was he inclined to point to her great weakness—her pride in her own sufficiency—while trying, through wit, to rescue both of them? Or, again, was he torn between conflicting thoughts and emotions, loyalties and appetites, hovering (which Nietzsche, who called him "the freest of all spirits," defined as his peculiar genius) between all the possibilities of what it might mean to be human—and to be redeemed, for he may never have abandoned belief in that possibility, among all the others. Enlightenment was a very seductive concept, often a prelude to pleasure, and just as often to disaster. Sterne liked nothing better than to dance on the edge of both, and in this may lie his true greatness as an author: that we will never be able fully to define his relationship with a concept such as Enlightenment.

[*See also* Literary Genres.]

BIBLIOGRAPHY

WORKS BY STERNE

The Florida Edition of the Works of Laurence Sterne. Vols. 1 and 2, *Tristram Shandy: The Text.* Edited by Melvyn New and Joan New. Gainesville, Fla., 1978. Vol. 3, *Tristram Shandy: The Notes*, edited by Melvyn New with Richard A. Davies and W. G. Day. 1984. Vols. 4 and 5, *The Sermons.* Edited by Melvyn New. 1996. The scholarly edition of Sterne's works, with two additional volumes (*A Sentimental Journey* and *The Letters*) planned.

A Sentimental Journey through France and Italy. Edited by Gardner D. Stout. Berkeley, Calif., 1967. The standard scholarly edition of this work until the new Florida edition.

Letters. Edited by Lewis Perry Curtis. Oxford, 1935. The standard scholarly edition of Sterne's letters until the new Florida edition.

WORKS ABOUT STERNE

Battestin, Martin C. "Sterne among the *Philosophes*: Body and Soul in *A Sentimental Journey*." *Eighteenth-Century Fiction* 7 (October 1994), 17–36. A representative argument for those who see Sterne as a forerunner of modernity.

Cash, Arthur H. *Laurence Sterne: The Early and Middle Years.* London, 1975.

Cash, Arthur H. *Laurence Sterne: The Later Years.* 2 vols. London, 1987. The standard and definitive biography.

Jefferson, D. W. "*Tristram Shandy* and the Tradition of Learned Wit." *Essays in Criticism* 1 (1951), 225–248. Still the best introduction to Sterne's reading.

Mullan, John. "Laurence Sterne and the 'Sociality' of the Novel." In *Sentiment and Sociability: The Language of Feeling in the Eighteenth Century*, pp. 147–200. Oxford, 1988. The best study available of a concern vital to Sterne, how to understand sentiment and sensibility in the eighteenth century.

New, Melvyn. *"Tristram Shandy": A Book for Free Spirits.* New York, 1994. An accessible reading of the work through the filter of Nietzsche's high praise.

New, Melvyn, ed. *Critical Essays on Laurence Sterne.* New York, 1998. Eighteen essays representing the best critical work on Sterne since 1980.

Wehrs, Donald R. "Sterne, Cervantes, Montaigne: Fideistic Skepticism and the Rhetoric of Desire." *Comparative Literature Studies* 25 (1988), 127–151. A rich discussion of Sterne's skeptical background.

MELVYN NEW

STEUART, JAMES (1713–1780), Scottish economist.

Steuart was the only son of Sir James Steuart (1681–1727) and Anne Dalrymple, the daughter of the lord president of the Court of Session, Scotland's highest court. James senior served as an MP in the Union Parliament and as solicitor-general, thus following in the footsteps of his own father, who at one time held the office of lord advocate.

Young James attended the parish school in North Berwick, entering Edinburgh University in 1725. He passed the bar examinations ten years later. It was expected that he too would enjoy a career in law, but in 1735 he embarked upon a foreign tour, which lasted for five years, during which time he visited Holland, France, Spain, and Italy. Steuart's visit to Rome had fateful consequences in that he became a committed Jacobite after meeting James Edward, known as the Old Pretender, and his son, Prince Charles, the claimant to the British throne.

While Steuart may have had doubts about the cause, he proved to be profoundly influential before and after the Jacobite rebels entered Edinburgh in September 1745, and was subsequently sent to France as ambassador. Steuart returned to Great Britain after the end of the Seven Years' War (1763), under the mistaken impression that he had been pardoned. In fact he was not granted clemency until 1771; possibly an indication of the fact that the government of the day continued to take him and his politics seriously.

Political exile and his foreign tour, allied with Steuart's energetic intelligence and linguistic ability, gave him a unique knowledge of conditions on the Continent, a knowledge that had a profound effect on the shape of his *Inquiry into the Principles of Political Oeconomy* (1767). The "historical clue" that Steuart found in David Hume's *Political Discourses* (1752) led him to develop an account of the origins and nature of the exchange economy and to elaborate upon the social and political consequences of such a structure. In particular, Steuart sought to describe a situation in which all goods and services command a price, and a high degree of interdependence exists between individuals and sectors of activity. It should be noted that the formal model laid out in *Inquiry into the Principles of Political Oeconomy*, completed by the summer of 1759, had been worked out by Steuart in isolation in Tübingen, Germany, and is essentially prephysiocratic in character.

His policy stance was equally distinctive in that Steuart showed a consistent interest in the problems of structural unemployment and regional imbalance—both in the *Inquiry into the Principles of Political Oeconomy* and in his *Considerations of the Interest of the County of Lanark in Scotland* (1769). He also advocated a managed grain market in his *Dissertation on the Policy of Grain; with a View to a Plan for Preventing Scarcity or Exorbitant Prices in the Common Markets of England* (1759). Steuart was also an advocate of the proposed Forth and Clyde Canal, which was intended to provide a link between the East and West coasts of Scotland, thus improving the market for wage goods and opening up further opportunities for trade with Europe.

With respect to economic policy in international trade, Steuart started from the premise that economic conditions are likely to vary between nations. He elaborated on the stages of "infant," "foreign," and "inland" trade, to each of which he ascribed a distinctive policy dimension, which included a defense of both free trade and protectionism as circumstances required.

In all these cases, Steuart found a place for state intervention in matters which he saw not simply as economic, but also as social and political. The perspective owed much to David Hume and to the French political economist Victor Riqueti, marquis de Mirabeau.

Toward the end of his life, Steuart wrote a series of letters on the American Revolution in which he advocated economic sanctions rather than military involvement. Steuart's appreciation of the need to protect relatively underdeveloped economies, when faced with competition from more advanced competitors, gained the approval of Alexander Hamilton, the defender of the interests of the infant American Republic.

Steuart had interests in addition to those in economics and state policy. Like others, he wrote on the reform of weights and measures (1759) and defended Sir Isaac Newton's *Chronology of the Ancient Kingdoms Amended* (1728) in his *Chronologie des Grecs* (1757). He also wrote critical works including *Observations on Dr. Beattie's Essay on the Nature and Immutability of Truth* (1775) and a critique of Paul-Henri Thiry d'Holbach's *System of Nature* (1779), a work which he believed had been written by Jean-Baptiste Mirabaud.

Steuart married Lady Frances Wemyss in 1743. Her brother, Lord Elcho, who remained a close friend, commanded Prince Charles's Life Guards in the Jacobite rebellion of 1745–1746. The surviving child of the marriage, also James (1744–1839), was the senior general of the British Army, notable for his reform of cavalry tactics. Steuart took the name of Steuart-Denham in 1773 when he inherited the estate of Westshields on the death of a relative, Archibald Denham.

[*See also* Economic Thought; Grain Trade; Hume, David; Moral Philosophy; Physiocracy; Scotland; Smith, Adam; *and* Turgot, Anne-Robert-Jacques.]

BIBLIOGRAPHY

Hont, I. "The Rich Country–Poor Country Debate in Scottish Political Economy." In *Wealth and Virtue: The Shaping of Political Economy in the Scottish Enlightenment*, edited by Hont and Ignatieff. Cambridge, 1983.

Hutchison, T. *Before Adam Smith*. Oxford, 1988.

Raynor, D., and A. S. Skinner. "Sir James Steuart: Nine Letters on the American Conflict, 1775–1778." *William and Mary Quarterly* 51 (1994).

Sen, S. R. *The Economics of Sir James Steuart*. London, 1957.

Steuart, James. *An Inquiry into the Principles of Political Oeconomy: Being an Essay on the Science of Domestic Policy in the Free Nations*. 2 vols. London, 1767. Repr., London, 1998, edited by Andrew Skinner, Noboru Kobayashi, and Hiroshi Mizuta.

Steuart, James. *Works Political, Metaphisical and Chronological*. 6 vols. London, 1805. See especially vol. 5, *Considerations on the Interest of the County of Lanark in Scotland: Which (in Several Respects) may be Applied to that of Great Britain* (1769), and *A Dissertation on the Policy of Grain, with a View to a Plan for Preventing Scarcity or Exorbitant Prices, in the Common Markets of England* (1759).

Tortajada, R., ed. *The Economics of James Steuart*. London, 1999.

ANDREW S. SKINNER

STEWART, DUGALD

STEWART, DUGALD (1753–1828), Scottish moral philosopher.

During his quarter century in the chair of moral philosophy at the University of Edinburgh (1785–1810), Stewart wrote on such an eclectic range of subjects, and with such inspiring effect, that he had become a transatlantic cultural figure by the time of his retirement. A pupil of Thomas Reid, he was first and perhaps foremost an effective popularizer of Scottish common sense philosophy. Stewart aimed to bring practical force to Reid's thinking by making it more readily teachable to the potential leaders of society. A charismatic lecturer, he attracted students in unprecedented numbers from England, continental Europe, and America, as well as from Scotland.

His chief work was the *Elements of the Philosophy of the Human Mind* (1792). He published it as a single volume in the midst of the French Revolution, then later revised and expanded the work, partly to respond to suspicions of Jacobinism and religious skepticism that mistakenly had been voiced against him. A second volume of the *Elements* appeared in 1814, and a third in 1826. Other influential writings included *Outlines of Moral Philosophy* (1793), *Philosophical Essays* (1810), and *Dissertation Exhibiting a General View of the Progress of Metaphysical, Ethical and Political Philosophy since the Revival of Letters in Europe* (1820), the last published as the introduction to another major Scottish enterprise, the *Encyclopaedia Britannica.* Stewart's lectures on political economy, although unpublished until 1850, had a powerful impact on and through the founders of the *Edinburgh Review*, the first and most influential of nineteenth-century British periodicals and a major vehicle for the popularization of the ideas of Adam Smith. His *Account of the Life and Writings of Adam Smith LL.D.* (1793) was also frequently reprinted as an introduction to nineteenth-century editions of Smith's work.

Although the main lines of Stewart's thinking derived from Reid's earlier efforts to counter modern philosophical skepticism, there were some important differences between the two. To begin with, Stewart was critical of Reid's use of the phrase "principles of common sense," because he thought it could be misunderstood as endorsing approaches to knowledge and morality different from those that could be acquired only through formal education. Stewart also believed that his own approach to moral philosophy was more practically oriented, faulting his teacher for not giving adequate attention to the importance of piecemeal reform and the education of far-sighted public leaders.

Living through the experience of the French Revolution and the Napoleonic wars, Stewart also was moved to reconsider some of the characteristic concerns of late-eighteenth century Scottish moral philosophy. Arguably the most important of these was his approach to the teaching of political economy. When Stewart decided to mount a separate course on political economy at the University of Edinburgh in 1799, he inverted a longstanding tradition in which discussion of the theory and forms of government had preceded political economy, on the grounds that law and government were a precondition for stable and social and economic life. Stewart's explanation for his inversion was that improvements in the human condition had come to depend more immediately on enlightened systems of political economy, whereas the role of particular forms of government in producing such systems was contingent and remote. He also argued that the popularization of the correct principles of political economy was a necessary precondition for making possible other improvements in forms of government.

A staunch Whig, Stewart, in his lectures on political economy, aimed to steer a middle course between enthusiasm for constitutional innovation, on the one hand, and political reaction, on the other. These lectures were given annually prior to his retirement in 1810. The interest they aroused was intense, and the usefulness of what he offered was widely appreciated, especially by three students who would go on to become the founders of the *Edinburgh Review*: Francis Jeffrey (1772–1850), Francis Horner (1778–1817), and Henry Brougham (1778–1868). All had attended Stewart's lectures between 1799 and 1801, and all maintained close personal contact with him over the following decades. While Smith's *Wealth of Nations* (1776) provided the framework for Stewart's understanding of political economy, he also covered a wide range of seventeenth- and eighteenth-century British and Continental works on the subject. The result was a carefully organized and invaluable mine of information and arguments that the reviewers would employ in debates of the period during and after the Napoleonic wars.

Present-day students of the Enlightenment see Stewart primarily as the most important early commentator on Adam Smith's work. During the first half of the nineteenth century, he was also a major influence on Pierre Paul Royer-Collard (1763–1845), Victor Cousin (1792–1867), and Théodore Jouffroy (1796–1842) in France; at the same time, his writings helped to establish common sense philosophy as the most widespread form of philosophy in America. Late-twentieth century philosophers, however, take only historical interest in his work.

[*See also* Economic Thought; Education, *subentry on* Reform and Experiments; Moral Philosophy; Scottish Common Sense Philosophy; *and* Smith, Adam.]

BIBLIOGRAPHY

Fontana, Biancamaria. *Rethinking the Politics of Commercial Society: The "Edinburgh Review," 1802–1832.* Cambridge, 1985.

Haakonssen, Knud. "From Moral Philosophy to Political Economy: The Contribution of Dugald Stewart." In *Philosophers of the Scottish*

Enlightenment. edited by Vincent Hope, pp. 211–233. Edinburgh, 1984.

Haakonssen, Knud. *Natural Law and Moral Philosophy: From Grotius to the Scottish Enlightenment*, Cambridge, 1996.

Madden, E. H. "Stewart's Enrichment of the Common Sense Tradition." *History of Philosophy Quarterly* 3.1 (1987), 45–63.

Phillipson, Nicholas. "The Pursuit of Virtue in the Scottish University Education: Dugald Stewart and Scottish Moral Philosophy in the Enlightenment." In *Universities, Society, and the Future*, edited by Nicholas Phillipson, pp. 82–101. Edinburgh, 1983.

Sher, Richard. "Professor of Virtue: The Social History of the Edinburgh Moral Philosophy Chair in the Eighteenth Century." In *Studies in the Philosophy of the Scottish Enlightenment*, edited by M. A. Stewart, pp. 87–126. Oxford, 1990.

Stewart, Dugald. *Collected Works of Dugald Stewart*. Edited by Sir William Hamilton. 11 vols. Bristol, U.K., 1994. Facsimile reprint of the 1854–1860 edition, introduced by Knud Haakonssen.

Winch, Donald. "The System of the North: Dugald Stewart and His Pupils." In *That Noble Science of Politics: A Study of Nineteenth-Century Intellectual History*, by Stefan Collini, Donald Winch, and John Burrow, pp. 23–61. Cambridge, 1983.

RICHARD F. TEICHGRAEBER III

STINSTRA, JOHANNES (1708–1790), Dutch Mennonite preacher.

Though a lifelong minister in a small town in the northern province of Friesland, Stinstra achieved renown both in the Netherlands and beyond through his involvement in the dissemination of Enlightenment thought. His contributions in this respect were threefold. The first was connected with his response to accusations of Socinianism (in Stinstra's case, this amounted to a denial of the traditional Christian doctrine of the Trinity) leveled at him by the Dutch Calvinist clergy, and his subsequent removal from office, by order of the Frisian authorities, in 1742. Stinstra upset the political and ecclesiastical establishment by formally offering the authorities a well-wrought text in which he adduced a variety of arguments in favor of freedom of religious worship (an English translation may be found in Van Eijnatten, 1998). In various writings, Stinstra drew ideas on liberty and toleration from such authors as the English philosopher John Locke, the Anglican bishop Benjamin Hoadly (1676–1761), the Dutch law scholar Gerard Noodt (1647–1725), and the Swiss-Dutch jurist Jean Barbeyrac (1674–1744). In these years he probably also translated a treatise on the unity of Christians by the Huguenot Pierre Coste (1668–1747), originally included in a French translation (1715) of Locke's *Reasonableness of Christianity*. Like other Dutch dissenters in this period, Stinstra followed developments in contemporary English thought and helped to introduce a number of latitudinarian and dissenting thinkers into the Netherlands. He advocated the mildly rationalist, anti-deist theology of the moral philosopher William Wollaston (1659/60–1724) and, above all, the Anglican theologian Samuel Clarke; he translated Clarke's sermons, as well as those of the Unitarian minister James Foster.

Stinstra's second contribution was related to the rise in Dutch Mennonite and Reformed communities of "enthusiasm" or "fanaticism." This emotional religiosity, influenced by German Moravianism (the so-called Herrnhuters), Anglo-American revivalism, and domestic Pietism, manifested itself especially in the 1730s and 1740s. In response, Stinstra in 1750 published a defense of rationalism in religion, virtually equating the work of the Holy Spirit with human ratiocination and putting the passions firmly under the control of reason. His book was received favorably abroad and was soon translated into French, German, and English.

Stinstra's third contribution to the dissemination of Enlightenment thought came with his eight-volume Dutch translation (1752–1755) of *Clarissa Harlowe*, a novel by the English writer Samuel Richardson. In his prefaces, which set the tone for the later reception of fictional literature in the Netherlands, Stinstra generally commented on the moral value of novels; he later supervised the translation of Richardson's *Charles Grandison*.

Stinstra was permitted to preach again in 1757 and continued his work as a pastor until his resignation in 1785. His last major publication was an examination of Old Testament prophecies concerning the Messiah. Stinstra remained true to the early latitudinarian Enlightenment he so admired in English writers, and he failed to adopt the more radical theologies developing in Germany in the second half of the eighteenth century. Similarly, he kept aloof from the democratic currents that set the Dutch Republic in turmoil during the 1780s.

[*See also* Latitudinarianism; Netherlands; Rationalism; Revealed Religion; *and* Translation.]

BIBLIOGRAPHY

Eijnatten, Joris van. *Mutua Christianorum Tolerantia: Irenicism and Toleration in the Netherlands: The Stinstra Affair 1740–1745*. Florence, 1998. Discusses Stinstra's defence of religious freedom and his role as an intermediary in the dissemination of Enlightenment thought.

Schings, H. J. *Melancholie und Aufklärung: Melancholiker und ihre Kritiker in Erfahrungs-seelenkunde und Literatur des 18. Jahrhunderts*. Stuttgart, 1977. A comprehensive discussion of fanaticism; see pp. 185–188 for an appreciative commentary on Stinstra's *Letter against Fanaticism*.

Slattery, W. C. *The Richardson-Stinstra Correspondence and Stinstra's Prefaces to Clarissa*. London and Amsterdam, 1969.

JORIS VAN EIJNATTEN

STOICISM was originally one of the most important

philosophical schools of antiquity. Samuel Johnson's dictionary defines *Stoicism* as the "opinions and maxims of the Stoicks." It also lists *stoically* and *stoick* ("of or belonging to the Stoicks; cold, stiff, austere, affecting to hold all things indifferent," referring to John Milton), *stoically* ("after the manner of the Stoicks; austerely; with pretended indifference to all things," referring to Brown), *stoicalness* ("the state of being stoical; the temper of a Stoic," referring to Scot), and *Stoick*, referring to Zeno of Citium as claiming that a wise man ought to be free of all passions, to be unmoved by joy or grief, and to consider all things to be governed by unavoidable necessity. Stoicism in the eighteenth century represented not just an ancient philosophical school but also a living doctrine that often had little to do with ancient Stoicism.

It is customary to distinguish between early, middle, and new, or Roman, Stoicism. Cicero (106–43 B.C.), Seneca (A.D. 1–65), Epictetus (A.D. c. 55–135), and Marcus Aurelius (A.D. 121–180) represent the Roman Stoicism that was decisive for the Enlightenment view of stoicism.

The virtuous or wise man was the central ideal of ancient Stoicism. Only the virtuous or wise man can be truly happy, since he lives "in accordance with nature" and is able to control his passions. He has attained calmness of mind (apathy). However, ethics was not the most fundamental discipline for the Stoics, who founded their philosophy on logic and physics. The ancient Stoics were materialists who believed that God, the logos or reason, pervaded the entire universe. Man was understood to be nothing but a "fragment torn from God." Stoicism may also be called "pantheism." One of its central problems is that of overcoming determinism.

Stoicism proved to be very adaptable. Its vocabulary survived in many theories. During the seventeenth century, Stoicism became so influential again in Protestant countries that one speaks of "Neostoicism." One of the most important of the new Stoics was Joest Lips (Lipsius, 1547–1606), for whom *constantia* became the central concept not only in ethics but also in political theory. His theory was further developed by Hugo Grotius (1583–1645) and Samuel Pufendorf (1632–1694).

In the eighteenth century Stoicism played a considerable role. Often it meant the acceptance of Neostoicism in opposition to Hobbesian materialism. Sometimes it meant the acceptance of certain ancient doctrines, but hardly ever did it involve materialism. Different philosophers adopted different aspects of the Stoic doctrine. Francis Hutcheson developed a theory of duties that is strongly reminiscent of ancient Stoicism. The perfectionism of Gottfried Wilhelm von Leibniz, Christian Wolff, and their followers also reflects a central idea of Stoicism. Adam Smith's "inner man" or impartial spectator also is indebted to Stoicism, as is Immanuel Kant's categorical imperative, which assigns moral worth only to actions whose maxims can become a universal law or which are done from duty, and his kingdom of ends is not only indebted to Leibniz but also to Stoic ideals. Still, more often than not stoicism meant nothing more than living austerely or living in accordance with strict rules, as for instance when one speaks of "Christian stoicism." While Hutcheson and Smith seem to have been genuinely fascinated by Stoic cosmology, as Christians, they could not accept its materialist or pantheist tendencies. David Hume's essay "The Stoic," on the other hand, meant to present a picture of "the man of action and virtue," is an attempt to show that the ancient Stoic doctrines point toward an enduring moral ideal of stoicism.

[*See also* Moral Philosophy.]

BIBLIOGRAPHY

Oestreich, Gerhard. "Calvinismus, Neustoizismus u. Preussentum." *Jahrbuch für die Geschichte Mittel- u. Ostdeutschlands* 5 (1956), 157–181.
Oestreich, Gerhard. *Neostoicism and the Early Modern State.* Cambridge and New York, 1982.

MANFRED KUEHN

STRUENSEE, JOHANN FRIEDRICH (1737–1772), Danish first minister and physician.

Struensee was a bourgeois German physician from Halle who, after some time as the town physician in Altona in Holstein, became physician to King Christian VII of Denmark in 1767. Struensee found that his king was more than a bit deranged. In 1769, the king and his entourage, which included Struensee, embarked on a tour of Germany, France, and England that kept them away from Copenhagen for two years. During this time, the young ruler and his wife developed a fondness and trust for the physician. When they returned to Denmark, the king, becoming progressively less sane and more inattentive to his queen, gave Struensee significant authority. By the autumn of that year, Struensee had ousted the former chief advisers, had abolished the privy council that had checked royal power, and had become secretary to the cabinet. He soon made this the central office in the administration of the kingdom and himself first minister. He had himself ennobled and later installed his brother as head of the treasury. He also persuaded the king to sign a decree that all laws must bear the minister's signature as well as the sovereign's. By the end of the year, he seemed securely in control of the government, which the king allowed him to run as he pleased. By then the queen was in love with him and they had probably begun to be intimate; her child, said also to be his, was born in 1771. Recklessness characterized Struensee's policies, but even in relatively enlightened Denmark, the pace of change could not be forced; moderation had to be used to effect changes in manners and institutions, a lesson that many enlightened rulers learned in hard ways.

Struensee's policies were modeled on the reforms of Frederick II (known as "the Great") and the policies advocated by the Physiocrats, then at the height of their popularity and influence. From the first, he learned to centralize the government and to curb the powers of the nobles. Abolishing the council of state got some of the greater nobility out of government and cleared the way for more reforms. Putting officials on fixed and stated salaries and abolishing perquisites made state service less attractive to many others, who were replaced by middle-class men owing loyalty only to the king and his minister. Others were cut from the payroll as sinecure offices were abolished. Struensee tried to make appointments dependent on merit and wanted to make nobility reflective of that too—as in theory it was often said to be. He reorganized the judicial system, which he made independent of the executive. He also reformed the laws, abolishing torture and the death penalty as Cesare Beccaria had recently recommended. The minister replaced the local governments of cities with state officials whom he expected to be less corrupt. He provided new rules for all the new or reformed agencies. He also cut many government expenses, including some at the court that had supported luxury trades, which then began to suffer. He tried to impose cuts in personal expenses on ordinary Danes, who, he thought, were spending too much on luxury items; they soon found that they had to have funerals at night so that expensive displays could be avoided.

Other changes looked to the economic theories of the Physiocrats. Struensee supported their notion of a "legal despotism"—that is, of a government that used only its constitutional powers, in accordance with natural law, for the good of its subjects. He freed trade from many restrictions. Petty regulations were voided, and he allowed the city gates of Copenhagen to remain open all night. He tried to cut taxes and to work toward a system that derived money more from taxes levied on land than from taxes on consumption items. He pursued foreign policies designed to keep Denmark neutral and trading with all nations.

Struensee's decrees included many more that dealt with other contentious issues. A deist, Struensee did not favor the established Lutheran Church and its clerics, who resented this deeply. He was willing to tolerate people of other confessions and was not eager to see church courts discipline offenders against morals—not even brothel-keepers. He eliminated the stigma of bastardy. Although he supported the building of schools, he was not eager for clerics to oversee them. In a Pietistic world, he seemed an outrageous fellow. To make matters worse, he thought that German, the language of the court, ought to become the language of the country in order to enrich the culture and make relations with some neighbors easier. He cut

the army list, and the Royal Guards mutinied against their disbanding. Peasants, whom he had tried to help, were not grateful, and the poor, whom he wished to relieve, were little more so.

By the end of 1771, the dowager queen and her younger son were ready to see the minister go. So were many nobles who had begun to plot against him because of the economic and social harm he had done them and because of the increasingly scandalous affair he was conducting with the queen. Clerics were against him. Ordinary Danes had no wish to learn German, and many resented the lower wages and higher prices that had come with the economic dislocations Struensee had caused. The oligarchies of the cities disliked him. Even reforms such as freeing the press, applauded by Voltaire in a poem, had produced a storm of public criticism. Many, not knowing the king was mad, thought the minister had restrained him and would oust him from the throne. They cared far more about that than about the public concerts and the opening of gardens and parks to the populace. Others thought Struensee dishonest, although he seems to have taken little money though much power for himself. He did not even try to manipulate public sentiment in his favor, apparently thinking his actions would soon be popular—a common delusion among the enlightened.

On the night of 16–17 January 1772, a group of nobles having the support of the dowager queen and her younger son broke into the king's bedroom and forced him to sign a warrant for Struensee's arrest. The queen was sent off to a castle under guard. Struensee was shortly thereafter tried and was convicted on 25 April 1772 of lèse majesté for usurping powers in violation of the constitution and for immoral conduct with the queen. He was publicly executed on 28 April 1772, in a manner that horrified many in Europe: the hand that had signed 2,200 decrees in sixteen months was cut off; he was beheaded, and his body was then broken on a wheel and quartered for public display in different places. It was a warning to the enlightened that, even in Denmark, they could not expect too much too fast.

[See also Aristocracy; Beccaria, Cesare; Censorship; Enlightened Despotism; Physiocracy; Scandinavia; and Tradition.]

BIBLIOGRAPHY

Cedergreen Bech, Svend. *Johann Friedrich, greve Struensee, 1737–1772.* Copenhagen, 1972. The most recent biography which draws on many earlier memoirs including some in French.

Reddaway, W. F. "Struensee and the Fall of Bernstorf." *English Historical Review* 27 (1912), 274–286.

Reddaway, W. F. "King Christian VII." *English Historical Review* 31 (1916), 274–286. Argues that Christian VII agreed with many of the reforms. Like the preceding entry, this is based partly on Struensee's confessions and on the records of his trial.

ROGER L. EMERSON

STUART, GILBERT (1743–1786), Scottish historian, critic, and political writer.

Stuart was born in Edinburgh, the eldest son of George Stuart, professor of humanity at Edinburgh University. Stuart grew up in the Old College buildings, where as a young man he worked in the library and attended classes. In 1764 he began an unhappy legal apprenticeship, during which time he wrote *An Historical Dissertation Concerning the Antiquity of the English Constitution* (1768). Written in the "conjectural" manner, this work summarizes the history of English liberty from the time of the first Britons to the Norman invasion. Implicit in Stuart's whiggish assertions was a challenge to David Hume, whose *History of England* Stuart found inaccurate and relativist, and not a good defense of British liberty.

Stuart, following many other Scots of his day, set off for London in 1769. He contributed articles to the *London Magazine* and the *Monthly Review*; he prepared several unfinished works for the press; and he wrote histories of the Isle of Man and of the city of Edinburgh, neither of which were published. After four years on Grubb Street, Stuart returned to Scotland in 1773 to establish the *Edinburgh Magazine and Review*, a monthly periodical of literature and politics in which he was assisted by William Smellie. Stuart's controversial new style of journalism—where the review itself served to incite praise or censure not only of the work in question, but also of its author—was not well received by the "polite" readership of the day. The periodical folded in August 1776.

Intemperate by nature and increasingly distanced from the intellectual milieu of Edinburgh because of the personal intensity of his views, Stuart returned to historical writing. His *View of Society in Europe* (1778) considers such topics as the concept of property, the roles of the sexes, and the place of religion in medieval times. It was his most successful work, appearing in several editions and translations. Two less popular books followed: the *Public Law of Scotland* (1779), an attack on the popular *History of Scotland* by William Robertson, whom Stuart believed had blocked his appointment to a professorship at Edinburgh University; and the *History of the Reformation of Religion in Scotland* (1780), also critical of Robertson.

Stuart's magnum opus, the *History of Mary Queen of Scots*, appeared in 1782. In opposition to Robertson's account of the same period, Stuart sought to revitalize the image of the queen. He wrote in a manner more sentimental and evocative than that practiced by the leading historians of the day. South of the border, this work achieved considerable praise.

Stuart returned to London in 1783 and recommenced writing for periodicals. A breakthrough came in 1785, when he was asked by Opposition leaders to edit the *Political Herald*. William Godwin and other able writers joined Stuart in an attack on the government of William Pitt and his minister Henry Dundas. However, Stuart's moment of glory was brief: illness, brought on by an intemperate lifestyle, hastened his death at the age of forty-three.

[*See also* Edinburgh; *and* Journals, Newspapers, and Gazettes, *subentry on* Great Britain.]

BIBLIOGRAPHY

Zachs, William. *Without Regard to Good Manners: A Biography of Gilbert Stuart, 1743–1786*. Edinburgh, 1992.

WILLIAM ZACHS

STURM UND DRANG. Sturm und Drang ("Storm and Stress"), a movement during the latter phase of the German Enlightenment from approximately 1769 to the mid-1780s, has been variously defined by literary critics and historians, from a simple continuation of Enlightenment ideals to a separate literary and philosophical tendency that often seemed not to bear much resemblance to the Enlightenment. The truth no doubt lies somewhere in the middle, but the variations in such efforts of definition are reflected in the movement itself, a literary phase clearly unique to Germany. Its exponents were equally varied: it attracted Goethe and Schiller, who were soon to become central to German literary culture; Jakob Michael Reinhold Lenz, who has become increasingly interesting to twentieth-century critics; and writers like Maler Müller, Heinrich Leopold Wagner, and Friedrich Maximilian Klinger, whose fame was limited primarily to their own time. The movement's name was in vogue in the early 1770s, before the drama by Klinger of that title appeared in 1776. Despite its strictly German milieu, influences on its development are to be found in England and France.

Traits of the Movement. The movement itself had several specific traits, among them the tendency for its members to cluster in loosely structured intellectual circles, and the remarkable focus on drama as the genre most favored by its writers. Goethe's and Schiller's early dramas, especially Goethe's *Götz von Berlichingen* (1773), and Schiller's *Die Räuber* (The Robbers, 1781) and *Kabale und Liebe* (Intrigue and Love, 1784), are products of this era, as are all of Lenz's so-called comedies, for example, *Der Hofmeister* (The Master of the Household, 1774) and *Die Soldaten* (The Soldiers, 1776). The Sturm und Drang writers who are less known today—Wagner, Klinger, and Müller, among others—also focused on the dramatic form: in 1776, Klinger published both *Die Zwillinge* and *Sturm und Drang*, (The Twins, Storm and Stress), Wagner, *Die Kindermörderin* (The Child-Murderess), and Müller, *Golo und Genoveva*. With the exception of Lenz's comedies, most of the Sturm und

German Authors. Friedrich Schiller reads to the elite of Weimar. Seated at left are the philosopher Johann Gottlieb Fichte, the philosopher Johann Gottfried Herder, and the poet and translator Karl Ludwig von Knebel. The poet Christoph Martin Wieland is seated in the center of the picture. Karl August, duke of Saxe-Weimar-Eisenach, in cocked hat, stands in front of the domed pavilion. Standing at right is Johann Wolfgang von Goethe. Lithograph by Ernst Fischer after a painting by the nineteenth-century history painter Theobald von Oer (1807–1885). (The Granger Collection, New York.)

Drang dramas are characterized by rebellious heroes who tend to die violently. Although women are present, often as model domestic heroines, there is also a group of characters generally known as *Machtweiber* ("women of power"), who tend to be aristocratic and sources of evil.

A typical prose work, Goethe's novel *Die Leiden des jungen Werthers* (The Sorrows of Young Werther, 1774), also appeared during this period, as did Lessing's prototypical Enlightenment drama *Nathan der Weise* (Nathan the Wise, 1779), which was published at a time when Sturm und Drang had essentially died out. Thus, the linear development of literary epochs and the neat pattern of one emerging from another are once again shown to be less than precise: Sturm und Drang intermingled with, reacted to, supplemented, and expanded on the ideas and concepts of the German Enlightenment, adding its own original turns but often echoing what had preceded it.

The ambiguities and contradictions that characterize Sturm und Drang also help to elucidate its various facets. A movement that seemed, at least on the surface, to stress the revolutionary potential of human individuals could hardly be expected to flourish in the absolutist states of eighteenth-century, with their exclusive court cultures restricted to the nobility. Unlike France, which in this era could definitely be labeled prerevolutionary, Germany produced fantasies about liberation and revolution that seem to have been acceptable only in literary form (Huyssen, 1980). The radicalizing and politicizing move of Sturm und Drang philosophy away from the idea of a well-ordered enlightened community and toward the unqualified autonomy of the individual was in a sense ironic because its circles formed in Strassburg, Frankfurt, and Göttingen, all far removed from the more politically active Berlin, Leipzig, and Hamburg. Even the continuation of the Enlightenment project of developing a bourgeois subjectivity seems strangely modified in Sturm und Drang dramatic heroes, many of whom are aristocratic and thus hardly different in that respect from the heroic type in the middle-class tragedies of Lessing and others. The outcomes of Sturm und Drang dramas also appear to contradict the revolutionary intent: there is often a certain tameness at the end, a return to the domestic sphere—or, as in *Werther*, the freedom and liberation expounded by the hero seem capable of resolution only in death. The final effect in much Sturm und Drang writing is one of pessimism, and not of constructive criticism, utopian dreams, or even social improvement beyond the usual Enlightenment aims. In addition, there is an overwhelming sense of confinement and limitation, not unexpected against a background of absolutist rule. Thus, even in the revolutionary writing represented here, the outside world interferes and controls the outcome.

Despite the absence of a directly equivalent movement in other European countries, Sturm und Drang was a part of the pan-European anti-absolutist intellectual and political crisis. Aside from the obvious influence of Shakespearean drama with its less rigid attention to classical details of form and unity, there are echoes of Graveyard poets like Edward Young; there is direct citation of "Ossian" in Goethe's *Werther*; and there are obvious borrowings from Jean-Jacques Rousseau's political and social philosophy. At the same time, Sturm und Drang was marked by its own peculiarly anti-political strains: as Huyssen has pointed out, the German revolutionary writings of this period were characterized neither by the rapid emancipation of the bourgeoisie from England's feudal past nor by the steadily progressive movement toward revolution that was evident in France.

If Sturm und Drang was not apt to imitate its neighbors in their more liberalizing political developments, however, it nevertheless echoed the search for subjectivity and inner growth characteristic of Pietism and the British "sensibility" of Laurence Sterne. Despite the fact that the so-called *Empfindsamkeit* ("sentimentality") that marked the later stages of Enlightenment also emphasized subjectivity, Sturm und Drang departed from the more cautious, evolutionary approach of the previous Enlightenment—eliciting, in fact, a debate in 1774, upon the appearance of *Werther*, in which Enlightenment proponents expressed a growing need to rein in and modify their previously propounded ideals of subjectivity. The Pietistic aim of separating the inner life from the outer, of drawing a line between private and public—although complementary to the Sturm und Drang goal of developing the autonomous individual—also was taken over in less than pure fashion and tended to clash with whatever forays into the public sphere of political change that the movement's proponents nominally propounded.

Ambiguities. Thus, any effort to define this movement is confronted with its ambiguities. Attempts to characterize it often have focused on such unifying factors as the Sturm und Drang drama (Huyssen, 1980), or the heroic male figure variously called the *Genie* (Sauder, 1980), the *Kraftmensch* (Leidner, 1989), or the *grosser Kerl* (Huyssen, 1980). Andreas Huyssen has attempted to place

an overriding structure on the era, dividing it into three moments of significant activity: the beginning of the 1770s, the early phase of intellectual circles forming in Strassburg, Frankfurt, and Göttingen; the middle phase, marked by what he calls the "year of the drama," 1776, when a number of important and characteristic dramas appeared; and the early 1780s, when Schiller's first three plays appeared. Other critics have selected particular dramas either to mark specific traits (Teraoka, 1984) or to point out the mixed nature of the movement. In recent years, however, much Sturm und Drang scholarship has ultimately problematized the simple linear relationship seen among Enlightenment, *Empfindsamkeit*, and Sturm und Drang, and has stressed the need for subtlety and nuance. As Alan Leidner states, for example, "to speak only of Sturm und Drang's spontaneity and immediacy is to tell only half the story, for such expressions are retracted, resolved, and condemned in a variety of ways" (1989, 179).

In the end, what marks this phase near the end of the German Enlightenment is, above all, the represented struggle of individuals whose striving toward autonomy and freedom often ends either in a chastened return to the safe but confining domestic sphere (Klinger's *Sturm und Drang*), or in madness, death (*Götz*), or disfigurement (*Hofmeister*). There is a stark contrast between the cries of dramatic characters for freedom and the dearth of references to actual political and social upheavals (such as the first division of Poland in 1772, or the famines of the early 1770s). As Gerrit Walther comments, "Sturm und Drang plays in German literature, but not in Germany" (quoted in Perels, 1988, 308.) The effort to reconcile often violent means with more noble ends seems destined to fail. The tensions between the individual and the community—whether a community of supporters or the wider contextual community of the state—are inevitable and unresolvable. The specifically German conditions of disparate, often warring principalities and expanding absolutist control, with no concept of a national literature, a national theater (something Lessing and others in the Enlightenment had urged), or a unified cultural perception, were not conducive to the freedom longed for by Goethe's Götz von Berlichingen or Schiller's Karl Moor.

The critique by Enlightenment proponents of the Sturm und Drang group generally centered on the latter's youth: its youthful emotionality and its rash excesses. There is some validity in this characterization, in that those works now labelled "Sturm und Drang" did emerge from the early writings of Herder (his *Journal meiner Reise* (1769) is often considered to mark the movement's beginning phase), the first major dramas of Schiller and Goethe, and the early writings of all of the participants. In subsequent years, the

Weimar Classical period, with its dispassionate remove from exuberant emotions, was viewed by many as a sign of progress toward a more "appropriate" manner of thinking and writing. Yet if we look at the ways in which Sturm und Drang both interacted with and reacted negatively to the earlier stages of the German Enlightenment, what we note in this phase is the sheer complexity of its literary and philosophical developments. Werther, although frequently read as a victim of his own extreme emotions, can argue dispassionately about the rationality of suicide. Goethe could structure *Götz von Berlichingen*, in its depiction of violence and rebellion, as nevertheless a consciously ordered and carefully composed work (Teraoka). Violence itself can be seen as justified within a carefully thought-out scheme of causation—certainly the case in Klinger's *Die Zwillinge*. Lenz could negate the violence-driven, almost anarchic hero of Sturm und Drang, and even eliminate him altogether in favor of heroes who, however parodically, accept responsibility for their actions.

Although Sturm und Drang can be seen as ambiguous and uncertain, its dramas represent a lively authenticity that had not been seen before in German plays. Its struggles to place the individual in the center of society, yet autonomous from it as well, go far beyond the well-meaning expressions of the earlier Enlightenment concerning the development of the bourgeois subject. Its colorful language and tone, in texts as various as Herder's *Journal* and Schiller's *Räuber* and *Kabale und Liebe*, allow for creative moves against the rigidities of Gottsched and the caution of many of its predecessors. The movement's efforts to refocus and reshape Enlightenment thought in its condemnation of smothering absolutist rule are the closest Germany got to any sort of political critique during the course of that century. That the movement was short-lived may well have been a result of the power of German absolutism, which was not challenged and openly attacked as was the case in France at the end of the 1780s. In the end, the very ambiguities that fragment any clear messages that Sturm und Drang presented make for its most intriguing aspects.

[*See also* Aufklärung; Goethe, Johann Wolfgang von; Romanticism; Schiller, Friedrich; Sensibility; *and* Theater, *subentries on* Literary Genre *and* Role of Theater.]

BIBLIOGRAPHY

Hinck, Walter, ed. *Sturm und Drang: Ein literaturwissenschaftliches Studienbuch*. Kronoberg, 1978.
Huyssen, Andreas. *Drama des Sturm und Drang: Kommentar zu einer Epoche*. Munich, 1980.
Karthaus, Ulrich, ed. *Sturm und Drang und Empfindsamkeit*. Stuttgart, 1976.
Leidner, Alan C. "A Titan in Extenuating Circumstances: Sturm und Drang and the *Kraftmensch*." *PMLA* 104 (1989), 178–189.
Mattenklott, Gert. *Melancholie in der Dramatik des Sturm und Drang*. Königstein, 1985.
Perels, Christoph, ed. *Sturm und Drang: Ausstellung im Frankfurter Goethe-Museum*. Frankfurt, 1988.
Prokop, Ulrike. "Der Mythos des Weiblichen und die Idee der Gleichheit in literarischen Entwürfen des frühen Bürgertums." In *Feministische Literaturwissenschaft: Dokumentation der Tagung in Hamburg vom Mai 1983*, edited by Inge Stefan and Sigrid Weigel, pp. 15–21. Berlin, 1984.
Sauder, Gerhard. "Geniekult im Sturm und Drang." In *Deutsche Aufklärung bis zur Französischen Revolution, 1680–1789*, edited by Rolf Grimminger, pp. 327–340. Munich, 1980.
Schmiedt, Helmut. "Wie revolutionär ist das Drama des Sturm und Drang?" *Jahrbuch der Schillergesellschaft* 29 (1985), 48–61.
Teraoka, Arlene Akiko. "Submerged Symmetry and Surface Chaos: The Structure of Goethe's *Götz von Berlichungen*." *Goethe Yearbook* 2 (1984), 13–41.
Wacker, Manfred, ed. *Sturm und Drang*. Darmstadt, 1985.

RUTH-ELLEN B. JOERES

SUBLIME. *See* Aesthetics.

SULZER, JOHANN GEORG (1720–1779), Swiss philosopher, aesthetician, and educationalist.

The son of a minister, Sulzer studied philosophy, mathematics, and botany as well as theology in Zurich. He was also exposed there to the teachings of the historian and aesthetician Johann Jakob Bodmer (1698–1793), with whom he shared some insights. After university, he worked as a private tutor and teacher in a variety of German academies until he retired as a result of ill health in 1773. He was elected to membership in the Royal Academy of Arts and Sciences of Berlin in 1750 and became the director of the philosophical section in 1775. This fact serves as clear confirmation of his status within the academic community, particularly among the core representatives of the Berlin Enlightenment.

His most famous publication was the *Allgemeine Theorie der schönen Künste* (General Theory of Fine Art, 2 volumes, 1771–1774). Intended originally as a German revision of Jacques Lacombe's *Dictionnaire portatif des beaux-arts* (Portable Dictionary of the Fine Arts, 1753), it became a much more substantial project, indeed an encyclopedia. It covers theoretical aesthetics, the aesthetic principles of individual visual art forms, music, and literature, and the history of the arts. Because of its encyclopedic nature, the text does not provide a systematic treatment of its various subject areas, although it is possible to identify some consistent principles. It is clear that Sulzer developed a tendency in aesthetics already identifiable in the work of Alexander Gottlieb Baumgarten (1714–1762) and Georg Friedrich Meier (1718–1777), among others, namely an emphasis on the importance of the receptive subject in the process of reception of art and in particular upon the role of the senses in facilitating that reception. Like many contemporary aestheticians, he was keen to establish the positive status of a field of study concerned primarily with confused representations (*verworrene Vorstellungen*) rather than with the clear representations of rationality. Furthermore, he wished to make clear that the senses need not necessarily be associated with the animal, the base, or the instinctive aspects of human nature, but could rather serve a higher aesthetic and ultimately moral purpose. To that extent, he can be seen as undermining the prescriptive object-based aesthetics of such powerful figures as Johann Christoph Gottsched (1700–1766), who, for example, sought to establish formal directives for the production of good—and so, in his terms, pseudo-French, neoclassical—drama.

For Sulzer, any attempt to derive aesthetic principles was, to begin with, an analysis of the process of the reception of art. This consisted in the arousal of the senses, the generation of aesthetic pleasure, the engagement of the soul, and so, ultimately, the awakening of "genius." Given the use of the last term, it is unsurprising that his work was to have an important influence upon the German literary movement known as the Sturm und Drang (conventionally translated as Storm and Stress) of the 1770s. This period in literary history, also referred to as the *Geniezeit* ("time of genius") was acutely concerned to discover new models for the creation and understanding of literature and to reject the models inherited from Gottsched. The writers of the Sturm und Drang, however, did find it difficult to incorporate some of the moralizing aspects of Sulzer's aesthetic into their more radical program. Given Sulzer's influence upon the radical end of the German literary scene, it is interesting that he himself translated the neoclassical aesthetician Johann Joachim Winckelmann (1717–1768). Winckelmann's aesthetics would superficially have had more in common with those of Gottsched. Yet Winckelmann was above all passionately receptive to art and was convinced that exposure to art could lead to moral improvement in the viewer. Sulzer certainly shared with Winckelmann the belief that art was fundamentally imitative of nature but at best could be representative of an ideal, a category confusingly identified by Winckelmann as *"ideal Natur"* ("ideal nature"). The best of art would need to operate upon the viewer/reader/listener in a twofold manner, through its overall unity and through the individual impacts of its component parts. In the perfect case, the subject would enter an active contemplative state located somewhere between subject and object, not determined entirely either by the object in question or entirely by the sentiments of the subject but mediating between the two. It is this contemplative state that generates good taste, defined as the ability to perceive the beautiful; it may produce a state of moral elevation.

Sulzer was particularly interested in music, and his work in this area exerted considerable influence on contemporary music pedagogy. Unsurprisingly, he saw song as more important than instrumental music and opera as the highest form of drama; it is certainly easy to see how the aesthetic impact of opera might be accounted for in his terms. The variety of individual musical, linguistic, and theatrical components of opera can, in the best cases, unite to form a fantastic whole.

As well as his *Allgemeine Theorie*, he produced a number of other philosophical texts with an emphasis upon aesthetics including *Versuch einiger moralischer Betrachtungen über die Werke der Natur* (Essays on a Moral Consideration of the Works of Nature, 1745) and *Unterredungen über die Schönheit der Natur* (Discussions on the Beauty of Nature, 1750); he also published more general philosophical texts such as *Vermischte philosophische Schriften* (Collected Philosophical Works, 2 volumes, 1773–1781).

There was also a more practical aspect to some of his work, associated with his activity as a teacher. He published a reader covering a wide range of material for grammar schools (Gymnasien) entitled *Vorübungen zur Erweckung der Aufmerksamkeit und des Nachdenkens* (Preliminary Exercises on Awakening Observance and Meditation, 1768). He also wrote on rhetoric and eloquence as in the *Theorie und Praktik der Beredsamkeit* (Theory and Practice of Eloquence, edited by Albrecht Kirchmayer, 1786), which appeared after his death. There would appear to be a clear connection between his philosophical and more broadly educational work; he sought to emphasize the necessity of naturalness (*Natürlichkeit*) in children's education in the hope of achieving a state of *Glückseligkeit* or rapture. In a similar way, art is derived from nature and can produce rapture.

[*See also* Aesthetics *and* Education.]

BIBLIOGRAPHY

Baker, Nancy Kovaleff, and Thomas Christensen, eds. *Aesthetics and the Art of Musical Composition in the German Enlightenment: Selected Writings of Johann Georg Sulzer and Heinrich Christoph Koch.* Cambridge and New York, 1995.
Dobai, Johannes. *Die bildenden Künste in J. G. Sulzers Ästhetik, seine "Allgemeine Theorie der Schönen Künste."* Winterthur, Switzerland, 1978.
Nivelle, Armand. *Kunst- und Dichtungstheorien zwischen Aufklärung und Klassik.* Berlin, 1960. First published as *Les théories esthétiques en allemagne de Baumgarten à Kant.* Paris, 1955.

JEFFREY MORRISON

SUPERSTITION. *See* Revealed Religion *and* Tradition.

SWEDEN. *See* Scandinavia.

SWEDENBORG, EMANUEL (1688–1772), Swedish scientist and mystic.

Swedenborg may be seen as a typical representative of the Enlightenment in many respects; at the same time, however, he exerted a considerable influence on the Romantic and Symbolist movements. After a career as a scientist and mining engineer, he underwent a deep religious crisis in the mid-1740s, which ended in a divine call to interpret the Bible and to found a new Christian church. Above all, he became famous for his visions of spirits and angels, on which he reported in numerous *memorabilia* interspersed in the theosophical works published in London and Amsterdam between 1749 and 1771. He was both adored and derided because of his pretensions to having free access to the world of spirits and to being capable of restoring the original truth of the Bible. One of the earliest and most devastating attacks came from no less a philosopher than Immanuel Kant, who voiced his disappointment at Swedenborg's *Arcana Coelestia* (Heavenly Secrets) in his *Träume eines Geistersehers* (Dreams of a Spirit-seer, 1766).

Swedenborg grew up in a clerical and intellectual milieu. His father was one of the leading figures of the

Emanuel Swedenborg. (Giraudon/Art Resource, NY.)

Church of Sweden, and professor of theology at Uppsala University and later bishop of Skara. As early as his student days, Swedenborg devoted himself to mathematics and technology; the autodidact inventor Christopher Polhem (1661–1751) was his greatest hero. During five years of travel in England, Holland, France, and Germany in the 1710s, he familiarized himself with developments in modern science and learned about many new inventions. In some of his letters, he even proposed his own fanciful designs for an airplane and a submarine.

After his return home, Swedenborg started publishing the first scientific journal in Sweden, *Daedalus hyperboreus* (1716–1718), which dealt mostly with the inventions of Polhem. He also found time to publish some minor works on geology and cosmology in Swedish, but he switched to Latin from the early 1720s on. He also used Latin, the language of the learned, in his theosophical works; as a consequence, Swedenborg became one of the best known Swedish writers internationally and was perceived as the very opposite of a popular preacher.

Philosophically, Swedenborg was inspired primarily by René Descartes, whose cosmology served as his point of departure. Eventually, he pushed himself hard to find a solution to the problem of the intercourse between the soul and the body, which arose out of Descartes's radical distinction between the spheres of thinking and extended matter. Inorganic nature was his focus of attention, culminating in the publication of three folio volumes in 1734, *Opera philosophica et mineralia* (Philosophical and Mineralogical Works). Swedenborg had learned from Descartes's *Principia philosophiae* that matter consists of indefinitely divisible particles in constant motion, and that the world of matter can be described exclusively by mechanical laws. He modified the model of his master, however, by claiming that the planets and the earth emerged from the solar mass (presaging the Kant-Laplace nebular theory), and by following the divisibility of matter to its absolute limit, the mathematical point. Being at the same time a mathematical concept and a material point of departure, this *punctum* was compared to the Roman god Janus with his two faces, a metaphor that Swedenborg was to make use of in physiological contexts later on, to illustrate the function of the cortical substance as a mediator between the blood in the arteries of the brain and the spiritual fluid in its finest fibers.

To his contemporaries, the two mineralogical volumes on copper and iron stood out as the most important parts of Swedenborg's work. It was the philosophical part, however, the *Principia Rerum Naturalium* (Principles of Natural Things), that provided the basis for his progress as a scientist and writer. In the same year, he also published *De Infinito* (On the Infinite), consisting of two essays. The first is devoted to the sensitive issue of how a scientist should deal with the metaphysical problem of the relations between the infinite and the world of matter. Swedenborg concluded this work with admonitions not to conflate the infinity of God with that of mathematics. The only safe way for acquiring knowledge of God, he maintained, is the one sanctioned by the Bible.

This declaration of faith, however, did not restrain Swedenborg from setting breathtaking goals for the continuation of his studies. In the second essay in *De Infinito*, he addressed the problem of the intercourse between soul and body, with the firm intent of applying the laws of mechanics to the mind. His intellectual efforts in the next years would be aimed at proving the immortality of the soul to the senses themselves—that is, empirically. This attempt had been anticipated in the 1710s, when Swedenborg, following Descartes and Polhem, tried to design a mechanistic model for the interrelations between soul and body as a series of vibrations in the nervous system.

Intense reading of anatomical and physiological literature in the decade before his religious crisis inspired Swedenborg to extend and revise this model. He was convinced that the soul must have its seat in the brain, and his attempts at finding its precise position have been particularly admired. Specialists have marveled at Swedenborg's ability to distinguish what seemed reasonable and useful in the enormous amount of data he had to deal with in the volumes he consulted, especially concerning the structure and function of the cortex, the hierarchy of the nervous system, the localization of the cerebrospinal fluid, and the function of the pituitary gland.

Swedenborg's research program forced him not only to collect countless data on the physiological basis of the mind, but also to look for refined philosophical concepts for interpreting them. In his extensive reading, Swedenborg displayed the aspiration for synthesis characteristic of his scientific work. He often declared that he was eagerly awaiting a thinker who would be able to combine the penetrating analytical power of the ancient philosophers with the empirical data of modern scientists—and, no doubt, this was an idealized self-portrait. He excerpted passages from the greatest philosophers of antiquity—Plato, Aristotle, and St. Augustine—as well as from modern rationalists such as Malebranche, Leibniz, and Christian Wolff.

Swedenborg first presented his concept of the human mind in the final chapter of *Oeconomia Regni Animalis* (Economy of the Animal Kingdom), the first of the three works that he published as a result of his far-reaching research program. He proposed a hierarchy of three levels: *anima*, the soul in the full sense of the word, which is in possession of all governing principles but unable to communicate directly with the lower functions; *mens rationalis*, the intellect and the seat of consciousness; and *animus*, the receptacle of the reports of the senses via the nerve fibers.

The scope of language is bound to the intellect, which means that what happens in *anima* remains inaccessible to scientific analysis. The aim of Swedenborg's research, however, was precisely to open the road to the innermost part of the mind. From his youth, he had been fascinated by the mathematical breakthroughs of the seventeenth century, and now he returned to an earlier dream: creating a kind of universal language analogous to analytical geometry and integral calculus. With the help of such an artificial language, it would be possible, he surmised, to formulate the laws of the relations between the spiritual dimension and the world of matter in a logically consistent way.

For a long time, Swedenborg adhered to his opinion that such a mathematical language might be constructed, and he made several attempts himself, but in the end he was forced to look for another solution. He found a substitute for it in his doctrine of correspondences and representations, which he presented in *Regnum Animale* I (The Animal Kingdom) in 1744, while discussing the function of the kidneys in the human body. His point of departure here was a Bible passage (Rev. 2:23) on the Lord's searching the loins and the hearts, from which Swedenborg concluded that the physical world is "purely symbolical" of the spiritual world. At the same time, he declared that he intended to publish a vocabulary with the help of which natural propositions might be transformed into spiritual correspondences.

This plan was never realized during his scientific period, but it became the basis of his voluminous theosophical writings after the end of his religious crisis. Primarily in Genesis, Exodus, and the Revelation of St. John, Swedenborg found a firm basis for the application of a decoding system of correspondences, which often seems far removed from the literal sense of the texts.

After the exegetic chapters in *Arcana Coelestia*, which he published from 1749 to 1756, Swedenborg inserted what he called *memorabilia*, scenes from the world of spirits and angels. Many of these refer to notes in a diary that he kept for more than fifteen years from 1747 onward. They confirm his claims to speak *ex auditis et visis*, from what he has heard and seen. From his visions, he came to believe that the wisdom and love of God flows as light and heat from the eternally shining sun, which is God's representation. In the divine *esse* (being), everything existed potentially before the birth of the cosmos; and man is the only being that can achieve the primary end of the Creation by acts of free will. Consequently, Swedenborg believed that the spiritual world is shaped in the form of a *Maximus Homo*, a universal human being in whose body every fiber consists of a specific community of spirits.

Heaven and Hell are successively expanding through the inflow of deceased souls, who after a while voluntarily join the company of whatever spirits they feel familiar with. For Swedenborg, Hell was not a place where sinners are permanently punished, nor did he grapple with original sin. To sin means that man removes himself from the love of God and fails in his responsibility to fulfill the ultimate end of Creation. Swedenborg put strong emphasis on this responsibility, the duty of being of use to all, and he believed it to be his own primary duty to restore to mankind the true meaning of the Word, which had been lost during centuries of spiritual darkness.

The high value ascribed to the concept of use in Swedenborg's theosophy has social implications well adapted to the era of Enlightenment. In spite of its hierarchical structure, there is a strong element of equality in his spiritual world: all of its inhabitants will turn to those communities that correspond most closely to their inmost feelings and moral qualities. This means that a mundane career does not count if it has not been built on real merits. It also explains why Swedenborg was attracted by the primitivism of the time and gave Africans a prominent position in the world of spirits: he believed that the original revelation of the Lord had been preserved somewhere in Africa. In Swedenborg's universal vision we may recognize the dream of his age for a just society.

As the founder of a new church, Swedenborg relied totally on the argumentative power of his writings and made no efforts to proselytize. Although he attracted some attention in his lifetime, it was not until the 1780s that the first New Church congregations were established in England. Through those congregations, the message of the New Jerusalem soon reached the United States. Since then, various American societies have made Swedenborg's theosophical writings accessible through translation in many languages, and have published a great number of commentaries. About twenty thousand pages of his original manuscripts are stored at the Royal Swedish Academy of Sciences in Stockholm, of which Swedenborg became a member in 1740.

Apart from his impact on the members of New Church societies, a few German Romantic philosophers, and the American Transcendentalists, Swedenborg has been most influential in literature. Johann Wolfgang von Goethe, William Blake, Samuel Taylor Coleridge, and Honoré de Balzac were among his early readers; by way of Charles Baudelaire, his doctrine of correspondence became a frequent reference for the Symbolists of the late nineteenth century. Swedenborg's presence can be felt in the works of outstanding modern writers like William Butler Yeats, Jorge Luis Borges, Czeslaw Milosz, and Martin Walser, as well as that of many of his compatriots—August Strindberg, Lars Gyllensten, and Kerstin Ekma.

[*See also* Mysticism; Natural Philosophy and Science; Revealed Religion; *and* Scandinavia.]

BIBLIOGRAPHY

Bergquist, Lars. *Swedenborgs hemlighet* [The Secret of Swedenborg]. Stockholm, 1999. A valuable modern biography, focused on the theosophical period.

Crasta, Francesca Maria. *La filosofia della natura di Emanuel Swedenborg*. Milan, 1999.

Emerson, Ralph Waldo. *Representative Men*. In this classic collection of essays from 1850 (many later editions), Swedenborg is presented as the representative mystic, which made a great impact on his literary reputation.

Hallengren, Anders. *Gallery of Mirrors: Reception of Swedenborgian Thought*. West Chester, Pa., 1998.

Jonsson, Inge. *Emanuel Swedenborg*. New York, 1971. (Revised edition, *Visionary Scientist: The Effects of Science and Philosophy on Swedenborg's Cosmography*, 1999.)

Lamm, Martin. *Swedenborg: En studie öfver hans utveckling till mystiker och andeskådare*. Stockholm, 1915. Still one of the most important monographs, translated into German in 1922 and French in 1936.

Sigstedt, Cyriel Odhner. *The Swedenborg Epic: The Life and Works of Emanuel Swedenborg*. New York, 1952. A comprehensive modern biography of great value.

Woofenden, William Ross. *Swedenborg Researcher's Manual*. Bryn Athyn, Pa., 1988. A useful manual containing data about Swedenborg's bibliography and an extensive list of collateral literature.

INGE JONSSON

SWIFT, JONATHAN (1667–1745), satirist, poet, and Christian critic of human sin and folly.

Swift was born in Dublin as a posthumous child. At the age of one, he was stolen by his nurse and taken to England; he did not return until the age of three. He was educated at Kilkenny College and Trinity College Dublin, from where, at the age of twenty-two, he entered the service of the ex-diplomat and man of letters Sir William Temple at Moor Park in England. He stayed with Temple for five years, completing his education by voracious reading, but becoming increasingly bitter at his patron's condescension. In 1694, he left and was ordained deacon of Kilroot; however, a reconciliation led him to return to Temple's service until Temple's death in 1699. The following year he was presented with the lucrative living at Laracor, worth £230 a year. Sometime during these years he wrote *A Tale of a Tub*, which he published in 1704. This is a masterpiece of paradox and parodied many fond Enlightenment notions. It caused Swift several later problems, but its satiric style, serious only where jesting, was never surpassed.

Swift returned to England several times on official embassies from the Church of Ireland, and in 1710 found favor with Robert Harley, leader of the new Tory administration. Soon he became a major literary light, defending the government in his regular *Examiner* articles, and *Conduct of the Allies* (1711) and other pamphlets. His circle quickly grew; John Arbuthnot, Alexander Pope, John Gay, and Viscount Bolingbroke became friends, while his former Whig attachments to Addison and Steele declined. This was the height of Swift's ambitions and in his *Journal to Stella*, he recorded every moment.

Queen Anne's death in 1714 led to disarray among her former ministers; the earl of Oxford (Robert Harley) was committed to the Tower, and Bolingbroke, having led the Jacobites in 1715, fled to France. Swift, installed as Dean of St. Patrick's Cathedral, Dublin, in 1713, retired there and, save for two brief visits to England in the late 1720s, remained there until his death in 1745. Increasingly deaf and miserable, he spent his time vexing those around him with his satires. His *Drapier's Letters* (1724), which attacked the English manipulation of Ireland's coinage, led to consternation among the governing class, and glee in the population of Ireland. There followed a period of pamphleteering urging reform of Ireland's status as a "depending kingdom." When these were ignored he retaliated with *A Modest Proposal* (1729), a brief pamphlet arguing, with faultless logic, that the chief marketable commodity that Ireland could supply was its children: "A young healthy child, well nursed, is at a year old a most delicious, nourishing and wholesome food, whether stewed, roasted, baked or boiled."

His chief satire, *Gulliver's Travels* (1726), was written at this time, and in it Swift sought various ways to tease and bamboozle the reader. First, he delights us with exquisitely vain miniatures of humanity in Lilliput; then he intimidates us, in Brobdingnag, with humans magnified so large that Gulliver is too frightened to recognize the sense they speak. Book Three is a kaleidoscope of parodic images, drawn mainly (but not exclusively) from Enlightenment ideals. Finally, he shocks by having sane and peaceful rationality represented by horses (Houyhnhnms), while the human beings (Yahoos) rage, riot, and hurl excrement. To Pope, he said the book proved the falsity of that definition *animal rationale* ["a rational animal"]; and to show it should be only *rationis capax* ["with the capacity for reason"]. Upon that great "foundation of Misanthropy," he said, "the whole building of my Travels is erected; And I never will have peace of mind till honest men are of my opinion." This was a truth that, like all Swift's truths, was false in as many ways as it was true. In *A Tale of a Tub*, he offered, as the sublime "point of felicity... the possession of being well deceived; the serene peaceful state of being a fool among knaves." But that was, characteristically, in a "Digression on Madness." He liked to be outrageous in his formulations, and was never more content than when his defiant notions mystified contemporaries. Pope was nonplussed by the many teasing ironies in *Verses on the Death of Dr. Swift* (1731) and carefully edited them out before sending it to be printed. Swift was not amused

and reinstated them; but did so with a chuckle, puzzling friends as well as enemies.

Swift claimed that Rabelais was his favorite author, and he liked to abuse Enlightenment authors, or lampoon their writings in his own parodic style. Characteristically, his satires confront us with the image of a monster in a maze. He leads us, with his plausible rhetoric, through a maze of conflicting definitions, only to abandon us before some terrifying image of ourselves as baby-eating politicians, or dung-throwing Yahoos. His favorite device is parody, and his artifice of irony is instinctive. Only by acknowledging our own self-love and sin can we acknowledge the essential humanity of Swift. He rests in St. Patrick's cathedral where, according to his own epitaph, "savage indignation can no more lacerate his heart."

[*See also* Counter-Enlightenment *and* Ireland.]

BIBLIOGRAPHY

WORKS BY SWIFT
Complete Poems. Edited by Pat Rogers. Harmondsworth, U.K., 1983.
Correspondence. Edited by Harold Williams. 5 vols. Oxford, 1963–1965.
Poems. Edited by Harold Williams. 2d ed. 3 vols. Oxford, 1958.
Prose Works. Edited by Herbert Davis, et al. 16 vols. Oxford, 1939–1974.

WORKS ABOUT SWIFT
Ehrenpreis, Irvin. *Swift, the Man, His Works, and the Age.* 3 vols. New York, 1962–1983.
Nokes, David. *Jonathan Swift, a Hypocrite Reversed: A Critical Biography.* Oxford, 1985.
Price, Martin. *Swift's Rhetorical Art.* New Haven, Conn., 1953.
Steele, Peter. *Jonathan Swift, Preacher and Jester.* Oxford, 1978.

DAVID NOKES

SWITZERLAND. The word *Switzerland* in the eighteenth century referred to the Confederation of the Thirteen Cantons, established between 1291 and 1513 and comprising Uri, Schwyz, Unterwalden, Lucerne, Zurich, Glarus, Zug, Bern, Solothurn, Fribourg, Basel, Shaffhousen, and Appenzell. Joined together for essentially defensive purposes, these cantons had little else in common. In addition, there was a group of smaller cities, regions, and provinces attached to the Confederation through various types of alliances and special relationships, which can also be considered under the umbrella term *Switzerland*. The Pays de Vaud, for example, was Bernese subject territory; the Principality of Neuchâtel was subject to the King of Prussia; Geneva was an independent city-state. Other allied, protected, or subject districts included the Gray Leagues, Toggenberg, Valais, Ticino, Aargau, and Thurgau. Taken together, these various cities and territories covered an area that coincides largely with present-day Switzerland. However, the many disparities that marked this region make it hard to define what it meant to be Swiss in the eighteenth century, and even harder to conceptualize a single Swiss Enlightenment.

One of the most important cleavages was undoubtedly the confessional one. Basel, Geneva, Bern, Schaffhausen, and Zurich had converted to Protestantism during the Reformation. Compounding this division, some cantons spoke French, others spoke German, and a variety of dialects existed. Different areas were ruled by different systems of government and sustained by different types of economies. There were remote mountain areas and predominantly rural cantons with economies based on traditional-style agriculture, and urban conglomerations with economies based on growing manufacturing and trade. Banking was quickly developing in Protestant cities like Zurich, Geneva, and Basel. All these disparities between regions help to explain why, as late as 1836, Alexis de Tocqueville is said to have remarked, "There are cantons; there is no Switzerland." Even in the eighteenth century, however, a growing number of people would have disagreed with that assessment.

Swiss Mountainscape. *Schmadribach Waterfall in the Lauterbrunn Valley*, painting by Joseph Anton Koch (1768–1839). (Museum der Bildenden Künste, Leipzig, Germany/Erich Lessing/Art Resource, NY.)

Between 1712 and 1798, the region we call Switzerland experienced a remarkable period of intellectual ferment and creativity. This renaissance of thought shared some of the main characteristics of the European Enlightenment. Ideas circulated quickly, owing to a flourishing publishing industry and book trade; journals of different types proliferated, as did learned and philanthropic societies, clubs, and salons. Masonic lodges sprang up in many areas. Two famous centers of enlightened conversation and sociability deserve special mention: the salon of Isabelle de Charrière in Colombier near Neuchâtel, and the chateau of Coppet near Geneva, home to Jacques Necker and his daughter, Germaine Necker de Staël. Both these places, with prominent women at their centers, attracted intellectuals from all over Europe and radiated new ideas outward. Therefore, in Switzerland, as elsewhere in eighteenth-century Europe, one can speak of the emergence of public opinion and, in particular, of a growing political and civic awareness of the need for reforms of various types.

Intellectual Contributions. Intellectual activity was most intense in the Protestant cities. Bern, Geneva, and Zurich had a particularly vibrant intellectual life, with Neuchâtel and Lausanne not far behind. This underscores one of the important characteristics of the Swiss Enlightenment: its friendly relations with Protestantism. A convincing argument has been made that the Enlightenment in Switzerland was an outgrowth of Calvinism in that it was based on what Swiss Protestants regarded as an enlightened faith. Already at the turn of the eighteenth century, Jean-Alphonse Turrettini (1671–1737) of Geneva, Jean-Frédéric Ostervald (1663–1737) of Neuchâtel, and Samuel Werenfels (1657–1740) of Basel had ushered in a less dogmatic, more moralistic brand of Calvinism far removed from the scholastic orthodoxy of the previous century. They preached a tolerant religion, optimistic about human potential, that sought to reconcile faith with reason and accorded a large space to individual conscience and natural theology. Jacob Vernet (1698–1789), the disciple of Turrettini in Geneva, befriended both Voltaire and Rousseau and undertook the publication of Montesquieu's *L'esprit des lois* in 1748.

This brand of Swiss Protestantism seems to have been particularly conducive to exploration in the natural sciences. Several well-connected Swiss researchers acquired international reputations through their work and discoveries in this field. The Genevan Abraham Trembley (1710–1784) studied freshwater polyps, foreshadowing modern research on tissue regeneration and grafting. His compatriot Charles Bonnet (1720–1793) made pioneering discoveries in the field of parthenogenesis (reproduction without fertilization) as well as notable contributions to botany and zoology; he is regarded as a founder of modern biology. Horace Benedict de Saussure (1740–1799), also from Geneva and the first person to climb Mont Blanc, is known for his discoveries in geology, mineralogy, and meteorology.

Other Swiss cities also had their illustrious scientists. Albrecht von Haller (1708–1777) of Bern was a renowned naturalist and physiologist, as well as a leading poet of his generation. In Zurich, scientific and medical research was pursued by Johann Caspar Lavater (1741–1801). In Basel, the Bernouilli family made important contributions in the field of pure and applied mathematics. Mention should also be made of the famous doctors Théodore Tronchin (1709–1781) of Geneva and Samuel-Auguste Tissot (1728–1797) of Lausanne. None of these men had any trouble reconciling their scientific research with their Christian beliefs; both Bonnet and Haller were vocal defenders of the Christian religion against its attackers, in particular against Voltaire. To them, as to other Swiss researchers, explorations in science and the exercise of reason revealed proofs of God's presence.

Switzerland also made important contributions in the fields of jurisprudence, political theory, and pedagogy. Jean Barbeyrac (1674–1744) taught natural law at the Academy of Lausanne and translated Hugo Grotius, Samuel Pufendorf, and Richard Cumberland into French. The Genevan patrician Jean-Jacques Burlamaqui (1694–1748) authored the influential *Principes du droit natural* and *Principes du droit politique* (Principles of Natural and Political Law, 1747 and 1751). Emerich de Vattel (1714–1767) of Neuchâtel made a notable contribution to international law with *Le droit des gens* (The Law of Nations, 1758). Jean-Jacques Rousseau (1712–1778), the famous "citizen of Geneva," authored the *Contrat social* in 1762. His hugely influential *Émile*, published the same year, was a seminal text in pedagogy; in Switzerland, it inspired Johann Heinrich Pestalozzi (1746–1827) of Zurich and Albertine Necker de Saussure (1766–1841) of Geneva to pursue the topic further. Johannes von Müller (1752–1809) of Schaffhausen and Isaac Iselin (1728–1782) of Basel deserve mention as important Swiss historians. Other Swiss authors, such as George Louis Schmid, Théodore Rilliet de Saussure, Jean-Louis Delolme, and Isaac Iselin actively participated in European debates on legislation and political economy. Historians now believe that Swiss authors like these were unique in their attempts to reconcile traditional republican and Christian standards of social justice with the imperatives of economic growth. For this reason, they came to occupy a central position in European debates on political economy. The essay competitions of the Economic Society of Bern were closely watched elsewhere in Europe.

Swiss Nationalism. It was also during the eighteenth century that a growing number of thinkers were led to explore the uniqueness of Switzerland and to affirm a distinctive Swiss character and national consciousness. Through the work of men like Béat de Muralt of Bern, Albrecht von Haller, and Jean-Jacques Rousseau, a "myth of Switzerland" was born and propagated. Béat de Muralt's *Lettres sur les Français et les Anglais* (1725) is widely recognized as a foundational text in this regard. In it, Muralt rejected French notions of "taste" and sophistication, openly criticizing what he instead regarded as French superficiality and decadence. The French were depicted as frivolous and hypocritical; by contrast, the Swiss were held up as an honest, simple people, protected by their mountains and living in uncorrupted freedom, frugality, and peace. The English were described flatteringly as the champions of liberty. Muralt's book, which anticipated many of the arguments of Voltaire's *Lettres philosophiques*, marked an important shift in intellectual allegiance from France to England that is a salient feature of both the Swiss Enlightenment and the burgeoning Swiss myth.

The anti-French sentiment integral to the construction of this Swiss myth was thereafter promoted by Albrecht von Haller. In 1732 he published his *Swiss Verses*, in which he expressed nostalgia for a virtuous and republican Switzerland while attacking the French mentality and way of life. In his famous poem, *The Alps*, Haller hailed the simplicity of the Swiss mountain people while denouncing the "refined madness" of the French. A chosen people, sheltered by their mountains, the Swiss were depicted as rustic, true, simple people, uncorrupted by worldly luxury. In this way, the Swiss Enlightenment contained within it not only an allegiance to religion but also a certain nostalgia for the past, an idealized regard for tradition and for the so-called authentic values associated with it.

This theme was elaborated by Rousseau in his *Discours* and *Lettre à d'Alembert*, and even more in his acclaimed novel *La nouvelle Héloïse*, in which the protagonists are admirers of Béat de Muralt. In Zurich, Muralt's ideas were further developed by Johann Jakob Bodmer (1698–1782) and Johann Jakob Breitinger (1701–1776), who edited a journal entitled *Die Discourse der Mahlern* (The Discourses of the Painters) modeled on Addison's *Spectator*. In it they polemicized against French taste and pleaded for the need to free the literary imagination. Stressing the importance of the "wonderful" in poetry, their literary criticism fostered both the revival of German letters and a pre-Romantic aesthetics. Once again, French values were rejected, this time in favor of a more German orientation. Bodmer's interests in national origins, medieval history, and literature, as well as linguistic particularities, also triggered a reawakened interest in the Swiss-German dialect. This attention to Swiss origins and the desire to promote both a Swiss national consciousness and much-needed reforms led to the creation of the Helvetic Society in 1761. While ostensibly preparing a history of Switzerland, its members tried to promote a unified outlook and Swissness, and to foster patriotism by glorifying Swiss history.

International Connections. Switzerland made a special contribution to the broader European Enlightenment as a mediator and facilitator of the spread of knowledge. Situated at the crossroads of France, Germany, and Italy, Switzerland constituted a nodal point where ideas met, interacted, and were often translated and then further disseminated across Europe. Geneva, Neuchâtel, and Yverdon were important publishing centers, and the Swiss maintained a thriving export trade in books banned in France. In Neuchâtel, the Société Typographique Neuchâteloise played a significant role from 1769 to 1789, publishing French authors like Louis-Sébastien Mercier, Paul-Henri Thiry d'Holbach, Rousseau, and Voltaire, as well as editions of the *Encyclopédie* of Denis Diderot and Jean Le Rond d'Alembert. The *Encyclopédie d'Yverdon* (1770–1780), directed by a Neapolitan convert to Protestantism, Fortunato de Felice (1723–1780), rejected the anticlericalism of the French *Encyclopédie* and attacked French philosophy from a liberal Protestant position. Appearing in fifty-eight volumes between 1770 and 1780, it sought to reconcile faith with reason and progress with tradition.

Conclusion. Although the Enlightenment in Switzerland tended to be the province of political elites and therefore had a conservative bent, Switzerland itself was not immune to political contestations. In particular, eighteenth-century Geneva can be seen as a veritable laboratory of political ideas, a highly charged intellectual context that inspired Rousseau's political theories. Other Swiss cities had their own political turmoil, and Swiss radicals and revolutionaries went on to play important roles abroad, notably in France and America. Thus, while there was a conservative Swiss Enlightenment, there was also a reaction, testifying to the fact that eighteenth-century Swiss intellectual history was as rich and varied as the territory of Switzerland and its people.

[*See also* Geneva; Haller, Albrecht von; Publishing; Rousseau, Jean-Jacques; *and* Trembley, Abraham.]

BIBLIOGRAPHY

Bircher, Martin, François Rosset, and Burbara Roth-Lochner, eds. *Travaux sur la Suisse des Lumières*. Vol. 1. Geneva, 1998. The first volume of a series dedicated to publishing recent scholarship on the Swiss Enlightenment.

Les conditions de la vie culturelle et intellectuelle en Suisse romande au temps des Lumières. In *Annales Benjamin Constant*, edited by Alain Dubois, Anne Hofmann, and François Rosset, vols. 18–19. Lausanne, 1996. Highlights the importance of French-Swiss debates for liberal thinkers like Benjamin Constant and Germaine de Staël.

Francillon, Roger, ed. *Histoire de la littérature en Suisse romande*. Vol. 1. Lausanne, 1996. The most up-to-date discussion available of French-Swiss intellectual and literary themes containing several chapters on the eighteenth century and a useful bibliography.

Im Hof, Ulrich. *Aufklärung in der Schweiz*. Bern, 1970. Somewhat outdated but still useful general discussion of the Swiss Enlightenment.

Kapossy, Béla, ed. *From Republicanism to Welfare Liberalism*. Special issue of *Schweizerische Zeitschrift für Geschichte* 50.3 (2000). Special issue on Swiss political economy. Covers eighteenth- and nineteenth-century Swiss debates on political economy.

Reill, Peter H. *The German Enlightenment and the Rise of Historicism*. Los Angeles, 1975. Contains good discussions of Swiss-German thinkers and argues for their importance to the Aufklärung.

Rosenblatt, Helena. *Rousseau and Geneva*. Cambridge, 1997. Describes the intellectual culture of eighteenth-century Geneva.

Taylor, Samuel. "The Enlightenment in Switzerland." In *The Enlightenment in National Context*, edited by Roy Porter and Mikulas Teich. Cambridge, 1981.

HELENA ROSENBLATT

T

TALES. Among the many literary genres associated with the Enlightenment, tales hold a prominent place. Fairy tales, Oriental tales, and philosophical tales are some of the best-known and most influential works of eighteenth-century Europe. Such tales found their fullest expression in seventeenth- and eighteenth-century France before spreading to other European countries. For this reason, the following article focuses primarily on the French *contes*.

To speak of tales is to speak of a truly heterogeneous genre, if indeed it is properly a genre at all. Even the various subsets of tales discussed here—literary fairy tales, Oriental tales, and philosophical tales—are notoriously difficult to define. The traits most frequently conjured up by the word "tales"—implausible plots and characters, brevity, use of oral storytelling as a narrative pretext, didacticism, or the topos of pleasure as instruction—are hardly infrequent in the Enlightenment avatars of the genre, but such traits are far from universal, and they occur in other genres as well.

Perhaps the most distinctive aspect of this broadly defined genre is revealed through the French word *conte* ("tale"), regularly found in titles. A tale evokes strict and easily identifiable formal and thematic conventions, and writers throughout the Enlightenment gleefully exploited and in many cases parodied such conventions. Paradoxically, then, the strictures of the genre invited experimentation. In many instances, such endeavors translated into literary and ideological subversion, as is attested by the reputations of prominent writers of tales such as Denis Diderot, Jean-Jacques Rousseau, and Voltaire. But there are notable exceptions as well. The far less radical (but formally innovative) narratives of Marie Le Prince de Beaumont and Jean-François Marmontel should remind us that the genre did not always purvey cutting-edge Enlightenment ideas.

Fairy Tales. The origins of Enlightenment tales, although multifaceted, owe much to the appearance of the modern literary fairy tale. To be sure, philosophical ferment and the evolution of the novel were at least equally significant, but the fashion of *contes de fées* ("fairy tale") in late seventeenth-century France was a decisive development. This genre, based not on elite, classical Greek and Roman models but on popular, modern French sources, cleared the way for importing into prose fiction other horizons, such as Orientalism and Enlightenment philosophy that gave birth to Oriental and philosophical tales.

Beyond these offshoots, the seventeenth- and eighteenth-century French literary fairy tale is significant in its own right. In two distinct waves (1690–1715 and 1722–1778), more than 250 fairy tales by forty-nine different authors were published, almost exclusively for adult consumption. The genre began as the written form of a society game played in mid-seventeenth-century Parisian salons and even at the court of Versailles, the object of which was to tell stories resembling those of nurses and governesses, but also incorporating elements from novels, plays, and operas. Dominated by women writers (notably Marie-Catherine d'Aulnoy, Rose de La Force, Marie-Jeanne L'Héritier de Villandon, and Henriette-Julie de Murat), the first wave of *contes de fées* put into place an aesthetic that was to be widely imitated and parodied later in the eighteenth century. The tales state from the very outset that the hero and heroine will ultimately triumph over their adversaries; they highlight the exemplary moral and social destiny of the heroic couple; and they establish the self-sufficiency of the marvelous universe. One notable collection of tales from the first wave, and the most famous of all collections of French fairy tales, does not subscribe to this aesthetic—the *Contes de ma mère l'oye* (Mother Goose Tales) of Charles Perrault (1691–1697). In spite of the numerous differences of style and content between Perrault's tales and those of the other fairy-tale writers of his time, all the late seventeenth century *contes de fées* belong to the Modern side in the contemporary Quarrel of Ancients and Moderns.

Eighteenth-century France witnessed a second wave of fairy tales. Many of these developed the stylistic and thematic precedents established earlier—for example, tales by Philippe de Caylus, Marie-Antoinette Fagnan, Louise Levesque, Catherine de Lintot, Mlle. de Lubert, Henri Pajon, and Gabrielle-Suzanne de Villeneuve. Others took the genre in different directions, including religious and political satire (Louis de Cahusac, Jacques Cazotte, Claude-Prosper de Crébillion *fils*, Charles Duclos, Charles de La Morlière, Rousseau, Henri-Charles

TALES

146 TALES

Mother Goose Tales. Frontispiece from *Contes de ma mère l'oye* (Mother Goose Tales) by Charles Perrault (1628–1702). (The Pierpont Morgan Library/Art Resource, NY.)

de Senneterre, Claude-Henri de Voisenon) and more or less explicit pornography (Cahusac, Crébillon, Senneterre, and Voisenon especially). That the last two categories often parody the fairy-tale form underscores the genre's contribution to the increasingly self-reflexive nature of eighteenth-century literature. Decidedly unsatirical and unparodic are the tales of Marie Le Prince de Beaumont, who defined a new (and thereafter dominant) use for the genre and inaugurated children's literature in France by writing moralizing stories explicitly for children.

Oriental Tales. Perhaps the single most important off-shoot of the eighteenth-century *conte de fées* is the Oriental tale. Appearing at the end of the first wave, Antoine Galland's immensely popular *Mille et une nuits* (Arabian Nights, 1704–1716) included the first and most influential version in a western European language of such stories as "Aladdin and the Magic Lamp," "Ali Baba," and "The Voyages of Sinbad." Galland's translation/adaptation also spawned stories that incorporate vaguely Oriental motifs, characters, and settings, such as works by Thomas-Simon

Gueullette and the abbé de Bignon, among many others. The vast numbers and immense popularity of these Oriental tales played a decisive role in the development of western European Orientalist stereotypes that found their way into literary works of philosophical and social critique, not least of which are Montesquieu's *Lettres persanes* (1721) and Voltaire's *Zadig* (1748).

Philosophical Tales. Philosophical tales, the third major category of Enlightenment tales, incorporate elements from both the *conte de fées* and the Oriental tale. They often feature implausible plots and not infrequently draw on the Oriental milieu popularized by the *Arabian Nights* and imitations of it. Yet the essence of philosophical tales lies elsewhere. In works by Voltaire, the consummate master of the genre, but also in those of Stanislas-Jean de Boufflers, Diderot, and even the marquis de Sade, narrative episodes combine to highlight a philosophical argument (for example, the opposition of societal constraints and individual happiness in *Candide*, 1759) through the kind of witty satire often associated with eighteenth-century Parisian salons. The plots of philosophical tales revolve around an extended voyage or a quest for a beloved, and the hero struggles against human stupidity, avarice, and suffering. In the end, these narratives are, as Thomas Kavanagh puts it, both "secular allegory and civic fable," the primary intent of which is to promote the power of reason. Individual happiness, these tales purport, can be attained only by wielding the arm of rational analysis for oneself. This idea, central to the Enlightenment, is but one of many notions that the philosophical tale made accessible to a broad public.

Subversion as Impetus for Tales. Perhaps the most important feature shared by all Enlightenment tales of all three types is their propensity to subvert literary, social, and philosophical norms. This is by no means to suggest that all of these tales are subversive, but rather to convey the polemical reputation of the genre, which, on balance, is deserved. From the earliest fairy tales to the late philosophical tales of Diderot and Voltaire, subversion is indeed an overriding motivation.

Precisely what is subverted and how this is accomplished vary according to the type of tale. The first wave of literary fairy tales takes on particular significance in the context of the Quarrel of Ancients and Moderns. Charles Perrault was the acknowledged leader of the "Moderns" and gained lasting popularity for his collection of tales. More significant, all the tales of the first "wave" are based (if only minimally and indirectly) on folkloric traditions and thereby reject the hegemony of classical models while asserting the validity of "indigenous" national sources for literary creation. At the same time, they resist, or at least redefine, the explicit didacticism often associated with the folktale. Hence, it is no exaggeration to say that the *contes de fées* are part of a far-reaching exploration of the nature and purpose of literature. They also reflect the changing composition of the literary field: the first wave was one of the few times a literary movement has been dominated by women. Through tales that closely resemble novels in style and content, these women gave expression to their collective and individual ambitions as writers and readers. As recent studies have argued (Hannon and Seifert), they also advocated, in various ways and to different degrees, a revision of women's roles in society.

Women continued to write fairy tales in the eighteenth century, but these tales did not dominate the second wave numerically. By this time, the *conte de fées* had entered the male literary mainstream, which it had not done before. Throughout the eighteenth century, the fairy-tale form itself was less subversive than the rewritings it occasioned in the guise of Oriental, satirical, and pornographic fictions. Although many eighteenth-century fairy tales deserve to be better known (for instance, Crébillon's *L'écumoire* [1734], La Morlière's *Angola* [1746], or Rousseau's "La Reine fantasque" [1754]), for the most part they did not have the same public impact that Oriental and philosophical tales had. In the long run, the very features that set the form apart—the romance-centered plots and obligatory magical characters—undoubtedly also limited their public appeal.

Central to the Oriental and philosophical tales are the themes of self-exploration and self-critique. Although hardly absent from fairy tales, these themes are given their most memorable expression in works such as *Lettres persanes*, *Micromégas* (1752), and *Candide*. In these tales, confrontations with the exotic Other, aliens from outer space, and a wide array of social and natural disasters lead readers to the conclusion that the self should be defined not through social conformity but rather through individual reflection. At the same time, the heroes' misadventures throughout the tale poke fun at—and thus subvert—the intolerance and tyranny of established beliefs and institutions. Humor was a key element of the Oriental tale and especially of the philosophical tale. The deft use of allusion, caricature, exaggeration, and insinuation enabled writers largely to circumvent the active censorship of the period and to publicize their ideas rather than being confined to the literary underground.

Like all subversion, that of the Enlightenment tales is not without its limits. Critics have inveighed against the aristocratic bias of seventeenth- and eighteenth-century French fairy tales (Robert), the exoticism of the Oriental tales (Lowe), and the bourgeois universalism of the philosophical tales (Barthes). More fundamentally, all these tales contribute to the myth of self-mastery that was so powerfully put into place by the Enlightenment. Nonetheless, these important objections should not cause us to lose sight of the genre's polemical import, especially in the context of eighteenth-century European culture. Not only did these works make philosophical debate accessible to readers otherwise unprepared to engage in it; but as Kavanagh has argued, they also militated for displacing the social by the personal and, thus, ideology by rational critique. That this critique has blind spots is incontrovertible and inevitable, but equally significant are the ideological blind spots that Enlightenment tales helped eighteenth-century readers recognize.

A Marginalized Genre. Eighteenth-century French literary fairy tales, Oriental tales, and philosophical tales endured a paradoxical fate. Popular in their own day, influential on writers of other Enlightenment and post-Enlightenment European countries (for instance, the German Romantic *Märchen* and Samuel Johnson), and, in a few instances, classics for students of literature (*Lettres persanes*, *Candide*), these genres have been unduly marginalized by literary critics, who have instead privileged the novel. Although such a bias is understandable in view of the prominence the novel gained throughout the eighteenth and nineteenth centuries, it obscures the different aesthetic to which the *conte* adheres. Whereas the novel endeavors to develop the psychology of its characters and to create the illusion of realism, the tale emphasizes style and assembles rapid and implausible episodes. Critics who apply the aesthetic criteria of the novel to tales have often failed to recognize that the latter seek to distance the reader from the narrative and to reinforce the necessity of interpretation and critique. Rereading Enlightenment tales through the lens of their own aesthetic, not the novel's, would allow us to recognize more fully the crucial role they played in the diffusion of Enlightenment ideas and in the subversion of pre-Revolutionary ideologies and institutions.

[*See also* Ancients and Moderns; Diderot, Denis; Literary Genres; Men and Women of Letters; Novel; Sociability; *and* Voltaire.]

BIBLIOGRAPHY

Barchilon, Jacques. *Le conte merveilleux français de 1690 à 1790: Cent ans de féerie et de poésie ignorées de l'histoire littéraire*. Paris, 1975.

Barthes, Roland. "Le dernier des écrivains heureux." In his *Essais critiques*, pp. 94–100. Paris, 1964.

Dufrénoy, Marie-Louise. *L'Orient romanesque en France*. Montréal, 1946.

Hannon, Patricia. *Fabulous Identities: Women's Fairy Tales in Seventeenth-Century France*. Amsterdam and Atlanta, 1998.

Kavanagh, Thomas. "Boufflers's *La Reine de Golconde* and the *conte philosophique*." *French Forum* 23.1 (1998), 5–21. Extremely useful synthesis and critique of approaches to the philosophical tale.

Keener, Frederick M. *The Chain of Becoming: The Philosophical Tale, the Novel, and a Neglected Realism of the Enlightenment: Swift, Montesquieu, Voltaire, Johnson, and Austen*. New York, 1983. A study of the interconnections between the philosophical tale and the novel.

Lowe, Lisa. *Critical Terrains: French and British Orientalisms*. Ithaca, N.Y., 1991.

May, Georges. *Les mille et une nuits d'Antoine Galland, ou le chef d'œuvre invisible*. Paris, 1986. A major reassessment of the *Thousand and One Nights* that argues for a reconsideration of late seventeenth- and early eighteenth-century French literary traditions.

Robert, Raymonde. *Le conte de fées littéraire en France de la fin du XVIIᵉ siècle à la fin du XVIIIᵉ siècle*. Nancy, France, 1982. A seminal study of the seventeenth- and eighteenth-century French literary fairy tales that incorporates folkloristic, narratological, and sociohistorical approaches.

Seifert, Lewis C. *Fairy Tales, Sexuality, and Gender in France, 1690–1715: Nostalgic Utopias*. Cambridge Studies in French, 55. Cambridge, 1996.

Van den Heuvel, Jacques. *Voltaire dans ses contes: De "Micromégas" à "L'Ingénu."* Paris, 1967. The most comprehensive study to date of Voltaire's *contes*.

Lewis C. Seifert

TAXONOMY. All human cultures separate local biodiversity into taxonomies whose basic level is that of the "generic species." Generic species often correspond to scientific species (for example, dog, apple tree); however, for phenomenally salient organisms, such as most vertebrates and many flowering plants, a scientific genus frequently has only one locally occurring species (for example, bear, oak). In addition to the spontaneous division of local flora and fauna into generic species, such groups have, according to Charles Darwin, "from the remotest period in ... history ... been classed in groups under groups. This classification [into higher- and lower-order groups, for example, tree / oak / white oak] is not arbitrary like the grouping of stars in constellations."

As in any native folk-biological inventory, ancient Greek and Roman naturalists contended with only five or six hundred local species. Because biological genus and species are often extensionally equivalent in any given locale, there was no conceptual basis for systematically distinguishing them. For Aristotle and Theophrastus, as for Dioscorides and Pliny, the term *atomon eidos*, or "species," referred to generic species (for example, eagle, dog, oak, wheat), whereas the term *megiston genos*, or "genus," referred to superordinate life forms (for example, bird, quadruped, tree, grass).

Europe's Age of Exploration introduced a multitude of new species. In 1694, the French naturalist Joseph Tournefort originated the genus concept as the ranked class immediately superordinate to that of the species. This allowed the reduction of species by an order of magnitude to equivalence classes that the mind could easily manage again (from roughly six thousand known species to six hundred genera). The place of a new species in the natural order of genera would be initially determined in either of two ways: (1) By empirical intuition, that is, readily visible morphological agreement with a European representative or some other preferred-type species of the genus; or (2) by intellectual intuition, that is, analytic agreement with the generic fructification (fruit and flower) according to the number, topological disposition, geometrical configuration, and magnitude of its constituent elements. Within this Cartesian framework, the one criterion would ultimately be commensurate with the other, allowing a mathematical reduction of the new species to its associated type by reason of their common fructification. In this way, the customary native knowledge of the folk naturalist would be rationally extended to a worldwide scale. Such was the aim of Carolus Linnaeus's 1735 "natural system."

Under John Locke's influence, in 1703, the English naturalist John Ray questioned whether fructification characters encoded the essential order of plant life. Analytic convenience might justify reliance on readily visible and numerable parts of the fruit and flower as a classificatory strategy, but there was no guarantee such analytic characters could be arranged into a preset combinatory system with absolute certainty. In the case of animals, reduction of visible parts to computable characters proved unwarranted.

The geometric rate of exploration and discovery further undermined the taxonomic priority of the genus. As awareness of new forms increased another order of magnitude, the family concept became the new basis for taxonomy. The family was itself rooted in local groupings that native folk implicitly recognize but seldom name, such as felines, equids, legumes, and umbellifers. The ancients called these *eide anonyma* or *genera innominata*. The local series of such groupings does not fully separate a local environment, but is riddled with gaps. A strategy emerged for closing them: Looking to other environments to complete local gaps, naturalists sought to discern a worldwide series that would cover the gaps in any and all environments. This would reduce the ever-increasing number of species and genera to a mnemonically manageable set of basic family plans that were still perceptually distinguishable. In 1751, Linnaeus dubbed this strategy "the natural method" for completing "family fragments."

French Enlightenment naturalists elaborated the natural method, favoring empiricism over rationalism. In 1763, Michel Adanson introduced the idea of classification by family resemblances *(air de famille)* for completing a worldwide family series, and in 1789, Antoine-Laurent Jussieu reduced the thousands of genera proposed since Tournefort to exactly one hundred families, but acknowledged this number to be more convenience than necessity. Jussieu's families became the standards of modern plant taxonomy. Extending the *méthode naturelle* to animals, including humans, Georges-Louis Leclerc de Buffon first identified family plans as lineages of temporally related species. This idea became crucial to the evolutionary thinking of Jean-Baptiste Lamarck and Charles Darwin. Although Enlightenment taxonomy kept biological science tied to the readily visible world of species, genera, and families, it provided a cognitively expedient morphological framework for initial exploration of the causal relations and history of species. Its success gave rise to taxonomies in many other fields as scholars worked to bring order to libraries, minerals, cultures, chemical compounds, language, and much else.

[See also Banks, Joseph; Botany; Buffon, George-Louis Leclerc de; Chemistry; Colonialism; Commerce and Trade; Linnaeus, Carolus; Natural History; North America; and South Seas.]

BIBLIOGRAPHY

Atran, Scott. Cognitive Foundations of Natural History: Towards an Anthropology of Science. Cambridge, 1990.

Burckhardt, Richard. The Spirit of System: Lamarck and Evolutionary Biology. Cambridge, Mass., 1977.

Frängsmyr, Tore, ed. Linnaeus: The Man and His Work. Berkeley, Calif., 1983.

Greene, Edward L. Landmarks of Historical Botany. 2 vols. Stanford, Calif., 1983.

Jacob, François. The Logic of Life. New York, 1973.

Lyon, John, and Phillip R. Sloan. From Natural History to the History of Nature: Readings from Buffon and His Critics. Notre Dame, Ind., 1981.

Mayr, Ernst. The Growth of Biological Thought. Cambridge, Mass., 1982.

Morton, A. G. History of Botanical Science. New York, 1981.

Raven, Peter, Brent Berlin, and Dennis Breedlove. "The Origins of Taxonomy." Science 174 (1971), 1210–1213.

Stevens, Peter F. The Development of Biological Systematics: Antoine-Laurent de Jussieu, Nature and the Natural System. New York, 1994.

SCOTT ATRAN

TAYLOR, JOHN (1753–1824), Virginia planter, agricultural reformer, and political philosopher.

Like many late-eighteenth-century American intellectuals, Taylor considered the newly created American republic a special place—a place where mankind, employing fresh principles springing from the new world environment, had the opportunity to create an entirely different kind of society, a society based on reason and talent. He confidently expected the ideals of popular sovereignty and personal autonomy to thrive within a world free of artificial distinctions. Shortly after the ratification of the Constitution, however, Taylor began to experience doubts about the future of American society. He believed that legislation enacted under the auspices of the new federal government awarded especial favors to capitalists at the expense of honest working people; he saw power and property being transferred from productive to unproductive classes within American society.

For the remainder of his life, Taylor ardently opposed the development of finance capitalism. His perception of the special quality of American politics and the manner in which he penetrated to the ethical and moral issues at the very center of the liberal world emerging around him found its clearest expression in his major work, An Inquiry into the Principles and Policies of the Government of the United States (1814). Here Taylor cut through the antiquated theory of a mixed polity comprised of monarchy, aristocracy, and democracy and offered a brilliant expression of the new conception of politics that emerged in America with the Revolution. The people were not divided into natural orders, but instead existed as a sovereign whole that distributed power among the various branches of the state and national governments, thereby preventing a dangerous accumulation of power in any particular branch of government. Then, following the writings of Adam Smith, Taylor grafted an idealized version of a market economy to these republican principles. Governments in America should foster the free exchange of goods produced by honest labor; they must never privilege one class over another by awarding it special favors. The Inquiry, however, clearly outlined how finance capitalism was creating a modern aristocracy of wealthy merchants, bankers, and financiers at the expense of honest labor. It portrayed a world based on the evil principles of avarice and ambition—under the aegis of the Constitution—rapidly displacing a society based on honest exchange and harmonious relationships.

Taylor occupies a strangely anomalous place in American intellectual history. Unlike most Enlightenment writers in America, Taylor assumed a pessimistic outlook; in his mind, America's golden age lay in the past, not in the future. Further, his major writings appeared long after the major points of the Constitution had been established and consequently appeared anachronistic. In addition, he never turned his critical abilities upon his own Virginia society. Instead, he equated the survival of slavery with the very existence of a natural, harmonious republican culture. As a result, Taylor's penetrating analysis of liberal capitalism was lost when it became entangled in a crabbed version of states' rights that led to secession and civil war.

[See also Political Philosophy.]

BIBLIOGRAPHY

For perceptive insights into various aspects of the thought of John Taylor, see Loren Baritz, City on a Hill: A History of Ideas and Myths in America (New York, 1964); Gordon S. Wood, The Creation of the American Republic, 1776–1787 (Chapel Hill, N.C., 1969); and Steven Watts, The Republic Reborn: War and the Making of Liberal America, 1790–1820 (Baltimore, 1985). Robert E. Shalhope integrates Taylor's life and thought in John Taylor of Caroline: Pastoral Republican (Columbia, S.C., 1980).

ROBERT E. SHALHOPE

TECHNOLOGY. Shaped by existing technologies and their attendant cultural systems, most notably those of the printed book, the Enlightenment engendered technological modernity by changing the relationship between the skills of the artisan and the overarching structures of knowledge to which these had previously been thought inferior. No longer understood as transcendentally ordered, human knowledge began to be seen as the temporal product of humanity's own contrivance and convention, at once natural and artificial, and as likely to be produced by an artisan as by a philosopher.

Experiments and Engineers. In many fields—textile carding and weaving, for instance—existing modes of skill diffusion and technical transfer continued, both within Europe and from beyond. A notable British example was the development of mechanical silk-throwing by John and Thomas Lombe in the 1710s, from an Italian adaptation of much older Chinese techniques. Our main story, however, opens with the dissemination of Newtonian mechanics, first within Britain itself, and then in continental Europe. Originating in the experimental procedures developed in the Royal Society of Robert Boyle and Isaac Newton, and thence broadcast by lecture and demonstration to the coffeehouses and mercantile mathematical academies of London, "applied Newtonianism" constituted a usable form and language of natural knowledge. English readers found in Newton's *Opticks* (1704) a manual of experimental practice. Thereafter, the chief architect of its dissemination, in which public demonstration was of paramount importance, was Newton's Huguenot associate John Theophilus Desaguliers (1683–1744), who came from Oxford University in 1712 to be the Royal Society's first curator of experiments.

Exhibited experiments exercised a persuasive power over the mind of the public, but equally important were the working connections formed between experimental philosophers, instrument makers, and the emerging community of practical engineers and entrepreneurs. Desaguliers and lecturers like him developed extensive networks linking experimentalists and their gentleman amateur patrons to the investments of stockjobbing promoters. Desaguliers's own patron from around 1720 to 1740, James Brydges, first duke of Chandos (1673–1744), belonged to this group of landowners and investors interested in finance, capitalized agriculture, mineral exploitation, and urban development. By the 1730s, these networks extended to voluntary agencies, such as hospitals, whose staffs and subscribers constituted part of the base of a distinctive provincial Enlightenment that aided in the countrywide diffusion of applied Newtonian teaching as the century progressed. In London, Royal Society philosophers and East End mathematical mechanists were brought together across a wide range of projects, such as the building of the new Westminster Bridge in the later 1730s, which utilized watchmaker-designed pile drivers. Engineering, metallurgical, and chemical linkages proliferated, running from London, where consistent materials were essential for the making of instruments, to other centers in the provinces. Among the most strategic of these were the crucible steel process developed in Sheffield (c. 1740–1750) by the Quaker horologist Benjamin Huntsman (1704–1776), and the development in metal machining of all kinds that is highlighted in the correspondence of the young James Watt (1736–1819). Especially important was the designed cutting of fine-pitch screw threads and gear trains, which stemmed from the navigational and cartographic demand for geared instruments that could be precisely calibrated. The celebrated horizontal cannon-boring machine of the Shropshire ironmaster John Wilkinson (1728–1808) may have solved the problem of cylinder leakage on the prototype Watt engine in 1774, but it was the pioneering work of the London instrument makers and lathe-men, notably Jesse Ramsden (1735–1800) and Henry Maudslay (1771–1831), that made possible the precision parts manufacture on which the full deployment of the Watt engine and its successors depended. It was in this competitive environment that specialized-parts production and finishing brought down the cost of nautical timekeeping, and so finally solved the longitude problem by enabling the navy and the East India Company to equip their ships with affordable successors to the magnificent, but unique, timekeepers of John Harrison (1693–1776).

These advances involved more than the "cutting edge" technology represented by the steam, or rather "atmospheric," engines of Thomas Savery (1650–1715) and Thomas Newcomen (1663–1729), for which Desaguliers was a chief advocate and an installation consultant. Throughout the two volumes of his *Course of Experimental Philosophy* (1734, 1744), Desaguliers insisted that a proper union of principle and practice was necessary for sound and cost-effective engineering of any kind. The reservoirs, mill dams, and waterwheels, to which stationary steam power remained largely ancillary into the mid-Victorian era (c. 1865), and even such ordinary equipment as the quarry carts that carried stone for the building of Bath, all required it. In the wake of rationalized engineering came rationalized business practices.

In Britain by the century's later years, when the fame of two of Desaguliers's most distinguished successors was drawing respectable families in the English midlands to exhibitions of the grand orrery or "Eidouranion" of Adam Walker (c. 1731–1821), the acme of Birmingham brasswork, and to the chemistry lectures of John Warltire (1739–1810), the earlier ethos of experiment had evolved into a widely diffused "culture of invention." Moreover,

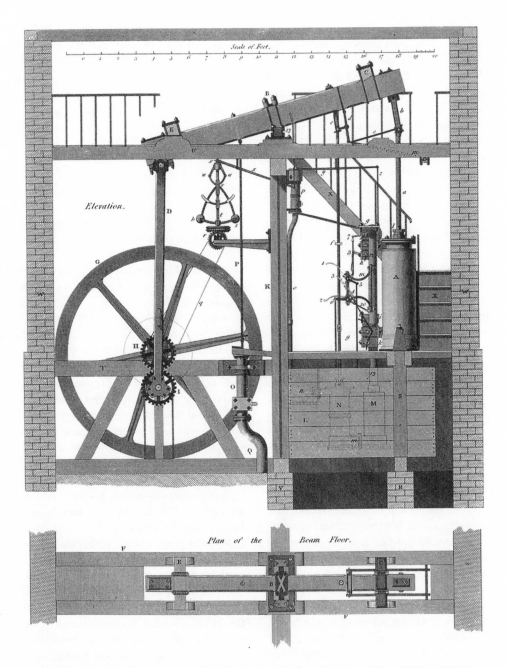

Technology. Single-acting steam engine by Matthew Boulton and James Watt, 1781 model. From Abrahm Rees's *Cyclopaedia* (London, 1820). (Ann Ronan Picture Library/Art Resource, NY.)

the sheer variety of skilled techniques pursued in the workshops of independent masters makes any attempt to distinguish systematically between inspired tinkering and "scientific" method ultimately impossible to sustain. Now, invention no longer meant simply the "finding" of facts benignly placed in nature for discoverable human use within limits ordained by divine Superior Wisdom. "Philosophers," it seemed, had themselves invented the way of inventing, the revolutionary potential of which alarmed the French industrial spies who were trying to

fathom it. What contemporaries were witnessing was the start of the epochal transition from an "advanced organic economy," still based on naturally occurring structural materials, to a "mineral energy economy," artifactually built and moved by the exploitation of coal, metals, and other geological reserves.

Art captured the varying responses. Poems such as Erasmus Darwin's Miltonic paean to "Unconquered Steam" praised the developments; those of William Blake, to say the least, did not. The profoundly ambiguous depictions of experimental demonstrations by the painter Joseph Wright of Derby (1734–1797), part domestic melodrama, part romantic sublime, leave the viewer uncertain. Industrial landscapes by Wright and others, including George Robertson (1742–1788) and such European counterparts as Per Hillestrom (1732–1816) and Leonard Defrance (1735–1805), show rather frightening changes. Whether the unbinding of Prometheus signified the advent of human perfectibility remained an open question. Erasmus Darwin looked forward unperturbed to the deep interpenetration of natural processes and human machination. Joseph Wright and others like him were not so sure.

European awareness of new technologies came remarkably quickly, but awareness did not necessarily mean the acceptance and implementation of them. Actual use depended upon many things including levels of literacy, fuel supplies, and effective demand for the products that were to be produced. One of the main transfer routes was between England and the Dutch Republic through the University of Leiden. Another was between the Newcastle area, southeast Scotland, and the Baltic countries, where the westernizing state-building ambitions of Peter the Great and Russo-Swedish rivalry during the Great Northern War increased interest and promoted inquiry and investment. Desaguliers was in Saint Petersburg in 1717–1718 building Savery steam engines; at nearly the same time, Swedes who had been in Newcastle, Edinburgh, and Fife adapted Newcomen engines to drive ore-crushing machinery. Peacetime diffusion was often equally rapid. After informal contacts during the Orleans Regency (1715–1723), the London Engine-Proprietors (largely members of the Royal Society) lobbied successfully for a patent to bring steam-pumping machinery to the Paris water supply in 1726–1727. The first French-built engine followed in 1731 in the Hainault coalfield. The imperial authorities in Vienna were equally interested in novelties. Ultimately, the area of most extensive and complete assimilation was in the Austrian Netherlands, where abundant coal stocks and extensive market access combined with favorable cultural and governmental conditions to produce a quasi-British entrepreneurial climate.

French Technological Innovation. It was France, however, where the word *engineer* denoted not the hybrid philosophical artisan of latitudinarian England and moderate Scotland, but a member of the army's *corps de genie*, which generated both the most strenuous and systematic commitment to a technological society; and, in the writings of Jean-Jacques Rousseau, the most searching critique of it. The Académie Royale des Sciences, founded by Jean-Baptiste Colbert in 1666, was initially committed to absolutist concepts of the use of knowledge, which showed only sporadic signs of changing before the 1740s. Natural knowledge was to be developed by and applied for the state, not by or for the many interests which had embraced it in Britain. Whatever the role of Newtonian popularizers like Voltaire and Émilie Le Tonnelier de Breteuil du Châtelet, or, as in Britain, experimental lecturers, such as Jean-Antoine Nollet (1700–1770), Newtonianism's institutional reception in France was fixed by the controversy over the shape of the Earth. This took place in the Académie Royale between the Cartesian astronomer Jacques Cassini (1677–1756) of the Paris Observatory, and the Newtonian astronomer Pierre-Louis Moreau de Maupertuis (1698–1759). The latter's vindication of Newtonian "truth" was offset by the academy's reassertion of its theoretically based authority over the development of French natural philosophy and its applications. Consequently, "public science," in the sense of an open and diverse working association between theory and practice, never developed in the ancien régime into the formative component of a more general culture such as it became in Britain. Paris had no counterpart to London's Royal Society of Arts, which despite its later title was in its origins unofficial, provincial, and somewhat associated with the opposition to the court of George II.

The main history of French technological innovation is thus one of delayed formal adoption of Newtonianism, still selectively determined by the priorities of the state and the constraints of precedence and patronage. At the practical level, however, this was offset by the cross-channel transference of know-how, as recent English advances in existing technologies were procured by industrial espionage and by suborning skilled workers. In this process women were as practically valuable as men, though the latter played the more prominent organizational role. Notable among them was the remarkable ex-Jacobite John Holker (1719–1786) of Manchester, who fled to Rouen and later became inspector-general of foreign manufactures. He founded a French industrial dynasty in textiles and chemicals. Another entrepreneur, from Birmingham, was the brass founder Michael Alcock (c. 1714–1775), who took light metal goods production to France in 1755.

After the reforming administration of Anne-Robert-Jacques Turgot (1774–1776), the French state became steadily and more comprehensively committed to scientific and technological solutions to its problems. During the optimistic 1780s something like a reverse grand tour developed as liberal young noblemen crossed the Channel to study English agriculture and see such works as the Soho plant of Matthew Boulton (1728–1809) and James Watt in Birmingham. Leading British manufacturers were then as interested in reaching new markets—they sometimes sent their own sons to complete their modern education on the Continent—as in keeping industrial spies off their premises. Nevertheless, local particularism, misdirected attempts to remedy the natural deficits that restricted France's steel production, even something as basic as the consequent chronic shortage of the hard steel hand files needed for the actual fitting of machinery, perpetuated a gap in France between public expectations of technology and its actual deployment. Differences should not, however, obscure a longer term convergence. In the later 1790s, the British state, like its Napoleonic rival, embraced a role in the technological application of science similar to that earlier upheld by Turgot's administration. The result was the Royal Institution, founded in 1799 in close association with the wartime government of William Pitt as the applied arm of the nation's scientific endeavors. There, Lavoisian chemistry was harmonized under the aegis of Sir Humphry Davy (1778–1829) with the structure and organization of existing British practice. The result recalls, in reverse, the Académie Royale's reception of Newtonianism over half a century before.

Technology and Society. The meanings that enlightened men and women attached to experiments, instruments, machines, and progress go far to restore to the last quarter of the eighteenth century the idea of an Industrial Revolution—an idea that much recent socioeconomic interpretation has sought to remove altogether. Reinstatement, however, does not mean that this technological change can be isolated from the inherited realities in which it occurred. In all cases, new technologies disrupted customary patterns of community and the organization of work. Technological changes often drew population away from older regions of rural protoindustry. Industrialization, thus, went hand in hand with a kind of deindustrialization. In typical settings, such as the West Riding of Yorkshire and the West Midlands hardware district, there were forms of settlement that were neither "urban" nor "rural" and modes of production that were neither "technological" nor traditionally "handcraft." Such changes bore on family formation and birth and mortality rates and thus had effects on population growth. Technology also affected the gendering of work. Because machine manufacture required technical knowledge and removed production from its previous domestic settings, the long-standing assumption has been that work became, conceptually and actually, predominantly masculine. This ignores the complex realities of change. In high-demand manufactures—block-printed textiles, for example—machine replacement of female labor in some aspects of production was offset by increased employment of women elsewhere. Whatever the effect of technology on the conceptual gendering of work, recent research shows that women significantly outnumbered men in the aggregate workforce of the early Industrial Revolution.

The Enlightenment saw a profound connection between technology and the arts but it had little precognition of the political economy of the factory and the rise of industrial modernity. Denis Diderot's *Encyclopédie* illustrated technical processes largely from a collection of plates commissioned decades previously by the Colbertian Académie Royale des Sciences. Many showed artisans in workshops hand-producing goods for the upper levels of a formally structured society, but none showed engine-driven "factory" machinery. Adam Smith illustrated the division of labor in his *Inquiry into the Nature and Causes of the Wealth of Nations* by the specialization of function in the making of pins; but even this famous example hardly began to grasp the scale of impending change in the modes of production. The larger social impact of technology was to preoccupy nineteenth-century thinkers as "the Machinery Question," but it did not greatly concern the contemporaries of Diderot and Smith.

The effects of technology were, however, at the crux of the debate on luxury that engaged moralists and political economists throughout the century. Enlightened thinkers tended to relate technology and the arts through Lockean psychology, which associated the representations of the world as empirically knowable with the world perceived as enjoyable. Learned as "taste," practical aesthetics thus rested on subjective sensations kept under the "objective" control of reason, understood as a secondary psychological process of calm discrimination in which primary responses were sifted and balanced. The importance of taste was reinforced by the new commercial relationship that technology inspired between original creation and an expanding culture of personal consumption supplied, not by original works of art, but by skilled replication in batch production runs based on standard patterns. Art now tended to become merely another commodity whose production and marketing made men and women more dependent on one another. At the core of the technological changes themselves, there thus remained an unresolvable tension between nature and artifice, freedom and dependence. It was this that Rousseau confronted.

If the proper study of mankind was man, his technology was part and parcel of that task. In its pursuit, the enlightened tried to order all human knowledge according to empirical reason. Sir Francis Bacon's original vision of the instauration of true knowledge had been aligned with temporal realities by providential assumptions about the ordained recovery of humanity's prelapsarian place in the Creation, governed by an explicitly Christian eschatology. In Britain, the attenuated substance of such transcendental assumptions survived. By around 1750, in the more antireligious and anticlerical context of the French Enlightenment, they had been eroded to the vanishing point. The possibility of a knowledge independent of the knower's language and culture had been for many effectively eliminated, leaving the enlightened no philosophical base beyond their own conventions on which to claim the improvability of the human condition. This was the predicament with which Rousseau struggled.

It would, however, be mistaken to conclude that Rousseau's critique was intrinsically antitechnological. Neither in his *Discours sur les arts et sciences* (Discourse on the Arts and Sciences, 1750), nor in his rebuttals of its critics, is there much reference to technology as such. His target was the meretricious abuse of the sciences and arts in pursuit of luxury, false self-fashioning, and the false erudition of small minds. This was amplified in *Émile* (1762), his treatise on education. In its third book he argued against the bogus social technology of formulaic book-learning oriented to the mannered performances of politeness and the rote repetition of standardized roles. He advocated a return to craft skills directly absorbed through the use of traditional hand tools in pursuit of self-sufficiency. The inculcation of higher concepts was to come through unmediated and spontaneous engagement with the natural world, learning through experiencing and doing. Only in this way could *techné* (practice) and *theória* (theory) be truly joined. In this, though ostensibly written in opposition to the credo of other *encyclopédistes*, Rousseau was arguably closer in spirit than his fellow contributors to the celebration of the artisans and artists to which Diderot's project aspired. Better, Rousseau said, to be a great cloth-maker than a fake Newton. Whether in the primal nobility of its first savage state, before the advent of property and false individualism divided *techné* from *theória*, or in its eventual recovery from that alienation through the *volonté générale* (general will) of the social contract, Rousseau's ideal humanity had surely known, and could again know, how to sustain its proper, self-sufficient nature.

Among *Émile*'s most enthusiastic readers were men like the members of the Lunar Society of Birmingham, provincial avatars of the British "culture of invention." For them, the marriage of science and technology offered limitless entry into Erasmus Darwin's "Temple of Nature." In this, the Industrial, French, and Romantic revolutions shared common ground. Resolution of the deep issues, which the Age of Enlightenment thereby passed to its successors, lies beyond this account. What remains is paradox. It was machining in the service of acoustics that created the valved brass instruments of the Romantic symphony orchestra and its nature-inspired music. Like Charles Babbage's calculating machines, the Victorian precursor of the computer, the Jacquard looms, which made the Pre-Raphaelite–inspired tapestries of William Morris available to discerning householders at the end of the nineteenth century, descended from the self-taught mechanist Jacques de Vaucanson of Lyon (1709–1782). Vaucanson's factory ventures in silk spinning were overshadowed by the fame of his automations, which fascinated Diderot, supplied Julien Offray de La Mettrie's materialist metaphor,

and offended Rousseau. The technological bonds between artist, artisan, machine, and the public endure. There is another legacy too, of which the problems of the French revolutionaries gave forewarning. For all that the information age now invokes Rousseau by hailing not the metropolis but the global village, the decentralized babel of "the postmodern condition" remains more redolent of his fallen *volonté de tous* (the will of all), aggregated from the separated wills of fragmented selves, than of the regained freedom of his *volonté générale*.

[*See also* Cabinets de Lecture; Chemistry; Cities; Commerce and Trade; Corporate and Estate Organization; Diderot, Denis; Encyclopedias; Encyclopédie; Exhibitions; Free Trade; Luxury; Popularization; Rousseau, Jean-Jacques; Turgot, Anne-Robert-Jacques; Watt, James; *and* Wedgwood, Josiah.]

BIBLIOGRAPHY

Alder, Ken. *Engineering the Revolution: Arms and Enlightenment in France, 1763–1815.* Princeton, N.J., 1997. This discusses the culture of engineering as an explicitly military and meritocratic vocation in ancien régime, revolutionary, and Napoleonic France but one distorted by ideology, expedience, and ingrained particularism.

Berg, Maxine. *The Age of Manufactures, 1700–1820: Industry, Innovation and Work in Britain.* 2d ed. London, 1994. Berg discusses the effects of technical change on family, community, and the organization of production in which women significantly outnumbered men in many processes, and consequently comprised over half the aggregate workforce.

Brewer, John, and Roy Porter, eds. *Consumption and the World of Goods, 1600–1800.* London, 1993. The first of three collaborative volumes on culture and consumption in the seventeenth and eighteenth centuries.

Clow, Archibald, and Nan Clow. *The Chemical Revolution: A Contribution to Social Technology.* London, 1952. Partially superseded by Golinski (below) but still valuable for its discussions of actual processes.

Gillispie, C. C. *Science and Polity in France at the End of the Old Regime.* Princeton, N.J., 1980.

Golinski, Jan. *Science as Public Culture: Chemistry and Enlightenment in Britain, 1760–1820.* Cambridge, 1992. Golinski and Stewart (below) reappraise the diffuse scientific activity of the eighteenth century, long regarded as representing a falling-off in inspiration after the epochal peaks attained by Boyle and Newton.

Harris, J. R. *Industrial Espionage and Technology Transfer: Britain and France in the Eighteenth Century.* Aldershot, Hants., U.K., and Brookfield, Vt., 1999. This result of a lifetime's archival work on the practical transference of technical knowledge grounds "technology" and "Enlightenment" in real people and places.

Hills, R. L. *Power from Steam: The History of the Stationary Steam Engine.* Cambridge, 1989.

Hills, R. L. "James Watt, Mechanical Engineer." *History of Technology* 18 (1996), 59–80. This and the above source are valuable for their details on Watt's early formation and his contacts with the London instrument makers.

Inkster, Ian. *Science and Technology in History: An Approach to Industrial Development.* Piscataway, N.J., 1991. A comparative history of the forms of industrialization across different cultures.

Jacob, M. C. *Scientific Culture and the Rise of the Industrial West.* New York and Oxford, 1997. Jacob intended to reach beyond historians to a larger audience and takes a controversial position on the singularity of Western technological development; readers should compare this with Berg.

Jones, Peter. "Living the Enlightenment and the French Revolution: James Watt, Matthew Boulton and Their Sons." *Historical Journal* 42 (1999), 157–182. Discusses Enlightenment assumptions of early industrial enterprise and the impact of the Revolution.

Kaplan, Steven, and Cynthia Koepp, eds. *Work in France*. Ithaca, N.Y., 1986. See especially the contributions by Sonenscher, Shepard, Koepp, and Sewell.

MacLeod, Christine. *Inventing the Industrial Revolution: The English Patent System, 1660–1800*. Cambridge, 1988. The evolution of the English patent system from a general register of privileges issued by Chancery under the Great Seal into the legal expression of a "culture of invention."

Money, John. *Experience and Identity: Birmingham and the West Midlands, 1760–1800*. Manchester and Montreal, 1977. The cultural, social, and political history of the West Midlands manufacturing region during the early decades of industrial change.

Musson, A. E., and Eric Robinson. *Science and Technology in the Industrial Revolution*. Manchester, 1969. The most important book of its generation on the subject. Its argument generated most of the questions that have since been addressed by Stewart and Golinski.

Scarfe, Norman, ed. *Innocent Espionage: The La Rochefoucauld Brothers' Tour of England in 1785*. Woodbridge, Suffolk, U.K., 1995. Remarkable as much for what these noble, physiocratic students of English agriculture and industry did not see, and for what they thought they saw at the point of economic transition, as for what they did see.

Singer, C., E. J. Holmyard, A. R. Hall, and F. G. Kilgour. *A History of Technology*. 8 vols. Oxford, 1954–1984. The relevant volumes of this compendious reference history are 3 (1957) and 4 (1958).

Stewart, Larry. *The Rise of Public Science: Rhetoric, Technology and Natural Philosophy in Newtonian Britain, 1660–1750*. Cambridge, 1992. The essential book on the Newtonian transformation in Britain.

Stewart, Larry. "A Meaning for Machines: Modernity, Utility and the Eighteenth-Century British Public." *Journal of Modern History* 70 (1998), 259–294. Especially interesting on the marriage of mathematics and mechanism among the London instrument makers.

Wrigley, E. A. *Continuity, Chance and Change: The Character of the Industrial Revolution in England*. Cambridge, 1988. Asserts the fundamental significance of the late-eighteenth-century transition from "advanced organic" to "mineral-based energy economy."

JOHN MONEY

THEATER. [*This entry contains two subentries:* Literary Genre *and* Role of Theater.]

Literary Genre

The best-known examples of Enlightenment thought are the essays, philosophical novels, and tracts produced during that era, but for the writers of the time, the theater was widely regarded as the expressive form most suited to the correction of manners and the promulgation of new ideas, and many of the leading Enlightenment figures were seriously involved with the theater. An interest in the moral utility of drama was an important part of traditional neoclassic thought, descended from the dictum of the Roman theorist Horace that the twin function of poetry was "to delight and to instruct." Thus the major late-seventeenth-century summaries of neoclassic theatrical theory, such as René Rapin's *Réflexions sur la poétique* (1674) and André Dacier's edition of Aristotle's *Poetics* (1697), considered poetry's principal end the serving of the public good by the improvement of manners. The dominance of French theatrical theory and practice guaranteed that these concerns would be carried on into the next century not only in France but in much of Europe, especially since they were reinforced by such leading Enlightenment figures as Voltaire and Denis Diderot.

Voltaire was not only a central figure in the Enlightenment generally but in the European theater of the eighteenth century; he was the author of fifty-six plays and innumerable critical statements on the theater, and the model for playwrights all over the Continent. In a letter of 1733, at the beginning of his career, Voltaire characterizes comedy and tragedy as lessons in virtue, reason, and proper behavior, and in his first major essays on drama, in the *Lettres anglaises ou philosophiques* (1734) and the preface to his tragedy *Sémiramis* (1748) he emphasized, even more than his neoclassic predecessors, the moral functions of theater, and particularly its importance in spreading the concerns of the Enlightenment: civilization, tolerance, benevolent royalism, and enlightened religion. The range of Voltaire's dramatic work extends into most of the genres of the period—comedy, tragedy, sentimental drama, even opera libretti—but typical of his most popular and successful works was a blending of spectacle, exoticism, and philosophical commentary on such matters as natural morality, human progress, religious toleration, and the nature of civilization. Among such works were his best-known tragedy, *Zaïre* (1732), a tragic love story set at the time of the Crusades and dealing with a cultural confrontation between representatives of Christianity and Islam; *Alzire* (1736), set in sixteenth-century Peru and depicting another cultural clash, that between the Indian natives and the conquering Spanish, as well as a debate over the proper conduct of a conquering race; and *Mahomet* (1741), portraying the prophet as an unscrupulous fanatic whose intolerance is countered by his more sympathetic and human opponents.

Although in these and other similar dramas Voltaire showed how the elevated figures of traditional serious drama could be used to illustrate moral and social messages, the major didactic drama of the early Enlightenment was more typically comedy, where the neoclassic practice of exposing to ridicule various types of social misfits was now turned toward the particular enemies of the Enlightenment. Religious mysticism was a particularly favored target. Thus, in Germany, Luise Gottsched, who with her husband Johann Christoph attempted to establish a modern German literary drama, ridiculed the emotionally based Pietist movement in her first play, *Die Pietisterey im Fischbeinrocke* (Pietism in Petticoats, 1763), while in Russia, Catherine II created an "anti-Masonic trilogy" of plays in 1785–1786, each showing a gullible family falling prey to the wiles of a visiting "mystic." Catherine, devoted to the work of Voltaire, shared his view of the theater as a mark of cultural sophistication as well as a school of public morals, and although she sent Voltaire her dramatic works anonymously (an easily penetrated subterfuge) she strongly and publicly supported the development of theater as a part of her program to bring Enlightenment thought and culture to Russia.

In France and elsewhere, however, the traditional comedy of ridicule tended to fall out of favor during the eighteenth century, to be challenged by a more realistic, more emotional, and more psychologically oriented comedy, as likely to solicit sympathetic tears as laughter. Although Voltaire created several works of this type, the real masters of the genre were Philippe Néricault Destouches and Pierre-Claude Nivelle de La Chaussée. Like their British contemporary Richard Steele, whose *The Conscious Lovers* (1722) is the best-known English example, Destouches and La Chaussée saw the emotional stimulus of their work not as an end in itself, but as an aid to moral instruction. The preface to La Chaussée's first work, *La fausse antipathie*, characterized the theater as a school where young people could gain lessons of wisdom and virtue while being entertained. The most enduring comic author of this period, Pierre Carlet de Chamblain de Marivaux, shares with Destouches and La Chausssée a central interest in the emotions, but his subtle studies of the expressions of young love had little direct social commentary, causing Voltaire and others to dismiss his works as gossamer trifles. In their delicate exploration of the shades of conversation and its hidden meanings, however, plays like *Le jeu de l'amour et du hasard* (The Game of Love and Chance, 1730) anticipate at least as much as the less mannered realistic dramas of Diderot, the drama of psychological realism that has so dominated the modern theater.

In their emphasis on the emotions and the utilization of the emotions as guides to virtue, the authors of "tearful" (*larmoyante*) comedy were clearly not so close to Voltaire as to the other dominant cultural figure of mid-eighteenth-century France, Jean-Jacques Rousseau. Rousseau, however, was far less supportive of the theater and indeed of almost all of the socially-oriented aspects of the Enlightenment than the urbane Voltaire. Although Rousseau created a number of theatrical works, including a popular comedy, *Narcisse* (1752) and operetta, *Le devin du village* (1753), he increasingly came to distrust the ability of the theater to improve the morals of its surrounding culture. Indeed he felt it more likely to pander to that society's weaknesses, a view that he elaborated at length in the century's best

known antitheatrical statement, the *Lettre à d'Alembert sur les spectacles* (1758), inspired by an article praising the theater as a school of civic virtue in the entry on Geneva in the seventh volume of the *Encyclopédie* (1757).

Denis Diderot shared Rousseau's moral enthusiasm and emphasis on a kind of natural morality superior to rational argument or social pressures, but Diderot, like Voltaire, remained convinced that this natural morality must be developed in social circumstances, and so he by no means shared Rousseau's suspicion of the theater as a social operation. On the contrary, the very period of Rousseau's famous attack on the theater saw Diderot involved in a far-reaching and original attempt to create a new kind of drama that would even more effectively serve as a tool for encouraging virtue and condemning vice. The dramatic theory and practice of Diderot marked a distinct shift in Enlightenment theater practice, particularly in the two countries most involved with Enlightenment drama, France and Germany.

Although Diderot remained strongly committed to the idea of a didactic stage, he took this in a new direction, turning from the neoclassic comedic tradition, with its stock characters, its tradition of "speaking names" ("Mrs. Sanctimonious" and "Lady Sneerwell") and its artificial and conventional patterns of action, to a new sort of serious theater, closer in tone, characters, and patterns of action to the "serious comedies" of Destouches and La Chaussée. This new form, which Diderot called the *drame*, he developed in his plays, *Le fils naturel* (1757) and *Le père de famille* (1758) and their accompanying defenses, *Les entretiens avec Dorval* and *Discours sur la poésie dramatique*. The purpose of these plays was still the reform of society, not by ridicule of exaggerated characters but by sympathetic interest in the actions of persons created to resemble as closely as possible members of the viewing public. This, Diderot argued, was the most effective means of moral instruction in the theater. As a precursor for such work, he cited not the earlier French attempts at a more realistic comedy but the English tragedy *The London Merchant* (1731) by George Lillo, the most successful of the early-eighteenth-century endeavors to create a domestic tragedy rather than one dealing with kings and princes, and also a work with a strong moral message.

Although Diderot's *Fils naturel* had little stage success, its impact throughout Enlightenment culture was enormous. Its fame spread quickly across France (where it appeared in twenty-five editions before 1800) and Europe, where it was translated into German, Russian, Italian, Dutch, Spanish, and Danish. Two of the leading French dramatists of the next generation both championed and extended Diderot's reorientation of socially engaged drama. Pierre-Augustin Caron de Beaumarchais, although best known for his two major comedies, *Le barbier de Séville* (1775) and *Le mariage de Figaro* (1784), began and ended his career with less familiar works directly in the Diderot tradition: his first two plays, *Eugénie* (1767) and *Les deux amis* (The Two Friends, 1770), and the final play in the Figaro trilogy, *La mère coupable* (The Guilty Mother, 1792). The *Essai sur le genre sérieux* that served as preface to *Eugénie* was one of the most important theoretical explanations and defenses of this new genre, whose aim, according to Beaumarchais, was to offer a morality more relevant than that of traditional tragedy, and more profound than that of traditional comedy.

An even more radical position was taken in the articles, essays, and plays of Louis-Sébastien Mercier, who condemned the whole French neoclassic tradition as corrupted by arbitrary and foolish regulation. Mercier firmly agreed with both Diderot and Beaumarchais that the aim of the drama should be social and moral improvement, and that this could best be achieved by the close imitation of everyday reality. On these grounds he attacked the traditional dramatic unities of time, place, and action, as well as the use of verse in serious drama, and his arguments, particularly as expressed in his key critical statement, *Du théâtre* (1773, translated into German in 1776), were an important influence on the proto-romantic German Sturm und Drang writers. Mercier's own forty-five plays, all written in prose, are varied in subject, but are for the most part both serious and socially engaged. Typical are *Le déserteur* (1771), a protest against war and compulsory military service, *Jean Hennuyer* (1772), one of the first French historical dramas as well as an early thesis play, and *La brouette du vinaigrier* (The Vinegar-Maker's Wheelbarrow, 1773), one of the first attempts at a sympathetic portrayal of the lower classes.

Diderot's influence was particularly important in Germany, due in large part to the work of Gotthold Ephraim Lessing, who translated both Diderot's plays and their prefaces in 1759. Lessing had already been attracted to a serious moral and realistic drama by English examples, and he found himself in close agreement with Diderot, whom he quotes often and highly approvingly in his major critical work on drama, the *Hamburgische Dramaturgie* (1767–1769). Although Lessing's verse epic, *Nathan der Weise* (1779), an allegory on religious tolerance, is probably today his best-known Enlightenment drama, his middle-class tragedies *Miss Sara Sampson* (1755) and *Emilia Galotti* (1772), written under the inspiration of Lillo and subsequently of Diderot, were far more popular and influential. The last major theoretical statement of Enlightenment theatrical principles in Germany was Friedrich Schiller's 1784 *Die Schaubühne als eine moralische Anstalt betrachtet* (The Stage Viewed as a Moral Institution), but the serious, realistic, middle-class drama reemerged after the romantic tide of the early nineteenth

century in the French social drama of Émile Augier and Alexandre Dumas *fils* and in the middle-class tragedies of Friedrich Hebbel in Germany, often complete with the moral orientation of their Enlightenment predecessors. In the next generation, the dramas of Henrik Ibsen's middle period, especially *A Doll's House* and *Ghosts*, made the middle-class drama of social concern Europe's dominant dramatic form.

[*See also* Aesthetics; Beaumarchais, Pierre-Augustin Caron de; Catherine II; Diderot, Denis; Gottsched, Johann Christoph; Lessing, Gotthold Ephraim; Marivaux, Pierre Carlet de Chamblain de; Rousseau, Jean-Jacques; Schiller, Friedrich; Sturm und Drang; *and* Voltaire.]

BIBLIOGRAPHY

Bruford, W. H. *Theatre, Drama, and Audience in Goethe's Germany.* London, 1950.
Bryson, Scott Stewart. *The Chastised Stage: Bourgeois Drama and the Exercise of Power.* Saratoga, Calif., 1991.
Carlson, Marvin. *Voltaire and the Theatre of the Eighteenth Century.* Westport, Conn., 1998.
Connon, Derek F. *Innovation and Renewal: A Study of the Theatrical Works of Diderot.* Oxford, 1989.
Hart, Gail Kathleen. *Tragedy in Paradise: Family and Gender Politics in German Bourgeois Tragedy, 1750–1850.* Columbia, S.C., 1996.
Hawkins, Frederick. *The French Stage in the Eighteenth Century.* 2 vols. London, 1888.
Hayes, Julie Candler. *Identity and Ideology: Diderot, Sade, and the Serious Genre.* Philadelphia, 1991.
Heitner, Robert R. *German Tragedy in the Age of Enlightenment.* Los Angeles, 1963.
Jourdain, Eleanor F. *Dramatic Theory and Practice in France, 1690–1808.* New York, 1968.
Lamport, Francis John. *German Classical Drama: Theatre, Humanity, and Nation, 1750–1870.* Cambridge, 1990.
Lancaster, H. Carrington. *French Tragedy in the Time of Louis XV and Voltaire.* 2 vols. Baltimore, 1950.
Nolte, Fred Otto. *The Early Middle Class Drama (1696–1774).* Lancaster, Pa., 1935.
Taylor, S. B. *The Theatre of the French and German Enlightenment.* Edinburgh, 1978.
Wade, Ira Owen. *The "Philosophe" in the French Drama of the Eighteenth Century.* Princeton, N.J., 1926.
Wellington, Marie A. *The Art of Voltaire's Theater: An Exploration of Possibility.* New York, 1987.

MARVIN CARLSON

Role of Theater

The prestige and popularity of theater in eighteenth-century Europe drew many Enlightenment authors to write for the stage, including Voltaire, Denis Diderot, and Gotthold Ephraim Lessing. Public performances of their work enabled authors to communicate Enlightenment ideas more widely than printed texts alone, and many playwrights embraced dramatic literature as an effective means to educate the public and improve social morality. In practice, the designs of playwrights and theorists were counterbalanced by the commercial necessities facing acting companies: paying spectators turned to the theater not so much for moral edification as for social purposes and for entertainment. As many new theaters were established beyond Paris and London, developments in architecture, repertory, and performance drew growing audiences throughout Europe and the colonies.

During the eighteenth century, as French theater reached the height of its influence across the Continent, few playwrights were as central to the French stage as Voltaire. This influential writer, critic, and philosophe first established his reputation as a man of letters in 1718 with the triumph of his tragedy *Oedipe* at the Comédie-Française. Success at the royal dramatic theater in Paris opened doors in high society, providing Voltaire (and many other French playwrights) with greater access to patronage and lucrative appointments. In Voltaire's lifetime, the Comédie-Française performed almost thirty of his works, and he became the most accomplished French tragic playwright of the century. Although Voltaire adamantly defended the French classical tradition, strictly adhering to the unities of time, place, and action in his plays, he introduced new geographical and historical settings in works such as *Mahomet, ou, Le fanatisme* (1741) to carry to the stage his crusade against religious extremism, tyranny, and cruelty. When royal actress Adrienne Lecouvreur died suddenly and was refused sacred burial because she had not renounced her "infamous" profession before her death, Voltaire spoke out against the church on behalf of French actors and actresses. Religious and social prejudice against the theater and actors had long been prevalent throughout Europe, but only in France did the Gallic church institutionalize this prejudice by excommunicating professional actors, who were not rehabilitated until the French Revolution.

Voltaire, Diderot, Jean-François Marmontel, and other playwrights countered hostility to theater by arguing that plays educated audiences, teaching them moral lessons by example. The purpose of theater, Diderot explained in the *Encyclopédie*, was "to stimulate virtue, inspire a horror of vice and expose folly." Many city officials in France supported theater on the more practical grounds that entertainment occupied the evening hours of the idle, forestalling greater evils such as gambling, troublemaking, and whoring. Under the influence of Diderot and his dramas of middle-class domestic life, plays increasingly engaged contemporary issues including marriages of inclination and family honor, appealing to sentiment rather than reason and often adopting a moralizing tone. The stage was also used to attack ideas and attitudes associated with the Enlightenment. In 1760 the Comédie-Française performed Charles Palissot de Montenoy's *Les philosophes*, a biting satire of Diderot and the *encyclopédistes* in which a Rousseau-inspired character appeared on the stage on all fours, eating lettuce. Public performances did not, however, raise many of the more radical aspects of Enlightenment thought, which could only be communicated in print. Playwrights were restricted by censorship, convention, and popular taste, while the theater companies selecting the plays faced commercial and political pressures of their own.

The most powerful criticisms of theater came from Jean-Jacques Rousseau's *Lettre à d'Alembert sur les spectacles* (1758), which raised important questions about the relationship between culture and society. In the article "Genève" in the *Encyclopédie*, Jean Le Rond d'Alembert had included a proposal that the city relax its prohibition and allow a municipal theater. Although Rousseau had previously written for the stage, to halt the expanding influence of the Parisian culture and manners that he considered corrupt, he responded with a wide-ranging indictment of theater. Rousseau denied that theater could change an individual, arguing that it only reinforced existing traits and was "good for the good and bad for the vicious." What audiences took away from a performance was not always what the playwright intended: even the most famous comedies and tragedies featured characters that might provide inspiration for wrongdoing. If plays were powerless to improve society, a theater could rapidly destroy Geneva's traditional life, encouraging idleness and luxury. Actors and especially actresses, immodest and paid to dissimulate, would corrupt Geneva's women and emasculate the men. Rousseau's rhetorical force renewed antitheater sentiment on social rather than religious grounds, and brought about the final break between Rousseau and the *encyclopédistes*.

In Paris, the three royally-privileged theaters—the Comédie-Française, the Comédie-Italienne, and the Paris Opera—benefited from monopolies over dramatic and operatic genres. These theaters harassed their unprivileged competitors, the popular theater troupes operating in the fairgrounds and on the boulevard, but took careful note of their popularity among elite and lower-class audiences alike. In 1762 the struggling royal Comédie-Italienne merged with the fairground Opéra-Comique, which had enjoyed tremendous popular success under the direction of composer-playwright Charles-Simon Favart. Boulevard entrepreneurs Nicolet and Audinot skirted monopolies by using puppetry, dance, pantomime, and other innovative techniques, while engaging in a critique of privilege and elite culture.

Urbanization and capital investment contributed to a significant expansion of public theater throughout France from the 1750s to the Revolution. Several dozen French cities built substantial municipal theaters, often replacing older stages in converted indoor tennis courts. Architect Jacques-Germain Soufflot revolutionized

THEATER: Role of Theater **159**

theater architecture with his neoclassical theater of Lyon, completed in 1756. Paris finally inaugurated several new theaters in the 1770s and 1780s; the aesthetic of monumental theater-temples culminated in Victor Louis's elegant Bordeaux theater, inaugurated in 1780. Many provincial cities contracted acting troupes to perform for part or all of the year, including cities in French colonies like Saint-Domingue (modern-day Haiti). Theaters became increasingly important social and cultural institutions, which brought together local elites and exposed new ideas to all who could afford entry.

Audiences became agents in the production of public opinion, especially as the theater became a space for political opposition. King Louis XVI and censors forbade performances of Pierre-Augustin Caron de Beaumarchais's *Le mariage de Figaro* on the grounds that it was politically dangerous, but public pressure in favor of the play grew and the king relented. When it finally opened in Paris in 1784, the comedy drew ecstatic crowds to see Figaro, a clever servant, outwit his aristocratic master. The French Revolution liberated theater from all monopolies in January 1791, and in that year more than twenty new theaters opened in Paris.

Theatrical Performer. Louise Contat (1760–1813) created the role of Suzanne in Beaumarchais's *Le mariage de Figaro*, first performed in 1784. Anonymous drawing, late eighteenth century. (Musée de la Ville de Paris, Musée Carnavalet/Giraudon/Art Resource, NY.)

In London, for much of the century, the royally-patented Drury Lane and Covent Garden theaters competed with the secondary stages at Goodman's Fields and Haymarket. After the 1737 Licensing Act imposed censorship and cracked down on these "illegitimate" theaters, their entrepreneurs went to creative lengths to keep the doors open. Actor and satirist Samuel Foote, for example, invited Haymarket patrons to drink tea and watch a "free" performance before Foote acquired a patent for the summer theater in 1766. Following David Garrick's London debut in 1741, the English stage was dominated for several decades by this remarkable leading actor, who was no less influential as a playwright and as the successful manager of the Drury Lane theater. Garrick promoted the revival of Shakespearean drama, restoring passages which had been cut from plays and reintroducing many of the Bard's works to the stage. In 1769 Garrick organized Shakespeare's Jubilee celebration at Stratford-upon-Avon, which (despite being rained out) reinforced Shakespeare's status as a British national icon.

Cities across Britain invested in municipal theaters in the 1750s and 1760s, with wealthier cities imitating the style of London's Drury Lane. Regional capitals typically contracted an acting company which based itself out of the city for several months, and toured local cities for the rest of the year. In 1768, in Norwich and Bath, the first provincial theaters were raised to the status of Theatre Royal, followed in the next decade by York, Liverpool, Manchester, and others. English actors toured the American colonies from Williamsburg to New York, and by 1740 Jamaica had a playhouse.

Italians remained the masters of opera and spectacle, providing singers, musicians, and composers for many European cities and courts, but the Italian dramatic stage did not enjoy the same success. Over the years, many of the greatest talents were lured away to the Comédie-Italienne in Paris, including actor-director Luigi Riccoboni, and even playwright Carlo Goldoni. With the popularity of lyric theater, however, especially the new *opera buffa* or comic opera, Italian acting companies proliferated. In Venice as many as fourteen theaters competed, and by the end of the century nearly all major Italian cities had a theater.

Politically and religiously fragmented, and slow to recover from the devastating Thirty Years' War, German states had not developed a dramatic literary tradition or theater industry like those in England, the Italian states, Spain, and France. In the eighteenth century, traveling German acting troupes performed *Haupt- und Staatsaktionen*, improvisational plays strongly influenced by the English and Italian traditions, on simple stages for popular audiences. German aristocrats, unwilling to patronize these lowbrow companies, embraced the more sophisticated Italian opera and French comedy and tragedy.

French theater became the predominant literary influence, and companies of French actors and actresses were hired at many German courts. In the 1720s and 1730s, author and critic Johann Christoph Gottsched began working to elevate popular German theater. He promoted a German dramatic literature based on French classicism, and encouraged formal, stiff acting, which became known as the Leipzig style. Gottsched's ideas were put into practice through collaboration with actress Friederike Caroline Neuber and her troupe, which ceremoniously "banished" Harlequin from the stage in 1737 and performed many French works in translation. Gottsched's reforms met with only mixed support from audiences and actors, but marked a first step toward developing a new genre.

Reacting against Gottsched's francophile sympathies, Lessing strove to free German culture from the overwhelming influence of France through the creation of a distinctively German literature. Lessing turned for inspiration to England, the self-conscious setting of his acclaimed bourgeois drama *Miss Sara Sampson* (1755). He employed specifically German settings in other plays which challenged social prejudice, criticized absolutism, and promoted religious toleration for Jews. Without the support of court theaters, struggling German playwrights often found it difficult to have their work performed. This began to change in 1766 when citizens of Hamburg came together to provide the city with a municipal German theater. Lessing collaborated with the new Hamburg National Theater in 1767, and as the critic for the theater, wrote the influential essays attacking French classicism that were published as *Hamburgische Dramaturgie*. Although the Hamburg National Theater was short-lived, it inspired others to support German culture: the first German court theater, featuring the troupe of actor Konrad Ekhof, was sponsored at Gotha in 1775. Just two years later Joseph II of Austria elevated Vienna's German-language theater to the status of the German National Theater; by the 1790s, there were more than thirty cities with German theater companies.

In the evening, as audiences across Europe gathered for performances, they entered theaters whose interior designs were typically based on Italian models. Private boxes were stacked two or more rows high around the perimeter of the auditorium. These prestigious seats, which attracted wealthy elite and middle-class patrons, did not usually provide the best view of the show, but they did afford a key perspective from which to see and be seen. The largest part of the audience occupied the pit, which provided benches for mixed crowds in England, while most pits in France offered only standing room for men. Packed into very close quarters, audience members were often boisterous and could become physically aggressive. As preperformance entertainment in London, audiences threw orange peels and other food onto the stage (or, when they missed, onto

other spectators). When the actors finally appeared, they were often crowded by audience members sitting on the stage, a practice that was not banished from the stage of the Comédie-Française until 1759. Tempers flared easily under these conditions. To control volatile crowds, soldiers were ultimately posted in French and English theaters, but even they could not guarantee order. The fate of a play and its actors was in the hands of this outspoken audience.

Professional acting began to receive attention as an art in the 1730s as authors including Riccoboni, Pierre Rémond de Sainte-Albine (whose work was adapted for English readers by John Hill), and Diderot developed theories of acting. Diderot's *Paradoxe sur le comédien* (published posthumously in 1830) argued that the best actors were detached from their roles and rational and calculating in their representation, a position still controversial today. Garrick and Mlle. Clairon broke with contemporary declamatory styles and theatrical gestures to introduce more "natural" styles of acting. Italians led developments in stage design and mechanics, introducing a more creative use of space with angled sets and producing increasingly sophisticated stage effects. By mid-century, costumes—typically luxurious displays of elite fashions—began to suggest historical eras, exotic locations, and class difference.

With the growth of municipal theaters across Europe, the position of director developed in the eighteenth century primarily as an entrepreneurial and managerial role. Increasingly, provincial actors began to work for directors on contract for a salary, rather than for a share of the profit. Theater companies extended unusual opportunities to women: women directed troupes, actresses might earn exceptionally high salaries, and women in the Comédie-Française participated in company decisions. In France and England, famous stars such as Henri Lekain of the Comédie-Française began to capitalize on provincial interest by organizing performance tours, enjoying unprecedented prestige and social acceptance and becoming national celebrities.

[*See also* Aufklärung; Literary Genres; Men and Women of Letters; *and* Philosophes.]

BIBLIOGRAPHY

Barish, Jonas. *The Antitheatrical Prejudice.* Berkeley, Calif., 1981. Includes chapters on the Catholic opposition in seventeenth-century France, religious and moral criticism of theater in England, and the Rousseau controversy.

Bruford, W. H. *Theatre, Drama, and Audience in Goethe's Germany.* London, 1950. A valuable survey of German theater in the eighteenth century.

Carlson, Marvin. *Theories of the Theatre: A Historical and Critical Survey from the Greeks to the Present.* Ithaca, N.Y., 1984. Chapters 8 to 11 discuss contemporary theoretical writings in English, French, and German.

Heitner, Robert. *German Tragedy in the Age of Enlightenment: A Study in the Development of Original Tragedies, 1724–1768.* Berkeley,

Calif., 1963. An excellent analysis of Gottsched, Lessing, and their cultural impact.

Isherwood, Robert. *Farce and Fantasy: Popular Entertainment in Eighteenth-Century Paris.* New York, 1986. Challenges the argument for a growing divide between popular and elite culture.

Lessing, G. E. *Hamburg Dramaturgy.* Translated by Helen Zimmern. New York, 1962. English translation of *Hamburgische Dramaturgie,* first published in 1769.

Nicoll, Allardyce. *A History of English Drama, 1660–1900.* 2d ed. Cambridge, 1952–1959. 6 vols. The classic, if now dated, survey of English dramatic literature. First three volumes address 1660–1800.

Nicoll, Allardyce. *The Garrick Stage: Theatres and Audience in the Eighteenth Century.* Manchester, 1980. An examination of theatrical production in England featuring dozens of contemporary images.

Ravel, Jeffrey. *The Contested Parterre: Public Theater and French Political Culture, 1680–1791.* Ithaca, N.Y., 1999. A history of pit audiences, demonstrating their influence in the definition of public opinion.

Rougemont, Martine de. *La vie théâtrale en France au XVIIIᵉ siècle.* Paris, 1988. A valuable overview that provides an extensive bibliography.

Rousseau, Jean-Jacques. *Politics and the Arts: Letter to M. d'Alembert on the Theatre.* Translated by Allan Bloom. Ithaca, N.Y., 1993. English translation of *Lettre à d'Alembert,* first published in 1758.

LAUREN CLAY

THEOLOGY. *See* Natural Religion *and* Revealed Religion.

THOMASIUS, CHRISTIAN

THOMASIUS, CHRISTIAN (1655–1728), German philosopher.

Thomasius is considered the founder of the German Enlightenment, to which he contributed mainly by a reform of practical philosophy. Although it was his interest in modern natural law that motivated him to take up the study of jurisprudence at Frankfurt an der Oder in 1675, it was not until around 1685 that he openly defended Samuel Pufendorf's (1632–1694) natural law theory, which was at the time vigorously opposed by orthodox Lutheran theologians. In 1688, Thomasius published his *Institutiones jurisprudentiae divinae,* modeled on Pufendorf's *De jure naturae et gentium* (1672). Like his predecessor, Thomasius established sociability (*socialitas*) as a basic principle of natural law; however, he considered divine jurisprudence to comprise not only natural law but also revealed law, at least as far as the latter applied to all men and concerned worldly happiness. In this way, he advocated the authority of jurisprudence in a domain traditionally claimed by theologians. Basing his argument on a comparative evaluation of natural and revealed law, he attempted to prove that polygamy was merely prohibited by revealed law and did not contradict natural law.

In 1688, Thomasius also published the *Introductio ad philosophiam aulicam,* a treatise on logic that sought to liberate philosophy from Scholasticism, the traditional form of academic philosophy, in order to make it useful at the courts, the centers of government. In the same year, he announced a lecture on propriety (*Wohlanständigkeit*) and prudence (*Lebensklugheit*), which he planned to deliver for the first time at the University of Leipzig in German. He had already provoked angry reactions from the Leipzig establishment with these activities, when he began to edit the critical monthly review *Monatsgespräche* (1688–1689) in the German language. Faced with unremitting hostility, he left Leipzig.

In 1690, Thomasius moved to Halle, in Prussia, where in 1694, he was among the founders of the first modern Protestant German university. Here he completed his massive effort to reform logic (*Einleitung zur Vernunftlehre* and *Ausübung der Vernunftlehre,* both 1691), in which he developed a critique of prejudices that is now considered a characteristic feature of the German Enlightenment. Thomasius demonstrated how prejudices, whose immediate origin he ascribed to credulous reason but whose ultimate cause he traced to the prejudices of the will, could be eradicated through a critical examination of traditional beliefs and opinions. Against Descartes's "skeptical" doubt, Thomasius invoked "eclectic" or "dogmatic" doubt, presupposing that there must be knowable truth. In his writings from early on, the term *eclecticism* referred to three methodological aspects of his philosophy: a critical examination of traditional opinions, liberation from "scholastic pedantry," and an awareness of the provisional state of one's own theory. Given Thomasius's belief that the liberation from prejudices ultimately depended on the moral improvement of the will, his logic was closely linked with his moral philosophy. He published two German treatises on ethics (*Einleitung zur Sittenlehre,* 1692; *Ausübung der Sittenlehre,* 1696), in which he defined virtue as love regulated by reason. Vice consisted of desires of the human will that were not directed by reason. He reduced these to three main passions: lust, ambition, and avarice.

Works on Natural Law. Thomasius's lecture on propriety and prudence as well as his ethics testify to his ambition not only to initiate a general reform of German civilization but also to inaugurate the moral improvement of the human will. In the mid-1690s, however, he underwent a moral and religious crisis that lasted several years, caused by the influence of Pietists such as August Hermann Francke and by his own increased awareness of the weakness of the human will. His second treatise on ethics thus led him to the conclusion that the corrupted will cannot be improved by reason alone, but only by the assistance of God's grace. Unlike the Pietists, however, Thomasius did not renounce reason in favor of faith. Instead, he developed a new foundation of natural law in accordance with his new psychological insight into the weakness of the human will.

As a result Thomasius published a second version of his theory of natural law (*Fundamenta juris naturae et gentium*, 1705), in which he tried to establish a system of universal moral norms based on common sense. Because he no longer presupposed that the will was determined by the dictates of reason, he looked to the passions of hope and fear as the starting points in directing the will. It was the function of wise men to direct foolish ones, either by advice (*consilium*) or by command (*imperium*). Advice and command could influence the will by pointing to the advantages and disadvantages or the rewards and punishments attached to a given action. This distinction between advice and command recalls Thomasius's first treatise on ethics, in which he had already introduced the important difference between unenforceable love and enforceable justice. In the *Fundamenta*, he distinguished between three sets of norms that led to peace and happiness: the enforceable rules of the just (*justum*) maintained "outward" peace; the unenforceable rules of the honest (*honestum*) led to "inward" peace; and the rules of the decorous or proper (*decorum*)—partly enforceable, partly unenforceable—contributed to inward as well as outward peace. Although Thomasius's tripartition of natural law was taken up by some of his followers, his doctrine of propriety did not survive as a substantial part of German natural law during the Enlightenment period, but it was later taken up in popular literature. It is his distinction between honesty (*honestum*) and justice (*justum*) that is commonly recognized as the first clearcut account of the distinction between moral and juridical law later elaborated by Kant.

In his treatises on natural law, Thomasius developed a contractual theory of the state that depended largely on Samuel Pufendorf's *De jure*. However, he considered public law not only as a systematic discipline but also as a historical one. The originality of his theory of the state lies in his new account of the history of the Holy Roman Empire, a portrayal that enabled him to acknowledge the sovereignty of the territorial princes while also recognizing the privileges of the emperor, which he considered merely as a historical, that is, contingent fact. In advocating the sovereignty of the territorial princes, Thomasius showed himself to be one of the founders of enlightened absolutism.

Reforms. Among the most important political and moral reforms to which Thomasius contributed by his teaching and writing were the abolition of torture and of witch trials and the granting of religious toleration. Criticizing the worldly ambitions of the Catholic clergy as well as of the Lutherans, he recommended that the church be subordinated to the state, and that the ruler grant liberty of conscience as well as liberty of inquiry, vital themes of the European Enlightenment.

[*See also* Aufklärung; Natural Law; Philosophy; Pietism; *and* Pufendorf, Samuel.]

BIBLIOGRAPHY

Hammerstein, Notker. *Jus und Historie: Ein Beitrag zur Geschichte des historischen Denkens an deutschen Universitäten im späten 17. und im 18. Jahrhundert*. Göttingen, 1972.

Holzhey, Helmut, and Simone Zurbuchen. "Christian Thomasius und der Beginn der deutschen Aufklärung." In *Grundriss der Geschichte der Philosophie: Reihe 17. Jahrhundert*, edited by Helmut Holzhey and Wilhelm Schmidt-Biggemann, vol. 4, pp. 1161–1202, 1216–1219. Basel, 2001. Provides a summary account of Thomasius's writings and ideas.

Lieberwirth, Rolf. *Christian Thomasius: Sein wissenschaftliches Lebenswerk, Eine Bibliographie*. Weimar, 1955.

Schneewind, J. B. *The Invention of Autonomy: A History of Modern Moral Philosophy*. Cambridge, 1998. See pp. 159–166.

Schneiders, Werner. *Naturrecht und Liebesethik: Zur Geschichte der praktischen Philosophie im Hinblick auf Christian Thomasius*. Hildesheim and New York, 1971.

Schneiders, Werner, ed. *Christian Thomasius (1655–1728). Interpretationen zu Werk und Wirkung*. Hamburg, 1989. Contains a bibliography of recent secondary sources.

Thomasius, Christian. *Ausgewählte Werke*. Edited by Werner Schneiders. Hildesheim, 1993–. 10 vols.

Vollhardt, Friedrich, ed. *Christian Thomasius (1655–1728): Neue Forschungen im Kontext der Frühaufklärung*. Tübingen, 1997.

WERNER SCHNEIDERS and
SIMONE ZURBUCHEN

TIME. *See* Natural Philosophy and Science *and* Physics.

TINDAL, MATTHEW

TINDAL, MATTHEW (1653–1732), English lawyer, political writer, and freethinker.

Tindal was educated at Oxford, where he was awarded a law fellowship (1678) and a doctorate in civil law (1685). After 1685, he occasionally resided at All Souls College, but otherwise in London. He converted to Roman Catholicism in the mid-1680s, but soon returned to the Anglican fold. His thought, like that of his friends John Toland and Anthony Collins, is strongly indebted to John Locke, to whom he wrote: "I have got more tru [sic] and useful knowledge by your writings than by all the books I ever read."

His dominant idea is the sovereignty of individual reason. He identifies its religious enemy as "priestcraft" which supports ecclesiastical establishments justified by divine right and which undermines reason by promoting mysteries, such as the Trinity, claimed to be "above human reason," but classed as fundamental articles of religion. Anticipating Toland's *Christianity not Mysterious* (1696), Tindal argues that Christianity's proper role is to remove mystery and superstition, not to entrench them. The point of the Reformation was to supplant arbitrary ecclesiastical power with individual reason or freethinking. Tindal defends the innocency of error in God's eyes when it results from sincerely conducted inquiry. For him, all legitimate authority, civil and ecclesiastical, is based upon the consent of the governed. On this foundation, he defends a free press and a wide-ranging toleration, which, like Locke's, embraces neither atheists nor Catholics. He is clear, however, that atheism is preferable to superstition.

Tindal's two most important works were *The Rights of the Christian Church Asserted* (1706) and *Christianity as Old as the Creation* (1730). Anthony Collins was widely regarded as having assisted him in writing both. *Rights* aims to refute the church's claim to a sovereign authority in religion, independent of the state, derived from Christ and vested in bishops. Any authority the church enjoys is derived from the state, whose object is to protect citizens in the peaceable enjoyment of their natural rights, not impose religion on them. Anonymously published, *Rights* was burned by order of the House of Commons in 1710.

Christianity as Old as the Creation, Tindal's most controversial work, was dubbed "the Deist's Bible." It examines the relation between natural and revealed religion. A centerpiece of its argument is its attack on Samuel Clarke's view that Deism or natural religion by itself is no longer defensible, although it had been before the Christian revelation. Clarke believed unaided human reason needs supplementation from revelation. For Tindal, Christianity is only defensible to the extent it republishes natural religion, the thesis expressed in the book's paradoxical title. Since God's moral law is simple, eternal, and discoverable by human reason, Tindal argues, God's goodness ensures that he can require nothing more of humans than reason can discover. The religion implied by this view, unencumbered by divisive creeds and ceremonies, consists entirely of duties, which humans owe their fellow creatures; God's perfection requires no other service to him. Revelation is superfluous and undermines reason's authority. Being veiled in allegorical language, it is obscurer and less complete than natural religion. Since revelations rely on external, probabilistic evidence such as miracles, revealed religion's foundation is not only evidentially weaker than natural religion, but lends itself to being corrupted by those seeking power. Revelation does not make good reason's deficiencies; on the contrary, reason is necessary to correct those of revelation. Tindal's thought aimed to liberate humanity. His influence proved more enduring in France and Germany than in Britain.

[*See also* Bible; Butler, Joseph; Clarke, Samuel; Collins, Anthony; Deism; Natural Religion; Reason; *and* Toland, John.]

BIBLIOGRAPHY

Leland, John. *View of the Principal Deistical Writers*. 3 vols. London, 1757; repr., New York, 1978. Vol. 1 surveys the notable attacks on *Christianity as Old as the Creation*.

Rivers, Isabel. *Reason, Grace, and Sentiment*. 2 vols. Cambridge, 1991–2000. Vol. 2 contains a valuable chapter on the true religion of nature.

Stephen, Leslie. *History of English Thought in the Eighteenth Century*. 2 vols. London, 1876. Vol. 1 has a lively account of *Christianity as Old as the Creation* and the controversy it generated.

Tindal, Matthew. *Christianity as Old as the Creation*. With an introduction by J. V. Price. Bristol, U.K., 1999. A reprint of Tindal's celebrated work.

Torrey, Norman. *Voltaire and the English Deists*. New Haven, Conn., 1930. Examines the parallels between Tindal's and Voltaire's critiques of Christian revelation.

JAMES DYBIKOWSKI

TISSOT, SAMUEL-AUGUSTE-ANDRÉ-DAVID
(1728–1797), Swiss physician.

Tissot was born in Grancy (Pays de Vaud) to an educated family. He studied at the Academy of Geneva and at the Medical Faculty of Montpellier, where he received his medical degree in 1749. He spent most of his medical career in Lausanne, Switzerland, except for some short journeys abroad and a two-year stay in Pavia, where he had been appointed professor of practical medicine by Grand Duke Leopold of Tuscany.

Tissot was an influential physician, not only in his home city and country but throughout Europe. He was in contact with the most prominent intellects of his time and participated in an extensive medical correspondence (the Tissot papers in Lausanne remain one of the best archives for the study of such medical communication in the 1700s). Tissot was the author of many medical works, and they provide a good survey of some important themes in Enlightenment medicine. His interest in the themes of sensibility and nervous phenomena was evident in his French translation of and his introduction to *Dissertation sur les parties sensibles et irritables des animaux* (1755), by his friend Albrecht von Haller, as well as in his *Traité des nerfs et de leurs maladies* (4 vols., 1778–1780).

Tissot was also concerned with improving public health. His *Inoculation justifiée* (1754), based according to him on facts and reasoning, was aimed at convincing the anti-inoculationists. Its publication led to a protracted quarrel with the Viennese physician Anton de Haen. A number of his other works, centered on similar concerns, were intended for a less specialized audience: *L'avis au peuple sur sa santé* (1761), *De la santé des gens de lettres* (1768), *Essai sur les maladies des gens du monde* (1770), as well as two books, written late in his life and left unpublished, on the diseases of women and children. With enlightened perspective, Tissot recommended self-education in health practices for different social classes and age categories, each one considered separately. His emphasis on medical education was a defense of medical integrity against charlatanism—the best way to help preserve his profession.

His treatise *L'onanisme* (1769; first published in Latin in 1758) must be seen in the same perspective. That work combines a somewhat Calvinistic morality with a medical rationality and a rhetoric aimed at persuading the reader of the disastrous consequences of masturbation for an individual as well as for society.

Tissot summarized the most significant themes of Enlightenment medicine. The fame of his medical practice, however, was exceptional: distinguished as well as modest people came to consult him or wrote to him from all over Europe. This fame can be gauged by his editorial success. His *Avis au peuple* and *L'onanisme* were continually reedited into the 1800s and translated into many languages. These, as well as a significant number of unpublished literary and philosophical texts, testify that the stylistic qualities of clear and convincing writing were fundamental attributes of a successful physician in the Age of the Enlightenment.

[*See also* Correspondence and Correspondents; Haller, Albrecht von; Inoculation and Vaccination; Medicine; *and* Switzerland.]

BIBLIOGRAPHY

Barras, Vincent, and Micheline Louis-Courvoisier, eds. *La médecine des Lumières: Tout autour de Tissot*. Geneva, 2001.

Emch-Dériaz, Antoinette. *Tissot. Physician of the Enlightenment*. New York, 1992.

Jordanova, Ludmilla. "The Popularization of Medicine: Tissot on Onanism." *Textual Practice* 1 (1987), 68–79.

Tarczylo, Théodore. "Prêtons la main à la nature: L'onanisme de Tissot." *Dix-huitième Siècle* 12 (1980), 79–96.

Teysseire, Daniel. "Aux origines de la médecine sociale et de la politique de la santé publique: *L'avis au peuple sur sa santé*." *Mots/Les langages du politique* 26 (1991), 47–64.

VINCENT BARRAS

TOLAND, JOHN (1670–1722), Irish theological and political writer.

Obscurely born, and raised a Roman Catholic in northwestern Ireland, Toland was educated as a protégé of Protestant divines at Glasgow, Edinburgh, and Leiden. When he migrated to England in 1694, he had ceased to be a Christian in any conventional sense. He was a prodigious linguist, a quick and fluent writer with protean intellectual interests, almost seductively charming when he chose to be, and frequently self-destructive. His acquaintances ranged from a few royals to the polymath Gottfried Wilhelm Leibniz and the Quaker William Penn. He died widely reviled and impoverished, a lodger in a carpenter's house outside London. Because of the variety, complexity, and routine anonymity of Toland's writings and his several self-refashionings, he has recently drawn increasing attention and differing interpretations.

Christianity Not Mysterious (1696) was the first major work that can be attributed to him with certainty. There he sought to complete the accommodation of Anglicanism and rationalism that he saw as implicit in the hermeneutics of some of the Latitudinarian divines and the contemporary Unitarian, or Socinian, tracts. The title of the book was accurately descriptive of its content. Although it propounded a severe epistemological naturalism without specifying its implications for metaphysics, it provoked a firestorm of obloquy. It was publicly burned in Dublin, whence Toland fled just ahead of the law. Thereafter, his writing was haunted by the memory of persecution. He knew the danger of treating fundamental religious issues with complete transparency. In his view, vulgar superstition, manipulated by omnipresent priestcraft, was inevitable and potentially lethal. Toland's optimism about the extent to which popular enlightenment was possible ebbed and flowed, but his anticlericalism was intense and persistent.

Dropping his plan for two books that would expose and vindicate what he believed was the rational content of the Gospel, he devoted himself mainly to political writings. He edited, or rewrote, the works of many of the seventeenth-century English republicans and became the biographer of a few of them including John Milton, James Harrington, and Edmund Ludlow. Central to Toland's project was the conviction that social hierarchy was inevitable and ramifying in its consequences. Without repudiating radical Whiggery, he effaced the democratic and other untimely aspirations of his chosen authors to make their ideas more respectable to his own contemporaries. He urged achieving a wider diffusion of power within the restricted English political nation more than expanding its ranks. His work effectively created the eighteenth-century republican canon in the British world. During this same period, he published investigations of apocrypha that seemed to subvert the authority of the canonical Bible, and he began a period of political intrigue, often as the agent of Robert Harley, later earl of Oxford. The latter effort remains largely impenetrable even today.

Theory of Philosophical Discretion. Drawing on the ancient Roman philosophers Cicero and Varro, Toland eventually accepted that theology must function at several levels, and that the best way of refining the English church into a proper civil theology was to reduce its quantity of myth. The result would be truthful, though not completely true, and would require that the wise elite use doses of allegory as an intellectual analgesic. In "Clidophorus; or of the Exoteric and Esoteric Philosophy, . . . : the one open and public, accommodated to popular Prejudices and the establish'd Religions; the other private and secret, wherein, to the few capable and discrete, was taught the real TRUTH stript of all disguises" (1720), Toland offered the fullest early-modern theory of philosophical discretion. At its heart was the ancient doctrine that, in every nation, there are a few reasonable guardians and the unreasonable many, whom they must guard.

Derived from various ancient sources interpreted with the aid of texts by Giordano Bruno, a sixteenth-century philosopher of divine immanence, and perhaps those of the seventeenth-century philosophers Hobbes and Spinoza, Toland's mature cosmology was naturalist and materialist. It was to be influential in France and elsewhere later in the eighteenth century. In the *Letters to Serena* (1704), he rejected the "Doctrin of Spirits" and insisted that, throughout history, all sages everywhere knew that motion was essential to matter and that matter-in-motion defined reality; that was the perennially true religion of the few reasonable guardians. The next year, he coined the English word *pantheist*. In 1709, in the decent obscurity of a Latin tract, he described Moses as an adept of the esoteric pantheism of ancient Egyptian priests. Another Latin book, *Pantheisticon* (1720), was Toland's penultimate discourse about religion. It describes the pantheistic tenets of a modern Socratic Society and includes their "philosophical canon." It is telling that the work has been interpreted both as an elaborate joke and as a precious window into the hidden world of Freemasonry.

[*See also* Deism; Freemasonry; Locke, John; Pantheism; Republicanism, *subentry on* Great Britain; *and* Revealed Religion.]

BIBLIOGRAPHY

Carabelli, Giancarlo. *Tolandiana: Materiali bibliografici per lo studio dell'opera e della fortuna di John Toland (1670–1722)*. 2 vols. Florence, 1975–1978. A work of enormous scholarship on which all contemporary studies of Toland depend.

Champion, J. A. I. *The Pillars of Priestcraft Shaken: The Church of England and Its Enemies, 1660–1730*. Cambridge, 1992. Situates Toland within his vigorously anticlerical rhetorical world.

Daniel, Stephen H. *John Toland: His Method, Manners, and Mind*. Kingston, Ont., 1984. A sympathetic, alert study of Toland's philosophical resonances.

Eagleton, Terry. *Crazy John and the Bishop and Other Essays on Irish Culture*. Notre Dame, Ind., 1998. Includes a theoretically informed discussion of the politics and aporia of Toland on language.

Giuntini, Chiara. *Panteismo e ideologia repubblicana: John Toland (1670–1722)*. Bologna, 1979. An intellectual biography that is particularly sensitive to Toland's thought in relation to early-modern science.

Jacob, Margaret C. *The Radical Enlightenment: Pantheists. Freemasons and Republicans*. London, 1981. Locates Toland as an early Freemason and progenitor of radical Enlightenment on the Continent.

Sullivan, Robert E. *John Toland and the Deist Controversy: A Study in Adaptations*. Cambridge, Mass., 1982.

ROBERT E. SULLIVAN

TOLERATION.

Few cultural lessons have been more difficult to learn than the value of toleration, accepting the existence of something to which one objects. That lesson was most effectively learned by much of Europe and America in the eighteenth century. The practice itself is possible—to say nothing of necessary—only where there are enduring conflicts among important doctrines and customs. Fear and hostility are often the initial reactions to what is now known as diversity, and they, in turn, generally give rise to attempts to eliminate opposition.

Defining Toleration. In its most extreme form, toleration requires that people remain content to live with what they find hateful. More moderate forms of toleration, where the objections are not so strong, demand only forbearance or indifference. Toleration is especially difficult to achieve and the battles leading to it are especially hard fought when religion and theology are at stake, for religious beliefs are at the very heart of people's self-conceptions, and it was from such religious conflicts that the doctrine of toleration emerged. This essay will therefore concentrate on religion and religious toleration.

In the early modern world, little was more sacred and fundamental than one's relationship to a deity, and nothing played so important a role in holding societies together as shared religious beliefs, to which the religious wars that swept across Europe after the Reformation are ample testimony. This was challenged by the rationalist and often antireligious philosophy of the eighteenth century. That philosophy obviously did not succeed in its extreme ambition of banishing religion altogether, but it was able to provide philosophic and practical bases for accommodation to the multiplicity of religious sects that continues to characterize the Western world.

The freedom of people to hold religious beliefs without fetters and to engage in the rituals and observances that follow from them are among the hallmarks of modernity and one of the most enduring legacies of the eighteenth century. The guarantee of that freedom is one of the fundamental standards by which states are evaluated. The guiding presumptions—widely shared in the West—are that religion is generally a matter of personal conscience and that religious practices that do not threaten the stability or security of the state ought not to be interfered with. In accord with this second presumption, when religious rituals are restricted or prohibited, it is on grounds of the social and political danger they pose, not their religious content. From the perspective of those whose activities are thus limited, however, the restrictions are direct interferences with their religions. (And, on the other side, from the perspective of those who must live in societies that do not suppress offensive religious practices, religious toleration is sometimes seen as the licensing of evil itself.)

"Religious toleration," strictly speaking, is a privilege that is granted by the state or some other powerful agency such as a dominant religion to a weak or minority religion and exists only so long as the grantor wishes. Historically, toleration often included restrictions and disabilities, such as limited access to the franchise and to office holding, inability to own land, and exclusion from educational institutions, all of which were designed to ensure that the dominant religion would remain in control. In most cases, religious toleration existed side by side with officially established churches within theocratic or confessional states.

"Religious liberty" frequently serves as an alternative name for "toleration," especially in the United States. The two are related but should be distinguished, for the claims of liberty are much stronger than those of toleration, even though arguments in their defense are similar. Religious liberty is a *right* of belief and practice that is presumed to exist prior to and independently of the state and is ultimately incompatible with official or established theology, for it rests upon the presumption that no religious beliefs or practices, no matter how popular and widespread, are entitled to occupy privileged statuses vis-à-vis others within a society. In these terms, groups might demand that states honor religious liberty, but they may only request toleration. Historically, liberty grew out of toleration, as dissident religious groups and their supporters pressed for the removal of the disabilities imposed upon religions that enjoyed mere toleration. The principle of liberty thus imposes the duty of tolerance upon the members of a society. Accordingly, one's freedom of belief carries with it the requirement that those who find it objectionable nonetheless tolerate it.

However lofty its ideals may seem today, toleration, often identified as "liberty of conscience" in the early modern period, was initially achieved rather more as the result of calculated attempts to minimize the sectarianism conflicts that were the legacy of the Protestant Reformations. It was rarely the consequence of principled commitments to openness, forbearance, and eventually rights. Although those principles had long existed, had their advocates, and were even put into practice outside the realms of politics and religion (see Remer, 1996, and Todd, 1987), the shift—gradual and sometimes grudging—from prudence to principles as the basis of toleration did not occur until the eighteenth century. The period during which the modern understandings of religious toleration and liberty took shape and principles replaced national interest as their primary justification is bounded at its beginning by the denial of toleration in France by the revocation of the Edict of Nantes (1685) and the publication of John Locke's *Letter Concerning Toleration* (1689) and at its end by the adoption of the First Amendment to the United States Constitution (1791) and the British removal of political restrictions on Roman Catholics (1830).

Toleration before the Enlightenment. Before the eighteenth century, persecution was more often the rule than was toleration. Long after the Reformation, most of the states of western Europe remained committed to religious uniformity and had officially established state churches. This was true even though these states almost always had religious minorities living within their boundaries. The members of these minorities were usually regarded as dissidents, if not heretics, who were to be eliminated, either through conversion (or reconversion) to the official church or by suppression. Even the American colonies, several of which were founded by people seeking to escape religious oppression in England, were rarely tolerant of religious minorities and often attempted to drive them out. The modern doctrine of religious toleration as a policy of permissive indifference gradually emerged from failures of these attempts to eliminate minorities and from the eighteenth-century triumph of some of the ideals of liberalism.

The practice of tolerating dissidents has a much longer but no less prudence-based history within Christianity. Both Saint Augustine and Thomas Aquinas defended a form of toleration as a means of religious education. The biblical injunction "Compel them to come in that my house may be filled" (Luke 14:23) was interpreted by both men as calling for the temporary tolerance of those who did not accept the teachings of the Roman Catholic Church and justifying what were, in effect, coercive attempts to reeducate their "erroneous" consciences. Those, however, who stubbornly persisted in their errors and did not accept the church's truth were ultimately persecuted. While it did not permanently eliminate objectionable beliefs, the Roman Catholic Church, on the whole, was able to contain them—at least until the Reformation. But the successes of Martin Luther, John Calvin, and their followers and imitators on the Continent and Henry VIII in England forever changed the religious face of the Western world.

The early Protestant reformers had claimed direct and accurate understanding of God's will and knowledge of religious truth that entitled and indeed required them to overthrow the corrupt "Romanish" church and to replace its teachings with their own doctrines. Few motives spurring action are stronger than the belief that one is in possession of the truth, religious truth in particular, and the several Reformation Protestant churches began their lives secure in that belief. They sought domination, not tolerance for themselves or the coexistence of differing Christian faiths. They were initially no more compromising in their rejection of Catholicism than the Roman church was in its attacks on them. Toleration emerged as a goal only where it was clear to Protestant denominations that they faced persecution and would not be permitted to worship according to their faiths. Some later sects, such as the Anabaptists, Quakers, English Independents (Congregationalists in America), Mennonites, and Methodists, to name a few, which for the most part were breakaway dissenters from mainstream Protestantism, were content with toleration, but they were more the exception than the rule.

For the most part, triumphant Protestants were no more tolerant of Catholicism or of other Protestant sects than previously ruling churches had been of them. There were exceptions: in England, the government of Oliver Cromwell granted limited tolerance to Protestants during the Protectorate and readmitted Jews to residence; Christians and Jews were granted a relatively wide tolerance in the Dutch Republic in the seventeenth century, even though the Reformed Church enjoyed a preferred status.

One of the most important political consequences of the Reformation was the emergence of the sovereign, territorial state as the locus of secular authority. This was, of course, a complex and extended process—that in many respects is still continuing—for which the Reformation was not singularly responsible. But the successful alliance of religious reformers and political rulers against the authority of the Roman Catholic Church played a fundamental role in recasting European politics. From the perspective of religious toleration, two factors emerged: first, Christianity was no longer structurally homogeneous; second, the determination of whether diverse or dissident Christian sects were to be permitted within one political territory was not the exclusive preserve of religious authority but increasingly required negotiation with the civil ruler. The form of settlement was different in each state.

Much of Scandinavia and many German states replaced Roman Catholicism with Lutheranism. Parts of Switzerland, the Netherlands, and Scotland converted to the new Calvinist theology. England, more for political than doctrinal reasons, adopted its own form of Protestantism, one that rejected the papacy but retained the parish organization, much of the structure, and many of the practices of Catholicism. Spain, the various principalities of Italy, and most of France remained Catholic. A great many French residents, however, including members of the nobility and the merchant classes, took up the religion of Geneva, as did substantial numbers of the English, who were dissatisfied with what they regarded as Roman Catholic residues in Anglicanism.

These conversions were not peaceful, and they were not thorough. In France, where the nature of state itself was seen to be at stake, bloody and protracted wars of religion between Protestants and Catholics led to the uneasy toleration of Calvinists announced in the Edict of Nantes (1598) that would be repealed in 1685. The English throne passed from Protestant to Catholic and back to Protestant hands (where, apart from the brief reign of James II from 1685 to 1688, it has remained), with persecution and some violence attending each transition. Because the head of the English state was also the titular head of the (Protestant) Church of England and had, among his or her entitlements, the power to appoint bishops, a Roman Catholic sovereign presented serious problems. One of the results of the Glorious Revolution of 1688, which ended the reign of James II, was the legislated protection of what became known as the "Protestant succession" through the 1701 Act of Settlement, which specifically excluded Roman Catholics from the throne. (For the text of the act, see Williams, 1960, 56–57.)

Except in the Netherlands, which has some claim to being regarded as the birthplace of the recognizably modern practice of religious toleration, conflict and various degrees of persecution were the order of the day throughout post-Reformation Europe. Even in the Netherlands, however, where the entitlement of citizens to practice the non-Catholic religions of their choice had been guaranteed since 1559 by the Union of Utrecht, the Reformed Church enjoyed a privileged status without being officially established. It had settled its own internal differences by expelling the liberal Remonstrants in 1619 at the Synod of Dort; its ministers were paid by the state, and its members had exclusive rights to hold public office.

Arguments for Toleration. Opposition to toleration persisted within the Reformed Church, some of whose members associated the practice with the liberals and with deism. In the 1640s Herman Noordkerk, a Lutheran lawyer in Amsterdam, summed up what would become one of the bases for toleration in the next century when he pointedly observed:

> Persecution is persecution, whether it stems from Rome, Augsberg, Geneva, or Dort! . . . Orthodoxy is a kind of lottery—it is the sentiment of the ruling party. Today your orthodoxy is in power, and, if the tables will be turned, mine will be tomorrow: then today's orthodoxy will have become heresy and awaits persecution just as much.
>
> (Quoted in van der Wall, 2000, 119.)

The Dutch debated toleration throughout the eighteenth century, as Calvinists remained hostile to Enlightenment values. Tolerance of other Protestant denominations was severely limited and would remain so until 1795—in the aftermath of the successful Batavian Revolution—when the privileges of the Reform Church were revoked in the name of the French Revolution's principles of "liberty, equality, and fraternity."

Toleration based on prudence and interest—the self-preservation of religious sects as well as the political and economic costs of continued persecution—was implicitly committed to a recognition that fundamental religious differences could not be resolved in their own terms. Behind this was a nonperfectionist realization that reason and persuasion did not necessarily change people's minds; the use of force might alter their behavior, but it would not influence their beliefs. This argument had been used by Thomas Hobbes in the 1640s and 1650s as the basis for attacks on religious heterodoxy. Acknowledging that individual consciences could not be coerced, Hobbes said that permitting people to act on the dictates of their consciences would lead to anarchy. His remedy, as stated in chapter 29 of his 1651 work *Leviathan; or the Matter, Forme, and Power of a Commonwealth, Ecclesiastical and Civil*, was to preserve the liberty of thought and "judgment" (which he equated with conscience) and to limit freedom of action to what the sovereign permitted.

On the other hand, John Locke implied in his *Letter Concerning Toleration* and his *Essay Concerning Human Understanding* (1690), prohibiting beliefs would be an invitation to false testimony. Another and more substantial of Locke's claims in the *Letter Concerning Toleration* was that the "business" of religion and that of the magistrate were altogether separate. Churches are concerned with salvation and the care of souls, he argued, and it is the job of states to protect people's lives and goods; the two should never meet, and the state should not hinder individuals in their pursuits of salvation:

> I esteem it above all things necessary to distinguish exactly the Business of Civil Government from that of Religion, and to settle the just Bounds that lie between the one and the other. If this be not done, there can be no end put to the Controversies that will be always arising between those that have, or at least pretend to have, on the one side, a Concernment for the Interest of Men's Souls, and, On the other side, a Care of the Commonwealth.
>
> The commonwealth Seems to me to be a Society of Men constituted only for the procuring, preserving, and advancing their own *civil interests*.
>
> (Locke, 1983, 236.)

Locke also stated his view that "a Church...I take to be a voluntary Society of Men, joining themselves together of their own accord, in order to the publick worshipping of God, in such a manner as they judge acceptable to him, and effectual to the salvation of their Souls" (Locke, 1983, 28).

Even stronger than Locke's sentiments was the insistence of William Popple, the translator of the *Letter Concerning Toleration*, who in his preface was as hard on the persecuted sects as he was on the government itself:

> Our Government has not only been partial in Matters of Religion; but those also who have suffered under that Partiality, and have therefore endeavoured by their Writings to vindicate their own Rights and Liberties, have for the most part done it upon narrow Principles, suited only to the Interests of their own Sects.
>
> This narrowness of Spirit on all sides has undoubtedly been the principal Occasion of our Miseries and Confusions. But whatever have been the Occasion, it is now high time to seek

for a thorow Cure. We have need of more generous Remedies than have yet been made use of in our Distemper....

> Absolute Liberty, Just and True Liberty, Equal and Impartial Liberty, is the thing we stand in need of. Now tho this has indeed been much talked of, I doubt it has not been much understood; I am sure not at all practiced, either by our Governours towards the People in general, or by any Dissenting Parties of the People towards one another.
>
> (Locke, 1983, 21.)

Because Popple did not sign the preface, these words were long taken to have been Locke's own sentiments, and as Popple implied, they are compatible with the arguments of the *Letter Concerning Toleration*. In many respects, the eighteenth century turned Popple's "absolute liberty" into an unyielding call not just for toleration but for liberty in general.

In these terms, many advocates of toleration agreed that attempts to coerce beliefs about something so sacred as one's relationship to God are always inappropriate. For a variety of reasons—some of them erroneous, no doubt—people will have diverse understandings of divinity, but within the limits of civility, they must be free to reason their ways to their own conclusions, and not simply about religion. This view was reinforced by and in turn gave added weight to a growing skepticism about knowledge in general and religious knowledge in particular as well as a commitment to what Baruch de Spinoza termed *libertas philosophandi*, the liberty to philosophize. The French Huguenot Pierre Bayle, living in exile in the Netherlands, went further yet and in 1686 insisted that the imposition of religious doctrines stood in the way of the search for truth. Thus, although Bayle and Locke were both Christians who advocated what amounted to a religious-based toleration that looked to the reconciliation of faith and reason, their doctrines tied toleration inseparably to the secular intellectual freedom, rejection of ideological authority, and anticlericalism that are characteristically associated with the eighteenth century.

Toleration Debated. In France, the elimination of toleration for Protestants in the revocation of the Edict of Nantes was the product of a belief among the Catholic leadership, shared by Louis XIV, that social and political stability were dependent upon religious uniformity. Protestants were seen as subversive republicans who threatened the survival of the nation. That same reliance upon religion as the source of national unity but without the animus toward Protestantism was the basis of Jean-Jacques Rousseau's reliance on "civil religion" in the penultimate chapter of his *Du contrat social* (1762). In that chapter he also shrewdly pointed out the deep paradox that inheres in toleration and observed that civil tolerance could not exist alongside religious intolerance:

> In my opinion, those who distinguish between civil and theological intolerance are mistaken. These two forms of

intolerance are inseparable. It is impossible to live in peace with people one believes to be damned; to love them would be to hate God who punishes them; it is an absolute duty either to redeem or to torture them. Whenever theological intolerance is admitted, it is bound to have some civil consequences, and when it does so, the sovereign no longer is sovereign, even in the temporal sphere; at this stage, the priests become the real masters, and kings are only their officers.

Now that there is not, and can no longer be, an exclusive national religion, all religions which themselves tolerate others must be tolerated, provided only that their dogmas contain nothing contrary to the duties of the citizen.

(Rousseau, 1968, 186–187.)

There was significant discussion of religious liberty and the rights of conscience in France throughout the eighteenth century. Despite a relatively rigid censorship of the press, Protestant works that originated outside the country were often permitted. Voltaire, in true conformity with the spirit of the French Enlightenment, said that the aim of tolerance should be to give people proper ideas about religion rather than to accept whatever they believed:

Such is the weakness of the human race, some such their perversity, that they would doubtless prefer to be subject to every conceivable superstition than to live without religion.... When men are bereft of sane ideas about divinity, false notions take their place, just as in times of economic depression counterfeit money circulates because reliable money is scarce.... Superstition is to religion what astrology is to astronomy, that is the very foolish daughter of a wise and intelligent mother. These two daughters have long held the entire world in subjection.

(Voltaire, 2000, 83.)

Nonetheless, a hostility to toleration persisted in France, and toleration was seen as representing "Enlightenment" and therefore Protestant values. In fact, advocates of toleration were often deists or skeptics who called upon society to adopt their principles. In 1787 Louis XVI granted a limited toleration to Huguenots with the Edict of Toleration, but it was not sufficient to stave off the Revolution. In 1789, at the height of that Revolution, the Declaration of the Rights of Man asserted, "No one shall be disquieted on account of his opinions, including his religious views, provided their manifestation does not disturb the public order established by law."

English discussions of toleration in the eighteenth century are especially instructive because that nation had gone further than any other in coming to terms with the religious heterogeneity that makes tolerance necessary as well as possible in the end. That peculiarly English accommodation was manifested both in laws and in informal practices. Despite the existence of the officially established Protestant Church of England and a virtual union of church and state, Roman Catholics and Protestant nonconformists and dissenters had long been included in the *political* nation. They participated

in elections, owned property, and in some cases retained noble titles even though they were not legally permitted to hold public office or to have churches of their own. The so-called Act of Toleration of 1689 allowed non-Anglican, Trinitarian Protestants—a category that excluded Roman Catholics, Quakers, and Socinians (as Unitarians were called)—to establish churches without fear of sanctions. But restrictions of the Test and Corporation Acts that limited office-holding to confessors in the established church were retained. (See Williams, 1960, 42–46, for the text of the Act.) The members of some of these sects wanted to be reunited with the Church of England, and negotiations had been under way for more than twenty years. But the Act of Toleration set the stage for their permanent exclusion, and by retaining the limitations of the Test and Corporation Acts, prepared the ground for a century-long debate on the place of religion within the constitutional structure of England. (See Schochet, 1996 and 2000.)

In the early part of the century, the celebratory anti-Catholicism—and anticlericalism—that had surrounded the Glorious Revolution gave way to concerns about safety of the established church and the security of the nation. Cries of "the Church in danger" were accompanied by calls for repeal of the Toleration Act itself. Fears from the period of the Restoration led to the branding of some of the sectarians as "fanatics" and "enthusiasts" who were seen as threats to social stability; behind this was a lingering alarm about the susceptibility of the masses to the appeals of unrestrained, passionate religion. Even Locke, the great champion of religious toleration and liberty, attacked "enthusiasm" in an addition to book 4 (chapter 19) of his *Essay Concerning Human Understanding*, as did his pupil the third earl of Shaftesbury in his 1707 "Letter Concerning Enthusiasm." David Hume, on the other hand, viewed religious enthusiasm as *a friend* to civil liberty (Hume, 1987, 78).

While Locke and Shaftesbury were troubled by what they saw as the excesses of toleration, they were not on the side of those who would have withdrawn or limited it. Both men believed in and appealed to the power of reason to overcome the dangerously seductive power of enthusiasm. And Locke at least would have sympathized with the dissenters and their liberal supporters within the Church of England who agitated for wider freedoms and for repeal of the Test and Corporation Acts and removal of the disabilities they imposed. Each of the several times that repeal was seriously proposed in Parliament, however, the opposition responded by defending the integrity of "the constitution."

The restrictions on Protestants of the Corporation and Test Acts were finally repealed in 1828 and those on Catholics in 1830, but nearly forty years earlier, that matter had been put to rest for Americans in Article VI of the U.S. Constitution, which declared, "no religious Test shall ever be required as a Qualification to any Office or public Trust under the United States." In better-known language, the First Amendment to the Constitution established religious liberty: "Congress shall make no law respecting an establishment of religion, or prohibiting the free exercise thereof."

Richard Price, in the tract that was to incite Edmund Burke to write his *Reflections on the Revolution in France*, numbered as the "First" of the worthy principles of the Glorious Revolution "the right to liberty of conscience in religious matters." Burke, who would have had no reason to disagree with at least that one of Price's sentiments, did insist that "the teachers who reformed our religion in England bore no sort of resemblance to your present reforming doctors in Paris," and then attacked what he saw as the hypocrisy of the assertions of religious freedom in France: "We hear these new teachers continually boasting of their spirit of toleration. That those persons should tolerate all opinions, who think none to be of estimation, is a matter of small merit. Equal neglect is not impartial kindness" (Burke, 1987, 131–132).

Thomas Paine, replying to Burke in his *The Rights of Man*, declared the following:

The French Constitution hath abolished or renounced *Toleration*, and *Intolerance* also, and hath established UNIVERSAL RIGHT OF CONSCIENCE.

Toleration is not the *opposite* of Intolerance, but is the *counterfeit* of it. Both are despotisms. The one assumes to itself the right of withholding Liberty of Conscience, and the other of granting it. The one is the Pope, armed with fire and faggot, and the other is the Pope selling or granting indulgences. The former is church and state, and the latter is church and traffic....

With respect to what are called denominations of religion, if every one is left to judge of his own religion, there is no such thing as a religion that is wrong; but if they are to judge of each other's religion, there is no such thing as a religion that is right; and therefore all the world is right, or all the world is wrong.

(Paine, 1985, 85–86.)

With Voltaire, Paine recognized that toleration was integral to a larger concern with the "civilizing" process and the expansion of reason. This was not simply an eighteenth-century goal but, as part of a more general conception of "progress," would continue well into the nineteenth century and form the basis of John Stuart Mill's *On Liberty*.

[See also Bayle, Pierre; Locke, John; Moral Philosophy; Natural Religion; Paine, Thomas; Political Philosophy; Revealed Religion; *and* Rousseau, Jean-Jacques.]

BIBLIOGRAPHY

Bayle, Pierre. *Commentaire philosophique sur ces paroles de Jésus-Christ, "Contrain-les d'entrer."* Translated as *Philosophical Commentary on the Words of Jesus Christ, "Compel Them to Come In."* 2 vols. London, 1708.

Burke, Edmund. *Reflections on the Revolution in France.* Edited by J. G. A. Pocock. Indianapolis, 1987.

Hume, David. *Essays Moral, Political, and Literary.* 2d ed. Edited by Eugene F. Miller. Indianapolis, 1987.

Kilcullen, John. *Sincerity and Truth: Essays on Arnauld, Bayle, and Toleration.* Oxford, 1988.

Locke, John. *Essay Concerning Human Understanding.* Edited by Peter H. Nidditch. Oxford, 1975.

Locke, John. *A Letter Concerning Toleration.* Translated by William Popple. Edited by James H. Tully. Indianapolis, 1983.

Paine, Thomas. *The Rights of Man.* Edited by Eric Foner. New York, 1985.

Remer, Gary. *Humanism and the Rhetoric of Toleration.* University Park, Pa., 1996.

Rousseau, Jean-Jacques. *The Social Contract.* Edited and translated by Maurice Cranston. New York, 1968.

Schochet, Gordon. "The Act of Toleration and the Failure of Comprehension: Persecution, Non-Conformity, and Religious Indifference." In *The World of William and Mary: Anglo-Dutch Perspectives on the Revolution of 1688–1689*, edited by Dale Hoak and M. Feingold, pp. 165–187 and 296–302. Stanford, Calif., 1996.

Schochet, Gordon. "Mandeville's *Free Thoughts* and the Eighteenth-Century Debate on 'Toleration' and the English Constitution." In *Mandeville and Augustan Ideas: New Essays*, edited by Charles W. A. Prior, pp. 35–50. Victoria, B.C., 2000.

Shaftesbury, Anthony Ashley Cooper, Earl of. "A Letter Concerning Enthusiasm." Incorporated into his *Characteristicks of Men, Manners, Opinions, Times* (1711). Edited by John W. Robertson. New York, 1967.

Todd, Margo. *Christian Humanism and the Puritan Social Order.* Cambridge, 1987.

Van der Wall, Ernestine. "Toleration and Enlightenment in the Dutch Republic." In *Toleration in Enlightenment Europe*, edited by Ole Peter Grell and Roy Porter. Cambridge, 2000.

Voltaire. *Treatise on Tolerance.* Reprinted in his *Treatise on Tolerance and Other Writings.* Edited by Simon Harvey. Cambridge, 2000.

Williams, E. N. *The Eighteenth-Century Constitution: Documents and Commentary.* Cambridge, 1960.

GORDON SCHOCHET

TORTURE. *See* Political Philosophy.

TOUSSAINT L'OUVERTURE, PIERRE DOMINIQUE (1746–1803), Haitian revolutionary leader.

Born in the French Caribbean colony of Saint-Domingue (now the Republic of Haiti), Toussaint l'Ouverture (or Louverture) rose from slavery to become governor of that colony. As a footman on the Breda plantation in the northern part of the island, Toussaint enjoyed a higher status than the other slaves toiling on the colony's plantations. He learned how to read and write and was familiar with herbal medicine. These skills later served him well as he rose to political prominence in Saint-Domingue.

Eighteenth-century Saint-Domingue was France's richest colony; its economy was closely linked with that of the ruling country, to which it exported sugar, molasses, coffee, indigo, and other merchandise. Agricultural and manufacturing activities in Saint-Domingue constituted about 40 percent of France's foreign trade and provided work for 20 percent of the kingdom's estimated 27 million people, while providing some 25 million livres annually in direct or indirect taxes.

This vast wealth was generated by a population of 500,000 African and Creole slaves. By law, the slaves, who formed the base of Saint-Domingue's society, were deprived of all human and civil rights. The Black Code of 1685, promulgated by Louis XIV's finance minister, Jean-Baptiste Colbert, defined them as just another category of property. Freedmen, numbering about 45,000, occupied the next level of the social pyramid. People of mixed European and African ancestry, they were largely an educated group. Although some of them owned plantations and slaves, they enjoyed no political rights and were forbidden to enter certain professions, such as medicine, or to marry whites. The whites formed the apex

Pierre Dominique Toussaint l'Ouverture. Engraving by J.-J.-G. Dulompre. (Bibliothèque Nationale, Paris/Giraudon/Art Resource, NY.)

of Saint-Domingue's society; though only about 30,000 in number, they exercised full control over the colony's economic and political life.

In 1789, the revolutionary National Constituent Assembly in Paris enacted a law granting the right to vote to all freedmen in France's colonies. This law created an almost irreconcilable divide between Saint-Domingue's freed people of color and the white population, which opposed any mulatto participation in the political life of the colony. This rift and the racial war that ensued caused deep political and economic changes in the colony's social fabric. The situation was exacerbated five years later, on 4 February 1794, when France's governing body, the National Convention, proclaimed the abolition of slavery in all of France's possessions. News of that decision was received in Saint-Domingue with a sense of outrage by whites and slave-owning mulattos alike, who saw it as a blow to the colony's race-based equilibrium as well as to their economic status and class privileges. To counter the Convention's decision, the white planters and, later, the mulattos sought to bring autonomy to the colony by enlisting Spanish and English support.

War in Saint-Domingue. As the shock wave of the French Revolution rolled over Europe, its fearful monarchs came to see France as an outlaw nation that should be contained and brought back into the old order. The war that subsequently engulfed western Europe spilled over into the Caribbean, an area of intense contention among France, England, and Spain, the colonial superpowers of the time. With their troops preoccupied in the European theater of war, these nations, aided by bands of escaped slaves or maroons (commanded by chiefs such as Jean-François, who fought for Spain, and Biassou, who fought on behalf of France), battled one another in a proxy war that ultimately had dramatic unintended consequences: the weakening of European influence in Saint-Domingue; the appearance of war-seasoned black leaders; and the emergence of Toussaint l'Ouverture, first as maroon leader and then as general-in-chief of France's colonial army.

Until the age of forty-seven, Toussaint avoided the disorders that ravaged Saint-Domingue. As trouble developed, he remained on Breda plantation in his position as footman to the plantation's overseer. He did not participate in the August 1791 slave uprising that burned and destroyed two-thirds of the plantations in the northern part of the colony. In November 1791, however, two years after the Declaration of the Rights of Man was adopted by the National Constituent Assembly, Toussaint left Breda and joined the maroon leader Biassou, whose troops were fighting against France under the Spanish banner. A brilliant strategist, he led the men under his command from victory to victory; a cunning politician as well, he fought successively on behalf of France, England, and Spain, and played the colonial powers against one another to serve his own interests. As early as 1793, while fighting under the Spanish banner, Toussaint offered his services to General Laveaux, commander of the French forces. Laveaux, however, refused to accept Toussaint's condition that France recognize the rights of the slaves to be free. When the National Convention proclaimed the abolition of slavery in February 1794, Toussaint abandoned Spain; the very next morning, with his 5,000-man army, he began his drive to push the Spaniards back to the eastern part of the island (now the Dominican Republic).

Toussaint in Power. Toussaint swiftly ascended to power. Because of the remoteness of France and the difficulty of obtaining reinforcements, Laveaux came to depend on him to counter white and mulatto challenges to France's political control over the colony. By 1796, Toussaint had successfully eliminated all internal opposition to Laveaux, who, in recognition of his services to France, named him lieutenant-governor of Saint-Domingue. In fact, Toussaint's ultimate goal was to wrest the colony from French control. Using outright manipulation, and crude military force, he systematically defeated all those who opposed his objectives. He subjugated the white and mulatto planters who had opposed the freeing of the slaves and had offered the colony to England and Spain; he checked Spanish and English ambitions for hegemony; and he unabashedly and systematically turned back every representative France named to represent it in the colony. In 1801, at the apex of his power, Toussaint signed a tripartite commercial treaty with the United States and England. To crown his achievement, Toussaint gave Saint-Domingue a constitution that named him governor for life and sent it to France, for recognition by the First Consul, Napoleon Bonaparte. It was a bold move toward declaring the colony's autonomy and consolidating his power. When Napoleon received Toussaint's constitution, he immediately perceived it as an act of rebellion against France and replied by sending a 54,000-man expeditionary force commanded by his brother-in-law, General Charles Leclerc. His secret instruction to Leclerc was to subdue Toussaint's forces, to deport the "rebel general" to France, and to reestablish slavery, which would be officially decreed by the First Consul on 20 May 1802.

On 1 February 1802, the expeditionary forces arrived in the port at Cap Français, Saint-Domingue's largest city. Leclerc immediately demanded the surrender of General Henri Christophe, the city's commanding officer. Christophe replied by carrying out Toussaint's previously issued orders to burn down the cities and the plantations and withdraw into the mountains, whence Toussaint planned to harass Leclerc's forces. In spite of some early victories, Toussaint lost the important battle of Ravines à Couleuvres (18 February 1802). This loss gave the French army access to the island's northern region—Toussaint's home base. Toussaint's resistance lasted three months, but in the end he could not contain the French assault. On 5 May 1802, he surrendered to Leclerc in Cap Français, bid farewell to his troops, and retired to his plantation in Ennery.

Deportation to France. Leclerc felt, however, that as long as Toussaint remained in Saint-Domingue he would constitute a smoldering ember that could rekindle the flame of revolt. Therefore, on 7 June 1802, following Napoleon's order, Leclerc had Toussaint arrested and deported to France. On 12 July, Toussaint arrived in the French port of Brest and, under heavy escort, traveled to the Fort de Joux in the Jura Mountains, where he was imprisoned. Subjected to the cold of the Jura, separated from his wife and children (who had also been deported to France), and denied all but the barest comforts, Toussaint soon fell ill, and on 7 April 1803, he was found dead in his cell. He was buried in the fort's cemetery; one of his sons, Isaac, later had his body exhumed and interred in the cemetery in Bordeaux, France. Upon embarking on the *Hero*, the fatefully named vessel that would transport him to France, Toussaint had uttered the famous words, "By overthrowing me, you have only cut off the trunk of the tree of freedom; it will grow back again, for its numerous roots run deep."

[*See also* Colonialism; Declaration of the Rights of Man; Diplomacy; France; French Revolution; Race; Slavery; *and* War and Military Theory.]

BIBLIOGRAPHY

Debien, Gabriel. *Les Colons de Saint Domingue et la révolution*. Paris, 1956.

Deschamps, Léon. *Histoire de la question coloniale en France*. Paris, 1891.

Dorsainville, Roger. *Toussaint Louverture ou la vocation de la liberté*. Paris, 1965.

Frostin, Charles. *Les Révoltes blanches à Saint Domingue au XVIIème et XVIIIème siècles*. Paris, 1975.

Garrett, Mitchell B. *The French Colonial Question*. Ann Arbor, Mich., 1916.

James, C. L. R. *The Black Jacobins: Toussaint Louverture and the San Domingo Revolution*. New York, 1962.

Lokke, Carl L. *France and the Colonial Question*. New York, 1932.

Schoelcher, Victor. *Vie de Toussaint Louverture*. Paris, 1982.

Seeber, Edward D. *Anti-Slavery Opinion in France during the Second Half of the Eighteenth Century*. New York, 1969.

Stein, Robert Louis. *The French Slave Trade*. Madison, Wis., 1979.

MARC A. CHRISTOPHE

TRADITION. The Enlightenment was a period in which optimism of various sorts took root and justified a break with ways that had been sanctioned by long usage. It was characterized, thus, by the criticism of traditions and by efforts to replace them with new ways of thinking and with new practices. It did this in nearly every field, but in doing so it usually built upon what had gone before. Other thinkers during the period of the Enlightenment, however, also found new uses for tradition, appealing to it to critique the ideas and values of the enlightened. When they did so, they often used the ideas of Enlightenment authors to criticize it.

The Erosion of Traditions. Every eighteenth-century European society, even in most of the Dutch provinces, was a peasant society in which the margin of subsistence tended to be very narrow. In such societies people simply cannot risk changing practices whose results are predictable and whose outcomes they understand. Peasant societies are inherently resistant to change and prize the ways of doing things which have existed from time immemorial—which meant, generally, at least beyond living memory. There was, then, no great incentive to plant new crops, adopt new technologies, or change the social context of their agrarian societies. One root of traditional attitudes thus lay close to the realities of everyday life. Until agrarian changes were demonstrated to have an ameliorative effect on peasant life, they were made only with difficulty and very slowly. As the article on agriculture in this work shows, most changes reflected slowly accreting innovations that went back into the seventeenth or even sixteenth centuries. The pace of change accelerated in the eighteenth century, particularly in Holland and Britain, parts of Italy, and France. As it did, the benefits of improved agriculture became clearer and more acceptable to the landowners, to the managers of the land, and eventually to those who worked it.

Economic changes. The rural experience was shared by town-dwellers. They often found that with innovative improvements, the prices for basic commodities fell a bit relative to their own wages. Towns also benefited from agricultural changes because they were dependent on the prosperity of the countryside, which produced the raw materials and supplied the principal market for their goods and services. Although agricultural reform uprooted some people and changed their lives for the worse, others found a place in growing cities where they had more cash in their pockets. Agrarian changes allowed for urban growth and often provided the labor needed for an expanded industrial base. At the lowest level of eighteenth-century life, there was often enough improvement and upward mobility to change the attitudes of ordinary people to life as they had first known it. They slowly became less resistant to change and less wedded to traditional ideas and ways.

Those changes were associated with the growth of social overhead capital or the facilities that supported the economy. In France much road building was undertaken by Louis XIV and continued into the eighteenth century.

At the same time a canal linking the Mediterranean and the Atlantic was built and other waterways were improved or created. In Britain a national improved road grid was in place by 1780, and by the end of the century there was a canal network that drastically reduced transport costs for many mine owners, manufacturers, and farmers. Docks, warehouses, market facilities, and public buildings had increased throughout the period, and even in war-ravaged areas of Europe there was, by 1790, on the whole, a general improvement in the infra-structural facilities that made for more flourishing economies. This, too, made men think that they were not living in the world of their fathers.

Law and administration. If one leaves the economic sphere and looks at the social landscape, in most places there were changes that affected individuals for the better. Places like the Scottish Highlands or Corsica were more peaceful and orderly by 1790 than they had ever been before. This was partly because economic ties linked such areas more closely to others that formerly had not mattered much to them, and partly because justice was administered more surely, less arbitrarily, and more fairly throughout most of Europe in 1790 than it had been in 1690. Trials in 1790 reflected the acceptance by lawyers of more stringent standards of evidence and proof, such as one finds in the thought of Montesquieu, Cesare Beccaria, or even William Blackstone (1723–1780). In 1790, the administration of justice was less likely to reflect the personal or class interests of a judge and more likely to be the application by a trained jurist of a rule imposed by an impersonal state. This is not to say that policing and punishments did not remain harsh (people could still be impaled and legally tortured in many other ways in some jurisdictions) or that governments anywhere allowed unbridled publication and free speech, but everywhere there was a change from the previous century. Better policing and justice were but symptomatic of the strengthening of states. With that phenomenon came more assurance that social stability could be retained without undue force, arbitrariness, or monstrous penalties for those who broke the rules.

Greater social and political stability allowed for the development of a larger public sphere, because governments no longer felt pressed to control everything, including personal thoughts, communications, speech, and associations. That was usually true in 1700, and certainly so in 1790. The explanations for all this lie as much in the strengthening of state institutions, such as those that gathered taxes and produced the states' monopoly of force, as in any other factor. By the end of Louis XIV's reign there were no hereditary officers left in control of important military organs like the cavalry or navy. Civil offices were still heritable, but there was in place an alternative administrative structure of appointed and removable *intendants, sub-délégués*, and lesser officials through which the centralized royal state executive controlled provinces. The judiciary had not been "nationalized," but Louis XV later tried to make it a royal bureaucracy, as kings elsewhere had done or were trying to do. In Britain this did not happen until 1747 (and then not to every court), and it was done only at considerable cost. Frederick II (known as "the Great") found it impossible to buy out his noble judges, but he did force them to qualify as lawyers or to exercise their duties through deputies who were qualified lawyers. This was a vast improvement over justice as it had been administered in many areas in 1700. All these changes sapped the viability of traditions of royal absolutism, feudal and noble rights, and vested interests in office, which could be defended not by arguments from utility and right but only from those relying on conceptions of property, history, and tradition.

Property since the ancient world had been seen as virtually untouchable without the permission of the owner, because each man had an equitable or natural law right in what he possessed, made, or appropriated from an unowned common. In the seventeenth century these ideas were restated by John Locke, but increasingly there was another conception of property rooted in Roman law, one that saw property as rooted in nature and equity, but as changing over time as societies changed. There was no property in herds or land until men ceased to be hunter-gatherers and became shepherds and farmers. This sort of property rested on agreements and customs, as David Hume argued, but it was also changeable as economic conditions changed and was subject to regulation and to legal definition by positive laws. As the great Scottish jurist James Dalrymple, Lord Stair (1619–1695), wrote before 1693, "So may the public consent of any people introduce ways of appropriation, as they find most convenient for the public good, and that either expressly by statute, or declaration of the legislative authority, or tacitly by consuetude." "Public sanction or common custom" determines what is to count as property and that ultimately is determined by "the ground of common utility" (*Institutions of the Law of Scotland*, book II, title 34–39.). What the people make, the people can change. That was as revolutionary a dictum as the defense of liberties of person and property offered by Locke, and just as subversive of the status quo. The Roman law conception of the origins of and the reasons for the regulation of property enunciated by Stair reappears in many thinkers of the Enlightenment, including Rousseau and Beccaria, and in the edicts of reforming rulers of the time. It was more important on the European continent than in England, but everywhere it justified changes, generally from above, in the name of the common interest.

Religious tradition and authority. These changes were concomitant with others that more often come to mind when tradition is discussed. Everyone in almost all European states in the period was expected to be a Christian. Every form of Christianity had its own version of tradition, and each had been subject to shocks that were still occurring and weakening the customary foundations of the various churches. If one looked to Roman Catholicism, the tradition that counted most was the magisterium, or teaching authority of the church, represented by councils or the pope speaking ex cathedra about doctrine and morality. The Roman Church claimed that it alone had the right to define the canon of holy books that composed the Bible and that partially defined the beliefs all Christians were to hold. The church's teaching authority rested on its traditions, whose purity was guaranteed and symbolized by the apostolic succession of its bishops, including the bishop of Rome who represented Peter upon whom Christ had built his church. Its teaching authority was ultimately traditional in nature and warranted tradition and traditions in a sort of circular fashion. For its severest and ever more vocal critics, those teachings of the church extended to a host of nonbiblical beliefs, some of which were little more than pious stories, while others, like the doctrines of the Trinity or transubstantiation, were the products of forgeries, interpolations, or the lucubrations of Christian philosophers writing during the Middle Ages.

The anticlericalism of the Middle Ages, reacting against an increasingly worldly church, blackened the character of clerics by seeking to show how self-interested and power-hungry they could be. This literature received permanent and well-read forms in works like *Encomium Moriae* (The Praise of Folly, 1510) and the *Colloquia* (complete in the 3d edition of 1526) of Erasmus (1466–1536). The first has had over six hundred editions and the second over three hundred, many before 1800. The popes' claims to moral and religious leadership became uncertain in the minds of many. Their authority suffered when they claimed too much, as in the bull *Unum Sanctum* (1302), and when schisms and divisions in the church between 1378 and 1414 left men free to choose between as many as three popes who all made traditional claims. Popes by then had also been subjected to the strictures and then to the regulation of councils that claimed to be the chief definers of doctrine and leaders of the Christian peoples. Conciliar claims were worked out, justified, and perpetuated by the followers of men like Marsilius of Padua (c. 1278–1342) or Jan Hus (c. 1369–1415), whose followers organized a sect that survived into the eighteenth century, and by a number of nominalist philosophers. When historians tried, as they did in the Renaissance, to reconstruct the early church, they often claimed to find that the bishop of Rome was but one bishop among many patriarchs, and that the early church did not in the least resemble the modern one, which had accumulated many institutions and practices unknown in fifth-century Antioch or Alexandria. Edward Gibbon's *History of the Decline and Fall of the Roman Empire* (1776–1788) was the eighteenth-century culmination of that attack on the history of the church; Gibbon sought to discredit its teaching authority by showing it as but another institution subject to all of the forces that affected any human institution—a point made earlier by a host of writers like the Catholic Servite friar Paolo Sarpi (1552–1623), whose *Istoria del Concilio Tridentino* (History of the Council of Trent, 1617) showed this to the satisfaction of the enlightened who everywhere read and approved the many editions and translations of his book.

Scholars also increasingly found that the canon was a complicated matter, indeed. There had been no final canonical selection of books in the Western church until the fourth century. When one was formed, it excluded the pseudoepigraphic Hebrew books and similar materials produced by various early Christians. This canon had not been there in the second century, when some early Church Fathers quoted as authoritative books that were now no longer regarded as having merit. Yet more dramatic, the canon accepted by the Western church was not that of the Russian, Coptic, or Armenian churches.

Critical scholars argued that it was not certain that the Bible accepted and authorized by Rome was in fact based on the best texts that might be found. Many believed that Corinthians 13:13, Matthew 28:19, and the Gospel of John 1:1 and 10:30 were later interpolations, because they did not all appear in every ancient manuscript. Erasmus had found 1 John 5:7, the Johannine Comma—a principal text supporting the doctrine of the Trinity—problematic, and he did not include it in the first edition of his New Testament (1516). Others suspected that John 14:15–26 was equally dubious. The doctrine of the Trinity as defined by Rome might not be correct. Since it was also a mystery, it could not be fully understood. Can we reasonably believe what is literally unintelligible? To believe that in the mass the wafer and wine miraculously become the body and blood of Christ is one thing; to explain this as the imposition of a new substance under the accidents or perceptible qualities of the bread and wine is to give an Aristotelian gloss to another mystery, one given status as a dogma only in 1215. To some extent the fate of Catholicism was captive to a philosophy whose prospects were limited.

All of the other churches, Orthodox and Protestant alike, had similar problems about the canon, the evolution of dogma, the sources of authority, and the status of those who claimed to teach authoritatively. The critical linguistic and historical issues were all canvassed during the Renaissance by the humanists, and questions of religious authority were discussed vibrantly during the Reformation by a host of thinkers who were good at finding motes in the eyes of others, but not the beams in their own. Anglicans, for example, thought they needed to authenticate their church by accepting the apostolic succession and claiming that their doctrines were those of the primitive Christians. Lutherans and Calvinists did so too, but for very different churches and theologies. Diversity and the strife between confessions further undercut traditional beliefs. By 1700 there had been nearly two hundred years of controversy about these issues among the faithful of many differing Christian churches. In such a situation it was hard to maintain the absolute certainty of one's religious traditions. Instead, one relied on establishment and the force of the state to ensure conformity to a single view within a limited territory. Those who, like Niccolò Machiavelli (1469–1527), thought religion a politically useful thing invented or supported as much for its uses as its truth, found in the politics of modern states and churches much to support their opinion.

Discussion of these and other similar problems persisted into the Enlightenment, when they affected more and more people. Higher literacy rates, more and cheaper books, and sensationalistic writing meant to appeal to a more vulgar readership gave such criticism ever greater currency. Further, the civil wars of the seventeenth century, which were everywhere marked by religious enthusiasm, made claims about power and religion more plausible. All this came together in a general assault on Christianity mounted by deists. Men like John Toland asked about the canon and why the *Gospel of Barnabas* had been excluded from it. He was quick to point out that the Johannine Comma had been an addition to the Bible, and that if his generation had been uncertain of the authorship of books in their own day, we could not be sure either of the authorship of books in the ancient world or of claims that we have the texts as they had been written by their putative authors. Toland was a fairly popular author, but he relied on the scholarship of men older and more erudite than himself—Pierre Bayle, Richard Simon, and various religious skeptics whose works usually were known only to savants. From such sources he extracted a host of seeming contradictions and absurdities. His usual answer as to why they had been accepted and fitted into orthodox Christianity was that they enhanced the power of priests who found it useful to keep their flocks in the dark about truth and the means of finding it. Critics like Toland were happy to ask, as had some of the orthodox: Where did Cain's wife come from? How could all the animals fit in the ark? Deists thought the answers that had been given were patently false or foolish. They reduced miracles to metaphors. For Toland, the pillar of fire by night and a cloud of smoke by day was only a poetic way of describing the great smudge-pot carried at the head of the column of Israelites as they wandered in the desert before they took the Holy Land by force. Here he was building on other scholars' work in seeing biblical language as poetic and metaphoric and not to be taken literally. Baruch de Spinoza in the 1670s had argued that one had to understand scriptural language in the context of the time and place where it was written. The biblical Hebrews, for him, were an ancient Near Eastern people and not the chosen of God. This line of thought would be pursued into the Enlightenment by numerous scholars, both Catholic and Protestant, some believers and others who doubted. Among them were Jean Astruc (1684–1766), Robert Lowth (1710–1787), William Warburton (1698–1779), Johann Gottfried Herder (1744–1803), and J. D. Michaelis (1717–1791). The cumulative effect was to call into question the foundations of Christianity and thus one of the great cultural institutions of the West.

New views of history. Just as the religious arguing among themselves undermined traditions of religious belief, the arguments of secular scholars undermined other notions that had given the past a primacy and authorized its recovery or perpetuation. One belief that had both Christian and classical roots was the idea that whatever was old was better than what was now obtained. God had made man good, but man had fallen. The story of the world was a story of decline, with only partial recoveries. The path of world history was, as Jonathan Edwards described it in 1743, a jagged line going generally downward. Was this so? Need it be so?

The Reformation had thrown up a variety of Christian sectaries who believed, like Joachim of Fiore (c. 1132–1202), that they lived at least potentially in a new age that would restore men and societies and bring this world again to the state in which God had intended it. The path of history might be reversed and historical optimism might replace a pessimism rooted in a set of traditional, but wrong, views. Those views had been picked up by Anabaptists in the 1530s, and they have lived on in radical Protestant sects into our own time. In the same years that Edwards was writing *A History of the Work of Redemption* (late 1730s), David Hartley was setting out a philosophy that purported to show that we could redeem mankind through education and social engineering. His views were accepted by English Dissenters like Joseph Priestley and by William Godwin, whose *Political Justice* (1793) was perhaps their most important intellectual manifestation. The quasi-millenarian writings of Thomas Paine during the French Revolution belong to the same train of thought. This was not exclusively Protestant: a millenarian strain also led to the Terror and its Republic of Virtue, showing that many Catholic Frenchmen were not untouched by similar notions. Catholicism, which embraced a doctrine of works, was perhaps more susceptible to this than

even dissenting Protestantism. In the works of a long string of Catholic-educated Frenchmen, one discerns a hope that the sinful world might be redeemed here and now or in the near future. This is a theme in various works by Denis Varaisse, Fénelon, the chevalier Ramsay, Anne-Robert-Jacques Turgot, baron d'Aulne (a one-time knight of Malta and the author of orations devoted to the progress of mankind given at the Sorbonne in 1750–1751), the abbé Mably, and the marquis de Condorcet, to cite only a few who held such views. It was also the aim of the Freemasons who, throughout Europe, from the 1730s on, were able to make their beliefs as masons square with a Christianity that was improving and optimistic. Theirs was not the unredeemed, unredeemable world of the Jansenists or of the Puritans. Rather, it resembled that of late eighteenth-century Unitarians and the nineteenth-century men of the social gospel. If men were saved and regenerate, given grace, or acquired grace in good works, then why could they not remake their world and improve it? To do so required that they shed traditional beliefs about the decline of all things since the Creation and the worsening of human nature and the settings in which it was displayed. If the path were upward, then the traditional view of degeneracy had to be abandoned.

In the classical myths, also, men live in an age unable to preserve an earlier innocence. Pandora's box, like Eve's apple, has been a bane to us all. Was the older always the better? By 1700, it was not at all clear that this was the case. Orthodox religious histories might reiterate such a claim, but there were other histories, going back to the Greeks, that claimed that men had progressed from the caves of the first barely human men and through stages of barbarism, pastoral agriculture, and farming to settle in cities and then to amalgamate into small and eventually large states. This story, which the histories of Greece and Rome, and then those of other peoples, seemed to establish, had become widely accepted by the early part of the eighteenth century. In one form or another it was to reappear in Vico, major Scottish writers, and in Condorcet. Its origin lay in part in the study of both the ancient past and the patterns of human development. Two places where the enlightened encountered such a history after 1730 was in *Ancient History* (12 vols., 1730) and *Roman History* (9 vols., 1738) by Charles Rollin (1661–1741), which became widely used textbooks for those studying the classical languages and literatures. His outlook also characterized the Parisian Académie des Inscriptions et Belles Lettres. The story of the progress of nations seemed to be confirmed by the differing stages of civilization to be found among the peoples of the world discovered by Europeans as they explored the globe. A new anthropology supported an ancient history.

The study of the ancients—and everyone educated studied them—contributed to the erosion of ideas about the superiority of the past and of tradition. Only in art were the ancients clearly better, in the minds of most by 1750; hence the notion that people should now seek to renew and emulate classicism. That program made it possible to think optimistically about a future for art where a Royal Academy might inculcate the standards to be followed in lectures such as those given by Sir Joshua Reynolds. In most cases, however, the future would be different from the past; the traditions that had guided men would no longer be useful, or at least, as useful. Religious controversy had weakened the hold of every confession; practical improvements had made it reasonable to think that times were getting better in unprecedented ways. Was there a method that could be followed to make all this happen? That was a question that had occurred to Francis Bacon (1561–1626) by the 1590s, and his answer was still of vital interest to minds of the Enlightenment.

Natural philosophy. Bacon had been sure that the world needed a new philosophy that would sweep away the detritus of the past and show how new, improving ideas and knowledge might be gathered and used. His skepticism about received knowledge, his hopes for the observational and experimental means of gaining and testing truths, and his belief that experiments should be followed by the implementation of the knowledge gained for the benefit of mankind—all transformed the outlook of growing numbers of men between 1626 and 1700. By the eighteenth century, this was accepted in some fashion as the prevailing view of every scientific academy in Europe. Further, this methodology, as it had been refined, developed, and applied by men like Boyle and Newton, had resulted in breathtaking achievements that put to shame much of the science of the last two millennia. The men of the Renaissance and Reformation had not called into question the presumed authority of the past; they had merely wanted to return to its pure ancient wisdom and religion. The men of the seventeenth-century scientific revolution generally knew there was no such thing to be found in the natural philosophies of Aristotle or most other ancient thinkers. Real knowledge was yet to be found, and it should be sought in every field.

The sciences of moving bodies, which as late as Galileo (1564–1642) had been divided into the circular motions of heavenly bodies and the straight-line motions of "sublunar" bodies, had been unified, mathematized, and later made into a science of great predictive power by Newton. Notions that had seemingly stood the test of time succumbed to experiments of Evangelista Torricelli (1608–1647), which created the very vacuum that Aristotelian nature "abhorred." The microscope, like the exotic animals that came back with explorers, vastly widened the created world and showed men plants unknown to Theophrastus and animals that his master, Aristotle, had

never seen. The systematic survey of the natural world that Bacon had recommended to natural historians had identified about 17,000 plant species in 1700—about three times the number of plants known in 1600. By 1800 the list of plants known to Europeans had grown by several hundred each year for a century. Many of these provided Europeans with new drugs and dyes. There had been progress in knowledge and understanding that could not be denied and that undercut the presumption that the opinions of ancients were authoritative or at least always to be considered. They no longer seemed so.

Moral philosophy. This was progress in natural philosophy, not in "science," as we might now call it. It was part of a systematic philosophy with wider epistemological and moral concerns to which it had to be related. What worked in the study of nature ought to work equally well in the study of everything else. Indeed, one ought to ask how one could more systematically pursue Bacon's vision and make its methodology both more rigorous and all-embracing. The first demand was met by a host of philosophers, not all of whom shared his empiricism, but who were all stirred by his achievements to rework their views in order to ground similar enterprises. Some looked back to Descartes, another great methodologist whose skepticism and interest in science equaled Bacon's, but whose efforts at systematization were even greater. Others, like John Locke, tried to show the origin, limits, extent, and certainty of all knowledge. His conclusions (that all knowledge of nature is derived from experience and reflection, and that it is limited by and extends no further than our experiences) affected every aspect of eighteenth-century intellectual work.

Implicit in this view was a denial that anything should be believed as true that did not have the warrant of experience. Revelation and tradition of themselves were of no account for Locke, although we ought to believe revelations and miracles that were vouched for by men of integrity whose evidence, when tried by the standards of the law courts, was found sound. The limits of our knowledge were indefinitely extendible, and the improvements that might be based on new knowledge had equally unknown limits. Probability, not the certainties of traditional authorities, became the guide to life. The task was to extend this knowledge through careful and well made observations, surveys, and experiments that could be verified and repeated. To make these means effective, no individual should be barred from their pursuit because of his political, religious, or other beliefs. The results should be freely published. Learned societies everywhere tended to admit men of differing faiths and philosophical outlooks and sometimes of quite diverse political views. None of that accorded well with traditional demands for conformity in religion, political belief, and loyalty, or for respect toward the philosophy of the ancients. If the world were to be improved, then it was to change through the newfound dynamism of new, not traditional, methods, technologies, and ideas.

To extend this set of methods into new fields became the program of many philosophers. To make morals scientific was the aim of Thomas Hobbes. To become the Newton of the moral sciences was the aim alike of Hume the agnostic and of the believer David Hartley. Adam Ferguson, Jeremy Bentham, and many more saw themselves as basing their moral science or political and social theories on an examination of the facts—the natural histories of men—which could then be used to ground explanations, base moral conclusions, or social policies. Hume's historical researches provided the evidence for his analytical conclusions about religion in the *Natural History of Religion* and various essays. The effect of this sort of study was to undermine the older conceptions of history as a literary and moralizing enterprise and to make it in the long run a handmaiden of the social sciences and not a story of the work of God in the Creation. At the same time Hume, like many others, found that his empirical analyses tended to make him something of a republican eager to establish, not a modern Sparta, but a state whose institutions balanced wealth, power, and authority in a mixed constitution that would give stability to a state whose citizens were free and productive. The new philosophy almost always entailed a new polity unlike that of the ancients or one's contemporaries.

The surveys of nature that Bacon envisioned enjoined men to search the whole world for novelties, which was just what his contemporaries had been doing. The well-known title page of one of his books, which shows a ship passing the Pillars of Hercules in search of knowledge, was plagiarized from a Spanish travel account of a few years earlier. Overseas exploration and discoveries also worked to undermine Western self-assurance and complacency. The Chinese had a society that seemed admirable in many ways even though it was not Christian. Voltaire used the reputed histories to argue for an older civilization in the East and for the relative lateness of the history contained in Genesis, which, by common agreement, went back only to about 4004 BC. Chinese history was said to record events of 72,000 years ago—so the Hebrew accounts of Creation and the revelation of the law to a chosen people were to be questioned and seen as unreliable. François Quesnay thought that Chinese government by mandarins, who had to pass civil service examinations, looked preferable to government by nobles and placemen in France, appointed for the political advantage of their patrons. Voltaire liked the seeming secularity of the morality which the Chinese were said to practice. On occasion he liked their religion, which seemed to have no hell and did not exhort men to

what he saw as the foolishness of Christian sects. He and the Physiocrats liked the social order and discipline of a people whose emperor honored agriculture by once a year ritually plowing a field. In certain moods, Voltaire seemed to like a world that rejected Western ways and religion as foolish.

What Voltaire found in the Chinese, other thinkers found in real or imagined others. Travel accounts were a means of shaking up those who believed in the rightness of their own ideas. Locke wrote the preface to a famous collection of voyages published by the Churchill brothers and left a remarkable account of his own journey to France in the 1670s. Real or imagined voyages flourished for the same reasons in the works of other philosophes including Bernard de Fontenelle, the chevalier Ramsay, Denis Diderot, François Jean, marquis de Chastellux, and Constantin-François de Volney, and it was not only the French who wrote them. Works like the letters of Lady Mary Wortley Montagu, detailing a trip to Constantinople, encouraged a tolerance of others and a new willingness to accept innovations from them. Other accounts, such as those of Captain Cook or Bougainville, revealed a world whose decorative arts were new and whose sexual mores called in question Christian ideas of chastity and marital fidelity. The other, the alien, if really pondered, offered a possibility of self-awareness that is seldom realized by those who stay isolated. All that also led to a grand questioning of tradition in the Enlightenment, but supporters of tradition were not without resources of their own.

Tradition Reaffirmed. When the Enlightenment was rejected, it was done sometimes in the name of traditional values. The Irishman Jonathan Swift thought of modern learning and the new science as morally useless and as generally contributing nothing of real use to the world. In his view, much had been promised and little had been delivered. Progress for him was an illusion. There is no point in prolonging life if we end as Struldbrugs, a lesson the world has yet to accept. There is little point in increasing literacy if the new readers read trash that encourages them, as Swift said, "to whore on and defy the parson." He lampooned the alleged rationality of men and found no real improvement to have been made in how they thought or acted. Progress would require a better human nature, which had not been produced and could not be had among sinful men. Swift saw in the Christian religion, in the form of English Episcopalianism, the moral values and message of salvation that alone was fit for men in this world. There was no point in transgressing the considered and tested wisdom of the ages and the revealed word of God. Swift's was not an unusual reaction: at the other end of the century, one could find it among the defenders of noble privilege, such as the Russian prince Mikhail Mikhailovich Shcherbatov (1733–1790).

Shcherbatov rejected much of the Enlightenment because it led to centralized control of the state and to the end of what he believed was the traditional power of the Russian aristocracy. Unlike Swift, he used the work of enlightened men such as Montesquieu, Rousseau, and Hume to defend an older Russia that was run by noblemen, was not corrupted by individualism and modernity, and had no desire to end customs that had proven their worth and value and whose replacement would yield chaos, not improvement. He believed that aristocratic power in the past had been exercised in the interest of all and had restrained a ruler who would be a despot if possible. He thought legitimate the traditions that allowed only the nobles and gentlemen to own land. Allowing the mercantile middle classes to become powerful was to make cash the only value that would be respected in a society increasingly driven by greed and forgetful of honor and righteousness. It should be not legislation but traditional custom and honor that bind a man to serve the state and to do right.

Russia needed a favorable balance of trade, and that would not be obtainable if luxuries were freely imported by merchants who cared little for the need to finance a strong state. Businessmen were less humane masters of serfs and employees than were the classes used to domination and bound and limited by traditions inculcating humane treatment of their underlings. It was not legislation that makes men good, but a change of heart; that is more likely to be brought about by traditional religion and morals than by all the rationalizing thought of Locke, Newton, Voltaire, or those westernizers with whom Shcherbatov sat on Catherine's legislative commission of 1767. After that, and the defeat it dealt him and his friends, he turned to history to find out more about the traditional Russia, which he continued to praise in preference to the modern world. He believed that Russian history, like all history, revealed a world of inequality. Inequality was a fact of life that could not be erased. To think otherwise was to accept a "sophistry of the present age." He cited Hume and Montesquieu in support of his views. Pugachov's rebellion in 1774, he thought, had been caused by even making a possibility of peasant emancipation. In religion he was not personally a devout Christian, but he firmly believed in Christianity for the masses who needed its restraint to achieve a moral life. Because the bright promises of the enlightened were sophistry, there was no good reason to abandon traditional ways for conditions that are untried and likely to result in a worse world than the one we have. He read all the enlightened but perversely used their arguments to defend a traditional order of things. Even d'Holbach interested him mainly for his defense of an absolute state.

Another kind of traditionalism was displayed by the reactionary writers who came, generally after the French Revolution, to defend the altars and the thrones of Europe—men like Joseph de Maistre and Louis de Bonald. These men used the skepticism of David Hume to refute the views of those whose ideas they abhorred. They also cited Hume's *History of England* to show that the removal of restraints on liberty, such as occurred for a few years in the period of the English Civil Wars, leads invariably to upsets, violence, anarchy, and the production of enthusiasts who deride religion and government and then fall prey to licentious behavior of every sort. Those who survived the French Revolution saw a similar pattern in France. The traditional sources of order—the church and state—were to them God-given agencies that fallen, violent, greedy men could not do without. To support such traditional pillars of society was the task of every right thinking man. Tradition embodied wisdom that we ignore to the peril of our very lives.

A traditionalism related to this, but distinct, arose in the works of Johann Georg Hamann (1730–1788). He too used Hume to show the fallibility of reason and a planned existence, but he went to the language and traditions of a people to discover what they really were and what they could develop into. No universal concepts or judgments could be used when talking about men. There were no "men" per se, but only Germans, Frenchmen, Hurons, or whatever. How they thought, wrote their poems, imagined God, and created their myths defines them, not some set of abstract Lockean or Kantian concepts, ideas, or theories of human nature. We are all formed by the languages we speak, and those are not translatable without remainder into one another. We cannot fully understand each other unless we speak the same language, share the same culture, and have the same traditions. He who would understand the Greeks must master not only their language but the Homeric books and all there is in them—in so far as we are able—and then intuit the soul of that wondrous people as best he can. We can never do it adequately, because we always project our own images and translate into our own words the realities of other lives.

To uproot traditions for some cosmopolitan daydream is to alienate a people from their true selves and to destroy something that God had created or allowed to flower in its own way to the enrichment of the world. If we would understand the world, we must understand the human world first in all its historical richness and then see the natural world as the poetry of a Creator who would have us enjoy the beauty of the created world and not make it a scene of human exploitation and domination. Those who study nature as dead matter described mathematically and seen as a realm to be used and improved, or who see the Bible as a linguistic entity to be analyzed into what is factual and metaphorical, or what belongs to one text or another, and not as the work of the Holy Spirit, miss the significance of both. Observing and keeping up traditions can save us from these errors. That was a message that was put in somewhat similar form by Herder and later accepted by many romantics. It is also a message that has affinities with the work of Edmund Burke.

Burke, writing on the French Revolution in 1790, found among the monsters of his world the sophisters, calculators, and economists whose great sin was that they sought to make utopias in an imperfect world. He had in mind men such as the English deists, the *encyclopédistes*, Diderot and d'Alembert, Rousseau, Condorcet, and Voltaire, whom he named and whose ideas, he believed, had provided the arguments for destructive revolutions. They were willing to see traditional loyalties dissolved as political myths and illusions were dispelled and the aura surrounding royalty dissipated. Utilitarian arguments, hasty innovations, the loss of warm sentiments projected on high political figures to whom we owe allegiance, all of these were the grounds for a utopian experiment doomed to fail because it loosened the bonds that held society together and occasioned a tragedy that Burke lived to see and describe in later works.

Burke's views of such forces are not so different from the social world described in Hume's *History of England* (1754–1761) and are also presented in his speeches in the impeachment trial of Warren Hastings. Hastings was indicted by Burke for, among other things, upsetting the people of Bengal by violating their customs, their laws, and their beliefs. Different though these may be from our own, they provide satisfactions that have a legitimacy and a worth that cannot be overlooked by those who would deal fairly with a subject people. These seemingly nonrational elements of life, when they concern indifferent matters and not essential rights, are what give life its value and structure and provide satisfaction to those who live within their confines. We should not destroy cultures in the mistaken belief that only our ways can lead to happiness and well-being.

Traditions had been criticized and had waned, but by 1815 many were back in fashion and were used to repress vigorously the enlightened, who persisted in their cosmopolitan dream of progress and social betterment among the ruins of war-ravaged Europe.

[*See also* Agriculture and Animal Husbandry; Cartesianism; China; Counter-Enlightenment; Deism; Empiricism; Natural Philosophy and Science; *and* Philosophy.]

BIBLIOGRAPHY

Beiser, Frederick C. *Enlightenment, Revolution, and Romanticism: The Genesis of Modern German Political Thought, 1790–1800.* Cambridge, Mass., 1992.

Bongie, Laurence. *David Hume, Prophet of Counter-Revolution.* Indianapolis, 1999. Interesting assessment of how the reading of Hume's works changed as radicalism and revolution appeared to verify his dark views of social rapid change.

Bouwsma, William J. "Anxiety and the Formation of Early Modern Culture." In *After the Reformation: Essays in Honor of J. H. Hexter*, edited by Barbara C. Malament. Philadelphia, 1980. pp. 215–246.

Brooke, John Hedley. *Science and Religion: Some Historical Perspectives.* Cambridge, 1991. This is not a study of the conflicts between religion and science but of their interaction, only a part of which was destructive of religion and tradition.

Gay, Peter. *The Enlightenment: An Interpretation*, vol. 1, *The Rise of Modern Paganism*. New York, 1966. Vol. 2, *The Science of Freedom*. New York, 1969. The first volume is concerned with the attack on Christianity, the second with efforts to rethink morals, politics, and the social sciences.

Glacken, Clarence J. *Traces on the Rhodian Shore: Nature and Culture in Western Thought from Ancient Times to the End of the Eighteenth Century*. Berkeley, Los Angeles, and London, 1967. A work about cultural change that is rich and more varied than its title suggests.

Israel, Jonathan I. *The Dutch Republic: Its Rise, Greatness, and Fall, 1477–1806.* Oxford, 1995. Touches on all the themes of this entry in one place or another and does so in a history of Europe's most developed country in the period.

Klinck, David. *The French Counterrevolutionary Theorist Louis de Bonald (1754–1840).* New York, 1996.

Kors, Alan Charles. *Atheism in France, 1650–1729*, vol. 1. *The Orthodox Sources of Disbelief.* Princeton, N.J., 1990. Kors shows how the arguments among Christians undermined belief in their religion and its traditions.

Lebrun, Richard. *Joseph de Maistre: An Intellectual Militant.* Montreal, 1988.

Manuel, Frank E. *The Broken Staff: Judaism through Christian Eyes.* Cambridge, Mass., 1992. This is a study of Judaism, not of the Old Testament, but it contains something of a history of the critique of that text and of a tradition closely aligned to Christianity.

Manuel, Frank E., and Fritzi P. Manuel. *Utopian Thought in the Western World.* Cambridge, Mass., 1979. An important study of the changing notions of utopia and the ways in which currents of thought have affected the period leading up to the Enlightenment.

O'Flaherty, James C. *The Quarrel of Reason with Itself: Essays on Hamann, Michaelis, Lessing, and Nietzsche.* Columbia, S.C., 1988. Particularly good on Hamann.

Pelikan, Jaroslav. *The Christian Tradition: A History of the Development of Doctrine.* 5 vols. Chicago and London, 1971–1989. A standard account of the doctrines of the Christian churches, how they evolved, and have been attacked and defended.

Pocock, J. G. A. *Barbarism and Religion*, vol. 1. *The Enlightenments of Edward Gibbon, 1737–1764*; vol. 2. *Narratives of Civil Government*. Cambridge, 1999. This broadly conceived study of the influences on Gibbon's *History* becomes something of a history of historiography and social thought, and in some senses a history of the Enlightenment.

Shapiro, Barbara J. *Probability and Certainty in Seventeenth-Century England: A Study of the Relationships between Natural Science, Religion, History, Law, and Literature.* Princeton, N.J., 1983. Just what it says it is.

Shcherbatov, Mikhail. *On the Corruption of Morals in Russia.* Edited and translated by A. Lentin. Cambridge, 1969. An extended example of how enlightened ideas, particularly those of Montesquieu and Hume, could be used to support the traditional role of the aristocracy in Russia.

Thomas, Keith. *Religion and the Decline of Magic.* New York, 1971. A brilliant study of the emergence of the way in which nature and its workings became de-spiritualized and made modern.

Todorov, Tzvetan. *La conquête de l'Amérique*. Paris, 1982. Translated by Richard Howard as *The Conquest of America: The Question of the Other*. New York, 1984.

ROGER L. EMERSON

TRANSLATION. The Enlightenment was the first attempt of Europe's Republic of Letters to conduct a cosmopolitan conversation without a "universal" language. In this respect, Latin was gone. By the early eighteenth century, important philosophers such as René Descartes and John Locke were being read in their native tongues or translated into other vernaculars. The Latin writings of Baruch de Spinoza, Samuel Pufendorf, and Isaac Newton were soon to stamp their unique marks on Enlightenment thought mostly through translations.

From Universal Language to Lingua Franca. Eighteenth-century philosophers writing in their own languages reached new audiences and benefited fellow thinkers through translation: David Hume, Jean-Jacques Rousseau, and Cesare Beccaria are seminal cases who reached broad European audiences. Imaginative literature written in living languages was diffused mostly in translation: in the mid-eighteenth century, the British authors Alexander Pope, Henry Fielding, Samuel Richardson, and Edward Young stamped their mark on the Continent through translations into French, German, and other languages. By the end of the century, Gotthold Ephraim Lessing, Johann Wolfgang von Goethe, and Friedrich Schiller began to acquire their European reputations in similar ways. Classical, medieval, and Renaissance authors, including Homer, Dante, and Shakespeare, made an impact on the Enlightenment through new translations, which themselves often ignited heated theoretical debates. It was largely through successful translations that Cervantes inspired literary circles in Copenhagen, Pope's works traveled to Saint Petersburg, William Robertson made his mark on German historiography, and Voltaire found readers in Budapest. Modern European languages obtained a new wealth of literary, scientific, and philosophical idioms. Toward the end of the century, national cultures were consciously being constructed, enriched, and even challenged to originality by means of translations. The theater, moving from a nomadic to a city-based existence and taking on national aspirations, was a great consumer of translations. Other Enlightenment institutions—journals, reading societies, and clandestine clubs—enabled translated books to mobilize new social and intellectual energies.

Europe's vernaculars had gathered strength as literary languages (and, in some cases, as scientific and philosophical languages) since the sixteenth century. Translations steadily multiplied from Latin into French, Italian, Spanish, English, and German, and to a lesser degree between these languages. Awareness of the complexities of translation and attempts to theorize it made parallel progress. By the early eighteenth century, the Latin scaffolding gave way and translations between vernaculars gained ascendancy for the first time in European history. After 1750, most scientific texts were no longer translated into Latin for international readership.

Other changes occurred in the balance of prominence among the modern languages. While French retained its cultural lead, other languages moved up and down the scale. English blossomed into continental recognition dramatically around 1750, becoming for the first time in its history a major origin-language in Europe's literary traffic. German, too, experienced an epochal transformation, rising to the position of a major host-language for new translations; by the end of the century, it was also an origin-language of great importance. Italian and Spanish, in contrast, lost their earlier prominence in both respects. By the end of the eighteenth century, newly awakened literary languages in central, northern, and eastern Europe launched ambitious projects of translation that led to the construction of their own national literatures in the century to come. Although quantitative data can be difficult to assemble, statistics from English, French, and German publishing suggest that translations rose to unprecedented levels in terms of number, diversity, speed of publication, and geographical diffusion. Translated texts were part of a general transformation of the European book industry. Their translators and publishers were members of a new social stratum of literati, a growing species of cultural mediators.

Translation was not indispensable for the diffusion of Enlightenment texts and ideas. Europe may have lost its universal language, but it gained a lingua franca. French was the cosmopolitan language of the well-bred, well-read and well-traveled throughout the century. Most French books received in non-Francophone parts of Europe were read in the original. The *Encyclopédie* of Diderot and d'Alembert reached the farthest outposts of the European Enlightenment, from Moscow to Lisbon, without the mediation of translators. French-language editions of Enlightenment works were regularly published even in non-Francophone countries. Adam Smith read his French mentors in their own tongue, members of the Enlightenment circle in Milan devoured Voltaire and Diderot in French, and Catherine II of Russia plagiarized Montesquieu in the original. If the Enlightenment could be conducted in French (as some historians have pretended it was)—or, when need be, in English, a language well understood by Voltaire and studiously perused by Lessing—then why was translation a crucial vehicle of diffusion?

The answer touches on the very nature of Enlightenment's social geography. French was not Latin, and the writers and the reading publics that made the backbone of Enlightenment culture were not Latinists. Many of the works conveying Enlightenment ideas could be written only in vernaculars; this was especially true of popularized science and philosophy, national histories, new imaginative literature deeply stamped by local landscape and idiom, travel books, and ethnography. Moreover, not all Enlightenment readers knew French, and many of its authors could not write it. Finally, even thinkers with a reasonable knowledge of other languages found translations easier to digest and to quote: Hume reportedly read Beccaria in the Italian original, but also in the abbé André Morellet's French translation.

Some seminal moments in the intellectual history of the eighteenth century therefore involved epoch-making translations of full texts or effective selections: we note Voltaire's quotations from Locke in his *Lettres philosophiques* (1734), his translation of Shakespeare's *Julius Caesar*, and his dissemination (which included the translation, chiefly by Mme. du Châtelet) of Newton's *Principia Mathematica*; the last, a classic case of variegated diffusion, brought Newton's ideas, via a network of retranslations, excerpts and popularizations, to a vast French-reading public. A similar case in the German Enlightenment is Johann Lorenz Schmidt's important rendering of Spinoza's *Ethics* in 1744.

Thanks to translations, the Republic of Letters could slowly evolve in some parts of Europe into an embryonic democracy of letters, where numerous people could read, but only one language. Having survived the loss of its universal language, Enlightenment thought became increasingly sensitive to linguistic and cultural differences and ever more dependent on translation. In this evolving scene, French was a crucial but temporary mediator, and under its dwindling shade, Europe's world of learning and literature reached multilingual maturity.

From a broad perspective, Enlightenment translation was a story of success. Not just the share of translations in Europe's ever-growing book industry and markets but also the increasing centrality of the very idea of translation are vital to an understanding of eighteenth-century European history. Enlightenment's fundamental ideas—progress, freedom of thought, universal humanity, and critical reasoning—proved highly translatable. Although formidable differentials were on the horizon, Europe's cosmopolitan legacy stood the first test of multilingual modernity.

Theories of Translation. Two approaches to linguistic theory underlie Enlightenment theories of translation. Descartes's rationalist theory of language assumed a universal similarity among all human languages, and therefore that all languages are, in principle, intertranslatable.

Another rationalist strand, represented by Beauzée's article "Langue" in the *Encyclopédie*, derived all European languages from one "primitive language," typically Hebrew. As the eighteenth century progressed, however, a particularist approach came to predominate. D'Alembert noted that languages "cannot all be used to express the same idea," and he pointed out "the diversity of their genius." The differences among languages—ancient and modern, European and extra-European, and even within Europe's boundaries—were increasingly acknowledged.

A decisive starting point for the Enlightenment debate on translation was the seventeenth-century French paradigm that subjected all translation to the aesthetic values and literary canons of the host (receiving, or "target") culture. Beginning with Nicolas Perrot d'Ablancourt's translations in the late seventeenth century, such texts were dubbed "the beautiful unfaithful." Original texts, primarily the classics, were to be translated into pleasant, smoothly readable, and stylistically familiar target texts. All aspects of the original—length and structure, verse and meter, terminology and metaphor, ideas and opinions—were fair objects for transformation.

Enlightenment discussion of translation was launched by important commentaries on the translator's art by several translators from ancient Greek and Roman, notably John Dryden in England and Anne Marie Dacier in France. Their ideas of the nature of translation paved the way for debates on language, truth, aesthetic values, and cultural differences that all went well beyond the scope of translation theory. Dryden distinguished between the two extremes of "metaphrase" (literal translation), and "imitation" (denoting the "excesses" caused by abandoning the original text); he rejected both in favor of a temperate, midway "paraphrase." Dacier, renowned translator of classical authors including Plato, Aristotle, Plutarch, and Horace, presented a theory of translation in the introduction to her famed rendering of the *Iliad* (1711). She called for a reserved faithfulness to the original spirit, preferring "noble" translation of the author's sense to "servile" verbal literalism, and subjecting translation to cultural differences, underlined by her abhorrence of some of Homer's images and characterizations.

Dryden and Dacier were followed by a line of self-reflective translators, many of them gifted writers and Enlightenment figures in their own right, who regarded translation as an important means of diffusing aesthetic standards and seminal ideas. Alexander Pope echoed Dryden's formula in the Preface to his translation of the *Iliad* (1715–1720), which drew directly on Dacier's French rendering. In his entry on translation for the *Encyclopédie*, Jean le Rond d'Alembert drew his readers' attention to the difficulties inherent in translation, voicing a preference for thoughtful "imitation" rather than literal rendering.

The abbé Prévost applied Dacier's refined discrimination to contemporary English literature: "I have suppressed English customs where they may appear shocking to other nations," he wrote in his translation of Richardson's *Pamela*.

The German Enlightenment launched its debate on translation with the competing approaches of Johann Christoph Gottsched (1700–1766) and his Swiss opponents, Johann Jakob Bodmer (1698–1783) and Johann Jakob Breitinger (1701–1776). Their debate, triggered by Bodmer's German translation of Milton's *Paradise Lost* (1732), shows the unique relevance of translation to the core of German aesthetics and literary theory. Gottsched aspired to submit all translations to "enlightened" standards of style. In terms largely similar to those of prevalent French theory, he claimed that translators ought to adapt original texts, if necessary, by various techniques to meet the demands of contemporary German literature. Breitinger retorted by defending the particular features of origin languages and demanding the visibility of original "thoughts." His line was radicalized by Friedrich Gottlieb Klopstock (1724–1803) and especially by Johann Gottfried Herder (1744–1803). The latter hailed the "gravity center" (*Schwerpunkt*) of all historical cultures and, by extension, the sanctity of their languages and the inviolability of original texts. Yet popularization, the Enlightenment's most common paradigm of diffusion, kept the host-oriented approach in the foreground. "If you want to influence the masses," wrote Goethe, "simple translation is always the best."

The common denominators of Enlightenment theories of translation should not, however, be obscured. It was widely accepted that a translator might take liberties in syntax, vocabulary, and structure. In commercial enterprises, such liberties were aimed at accommodating the publishers' demand to attract readers in the host language, especially French, by appealing to their tastes. More reflective and independent translators, less dependent on the whims of the market, professed taking poetic liberties to transmit the author's voice as well as possible.

At the close of the eighteenth century, Alexander Tytler published his *Essay on the Principles of Translation* (1791), in which he attacked Dryden's approval of paraphrase and the ensuing liberties taken by eighteenth-century translators. Departing from the mainstream eighteenth-century creed, Tytler requested a rigorous loyalty to the original text in matters of vocabulary, style, and ideas. His own translations of Petrarch from Italian (1784) and of Schiller from German (1792) exemplified the new standards. Tytler heralded the onset of a (mostly German-inspired) Romantic emphasis on the integrity and vocal uniqueness of origin languages. Herder's theoretical works and new German translations of Homer (by Voss), Dante and Shakespeare (by Schlegel) and Cervantes (by Tieck) marked a culmination of the "faithful" strand of Enlightenment translation theory, shifting it from the author's "spirit" to his very words. Romantic translators turned from the Enlightenment not so much in their poetic shift (which flowed from an important undercurrent of Enlightenment thought itself) as in their abandonment of Enlightenment texts as candidates for translation.

Geography of Translation: Centers and Major Trajectories. Europe's great centers of translation were Paris, London, and (from about 1760) Leipzig and environs; the last was also a hub of circulation through its book fair and its academic, literary and journalistic connections. Important secondary centers of multilingual translation included Zurich, Amsterdam (and other Dutch cities), and Hamburg. Other cities producing significant numbers of translations into the local language included Lisbon, Naples, Dublin, Edinburgh, Copenhagen, Stockholm, Berlin, and Saint Petersburg. The seven hundred publishers of translated works counted by Bernhard Fabian in the German lands worked in small towns as well as larger cities.

Several centers merit attention not necessarily for the volume of translations they produced but for their cultural significance as trend-setters. An industry of publication and translation developed in Leipzig, issuing translations not only into German but also into French and several other languages, even into the nascent modern Greek. It was also a bastion of translation theory, with Gottsched and his circle in residence. Zurich, home to Gottsched's theoretical opponents Bodmer and Breitinger, was a multilingual nucleus of the Swiss network of cultural mediation, both French-German intermediary and English-German. By midcentury, the Zurich publishers were among the first to insist on the merit of direct translation between the origin and the host languages. Hamburg became another meeting point for French, English and German; its geographic and economic orientation gave it a unique advantage for becoming an Anglo-German intermediary. It was a major gateway for importation of new English books into the Holy Roman Empire. Especially in the last four decades of the century, the speedy arrival of new books from Britain (notably the central writings of the Scottish Enlightenment) was followed by prompt publication of German translations.

The multilingual publishing history of the Dutch Republic preceded the Enlightenment by a century and more and also pioneered the abandonment of Latin publication. Amsterdam was a center of translation into French as well as Dutch, thanks to the influx of erudite Huguenots after the revocation of the Edict of Nantes (1685). Demand for translations into Dutch nevertheless grew rapidly. Elsewhere, translations were commissioned by rulers and by scholarly institutions. Catherine the Great set up a commission to explore, propose, and perform a wide-ranging translation project from European languages into Russian. A translation seminar was launched at the University of Moscow a decade later. Several other universities and academies were particularly important for intercultural mediation. At Göttingen, Anglophile professors and students came in touch with British colleagues and with English books. The University of Copenhagen, where Swedes, Finns, and Icelanders encountered the latest trends in European literature, educated several leading translators.

The history of eighteenth-century translation is primarily the drama of two languages: French, Europe's almost unrivaled lingua franca, and English, a newcomer to the cosmopolitan scene that rose to challenge French in essential areas of cultural creativity. The interplay between French and English was complex and subtle. The French Enlightenment owed its early flowering to Voltaire's and Montesquieu's discovery of English politics, literature, science, and philosophy. The French language became a vehicle for transmitting English authors into other major European languages. After 1750, however, British influence began to vie with French and in some respects overcame it. From the perspective of the late German Enlightenment, for example, French was no longer the magnanimous mediator of English style and ideas, but their vanquished adversary. Direct translations from English were now the rule, and French mediation was abandoned or held in suspicion.

Almost every important Enlightenment work not originally written in French was translated into it. Around the mid-eighteenth century, interest in France shifted from "beautiful" translations of classical texts to modern works, literary and scientific. English was the main origin language, though only a handful of English works had been translated into French during the seventeenth century, compared with some five hundred in the eighteenth. Voltaire's role as pioneering intermediary between English and French cultures was coupled with Diderot's keen interest in English literature and in cultural aspects of translation. Shakespeare, Pope, Richardson, and Hume were initially read on the Continent in French translation more than in any other language, including the original English. Translations into French from Italian were significantly fewer, among them Antoine de Rivarol's rendering of Dante's *Divine Comedy* and Morellet's translation of Beccaria's *Dei delitti e delle pene*. Toward the end of the century, German became an important origin language.

By contrast, translations *from* French into other European languages marked the lines where the formidable strength of French culture overtook the considerable expanse of the French language. The profusion of translations from French, beginning in the early

Enlightenment with Bayle and especially Fénelon, peaked with the writings of Voltaire, Montesquieu, and Rousseau. Among the most popular were Montesquieu's *Lettres persanes* and Voltaire's *Candide* and *Zaïre*. Beside numerous reprints of the original French editions, these works were repeatedly translated into Italian and German, followed by many other European languages. More scholarly works, such as Montesquieu's *L'esprit des lois*, were less frequently translated. No full translation was made of the *Encyclopédie*, widely circulated in Europe in the original French. Another channel of French predominance, unique to the eighteenth century in its popularity, was the "secondary translation" of texts initially translated into French, most often from English, and retranslated into an array of other languages, including Portuguese, Polish, Russian, Swedish, and Hungarian.

It was a mark of the maturity and independence of German culture when, during the second half of the century, secondary translation was largely abandoned in favor of direct and more source-oriented renderings. The change of the tide was marked by direct German translations of Shakespeare's plays. Edward Young's *Conjectures on Original Composition* (1759) was translated into German soon after its original publication. Shakespeare and Young, far removed from the rules of French classicism, paved the way for an era of fruitful British-German cultural exchange that defiantly circumvented France. The last four decades of the century saw a tide of prompt, well-informed, and intensely discussed German publications of translated English poetry, drama, and novels, as well as a broad range of theoretical texts in moral philosophy, aesthetics and political economy. Translations from English into German, though never outnumbering the French, left all other languages far behind. More than any other European culture, the German Enlightenment transformed its literary standards under the guidance of translated texts. The British inspiration was not just a matter of rearranging the translated canon but of rethinking what translation (and all writing) must perform. The English and Scottish influences make it clear that objection to French classicism was by no means an anti-Enlightenment approach: imagination and sentiment were at home in the aesthetic theory of Young, Blair, and Burke, all avidly read in German.

Translations of Enlightenment texts into English remained predominantly from French. Toward the end of the century, however, German became a major source language for both direct and secondary translations, first in eastern and northern European cultures and later in the west. Klopstock's poetry was translated into Icelandic, and *Hamlet* was indirectly translated into Polish and Hungarian via a German translation.

Direct translations between more minor languages were relatively few, most notably between Italian and Spanish.

Italian also served as a mediator for indirect Spanish translations of such works as *Ossian*. Translations from non-European languages were similarly sparse, but of great importance. The *Arabian Nights*, translated into French by Antoine Galland in the early eighteenth century, inspired the Orientalist fables of Montesquieu and Voltaire. The Qur'an was translated into English by George Sale in 1734.

At the receiving end, the host languages were diverse: Russian, Portuguese, Italian, Greek, Finnish, and Croat are but a sample. These languages were, in various degrees, affected by the translated texts and influenced by new literary standards and ideas. Translation, the tool of a new Enlightenment cosmopolitanism, eventually became the medium (and target) of new linguistic self-awareness and cultural nationalism.

In Italy, where Latin remained the language of science and theory longer than in other parts of Europe, interest in French culture rose dramatically at the beginning of the eighteenth century, and translations in Enlightenment context gathered pace in the second half of the century. Voltaire, Diderot, d'Alembert, and Rousseau made important contributions to Italian intellectual history both in the original French and in Italian translations. British sources were important to two leading groups of the Italian Enlightenment. In Milan, the journal *Il Caffè* was modeled on the *Spectator*, and its contributors, Pietro and Alessandro Verri and Cesare Beccaria, quoted extensively from English and Scottish works with a special emphasis on Hume's philosophy, politics, and history. In Naples, political economists read Scottish works in French translations.

Types of Books, Authors, and Disciplines Translated. The Enlightenment translation market was different from all predecessors in its appeal to a new and broad readership comprised of women and men, aristocrat and bourgeois, readers of high erudition and basic literacy. This expansion of audiences brought to the fore novels, plays, poetry, geography, ethnography, and travel books, as well as philosophy in the Enlightenment vein, history, art theory, and popular science. All these categories, along with medicine and theology, are represented in the list of translations from French and English into German cataloged for the Leipzig Easter book fair in the peak era of 1765–1785.

New translations of the classics reached audiences not versed in Latin and served Enlightenment authors for quotation and discussion. Even an excellent Latinist like the Scots philosopher Adam Ferguson preferred to quote, when possible, from a good contemporary translation such as Elizabeth Carter's rendering of Epictetus, rather than use the original.

Enlightenment translations of poetry include several shining exceptions in the history of this particularly untranslatable genre: those of Alexander Pope (especially the *Essay on Man*), Edward Young's *Night Thoughts*, and Macpherson's *Ossian*. Drama, in verse and prose, was widely translated and often fiercely adapted to host cultures. The newly discovered Shakespeare, followed by plays of the German Sturm und Drang movement and Schiller, transformed European stages and inspired numerous imitations.

The popularity of translated philosophical works can be attributed to the popular and witty style of the philosophes, but also to the relative accessibility of the more demanding works of Hume and Kant. An early landmark of the vernacular turn was the decision of the editors of Spinoza's complete works, published posthumously, to issue Dutch translations alongside the Latin originals; French and German versions soon followed. By the mid-eighteenth century, some philosophical works, such as Locke's *Some Thoughts Concerning the Education of Children* (1693, with five German translations during the eighteenth century) and Hume's *Enquiry concerning Human Understanding*, did well in translation. British political philosophy, notably Locke's *Two Treatises of Government* (1690), fared better in French than in German. Scottish moral philosophy, aesthetic theory, and historiography were far more successful in German translation than were Scottish discussions of politics. Political economy became popular during the last phase of the Enlightenment, with James Stewart's *Oeconomy* a bestseller in German translation.

Works in the natural sciences were translated sporadically, often with an emphasis on practical manuals such as agriculture, gardening and beekeeping. The most important single theoretical text was Newton's *Principia Mathematica*, mediated on the Continent by Voltaire and translated into French largely by Gabrielle-Émilie du Châtelet (1756). Translation was also instrumental in the spread of popularized Newtonianism; Francesco Algarotti's *Newtoniamismo per le dame* (1737) promptly made its way to Newton's homeland as *Sir Isaac Newton's Philosophy Explain'd for the Use of the Ladies* (1739). Medicine was highly translatable: a lavish edition of Smellie's *Anatomy* was produced in Nuremberg, and the Göttingen publishers Vandenhoeck and Ruprecht launched a broad translation project of British medical works and translated the *Transactions* of the Royal Society of Edinburgh.

Beyond the realm of books lay that of periodical publications. The most translated and copied Enlightenment periodicals were Steele and Addison's *Tatler* and *Spectator*, eagerly read, emulated, translated, and pirated by German and Italian writers in the early and middle decades of the eighteenth century.

The most interesting question is not who were the most translated authors, but who were the authors most effective in translation. Seen in this light, it was British authors—from Shakespeare to Smith, from Newton to Hume and from Addison to Burke—who made the greatest impact on Enlightenment theory and art through the medium of translation.

Economics of Translation: Print Culture, Distribution, Rights, and Piracy. The two prime movers of eighteenth-century translation were the publishing house and the independent translator. Such publishers as Vandenhoeck and Ruprecht in Göttingen and Philip Erasmus Reich of the house of Weidmann in Leipzig put great efforts into preliminary research, selection, commissioning, supervising, editing, and marketing translated works. The Société Typographique de Neuchâtel (STN), of which the fullest documentation has survived, exemplifies these efforts in its own modest translation project from German into French.

Copyright legislation was in its infancy in Britain and in France, and no protection was given in regard to international publishing, including translations. Book piracy in the form of unauthorized reprints (of both originals and translations) was widely practiced in areas such as southern Germany, Switzerland, Austria, and Ireland. When it came to translations, piracy was the norm all over Europe. Even when authors were given notice of translation, earnings were not forthcoming. In general, although the Enlightenment emphasis on literary fame heralded a new concept of intellectual property, few publishers of translations upheld the new notion of copyright.

Translators were most often employed on a freelance basis. More rarely they were "in house," or even partners. A select few, such as Dryden, could obtain good pay for their work. Pope, in his prime, earned some £4,000 for his *Iliad* and a similar sum for his *Odyssey*. Although many translations were commissioned by publishers on pure economic grounds, others were created as a gentlemanly pastime or a scholarly effort.

Large publishers used an international network of correspondents reporting on new books worthy of translation, readers' preferences, and the reception of recent translations. A few firms employed consultants, at times translators themselves. Publishers often advertised translations and marketed them through catalogs and correspondence with book traders. Royal and imperial protection was at times obtained for selected books. In several parts of Europe, translation was encouraged by learned institutions, such as Arcadia, the Roman Academy of Letters, which produced important new Italian versions of the classics.

One measure of a translation's success was the number and spread of reprints, pirated editions, and retranslations. Many of the English translations of French Enlightenment works published in Dublin were reprints from London publishers; the Basle house of Tourneissen specialized in reprints; Shakespeare's plays, Richardson's novels, Pope's poetry, and certain works by Hume and Smith were retranslated into the same language, sometimes within less than a decade.

In physical terms, translated books tended to have good design and typography, sometimes replete with engraved title pages and illustrations, but inferior paper and binding. Editions could run to some 1,000 copies; few translations reached more than two editions.

Translators. Some of the Enlightenment's greatest contributors were enthusiastic and prolific translators, among them Voltaire, Pope, and Lessing. The caliber of its translators at times foretold and affected a book's success in translation: the earliest translations of *Clarissa* into German and French were made by two renowned men of letters, Johann David Michaelis and Prévost, respectively. Lessing translated Hutcheson's *System of Moral Philosophy*. Macpherson's Ossianic poetry was translated into Polish (via the French) by the renowned poet Ignacy Krasicki, and into Italian by the famed Melchiorre Cesarotti.

Beyond the celebrated names, however, labored thousands of little-known translators in several dozen cities and towns, carrying out the massive labor of Europe's growing translation industry. Some worked anonymously, and others had only their initials printed on the book's title page. Among them were university professors, freelance lecturers and students, clerics, clerks, and minor government employees. Many of them were struggling self-employed literati.

A few translators understood their profession as an art, or even a vocation of religious intensity, and undertook close correspondence with authors, but relations between translators and authors were usually prosaic, and most often nonexistent. Few translators had any personal contact with the authors they translated or any business connection with the original publisher of the work.

Eighteenth-century book reviewers were keenly aware of the merits and deficiencies of translators. Some publishers, like STN, took pride in the exceptional quality of their translations. Historians now attempt to measure "good" against "bad" translations as indicators of the success of a particular book or edition. Inadequate translation is sometimes blamed for the obscurity of Adam Smith's *Wealth of Nations* in its early German edition (1776–1778), and a brilliant second translation by Christian Garve, with an enlightening preface (1794–1796), is seen as a key factor in Smith's somewhat belated German success.

Women translators, not unknown in previous times, broke new ground in the Enlightenment. Aphra Behn and Anne Dacier dared to tackle the classics. Dacier, whose work inspired Pope's own translation of Homer, was derided for her gender by some of his critics. Elizabeth Carter provided a first complete English rendering of Epictetus (1749–1752). Charlotte Brooke published the first collection of translated Gaelic poetry from Ireland (1789). The prolific Dutch writer Betje Wolff found time to translate twenty-three works from English, French, and German.

Cross-Fertilization of Literary Forms and the Rise of Modern National Cultures. The cultural dominance of France meant that French translations were typically host-oriented, and most translators willing and even eager to adapt the origin texts to French grammatical, semantic, and aesthetic standards. For a German Enlightenment author like Friedrich Nicolai, such adaptations, even of his own work, were a necessary tool for the broad dissemination of Enlightenment ideas. He nevertheless warned of the French tendency to expect all books to be "dressed *à la française*" and to "merely admire themselves in us" (Freedman, p. 96). Even as Nicolai wrote this in the 1770s, however, change was in the air. Adam Ferguson, visiting Voltaire in Ferney in the same period, was congratulated by the aged philosophe for "civilizing the Russians" through his translated history and philosophy books, but Enlightenment translations did not follow Voltaire's imperative. Rather than universally spreading the Voltairean idea of Reason or the Scottish idea of historical progress, translations increasingly encouraged the birth of modern national literatures and cultures. While strong national literatures, supported by late Enlightenment ethnography and anthropology, paid growing respect to source languages and origin cultures, secondary or nascent national literatures were fiercely host-oriented, adapting translated texts to their needs. Translations thus played an important part in the birth of modern literature in Polish and Rumanian. The literary modernization of two ancient languages, Greek and Hebrew, was substantially fed by translations.

Translators—and some publishers—were among the first to notice new intercultural sensitivities. The late Enlightenment opposition to French cultural domination was shared by German, Dutch, and Scandinavian mediators of texts. At the same time, the map of translations highlighted cultural hierarchies and unequal exchanges: "Klopstock, our more than Milton . . . [is] wholly unknown to Your country, or, what is still worse, quite disguised in the most abominable translation," wrote a German translator to his English correspondent. Since Milton was at that time a household name among literate Germans, the injustice seemed great.

Shifts of political loyalty were also reflected in translation trends: Americans read French works in translations, mostly imported from London and Edinburgh, that enhanced their sense of cultural autonomy and supported political radicalization. In *The Rights of the British Colonies Asserted and Proved* (1764), James Otis translated

and quoted passages from Rousseau's *Contrat social*, buttressing anti-English political sentiments. Revolutionary pamphleteers followed the same example, using Montesquieu and other French writers alongside Rousseau.

Translations enabled cultural shifts of emphasis though the discovery of fringe cultures. Macpherson's Ossianic pseudo-translation, despite the bitter controversy over its authenticity, opened a new horizon for Celtic literature; translations appeared from Welsh into English by Evans Evans, and Charlotte Brook compiled an anthology of translations from Irish Gaelic poetry (1789). In Germany, enthusiasm for Celtic and Nordic sources and emphasis on the integrity of origin languages dovetailed with conscious cultural patriotism. Translation could be recruited to bolster the German literary revival by making a large pool of the best world literature available to local readers and writers.

Finally, translation could also channel cultural hostility and self-centeredness. As such, it took two forms: a negative attitude to translations, or a brusquely instrumental attitude to languages and texts of origin. Toward the end of the century, a new undertone of national defiance crept into even the linguistically open Dutch culture. Dutch literati engaged in a prolonged debate on the merits of their culture's openness to an "all-engulfing ocean of translations" (Baker, 398). In Poland, translations were seen as building blocks of a new national culture and free adaptations were made, at times dropping all reference to the original texts and masquerading as originals. Stylistic "improvement" and the exchange of prose and verse were frequent.

Practices of translation thus belong both to the rise of Enlightenment and to its demise. Shifts in both the theory and the body of translated texts accompanied the late eighteenth century retreat from universalism and the rise of cultural and political nationalism. Yet continuities are no less important. Voltaire, Rousseau, and Pope were not translated for the use of latecomer Enlightenments, such as the Jewish and other eastern European variants, until the first half of the nineteenth century. Conversely, cultural pluralism, respect for source languages, and sensitivity to "untranslatable" words and semantic uniqueness, often associated with Romanticism, are deeply rooted in the Enlightenment debates on the practice and theory of translation.

[*See also* Language Theories; Print Culture; Publishing; Reading and Reading Practices; *and* Republic of Letters.]

BIBLIOGRAPHY

Baker, Mona, ed. *Routledge Encyclopedia of Translation Studies*. London and New York, 1998. A groundbreaking enterprise, good on translation theory and major trajectories, but tending to neglect the material, social, and economic histories of print and translation.

Barber, Giles, and Bernhard Fabian, eds. *Buch und Buchhandel in Europa im achtzehnten Jahrhundert / The Book and the Book Trade in Eighteenth-Century Europe*. Hamburg, 1977.

Beebee, Thomas O. *Clarissa on the Continent: Translation and Seduction*. University Park, Penn., and London, 1990.

Carpenter, K. E. *Dialogue in Political Economy: Translations from and into German in the Eighteenth Century*. Boston, 1977.

Fabian, Bernard. *The English Book in Eighteenth-Century Germany*. London, 1992.

Gargett, Graham, and Geraldine Sheridan, eds. *Ireland and the French Enlightenment, 1700–1800*. New York, 1999. Contains a detailed account of French books translated in Ireland.

Graeber, Wilhelm, and Geneviève Roche. *Englische Literatur des 17. und 18. Jahrhunderts in französischer Übersetzung und deutscher Weiterübersetzung: Eine kommentierte Bibliographie*. Tübingen, Germany, 1988. A pioneering study of "secondary translation."

Ischreyt, Heinz. "Buchhandel und Buchhändler im nordosteuropäischen Kommunikationssystem (1762–1797)." In Barber and Fabian, 1977, pp. 249–270.

Kiesel, Helmuth, and Paul Münch. *Gesellschaft und Literatur im 18. Jahrhundert: Voraussetzungen und Entstehung des literarischen Markts in Deutschland*. Munich, 1977.

Kontler, László. "William Robertson and His German Audience on European and Non-European Civilisations." *Scottish Historical Review* 80 (2001), 63–89. An innovative analysis of the reception of major Enlightenment texts through translation.

Korshin, Paul J., ed. *The Widening Circle: Essays on the Circulation of Literature in Eighteenth-Century Europe*. Philadelphia, 1976.

Munck, Thomas. *The Enlightenment: A Comparative Social History, 1721–1794*. London, 2000.

Oz-Salzberger, Fania. *Translating the Enlightenment: Scottish Civic Discourse in Eighteenth-Century Germany*. Oxford, 1995. Case study of the translation and mistranslation of historical and political texts.

Price, L. M. *English Literature in German*. Berkeley and Los Angeles, 1953.

Price, Mary Bell, and Lawrence Marsden Price. *The Publication of English Humaniora in Germany in the Eighteenth Century*. Berkeley, Calif., 1934. Useful, though incomplete, checklist of English-German translations.

Venuti, Lawrence. *The Translator's Invisibility: A History of Translation*. London, 1995.

Ward, Albert. *Book Production, Fiction, and the German Reading Public, 1740–1800*. Oxford, 1974.

FANIA OZ-SALZBERGER

TRAVEL LITERATURE. In the eighteenth century, travel literature was characterized by several typical aspects, which may be represented in the paradigmatic figures of the "philosophical traveler," the "sentimental traveler," and the "scientific traveler," each reflecting a distinctive concern of the Enlightenment. These aspects were often combined to form the complex perspective of individual eighteenth-century travelers, and the amalgam further produced the uniquely modern perspective of the "civilized traveler," passing judgment on lands and peoples with reference to the newly articulated standard of civilization.

The Philosophical Traveler. The importance of travel literature in the Enlightenment may be judged from the fundamental influence of two celebrated publications of the early eighteenth century, both works of fiction: Montesquieu's *Lettres persanes* (1721) and Jonathan Swift's *Gulliver's Travels* (1726). Both focused on the experiences of fictional travelers—the peripatetic Persians Usbek and Rica, and the eponymous Gulliver. Gulliver visited imaginary lands, like those of the little Lilliputians, the giants of Brobdingnag, and the equine Houyhnhnms, while Usbek visited the real and recognizable land of France, which nevertheless appeared completely alien to him. The philosophical point of these two works of travel literature concerned, above all, the importance of perspective in the evaluation of lands and peoples; they emphasized the variety of customs and the relative nature of their merits. "Rica and I are perhaps the first Persians to have left our country for love of knowledge," writes Usbek, who soon finds himself in France, wondering why Muslims like himself are forbidden to eat pork. Rica generalizes radically on the relativity of customs: "It seems to me, Usbek, that all our judgments are made with reference covertly to ourselves. I do not find it surprising that the Negroes paint the devil sparkling white, and their gods black as coal." This line of reasoning leads to the conclusion that "if triangles had a god, they would give him three sides." French readers were thus encouraged to follow the intellectual example of the traveling Persians and to think critically about social and religious prejudices in France. Furthermore, both Swift and Montesquieu made use of the traveler's perspective for the political purpose of satirizing their own societies, as described by an astonished visitor; even the Lilliputians, with their dispute over how to break open an egg, were miniature caricatures of petty Europeans, who disputed over religious differences that would have seemed equally trivial from an alien perspective. Thus, from the earliest generation of the Enlightenment, the figure of the traveler provided the ideal literary vehicle for representing the spirit of philosophical criticism.

The voyages of discovery in the sixteenth and seventeenth centuries, resulting in vastly expanded knowledge of the world, provided the philosophes of the Enlightenment with published accounts of lands and peoples from which to study what Edmund Burke, in 1777, called the "Great Map of Mankind." *Gulliver's Travels* itself appeared as an absurd philosophical parody of a voyage of discovery, complete with a mock map to show the geographical position of Lilliput with respect to Sumatra; the discovery of Brobdingnag proved "that our Geographers of Europe are in a great Error, by supposing nothing but Sea between Japan and California." Works such as Hakluyt's sixteenth-century *Principal Navigations*, which was constantly republished, as well as seventeenth-century Jesuit accounts of Asia and America, offered eighteenth-century writers information about the most remote lands without

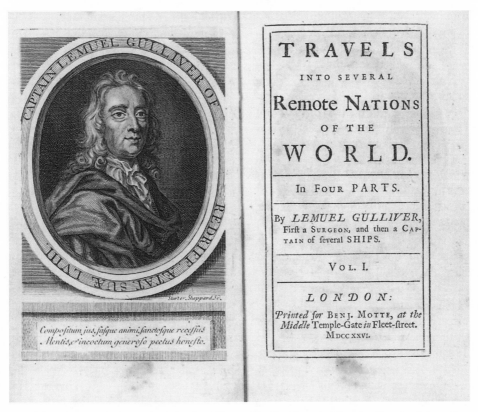

Imaginary Travel. Frontispiece to and title page of *Gulliver's Travels* by Jonathan Swift (London, 1726). (Rare Books and Special Collections Division, Library of Congress.)

imposing the hardship of travel. Rousseau, in the *Discours sur l'origine de l'inégalité*, was able to speculate about the life of the savage Carib without ever getting anywhere near the Caribbean, while Adam Smith, in the *Wealth of Nations*, was able to cite patterns of economy and society from China to Peru. Voltaire's library included numerous collections of voyages, enabling him to write the universal history of customs without feeling the need to travel. Catherine the Great purchased his library after his death, and the volumes can still be seen today in Saint Petersburg, a city Voltaire never visited in spite of his lifelong interest in Russia.

It was a very modest voyage from France to England that became the occasion for establishing Voltaire's career as a social and political critic, with the *Lettres philosophiques* (1734). Writing about England from his personal experience and comparing it with France enabled him to formulate fundamental enlightened ideals like religious toleration. Voltaire clearly appreciated that travel, which permitted the comparison of laws, customs, institutions, and societies, was perfectly adapted to the spirit of philosophical criticism. In 1731, he published the *Histoire de Charles XII*, also a kind of travel literature; Charles himself, the conquering Swedish king, traveled across the map of Europe, and Voltaire had to set the scenes in

lands relatively unfamiliar to his readers. Charles fought in Poland, Russia, and Ukraine, where he was defeated by Peter the Great at Poltava in 1709, and then found refuge among the Tartars and the Turks; Voltaire's account thus became the Enlightenment's introduction to the concept of "Eastern Europe," as these lands and peoples were placed in literary alignment according to the principle of relative backwardness. The author himself traveled only vicariously along the route of his historical hero, but philosophically illuminated the terrain by offering enlightened commentary.

Voltaire would eventually take the peripatetic protagonist as the natural focus for a philosophical fable. In *Candide* (1759), the hero travels from Westphalia to Portugal to Paraguay, to the utopian kingdom of El Dorado, and back again through Europe to Constantinople, discovering that the same philosophical lessons can be learned in every clime. Also in 1759, Samuel Johnson followed the fictional Rasselas around Abyssinia and Egypt; years before, Johnson had translated into English the Jesuit Jerome Lobo's *Voyage historique d'Abyssinie* as *A Voyage to Abyssinia*. In 1776, the Polish philosophe Ignacy Krasicki sent his fictional hero, Nicholas Wisdom, from Warsaw to Paris to the Cape of Good Hope, and eventually to the island utopia of Nipu. In fiction, travel provided the occasion for philosophical education. In the real world of the eighteenth century, travel around Europe was a recognized educational course for young men, of whom the most institutionalized cohort were the travelers on the English Grand Tour of France and Italy. The young Russian writer Nicholas Karamzin followed a less well-established route from Moscow through Germany and Switzerland, reaching France and England in 1790, and discovering that "the path to education and enlightenment is the same for all nations." His *Pisma russkogo puteshestvennika* (Letters of a Russian Traveler) began to appear in Russia in 1791, after his return. Fictional figures like Candide traveled more widely around the world and learned more pointedly philosophical lessons, but actual travelers similarly circulated around Europe to broaden their experience and deepen their insight in the age of Enlightenment.

The Sentimental Traveler. Laurence Sterne's *Sentimental Journey* (1768) presented, with some ironic absurdity, a traveling narrator who seemed more focused on himself and his sentiments than on any observation of France and Italy. It was intended partly as parody of the Grand Tour, but Sterne drew attention to an important aspect of travel literature at midcentury: its increasing emphasis on the personality and sensibility of the traveler, whose education on the road was inevitably personal and sentimental as well as philosophical. Karamzin, for instance, responded to Paris with self-conscious sentimental intensity: "I am in Paris! This thought produces in my soul a kind of peculiar agitated, inexplicable, delightful sensation." That sensation conditioned his observations of every sight in the city.

Lady Mary Wortley Montagu traveled to Constantinople in 1717, when her husband became the English ambassador there, but her *Turkish Embassy Letters* were not published until 1763, the year after her death. The success of the book followed not only from her detailed observation of exotic customs and circumstances but also from the inviting intimacy of her epistolary style, as when she brought her readers with her into the Ottoman baths of Sofia and evoked the naked charms of the other female bathers. The fact that it was a woman narrating her travels gave the letters of Lady Mary a distinctive personal appeal to her readers, demonstrating the special sensibility of a woman observing alien customs at a time when travel writing was more often the work of men. She herself was very much a presence in the letters, as when she wrote from Adrianople: "I will try to awaken your gratitude by giving you a full and true relation of the novelties of this place, none of which would surprise you more than a sight of my person as I am now in my Turkish habit, though I believe you would be of my opinion that 'tis admirably becoming." Other Englishwomen would also write about their travels in the eighteenth century, like Hester Thrale Piozzi, whose account of France, Italy, and Germany appeared in 1789, as did Lady Elizabeth Craven's even more adventurous *Journey through the Crimea to Constantinople*. Lady Craven admitted the importance of the sentimental traveler's "fancy" and "imagination," well aware, as she set out from Constantinople to traverse Bulgaria, Wallachia, and Transylvania, that "most women would be frightened with the journey I am taking." She carried with her two little pistols and a strong sense of herself.

The masterpiece of sentimental travel literature was Goethe's *Italienische Reise* (Italian Voyage), which freed the genre from the shadow of Sterne's irony. The already celebrated German poet and dramatist traveled in Italy between 1786 and 1788, keeping a detailed diary, though the complete book was not finally prepared for publication until thirty years later. Goethe's observations of Italy, Italians, and Italian art were profoundly imbued with his own poetic sentiments and emotional surges. Arriving in Rome, he reflected on the "long, solitary journey in search of the focal point toward which I was drawn by an irresistible desire." He exclaimed at the intensity with which the Pantheon, the Apollo Belvedere, and the Sistine Chapel had "captivated my mind and heart," while distinguishing himself from less engaged, more superficial travelers. Goethe emphasized the importance of the individual traveler's response to foreign scenes, and he declared his own to be so powerful that "I count the day when I entered Rome as my second natal day, a true rebirth." In his account of the Roman Carnival, first published in 1789, he reflected on the Italian experience of "the most intense and extreme pleasures." For Goethe, sentimental travel became the occasion for spiritual renewal, while his aesthetic response to Italy also inspired him with the virtues of classicism in verse and drama. Interestingly, Goethe himself could become an object of sentimental travel; when Karamzin came to Weimar in 1789, he wrote, "Last night, as I passed Goethe's house, I saw him through the window. I stood and looked at him for about a minute. What a serious Grecian face!" Whether observing Goethe's classical features or Rome's classical sculptures, the sentimental traveler supplied the exclamatory element of personal intensity.

Casanova, writing his memoirs in the 1780s and 1790s, recounted the history of his sexual adventures in the form of a travel narrative, following an autobiographical itinerary across the map of Europe from Venice and Paris to Warsaw and Saint Petersburg. The catalog of his exploits received its variety from the changing geographical scenes, while the ambulatory adventurer not only pursued his successful seductions but also explored the sentimental experience of his own libertinism. Sade, composing pornographic fictions in the same period, kept his libertine protagonists often in motion, as they sought to satisfy and describe their violently obscene sentiments. In the *Histoire de Juliette*, published in 1798, a voyager reports that "from Astrakhan we moved toward Tiflis, killing, pillaging, fucking, ravaging all that crossed our path." The repetitive conquests of the sexual adventurer required fresh victims in new terrain to demonstrate the philosophical consistency of libertinism. In Casanova's memoirs and Sade's novels, the sentimental traveler took to an erotic extreme the narrative emphasis on himself, his own emotions, and his own sensations.

The Scientific Traveler. In 1768, the most celebrated scientific expeditions of the eighteenth century commenced with the departure of James Cook from England, commanding the *Endeavour* on this the first of his three expeditions of Pacific exploration; the last would end in 1779, with his murder by Hawaiians. Cook's voyages in the Pacific largely completed the remapping of the world that began with Columbus's Atlantic voyages at the end of the fifteenth century. Though Cook was authorized to raise the British flag on islands that he discovered, like Hawaii, the notable emphasis on scientific concerns made his expeditions distinctively enlightened in character, in contrast to the overwhelmingly imperial and religious purposes of discovery in previous centuries. Of course, scientific knowledge of island cartography, indigenous populations, or natural resources was not without potential imperial significance for England.

Cook's initial assignment on the first voyage was to observe the transit of Venus in 1769 from the vantage point of Tahiti, a task sponsored by the Royal Society as part of an international astronomical enterprise. His other principal purpose was to search for the undiscovered Southern Continent that was supposed to lie somewhere in the Pacific. As he voyaged from island to island, he was "carefully to observe the Nature of the Soil, and the Products thereof; the Beasts and Fowls that inhabit or frequent it"; he was also to take specimens of minerals and seeds, and "to observe the Genius, Temper, Disposition and Number of the Natives." A team of scientists sailed with Cook, including an astronomer and several naturalists; Cook himself was a careful scientific cartographer, mapping large parts of the coasts of New Zealand and Australia during the first voyage. During the second voyage, Cook sailed as far south as the Antarctic Circle, and on the third voyage, after making the first European visit to Hawaii, he sailed north to Alaska. It was also on Cook's voyages that John Harrison's invention, the marine chronometer, could be tested for calculating longitude at sea, thus providing the technological means for consolidating cartographic advances. The published accounts of Cook's explorations were of great public interest, beginning with John Hawkesworth's editing of the records of

the first voyage in 1773. Cook's journals reported detailed observations of the peoples he encountered; for instance, he commented with attempted scientific precision on the tattoos of the Tahitians, the implements of the Maoris, and the ornaments of the Australian Aborigines.

Tahiti had been discovered in 1767 by Samuel Wallis, who claimed and named the island for George III. The Tahitians, who had hitherto had no contact with Europeans, became an object of fascination to Europe for the rest of the century, offering a glimpse of what was sometimes imagined to resemble the idyllic state of nature. The French explorer Louis-Antoine de Bougainville visited Tahiti in 1768 and brought back to France an authentic Tahitian, Ahu-toru, who was presented as a specimen of Pacific savagery in the salons of Paris. Bougainville also published an account of his voyage in 1771, which inspired Diderot to write, in 1773, a fictional "Supplément du Voyage de Bougainville," using the supposed sexual morals of Tahiti as a means of questioning the conventional morality of Europe. For the Enlightenment in Europe, the encounter with the Tahitians made it possible to consider philosophically matters of custom, but also to try to establish the principles of scientific anthropology.

In 1774, the Paduan natural historian Alberto Fortis published his *Viaggio in Dalmazia*, which promptly translated into English, French, and German. It set forth the geology and natural history of Dalmatia, together with an anthropological account of the primitive customs of its inhabitants, the pastoral population of the inland mountains, called Morlacchi. Dalmatia was not nearly so remote as Tahiti, though the Morlacchi seemed almost as exotic as the Tahitians, and Fortis demonstrated the importance of scientific travel for the detailed description of customs. The word "anthropology" took on its modern meaning in French in 1788 with the publication by Alexandre-César Chavannes of *Anthropologie ou Science génerale de l'homme*; in 1798, Immanuel Kant published *Anthropologie in pragmatischer Hinsicht* (Anthropology in Pragmatic Consideration). The emergence and development of the discipline was conditioned by the reports of scientific travelers. Georg Forster, who had traveled on Cook's second voyage, debated with Kant and Herder over the significance of race. The American John Ledyard, who accompanied Cook on the third voyage, traveled alone in Siberia in 1787, sponsored in part by Thomas Jefferson, and attempted to establish scientifically the similarity between Siberian Tartars and American Indians through the measurement of facial features and the study of customs.

Scientific travel in the late eighteenth century was also important for the gathering of literary texts and the study of linguistic relations, especially in the creation of the scholarly field of Orientalism. Abraham-Hyacinthe Anquetil-Duperron made pioneering translations of Asian religious texts, beginning with the Zoroastrian *Zend Avesta* in 1771, and he traveled to India to study Sanskrit. William Jones also went to India to pursue Sanskrit studies, founding the Asiatic Society of Bengal in 1784. Jones then proposed the Indo-European linguistic relation between Sanskrit and Greek. Carsten Niebuhr, who participated in a Danish scientific expedition to the Ottoman Near East, published his *Beschriebung von Arabien* (Description of Arabia) in 1772; the French traveler Constantin-François Volney attempted to follow that example with a scientifically encyclopedic description of his own *Voyage en Égypte et en Syrie* (1787). During the French Revolution, Volney composed for the revolutionary government a questionnaire to be used by traveling commissioners for the methodical collection of information about the entire country of France; his models included not only his own account of Egypt and Syria, but also the English traveler Arthur Young's economically oriented *Travels in France* (1792). Volney then produced a similar questionnaire to be used by French diplomats for the purpose of scientifically harvesting knowledge of the whole world.

The Civilized Traveler. The modern concept of *civilization*, which began to be employed in the middle of the eighteenth century, was directly relevant to the experience of the enlightened traveler. The civilized traveler brought together the viewpoints of the philosophical traveler, with a penchant for critical comparisons; of the sentimental traveler, who made himself or herself the focus of new experience; and of the scientific traveler, who aspired to perfect empirical observation of places, languages, and customs. The civilized traveler possessed a conviction of a hierarchy of lands and peoples and presumed to make an enlightened evaluation of relative development.

The French physiocrat Lemercier de la Rivière, after serving as royal intendant in Martinique, traveled to Russia in 1767 with the civilizing conviction that he could recommend the total transformation of Russian society and government. He declared that "everything remains to be done in that land; or to say it better still, everything remains to be undone and redone." Catherine the Great, offended by his presumption, wrote to Voltaire that Lemercier seemed to think "we walked on four paws," and that he "politely gave himself the trouble of coming from Martinique to stand us up on our hind feet." Years later, she still recalled that he had "got it in his head that I had called him to help me govern the empire, to draw us out of the darkness of barbarism by the expansiveness of his lights." The civilized traveler set up to judge the barbarism of others, and he did not hesitate to make recommendations on the basis of his supposedly more enlightened perspective. *The Travels and Surprising Adventures of Baron Munchausen* (1785), a novel by the German Rudolf Erich Raspe that was later advertised as

"Gulliver Revived," was vastly successful as a parody of boastful fantasy in travel literature. Munchausen enthusiastically undertook preposterous civilizing projects; in one adventure, he put Russians and Turks to work building a canal at Suez, "to facilitate commerce and civilization."

The Englishman William Coxe traveled as a tutor on an unusually extended educational Grand Tour, and in 1784 he published an account of his travels in Poland, Russia, Sweden, and Denmark. In Russia especially, he attempted to measure the degree of civilization with reference to a variety of factors, from technology and transport to costumes and customs. On the road from Moscow to Saint Petersburg, he testified to the discernment of the civilized traveler: "The backwardness of the Russian peasants in the mechanical arts, when compared with those of the other European nations, is visible to a superficial observer. As we approached Petersburg, and nearer the civilized parts of Europe, the villagers were better furnished with the conveniences of life, and further advanced in the knowledge of the necessary arts." Coxe's conclusion concerning the Russians was that "their progress towards civilization is very inconsiderable, and many instances of the grossest barbarism fell under our observation." The traveler thus made his own observations into a civilized verdict on the visited terrain. In fact, in 1790 the enlightened Russian writer Alexander Radishchev published his criticisms of his own country under the title *Puteshestvie iz Peterburga v Moskvu* (A Journey from Saint Petersburg to Moscow). John Ledyard, traveling from Saint Petersburg into Siberia, claimed to discern a calibrated scale of civilized aspects in the peoples he encountered: "The nice gradation by which I pass from Civilization to Incivilization appears in everything: their manners, their dress, their language, and particularly that remarkable and important circumstance of Colour."

The indexes of civilization were devised by the traveling observer and might range from weighty economic concerns to petty matters of comfort in accommodations. James Boswell, who made his literary reputation as a traveler, writing in 1768 about his interviews on Corsica with Pasquale Paoli, and in 1773 on his tour of the Hebrides with Samuel Johnson, was not above complaining about the quality of lodgings on other travels. In 1764, he lamented in verse:

> Here am I, sitting in a German inn.
> Where I may penance do for many a sin,
> For I am pestered with a thousand flies,
> Who flap and buzz about my nose and eyes.

Sterne, in *A Sentimental Journey*, satirized the discontented traveler: "The learned Smelfungus traveled from Boulogne to Paris—from Paris to Rome—and so on—but he set out with the spleen and jaundice, and every object he passed by was discoloured or distorted—He wrote an account of them, but 'twas nothing but the account of his miserable feelings." Smelfungus was none other than Tobias Smollett, who had published his *Travels through France and Italy* in 1766. It was not remarkable in the eighteenth century for travelers to complain about conditions on the road, but for the civilized traveler, the amenities of accommodation could be inseparable from what they considered uncivilized in foreign parts. This was very clear in Coxe's complaints about lodgings in Poland, "where the only places of reception for travellers were hovels, belonging to Jews, totally destitute of furniture." The absence of furniture was consistent with his general image of poverty and backwardness: "Our only bed was straw thrown upon the ground, and we thought ourselves happy when we could procure it clean. Even we, who were by no means delicate, and who had long been accustomed to put up with all inconveniences, found ourselves distressed in this land of desolation." Poland was represented negatively according to the evolving idea of eastern Europe as a domain of backwardness, but Arthur Young was similarly censorious about some of the inns he found in France: "What are we to think of a country that has made, in the eighteenth century, no better provisions for its travellers?" The civilized traveler in the age of Enlightenment was ready to draw sweeping conclusions even from petty personal discomforts.

There was no problem with the comfort of accommodations when Catherine the Great sailed down the Dnieper River in 1787 to visit the Crimean Peninsula, recently annexed by Russia, but this internationally celebrated eighteenth-century voyage also involved concern for the civilized appearance of peoples and landscapes. This was the occasion for the creation of "Potemkin villages" by Prince Grigory Potemkin; according to the French ambassador, Louis-Philippe de Ségur, who accompanied Catherine and helped to publicize her voyage, the banks of the Dnieper were "so ornamented and disguised" as to produce the illusion of civilized cities and gardens. Later, as the travelers crossed the steppe, Ségur found lands "upon which civilization seeks to extend its conquests and labors"; finally, in the Crimea itself, Catherine appeared as the enlightened monarch who would bring the benefits of civilization to her uncivilized subjects. The celebrated traveler could personify the Enlightenment even in Paris—for instance, when Voltaire returned to Paris in 1778, the year of his death, or when Benjamin Franklin came to the French capital as the representative of the American revolutionary cause.

More usually, however, it was the celebrated traveler setting out from Paris who represented the Enlightenment in supposedly less civilized parts. When Mme. Geoffrin left her Parisian salon on a voyage to Warsaw in 1766, to visit her adoptive "son," Stanisław August, king of Poland, he wished that he could provide "beautiful roads, beautiful

bridges, good lodgings, in short all that it would require to keep you from saying: 'Ah! what a nasty kingdom is the kingdom of my son!'" The civilized traveler implicitly condescended in making her visit, and Stanisław August hailed Mme. Geoffrin "descending as if from a planet" when she traveled from Paris to Warsaw.

The most famous voyage of a philosophe was that of Diderot, setting out from Paris for Saint Petersburg in 1773, to visit Catherine. "All my life I will congratulate myself on the voyage to Petersburg," wrote Diderot, addressing Catherine, but in fact, he felt some ambivalence about the whole phenomenon of travel. In a passage composed for the abbé Raynal's history of the Indies, Diderot reflected that "the greater the distance from the capital, the further the mask of the traveler's identity slips from his face," effacing his national sense of self, until finally "all that he preserves of his homeland are the principles and prejudices which authorize or excuse his conduct." Those principles and prejudices could be interpreted as the conviction of civilization, but even that became equivocal in the fictional Tahiti that Diderot described, where the chaplain's sexual principles were ultimately overwhelmed by the seductive reasoning of the Tahitians. Diderot never visited Tahiti, of course, but Saint Petersburg was an adventurous destination in itself, and he felt called to make some civilized recommendations for Russia. "To civilize all at once such an enormous country seems to me a project beyond human forces," he reflected, and he advised Catherine to begin with a model district of the Russian empire, and "to execute a plan of civilization" within that designated territory. He declared that "this district would be, by its relation to the rest of the empire, what France is in Europe relative to the countries that surround it." The civilized traveler who voyaged from France to Russia discovered a pattern of relations and relative degrees that ordered the map of Europe according to the principles and prejudices of civilization.

[*See also* Grand Tour *and* Utopianism.]

BIBLIOGRAPHY

Adams, Percy G. *Travelers and Travel Liars, 1660–1800*. Berkeley, Calif., 1962. A study of the relation between real and pretended travels, between truth and falsehood in travel literature.

Beaglehole, J. C. *The Life of Captain James Cook*. Stanford, Calif., 1974. A comprehensive study of Cook's voyages.

Black, Jeremy. *The British Abroad: The Grand Tour in the Eighteenth Century*. Stroud, U.K., and New York, 1992. A study of English travelers to the Continent, with emphasis on the experience and conditions of travel.

Cross, Anthony. *By the Banks of the Neva: Chapters from the Lives and Careers of the British in Eighteenth-Century Russia*. Cambridge, 1997. An erudite study of the experience of Russia by Englishmen abroad.

Dolan, Brian. *Exploring European Frontiers: British Travellers in the Age of Enlightenment*. New York, 2000. A study of travelers to

Scandinavia, Russia, and Greece, on the northern, eastern, and southern frontiers of Europe.

Duchet, Michèle. *Anthropologie et histoire au siècle des lumières: Buffon, Voltaire, Rousseau, Helvétius, Diderot.* Paris, 1971. A study of the anthropological conceptions of the philosophes, based on the Enlightenment's understanding of cultures and societies.

Lough, John. *France on the Eve of the Revolution: British Travellers' Observations 1763–1788.* Chicago, 1987. A study of how the British perceived pre-Revolutionary France.

Mączak, Antoni. *Travel in Early Modern Europe.* Translated by Ursula Phillips. Cambridge, 1995. English translation of *Życie codzienne w podróżach po Europie w XVI i XVII wieku* (1980), an important study of conditions of travel in Europe, especially in the sixteenth and seventeenth centuries, but with much relevance for the eighteenth century as well.

Marshall, P. J., and Glyndwr Williams. *The Great Map of Mankind: British Perceptions of the World in the Age of Enlightenment.* London, 1982. A comprehensive study of British views of Asia, Africa, America, and the Pacific.

Pagden, Anthony. *European Encounters with the New World: From Renaissance to Romanticism.* New Haven, Conn., 1993. A brilliant study of how Europe interpreted the New World of America; chaps. 3–5 address eighteenth-century issues.

Redford, Bruce. *Venice and the Grand Tour.* New Haven, Conn., 1996. A study of the significance of the Venetian experience for British travelers.

Schwab, Raymond. *The Oriental Renaissance: Europe's Rediscovery of India and the East 1680–1880.* Translated by Gene-Patterson Black and Victor Reinking. New York, 1984. Translation of *La Renaissance orientale* (1950), a pioneering study of Orientalism, of how Europe acquired and articulated its knowledge about Asia.

Smith, Bernard. *European Vision and the South Pacific.* New Haven, Conn., 1985. A study of artistic images and conceptions of the Pacific islands and Australia, with the first six chapters addressing eighteenth-century issues, including Cook's voyages.

Stagl, Justin. *A History of Curiosity: The Theory of Travel, 1550–1800.* Chur, Switzerland, 1995. A study of ideas about the phenomenon of travel itself; chaps. 4–7 discuss eighteenth-century developments.

Stroev, Alexandre. *Les aventuriers des lumières.* Paris, 1997. A study of eighteenth-century adventurers, who were largely traveling adventurers.

Wolff, Larry. *Inventing Eastern Europe: The Map of Civilization on the Mind of the Enlightenment.* Stanford, Calif., 1994. A study of how the Enlightenment came to think of Europe as divided into Eastern Europe and Western Europe, with much discussion of the accounts of travelers.

LARRY WOLFF

TREMBLEY, ABRAHAM (1710–1784), Swiss scientist, philosopher, and tutor to Dutch and British nobility, sometimes called the father of experimental zoology.

In 1744, Trembley published his *Mémoires*, in which he described his tradition-shattering studies on the freshwater hydra, or polyp. This beautifully illustrated treatise described systematic and meticulous observations and ingenious experiments; strikingly, he relied mostly on such simple instruments as a magnifying glass and a boar's hair probe. Trembley's findings included such then-startling phenomena as the regeneration of a complete animal, asexual reproduction in animals, and the grafting of animal tissue. His discoveries created a furor in the universities, academies, and salons of Europe, where the theological and philosophical implications of his work were hotly debated. They also fed an already existing passion of the time for studying lower forms of life, and they set a new standard in such studies for objectivity, elegance, and repeatability in experimentation.

A member of a prominent French Huguenot family in Geneva, Trembley, with his relative and collaborator, Charles Bonnet, grew up during the intellectual flowering of his native city. As a student, he wrote a thesis on the calculus. While residing temporarily in Leiden (Netherlands), he came into close contact with such distinguished scientists as Willem Jacob 'sGravesande and Bernard Albinus. Yet Trembley made his momentous discoveries outside the Dutch university milieu, while he was employed as tutor-in-residence for the sons of Count William Bentinck of The Hague, in their country mansion at Sorgvliet.

In 1740, Trembley initiated a correspondence with the great French scientist, René-Antoine Ferchault de Réaumur, who brought Trembley's work before the French king, the royal court, and the Académie Royale des Sciences. Through similar support from Count Bentinck, the duke of Richmond, and the Royal Society of London's president Martin Folkes, this obscure tutor was elected a Fellow of the Royal Society of London in 1743 and received its prestigious Copley Medal. Later, Trembley's involvements increasingly turned to politics, diplomacy, education, moral philosophy, and religion. Leaving Bentinck's household in 1747, he went to England, where he developed a strong relationship with the duke of Richmond. Through the duke's good offices, Trembley participated in continental peace negotiations. Upon the duke's death, Trembley took charge of Richmond's fifteen-year-old son; again Trembley was tutor to the nobility. For four years he led the young Duke Charles on the customary Grand Tour of Europe, meeting with Enlightenment luminaries.

When Trembley returned to Geneva with a handsome endowment from the king of England and the young duke, he was forty-six; he married, fathered five children, and immersed himself in close personal oversight of their rearing and education. From this time came Trembley's four books on religion, philosophy, and education, which project a deeply held nonsectarian Christian faith. Arguing for the study of nature as a means of glorifying God, Trembley rejected both the widely practiced theoretical system-making of his era and Voltaire's rationalism, asserting that in the grand design of the Infinite, all things were possible, and that "Nature must be explained by Nature and not by our own views."

[*See also* Natural History; Scientific Instruments; *and* Zoology.]

BIBLIOGRAPHY

Baker, John R. *Abraham Trembley of Geneva*. London, 1952. Definitive biography of Trembley; though out of print, available in major libraries.

Dawson, Virginia P. *Nature's Enigma: The Problem of the Polyp in the Letters of Bonnet, Trembley, and Réaumur*. Philadelphia, 1987. Provides excellent historical context with analysis of archival materials.

Lenhoff, Howard M., and Sylvia G. Lenhoff. "Trembley's Polyps." *Scientific American* 256 (1988), 108–113. For the general reader, the most readily available account of Trembley's contributions, with seven illustrations.

Lenhoff, Howard M., and Pierre Tardent, eds. *From Trembley's Polyps to New Directions in Research on Hydra: Proceedings of a Symposium Honoring Abraham Trembley (1710–1784)*. In *Archives des sciences*, 38.3. Geneva, 1985. Includes such topics as Trembley's influence on the development of the aquatic microscope; Trembley's rhetoric of proof and persuasion; the influence of Dutch science on Trembley; and the relation of Trembley's discoveries to theories of the "Chain of Being."

Lenhoff, Sylvia G., and Howard M. Lenhoff. *Hydra and the Birth of Experimental Biology, 1744: Abraham Trembley's Mémoires Concerning the Polyps*. Pacific Grove, Calif., 1986. In two parts; book 1 offers a scientific overview and interpretation, as well as historical background for book 2, the only published English translation of the *Mémoires*. Also contains copies of the thirteen engraved fold-out plates from Trembley's original.

SYLVIA G. LENHOFF and
HOWARD M. LENHOFF

TRUMBULL, JOHN (1756–1843), American artist.

Trumbull was born in Lebanon, Connecticut, into one of the most prominent families in the colony. This eventually gave him easy access to the most important players in the dramatic events of his lifetime, which he recorded in the greatest series of war paintings ever created by an American artist: eight scenes depicting crucial events in the American War of Independence.

After serving in several campaigns of the war, he sailed for England in 1780 to study art with Benjamin West, and possibly to carry out a secret mission. He was arrested as a spy and sent to prison, but was released and expelled from the country. As soon as the treaty of peace made it possible, he returned to London and Benjamin West. There he began the first of the Independence paintings, *The Death of General Warren at the Battle of Bunker's Hill, 17 June 1775*, followed by *The Death of General Montgomery in the Attack on Quebec, 31 December 1775*.

In 1786, Trumbull visited Thomas Jefferson, then minister to France, with whose advice he planned *The Declaration of Independence, 4 July 1776*. Returning to London, he began work on this and three others in the series, *The Capture of the Hessians at Trenton, 26 December 1776*; *The Death of General Mercer at the Battle of Princeton, 3 January 1777*; and *The Surrender of Lord Cornwallis at Yorktown, 19 October 1781*.

Trumbull returned to the United States at the end of 1789, where he traveled along the Atlantic seaboard to "collect heads" for his history series. In 1793, when the young woman he hoped to marry, Harriet Wadsworth, died, he returned to London as John Jay's assistant on the Jay Treaty Commission. For the next six years Trumbull abandoned his art career, but returned to it in 1800 when he married Sarah Hope Harvey and returned to the United States where he became a successful portrait painter of New York's civic leaders. The final stage of his career began in 1815, when he successfully petitioned the U.S. Congress to commission four of his Independence scenes for the central rotunda of the Capitol, which was being rebuilt after its partial destruction in the War of 1812. In 1826, President John Quincy Adams viewed the finished paintings, greatly enlarged from the originals (approximately 20 by 30 inches) to 144 by 216 inches each, with life-size figures: *The Declaration of Independence, The Surrender of General Burgoyne at Saratoga, The Surrender of Lord Cornwallis at Yorktown*, and *The Resignation of General Washington*. (The entire series of small-size works is in the Yale University Art Gallery.)

In seeking to achieve virtual reality in depicting historical events and persons through research, Trumbull adhered to the Enlightenment's proposition that truth is attainable by means of scientific, objective methods. Trumbull's overall theme throughout the Independence series is rooted in the Enlightenment conception of virtue as the servant of liberty: The scenes depict men risking or sacrificing their lives to overthrow monarchy and establish a republic. As such, they represent the Enlightenment conception of liberty as an artifact of culture, fashioned by the virtue of human beings in pursuit of happiness in an orderly society ruled by law.

[*See also* American Revolution *and* Painting.]

BIBLIOGRAPHY

Cooper, Helen, Patricia Mullan Burnham, Martin Price, Jules David Prown, Oswaldo Rodriquez Roque, Egon Verheyen, and Bryan Wolf. *John Trumbull, The Hand and Spirit of a Painter*. New Haven, Conn., 1982. A catalog published in conjunction with the exhibition under the same name, 28 October 1982–16 January 1983, with essays by the collaborators on the various categories of Trumbull's subject matter: history, portraits, religion, landscape, literature and allegory, and architectural designs.

Jaffe, Irma B. *John Trumbull: Patriot-Artist of the American Revolution*. Boston, 1975. The only full-length study of the life and works of Trumbull. Includes sixteen color illustrations including all eight of the Independence paintings plus 205 in black and white, and a fully annotated catalog of all works illustrated.

Sizer, Theodore. *The Works of Colonel John Trumbull*. New Haven, Conn., 1950; revised edition, 1967. The first catalog of John Trumbull's entire oeuvre in all media; 275 works illustrated in black and white.

Trumbull, John. *Autobiography, Reminiscences and Letters by John Trumbull from 1756 to 1841*. New York and London, 1841. An interleaved copy of this *Autobiography*, bound into 3 volumes, is in the Yale University Library, Franklin Collection. Compiled by Charles Allen Munn, it contains letters to him from Jefferson, Adams, and others, together with memorabilia.

Trumbull, John. *The Autobiography of Colonel John Trumbull.* Edited by Theodore Sizer. New Haven, Conn., 1953.

IRMA B. JAFFE

TUCKER, ST. GEORGE (1752–1827), American judge, writer, and law professor.

St. George Tucker was born near Port Royal, Bermuda, to Henry Tucker and Anne Butterfield Tucker on 29 June 1752. He emigrated to Williamsburg, Virginia, in 1771 to attend the College of William and Mary.

In the Virginia capital, Tucker came under the tutelage of the jurist George Wythe. In 1774, Tucker won appointment as a county court clerk, just as Virginia's courts were closed down in the American Revolution. At the outbreak of hostilities, Tucker joined his brother in a scheme to smuggle war matériel from loyal Bermuda to South Carolina and Virginia. He profited handsomely from his wartime smuggling. Tucker married Frances Bland Randolph in 1777. Mrs. Tucker was a relative of many eminent Virginians, and her late husband linked her to Virginia's leading family. In the 1780s, Tucker practiced law and served as the commonwealth's attorney for Chesterfield County (outside Richmond). He decided in 1786 to focus his energies on legal practice before the state's highest courts, which required him to surrender his offices. Widowed in 1788, Tucker took a position on the General Court.

Also in 1788, Tucker opposed ratification of the federal constitution. He had been appointed to the Annapolis Convention of 1786 on the basis of a trade-related pamphlet he published in 1785, but his state-centered views could not be reconciled with the unamended constitution. In 1790, Tucker succeeded Wythe as William and Mary's professor of law. In 1791, he married Lelia Skipwith Carter, another widow of an elite Virginian; their three children died in childhood. Tucker lent his pen to the Republican side in their 1790s political dispute with the Federalists.

In 1803, Tucker accepted election to the Virginia Court of Appeals. First, however, he published his republican edition of Sir William Blackstone's *Commentaries on the Laws of England,* adding hundreds of pages of appendices to the monumental English work "correcting" elements unsuited to a republic. Tucker's appendices on matters such as the right to emigrate, the Virginia constitution, and the United States constitution were in the tradition of republican thought established by Virginia pamphleteers in the Imperial Crisis. To a large extent, Tucker simply appropriated the work of various American and European Enlightenment figures (particularly Thomas Jefferson)—often, in the style of the day, without attribution. His book became a staple of American legal education almost immediately.

One appendix to Tucker's Blackstone reprinted Tucker's 1796 proposal for the gradual abolition of slavery. Patterned on statutes adopted in several northern states, Tucker's was the only detailed proposal of its kind in Revolutionary Virginia. Following Jefferson, Tucker envisioned the deportation from Virginia of all freedmen. Unlike Wythe, Tucker insisted that the judiciary could not abolish slavery in Virginia absent a specific legislative enactment.

On Virginia's highest court, Tucker clashed with his colleague Spencer Roane. Roane remained devoted to a jurisprudential vision grounded in tradition, while Tucker wanted to see law develop along scientific lines. Tiring of the personal acrimony, Tucker resigned in 1811. Within two months, President James Madison appointed Tucker Virginia's federal district judge.

Tucker's poetry, a staple of his correspondence throughout his life, demonstrated a real linguistic gift. It revealed a man at once as sentimental as Jefferson and, on the other hand, devoted to a traditional British Protestantism. Tucker also devoted some quite humorous yet philosophically powerful lines to the slavery question.

In 1825, an ailing Tucker resigned from the bench. He died at the home of his stepdaughter in western Virginia on 10 November 1827.

[*See also* Slavery.]

BIBLIOGRAPHY

Most of Tucker's papers are in the Tucker-Coleman Collection in the Swem Library at the College of William and Mary. Related collections are scattered hither and yon.

Gutzman, K. R. Constantine. "Jefferson's Draft Declaration of Independence, Richard Bland, and the Revolutionary Legacy: Giving Credit Where Credit Is Due." *The Journal of the Historical Society* 1 (2001), 137–154. Describes the colonial Virginia constitutional theory on which Tucker based the constitutional teaching of his republican Blackstone.

Haldane Coleman, Mary. *St. George Tucker: Citizen of No Mean City.* Richmond, Va., 1938. Portrait of Tucker by a relative.

Hamilton, Phillip. "Revolutionary Principles and Family Loyalty: Slavery's Transformation in the St. George Tucker Household of Early National Virginia." *William and Mary Quarterly,* 3 ser. 55 (1998), 531–556. Captures Tucker's changing relationship to slavery.

Miller, F. Thornton. *Judges and Juries versus the Law: Virginia's Provincial Legal Perspective, 1783–1828.* Charlottesville, Va., 1994. Contains information on the Virginia judiciary in Tucker's day as well as a description of the Tucker-Roane feud.

Prince, Willaim S., ed. *The Poems of St. George Tucker of Williamsburg, Virginia, 1752–1827.* New York, 1977.

Shepard, E. Lee. "St. George Tucker." *American National Biography* 21 (1999), 907–908.

Tucker, St. George. *View of the Constitution of the United States: With Selected Writings.* Indianapolis, Ind., 1999. Contains selected appendices to Tucker's edition of Blackstone.

K. R. CONSTANTINE GUTZMAN

TÚPAC AMARU (José Gabriel Condorcanqui, 1738–1781), Inca leader of the Great Andean Rebellion of 1780–1783.

Born in Surimana, Tinta, about fifty miles southeast of Cuzco, José Gabriel was the son of Miguel Condorcanqui, a *cacique* (intermediary between indigenous Andean society and the Spanish state) of three towns, and Rosa Noguera, a direct descendant of Túpac Amaru, a leading figure in the Inca Kingdom during the early European contact period. As a result of his lineage, José Gabriel led a relatively privileged life. After he was orphaned in 1750, his aunt and uncle raised him and tutored him in Inca history. As a child, he was educated by Jesuit priests at the prestigious San Francisco de Borja school for the children of *caciques* in Cuzco. In 1760, at sixteen, he married Micaela Bastidas; they had three sons.

In his mid-twenties, José Gabriel inherited the title of *cacique*, along with 350 mules he used to transport goods throughout the region. This gave him the opportunity to travel and observe the increasing abuses the Spanish colonial government was inflicting on the local indigenous population. Indian men were forced to labor in the *mita* (corvée labor) system in the Andean silver mines and to purchase unwanted and overpriced materials by the *reparto* (distribution of merchandise) system. In 1777, José Gabriel traveled to the colonial capital, Lima, to ask the government for immunity for his region from the *mita*. He also asked them to recognize him as marques de Oropesa, a title given to the heirs of the Inca. He cited as inspiration the sixteenth-century *Cronicas reales* by Inca Garcilaso de la Vega, which chronicled the past greatness of the Incas. José Antonio de Areche, Spain's leading representative in the colony, denied both requests. José Gabriel's dual contact with indigenous and Spanish cultures helped to shape the ideology that would convince him to lead a rebellion against Spanish rule.

It is believed that José Gabriel's early contact with the Jesuits introduced him to the scholasticism many of them embraced; the order was expelled from Latin America in 1767. His year in Lima in 1777 introduced him to the ideas of the Enlightenment. As the historian Charles Walker has noted, José Gabriel stayed near and apparently frequented the University of San Marcos, where he was able to read and discuss the writings of Montesquieu, Jean-Jacques Rousseau, and John Locke with little censorship. More important than any European influences were his learning in the history of his people and his experience of the immediate abuses by the Spaniards of both indigenous peoples and *mestizos* (mixed-race people).

After failing to obtain concessions from the Spanish colonial government, José Gabriel returned to Tinta in 1778. There, he saw increasing tension, created in part by the implementation of the Spanish Bourbon reforms. New policies created more customshouses to collect higher taxes and extended requirements for tribute payment to mestizos and many creoles (American-born Spaniards). During the next two years, José Gabriel prepared to revolt against the system; by late 1780, he had his plan in place.

The Great Andean Rebellion began on 4 November 1780, when José Gabriel took the name of Túpac Amaru and ambushed the local *corregidor* (Spanish provincial governor), Antonio de Arriaga. After a hasty trial in which Arriaga was accused of corruption and abuses of the *repartos*, he was hanged on 10 November in the name of the Spanish crown. Although it was clear that Túpac Amaru wanted to do away with the abuses and corruption of Spanish colonialism, there is debate as to whether the goal of the rebellion was reformist or revolutionary. At the beginning, as indicated by his proclamation at the execution of the *corregidor*, Túpac Amaru claimed the rebellion was in the name of the Spanish crown and against local abuses. As news spread of the mounting rebellion, the number of his allies in the immediate region increased and his rhetoric became more indigenous and nationalist. Meanwhile, royalist forces and indigenous groups loyal to them prepared for battle.

In the early stages of the campaign, Túpac Amaru and his allies achieved important victories. On 18 November, they defeated royalist forces sent from Cuzco. Túpac Amaru and his forces then proceeded south, where they captured the cities of Lampa and Azangaro. As his victories mounted, so did his allies; by January 1781, he was able to assemble between forty and sixty thousand troops. Although he and his troops besieged Cuzco for a week, they were unsuccessful. In the face of increasing violence and ethnic fervor, many of Túpac Amaru's creole and *mestizo* allies began to withdraw their support. Much of the support for the rebellion came from Túpac Amaru's immediate region and those adjacent to it, but other *caciques* helped the Spaniards defend Cuzco.

Shortly after their defeat at Cuzco, Túpac Amaru lost control of his home region, Tinta. After numerous defeats at the hands of royalist troops and their indigenous allies, Túpac Amaru was betrayed and captured, along with his wife and several other close aides, on 6 April 1781. After being brutally tortured, they were executed on 18 May.

Although Túpac Amaru's aims were never clear, the Great Andean Rebellion shook the foundations of Spanish colonial society. The rebellion did not succeed in overthrowing the Spanish colonial government, but it did raise the consciousness of the indigenous Quechua people, and it forced the Spanish to moderate their exactions for fear of another rebellion. More important, Túpac Amaru gave indigenous people someone to look up to with pride. His ideology was shaped by his life experiences. Although neo-Inca nationalism was his most obvious ideological influence, the Enlightenment also inspired him indirectly. It was, however, less the writings of Enlightenment thinkers than the implementation of the Bourbon Reforms—a program shaped by the Enlightenment—with its increased oppression of the indigenous populations of Peru, that set Túpac Amaru's ideological agenda.

[*See also* Colonialism; Latin America; *and* Spain.]

BIBLIOGRAPHY

Fisher, Lillian Estelle. *The Last Inca Revolt, 1780–1783*. Norman, Okla., 1966.

Lewin, Boleslao. *La rebelíon de Túpac Amaru y los orígenes de la Independencia de Hispanoamérica*. 3d ed. Buenos Aires, 1967. Argues that the Túpac Amaru Rebellion was the beginning of the fight for Spanish-American independence from Spain.

O'Phelan Godoy, Scarlett. *Rebellion and Revolts in Eighteenth-Century Peru and Upper Peru*. Vienna, 1985. Argues that the Túpac Amaru rebellion was an attempt to reach a balance between the "return to Inca" and a society with *mestizos* and creoles.

Stavig, Ward. *The World of Túpac Amaru: Conflict, Community, and Identity in Colonial Peru*. Lincoln, Nebr., 1999. Looks at community and identity among various indigenous groups leading to the Túpac Amaru rebellion.

Walker, Charles F. *Smoldering Ashes: Cuzco and the Creation of the Republic of Peru, 1780–1840*. Durham, N.C., 1999. Important work that addresses the Túpac Amaru rebellion and its impact from an indigenous perspective.

ABRAHAM M. SMITH

TURGOT, ANNE-ROBERT-JACQUES, baron de l'Aulne (1727–1781), French philosopher, economist, and administrator.

Turgot was born in 1727 to a distinguished Norman family with a long history of administrative service to the French monarchy. He was educated at the Collège Duplessis and then at the Collège de Bourgogne, where he fell under the influence of the abbé Sigorgne, who introduced him to Newtonian physics and Lockean sensationalism. As a student with wide-ranging interests, Turgot read Montesquieu and Voltaire, yet he never identified himself entirely with any sect, including that of the philosophes. Despite his early exposure to Enlightenment literature, Turgot's first intended vocation was the church, and his earliest associations were with the "devout party," which opposed Jansenism and the faction of the king's mistress, Mme. de Pompadour. These devout associations were strengthened at the seminary of Saint-Sulpice, which Turgot entered in 1743. In 1748, he helped circulate defamatory verses against Pompadour, whom the devout party blamed for the forcible exile of the popular Stuart prince, Charles Edward.

By this date, Turgot had begun to develop a philosophical history of civilization that contained the intellectual germs of his many future projects. This historical vision was sketched out in two Latin orations that Turgot presented in 1750 to the Sorbonne, where he had enrolled the year before to prepare his *license*. Turgot's central thesis was that, amid all the chaos and conflict of the centuries, humankind's innate tendency to reassociate sensations in new combinations had produced a fairly steady stream of moral and technical progress. Although Turgot attributed the generation of new ideas principally to the few geniuses scattered over many times and places, he emphasized the importance of varied experience as the source of intellectual grist for the genial mind to work on. For the ever restless Turgot, the chief obstacle to human progress was not superstition, error, or social instability, but routine and sectarianism, which had constricted the vitalizing flow of fresh empirical data to the human mind. Despotism also stood condemned, because by constricting human liberty and enforcing orthodoxy, it, too, straitjacketed human development. Turgot's advocacy of Lockean epistemology, historical progressivism, and freedom put him in the mainstream of Enlightenment thought, but these views were balanced by a strong belief in the historically liberating role of the church that was atypical of the philosophes.

Career in Government Service. In 1751, Turgot made an abrupt career shift, abandoning the church for the government, reverting to family tradition. In 1752, he became attached to the Parlement (sovereign court) of Paris, first

Turgot. Anonymous portrait, eighteenth century. (Châteaux de Versailles et de Trianon, Versailles, France/Giraudon/Art Resource, NY.)

as substitute *procureur-général* and then as *conseiller*. In 1753, he bought a venal office as *maître de requêtes*, which placed him more fully within the royal administration. (A venal office was a government charge to exercise a public function that was sold to individuals as property; *maîtres des requêtes* were magistrates who dealt primarily with the preparation, examination, and adjudication of petitions and cases brought before the royal council.) His earliest duties included service on a special court erected to replace the parlement, which had been temporarily exiled for defending Jansenism. His writings on this controversy reveal a Molinist belief in free will that recalled devout theology, but this belief was used to support an argument for religious tolerance that was more in harmony with Jansenist positions.

Not unduly burdened by his administrative obligations, Turgot spent much of the period until 1761 writing on a wide variety of topics and cultivating his intellectual and social contacts in Paris. He frequented the salon of Mme. Geoffrin, where he associated with such Enlightenment luminaries as d'Holbach, Grimm, d'Alembert, Hume, and, above all, Condorcet and Julie de Lespinasse, both of whom became close friends. These contacts led to his collaboration on the *Encyclopédie*, for which Turgot wrote articles on "Étymologie," "Existence," "Expansibilité," "Foires et marchés," and "Fondations." Turgot, however, maintained a certain distance from Enlightenment circles, whose religious heterodoxy he did not share, fearing that too close an association might hurt his chances for promotion. In the late 1750s, he also became an associate (although, characteristically, never a full member) of the physiocratic circle around François Quesnay, and he made provincial inspection tours with the progressive administrator Vincent de Gournay. In succeeding years, Turgot elaborated his own economic views, arguing strenuously for the removal of state controls on grain sales as a method for stabilizing prices.

Turgot got his chance to put his theories to work when he was appointed *intendant* of Limousin in 1761. Hardly the post he coveted, the intendancy nonetheless allowed him to conduct reform experiments in rationalizing tax assessments, building roads, promoting agricultural innovation, organizing poor relief, and liberalizing the grain trade. On Louis XVI's accession in 1774, Turgot was made minister of the marine. He owed this promotion partly to his reputation for honesty and competence and partly to his devout connections with the new king's chief adviser, Jean Frédéric Phélypeaux, comte de Maurepas. Almost immediately, however, he left this office to become controller-general, the monarchy's principal financial officer. To manage the government's large debts, Turgot resorted to policies he had long advocated: tax reforms, administrative economies, and especially stimulation of the economy through liberalization of the grain trade and the abolition of the guilds. Behind these changes lay a broader political vision of enlightened absolutism. In the *Mémoire sur les municipalités*, drafted with Pierre-Samuel du Pont de Nemours in 1775, Turgot pointed out that France had no constitution to coordinate its operations. To rationalize the state, Turgot proposed a system of national education and a series of assemblies composed of property-holders to advise the government. In this way, he contended, individual rights would be reconciled with the general good.

Dismissal from Office. Turgot did not stay in office long enough to institute this larger program of political reform. His economic proposals were enacted, but during a period of poor harvests and a cattle plague; the scarcities led to a peasant uprising known as the "Flour War," which was blamed on his policies. Far more responsible for Turgot's dismissal, however, was the loss of credit he suffered within the government. The parlements opposed the abolition of the guilds; the queen, an early supporter, came to resent his support for her adversary Maurepas; and Maurepas and the king were offended by Turgot's insensitive meddling in matters outside his domain, especially foreign policy. In May 1776—after less than two years in office—Turgot was dismissed, much to the dismay of his friends. He spent his last five years in retirement, following closely the unfolding of the American Revolution, with which he strongly sympathized.

Despite its setbacks, Turgot's career provides strong evidence against the common view that Enlightenment theorists were isolated from political reality. Turgot may have lacked the tact to make his ministry a success, and his policies may have been misguided; yet for fifteen years he faced the daily business of imposing his rationalist visions on often intractable forces, and his tireless devotion to government administration undoubtedly restricted his intellectual output. His most important political heir was his friend and biographer, Condorcet, who carried forward many of Turgot's views into the French Revolution.

[*See also* Condorcet, Jean-Antoine-Nicolas de Caritat; Encyclopédie; *and* Physiocracy.]

BIBLIOGRAPHY

WORKS BY TURGOT
Oeuvres de Turgot et documents le concernant. Edited by Gustave Schelle. 5 vols. Glashütten im Taunus, 1972. Comprehensive collection of Turgot's works, with extensive commentary.

WORKS ABOUT TURGOT
Cavanaugh, Gerald J. "Turgot: The Rejection of Enlightened Despotism." *French Historical Studies* 6 (1969), 31–58.

Dakin, Douglas. *Turgot and the "Ancien Régime" in France*. New York, 1965. The standard political biography, now badly in need of updating.

Faure, Edgar. *La disgrâce de Turgot*. N.P., 1961. The best study to date of Turgot's ministry.

Laugier, Lucien. *Turgot: ou, Le mythe des réformes*. Paris, 1979.
Manuel, Frank E. *The Prophets of Paris: Turgot, Condorcet, Saint-Simon, Fourier, and Comte*. New York, 1965. The chapter dealing with Turgot places him at the beginning of a distinguished line of political and social visionaries.

THOMAS E. KAISER

TUTORING. Although tutoring was not a form of education that was used exclusively by the nobility, since other social classes also employed tutors, it is indeed clear that it was one of the essential ways in which the nobility sought to transmit values of lineage, religion, and morality in the bosom of the aristocratic household. The tutor played an ambiguous role because he belonged to the domestic class, yet fulfilled a unique role. He was attached to his master as much by loyal relations of man to man as by a relation of employer to wage-earner. Jean-Jacques Rousseau, who had been an unsuccessful tutor for the Mably family, doubtless expressed best the tension and opposition that could exist between the awareness that talented tutors had of their intellectual worth, their hopes to achieve recognition, and the concrete reality of their situation, which placed them in the same social category as a mercenary or a valet.

In the eighteenth century, many theoretical treatises were written on education. They emphasized that three qualities were required of a good tutor. First, he must have a good character and morals, meaning the "virtues" of his station. This is why, in Catholic countries, the tutor was usually a young priest who had just completed his university studies. Second, he must be well educated. It was less important for him to be an erudite specialist in Latin or metaphysics than to be educated in all sciences—from classical humanities to history, geography, and mathematics. Further, he must be capable of leading and guiding young minds to understand this knowledge. Third, he had to know how to adapt to the world of his students. He had to show, as Charles Rollin, rector of the University of Paris, wrote, "a certain politeness and *savoir-vivre* everywhere so that his young pupil would learn to form his mind and manners from his influence."

Usually parents seem to have been extremely careful in their choice of a tutor for their children. They would often find one through relations or recommendations. Parents regularly solicited principals and professors of the colleges of the University of Paris to find them a proper tutor. For example, this was how Charles Rollin could work for the duke of Arenberg, who belonged to one of the most influential families in the Netherlands. Quite often, the candidates were talented young clergymen who were waiting for an ecclesiastical appointment. However, at the end of the eighteenth century, more tutors tended to come from the laity, as witnessed by the numerous French and Swiss laypeople employed by the families of the Russian aristocracy. Furthermore, in the eighteenth century, the education of the nobility tended to combine the practice of tutoring with education in a *collège*. In many establishments for the nobility, the offspring of a large family could benefit from a "private tutor," known as the "tutor of the room," who lived with them throughout their studies in the *collège*.

With this original system, based on emulation, public education could be combined with private instruction in subjects that were not taught in public courses. These private tutors enjoyed the privilege of using rooms with chimneys, while the rest of the inhabitants had to endure cold winters in frigid sleeping quarters and there contracted chilblains. The expense of this method of tutoring restricted it to those with the privilege of wealth. Such mixed methods, where the private tutor was associated with the teaching of the *collège* and with worldly teaching methods, were rather similar to methods used at Oxford University. There, tutors were usually younger than thirty years old, and were chosen after extremely careful selection by the fellows of the colleges having the largest aristocratic clientele (Christ Church, Trinity, Queen's, and Magdalen College). Further, the role of the tutor in the Grand Tour of the young aristocrat across Europe cannot be overemphasized. The trip to the Italian peninsula was especially important, as it crowned and concluded the cycle of aristocratic education. These young pupils' ability to become adults depended on the firmness or weakness of their relationship to the tutor. Of course, the success or failure of the journey also depended on the relationship the tutor had with parents, and on the authority they delegated to him. The trip was a rite of initiation into the world, in every sense of the term.

It is difficult to capture the figure of the tutor for two reasons. First, tutors were temporary and mobile. Second, most of the papers that would shed light on them are not publicly available. Tutoring was, for these brilliant young men, a period of waiting, either to enter the Republic of Letters, to become *collège* professors, or to undertake a clerical career by securing a benefice. Furthermore, for those who became tutors, it could be difficult to accept subordination to and dependence vis-à-vis parents who were privileged simply by the fact of their birth, at a time when the literary field was becoming autonomous and the "man of letters" was being born.

[*See also* Education, *subentry on* Pedagogical Thought and Practice; *and* Aristocracy, *subentry on* Cultural Contributions.]

BIBLIOGRAPHY
Becchi, E., and D. Julia. *Histoire de l'enfance en Occident*, vol. 2, *Du XVIIIᵉ siècle à nos jours*. Paris, 1998, pp. 72–85.

Bely, L. "L'élève et le monde: Essai sur l'éducation des Lumières d'après les mémoires autobiographiques du temps." *Revue d'Histoire Moderne et Contemporaine* 28 (1981), 3–35.

Fertig, L. *Die Hofmeister: Ein Beitrag zur Geschichte des Lehrerstandes und der Bürgerintelligenz.* Stuttgart, 1979.

The History of the University of Oxford, vol. 4, *Seventeenth-Century Oxford.* Edited by Nicholas Tyacke. Oxford, 1997, pp. 62–78. Vol. 5, *The Eighteenth Century.* Edited by L. S. Sutherland and L. G. Mitchell. Oxford, 1986, pp. 227–268.

Motley, M. *Becoming a French Aristocrat: The Education of the French Nobility, 1580–1715.* Princeton, N.J., 1990.

Roche, D. "Le précepteur dans la noblesse française: Instituteur privilégié ou domestique." In *Problèmes d'histoire de l'éducation: Actes des séminaires organisés par l'École Française de Rome et l'Università di Roma-La Sapienza.* Rome, 1988, pp. 13–36.

DOMINIQUE JULIA

Translated from French by Susan Romanosky

TYRANNY. *See* Despotism *and* Political Philosophy.

TYSSOT DE PATOT, SIMON (1655–1738), Huguenot freethinker, mathematician, and author.

Born in London, Tyssot was reared in France until 1664, when his family moved to Delft, in Holland. He finally settled in Deventer (1680), where he initially ran a French school; he was eventually appointed professor of mathematics at that city's École Illustre (1699). He made his most significant contribution to the Enlightenment with the anonymous publication of an imaginary voyage, *Voyages et avantures de Jaques Massé,* dated 1710 but probably published in the Hague between 1714 and 1717.

The imaginary voyage may be defined as a heuristic fictional tale, purporting to be the story of a real journey, inspired by the published travel journals of true voyages of discovery of other countries and civilizations undertaken by Europeans since the Renaissance. As is characteristic of the genre, *Jaques Massé* is a first-person narrative with a circular narrative structure, which facilitates the ideological confrontation of the narrator's value system, or that of the culture of origin, with those of the places visited and the people met or discovered. The eponymous narrator-traveler leaves his country of origin, France, and undertakes three journeys, two of which end in shipwreck. The second occurs at sixty degrees longitude, and forty-four degrees latitude, that is, on the coast of the Austral Land so beloved of imaginary voyages in the early modern period. The ten chapters devoted to the description of this new world contain two robinsonade episodes (desert island experiences, in this case collective rather than individual) and the discovery of a utopian society by Massé and a fellow crew member who journey to the interior.

Massé describes the rational, geometrical topography of this utopia, and, as he sees it, its equally rational pyramidal political structure, which culminates in a paternalistic and benign monarchy. He also dwells on the ceremonies and customs of the inhabitants, their religion (which is deist), and the rudiments of their language, which he presents as ideal because it is logical and simple and therefore easy to learn. Tyssot is less interested in the imaginative creation of a utopia, however, than in using Massé's encounters with key political and religious figures in this world and on his other journeys (the Wandering Jew, a Protestant surgeon, a Chinese sage, and a French atheist) to develop a rationalist critique of the Jewish and Christian revelation which is as virulent as any to be found in the clandestine manuscripts of the time. The Creation, the resurrection, the immateriality and immortality of the soul, miracles, Hell, and the biblical narratives are dismissed as fables and pious frauds. The Chinese sage (a professed deist and disciple of Spinoza) and the French atheist both recommend toleration and conformity to the dominant religion. The French atheist also tells Massé the fable of the bees, a patent satire of the biblical redemption narrative. It was only the anonymity of *Jaques Massé* that protected Tyssot from official censure. In 1726, he published under his own name two volumes of selected letters which contained milder expressions of similar ideas. The conservative Calvinist magistrates and church leaders of Deventer proceeded against him and, in the summer of 1727, he was dismissed from his position at the École Illustre on charges of blasphemy, impiety, and Spinozism. They could do nothing, however, to prevent his considerable appeal to eighteenth-century readers in France, England, and Germany, where editions and translations of *Jaques Massé* were published, to be read by, among others, Montesquieu, Swift, and Voltaire.

[*See also* Novel; Spinoza, Baruch de; Toleration; Travel Literature; *and* Utopianism.]

BIBLIOGRAPHY

Knowlson, J. R. "The Ideal Languages of Veiras, Foigny and Tyssot de Patot." *Journal of the History of Ideas* 24 (1963), 269–278.

McKee, D. R. *Simon Tyssot de Patot and the Seventeenth-Century Background of Critical Deism.* Baltimore, London, and Oxford, 1941. Dated but still useful survey.

Racault, M. *L'utopie narrative en France et en Angleterre, 1675–1761.* Oxford, 1991. The most authoritative critical survey of imaginary voyages with a particular focus on utopias, pp. 395–405.

Rosenberg, A. *Tyssot de Patot and His Work (1655–1738).* The Hague, 1972. Still the most authoritative biography.

Tyssot de Patot, S. *Voyages et avantures de Jaques Massé.* Edited by A. Rosenberg. Paris and Oxford, 1993. A modern transcript of the text with a short introduction, but unfortunately no annotation.

RUTH WHELAN

U

ULTRAMONTANISM. The word "ultramontane" means "beyond the mountains," and specifically south of the Alps. In the eighteenth century, it took on a polemical connotation, especially in France, Austria, and Germany, where it was used to designate Catholic groups in Europe, and particularly in Italy, that sided with Rome in contemporary political and ecclesiological controversies and that defended a form of Catholicism that was pro-papal, authoritarian, and also anti-patriotic, inasmuch as it undermined the prerogatives of the state.

In France, the ultramontane and pro-Jesuit faction led the battle against the Gallican tradition and against Jansenism. The defeat of the Jansenists was sealed by the papal bull *Unigenitus* (8 September 1713), but this in turn gave impetus to French episcopalism (defense of the independent rights of a bishop) and parochialism (defense of the independent rights of a parish), and it opened the way to the bitter political-religious conflicts of the second half of the century. Ultramontanists fought on two fronts: externally, against modern culture; and within the Catholic world, to secure papal primacy once and for all.

The publication at Frankfurt in 1763 of *De statu ecclesiae et legitima potestate Romani Pontificis* (On the Status of the Church and the Legitimate Powers of the Roman Pontiff) by Justinius Febronius (the pseudonym of Johann Nikolaus von Hontheim), which demanded collegiality in church government and affirmed the rights of bishops, provoked a determined reaction from Rome and the ultramontanists. In numerous polemical works maintaining the rights of the Holy See, Italian authors such as Pietro Ballerini, Tommaso Maria Mamachi, Francesco Antonio Zaccaria, and Giovanni Marchetti distinguished themselves. There was also an outburst of diplomatic activity and correspondence that activated an international network of learned authors and ecclesiastics who were faithful to Rome and had the capacity to make up for the loss caused by the suppression of the Jesuits in 1773.

For the defenders of papal primacy, the real battle was not so much against the Enlightenment as against the enemy within, those Catholic authors who gave voice to the drive for reform and attacked the ecclesiastical structure on institutional and disciplinary planes. In central and northern Europe, the strands of this international network were woven by one of the outstanding personalities of ultramontanism, Giuseppe Garampi, papal nuncio at Vienna from 1776 to 1785 (when he was made a cardinal). Garampi established a genuine espionage system within the imperial court and sought in every way to block reformist Habsburg policy toward the church and to have the imperial censor ban books and authors critical of the papacy. His first success was a retraction from von Hontheim himself in 1778. He collaborated closely with authors abroad, even sending funds for the publication of works by scholars such as Franz Heinrich Beck; Jean Pey, author of pro-curial works such as *La verité de la religion, prouvée à un déiste* (The Truth of Religion Demonstrated to a Deist, Paris, 1770) and *De l'autorité des deux puissances* (On the Authority of the Two Powers, Strasbourg, 1780); the ex-Jesuit journalist François-Xavier de Feller, author of the *Journal historique et littéraire*: and the anti-Enlightenment writer Nicolas-Sylvestre Bergier, author of *Traité historique et dogmatique de la vraie religion, avec la réfutation des erreurs* (Historical and Dogmatic Treatise on True Religion, with a Refutation of Errors, Paris, 1780).

The turning point for ultramontanism came in the 1780s, which saw a jurisdictionalist and anti-ecclesiastical offensive by the European sovereigns, most notably as Josephinism, a fundamental shift to a policy of radical reform in Austria. This attempt to create a national church within the ambit of the Habsburg monarchy was imitated in Tuscany at the initiative of the grand duke Leopold and with the support of Italian Jansenists. The first response from Rome was an attempt at negotiation, with the visit of Pius VI to Vienna. When that failed, Rome adopted a harder line, manifested in a burst of ultramontanist publication to spread pro-papal propaganda. A frontal challenge to the papacy came from Josephinist literature, culminating in the publication at Vienna in 1782 of the anti-papal pamphlet *Was ist der Papst?* (What Is the Pope?) by Joseph Valentin Eybel, the high point of eighteenth-century episcopalist theory.

In response, ultramontanists deployed all the structures organizing intellectual life and guiding public opinion, especially the press, in a militant campaign. Indeed, one of the most effective strategies of Catholic reconquest adopted by the ultramontane wing against the onslaught of the modern world was to turn the weapons used by the Enlightenment back on it, and subsequently on the French Revolution. The *Giornale Ecclesiastico di Roma* (Ecclesiastical Journal of Rome, 1785–1798) was the first periodical publication of a semi-official kind to speak for the Roman Curia, faithfully relaying its directives against the adversaries of Roman Catholicism while seeking to bring Catholics sympathetic to reform movements back to support of the pope. The same purpose was served by the Accademia di Religione Cattolica, founded at Rome in 1800, and by the revival, with a conservative and anti-modern twist, of the kind of secret society typified by the Freemasons—for example, the ultramontane "Christian friendship" societies.

Yet another instrument of the determined strategy of curial ultramontanism, one fully supported by Pius VI, was an enhanced emphasis on popular religiosity. Spectacular and emotional devotions like the Via Crucis, the Sacred Heart of Jesus, and the devotion to Mary, as well as new saints' cults, reinforced the hegemony of the church over society by strengthening its bond with the lower classes and with women.

With the French Revolution, ultramontanism's attempt to influence public opinion took a vehement anti-revolutionary form, supporting Rome's condemnation of the Civil Constitution of the Clergy (1791), which was portrayed as an offshoot of Jansenism, and of the synod held in 1794 at Pistoia in Tuscany, which attempted to empower parishes. The ultramontane campaign progressed to the view that there was an anti-Catholic plot, a view spread by the ex-Jesuit Augustin Barruel in his *Histoire du clergé de France pendant la Revolution* (History of the Clergy of France during the Revolution, London, 1796).

A strain of thought emphasizing the political and social utility of religion, already found in anti-Enlightenment apologetics, was also gaining ground. The church was portrayed as indispensable because of its capacity to reinforce all forms of government by supplying legitimacy, security, stability, and social cohesion. This proposition—along with support for the absolute authority of the pope from a theocratic perspective, a program to reconstruct the moral and social order that had been subverted by the Enlightenment and the Revolution, and heightened devotionalism—would be relaunched during the Bourbon restoration by the reactionary and intransigent Catholicism of the nineteenth century, and in the writings of Joseph de Maistre, Albrecht von Haller, Louis de Bonald, and Félicité Lamennais. The *Syllabus of Errors* (1864) and the dogma of papal infallibility proclaimed by Pius IX (1870) would be the eventual outcome.

[*See also* Austria; French Revolution; Josephinism; Pius VII; Revealed Religion; *and* Roman Catholicism.]

BIBLIOGRAPHY

Caffiero, Marina. *La politica della santità: Nascita di un culto nell'età dei Lumi*. Rome and Bari, 1996.

Caffiero, Marina. *Religione e modernità in Italia (secoli XVII–XIX)*. Pisa and Rome, 2000.

Caffiero, Marina. "Pio VI." In *Enciclopedia dei Papi*, vol. 2. Rome, 2000.

Menozzi, Daniele. "Tra riforma e restaurazione: Dalla crisi della società cristiana al mito della cristianità medievale (1758–1848)." In *La Chiesa e il potere politico dal Medioevo all'età contemporanea*, edited by Giorgio Chittolini and Giovanni Miccoli, pp. 767–806. Turin, 1986.

Omodeo, Adolfo. *Studi sull'età della Restaurazione*. Turin, 1970.

Pignatelli, Giuseppe. *Aspetti della propaganda cattolica a Roma da Pio VI a Leone XII*. Rome, 1974.

Rosa, Mario. *Politica e religione nel '700 europeo*. Florence, 1974.

Vanysacker, Dries. *Cardinal Giuseppe Garampi (1725–1792): An Enlightened Ultramontane*. Brussels and Rome, 1995.

Verucci, Guido. *Félicité Lamennais: Dal Cattolicesimo autoritario al radicalismo democratico*. Naples, 1963.

Verucci, Guido. *I cattolici e il liberalismo: Dalle "Amicizie cristiane" al modernismo*. Padua, 1968.

MARINA CAFFIERO
Translated by William McCuaig

UNIGENITUS. *See* Jansenism *and* Revealed Religion.

UNITARIANISM. *See* Socinianism.

UNIVERSITIES. For most of the eighteenth century there were some 150 universities in Europe and a further fifteen or so in the Americas, including the university colleges in the English colonies. Apart from the forty or so medieval foundations, nearly all had been founded in the period from 1400 to 1700, especially between the years 1550 and 1650. In an era that witnessed the growth of the territorial and confessional state, even the most petty prince wanted his own university in which the servants of state and church could be appropriately reared. By 1700 the early-modern university map was all but full. In the Age of the Enlightenment a number of existing universities, such as Edinburgh, rose to a novel intellectual prominence, but the only significant foundations outside Russia and the new United States were at Halle (1693–1694) and Göttingen (1733, 1737). The first Russian university was founded at Moscow in 1755; Alexander I added another five in 1803. The coming of independence to Britain's North American colonies resulted in a plethora of new foundations over the following decades, notably Thomas Jefferson's University of Virginia, opened in 1825.

The University System. Virtually all universities in the eighteenth century were independent, corporate institutions, theoretically confessionally closed and exclusively

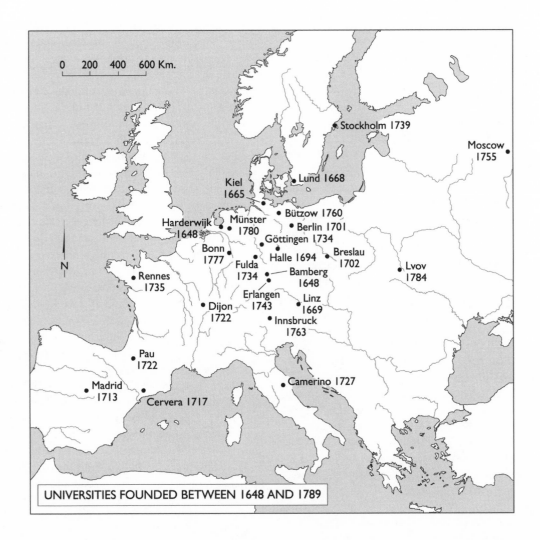

UNIVERSITIES FOUNDED BETWEEN 1648 AND 1789

male. Uniformly, their raison d'être was teaching rather than research. By tradition universities specialized in providing tuition in one or more of the four recognized sciences—philosophy, theology, law, and medicine. Until the end of the sixteenth century universities had had a monopoly in science teaching, but in the eighteenth century they faced increasing competition from rival institutions, such as the English and Irish Dissenting Academies. What differentiated universities from rival centers of education was their privilege of granting degrees. As a degree was increasingly an essential passport to a career in the learned professions all over the European world, this monopoly right ensured universities a competitive edge in the educational marketplace. Even so, few universities were of any significant size, which would suggest that provision was excessive. Oxford, Cambridge, Naples, Paris, Halle, and Leipzig were among only a handful of universities in the middle of the century boasting five hundred students or more; Salamanca was probably the largest with a roll of twenty-three hundred.

Many universities were small institutions with fewer than one hundred students.

The universities of the eighteenth century divide into two groups according to their relative commitment to philosophy. Historically, philosophy was the quintessential university science. Treated as propaedeutic, or preparatory, the study of its four component parts—logic, ethics, physics or natural philosophy, and metaphysics—was supposed to provide the analytical tools and conceptual apparatus needed to pursue the three "higher" professional sciences. In consequence, philosophy or arts was usually the most populous, if not the most prestigious, faculty. In most Catholic universities, however, philosophy's wings had been seriously clipped by 1700. All over Europe most university entrants had previously attended feeder schools, such as England's Eton or Winchester, where they were principally instructed in the classical humanities and taught to read, write, and speak Latin fluently. In Catholic countries, however, where these schools were generally run by the regular orders, especially the Jesuits, the curriculum had been extended to include philosophy. As a result, many faculties of arts in Catholic universities ceased to have any pedagogical function and became simple examining boards. In Protestant states, in contrast, university arts courses of three to four years' duration continued to flourish and usually included the study of rhetoric and higher Greek as well as the four philosophical sciences. Indeed, in England and its North American colonies, where entry to the learned careers was not yet professionalized, the curriculum was almost exclusively arts based.

Irrespective of this fundamental structural division, teaching methods and examination procedures were much the same across the university system. The principal language of the classroom and the examination hall was Latin—hence the need for long years of prior instruction in the tongue before beginning the study of philosophy. Tuition was normally given through hour-long lectures. For half the time, the professor would read from a prepared text at dictation speed; for the last thirty minutes he would extemporize, developing the more abstruse and difficult points. Lectures were mainly composed in a time-honored scholastic format around a difficult *quaestio*, or question. In conveying theoretical knowledge, it was not customary to use visual aids, even a blackboard. Professors seldom allowed time for questions. At the beginning of the eighteenth century, only students who lived in residential colleges or seminaries, or who had paid for private tuition outside the formal curriculum, had access to more informal forms of learning.

Examinations universally took the form of question and answer sessions before a jury and the oral defense of a dissertation before a graduand's teachers and peers. As professors frequently depended heavily on examination fees to boost their income, these jousts were serious occasions in only a handful of universities. In law faculties especially, the questioning was perfunctory, the theses prepared by a professor or copied, and success assured. At Cambridge in the course of the century an attempt was made at least to differentiate candidates by dividing arts graduands into "pass" and "honors" men, and to rank the latter according to performance. At about the same time, Paris—one of the few major Catholic universities with a functioning faculty of arts—moved to secure the quality of its arts teaching by insisting that professors, in addition to taking a degree, henceforth pass a written examination, the first of its kind, called the *agrégation*. These, though, were exceptionally bold and innovative gestures in a notoriously venal world.

Criticisms of the System. Not surprisingly, in the eighteenth century, an age that placed a premium on utility and merit and looked askance at corruption, the universities and their feeder schools were the target of growing criticism. Denis Diderot and Jean Le Rond d'Alembert in France, Vicesimus Knox in England, and Joachim Heinrich Campe in Germany were just a few of the educational pundits who viewed the system with a jaundiced eye. The reformers were unconcerned that the universities were almost exclusively teaching institutions. To the extent that the critics had a concept of research, they associated knowledge creation with a separate institution, the fast-proliferating, state-protected learned academy. What they objected to principally was the curriculum and its method of delivery. On the one hand, critics objected to the predominance of Latin as a medium of communication and agitated for its replacement by the vernacular. Thereby, it was argued, the feeder schools could devote their time to more useful subjects, such as modern languages and mathematics. On the other hand, reformers wanted the university curriculum to become more practical and relevant. As, in their opinion, much of the traditional content of logic, ethics, and metaphysics was arid and pointless, they demanded that the philosophy course give primary emphasis to the work of the moderns in the natural sciences. Similarly, professors of theology, law, and medicine were urged to abandon their emphasis on theoretical speculation and concentrate on inculcating their charges with practical and certain knowledge, wherever possible using more stimulating methods of teaching. As Diderot's reform plan, presented to Catherine the Great in 1775–1776, makes particularly clear, the enlightened university was not to be an ivory tower but a school for good and useful citizens.

Although these Enlightened critics gained the ear of many rulers and their advisers in the second half of the century, there was no fundamental change to the system before the French Revolution. Rulers preferred to establish alternative centers of practical learning—surgical colleges, military academies, mining schools, and so on—rather than subject the universities to thoroughgoing reform.

It would be wrong, however, to conclude that in consequence universities in the eighteenth century were moribund institutions immune to contemporary intellectual developments. A number of leading philosophers in Protestant countries—notably Adam Smith (1723–1790) and Immanuel Kant (1724–1804)—were university professors. Even if they kept their most radical and original thoughts out of their lectures, the fact that they were able and content to occupy an academic post for a large part of their life suggests that some universities at least were more dynamic institutions than contemporary polemic maintained. In fact, within its traditional corporative and confessional carapace, the system as a whole changed quite significantly over the century.

Changes in the System. In most, if not all, Protestant countries the universities became much more open institutions as the century progressed. In the early part of the century, in both the Protestant and Catholic worlds, the universities were dominated by doctrinaire faculty theologians who allowed their colleagues in other disciplines only a limited freedom of expression. The Arian William Whiston (1667–1752) was ejected from the Lucasian chair of mathematics at Anglican Cambridge in 1710; the philosopher Christian Wolff (1679–1754) was forced to leave Lutheran Halle in 1731 because of his admiration for Confucian ethics. By the middle of the century, however, the climate was very different. When the new Hanoverian university of Göttingen was founded in 1733, it was specifically established as a multiconfessional institution. Although it boasted a faculty of theology, its Lutheran members were forbidden to fashion and enforce a party line. According to the 1737 statutes, professors in all faculties could choose their own textbooks and organize their courses as they pleased, provided they taught nothing contrary to the Christian religion, morals, and the state. Other Protestant universities never erected academic freedom into a statutory fact, but the principle quickly gained tacit acceptance everywhere.

In consequence, the confessional and regional character of the most open Protestant universities was steadily eroded. Göttingen in particular attracted a stream of dynamic and talented teachers, such as the botanist and physiologist Albrecht von Haller (1708–1777), the naturalist Johann Friedrich Blumenbach (1752–1840), and the electrical experimenter and geologist Georg Christoph Lichtenberg (1742–1799). So too did the Scottish universities, especially Edinburgh, whose faculty included three of the leading members of the European Enlightenment, the moral philosopher and economist Adam Smith, the moral philosopher and historian Adam Ferguson (1723–1816), and the philosopher of the mind Dugald Stewart (1753–1828). Unlike most university professors in the past, such figures were active researchers. They helped to develop a new concept of the university as a center of knowledge creation, not just a center of learning. Göttingen soon had its own scientific society with its own published transactions, distinct from the Elector's academy to which the professors also belonged. University societies of one kind or another began to appear all over Protestant Germany, often devoted to standardizing and promoting the German vernacular as a literary language. Many were dilettante social gatherings, but some were embryonic research seminars, such as the regular meetings for prospective classics teachers organized by Friedrich August Wolf (1759–1824) at Halle at the turn of the nineteenth century. The professors, too, often played a leading role in promoting organs of enlightened sociability in the local town, such as Masonic societies and lending libraries. The most energetic, like the Helmstedt chemist Lorenz Crell, even attempted to organize their disciplinary colleagues in and out of the university world into a national community.

Transformation of the Curriculum. In both Catholic and Protestant countries, moreover, even if the university system remained relatively closed, the curriculum was everywhere slowly transformed. Although the emphasis remained primarily on aural learning and the inculcation of theoretical knowledge, the system proved highly adaptive. Across the century, especially after 1750, the universities, often on their own initiative, proved remarkably adept at meeting the challenge of the Enlightenment by integrating new material and methods of teaching within the existing curricular structure.

Accelerating change was visible at every level, even in the language teaching of the feeder schools. Although the lengthy study of Latin and Greek remained de rigueur for university entrance, grammar schools, colleges, and gymnasiums eventually accepted the need to devote some time to teaching the native vernacular, other modern languages, history, geography, and elementary mathematics. In this regard the suppression of the Jesuit Order in 1773 proved particularly decisive in Catholic countries. While their schools tended to be taken over by other regular orders, one in particular—the Piarists, prominent in eastern Europe—played an important role in broadening the curriculum.

Philosophy. The study of philosophy in and outside the faculty of arts was even more radically altered. Traditionally the course was built around the study of the Aristotelian corpus, but by the second half of the eighteenth century the Peripatetics had been largely dethroned everywhere, albeit belatedly in Poland, the Austrian empire, and on the Iberian Peninsula. In the English-speaking world at the beginning of the century, Aristotle was immediately replaced by John Locke and Isaac Newton. In the colleges and universities of France and Protestant northern Europe, on the other hand, the first part of the century saw Aristotle initially give way to Descartes. Courses in physics followed closely René Descartes's own formulation of the mechanical philosophy, while the study of logic, ethics, and metaphysics reflected the ideas of the neo-Cartesians Nicolas Malebranche and Christian Wolff. Locke's and Newton's critiques of Cartesian philosophy were almost entirely ignored. Gradually, however, philosophy courses on the Continent too came under the Englishmen's spell. First in the Netherlands, then in parts of Italy and finally, after 1760, in every part of the European world, even Spanish America, Lockean empiricism and the universal law of gravitation were adopted as the new philosophical orthodoxy.

The detailed content of the new philosophy course was continually refined in the light of contemporary research. In the second half of the century especially, professors were well informed about contemporary developments in the philosophical sciences and discussed the new material in their lectures, whatever the provenance. Active researchers among the professoriat, moreover, were seldom afraid to incorporate their original thoughts into their lessons, toned down where necessary to accommodate tender consciences. Once in the public domain, new ideas formulated in one institution quickly spread across part, if not all, of the university system.

Also, for the first time since the late Middle Ages, a number of professors became international stars. The "common sense" school of philosophy, for instance, developed by the Aberdeen professor Thomas Reid (1710–1796) and his Scottish university colleagues, did not remain confined to the Caledonian classroom but was quickly transported to the German Protestant universities; so too was Ferguson's robust development of Francis Hutcheson's moral sense theory. Even Kant's categorical imperative, initially formulated in the comparative isolation of the tiny university of Königsberg, spread quickly in the 1790s through the universities of the Holy Roman Empire (even gaining a foothold in Catholic Würzburg).

What enabled such rapid transmission was the willingness of university professors of philosophy to commit their ideas to print, a hitherto relatively uncommon phenomenon. Admittedly, enthusiastic students often played a significant role in the first stages of transmission, too. The Scottish university Enlightenment was in part popularized on the Continent by dint of the fact that Edinburgh University was visited by a growing number of foreigners, such as the Swiss Benjamin Constant in 1783–1785. Ultimately, though, what drew the young Constant and others to the "Athens of the North" was the university's rising reputation forged by the publishing record of its professors in the form of treatises and textbooks.

New teaching methods. The abandonment of Aristotle was accompanied to a certain extent by changes in the method of teaching philosophy. First, it became increasingly common for separate professors to be appointed for the moral and physical sciences, in recognition of the fact that philosophy was becoming too capacious a science for one man to master successfully. Second, in some universities, notably in Scotland, it became customary to lecture in the vernacular. Third, an important element of visual learning was introduced into the course of physics. While lectures in logic, ethics, and metaphysics continued to be taught ex cathedra, the conversion to a Newtonian natural philosophy was usually accompanied by the development of a new type of course based on experiments. This reflected the fact that students (and professors) largely lacked the mathematical expertise to follow Newton's own arguments in the *Principia*. Instead, professors adopted the practice, initiated by the Scot John Keill (1671–1721) at Oxford at the turn of the century, of demonstrating the validity of Newton's conclusions, using devices that were not always up to the task. The new physics course was colorful, but not always expertly handled. The purchase of the necessary equipment demanded a considerable outlay, especially for an electric machine—Marischal College Aberdeen in 1725–1726 tried to raise the money by public donation—and the professor, however intellectually eminent, could not always get the apparatus to work. When Jeremy Bentham attended the experimental physics course of the astronomer Nathaniel Bliss (1700–1764) at Oxford in 1763, he wrote to his father that scarcely a single experiment had been successful. Highly competent professors, such as John Anderson (1726–1796) of Glasgow or Alessandro Volta (1745–1827) of Pavia were probably few and far between.

In one country in Europe, however, Newton was never introduced to students by experiments. This was France, where the physics course remained built around the

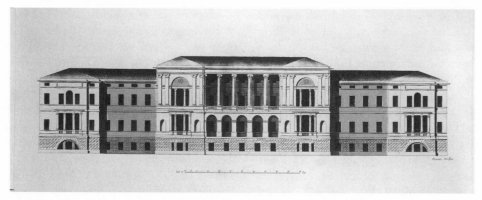

University Building. Design of the south front of the new building for the University of Edinburgh by Robert Adam (1728–1792). (Prints and Photographs Division, Library of Congress.)

traditional *dictée* until the Revolution. Colleges provided courses in experimental physics, but only in the summer months after the magisterial course was completed. In France, however, Newtonianism was taught much more rigorously because the course was mathematically based. As a result, French philosophy students had to undergo a crash course in mathematics, which took them from the elements to calculus in the space of three months, in order to prepare them for the ordeal ahead. Not surprisingly, France at the turn of the nineteenth century was the center of mathematical physics par excellence. Pierre-Simon de Laplace could never have perfected the Newtonian system and extended mathematical physics into new areas such as heat and light without the extremely sophisticated physics education he had received as a boy at the University of Caen at the hands of Christophe Gabled (1734–1782). Newton's own university, Cambridge, unique among the eighteenth-century universities of the British Isles, had a similar commitment to mathematical physics. At Cambridge, though, the sifting mechanism of the tutorial system ensured that only the brightest students were ever educated in the mysteries of higher mathematics and taken through the *Principia*.

Curricular Adjustments in the Higher Faculties. In both Catholic and Protestant states, important adjustments were gradually made to the traditional curriculum of the three higher faculties as well.

Theology. Until the turn of the nineteenth century, theology courses everywhere may have remained dedicated to the defense of confessional orthodoxy, but this did not mean that teaching remained necessarily locked in a scholastic straitjacket. At the new University of Halle, led by the Pietist August Hermann Francke, professors of theology developed a much more textually oriented course, based on the elucidation of the Bible, rather than the rational analysis of theological concepts. A similar approach was adopted in many other Protestant universities across the century, thereby stilling the criticisms that theology had become a science of words.

In Catholic universities, in contrast, scholastic theology continued to reign supreme. Even there, though, professors paid token homage to the Enlightenment god of utility: throughout the century the authors of theological manuals prided themselves on their ability to produce ever simpler and more focused justifications of their confessional stance. Moreover, across the confessional divide, professors realized that Christianity *tout court* faced a novel challenge from freethinking critics that had to be met. Theology courses therefore began to include the study of Christian apologetics, which demonstrated the limits of natural religion and the necessity and plausibility of Christian Revelation. In the support classes provided by the Paris seminary of Saint-Sulpice for students at the Sorbonne, seminars were even conducted on passages from Georges-Louis Leclerc de Buffon, Jean-Jacques Rousseau, and Diderot.

Law. Similarly limited, if more far-reaching, changes occurred in the faculties of law. If the staple diet of a law student remained Roman law (along with canon law in Catholic countries), there was a novel recognition that future barristers needed classroom training in the actual laws of the land. As a result, from Spain to Scotland courses delivered significantly in the vernacular were instituted in customary and state law. In German-speaking territories the curricular changes were particularly extensive. Thanks in particular to the influence of the historicist legal studies of the Halle professor Christian Thomasius (1655–1728), first Protestant northern Germany and then the Catholic south came to accept the limited importance of Roman law for the development of the institutions of the Holy Roman Empire. This devalued the traditional belief that civil law was the law of reason against which all other legal systems could be judged, and encouraged not only the establishment of courses in specifically German public law but also the separate study of natural law and human rights.

Thomasius too helped promote the completely novel university discipline of *Staatswissenschaft*, or cameralism. Aware that many law students would end up as government officials, and committed to the quasi-Aristotelian idea that the state should be a vehicle for moral and material improvement, he believed that legal training should also include a course in economic and fiscal management. The first separate chairs in cameralism were founded at the Prussian universities of Halle and Frankfurt on the Oder in 1727, and the new science given its fullest statement by Johann Heinrich Gottlob Justi (1717–1771) at Göttingen. Cameralism, though, was very much a German academic fad. Elsewhere in Europe, chairs in the discipline were only founded in Sweden.

Medicine. Changes in medical teaching were far more extensive. At the beginning of the century most medical faculties were dormant: there were only a handful of dynamic faculties, notably Padua, Paris, Montpellier, and Leiden. A century later, however, medicine had become an entrenched subject in many more universities, a reflection of the growing demand for trained physicians in an age obsessed with its health. In the second half of the century there were additional important centers of medical learning at Halle, Göttingen, Edinburgh, Vienna, and Valencia, and medical schools were being established in even the most isolated parts of the European world. The first chair of medicine in North America was established in 1765 at the College of Philadelphia, and even the University of Buda (formerly at Trnava) had a faculty from 1769.

Although the bias of the medical curriculum remained heavily theoretical everywhere, its epistemological underpinning underwent a complete revolution. Like the course in philosophy, medicine in the last decades of the seventeenth century was still in the grip of its classical past: courses virtually everywhere were principally inspired by the ideas of Galen. Within a few decades, however, professors of medicine had embraced the mechanical philosophy as warmly as their philosophical colleagues and aligned their teaching with the dominant medical paradigm outside the classroom.

On the other hand, beginning in the middle of the century, they too had their Newtonian epiphany. Increasing numbers rejected a mechanical model of the human body as simplistic and experientially untenable, argued that organic and inert matter operated according to separate laws, and came out in favor of the medical doctrine of vitalism. Unlike iatromechanism, vitalism was a medical philosophy created inside the university system. As researchers and theoreticians, medical professors across the European world played an important role in exposing the limitations of mechanism and devising an alternative model. The discovery of irritability by the Göttingen professor Albrecht von Haller helped provide empirical support to the vitalist critique, and Paul-Joseph Barthez (1734–1806) at Montpellier and William Cullen (1710–1790) at Edinburgh gave it theoretical coherence.

The medical faculties were also notable for the space they afforded visual learning. By the end of the sixteenth century the leading medical centers were already giving practical courses in anatomy, botany, surgery, and pharmacy. Even a century later, however, such courses were not commonplace, and facilities could be poor. At Paris, for instance, faculty doctors anatomized in the open air until a wooden amphitheater was built in 1617. In the eighteenth century, in contrast, as the number of functioning faculties expanded, so did the commitment to practical learning. Anatomies were even performed regularly at the hitherto dormant medical faculty of the University of Mexico beginning in the 1770s. Furthermore, the range of practical courses offered was frequently extended to include the new disciplines of chemistry and natural history. In German universities, for instance, there were twenty-eight medical professors entrusted with teaching chemistry by 1780. By the final quarter of the eighteenth century even official courses in clinical medicine attached to local hospitals were being established in a handful of faculties, notably Edinburgh, Pavia, and Vienna.

However, the significance of these developments should not be overstated. Throughout the century the practical medical sciences were seen as descriptive rather than analytical disciplines. They were taught independently of the theoretical meat of the course, treated as being of marginal importance, and seldom examined. If a number of professors—notably Cullen and Joseph Black (1728–1799) at Edinburgh—developed their experimental chemistry course into the novel analytical study of the structure of matter, they were exceptional. Furthermore, the practical courses were often poorly taught. Although a number of professors in these practical disciplines were highly creative scientists who added more than most university professors to the sum of knowledge—one thinks of the botanist Carolus Linnaeus (1707–1778) at Uppsala or the Leiden anatomist Bernard Siegfried Albinus (1697–1770)—this was frequently not the case. As the practical courses were of a low status, they tended to be taught by the most junior professors. In the mid-eighteenth century Gabriel-François Venel (1723–1775) was the most skillful chemist in France: at the Montpellier faculty, however, his seniority dictated that he lecture on hygiene. Above all, however important the role of the practical courses in a given faculty, students almost never had the opportunity for the hands-on learning so prized in the Age of the Enlightenment. As a result, many medical graduates received their most valuable practical training, especially in bedside care, from the plethora of private courses that sprang up in large European cities such as London and Paris to fill the gap.

Systemic Changes Following the French Revolution. From what has been said, it is clear that the universities played a more positive role in the Enlightenment than their contemporary critics allowed. Although they fell short of the philosophe ideal, at the very least they eventually accommodated key aspects of Enlightenment ideology within the curriculum and thereby aided the popularization and even the crystallization of the movement. In the maelstrom of 1789, however, accommodation counted for nothing. When the overthrow of the French ancien régime opened up unparalleled opportunities for the wholesale reform of all institutions on Enlightened lines, the revolutionaries were quick to turn their attention to higher education. Under the chairmanship of Charles-Maurice de Talleyrand-Périgord, the educational committee of the National Assembly drew up a proposal that envisaged completely abolishing the existing university system of higher faculties and replacing it with a series of independent professional schools. Even if the Talleyrand plan was never implemented, it was the inspiration behind a series of governmental measures over the next two decades. In September 1793 the French universities and their feeder colleges were abolished, while in the winter of 1794–1795 new professional schools in medicine and in officer and teacher training (the École Polytechnique and the École Normale) were opened with suitably enlightened curricula and French as the classroom language. Napoleon continued the rebuilding process. Although he put an end to attempts to create a new type of secondary school dedicated to the teaching of mathematics and natural science, and reemphasized the value of a classical education for the young, he remained opposed to the reconstitution of the traditional university. Thus, in 1802 the emperor established a number of independent law schools. Then in 1808 he founded the first separate faculties of science and letters outside Russia (where they had existed since 1803). In the same year, he created a number of Catholic and Protestant theology schools, and revived the defunct École Normale. Finally, all but the École Polytechnique and its affiliated specialist military schools were placed under one novel institutional umbrella, the Université Impériale, controlled by a civil servant.

As the French under Napoleon gradually occupied most of continental Europe, a similar hatchet was wielded against the university systems of other European states, although the edge was usually more blunt. Everywhere either universities were shut down altogether or their theology faculties closed and the remaining faculties transformed into same-site professional schools. Indeed, had Napoleon successfully established his empire, the traditional idea of a university as an integrated center of universal learning might quickly have withered. As it was, if a number of Europe's famous universities remained closed for good—notably Ximénez's Alcalá and Martin Luther's Wittenberg—the Restoration era saw the resurrection of the ancien-régime university, albeit shorn of many of its corporate privileges. Only in France did the experiment with the independent professional school take permanent root, where it lasted until the 1890s. In fact, in an important respect the real turning point in the history of the eighteenth-century university only came with Napoleon's defeat and the resurgence of Prussia's influence in northern Germany. While for twenty years the marauding French had been turning the university map of Europe upside down, a new vision of the old institution had matured in the one German state that had largely escaped long-term French occupation.

The Humboldtian University. In the traditional university, philosophy, if taught at all, had been the poor relation of the system. Immanuel Kant, who himself had done so much to revolutionize the teaching of the science in the German-speaking world of the 1790s, argued strenuously in his *Streit der Facultäten* of 1798 that philosophy should rather be elevated to the queen of the sciences. He accepted, like the French revolutionaries whom he admired, that the curriculum of the higher faculties could be supervised by the state, since the state through its duty to maintain the security of its citizens had an interest in the ideology of the professions. The state, however, had an equal duty to give professors in the philosophy faculty total freedom to pursue truth. Kant's Idealist followers

took up his cry, but developed his argument in favor of professorial autonomy to include even the theology faculty. When the Idealist Prussian minister of education, Wilhelm von Humboldt established the new University of Berlin in 1810, he created a traditional four-faculty institution, but also the first university whose professors in all faculties were statutorily expected to pursue research as well as teach. Although the moral and natural sciences continued to be lumped together under a single institutional umbrella, individual subject professors within the faculty of philosophy were free to teach what they liked, and philosophy students free to attend what classes they pleased.

Humboldt's conception of the Idealist university was never fully realized. Many universities in Germany and the rest of the European and American world gradually adopted his ideas in the following century (such as the Harvard of Charles William Eliot), but never accepted his Idealist commitment to the unity of knowledge. Within the segregated space of the research seminar, separate disciplines evolved their own research cultures under a common institutional umbrella. Nor can the University of Berlin be seen as an Enlightenment institution. The eighteenth-century philosophes were too wedded to the institutional separation of teaching and research for the Humboldtian ideal to be the direct inspiration of their critique. On the other hand, the secular, freethinking Humboldtian university was an ideal environment in which Enlightenment values could flourish. More permanent and capacious than the salon, less utilitarian than the academy, the Humboldtian university was an institution the philosophes desperately needed to turn Kant's "Age of Enlightenment" into an "enlightened age." It is appropriate that a professor who spent his entire life in Königsberg, the one giant of the Enlightenment who made the university his permanent adult home and from within its confines keenly recognized the Enlightenment's limited purchase on contemporary society, should have perceived how an archetypal ancien-régime institution might hold the key to modernity.

[*See also* Diderot, Denis; Education, *subentries on* Pedagogical Thought and Practice *and* Reform and Experiments; Humboldt, Wilhelm von; Medicine, *subentry on* Theories of Medicine; *and* Philosophy.]

BIBLIOGRAPHY

GENERAL

Julia, Dominique, Jacques Revel, and Roger Chartier, eds. *Les Universités européennes du XVIᵉ au XVIIIᵉ siècle: histoire sociale des populations étudiantes.* 2 vols. Paris, 1986–1989.

Leith, James A., ed. "Facets of Education in the Eighteenth Century." *Studies on Voltaire and the Eighteenth Century*, 167. Oxford, 1977.

Ridder-Symoens, Hilde de, ed. *A History of the University in Europe*, vol. 2, *Universities in Early Modern Europe (1500–1800).* Cambridge, 1996.

BRITISH ISLES

Bill, E. G. W. *Education at Christ Church, Oxford, 1600–1800*. Oxford, 1988.

Gascoigne, John. *Cambridge in the Age of the Enlightenment: Science, Religion, and Politics from the Restoration to the French Revolution*. Cambridge, 1989.

McDowell, R. B., and D. A. Webb. *Trinity College Dublin, 1592–1952: An Academic History*. Dublin, 1982.

Midgeley, Graham. *University Life in Eighteenth-Century Oxford*. New Haven, Conn., 1996.

Rosner, Lisa M. *Medical Education in the Age of Improvement: Edinburgh Students and Apprentices, 1760–1826*. Edinburgh, 1991.

Searby, Peter. *A History of the University of Cambridge (1750–1870)*. Cambridge, 1997.

Sutherland, L. S., and L. G. Mitchell, eds. *The History of the University of Oxford*, vol. 5, *The Eighteenth Century*. Oxford, 1986.

Wood, Paul B. *The Aberdeen Enlightenment: The Arts Curriculum in the Eighteenth Century*. Aberdeen, Scotland, 1993.

FRANCE

Brockliss, L. W. B. *French Higher Education in the Seventeenth and Eighteenth Centuries: A Cultural History*. Oxford, 1987.

GERMANY

Hammerstein, N. *Jus und Historie: Ein Beitrag zur Geschichte des Historischen Denkens an Deutschen Universitäten im Spaten 17 und im 18 Jahrhundert*. Göttingen, Germany, 1972.

La Vopa, Anthony J. *Grace, Talent and Merit: Poor Students, Clerical Careers and Professional Ideology in Eighteenth-Century Germany*. Cambridge, 1988.

McClelland, Charles E. *State, Society, and University in Germany, 1700–1914*. Cambridge, 1980.

NETHERLANDS

Frijhoof, W. Th. M. *La Societe Neerlandaise et ses Graudes, 1575–1814*. Amsterdam, 1981.

Ruestow, E. G. *Physics at Seventeenth and Eighteenth-Century Leiden*. The Hague, 1973.

Vanpaemel, G. *Echo's van een Wetenschappelijke Revolutie: De Mechanistische Natuurwetenschap aan de Leuvense Artesfaculteit (1650–1797)*. Brussels, 1986.

SPAIN

Addy, G. M. *The Enlightenment in the University of Salamanca*. Durham, N.C., 1966.

Albinea, S. *Universida e Ilustración: Valencia en la epoca de Carlos III*. Valencia, 1988.

Peset, M. and J.-L. *La Universidad Española, Siglos XVIII y XIX: Despotismo ilustrado y revolución Liberal*. Madrid, 1974.

LAURENCE BROCKLISS

USURY. *See* Economic Thought.

UTILITARIANISM. Utilitarianism is the normative moral theory according to which an action is morally right if and only if the consequences of that action produce the greatest good for the greatest number of people. It is ultimately an alternative to both rationalism and sentimentalism in ethics and an attempt to put ethics on an empirical basis.

Defining Utilitarianism. Utilitarianism focuses primarily on the question of what makes any kind of act morally right or wrong and is concerned only secondarily with the evaluation of the moral agent and his character. For this reason it is little very interested in the motives of the agent. Though some have spoken of "egoistic utilitarianism" and distinguished it from "universalistic utilitarianism," this seems to be a mistake simply because the focus is on the acts and not on the motives. Put differently, utilitarianism is an act-centered theory and not an agent-centered theory.

Furthermore, it is a kind of consequentialist, or teleological, theory, for which the morality of an act does not consist in any intrinsic quality of the act, but in what follows from it. If the consequences lead to more good than bad (or tend toward leading to more good than bad), the act is considered good; if the reverse is the case, then it is bad. This is sometimes called the consequentialist principle. Utilitarians tend to be hedonists, that is, thinkers who define good as pleasure and evil as pain. This is sometimes called the hedonist principle and the greatest happiness principle is said to be a combination of the consequentialist and the hedonist principles. Utilitarians need not be hedonists, however. Indeed, many modern utilitarians have moved away from such a simple view. One might consider things other than pleasure as intrinsically good, and there are, for instance, ideal, welfare, and even motive utilitarians.

The most famous utilitarian is John Stuart Mill (1806–1873). He may be said to have formulated the best-known and most influential statement of the utilitarian position. He counted himself among the "creed" that accepts "utility" or the "greatest happiness principle" as the foundation of morals, considering actions right in proportion to the degree to which they tend to promote happiness and considering them wrong as they tend to promote the reverse of happiness. Mill thought that he was the first to use the word "utilitarian" in ethics, adapting it from a passage in John Galt's *Annals of the Parish* (1821), in which Galt warned his parishioners not to secede from Christianity to become Utilitarians, because Christianity taught them to do everything that the "newfangled doctrine of utility" pretended. Mill apparently did not know that Jeremy Bentham had already used the word "utilitarianism" in 1809 in a letter to Pierre-Étienne-Louis Dumont. Whatever the origins of the word, however, Mill did not think he was formulating a new theory but that he was developing what many writers from Epicurus to Bentham had already tried to say.

Neither Thomas Hobbes (1588–1679) nor Bernard Mandeville (1670–1733) was a utilitarian, even if some, such as Adam Smith, attributed such a theory to them. Both put forward a form of egoism that is opposed to the altruism presupposed by utilitarian theories. Still, since utility played such a central role for both Hobbes and Mandeville in moral philosophy, they are also important in this context. In their view, people enter into the social contract because it is ultimately useful to them. They want to live in peace and security, and the government is given the power to institute and enforce laws because this is better than life in the state of nature. *The Fable of the Bees* (1714, enl. ed. 1723, 1728), an enlarged version of his poem *The Grumbling Hive* (1705), became the target of many defenders of virtue in the eighteenth century. Mandeville claimed that the most important motive within a commercial and industrial society is the self-seeking effort of individuals. "Private vices are public benefits." Though his moral theory tends toward a moral sense theory, his claim that utility or public benefit was a most important consideration in discussion of moral and political matters makes him a precursor of utilitarianism.

Enlightenment Utilitarianism. During the period of the Enlightenment, and indeed throughout most of the eighteenth century, there were several well-known philosophers who accepted a version of utilitarianism. Thus, by 1700, Leibniz had already stated the "greatest happiness principle" very clearly: "To act in accordance with supreme reason is to act in such a manner that the greatest quantity of good available is obtained for the greatest multitude possible and that as much felicity is diffused as the reason of things can bear" (quoted according to Joachim Hruschka, "The Greatest Happiness Principle"). We cannot be sure whether Leibniz accepted this theory or not. In any case, the moral philosophy of Christian Wolff and his followers also has definite utilitarian aspects and was for that reason criticized by Immanuel Kant.

The most important developments concerning utilitarianism, however, took place in Great Britain. Francis Hutcheson, who may have been influenced by Leibniz, argued in *An Inquiry into the Original of Our Ideas of Beauty and Virtue* (1725) that it was possible to develop a felicific calculus or a universal rule that would allow us "to compute the morality of any actions with all their circumstances." The first axiom states that the moral importance of an agent or "the quantity of public good he produces" has to do with the relation of his benevolence and his abilities. The second maintains that when the abilities of two agents are equal, the moments of public good are proportioned to the degree of benevolence of the agent and if the degree of benevolence is the same, then the quantities of good are identical with the abilities. The third axiom amounts to the claim that the greater the ability, the smaller the virtue exhibited "in any given moment of good produced," whereas the fourth compares the consequences of actions, considering whether they benefit

ourselves and are harmful to the public, harmful for ourselves but good to the public, useful to ourselves and others, or harmful to ourselves and others.

This discussion was not well received, however. Since it was in many ways no more than an illustration of a certain kind of reasoning and perhaps even an aside, Hutcheson eliminated it in the third edition of 1729. To count Hutcheson among the utilitarians would clearly be a mistake, in any case. His concerns ultimately lay elsewhere. Morality is not simply founded on considerations of utility or the consequences of our actions. We must also consider the moral sense or our moral sentiments. An action may be formally good when it tends to contribute to the good of society, but it is formally good only when it flows from good affection. Motives play a central part in his theory. Furthermore, his theory cannot be called hedonistic. Nor is it the kind of action-centered theory that is put forward by classical utilitarianism. The focus of concern remains ultimately the moral agent and his moral character. Hutcheson's excision of the offensive passage did not end the discussion, however. Thomas Reid criticized it as late as 1748 in his first publication, "An Essay on Quantity Occasioned by Reading a Treatise in which simple and Compound Ratios are Applied to Virtue and Merit," arguing that virtue and merit do not belong among the kinds of things that can be measured.

John Gay (1699–1745), a critic of Hutcheson who argued that the moral sense is not natural sense, may also be said to have tried to combine a religiously motivated ethics with a kind of utilitarianism. Thus he argued that virtue is "conformity to a rule of life directing the action of all rational creatures with respect to each other's happiness" because God's benevolence implies that he wills the happiness of human beings. To find out God's will we need therefore only determine what would make others happy.

David Hume (1711–1776), who followed Hutcheson in many ways, proposed in his *Enquiry Concerning the Principles of Morals* to answer the question of whether "public utility is the sole origin of justice" and whether "reflections on the beneficial consequences of this virtue are the sole foundation of its merit." His answer was a resounding "yes": "the rules of equity or justice depend entirely on the particular state and condition, in which men are placed, and owe their origin and existence to that utility, which results to the public from their strict and regular observance" (*Enquiry Concerning the Principles of Morals*, ed. Tom L. Beauchamp, Oxford, 1998, p. 86). Justice made useless is thus a contradiction in terms. Though Hume is often counted among the precursors of classical utilitarianism, it would be a mistake to identify his position with utilitarianism, for in section five he shows that for him utility is not the foundation of morality.

Indeed, it is perhaps not even the ultimate foundation of justice, because we must discuss the question of why utility pleases. For both Hutcheson and Hume, it is the moral sense or our natural sentiments that form the ultimate foundation of morality. If considerations of utility were ultimate, reason would have to be the final arbiter in moral matters, and that is a position Hume could not accept. In this regard, Hume's position resembles that of Hutcheson. In another respect it is rather different, however—whereas Hutcheson thought that both his moral-sense theory and his musings about utility were quite compatible with a basically Christian position on morals, Hume's public utility is meant to provide an alternative to Christian morality. Indeed, when Hume argues that justice is very much like "superstition" and that the only thing that separates it from the latter is its utility, he makes this critique explicit. His position is—in this respect very much like that of classical utilitarianism—thoroughly naturalistic and secular. It is also closely allied with his empiricism. Still, he does not identify utility with contributing to the greatest happiness.

David Hartley (1705–1757) and Joseph Priestley (1733–1804), who are mainly known for their associationist psychology and their advocacy of materialism and determinism, also tended toward a form of utilitarianism. Thus, Priestley wished to avoid judgments about the blame- or praiseworthiness of people and thought it better to judge whether they were determined by good or bad principles. To determine which principles are good and which ones are bad, he asked whether they could lead to general happiness or not.

The materialist Claude-Adrien Hélvetius (1715–1771), who tried to show in his *De l'esprit* of 1758 that human beings should be influenced to further public utility and that it was regrettable that most people did not know that the public utility and the general happiness should be the measure of all good in human action, was probably influenced by Hume in these views. His idea that an excellent dictionary that precisely determined the meaning of good might help people in seeing the importance of public utility was probably just as naïve as his belief that such a dictionary would end the discussion about the nature of good. He was not alone in believing this, nor was he alone in his view that general happiness is one of the essential aims of morality. Paul-Henry Thiry d'Holbach (1723–1789), for instance, held a similar view, claiming that one's own happiness was essentially connected with the happiness of others. It would be a stretch, however, to call such theories "utilitarian" in any but the very vaguest sense.

Cesare Beccaria (1738–1794), whose book *Dei deletti e delle pene* (On Crimes and Punishments) of 1764 criticizes the treatment of criminals, argues that punishment should serve to deter criminal acts and help in the protection of society. The highest good was for him the greatest good of the greatest number of people. Therefore punishment should fit the crime and should be public, prompt, necessary, the least possible, and proportionate to the crime. He may be said to have used the principle of utility in a proposal to reform the administration of punishment.

Jeremy Bentham. However, the classical statement of the utilitarian doctrine can be found in Jeremy Bentham's *An Introduction to the Principles of Moral and Legislation* (first printed in 1780, but published only in 1789), which puts forward an uncompromising version of utilitarianism. Bentham himself says that he had learned the importance of utility as the criterion of all virtue from Hume's *Treatise*, but he also had learned from Beccaria and Priestley about the "greatest happiness of the greatest number."

Bentham is a hedonist without apology. Nature has given us two sovereign masters, whom we cannot escape, however much we try. These are pleasure and pain, and on these the principle of utility is based. It states that we should approve and disapprove of every action in accordance with "the tendency, which it appears to have to augment or diminish the happiness of the party whose interest is in question." The party whose interest is in question can be an individual or a community, but the community is not some kind of fictitious body but the sum of the individuals who compose it. Bentham stresses this individualism by emphasizing that it makes no sense to speak of community interests apart from individual interests. Furthermore, everyone is to count as one, and no one is to count for more as one. This shows not only that Bentham's utilitarianism has nothing in common with egoism (because I am not allowed to give my own interests a greater value than those of others), but also that his utilitarianism is essentially a democratic theory, meant to provide an instrument for social reform.

Since the only thing that counts in the determination of the rightness or wrongness of an action is its tendency to produce pleasure and pain in individuals, Bentham feels it necessary to spend a great deal of time in discussing pleasure. While there are many different kinds of pleasure, it is ultimately only the quantity of pleasure that counts. Contrary to what Reid may have thought, pleasures can be measured and they can be compared. Therefore, we can calculate in particular cases what will tend to bring about the greatest pleasure. When we measure the values of a pleasure, we must consider its intensity, its duration, its certainty or uncertainty, as well as how close or how remote it is. Other considerations concern its fecundity—that is, the degree of likelihood that a certain pleasure will lead to more pleasure or to pain—the purity of any pleasure, and, in case of several persons, the extent of pleasure. It would be a mistake to view the principle of utility and the calculation of degrees of pleasure as criteria that we must apply in every moral decision or as rules that should actually motivate us. Rather, they should form guidelines for evaluating the acts performed by others and ourselves.

The principle of utility is for Bentham a basic principle. As such it cannot be proved. Nor should one try to prove it. All that is necessary is to show that it is actually the principle according to which we act when we act morally. The great rivals of the principle of utility are, however, the religious principle of asceticism and the principle of sympathy and antipathy. The first is always opposed to the principle of utility, the other only sometimes.

However, the principle of asceticism cannot be pursued consistently and is therefore not alternative to the principle of utility, which can be consistently followed and as a matter of fact has always been implicitly followed by most people, at least according to Bentham. The principle of sympathy and antipathy, which is essentially a critical expression of the appeal to moral sentiments or a moral sense, is to Bentham only a principle in name. It is really not much more than the expression of caprice. While it is not always opposed to the principle of utility, it is an attempt to cover up its hold on us. At the same time, Bentham rejects the validity of any appeal to the will of God, claiming that whatever will be determined to be right by the utility principle will also be in accordance with divine will, and that we can in any case only know the presumptive will of God, and not what is his real will. However much he may have learned from Gay, for instance, he does not think that morality needs theology.

William Paley (1743–1805) had argued in his *The Principles of Moral and Political Philosophy* of 1785 that God's will could be ascertained either through scripture or through the light of nature, and that the latter allowed us to determine whether an act is right or wrong by its tendency "to promote or diminish human happiness," since it is God's will that human beings live happily. Virtue is "the doing good to mankind, in obedience to the will of God for the sake of everlasting happiness. His position, which resembles that of Gay and Abraham Tucker, whose *Light of Nature Pursued* (1768) also pursues a religious utilitarianism, shows that utilitarianism is not necessarily antireligious. Nevertheless, Bentham later used the principle of utility as an instrument for eradicating religious belief. Another thinker for whom utilitarianism went hand in hand with a rejection of Christianity was William Godwin (1751–1836). He had lost his faith as a result of reading Helvétius and d'Holbach. In his moral and political philosophy he came under the influence of Hume. Thus, he both argued in his *Enquiry Concerning Political Justice* (1793) that moral reasoning is essentially nothing more than the attempt to awaken certain feelings and endorsed the greatest happiness principle as an ultimate moral principle that cannot be derived from egoism. Very much like Bentham, he rejected natural rights.

While utilitarianism had a history both before the period of the Enlightenment and after, it may be said to have been intimately connected to many of its central concerns. Indeed, insofar as it is concerned with the improvement of mankind and with the emancipation of citizens from the authority of church and state, it was a powerful weapon in showing that we need no transcendent justification for our moral judgments. While quite compatible with divine command theories, it could also be employed to show that they are superfluous.

[*See also* Beccaria, Cesare; Bentham, Jeremy; Helvétius, Claude-Adrien; Human Nature; Hume, David; Hutcheson, Francis; *and* Moral Philosophy.]

BIBLIOGRAPHY

Berry, Christopher J. *Social Theory of the Scottish Enlightenment.* Edinburgh, 1997.
Chitnis, A. C. "The Scottish Enlightenment in the Age of Galt." In *John Galt, 1779–1979,* edited by Christopher Whatley, pp. 31–63. Edinburgh, 1979.
Crimmins, James E. *Secular Utilitarianism: Social Science and the Critique of Religion in the Thought of Jeremy Bentham.* Oxford, 1990.
Hope, Vincent. *Virtue by Consensus.* Oxford, 1989.
Hruschka, Joachim. "The Greatest Happiness Principle and Other Early German Anticipations of Utilitarian Theory." *Utilitas* 3 (1991), 165–177.
Leslie, Stephen. *The English Utilitarians.* 3 vols. New York and London, 1900.
Norton, David Fate. *David Hume: Common-Sense Moralist and Sceptical Metaphysician.* Princeton, N.J., 1982.
Sidgwick, Henry. *Outlines of the History of Ethics.* London, 1902.

MANFRED KUEHN

UTOPIANISM. In 1789, at the beginning of the French Revolution, the future Jacobin revolutionary Thomas Rousseau published a new edition of Sir Thomas More's *Utopia* as a guide to France's new reformers—the fourth French translation to appear in the eighteenth century. The majority of published "utopias" (the word comes from More's name for his imaginary country, which means "no place" in Greek) in the century are not seriously concerned with reform, however, and much less with revolution. They are primarily popular novels, intended to divert, in which the adventures of heroes and heroines all but drown out the didactic element.

The Enlightenment pursuit of a science of society nevertheless invoked utopian speculation in the attempt to establish the natural laws of human conduct. Charles de Secondat Montesquieu (1689–1755) approached the task empirically, through long years of comparative study of actual human societies; others preferred a shorter route, stripping away the accretions of existing society and civilization to reveal the pristine natural man beneath. This was, in its purest form, the method of Rousseau. Rousseau wrote in 1755, in the conclusion to his *Discours sur l'origine de l'inégalité*: "I have tried to expose the origin and progress of inequality, the establishment and abuse of political societies, in so far as these things can be deduced from the nature of man by the sole light of reason."

The Enlightenment was aware of some empirical evidence for "the nature of man": travelers' accounts of noble savages in the Americas and the Pacific, or the Jesuit *Relations* with their evocation of the uncorrupted natives of North America and the malleable Guaranís of the Paraguayan mission-state. What was chiefly lacking was experimental data. In his personal journal, the marquis d'Argenson suggested one appealing solution: princes might profitably set up menageries of contented human beings to match their modish collections of exotic animals. Failing actual experiments, such menageries could be constructed more readily and cheaply in the imagination.

Types. The serious utopias of the Enlightenment were, in fact, experimental models for testing deduced theories of human nature and of the kind of society that would best fit that nature. It was vital that such utopias should be isolated from the existing world, the here and now. This isolation could be managed in four main ways. First, there were historically based utopias placed in the remote past. The most notable of these, and probably the most read of all eighteenth-century utopias, was François de Fénelon's *Télémaque*, first published in 1699 and reprinted many times; its "Boetica" is situated in ancient western Spain and inhabited by communist shepherd families still living in Hesiod's Golden Age. Powerful echoes of the pastoral utopia recurred throughout the century. In 1766, Nicolas Boulanger's *L'antiquité dévoilé* (Antiquity Unveiled) borrowed from Plato's account of primitive and benevolent man to transmute the Golden Age from myth into history. In 1740, Charles Rollin's *Histoire ancienne* had done the same for Plutarch and Lycurgus's Spartan communism. Other ancient sources of supposed utopian wisdom were cited: the laws of King Minos of Crete, and the reforms of Séthos of Thebes, enshrined in the abbé Terrasson's 1731 novel of that name.

More popular were geographical utopias. The simplest form was the robinsonade, a genre whose name was borrowed from Daniel Defoe's *Robinson Crusoe*. What could be more convenient than actually to remove a man from society and allow him to rediscover his true nature and capacities, and then, perhaps with the help of a convenient girl Friday, to start a family and build a human society from scratch, based on truly natural laws? This happens, for example, in Guillaume Grivel's *L'île inconnu* (The Unknown Isle), published in the 1780s; there was a host of other versions in British, German, Italian, and French literature. In 1782, Thomas Spence's *Supplement to the History of Robinson Crusoe* created a democratic English utopia without landowners, following a revolution in "Crusonia."

Quite apart from the robinsonades, exotic islands—often in the South Seas—had a natural fascination for utopians who, like Thomas More himself, felt the need to present a closed, self-sufficient society in full operation. This was sometimes done through the fictional reports of an unfortunate castaway, such as the abbé Morelly's celebrated Pilpaï, whose *Basiliade*, or account of his shipwreck, appeared in 1753. In other works, the hero was an intrepid voyager; few were as intrepid as Restif de la Bretonne's, Victorin, who, in *La Découverte australe par un homme volant* (Southern Discovery by a Flying Man, 1781) flitted between a variety of utopias in a pedal-operated flying machine before arriving at the ultimate Australian utopia of Megapatagonia. The most popular German language utopia, Johann Gottfried's *Insel Kelsenburg* (1731–1743), belongs in this category. Often, however, the favored location of a utopia was in North America. Cleveland, the eponymous hero of a novel by the abbé Prévost (1697–1763), visits three distinct American utopias: one inhabited by noble red men, one by Huguenots, and one by scientists.

Occasionally, more exotic settings appear. In 1788, Giacomo Casanova produced five volumes of *Icosaméron*, whose Protocosmos, like the vegetarian utopia of the anonymous English *A Voyage to the World in the Centre of the Earth* (1755), is situated deep underground. In 1750, the chevalier de Béthune set his imaginary world on the planet Mercury.

In another category are utopias that are isolated because they are purely hypothetical constructions rooted in neither time nor place. Simply visions of what ought to be, such utopias are usually built around detailed codes of laws or regulations. They evince the fascination of the eighteenth century with the notion of the all-powerful legislator in the mold of Lycurgus and Solon, as well as the prevailing conviction that human behavior may be fundamentally changed by legal decree. Morelly's *Code de la nature* (1755) explained the theory behind the *Basiliade*, his South Sea island romance, with the aid of several score of decrees; Restif de la Bretonne's trilogy—*Les gynographes* (1777), *L'andrographe* (1782), and *Le thesmographe* (1789)—includes extensive lists of laws and regulations. Rousseau's *Projet d'un constitution pour la Corse* (written in 1765, but not published until the nineteenth century) is another legalistic utopia.

The final utopian category is that in which the utopia is placed in the remote future. In 1771, Louis-Sebastien

Mercier completed his novel *L'an deux mille quatre cent quarante (A.D. 2440)*, in which a sleeper awakes in the twenty-fifth century, into a better Paris, a better France, and a better world. To Mercier belongs the distinction of pioneering the first voyage of this kind into the future, and thus of being the remote precursor of Edward Bellamy's and William Morris's nineteenth-century "euchronias," or time-travelers' utopias.

Intents and Effects. The preceding short general survey and catalog raise many contingent questions. Which were the popular, the important, and the influential utopias? Who read utopian literature in the eighteenth century? Which elements in the utopian tradition did they find most absorbing or stimulating? The answers must be impressionistic and subjective. The kinds of utopias were many—feudal, bourgeois, and Physiocratic as well as communistic. The standpoint of the observer, now as in the eighteenth century, will determine which utopian ideas seem truly important.

A literary critic might feel that baron Wollmar's island of Clarens, where the characters of Rousseau's *La nouvelle Héloïse* explore the natural morality of human relationships, was the most significant island utopia of the century. Jeremy Bentham frequently used the word *Utopia* to describe his plan of 1796–1797 to herd the English poor into a network of "Panopticon Houses of Industry." A feminist might give more weight to Louis Rustaing de Saint-Jory's account of the island of Manghalour, described in *Les femmes militaires* (1736), in which there is total equality of the sexes in education, warfare, love, and government. One of the most striking features of eighteenth-century utopian thought is the exploration of a variety of secular patterns and domestic arrangements, generally quite at variance with the prevailing monogamous, patriarchal, sacramental family order of contemporary Europe. In the communist utopia constructed by Léger-Marie Deschamps (1716–1774), an atheistical Benedictine monk, there is no giving away in marriage, and men and women couple as they see fit without asserting proprietary rights; on David Thomson's *Ile de la raison* (1757), eight men and four women cohabit in a group marriage. For all that, sexual liberation is hardly the message of the more influential utopias. Where all other hierarchy is stripped away as artificial, patriarchy reigns undisturbed in Morelly's *Code de la nature*; the question of the structure of the family is never broached. Restif's prescriptions for the education of women in *Les gynographes* reflect deep and serious anxieties: in Rousseauist tradition, boys are to be given the maximum freedom of physical action, but girls are to be tightly swaddled from birth to accustom them to their destiny of relentless control and subordination; they are to be given no intellectual training, not even in basic literacy, and no instruction

in the higher arts, since this might divert them from the primary task of pleasing their husbands.

Restif's friend Sébastien Mercier was less pathological in his reaction to perceived threats of the breakdown of the traditional family; even in his twenty-fifth century, however, women will still be "all submitted to the duties their sex imposes on them." They will have abandoned music and dancing for the study of "housekeeping, the art of pleasing their husbands and raising their children."

From these engaging perspectives we are recalled by the dour reminder of Marxists that the overriding reality of the eighteenth century was a class society of feudal exploitation. Thus, one touchstone for evaluating the utopias of the age must be the extent to which they illuminate, criticize, and seek to transcend the conflicts of that society. For Franco Venturi, the important thing is not to follow ideas back to their origins, however fascinating that pursuit, but to examine their function in the history of the eighteenth century. For Venturi, one of the more significant functions of utopia in that period was to give birth to modern communism: "In the past, the idea of communism appeared to be sporadic and isolated. Now, for the first time, it was the origin of a current of thought."

There is no doubt that one widespread, almost overwhelming conclusion drawn by the Enlightenment from the contemplation of man's true nature—whether made clear by the memory of the Golden Age of the past, by the forests of the noble savage, or by the rational precincts of Utopia—was that man was a social being, born for free and willing cooperation with his fellows in a condition of equality. The utopias of Morelly and of Restif de la Bretonne were merely the most notable examples of the corollary, an attempt to demonstrate that the shape of society that must inevitably result is a state of organized communism.

The abbé Morelly's *Code de la nature* is the most significant of the communist utopias. Published anonymously in 1755, it made an immediate impact. A Touraine nobleman, the marquis d'Argenson, hailed the *Code* promptly as "the book of books" and found it immensely superior to Montesquieu's *L'esprit des lois*. Though this is a curious assessment of a desperately solemn, graceless publication, it is hard not to see the *Code de la nature* as the central achievement of Enlightenment utopianism.

It is certainly worth a closer analysis. The *Code* begins with a long preface that confutes present practice and elucidates correct first principles. As the title implies, the objective is to distinguish a natural code of conduct from the absurdities of accepted morality.

The first, fundamental, and sacred law of the *Code* outlaws private property; the second makes the subsistence of everyone a public charge; and the third orders all to contribute to the community according to strength, talents, and age. Thereafter it becomes a matter of detail, of "counting things and persons." Items of immediate consumption are distributed freely in the public squares; others are stored in common warehouses against future need. There are public workshops and stores for all tools. Houses for each family and clothes for each individual are provided. There is a public educational system for boys *and* girls. There are free hospitals and old people's homes. A rotating hierarchy of administration chosen by lot from among all "fathers of families" plans and directs the labor of all inhabitants.

There are no hereditary nobles, no landlords, no lawyers, and no priests in Morelly's utopia. There are no moneylenders or merchants, and, of course, no factory owners or factory workers. There are only peasants in the fields, artisans in the workshops, and administrators in the offices.

Throughout, a deadening uniformity is evident. All houses and quarters of the city are of exactly the same design; all young men wear vocational uniforms until they are thirty. Marriage is compulsory. The city contains no theaters, concert halls, cafés, dance halls, or gambling houses. It is a regimented, gray, but adequate life in which happiness is defined as having enough to eat, clothing, and a place to sleep.

Gracchus Babeuf and Filippo Buonarroti, the communist leaders of the French revolutionary Conspiracy of the Equals of 1796, adapted and incorporated many of the features of the *Code de la nature* in their plans for the new France that would be born from their uprising: the abolition of property and of money; free distribution of comestibles and clothing and other products by the administrators of state warehouses; adequate housing and free education; the direction of labor; and stringent penalties for the idle and politically intransigent. In turn, the outlines of the Babouvist utopia were passed down to the nineteenth century in Buonarroti's account of the Conspiracy (published, with documents, in 1828), an inspiration for future communists down to the twentieth century.

Contemporaries might have been forgiven for seeing in the failure of the 1796 conspiracy a vindication of Morelly's original pessimistic assessment: that in western Europe property was too firmly entrenched, and a return to the Golden Age was no longer among the possibilities. There remained only the other direction to travel: forward to the twenty-fifth century. Mercier's utopia *L'an 2440 A.D.* did not foreshadow pulling down existing society to return to a natural order. Instead, Mercier contemplated the reforms that seemed rational, desirable, and above all possible in his day, and he conjectured—reasonably enough—that, given six hundred years, most would be accomplished. Mercier's imagined Paris has been replanned with wide boulevards, pedestrian malls, clean, well-lit streets, and a free public water supply. Extremes of wealth and poverty have disappeared. The state funds health care for the poor and provides welfare relief. Politically, the hereditary nobility has disappeared and a democratic king presides over a constitutional monarchy. Arbitrary imprisonment and torture are unknown, and swift and humane justice is administered by courts inspired by the Italian reformer Cesare Beccaria's principles. All this has been achieved peacefully through the benevolent actions of a philosophical ruler. Confident, reformist optimism was thus also a legacy of Enlightenment utopianism.

[*See also* Architecture; Cities; Fénelon, François-Armand de Salignac de La Mothe; Godwin, William; Literary Genres; Malthus, Thomas Robert; Novel; Optimism, Philosophical; Political Philosophy; Price, Richard; Progress; Rousseau, Jean-Jacques; *and* Wallace, Robert.]

BIBLIOGRAPHY

Chinard, Gilbert. *L'Amérique et le rêve exotique dans la littérature française au XVIIe et au XVIIIe siècle.* Paris, 1934.

Droz, Jacques, ed. *Histoire générale du socialisme.* 4 vols. Paris, 1972–1978. See especially vol. 1, pp. 103–194, Albert Soboul's "Lumières, critique sociale et utopie pendant le XVIIIe siècle français." French utopias exclusively.

Kamenka, Eugene, ed. *Utopias: Papers from the Annual Symposium of the Australian Academy of the Humanities.* Oxford, 1987. Chapters 2–4 deal with the Enlightenment era. Includes British utopias.

Manuel, Frank Edward, and Fritzie P. Manuel. *Utopian Thought in the Western World.* Cambridge, Mass., 1979. Chapters 16–23 deal with the Enlightenment.

Poster, Mark. *The Utopian Thought of Restif de la Bretonne.* New York, 1971.

Rose, Robert Barrie. *Gracchus Babeuf: The First Revolutionary Communist.* Stanford, Calif., 1978.

Talmon, J. L. *The Origins of Totalitarian Democracy.* London, 1952.

Tower, Sargent Lyman. *British and American Utopian Literature, 1516–1985: An Annotated, Chronological Bibliography.* New York and London, 1988. pp. 17–33 cover the eighteenth century. Non-French utopias.

Venturi, Franco. *Utopia and Reform in the Enlightenment.* Cambridge, 1971.

R. B. ROSE

V

VERRI, ALESSANDRO (1741–1816), Italian jurist and writer.

After taking his degree in jurisprudence at the University of Pavia in 1760, Verri was accepted (at a very young age) to the college of noble legal professionals in Milan, and held the post of "protector of jailed prisoners." Guided by his older brother Pietro, he took part in the intellectual discourse of the Accademia dei Pugni, and opened up to the culture of the Enlightenment. Between 1763 and 1766 he wrote, but did not publish, a *Saggio di morale cristiana* (Essay in Christian Morality) and an ample *Saggio sulla storia d'Italia dalla fondazione di Roma fino alla metà del nostro secolo* (Essay on the History of Italy from the Foundation of Rome to the Middle of Our Century; commonly given the short title *Storia d'Italia*, 2001). The latter work, written for a general readership, echoed Verri's reading of Voltaire and Montesquieu, but also bears the stamp of a meticulous erudition inspired by Lodovico Antonio Muratori, and reflects a keen interest in the "primitive" and the "barbaric" derived from the *Scienza nuova* of Giambattista Vico.

Verri was the most lively contributor to the paper *Il Caffè*, and the one most endowed with journalistic talent. In some of his articles he aimed to rejuvenate the culture by proposing a more modern idea of the role of the intellectual, of literary prose, and of the language itself. In others, he developed a radical critique of Roman law and the juridical systems of his time, probing the limits of natural law theory, against which he set a utilitarian philosophy built around the ideals of moderation and a virtuous life. In accordance with Enlightenment thought, he set forth an ideal of man as sensitive, free, and actively working to transform reality.

Some of his writings, however, reflect an unresolved tension between enthusiasm and reason, between passion and "cold logic," along with a suspicion that the violent motions of the soul might act to destabilize the inner harmony of the person.

A sojourn in Paris and London in 1766–1767 had the effect of heightening this uncertainty. The philosophe circles with whom he came in contact repelled him with their tone of fanaticism and with the prevailing attitude of derision toward religion: Verri was present, astonished and appalled, at a private reading of the *Système de la Nature* at d'Holbach's house. London, in contrast, seemed to him a symbol of a cohesive and stable civil society, and of a tranquil and reasonable way of life—an impression that abetted his choice of David Hume, with his detached skepticism, as the champion of a "gentle philosophy."

Rather than return to Milan, Alessandro Verri settled in Rome for the rest of his life, drawn by his relationship with the marquise Margherita Boccapadule Gentili, and by a desire to live independently of his family. By 1770 he had come to a position that differed from that of his own years at *Il Caffè*, and from that of his brother Pietro, with whom he engaged in an epistolary dialogue that constitutes the most important exchange of letters in eighteenth-century Italy. Under the influence of Rome, he took up classical studies again, translated Shakespeare's *Hamlet* and *Othello*, became more interested in art and theater, and gave up his ironic style, for one founded on a neoclassical ideal of elegance and clarity exemplified by Greek models.

Aside from minor writings, his Roman years yielded two tragedies (*Pantea* and *La congiura di Milano*), published under the title *Tentativi drammatici* (Attempts at Drama, Leghorn, 1779) and three novels: *Le avventure di Saffo, poetessa di Mitilene* (The Adventures of Sappho, Poetess of Mytilene, 1780); *Le notti romane* (Roman Nights, 1792–1804), which enjoyed enormous success in Italy and abroad; and *La vita di Erostrato* (The Life of Erostratus, 1815). These works are overcast by an increasingly dark and pessimistic vision of history and human destiny; they plumb deeply in exploring the irrational as an ineliminable component of the moral world; and they accumulate a sort of catalog, in the tones and tints a vision typical of the romantic era that was commencing, of the disorders of the modern world, in which passion and enthusiasm are seen as morbid and pathological phenomena that have negative effects on the social fabric. In *Le vicende memorabili dal 1789 al 1801* (The Memorable Events of 1789–1801, written in the first decade of the nineteenth century and published posthumously at Milan, 1858), Alessandro Verri arrived at a counterrevolutionary and reactionary position. He rejected modern culture and the Enlightenment idea of the continuous progress of knowledge, and attacked the philosophes as the direct instigators of the wave of revolution that had overturned all order, all values, and all certainty.

[*See also* Academies, *subentry on* Italy; Beccaria, Cesare; Economic Thought; Italy; Milan; Political Philosophy; *and* Verri, Pietro.]

BIBLIOGRAPHY

Il Caffè (1764–1766). Edited by Gianni Francioni and Sergio Romagnoli. Turin, 1993; repr., 1998.

Carteggio di Pietro e di Alessandro Verri. Edited by Alessandro Giulini, Emanuele Greppi, Francesco Novati, and Giovanni Seregni, 12 vols. Milan, 1910–1942.

Cerruti, Marco. *Neoclassici e giacobini*. Milan, 1969. See especially "Alessandro Verri fra storia e bellezza," pp. 17–114.

Cicora, Fabrizio. *Alessandro Verri. Sperimentazione e autocensura*. Bologna, 1982.

Verri, Alessandro. *I romanzi*. Edited by Luciana Martinelli. Ravenna, 1975.

Verri, Alessandro. *Saggio Sulla storia d'Italia*. Edited by Barbara Scalvini. Rome, 2001.

GIANNI FRANCIONI
Translated from Italian by William McCuaig

VERRI, PIETRO (1728–1797), Italian writer, philosopher, and economist.

The eldest son of Count Gabriele Verri, a conservative jurist and authoritative member of the Senate of Milan, Pietro Verri was educated by the Barnabites in Milan, the Piarists in Rome, and finally by the Jesuits at the Collegio dei Nobili in Parma. He refused to undertake the legal career his parents intended for him. Instead, he joined the Accademia dei Trasformati in Milan, and under their influence developed a marked interest in the theater, siding with Carlo Goldoni in the controversy that swirled around the Venetian playwright in those years. His adhesion to the Enlightenment, already perceptible in his writings on the theater and in other unpublished texts, inspired him to launch a series of satirical almanacs (*Il Gran Zoroastro*, Milan, 1758, 1759; Lugano, 1762; Lucca, 1764; *Il Mal di Milza*, Lugano, 1764) in which he fought against popular beliefs and superstitions and promulgated ideas based on the progress of the sciences. Fleeing the confined social environment and arid culture of Lombardy, Verri volunteered in 1759 to fight with the Austrian army against Prussia. There, he made the acquaintance of the English economist Henry Lloyd, which prompted him to study economics; the upshot was a work infused with the principles of mercantilism, *Elementi del commercio* (Elements of Trade, drafted at Vienna in 1760 and published later in *Il Caffè*).

Upon returning to Milan in 1761, Verri left the Trasformati, and together with his brother Alessandro, Cesare Beccaria, and a few others, founded the Accademia dei Pugni, which became the scene of animated discussions

and readings of the works of Rousseau, Voltaire, Helvétius, Montesquieu, and major contemporary authors. In 1763, he completed a large work, *Considerazioni sul commercio dello Stato di Milano* (Considerations on Trade in the State of Milan), which he did not publish, but did submit to the court at Vienna, in which he investigated the extreme decadence of the economy of Lombardy from the time of the Spanish domination. It contained the outline of a program of wide economic and political reform, which included detailed proposals concerning freedom of trade, the elimination of guilds, fiscal administration, and the reorganization of the councils responsible for managing the economy.

The ethical grounding of the political program that Verri was working out was entrusted to a small work, rich in autobiographical insights, *Meditazioni sulla felicità* (Meditations on Happiness; Leghorn, 1763). In it Verri established a necessary connection between the search for individual happiness and the requirement of collective happiness: "the well-being of each one who cooperates to form society" becomes more certain to the degree that "public happiness, meaning the greatest possible happiness shared out with the greatest possible degree of equality" is realized. This was the first statement in the Italian language of a principle posited by Francis Hutcheson in his *Inquiry into the original of our Ideas of Beauty and Virtue* (1725), and destined to become the core idea of the utilitarianism of Jeremy Bentham. The same utilitarian slogan figures in the important book that the "école de Milan," as Voltaire called it, produced the following year: Cesare Beccaria's *Dei delitti e delle pene*, to which Pietro Verri made a considerable contribution, not only suggesting the topic to Beccaria, but transcribing, correcting, and amply reworking the text, and finally supervising its publication at Leghorn in 1764.

Verri was also the originator and organizer of, and major contributor to, the journal *Il Caffè* (1764–1766), which was inspired by Joseph Addison's *Spectator*. The "brief and varied articles" promised in the subtitle of this periodical avoided direct commentary on political and religious questions, for Verri was careful to tone down the more extreme positions taken in his own drafts and those of the other collaborators so as not to get into trouble with the censor. *Il Caffè* ranged over a broad spectrum, including philosophy and economics, law and literature, ethics and the sciences, alternating light or satirical pieces with more serious dissertations. It was distinguished by the battle (waged principally by Alessandro Verri) for the renewal of the legal system and against the Roman and natural law traditions; by its attack on the ethos and the privileges of the institutionalized Milanese patriciate, with the aim of promoting a reform of the nobility, in which the ideology of honor would be replaced by the principles of virtue, merit, and competence; by the proclamation of a model of economic development built around an unencumbered market capable of bringing about a redistribution of wealth through the free circulation of goods and money; and by the rejection of pedantic erudition in the name of a new culture and an ideal of the man of letters immersed in his own age. The entire project of *Il Caffè* was grounded in support for the "enlightened" policy of reform that the Habsburg monarchy was conducting against the traditional intermediate bodies and privileged social strata.

The birth of *Il Caffè* in June 1764 was preceded by the nomination, a few months earlier, of Pietro Verri to membership of a board charged with reforming the system of collecting indirect taxes in the form of duties, the so-called "Ferma," which had until then been wholly farmed out to private entrepreneurs who profited richly from it. In November 1765, after earning support for his proposals to bring the collection of duties under the royal administration, Verri was named a member of the newly created supreme economic council, and superintendent of the Ferma. Years of hard work followed, during which Verri dealt with duties and taxes, the abolition of the guilds, and the liberalization of the grain trade; on the last subject he wrote a limpid analysis in 1768, *Riflessioni sulle leggi vincolanti principalmente nel commercio dei grani* (Reflections on Restrictive Laws, Principally in the Grain Trade, which he only published in 1796).

Verri's economic thought was given its mature exposition in his *Meditazioni sulla economia politica* (Meditations on Political Economy, Leghorn, 1771). This work firmly embraces free trade, and anticipates (especially the concept of money as a universal commodity, the theory of value, and the dynamics of the laws of the marketplace) the *Wealth of Nations* of Adam Smith. In the year it was published, however, the institutions of Lombardy were reorganized at the command of Vienna, and the supreme economic council was abolished, and replaced by a Cameral Magistracy with responsibility for the state's finances and the economy. Verri suffered the sharp disappointment of seeing his reform proposals turned down and his career hopes frustrated: Gian Rinaldo Carli was named president of the new magistracy, while Verri was made a simple councillor. Even promotion to the vice presidency in 1772, and to the rank of councillor of state in 1773, were not enough to counterbalance the real loss of political power by a man who had aimed to become the sole person in charge of the finances of the state of Milan. Thus began a gradual withdrawal on his part, and a reawakening of his own private life, evident in his plunge back into studies, and in his marriage in 1776 to Maria Castiglioni, who bore him a daughter, Teresa, in 1777.

The 1770s saw the publication of his *Idee sull'indole del piacere* (Ideas on the Character of Pleasure, Leghorn, 1773 and Milan, 1774) and the reordering of materials he had been accumulating since the 1760s into the *Osservazioni sulla tortura* (Observations on Torture, 1776–1777), in which he renewed Beccaria's appeal against intolerance and the useless cruelties of the justice system. Verri did not publish this work, which appeared posthumously, partly to avoid an open clash with his father, who was a strong believer in judicial torture. In 1778, he began work on a *Storia di Milano* (History of Milan; vol. 1, Milan, 1783; vol. 2, posthumous, Milan, 1798). In the same year he again took up his youthful *Meditazioni sulla felicità* and prepared a longer and more organic version, which he published together with his essays on political economy and pleasure in a single volume: *Discorsi sull'indole del piacere e del dolore, sulla felicità e sulla economia politica* (Milan, 1781). The *Discorsi* show a clear shift in his philosophical stance. In the short text of 1763, happiness is seen by Verri as securely attainable; but by 1781 he maintained that "pure and constant felicity cannot be for man, while on the contrary misery and unhappiness can." The concepts of pleasure and pain were also redefined: pleasure is no more than a "sudden cessation of pain," but at the same time Verri takes pain to be "the only thing that drives the human race," giving rise to everything that man can positively realize: the arts, industry, the sciences.

At the end of 1780, the death of Maria Teresa and the rise of Joseph II led to Verri's promotion to the presidency of the Cameral Magistracy—which was, however, given reduced responsibilities. Verri supported the policies of Joseph II with renewed ardor, especially the ecclesiastical reforms, in furtherance of which he composed a *Dialogo fra Pio VI e Giuseppe II in Vienna* (Dialogue between Pius VI and Joseph II in Vienna, 1782, still unpublished). He was for several years a resolute defender of "enlightened despotism," until the speed and force of the reforming process (which was directed with a heavy hand by the emperor) caused him to doubt the value of governmental measures that broke with the customs and mentality of the population to whom they were directed. His defection was certainly influenced by his sudden forced retirement in 1786, at the height of Joseph II's reforms, when the Milanese Senate and the Cameral Magistracy were suppressed and replaced by a Supreme Tribunal of Justice and a Government Council. In the *Pensieri politici sulle operazioni fatte in Milano nel 1786* (Political Thoughts on the Measures Taken in Milan in 1786, as yet unpublished) he broke for good with the policy of "enlightened despotism." The death of Joseph II in 1790 and the ascent to the throne of his brother Leopold II resulted in the abolition of the most controversial of Joseph II's reforms; and particularly, in the creation of a

Social Deputation that was meant to transmit the desires of the state of Milan to the Habsburg throne. Although Verri hoped to be a member, he was excluded by his fellow citizens. So instead he confided his judgment on the political situation to the written page, assembling a private collection (entitled *Idee politiche del conte Pietro Verri, da non pubblicarsi* [Political Ideas of Count Pietro Verri, not to be published]) of texts from the 1780s and new writings composed in that year (*Pensieri sullo Stato politico del Milanese nel 1790: Orazione funebre per Giuseppe II imperatore e re; Dialogue des morts: le Roi Frédéric et Voltaire: Dialogo fra l'Imperatore Giuseppe II ed un filosofo*), all of them converging on an ideal of moderate monarchy. Verri did not exclude that evolution beyond absolutism might be achieved with the consent of the monarch himself by a gradual process, although in his *Primi elementi per somministrare al popolo delle nozioni tendenti alla pubblica felicità* (First Elements in Order to Imbue the People with Notions Tending to the Public Happiness, 1791–1792, but published posthumously) he realistically acknowledged the inevitability of a popular revolution. For that matter, he had already greeted the French Revolution with favor in *Alcuni pensieri sulla rivoluzione accaduta in Francia* (A Few Thoughts on the Revolution That Has Taken Place in France, 1789, but published in 1928).

In 1792–1793, Pietro Verri returned to politics as a member of the Decurional Council of Milan. Napoleon Bonaparte's entry into Milan in 1796 led to the creation of a new republican municipal council, of which he became a member. During this period he drafted a brief *Storia dell'invasione dei francesi repubblicani nel Milanese* (History of the Invasion of the Milanese Territory by the French Republicans) and resumed journalism with contributions to *Il termometro politico della Lombardia* (The Political Thermometer of Lombardy). At the beginning of 1797 he became a member of the Society for Public Education and president of the Council of Forty created at the request of Bonaparte. In one of his last writings, *Lettera del filosofo NN al monarca NN* (Letter from an Anonymous Philosopher to an Anonymous Monarch, 1797) he emphasized yet again the need to elect a senate with legislative functions, "then equip the people with arms and organize a national militia, and finally publish a democratic constitution." Death came to Pietro Verri during the night of 28–29 May 1797, while the municipal council of Milan was in session.

[*See also* Academies, *subentry on* Italy; Beccaria, Cesare; Economic Thought; Italy; Milan; Political Philosophy; *and* Verri, Alessandro.]

BIBLIOGRAPHY

WORKS BY VERRI

Il Caffè (1764–1766). Edited by Gianni Francioni and Sergio Romagnoli. Turin, 1993; repr., 1998.

Carteggio di Pietro e di Alessandro Verri. Edited by Alessandro Giulini, Emanuele Greppi, Francesco Novati, and Giovanni Seregni, 12 vols. Milan, 1910–1942.
Considerazioni sul commercio dello Stato di Milano. Edited by Carlo Antonio Vianello. Milan, 1939.
Delle nozioni tendenti alla pubblica felicità. Edited by Gennaro Barbarisi. Rome, 1994.
Del piacere e del dolore ed altri scritti di filosofia ed economia. Edited by Renzo De Felice. Milan, 1964.
"Manoscritto" per Teresa. Edited by Gennaro Barbarisi. Rome, 1983.
Meditazioni sulla felicità. Edited by Gianni Francioni. Como Pavia, 1996.
Osservazioni sulla tortura. Edited by Gennaro Barbarisi. Milan, 1985.
Scritti vari. Edited by Giulio Carcano, 2 vols. Florence, 1854.
Storia di Milano. Edited by Enzo Ronconi, 2 vols. Florence, 1963.

WORKS ABOUT VERRI

Baia Curioni, Stefano. *Per sconfiggere l'oblio: Saggi e documenti sulla formazione intellettuale di Pietro Verri*. Milan, 1988.
Pietro Verri e il suo tempo. Edited by Carlo Capra. Milan, 1999. Assembles the papers delivered at a scholarly conference held in Milan in 1997; the most up-to-date and useful interpretive guide to Verri's thought.
Capra, Carlo. *I progressi della ragione: Vita di Pietro Verri*. Bologna, 2002.
Moloney, Brian. "The *Discorsi* of Pietro Verri: Genesis and Revision." *Studies on Voltaire* 56 (1967), 893–906.
Panizza, Giorgio, and Barbara Costa. *L'Archivio Verri*. Milan, 1997. A guide to the archive of Pietro Verri's papers, which contains numerous unpublished manuscripts and is held at the Fondazione Raffaele Mattioli in Milan.
Sala Di Felice, Elena. *Felicità e morale in Pietro Verri*. Padua, 1970.
Scianatico, Giovanna. *L'ultimo Verri: Dall'Antico Regime alla Rivoluzione*. Naples, 1990.
Valeri, Nino. *Pietro Verri*. Milan, 1937; repr., Florence, 1969. Partly outdated but still useful biography.
Venturi, Franco. *Settecento riformatore*. Vol. 1, *Da Muratori a Beccaria*. Turin, 1969; repr., 1971. See chapter 9, "La Milano del *Caffè*."
Venturi, Franco. *Settecento riformatore*. Vol. 5.1, *L'Italia dei Lumi*. Turin, 1987. See chapter 3, "Gli uomini delle riforme: la Lombardia." The best overview of the Enlightenment in Lombardy.

GIANNI FRANCIONI

Translated from Italian by William McCuaig

VICO, GIAMBATTISTA (1668–1744), Italian philosopher of history, law, and mythology.

Vico was born and lived his entire life in Naples, except for nine years (1686–1695) spent as tutor to the Rocca family at their castle at Vatolla, south of Naples, and traveling with them periodically to their residences in Portici and Naples. Vico was professor of Latin eloquence (rhetoric) at the University of Naples from 1699–1741. Vico regarded himself as an autodidact, having withdrawn from grammar school and later from the university to study on his own. He nominally received an L. L. D. from the University of Naples (Salerno) in 1694. In 1734, he served as head of the university delegation to congratulate

Charles of Bourbon on conquering the Kingdom of Naples; the following year he was appointed royal historiographer.

As part of his duties during the first years of his professorship, he delivered six orations to inaugurate the university's academic year (1699–1707). These concerned the ideal of self-knowledge and the importance of liberal education for the state and the individual. A seventh oration was published in 1709 as Vico's first book, *De nostri temporis studiorum ratione* (On the Study Methods of Our Time), which is an evaluation of the merits of both ancient and modern conceptions of education—rhetoric, poetry, and civil wisdom versus analytic geometry, science, and methodology. The following year Vico published the first of a three-part work, *De antiquissima Italorum sapientia* (On the Most Ancient Wisdom of the Italians), in which he derived a metaphysics from etymologies of the Latin language; he intended to counter the rationalism of Descartes's metaphysics. This work began with Vico's famous claim that "the true is the same as the made," his principle of *verum ipsum factum*. This work on metaphysics was to be followed by one on physics and a third on ethics, neither of which was written, although Vico wrote a work, now lost, *De aequilibrio corporis animantis* (On the Equilibrium of the Living Bodies) related to the second part of this project.

In 1720–1722 Vico wrote two works in Latin with an elaborate set of notes, all grouped under the Italian title *Il diritto universale* (Universal Law). This was written in preparation for obtaining the chair of civil law at the university, but Vico's loss of the competition for the chair, in 1723, was the decisive event in his career. In a chapter of this work, Vico had sketched his conception of a new science that would show the principles of the origin and development of the world of nations. With his defeat, he felt free both to write in Italian instead of academic Latin and to develop this conception into a major work. The first version of his *Scienza nuova* (New Science) appeared in 1725. A second, fully rewritten version appeared in 1730. Vico was revising this second edition at the time of his death, and it appeared as *Principi di Scienza nuova d'intorno alla comune natura delle nazioni* (Principles of New Science Concerning the Common Nature of Nations, 1744). Vico took the title of his major work from Francis Bacon's *Novum Organon* and Galileo's *Dialoghi delle nuove scienze*.

Against the seventeenth-century natural-law theorists—Thomas Hobbes, Hugo Grotius, Samuel Pufendorf, and John Selden—Vico advanced a conception of ideal eternal history in which all gentile nations develop in cycles of *corsi* and *ricorsi*. Instead of understanding a nation as originating through a covenant among individuals that transforms them from barbarism into civil society, Vico understood each nation as developing through three ages. The first was the age of gods, in which all of nature and basic social relations are ordered in terms of divine personalities and powers. This was succeeded by the age of heroes who embodied in their characters and deeds the virtues upon which civility is based.

Vico understood these two ages in terms of an analysis of myth or "poetic wisdom" (*sapienza poetica*). He regarded all myths as having a common form of thought, which he termed "imaginative universals" (*universali fantastici*), in which particulars appeared as embodied universal meanings grasped through the power of imagination (*fantasia*). The third age was that of humans, in which all was understood in completely human terms. The society of this age was based on written law instead of custom, and thought depended upon abstract or "intelligible universals" (*universali intelligibili*). As a nation lost touch with the imaginative and vital senses of the world that characterized its origin and became one-sidedly rationalistic, it declined and disintegrated, only to rise again in a *ricorso* of three ages. Vico understood all of the human world to depend upon three "principles of humanity"—religion, marriage, and burial. These were the basis of "the great city of the human race," within which each of the nations developed through the ages at its own pace. For Vico, the course the nations run in these ages involved three respective kinds of human nature, as well as customs, natural law, governments, languages, characters, jurisprudence, authority, and reason.

While writing his first *New Science*, Vico responded to an invitation from a new Venetian journal to write his autobiography. It appeared in the inaugural issue of *Raccolta d'opusculi scientifici e filologici* (1728). Vico continued his autobiography in 1731. In so doing, he applied to the recounting of his own life the principles of history he had discovered in *New Science*. By applying the genetic method of understanding to his own development, Vico invented the modern conception of intellectual autobiography.

Throughout his career Vico continued his defense of humanistic education, restating its ideals in an oration, "On the Heroic Mind" (1732), and in his last philosophical statement, an address to the Academy of Oziosi on "The Academies and the Relation between Philosophy and Eloquence" (1737). Within Vico's corpus there survive a number of important letters describing the intellectual climate of the Naples of his day and the reception of *New Science* as well as a wide range of occasional and commissioned pieces—orations, poems, and inscriptions commemorating marriages, deaths, and events in the lives of prominent persons in Naples. Vico also wrote a commissioned biography, *De rebus gestis Antonii Caraphaei* (Life of Antonio Carafa, 1716), the general in the Austrian service who had ruled Hungary.

There are several distinct views of the relation of Vico's thought to his time and to the history of ideas generally. The first of these, which established itself as the standard view for the first half of the twentieth century, is that of Benedetto Croce (1866–1952) and, in connection with Croce, of the British idealist Robin George Collingwood (1889–1943). Croce saw Vico as the nineteenth century in germ, as the forerunner of German idealism, and as the Italian Hegel, specifically regarding the *New Science* as having considerable affinity to Hegel's *Die Phänomenologie des Geistes* (Phenomenology of Spirit, 1807) as well as considering them both as founders of the philosophy of history. There is no evidence that Hegel read Vico, nor does Croce claim this.

Underlying Croce's view is the interpretation of Vico made by Francesco De Sanctis (1817–1883) that Vico is the inheritor of Renaissance humanism, a Platonic-Christian continuator of Marsilio Ficino and Pico della Mirandola. The Italian Hegelian Giovanni Gentile (1875–1944) also shared this view. De Sanctis sees Vico as estranged from his time because of this humanism. In this interpretation, Vico as a reactionary became a revolutionary who was a forebear of the nineteenth century's philosophy of history.

Isaiah Berlin (1909–1997) connected Vico with Johann Gottfried Herder (1744–1803) rather than with Hegel and nineteenth-century idealism. Berlin understood Vico in terms of a Counter-Enlightenment identified with Herder and, very strongly, with Johann Georg Hamann (1730–1788) and his attacks on the existence of undeniable rational truths, on the idea of "pure" reason, and on the attempts to discover a natural religion. Berlin holds that Vico's ideas, had they been fully known, would have been central to the Counter-Enlightenment. Hamann was aware of Vico and wrote a letter to Herder mentioning him. Herder first discussed Vico in his *Briefe zur Beförderung der Humanität* (Letters in Furtherance of Humanity, 1797), although he knew of Vico, at least through Hamann's letter, before he wrote his *Ideen zur Philosophie der Geschichte der Menschheit* (Ideas toward the Philosophy of the History of Mankind, 1784–1787). Vico, with Herder, stands opposed to the widespread Enlightenment view held to varying degrees by Voltaire, Diderot, Helvétius, d'Holbach, and Condorcet, that there is only universal civilization, which various nations can represent at the zenith of their development. Vico understood each nation as developing in its own terms, held together by its own language, customs, and laws within the cycles of his ideal eternal history.

Those who heard of Vico in the French Enlightenment largely saw him as only the representative of a long line of Neapolitan jurisconsults. They were not generally aware of his doctrines of history or knowledge. Berlin holds that Vico's genius lies not primarily in his philosophy of history but in his conception of knowledge that opposes the Enlightenment ideal that there is only one structure of reality that, at least in principle, can be described by one rational method and put into a logically perfect language from which a perfect mode of thought and a perfect society can be formed. In contrast, Vico understood that knowledge and laws are made under certain conditions at certain times and develop through a combination of imagination, reason, and authority.

Eugenio Garin (b. 1909), the Italian historian of philosophy and the Renaissance, argued that Vico is not a man out of his own time and that he cannot be understood simply as an imitation of the Renaissance themes of Christian Platonism or as a little-known formulator of the ideas of the Counter-Enlightenment. Garin claimed that Vico belongs completely at the center of the great discussion of the eighteenth century about the necessity of organizing a tree of the sciences, of constructing new systems of encyclopedias, and of articulating the link between the investigation of nature and the investigation of man. Vico's aim was to discover a new foundation of knowledge. Garin holds that through his *verum ipsum factum* principle, Vico wished to break the link established by the Cartesians between physics and mathematics. Vico held that all knowledge, including mathematics, is "made," clearing the way for physics to become experimental physics. A science of the human world is then possible as something made. Since the institutions of the human world are themselves made, nothing in principle stands in the way of the human having a sound knowledge of its own constructions. Thus a science of the human is fully possible.

The philosopher and Renaissance scholar Ernesto Grassi (1902–1991) emphasized Vico's connection to rhetoric and topical philosophy as against critical philosophy. Grassi focused on Vico's criticism of both Descartes's alienation of the humanities in *Discourse on Method* and his claim of a single rationalistic method for all knowledge. Descartes established modern philosophy on the basis of a conception of the *ars critica* and banished from true knowledge all that was classically attributed to the *ars topica*. Descartes thus eliminated all reasoning that since Aristotle had been understood to proceed from opinion, from communal sensibility, and from probability. The *ars topica* in the Renaissance was associated with poetry, rhetoric, the arts of memory, metaphor, and *ingenium* ("ingenuity," "wit"), all the forms of thought necessary for politics, human conduct, aesthetics, and the law.

Grassi saw Vico as the summary figure of Renaissance humanism, not so much by continuing Christian Platonism and metaphysics as by formulating a theory of history and knowledge based on the connections among poetry, rhetoric, and Renaissance philosophy. Grassi connected

Vico not to Hegel or Herder, but to Heidegger. He drew connections between Vico's notion of poetic wisdom and Heidegger's conception of poetry. Specifically, Grassi saw similarities between Heidegger's conception of *Lichtung* ("clearing") and Vico's conception of *luce* ("light") that is crucial for the first age of a nation by the clearing of places in the great forests of the earth to establish cities and altars on which the founders of the first families take the auspices of the gods. Grassi, at one time a junior colleague of Heidegger, did not regard Heidegger's well-known attacks on humanism as applying to these connections. Grassi regarded Vico as a figure opposed not only to Enlightenment ideals but also to those of a twentieth-century technological society and rationalistic philosophy. Grassi's Vico is a primary source for revitalizing the connection between, on the one hand, the rhetorical and senses of language that are needed for the formation of human society and its continued cohesion, and, on the other, the philosophical senses of Being and the world that depend upon thought and reason. Vico's work, thus, has forced deep consideration of the Enlightenment, of its central concerns, and of its relationship to its predecessors and its heirs.

[*See also* Cartesianism; Hamann, Johann Georg; Herder, Johann Gottfried; Hobbes, Thomas; Natural Law; *and* Pufendorf, Samuel.]

BIBLIOGRAPHY

WORKS BY VICO

The Autobiography of Giambattista Vico. Translated by Max Harold Fisch and Thomas Goddard Bergin. Ithaca, N.Y., 1944; repr., 1975. Contains as its introduction one of the best short treatments of Vico's philosophy and its influence on later thought.
The New Science of Giambattista Vico. Translated by Thomas Goddard Bergin and Max Harold Fisch. Ithaca, N.Y., 1948; repr., 1984. Unabridged edition, including their translation of Vico's "Practic of the New Science." Full translation of Vico's major work.
On the Study Methods of Our Time. Translated by Elio Gianturco. Ithaca, N.Y., revised edition 1965; 1990. New edition includes a translation by Donald Phillip Verene of Vico's "The Academies and the Relation between Philosophy and Eloquence." The central work of Vico's pedagogical philosophy.
On the Most Ancient Wisdom of the Italians, Unearthed from the Origins of the Latin Language. Including the Disputations with the *Giornale de' Letterati d' Italia.* Translated by Lucia M. Palmer. Ithaca, N.Y., and London, 1988. Vico's attack on Descartes' metaphysics, based on his principle of *verum ipsum factum.*
Opere di G. B. Vico. Edited by Andrea Battistini. Milan, 1990. A recent edition of Vico's major works, containing an excellent up-to-date commentary.
On Humanistic Education: Six Inaugural Orations (1699–1707). Translated by Giorgio A. Pinton and Arthur W. Shippee. Ithaca, N.Y., 1993. Vico's first works, the background for the *Study Methods* (see above).

WORKS ABOUT VICO

Berlin, Isaiah. *Vico and Herder: Two Studies in the History of Ideas.* London and New York, 1976. An analysis of Vico as a figure of the Counter-Enlightenment.

Croce, Benedetto. *The Philosophy of Giambattista Vico.* Translated by R. G. Collingwood. London, 1913; repr., 1964. The standard work of Croce on Vico.
Garin, Eugenio. "Vico and the Heritage of Renaissance Thought." Translated by B. A. Haddock. In *Vico: Past and Present,* edited by Giorgio Tagliacozzo, vol. 1, pp. 99–116. Atlantic Highlands, N. J., 1981. Statement of Garin's argument that Vico's *New Science* is closely related to the problems of his age.
Grassi, Ernesto. *Vico and Humanism: Essays on Vico, Heidegger, and Rhetoric.* New York and Bern, 1990. Reprints Grassi's central essays on Vico and his connection to Renaissance rhetoric as well as to Heidegger's conception of poetry.
Stone, Harold S. *Vico's Cultural History: The Production and Transmission of Ideas in Naples, 1685–1750.* Leiden, 1997. The only book-length study in English on Vico's relation to the intellectual culture of Naples.
Verene, Donald Phillip. *Vico's Science of Imagination.* Ithaca, N.Y., 1981; repr., 1991. A study of the fundamentals of Vico's philosophy.
Verene, Donald Phillip. *The New Art of Autobiography: An Essay on the "Life of Giambattista Vico Written by Himself."* Oxford, 1991. A study of Vico's autobiography as the verification of his principles of history.
Verene, Molly Black, ed. *Vico: A Bibliography of Works in English from 1884 to 1994.* Bowling Green, Ohio, 1994. Bibliography of all works on and by Vico in English, including citations to Vico in a wide range of works in the humanities and social sciences. Includes a guide to bibliographies of work on Vico in all other languages. Annual bibliographic updates appear in the journal *New Vico Studies* (1983–).

DONALD PHILLIP VERENE

VIRTUE. Virtue, like many other ideas, had a long history prior to the Enlightenment. This history involves two intertwined strands of thought, both traceable to the Greek philosopher Aristotle (384–322 BCE). The first focuses on human character, which should properly exhibit and embody the four cardinal virtues of justice, wisdom, temperance, and fortitude. This vocabulary later became overlaid with, or incorporated within, a Christian discourse that features faith, hope, and love (of God, of our neighbors, and of ourselves). The second strand focuses more explicitly on the public or political realm; here, virtue is a commitment or disposition to foster and defend the common good. In the Enlightenment, these strands kept their interlocked character, sharing in broad terms a concern with the relation between morality and self-interest. However, it is fair to say that the proponents of the first strand, until it received a significant reworking late in the eighteenth century by the German philosopher Immanuel Kant (1724–1804), exhibited a rough consensus in opposing "selfish" systems and retaining the closeness of the link between virtue and religion. By contrast, the second strand was the focus of a more intense debate. This article will concentrate on this latter element. The key question that echoed throughout the Enlightenment was: Does commercial society with its seeming reliance on self-interest constitute a threat to moral or civic virtue, or is a "new" form of society calling forth a new, more appropriate schedule of virtuous conduct?

The Mandevillean Challenge. A focal text in the Enlightenment debate over the meaning of virtue is a work by the Dutch-born physician and essayist Bernard Mandeville (1670–1733), *Fable of the Bees* (1714). What made this composite work of verse and extensive commentary important was that Mandeville was regarded not only as both the prime exponent of the selfish philosophy—the successor in notoriety to the English philosopher Thomas Hobbes (1588–1679)—but also as an advocate of the merits of commerce. Mandeville's main aim was the identification of a contradiction between theory and practice. He claimed to have demonstrated that it is impossible to enjoy the benefits of an elegant and comfortable life, as they are experienced by the members of industrious and prosperous nations, while simultaneously leading a virtuous and innocent life as prescribed either by strict Christian teaching or by the philosophical version of the good life, especially in its popular Stoic form. He wished to expose the intellectual inconsistency of those moralists who decried the avarice, self-indulgence, and weakness of an opulent and flourishing society but who still desired the benefits of material prosperity.

Mandeville's contemporaries read this to mean that he was accusing all virtuous individuals of being practicing hypocrites. Beyond this, he was interpreted as arguing that the benefits of industry and wealth are associated with certain inextirpatable vices, not with virtues. This broke the links in an accepted causal chain. Beneficial effects, like industry, were supposed to follow from appropriately worthy causes; virtue thus begat its own reward, whereas vice produced bad effects. This notion was reinforced by the link with religion. For example, the Irish bishop George Berkeley (1685–1753) maintained that religion is cherished because it is impossible for a nation to thrive without virtue (*Ruin of Great Britain*, 1721), and the Anglican clergyman William Paley (1743–1805) defined virtue as "doing good to mankind in obedience to the will of God" (*Principles of Moral and Political Philosophy*, 1786). In essence, a good and Christian society comprises virtuous individuals performing good deeds. Mandeville had no quarrel with this, so long as the "good society" meant one where comfort and luxury were absent; but once these, and the values they represent, are admitted into the definition of a "good society" (as the evidence of the actual practice of men now reveals to be the case), then the supposed vices of pride, avarice, envy, vanity, must also be allowed.

The significance of Mandeville's challenge can be appreciated by noting how deep-rooted the conventions were that he was ridiculing. The "natural life" was the (neo)-classical "simple" or Christian ascetic life. Those who live a virtuous, simple life, it was claimed, will not be poor because poverty is experienced only by those who have exceeded nature's bounds—that is, by those who desire more. According to this approach, the definitive characteristic of desires that focus on the body—on what the Scottish philosopher David Hume (1711–1776) called "a more splendid way of life" in which the senses are gratified—is that they are boundless. Since bodily desires have no natural limit, there is no resting place for them. Viewed from that perspective, life will always appear too short, and those who see matters in this light will become "soft" and afraid of death. Such fear is unmanly. That gendered language was not accidental: those unable to endure hardship and to act courageously (with Latin *virtus*, or Greek *andreia*) in the definitively masculine (as a "man," *vir*, *aner/andra*) fashion were seen as effeminate. To live effeminately or luxuriously (the terms were synonyms) is to devote oneself to the pleasures of self-indulgence and avarice.

Such a life has significant social consequences. The strength (*virtus*) or virility of a state depends on the virtues of its citizens, as the Genevan republican theorist and essayist Jean-Jacques Rousseau (1712–1778) maintained throughout his writings. A society where luxury is established and where commerce is the dominant enterprise will devote itself to private ends, and effeminate men will fail to exhibit virtue; they will be unwilling to act (and fight) for the public good. This society, it follows, will be militarily weak. Commerce breeds cowards. Commerce was further suspect because of the uncertainty or risk that lies at its core: there is no guarantee that the merchant will be able to sell his goods. A system resting on nothing more tangible than belief, opinion, and expectation seemed clearly too insubstantial to support a social order. These views were fueled by spectacular financial collapses, such as the mid-seventeenth-century Dutch "tulipomania," the Darien scheme to establish a Scottish colony, and, in the 1720s, the South Sea Bubble in England and John Law's scheme in France. These events were judged to be symptomatic of deep structural flaws in any society in which such disasters could happen.

The touchstone of this judgment was the presence of a contrasting model, personified by the independent landowner or country gentleman. This individual's landed property gave him stability and greater security and certainty. In sharp and deliberate contrast to the fluidity of a money economy, the giddy whirl of fashion, and the evanescence of profit, the landowner with his commitment to a fixed place could practice what the Irish-born British parliamentarian Edmund Burke (1729–1797) called the great masculine virtues of constancy, gravity, magnanimity, fortitude, fidelity, and firmness (*Speech on American Taxation*, 1774). To these thoroughly estimable traits could be contrasted the proverbial unreliability of women; their fickleness—their "prerogative to change their mind"—symbolized evocatively the inconstancy of commercial life.

To defend commerce meant dissociating it from its role as a source of corruption and a threat to virtue. A number of strategies were developed to achieve that end, the effect of which was to produce a reevaluation or rescheduling of virtues.

The Decline of Courage and Rise of Punctuality. Charles de Secondat Montesquieu (1689–1755), in his enormously influential *L'esprit des lois* (1748), commented that the natural effect of commerce is to lead to peace (book 20). This is indicative of a shift away from martial virtues like courage and values like glory to what the Scottish philosopher and political economist Adam Smith, in his *Theory of Moral Sentiments* (1759), following Montesquieu's terminology, labeled the "gentle virtues" of decency, modesty, and moderation. In *Lectures on Jurisprudence*, the student-recorded version of his Glasgow University lectures in the 1760s, Smith was more precise, identifying probity and punctuality as the principal virtues of a commercial nation (where the greater part of the people are merchants). Smith was not alone. Adam Ferguson (1723–1816), professor of moral philosophy at Edinburgh University, with whom Smith did not always agree, referred to punctuality and fair-dealing as the system of manners of merchants (*Essay on the History of Civil Society*, 1767). In these circumstances, courage can have only a limited role to play. Valor and fortitude only really "count" in circumstances where warfare is endemic, such as in savage society or the early Roman Republic. Speaking of the latter, Claude Helvétius (1715–1771) noted that glory for early Romans was the prize of virtuous action, which he contrasted with the quieter virtues of his own day's respectable, civilized man (*honnête homme*) (*De l'esprit* [On Mind], 1758, Discourse 3).

This contrast was mirrored in a shift in the arena of activity from the public world of politics and war to the private and peaceful realm of industry. In *Of Refinement in the Arts* (1752), Hume declared ages of refinement to be the "happiest and most virtuous." For him, happiness has three components—repose, pleasure, and action—and of these, the last is crucial. The first is merely derivative, valued only as a break from action; the second is integrally connected with action because "being occupied" is itself enjoyable. Humans are roused to activity or industry by a desire for a better, more comfortable way of life than that enjoyed by their ancestors (*Of Commerce*, 1752). This greater comfort manifests itself in refinement of behavior and manners. The more refined a people become, the more they are able to cultivate the pleasures of the mind and body. These pleasures are now associated with virtue and not set against it as the "severe moralists," as Hume called them (naming the Roman historian Sallust as an example) would have it. In addition, there is an increase in sociability, including gallantry toward women. In an implicit rebuke of the country gentleman, this sociability is a product of the increased density of population as they flock into cities, which rather than being the nurseries of "debauchery and voluptuousness" are the source of civility and civilization. Hume summed up these improvements by stating that "industry, knowledge and humanity" are indissolubly linked together and are the prerogative of what he explicitly called "the more luxurious ages."

Hume's reference to "humanity" carries considerable weight. He associates it here with increased conversation and improvement in "temper," or emotional dispositions. These are accompanied by a heightened sensitivity. By contrast, barbarians lack humanity and are brutal, cruel, and bloodthirsty. Smith noted (*Moral Sentiments*, book 5) how savages torture their victims and steel themselves not to express emotion when they are being tortured; such hardiness diminishes their humanity. Their self-command, compared to that exercised by civilized peoples, is more a matter of repression, which when released results in violence and fearful bloodshed. The peaceful humanity of a commercial people, along with their truthfulness and justice, is rewarded with the confidence (a crucial attribute in a commercial society) and esteem of their fellows. Because Smith's moral theory hinges on responsiveness to others (society acts as a mirror within which we see and from which we learn how to make proper judgments), these virtues will establish themselves; the desire to be seen as trustworthy, for example, instills trustworthiness.

In another context, however, the rhetoric of the virtuous, "innocent" savage could be employed as part of a critique of the falsity of hypocritical Christian civilization. Denis Diderot (1713–1784), editor-in-chief of the *Encyclopédie* published between 1751 and 1772, exploited this line of attack in his commentary (published 1796) on L.A. de Bougainville's record of his circumnavigation. As a pretext for his argument, Diderot fastened onto Bougainville's account of Tahiti. Rather than follow nature and live a happy life like the Tahitians, Europeans have, largely for religious reasons, attached the labels of virtue and vice to activities, like those associated with sex, that are not properly subject to moral judgment. In like fashion, Voltaire (1694–1778), the quintessential Enlightenment freethinker, inveighed against dogma and superstition as inimical to virtue. In order to be genuine, virtue has to be socially useful; it must enhance the public good (*Dictionnaire philosophique*, 1764). Others, like the baron d'Holbach (1723–1789), another militant French freethinker, identified as true virtues only those that add to public felicity (*Le Bon-Sens*, 1772). Virtue had always had this public or political character; however, that too underwent a change.

Political Virtue from Participation to Justice. Despite Montesquieu's unique tripartite reclassification of constitutions into republics, monarchies, and tyrannies, he reiterated the received wisdom about the first of these. Each of the three types has its own distinctive "spring" (*ressort*), and in republican, or free, governments, this is identified as "virtue" (book 3). This is political virtue, though it is also moral virtue in the sense that it points toward the general good. Later, this virtue is declared to be a feeling, not a matter of knowledge, and is embodied in patriotism (book 5). More precisely, love of the republic is love of equality and frugality; the former limits ambition to the single desire to render more services to one's country than do other citizens, and the latter limits the desire to possess that which is necessary for family support. The appropriate system of laws is one that would foster these virtues through, for example, regulation of the inheritance and extent of landed property. To eighteenth-century subscribers to the republican tradition, frugality and political equality were threatened by commerce and luxury. The growth of commerce not only enfeebled moral character, making a frugal lifestyle unpalatable, but it also undermined the political solidarity and commitment that can be attained only through shared participation in the public arena (*res publica*). Citizens should exhibit both civic and martial virtues in pursuit of the public good, the latter through membership in a citizen militia.

The crux of this distinctively republican or political conception of virtue is that humans (that is, males) realize themselves in political action; Aristotle's dictum that man is a political animal is the canonical text. In the Enlightenment, the most illustrious exponent of this view was Rousseau. For him, the essence of political virtue lay in the citizen willing the general will—that is, willing the common good as an indivisible part of the individual's own good. This can occur only where there is direct participation by all citizens without exception in sovereign decisions, and where there is political equality and economic independence (see *Discours sur l'oeconomie politique*, 1755; *Du contrat social*, 1766). Though not necessarily in his terms, Rousseau's defense of republican virtue was echoed throughout the Enlightenment, notably in America, where the establishment of a republic was more than a rhetorical conceit, and where there was a self-conscious endeavor to deal with the conditions of citizenship. As Thomas Jefferson manifested in both thought and deed, this was consistent with slave-ownership and the exclusion of women—as it had been in the ancient world.

The writer best known for contesting the maleness of republican virtue is Mary Wollstonecraft (1759–1797) in her *Vindication of the Rights of Woman* (1792).

Though influenced by Rousseau's educational treatise *Émile* (1766), she fiercely attacked his view of women as properly nonpolitical. She sought to redefine virtue so that, for a woman, it was not focused on her sex. Women, she argued, cannot be virtuous until they are free to use their reason and are educated accordingly. In this way, Wollstonecraft took issue with the notion that docility, chastity, and modesty define female virtue.

Just as the defense of commerce reevaluated the merit of glory and honor, so a central part of commerce's vindication was a reevaluation of the virtue of direct political participation. There was a shift away from participatory action to adherence to rules, so that justice, one of the original cardinal virtues, attained new primacy. For Diderot, there was properly only one virtue, and that was justice; the "invariable rules of justice" were identical with the common interest (*Histoire philosophique des Deux Indes*, 1783). Perhaps not surprisingly, in view of their articulated defense of commerce, both Hume and Smith were prominent exponents of this approach to justice—and, by extension, to the proper role of the magistrate.

For Hume, justice is an artificial virtue (*Treatise of Human Nature*, 1739/40, book 3). By this, he meant that it is the product of human conventions or agreements. Though conventional, it is not contingent but necessary. The source of this necessity lies in the conjunction of two sets of facts: humans, though not selfish in Mandeville's or Hobbes's sense, do have only a limited generosity; and there is relative scarcity of desired goods. The presence of these ineliminable facts means that, without justice, society "must immediately dissolve." Justice is thus useful. What makes it also a virtue is Hume's position that morality is a matter of feeling, not of reason. Accordingly, what induces pain, such as acts prejudicial to social order (injustice), will be called a vice, and what supports order—preeminently, justice—will be deemed a virtue. The content of justice is a system of rules: stability of possession, its transfer by consent, and promise-keeping.

Although Hume's terminology was not accepted (indeed, he himself dropped the word "artificial" in his later versions), the preconditional necessity of justice was commonplace. That justice manifests itself in invariable rule-following is indicative of its operation in a commercial society, because stable expectations are necessary for markets to operate. Without confidence in consistent regulation, there is little point—as Smith demonstrated in the *Wealth of Nations* (1776)—in specialization, the source of commercial opulence (and of military effectiveness, since a professional army is superior to any citizen militia). Hence it is, as historically informed Enlightenment thinkers such as Jean-François Melon (1675–1738), Antonio Genovesi (1713–1769), and Anne-Robert Turgot

(1727–1781) could see, that hunter-gatherers were miserably poor. This poverty is not the mother of virtue, as the late seventeenth century republican theorist Algernon Sydney styled it in his *Discourses Concerning Government* (1698); instead, it produces the abandonment of infants, the aged, and the infirm to the elements (see Smith's Introduction to the *Wealth of Nations*). There is nothing virtuous about that policy, which offends the Enlightenment virtue of humanity.

If justice is now the prime political virtue, then the preeminent task of the magistrate is to enforce it, and that of citizens to adhere to it. This adherence is enforceable, so justice is a strict virtue, but it is essentially negative: refraining from injustice and following the rules. Again, an implicit critique of direct political virtue can be detected. Hume, for example, criticized Sparta, the classical paradigm of a military regime founded on hard, austere virtues. Sparta, he wrote, was unworthy of emulation because its vaunted virtue and military prowess rested on slavery, and slavery, if nothing else, is "disadvantageous" to "happiness" (*Of the Populousness of Ancient Nations*, 1752). Beyond that, a Spartan devotion to the public good is unrealistic; it runs against the grain of human nature. Two noteworthy consequences follow. First, political virtue is too fragile a base on which to erect a system of government; and second, this means that, in the normal run of things, governments must govern their subjects by those passions that most effectively animate them.

Because humans always act in conformity with their interests, legislation, as Helvétius directed, should assign punishments to vice and rewards to virtue, so that all individuals will find it in their interest to be virtuous (*De l'homme* [*On Man*], 1773). There is the possibility of scientific precision here, and the English legal theorist Jeremy Bentham (1748–1832) attempted to achieve it in *Principles of Morals and Legislation* (1789). The cornerstone of this endeavor was his principle of utility, which he based on regarding pleasure and pain as the sovereign masters of human behavior. These determine both what we do and what we ought to do. On this basis, virtue refers either to the happiness of the agent (prudence) or to that of others (benevolence). Building on the stable foundations of a science of human nature, it can now be held that the golden age of virtue lies not in the past but in the future. The marquis de Condorcet (1743–1794), a mathematician and philosopher, expected that virtue, in indissoluble conjunction with truth and happiness, will be truly realized when the sun shines only on free men knowing no master but their own reason (*Des progrès de l'esprit humain*, 1793).

Moral Virtue and Self-Interest. Mandeville's attack on hypocrisy was interpreted as the claim that all virtue was an invention and was thus unnatural. This was assailed throughout the early and middle decades of the eighteenth century. The "naturalness of virtue" was insisted on. This meant that virtuousness was an indisputable empirical fact of human nature, because all available historical and ethnographic evidence showed that humans acted morally. Of course, they were self-interested, but, as Bishop Joseph Butler (1692–1752) argued in a series of sermons (1726), private interest and virtuous conduct were not opposed but rooted in human nature. Indeed, we would be unable to justify the pursuit of virtue to ourselves if it were not seen to be conducive to our happiness. Perhaps the most persistent and insistent critic of Mandeville was the Glasgow professor Francis Hutcheson (1694–1746). He identified in the constitution of human nature the possession of a moral sense, and he held that what is approved by this sense is called "virtue." Other theorists might dispute that source and, like Butler, contest Hutcheson's view that benevolence comprises the entirety of virtue; but it was generally accepted that humans are constituted to condemn falsehood, violence, and injustice as vices, and to commend benevolence and prudence as virtues.

Hutcheson's anti-Mandevillean naturalism and Hume's more nuanced version are, along with Helvétius's programmatic pleasure/pain approach, among the progenitors of utilitarianism identified by Jeremy Bentham. Although utilitarianism in some guise was in many ways the dominant moral philosophy of the Enlightenment, its intellectual cogency was found wanting by Immanuel Kant (1724–1804). Kant had been aroused by reading Hume to develop a new, non-empiricist epistemology; and, as part of his thoroughgoing rethinking of philosophical foundations, he also articulated a new non-empiricist account of virtue.

Kant's most systematic treatment appears in his *Grundlegung der Metaphysik der Sitten* (part 2, 1797). The doctrine of virtue (as he called it) deals not with duties that are imposed by external laws (which is the sphere of the doctrine of right), but with those that are internally imposed. This self-imposition is definitive of free agency; and, for Kant, the naturalism of utilitarianism, based in the physical responsiveness of pleasure and pain, is an obstacle to freedom. Kant thus identified virtue with successful resistance to what opposes the moral disposition—that is, to the performance of one's duties for duty's sake. Humans act dutifully, or virtuously, when the ends of their actions are moral ends. These ends have no source other than their free will. Hence, contrary to the empiricism of Hutcheson or Hume, virtue is not the outcome of a sense or a feeling; contrary to the Aristotelian tradition, neither is it a habitual striking of the mean between vices; rather, it is self-constraint in accordance with the principle of freedom. Elsewhere, Kant, exhibiting his debt to Rousseau, identified this principle with republican government, but he also upheld the historical argument that savage life represents a degraded, virtue-deficient form of human existence, and that the spirit of commerce is incompatible with war (*Zum ewigen Frieden*, 1795). In his own unique way, Kant can thus be seen to embody the interwoven discourses on virtue found in the Enlightenment.

[*See also* Human Nature; Moral Philosophy; *and* Political Philosophy.]

BIBLIOGRAPHY

Berry, Christopher J. *Social Theory of the Scottish Enlightenment*. Edinburgh, 1997. An accessible overview with chapters on the debate over commercial society and Scottish moral theory.

Blum, Carol. *Diderot: The Virtue of a Philosopher*. London, 1974. An intellectual biography that focuses on Diderot's concept of virtue and his need to experience himself as a virtuous man.

Burtt, Shelley. *Virtue Transformed: Political Argument in England, 1688–1740*. Cambridge, 1992. Charts and argues for the emergence of a privately oriented civic virtue.

Crocker, Lester. *Nature and Culture: Ethical Thought in the French Enlightenment*. Baltimore, 1963. Occasionally hostile overview of the identified central moral problem of how to socialize the egoistic individual.

Darwall, Stephen. *The British Moralists and the Internal 'Ought'*. Cambridge, 1995. Detailed analysis of British discourse up to and including Hume.

Dent, N. J. H. *Rousseau*. Oxford, 1988. An informed overview of Rousseau's key arguments.

Griswold, Charles L., Jr. *Adam Smith and the Virtues of Enlightenment*. Cambridge, 1999. The most thorough analysis of Smith's *Moral Sentiments* available.

Hope, Vincent. *Virtue by Consensus*. Oxford, 1989. Careful internal critique of Hutcheson, Hume, and Smith.

Hundert, E. G. *The Enlightenment's "Fable": Bernard Mandeville and the Discovery of Society*. Cambridge, 1994. Useful collection of linked essays discussing Mandeville and his influence.

Lyons, David. *In the Interest of the Governed*. Oxford, 1973. A study of Bentham's moral and legal theory.

MacIntyre, Alasdair. *After Virtue: A Study in Moral Theory*. 2d ed. London, 1985. A controversial account of the failure of what he calls the "Enlightenment Project" to establish a secure foundation for morality.

MacIntyre, Alasdair. *Whose Justice? Which Rationality?* London, 1988. Continues the broad theme of *After Virtue* but pays special attention to the debate in Scotland.

Norton, David Fate. *David Hume: Common-Sense Moralist and Sceptical Metaphysician*. Princeton, N.J., 1982. A careful, contextual argument for Hume as moral realist, a mitigated naturalist.

Pocock, J. G. A. *Virtue, Commerce and History*. Cambridge, 1985. Pocock is the scholar who has done most to resurrect the interest in civic virtue; these essays focus on the eighteenth century.

Sapiro, Virginia. *A Vindication of Political Virtue: The Political Theory of Mary Wollstonecraft*. Chicago, 1992. A measured feminist interpretation placing her in a tradition of democratic thought.

Schneewind, J. B. *The Invention of Autonomy*. Cambridge, 1998. A comprehensive exegetical history of moral theory from the Renaissance to Kant.

Sullivan, Roger J. *Immanuel Kant's Moral Theory*. Cambridge, 1989. A thorough expository account of the range of Kant's writings on morality.

Viroli, Maurizio. *Jean-Jacques Rousseau and the "Well-Ordered Society."* Cambridge, 1988. Treats Rousseau's thought as one of the last expressions of classical republicanism.

CHRISTOPHER J. BERRY

VIRTUOSI. In the sixteenth and early seventeenth centuries, boys had flocked to the universities to study subjects that they expected to fit them for employment and to teach them about a world that was rapidly changing. These students had been drilled in the classics and could bring to their studies a knowledge of many aspects of the ancient world. Some who became physicians were interested in botany, astrology, and astronomy; they usually had some training in mathematics and natural philosophy. Many others who became lawyers were more interested in history. Since the 1540s, the widespread interest in history and its methods had been related to the construction of histories of Rome, Greece, and then of modern states, some of which were only then taking shape. The modern histories excited men because it was widely believed they could be used to uphold contentious political and religious positions. Another interest, in ancient art and the standards that still defined good art, tied some scholars to earlier humanists and literary men. Most educated men had also absorbed the medieval lesson that all natural things were related to a creative God who was best described in the Christian revelation, which some saw as ongoing or, at least, a revelation that was being progressively better understood. Others founded a natural theology on the order of the natural world. The Renaissance had thus generally broadened conceptions of knowledge and had made it more polite. Out of this complex mixture there emerged the concept and life of the "Virtuoso."

The word *virtuoso* first came into the English language in the mid-seventeenth century when it denoted those who were curious about and collected information and objects of almost every kind. The virtuosi built upon this foundation, but they accepted the need to find out new things in every field. This made them receptive to the skeptical, empirical, and improving messages conveyed by Francis Bacon (1561–1626) and the innovating but not always utopian messages of pansophists such as Johann Valentin Andreae (1586–1654) or Jan Amos Comenius (1592–1670). Bacon urged men to collect information on everything; or, as he said, to write the natural histories of inanimate objects, plants, animals, and processes of all kinds. That required classification of data deriving from the ancients but also from their own and from the new worlds being discovered and explored overseas. Having found and sorted things, one should attempt to understand and explain these things causally, relating them to one another, but also to the Creator. Bacon also thought that his natural histories found parallels in civil and ecclesiastical histories where thinkers needed critically to gather the facts and come to a better understanding of men and their societies over time. From all that would come knowledge purged of the errors of the past, reorganized, and expanded by the searches and experiments of the learned. This knowledge could then be used to control and dominate nature for the benefit of mankind, an activity that would also require new institutions. Most of the virtuosi accepted such a program, although many did not take it from the works of Bacon.

Virtuosi had not existed in numbers much before 1600; fifty years later they were numerous enough to be named and even ridiculed because most of them were collectors of what seemed to many to be useless objects. The Copenhagen museum (1630–1654) or cabinet of Ole Worm, M.D. (1588–1654), was the subject of a famous Dutch print of 1655. It contained a great array of minerals, chemicals, dried plant specimens, stuffed animals, skeletons and anatomical preparations, and artifacts such as an Eskimo's clothing, kayak, and weapons. It contained Danish archaeological artifacts, some instruments, and pieces that belonged more to the fine arts than to collections of natural curiosities. Greater museums, formed at courts, colleges, or in learned societies, such as that of Athanasius Kircher (1602–1680), in the Roman college of his Jesuit order, were not much different save in size and variety. The virtuosi were among the creators of the museums and learned societies.

By the end of the seventeenth century, the virtuosi had managed to make themselves both conspicuous and useful. They filled an increasing number of offices from which knowledge could be advanced and made to change the world. Such men also gave popularity and status to learning. In Paris, these men included many of the amateurs and academicians who supported and disseminated new ideas. This was equally true in London and other centers with scientific and antiquarian societies. The Irish physician and naturalist Sir Hans Sloane, M.D. (1660–1753), who lived in London, was active in antiquarian, historical, botanical, and natural history societies and in improving groups throughout his very long life. This royal physician and secretary and president of the Royal Society of London amassed an astonishing collection of things of every sort. His library alone totaled some fifty thousand books. Sloane's collections made important contributions in Britain to natural history and even ethnology. They became the basis for the collections of the British Museum, of which he must be regarded as the true founder. His career overlapped those of many of the enlightened who, when they visited him, as many did, would have seen little difference between his concerns and their own.

The Enlightenment inherited from the virtuosi interests in science and its methods and a belief that the acquisition of new knowledge was important if improvements were to be made. These beliefs greatly influenced the early stages of the Enlightenment throughout Europe. The enlightened benefited from the virtuosi's institution-building and collecting. The enlightened pushed further their acceptance of a measure of tolerance and secularization as the price of cooperation among scholars and progress in the studies that interested them. The Enlightenment retained until its end their generally encyclopedic and holistic view of knowledge, prizing that above narrow specializations and insisting that it be purged of error. The enlightened also tended to retain the belief that science had religious and moral implications that were among its most important features. The ranks of the virtuosi included many amateurs who found that the knowledge they prized was not incompatible with politeness and refinement. That too was an attitude widely held by the enlightened who by the end of the eighteenth century had begun to think of the virtuosi as connoisseurs concerned primarily with works of art of antiquities.

[*See also* Aesthetics; Archaeology; Aristocracy, *subentry on* Cultural Contributions; Clerk, John; Clubs and Societies; Erskine, David Steuart; Exhibitions; Jefferson, Thomas; Natural Philosophy and Science; *and* Salons.]

BIBLIOGRAPHY

Emerson, Roger L. "Sir Robert Sibbald, Kt., the Royal Society of Scotland and the Origins of the Scottish Enlightenment." *Annals of Science* 45 (1988), 41–72. This looks at a virtuoso in a provincial setting and traces much of the Scottish Enlightenment to his concerns.

Levine, Joseph M. *Dr. Woodward's Shield: History, Science, and Satire in Augustan England*. Berkeley and Los Angeles, 1977. An account of Sloane's rival whose career was almost as interesting and in which history was more important.

MacGregor, Arthur. *Sir Hans Sloane: Collector, Scientist, Antiquary*. London, 1994. This is a profusely annotated collection of essays on all aspects of Sloane's career.

Manuel, Frank E., and Fritzie P. *Utopian thought in the Western World*. Cambridge, Mass., 1979, pp. 203–331. This section deals with the pansophist and Baconian contributions to a new mind-set in Europe.

Pomian, Krzystof. *Collectors and Curiosities: Paris and Venice, 1500–1800*. Cambridge, 1990.

Webster, Charles. *The Great Instauration*. London, 1975. A brilliant account of the English Baconians.

Whitaker, Kate. "The Culture of Curiosity." In *The Cultures of Natural History*, edited by N. Jardine, J. A. Secord, and E.C. Spary, pp. 75–90. Cambridge, 1996.

ROGER L. EMERSON

VITALISM. The term *vitalism* designates the physiological theories that attribute the phenomena of life neither to matter, nor to the soul, but to an intermediary principle possessing properties of its own. During the second half of the eighteenth century, vitalism was professed in various institutions at the same time that the comparative study of living beings fostered the advent of biology. The methodologies involved in vitalism ranged from the empirical to the metaphysical, and they linked observations and experiments with speculative hypotheses. The vitalist physiologies exerted considerable influence on such philosophes as Denis Diderot, Charles Bonnet, Immanuel Kant, and Friedrich Wilhelm Joseph von Schelling.

In the early 1700s, mainstream physiology was mechanistic. The circumstance that triggered the advent of vitalism was the identification in 1752 by the Swiss physiologist Albrecht von Haller (1708–1777) of irritability and sensibility (sensitivity) as vital properties that emerged from special configurations of fibers, the presumed elementary structures of organic bodies. Though not a vitalist, Haller postulated a special inherent force of muscle fibers producing autonomous contractile motions that were independent of any central sensitive determination. Sensibility seemed likewise to depend on a network of nerve fibers centrally connected to the brain (in strict correlation with the psychic functions). The physiological forces involved in both cases were neither subordinate to the psyche nor derived from the physical and chemical features of the fibers. Haller shrank from deciding on the cause of these vital properties, but he presumed that the laws regulating physiological processes still belonged to a physics of organic bodies. His followers deviated considerably from this cautious stand.

The three main centers for the emergence of vitalism were Montpellier in France, Göttingen in Germany, and the medical schools of Scotland. At Montpellier, medical practitioners and theorists tried to combine microstructuralist and animist influences with the ancient Greek medical tradition of Hippocrates. This movement was initiated by the physicians Henri Fouquet (1727–1806), Jean-Jacques Ménuret de Chambaud (1733–1815), and Théophile Bordeu (1722–1776), who contributed to the *Encyclopédie* and inspired the biological aspects of Denis Diderot's thought. Bordeu, in his *Recherches anatomiques sur la position des glandes et leur action* (1752), developed the notion that the life of an organism consists of a harmony of actions between its different parts, each of which depends on its respective sensibility; reacting to stimulations, these sensibilities are responsible for all processes of health and illness. Such a physiology posits an architecture of fetal nervous filaments that issue from an embryo's primordial fiber: this complex network determines and coordinates organic processes by means of the various adaptative operations of organic sensibility. Fouquet, in his article "Sensibilité" in the *Encyclopédie*, wrote: "Sensibility being apportioned to each organic part of the body, each organ feels and lives in its own manner, and the

combination and sum of these particular lives makes the general life, in the same way that the harmony, symmetry and arrangement of these small lives produces health" (1765, vol. 15, p. 42b). The Montpellier paradigm culminated in the *Nouveaux éléments de la science de l'homme* (1778) of the physician Paul-Joseph Barthez (1734–1806). According to him, physiological functions manifested considerable autonomy in the way they utilized and modified organic conditions to maintain an adequate level of vital dynamism. *Vital principle* is his term to denote this correlation of the sensitive and motive vital forces that form the unity of an organism. These forces are to be conceived as experimental causes reflecting the "sympathies" and "synergies" that characterize the correlations of physiological and pathological phenomena. The two types of forces forming the system of the vital principle are acting forces, which implement the processes of organic life in the various parts, and radical forces, which regulate and preserve the changing balance of acting forces needed for maintaining an organism's integrity.

German vitalism derived from other theories. The naturalist Caspar Friedrich Wolff (1733–1794) in his *Theoria generationis* (1759) restored epigenesis, which supposed that an essential force organized complex organisms from an amorphous blend of seeds. The physician Friedrich Kasimir Medicus (1736–1808) in his *Von der Lebenskraft* (1774) tried to demonstrate that a specific principle of vital impulse counters the dissolving effect of mechanical processes in organic components and coordinates physiological processes. The main German vitalist theory was that of Johann Friedrich Blumenbach (1752–1840). In his memoir *Über den Bildungstrieb und das Zeugungsgeschäfte* (1781), this renowned Göttingen physiologist and naturalist argued that the formation of the organism required a force capable of prefiguring the structural and functional organization to be achieved, a force that embodied a kind of immanent plan and implemented it by adjusting to external and internal circumstances that affected the organic development. This "formative disposition" (*Bildungstrieb*) produced the various vital forces related to specific organic structures, and it governed their interactions for the sake of the whole. The formative disposition, thus understood, accomplished a finality of internal organization.

This finality is precisely the type of relation that Immanuel Kant (1724–1804) in his *Kritik der Urteilskraft* (1790) derived from the reflective activity of the judging mind and that he deemed indispensable to regulate our comprehension of "organized and self-organizing bodies," all parts of which acted respectively as ends and means for the sake of the whole, under the guidance of a formative force. Kant's positive appraisal of Blumenbachian vitalism stimulated new speculative tendencies in German philosophy and biology, usually classified as *Naturphilosophie* and Romantic science. Schelling, in his treatise *Von der Weltseele* (1798), criticizes Kant for having restricted the vital force to a mere hypothetical representation of the cause of vital phenomena, that is, as a mere fiction of reflective judgment. Instead, the philosophy of nature must conceptualize a "free interplay of forces" that presents to transcendental intuition the very essence of life, both in its autonomy and in its constant resistance to external influences. Romantic science, as represented by the scientific works of Johann Wolgang von Goethe, appealed to the theoretical schemes or principles that could unify the several orders of natural phenomena and express their integrative hierarchy from the inorganic to the spiritual level. Such abstract representations occasioned a variety of particular models to account for the physiological processes that encompass the various life forms. In this way, such models helped to create the foundations of the new science of biology.

In the Anglo-Saxon world, the Scottish physician and comparative anatomist John Hunter (1728–1793) was probably the most influential vitalist. In his *Lectures on the Principles of Surgery* (1786–1787) and *Treatise on the Blood, Inflammation, and Gun-shot Wounds* (1793), Hunter affirmed the absolute irreducibility of vital phenomena and framed a theory of the vital principle. Organic matter is endowed with special powers and modes of action for both preservation and reproduction. His concept of vital principle signified an autonomous agent that produced and regulated organic phenomena independently from the organization into which it fitted. This agent was present in the least organic components, which had elementary vital powers, and diffused their action to neighboring parts and associated themselves for the sake of higher level functions. There were thus two kinds of functions: those consisting of the common actions of the various parts, such as growth, assimilation, and disassimilation; and those consisting of the global actions of specialized organs, such as digestion, circulation, respiration, sensibility, conscious awareness, and voluntary motion. The complex organic systems resulted from a combination of the powers of elementary parts, but they supported in their turn the basic operations of life. The vital principle was at once segmented and unified, insofar as it represented the integrative activity of complex organisms. Well supported by a variety of observations in comparative anatomy, Hunter's vitalism exerted considerable influence on the early developments of experimental physiology at the turn of the nineteenth century. His influence can be definitely traced, for example, in the French anatomist and physiologist Xavier Bichat's *Recherches physiologiques sur la vie et la mort* (1801).

[*See also* Academies; Life Sciences; Medicine, *subentry on* Theories of Medicine; Spontaneous Generation; *and* Zoology.]

BIBLIOGRAPHY

Cimino, Guido, and François Duchesneau, eds. *Vitalism from Haller to the Cell Theory*. Florence, 1997. Essays that document the various aspects of vitalism in the life sciences between 1750 and 1850.

Cross, S. J. "John Hunter, the Animal Oeconomy, and Late-Eighteenth-Century Physiology." *Studies in History of Biology* 5 (1981), 1–110. Presentation of the diverse aspects of Hunter's conception of the living.

Duchesneau, François. *La physiologie des Lumières: Empirisme, modèles et théories*. The Hague, 1982. The most comprehensive study available on the evolution of physiological theories in the eighteenth century.

Duchesneau, François. "Vitalism in Late Eighteenth Century Physiology: The Cases of Barthez, Blumenbach and John Hunter." In *William Hunter and the Eighteenth Century Medical World*, edited by William F. Bynum and Roy Porter, pp. 259–295. Cambridge, 1985. A comparison that emphasizes the common features of the principal vitalist doctrines of the Enlightenment.

Hall, Thomas S. *Ideas of Life and Matter: Studies in the History of General Physiology*. Chicago, 1969. Presentation of the history of physiology; sections 28–35 are concerned with the reappraisal of vitalism.

Kaitaro, Timo. *Diderot's Holism: Philosophical Anti-reductionism and Its Medical Background*. Frankfurt, Germany, 1997.

Lenoir, Timothy. "The Göttingen School and the Development of Transcendental Naturphilosophie." *Studies in History of Biology* 5 (1981), 111–205. The best available general presentation of the relationship of *Naturphilosophie* with the life sciences.

Lenoir, Timothy. *The Strategy of Life: Teleology and Mechanics in Nineteenth-Century German Biology*. Dordrecht, Netherlands, 1982. Chapter 1 is devoted to the relationship between Blumenbach and Kant.

Roe, Shirley A. *Matter, Life, and Generation: Eighteenth-Century Embryology and the Haller–Wolff Debate*. Cambridge, 1981. Presentation of the theory of generation at the turning point of Wolff's restoration of epigenesis.

Williams, Elizabeth A. *The Physical and the Moral: Anthropology, Physiology, and Philosophical Medicine in France, 1750–1850*. Cambridge, 1994. Chapters 1 and 2 describe the evolution of French vitalism in the eighteenth century.

FRANÇOIS DUCHESNEAU

VOLNEY, CONSTANTIN-FRANÇOIS DE CHASSEBOEUF (1757–1820), French political philosopher and anthropologist.

The man of letters who is now known by his pen name, Volney, was born to Jacques-René Chasseboeuf and Jeanne Gigault de la Giraudais in Craon, now in the department of Mayenne. His mother died when her son was not yet two, and his father did not show much tenderness toward the boy, who was sent away to school at the age of seven. His lonely, self-centered childhood was to influence his way of life as well as his studies. At school, he showed a keen interest in Hebrew and Oriental languages. In 1780, he attended a course in Arabic while beginning medical studies that he never completed.

The youth, now using the name Boisgirais (which his father had substituted for the somewhat comical family surname), was in Paris in the 1780s. There he met the baron d'Holbach and was included in the "Groupe d'Auteuil" meeting at the home of Mme. Helvétius: Georges Cabanis, père Lefebvre, abbé Lefebre Laroche, and Dominique Garat. This intellectual circle helped him form his moral basis and his idea of man. In the same salon, he became friends with Benjamin Franklin.

In 1782, Boisgirais traveled in the Middle East and Egypt, serving his apprenticeship as a traveler and ethnologist; all his works bear the mark of this experience. He published *Voyage en Syrie et en Égypte, pendant les années 1783, 1784 et 1785* in 1787, adopting his pen name Volney, which he compounded of the name of Voltaire and of Voltaire's home, Ferney. In April 1785, he returned to Paris, where he met Thomas Jefferson, who was his friend and correspondent for many years. In 1788, Volney published *Considérations sur la guerre des Turcs* (On the Turkish War).

On the eve of the French Revolution, in the Rennes newspaper *La Sentinelle du Peuple*, Volney wrote a vigorous polemic against a nobility attached to its privileges and its titles. On 11 March 1789, he was elected member of the Tiers-État for the province of Anjou at the Constituent Assembly. There, he defended the rights of foreign peoples and later strongly opposed the conquests made by the Revolution. Still later, he campaigned against Napoleon's project to annex Louisiana.

Volney's most famous book, *Les ruines, ou, Méditation sur les révolutions des empires* (1791), is a true philosophical testament inspired by his travels in the East. While staying in Corsica (January 1792–February 1793), he tried to implement one of his numerous agricultural projects. There, too, he befriended a then obscure officer, Napoleon Bonaparte. Volney wrote *La loi naturelle ou Catéchisme du Citoyen* (Natural Law, or the Citizen's Catechism) during a few months' stay in western France, where he had been sent as a superintendent-observer by the ideologist Garat, then home office minister. This catechism, based on reason and not on faith, aimed to promote a morality free from all prejudice. On 16 November 1793, Volney was arrested and imprisoned, just when he had decided to leave France for the United States. He was liberated after the Thermidor coup.

At the beginning of 1795, Volney began a series of Lectures of History at the École Normale de l'An III, one of the most original of the French Republic's educational institutions. He introduced a spirit of criticism where authority alone had reigned. The École Normale, however, closed in May 1795. During this period, Volney was also working on his *Simplification des langues orientales*.

On 12 July 1795, Volney set sail to the United States, where he stayed for about three years, traveling extensively. In January 1797, he was elected a member of the American Philosophical Society. In 1791, he had suggested the creation of a museum of ethnography in the Louvre, and he attended with the keenest interest several meetings of the society at which American scholars and explorers displayed artifacts, ritual clothing, and shamanic masks from various Indian tribes, and discussed Indian musical rites and ceremonies. Volney embarked for Europe in June 1798; he maintained a correspondence with Jefferson.

Like the other Ideologues, Volney had thought that supporting Napoleon would save freedom, but he soon discovered he had helped to set up a military despotism. He then devoted himself, above all, to his work. He published *Le tableau du climat et du sol des États-Unis* (A View of the Soil and Climate of the United States of America) in 1803, and *Nouvelles recherches sur l'histoire ancienne* (New Researches on Ancient History, 1813). His last book was *L'histoire de Samuel, inventeur du sacre des rois* (History of Samuel, Inventor of the Rite of Kings, 1819), fed by his experience in Egypt and Syria, which opened the way to an anthropological interpretation of the Bible. Volney died in Paris. His *Vues nouvelles sur l'enseignement des langues orientales* (New Views on the Teaching of Oriental Languages) was published in 1826.

Volney was in essence a man of the Enlightenment. His rationalism, his distrust of all forms of prejudices, his hostility against dogmas, his faith in progress, his open mind for alternative ideas, and his deep concern for the investigation of facts made him a true disciple of Diderot, Helvétius, and d'Holbach. Volney, however, thought differently from his predecessors on several important points and opened the way for the development of ethnology and cross-cultural psychology. He broke with the speculative anthropology of the Enlightenment, which theorized about "primitive" cultures without actually knowing them. He learned the languages of the people whom he was observing by mixing and living with them. This made him conscious of Western prejudices, which he analyzed with clarity. As early as his stay in Egypt and Syria, he was aware of the importance of using the comparative method to distinguish the universal from the particular.

The Revolution, and the Empire with its train of wars and conquests, changed the philosophy of Volney and of most of the Ideologues. In the New World, Volney discovered indigenes whose social structures had been destroyed by colonialism—who had lost their culture and had been torn from their traditional surroundings. In Europe, wars, intermarriage, and migrations had revealed the importance of social and cultural adaptation to new social realities. Volney was one of the first Europeans to understand the importance of the scientific study of acculturation, but he came too early. The colonialist nineteenth century, influenced by racialist doctrine, would forget the Ideologues. Our era of massive migration may rediscover them.

Volney questioned a number of inherited ideas which, he said, flattered the Europeans. In particular, he refuted the idea that climate played a preponderant role in the formation of national characteristics. The pages he dedicated to the problem, based on the comparative method, are among the most convincing he wrote. Volney understood the importance of socialization in the family, group, and tribe in the process of cultural acquisition and transmission. He was a precursor not only of cross-cultural psychology but also of psychological anthropology. For example, he clearly contrasted the cultural personalities of the Franco-Canadian and Anglo-Saxon communities living on the Wabash River, in the same climate, with rather similar diets. Culture, he believed, is not transmitted biologically; the causes of differences are to be traced in early influence in the family.

Recent developments in human studies suggest an opportunity for a rediscovery of Volney. New studies of his works and those of other forgotten Ideologues should improve the recently tarnished image of the French Enlightenment, whose end some historians wrongly place at the death of Diderot.

[*See also* American Philosophical Society; Asia; French Revolution; Idéologues; *and* Native Americans.]

BIBLIOGRAPHY

WORKS BY VOLNEY
Ocuvres Complètes. Paris, 1821.
Travels through Syria and Egypt in the Years 1783, 1784 and 1785. English translation, London, 1788.
A View of the Soil and Climate of the United States of America. Translated by C. B. Brown. Philadelphia, 1804. English translation of *Tableau du Climat et du Sol des États-Unis*, first published in 1803.

STUDIES
Chinard, Gilbert. *Volney et l'Amérique d'après des documents et sa correspondance avec Jefferson* (Johns Hopkins Studies in Romance Literatures and Languages, 1). Baltimore, 1923.
Gaulmier, Jean. *L'Idéologue Volney (1757–1820): Contribution à l'histoire de l'Orientalisme*. Paris, 1980. First published in 1952. Essential.
Gusdorf, Georges. *La conscience Révolutionnaire: Les Idéologues*. Paris, 1978.
Moravia, Sergio. *Il Pensiero degli Idéologues*. Florence, 1974.
Matucci, Mario, ed. *Gli "Idéologues" e la Rivoluzione*. Pisa, 1991.
Mauviel, Maurice. "L'Anthropologie des Idéologues, une rupture épistémologique?" In *Idéologie, Grammaire-Écoles centrales, Colloque organisé par le Romanisches Seminar, Universität Tübingen Avril 2001*. Forthcoming.
Roussel, Jean, ed. *L'Héritage des Lumières: Volney et les Idéologues*. Angers, 1988.

MAURICE MAUVIEL

VOLTAIRE, pseudonym of François-Marie Arouet (1694–1778), French writer.

"The age of Voltaire" has become synonymous with "the Enlightenment," but although Voltaire's eminence as a philosophe is self-evident, the precise originality of his thought and writings is less easily defined. Born in Paris into a wealthy bourgeois family, he was a brilliant pupil of the Jesuits. His rejection of his father's attempts to guide him into a career in the law was sealed in 1718, when he invented a new name for himself: Voltaire is an anagram of Arouet *l(e) j(eune)* (the verb *volter*, "to turn abruptly," evoking perhaps a playful or "volatile" quality); de Voltaire, with the addition of the aristocratic preposition, is an early sign of his social ambition.

Early Life and Works. In the same year that he coined his new name, Voltaire enjoyed his first major literary success when his tragedy *Œdipe* was staged by the Comédie Française. Meanwhile, he was working on an epic poem that had as its protagonist Henri IV, the much-loved French monarch who brought France's civil wars to a close, and who, in Voltaire's treatment, becomes a forerunner of religious toleration; *La Ligue* (later enlarged to become *La Henriade*) was first published in 1723. His

Voltaire. Portrait (c. 1736) after a painting by Maurice-Quentin de La Tour. (Châteaux de Versailles et de Trianon, Versailles, France/Gérard Blot/Giraudon/Art Resource, NY.)

reputation as a poet and dramatist was now comfortably established, and he decided to travel to England to oversee the publishing of the definitive edition of *La Henriade*. His departure for London was precipitated when he unwisely became involved in a humiliating argument with an aristocrat, who had him briefly interned in the Bastille.

Voltaire arrived in London in the autumn of 1726, and what had begun partly as self-imposed exile became a crucially formative period for him. He learned English and mixed with a number of figures prominent in England's political and cultural life. An old saw has it that Voltaire "came to England a poet and left it a philosopher." In truth, he was a philosopher before coming to England, and it would be more accurate to say that Voltaire came to England a poet and left it a prose writer. Voltaire thought of himself first and foremost as a poet, and during his long life he would never abandon the writing of verse, for which he had a remarkable facility (many of his letters are sprinkled with seemingly spontaneous passages of verse). In England, however, he came into contact with models of prose unlike those to which he was accustomed in France: Swift's *Gulliver's Travels*, for example, which Voltaire read on first publication, or Addison's *Spectator*, a periodical he used in order to learn to read English. It is hardly coincidental, therefore, that before returning to France in 1728, Voltaire began writing his first two major essays in prose: a history, the *Histoire de Charles XII*; and a book about the English that is now best known under the title *Lettres philosophiques*, but first published in English translation (London, 1733) as the *Letters Concerning the English Nation*.

The furor created by the publication in France in 1734 of the *Lettres philosophiques* led Voltaire to leave Paris and take refuge in the château of his mistress, Mme. du Châtelet, at Cirey-en-Champagne. From 1734 until Mme. du Châtelet's death in 1749, this was his haven from the world. During this period, he studied and wrote intensively in a wide variety of areas, including science (*Eléments de la philosophie de Newton*, 1738), poetry (*Le mondain*, 1736), drama (*Mahomet*, 1741), and fiction (*Zadig*, 1747). In the 1740s, Voltaire was briefly on better terms with the court: he was made royal historiographer in 1745, and the following year, after several failed attempts, he was finally elected to the Académie Française. He had turned fifty and was now the leading poet and dramatist of his day; perhaps even Voltaire did not imagine that the works that would make him even more celebrated still lay in the future.

An initially idyllic interlude was provided by Voltaire's stay at the court of Potsdam (1750–1753), and in 1752 he published both *Le siècle de Louis XIV* and *Micromégas*. Throughout his career, however, Voltaire was prone to involvement in literary quarrels, and Berlin was no exception; his attack on Pierre-Louis de Maupertuis, president of the Berlin Academy, caused Frederick II to lose patience with him. Voltaire left Berlin in a flurry of mutual recriminations, and although these were later forgotten, Voltaire's dream of having found the ideal enlightened monarch were definitively shattered. His correspondence with Frederick, which had begun in 1736 when the latter was still crown prince, survived and, after a hiatus, it continued until Voltaire's death; they corresponded on literary and philosophical matters, and Voltaire sent Frederick many of his works in manuscript. Their exchange of more than seven hundred letters remains as an extraordinary literary achievement in its own right.

Later Life and Works. In January 1755, after a period of wandering, Voltaire acquired a property in Geneva which he called "Les Délices." A new and more settled phase now began as, at the age of sixty-one, he became master of his own house for the first time: in a letter of March that year, he wrote that "I am finally leading the life of a patriarch." The Lisbon earthquake of November 1755 may have disturbed his philosophical certainties and caused him to doubt the Leibnizian optimism that Alexander Pope had helped to popularize, but it did not disturb his new-found personal happiness. His *Poème sur le désastre de Lisbonne* appeared within weeks of the earthquake, and it is revealing that his instant literary response should have been in verse. His prose response to the catastrophe, in *Candide*, took longer to mature and was published in 1759. In the meantime, he had written articles for the *Encyclopédie* of Diderot and d'Alembert, and in 1756 he published his univeral history, the *Essai sur les moeurs*.

In 1757, d'Alembert's critical article "Genève" in the *Encyclopédie* had provoked a scandal in that city. Geneva turned out not to be the model republic that Voltaire had imagined or hoped it was, and after a number of tussles with clerical authority, he resolved to leave the city. A return to Paris would not have been welcomed by the government, so he purchased a house and estate at Ferney, where he installed himself in 1760—on French soil now, but within striking distance of the border. It was in this symbolically marginal position that Voltaire was to live for the rest of his life. Henceforth he would play the part of the *seigneur*, caring for his estate and even building a church for the villagers: it bears the deist (and immodest) inscription *Deo erexit Voltaire*. This new-found role did not mean that, like Candide, Voltaire had found happiness in cultivating his garden and in ignoring the world beyond. On the contrary, it was in 1760 that Voltaire first issued the rallying cry with which he would henceforth sign many of his letters: *Écrasons l'infâme* ("Crush the Infamy"). The stability of his base at Ferney seems to have given Voltaire the opportunity over the following years to launch and encourage the campaigns that soon made him the most famous writer in Europe.

The Calas affair was a defining moment in this crusade for tolerance. The Huguenot Jean Calas was tortured and broken on the wheel in 1762 after being found guilty, on the basis of dubious evidence, of murdering his son. Voltaire successfully led a determined campaign to clear Calas's name, writing many letters and publishing a number of works, including *Traité sur la tolérance* (1763). Other campaigns followed—a successful one to obtain the rehabilitation of another Huguenot family, the Sirvens, accused of having murdered a daughter recently converted to Catholicism, and an unsuccessful one to achieve a pardon for a nineteen-year-old man, La Barre, condemned to be burned at the stake for having committed certain trivial acts of sacrilege (and for having in his possession a copy of Voltaire's *Dictionnaire philosophique*). These struggles brought Voltaire to even greater public prominence, and it in no way diminishes his undoubted determination and courage to say that he obviously relished his new role: in a letter of 1766, he wrote to a friend, "Oh how I love this philosophy of action and goodwill."

Although many of Voltaire's later writings concerned his crusade for tolerance and justice, he continued to write in a wide variety of forms, from tragedy to biblical criticism, and from satire to short fiction (*L'ingénu*, 1767; *Le taureau blanc*, 1773). In February 1778, Voltaire was persuaded by his friends to make a symbolic return to Paris, ostensibly to oversee preparations to stage his latest tragedy, *Irène*. It was the first time he had set foot in the capital since 1750, and he was received in triumph. A succession of friends called on him, and despite his deteriorating health, he attended a performance of his new play at the Comédie Française, in the course of which his bust was crowned on stage with a laurel wreath. His health did not permit his return to Ferney, and he died in Paris two months later. Even in death, Voltaire, a celebrated amateur actor, seemed to have stage-managed his departure from the scene so as to gain maximum publicity.

Voltaire's Legacy. Voltaire's afterlife is complex, his reputation changing with successive regimes. The French Revolution looked back to him as a heroic precursor of its struggle, and in 1791 his remains were brought back to Paris and with great ceremony placed in the Panthéon. For much of the nineteenth century, the name of Voltaire was synonymous with anticlericalism, and the philosophe was widely, if implausibly, seen as an Antichrist. In the wake of the Dreyfus affair, Voltaire's reputation as a crusader for tolerance was reemphasized, and in the latter years of the Third Republic, under the influence of

the Sorbonne literary historian Gustave Lanson, Voltaire became a fixture of the republican school and university curriculum. The latter half of the twentieth century has taken a more nuanced approach to Voltaire's religious views, especially in the wake of René Pomeau's *La religion de Voltaire*, which stresses the depth of Voltaire's deist convictions.

Editions. In a career that stretched over sixty years, Voltaire's extant writings ran, it has been estimated, to some fifteen million words: everything concerning the *œuvre* seems larger than life, and it is hard to make any simple assessment of it. "Complete" editions appeared in Voltaire's lifetime; the last, published by Cramer in Geneva in 1775, ran to forty volumes (the so-called *édition encadrée*). The first complete edition of Voltaire's writings after his death, known at the Kehl edition, was published on the eve of the Revolution (1785–1789) in seventy octavo volumes (there was also a duodecimo edition in ninety-two volumes). Many complete editions followed in the nineteenth century, culminating in the Moland edition (1877–1883) in fifty-two volumes, which remains—pending the completion of the Oxford edition—the standard edition of reference. Theodore Besterman's "definitive" edition of Voltaire's correspondence (1968–1977) includes more than 15,000 letters, but these surviving letters must represent only a fraction of the total number written by Voltaire in his lifetime, probably in excess of 40,000. This edition is part of the larger *Complete Works of Voltaire*, a complete and critical edition of all Voltaire's writings currently being published by the Voltaire Foundation in Oxford; when complete, it will exceed two hundred volumes.

Voltaire and Enlightenment. Voltaire's contribution to the history of Enlightenment philosophy is minimal, and he cannot be considered a significant or original thinker. In terms of the history of ideas, his single most important achievement was to have helped in the 1730s to introduce the thought of Newton and Locke to France (and so to the rest of the Continent); and even this achievement is, as Jonathan Israel has shown, hardly as radical as has sometimes been thought: the English thinkers in question served essentially as a deistic bulwark against the more radical (atheistic) currents of thought in the Spinozist tradition. Voltaire's deist beliefs, reiterated throughout his life, came to appear increasingly outmoded and defensive as he grew older and as he became more and more exercised by the spread of atheism. Voltaire's failure to produce an original philosophy was, in a sense, counterbalanced by his deliberate cultivation of a philosophy of action; his "common sense" crusade against superstition and prejudice and in favor of religious toleration was his single greatest contribution to the progress of Enlightenment. "Rousseau writes for writing's sake," he declared in a letter of 1767, "I write to act."

It was therefore Voltaire's literary and rhetorical contributions to the Enlightenment that were truly unique. Interested neither in music (like Rousseau) nor in art (like Diderot), Voltaire was fundamentally a man of language. Through force of style, through skillful choice of literary genre, and through the accomplished manipulation of the book market, he found means of popularizing and promulgating ideas that until then had generally been clandestine. The range of his writing is immense, embracing virtually every genre. In verse, he wrote in every form—epic poetry, ode, satire, and epistle, and even occasional and light verse; his drama, also written in verse, includes both comedies and tragedies (and although the tragedies have not survived in the modern theater, many live on in opera; for example, Rossini's *Semiramide* and *Tancredi*). It is above all the prose works with which modern readers are familiar, and again the writings cover a wide spectrum: histories, polemical satires, pamphlets of all types, dialogues, short fictions or *contes*, and letters both real and fictive. The conspicuous absentee from this list is the novel, a genre that, like the prose *drame*, Voltaire thought base and trivial. To understand the strength of his dislike for these "new" genres, we need to remember that Voltaire was a product of the late seventeenth century, the moment of the Quarrel between Ancients and Moderns, and this literary debate continued to influence his aesthetic views all through his life. Controversial religious and political views were often expressed in the literary forms (classical tragedy, the verse satire) perfected in the seventeenth century; the "conservatism" of these forms seems, to modern readers at least, to compromise the content, though this apparent traditionalism may in fact have helped Voltaire mask the originality of his enterprise: it is at least arguable that in a work such as *Zaïre* (1732), the form of the classical tragedy made its ideas of religious toleration more palatable.

Yet this would also be a simplification, for notwithstanding his apparent literary conservatism, Voltaire was in fact a relentless reformer and experimenter with literary genres, innovative almost despite himself, particularly in the domain of prose. Although he never turned his back on verse drama and philosophical poetry, he experimented with different forms of historical writing and tried his hand at different styles of prose fiction. Above all, he seems to have discovered late in his career the satirical and polemical uses of the fragment, notably in his alphabetic works, the *Dictionnaire philosophique portatif* (1764), containing 73 articles in its first edition, and the *Questions sur l'Encyclopédie* (1770–1772). The latter work, whose first edition contained 423 articles in nine octavo volumes, is a vast and challenging compendium of his thought and ranks among Voltaire's unrecognized masterpieces. When he died, Voltaire was working on what would have been his third "philosophical" dictionary, *L'opinion en alphabet*.

Voltaire's ironic, fast-moving, deceptively simple style makes him one of the greatest stylists of the French language. All his life, Voltaire loved to act in his own plays, and this fondness for role-playing carried through into all his writings. He used something like 175 different pseudonyms in the course of his career, and his writing is characterized by a proliferation of different personae and voices. The reader is constantly drawn into dialogue—by a footnote that contradicts the text, or by one voice in the text that argues against another. The use of the mask is so relentless and the presence of humor, irony, and satire so pervasive that the reader has finally no idea of where the "real" Voltaire is. His autobiographical writings are few and entirely unrevealing: as the title of his *Commentaire historique sur les œuvres de l'auteur de la Henriade* suggests, it is his writings alone that constitute their author's identity.

In fact, we rarely know with certainty what Voltaire truly thought or believed; what mattered to him was the impact of what he wrote. The great crusades of the 1760s taught him to appreciate the importance of public opinion, and in popularizing the clandestine ideas of the early part of the century, he played the role of the journalist. He may have been old-fashioned in his nostalgia for the classicism of the previous century, but he was wholly of his day in his consummate understanding of the medium of publishing. He manipulated the book trade to achieve maximum publicity for his ideas, and he well understood the importance of what he called "the portable." In 1766, Voltaire wrote to d'Alembert: "Twenty in-folio volumes will never cause a revolution; it's the little portable books at thirty *sous* which are to be feared."

Voltaire was also modern in the way he invented himself by fashioning a public image out of his adopted name. As the patriarch of Ferney, he turned himself into an institution whose fame reached across Europe. As an engaged and militant intellectual, he stood at the beginning of a French tradition that looked forward to Émile Zola and to Jean-Paul Sartre, and in modern republican France his name stands as a cultural icon, a symbol of rationalism and the defense of tolerance. Voltaire was a man of paradoxes: the bourgeois who as *de* Voltaire gave himself aristocratic pretensions, but who as plain Voltaire later became a hero of the Revolution; the conservative in aesthetic matters who appeared as a radical in religious and political issues. He was, above all, the master ironist, who, perhaps more than any other writer, gave to the Enlightenment its characteristic and defining tone of voice.

[*See also* Châtelet, Émilie Le Tonnelier de Breteuil du; Deism; Letters; Literary Genres; Men and Women of Letters; Philosophes; Publishing; *and* Toleration.]

BIBLIOGRAPHY

WORKS BY VOLTAIRE

Candide and Other Stories. Translated by R. Pearson. Oxford, 1990. Also includes *Micromégas, Zadig, The Ingenu,* and *The White Bull.*

Candide, Zadig, and Selected Stories. Translated by D. M. Frame, introduction by J. Iverson. New York, 2001. Includes fourteen other short fictions.

Letters Concerning the English Nation. Edited by N. Cronk. Oxford, 1994. A critical edition of the translation by John Lockman, first published in London in 1733, in advance of the French edition of the *Lettres philosophiques.*

Philosophical Dictionary. Translated by T. Besterman. Harmondsworth, 1971.

Treatise on Tolerance and Other Texts. Translated by B. Masters and S. Harvey. Cambridge, 2000.

STUDIES

Aldridge, A. Owen. *Voltaire and the Century of Light.* Princeton, N.J., 1975. A highly readable account of Voltaire's life and writings.

Bird, Stephen. *Reinventing Voltaire: The Politics of Commemoration in Nineteenth-Century France.* (Studies on Voltaire and the Eighteenth Century, 2000.) Oxford, 2000.

Brumfitt, J. H. *Voltaire Historian.* Oxford, 1958. A pioneering study of Voltaire's historical writings.

Cotoni, Marie-Hélène. *L'exégèse du Nouveau Testament dans la philosophie française du XVIIIᵉ siècle.* (Studies on Voltaire and the Eighteenth Century, 220.) Oxford, 1984. Major contribution to the study of Voltaire and the Bible.

Dawson, Deirdre. *Voltaire's Correspondence: An Epistolary Novel.* New York, 1994. One of the ten studies of Voltaire's correspondence.

Gay, Peter. *Voltaire's Politics: The Poet as Realist.* Princeton, 1959. Classic study of Voltaire's political thought.

Gray, John. *Voltaire: Voltaire and Enlightenment.* London, 1998. A brief account of Voltaire's achievement as a philosopher.

Israel, Jonathan I. *Radical Enlightenment: Philosophy and the Making of Modernity 1650–1750.* Oxford, 2001. Chapter 27, "Anglomania: The 'Triumph' of Newton and Locke," situates Voltaire's contribution to the spread of English ideas in France.

Mervaud, Christiane. *Voltaire et Frédéric II: Une dramaturgie des Lumières.* (Studies on Voltaire and the Eighteenth Century, 234.) Oxford, 1985. Definitive study of the complex relationship between Voltaire and Frederick.

Moureaux, José-Michel. "Voltaire apôtre: de la parodie au mimétisme." *Poétique* 66 (1986), 159–177. Remarkable study of Voltaire's polemical appropriation of religious discourse.

Naves, Raymond. *Le goût de Voltaire.* Paris, 1938; repr., Geneva, 1967. Still the definitive account of Voltaire's aesthetic thought.

Pearson, Roger. *The Fables of Reason: A Study of Voltaire's contes philosophiques.* Oxford, 1993. The best critical study in English of the *contes.*

Pomeau, René. *La religion de Voltaire.* Revised ed., Paris, 1969. First published in 1956, an influential study that emphasizes the importance of deist belief in Voltaire's writings.

Pomeau, René, and others. *Voltaire en son temps.* Rev. ed., 2 vols. Oxford, 1995. The most complete biographical account, with detailed index.

Ridgway, Ronald. *Voltaire and Sensibility.* Montreal, 1973. Important study of a neglected subject.

Rousseau, André-Michel. *L'Angleterre et Voltaire.* (Studies on Voltaire and the Eighteenth Century, 145–147.) 3 vols. Oxford, 1976. Most detailed account of Voltaire in England.

Trousson, Raymond, and Jeroom Vercruysse, eds. *Dictionnaire de Voltaire.* Paris, 2002. The most extensive reference work on Voltaire's life and writings.

NICHOLAS CRONK

W–Z

WALLACE, ROBERT (1697–1771), Scottish cleric, Moderate, and philosopher.

Wallace attended the arts courses at Edinburgh University (1711–1715) and the Divinity Hall (1715–1722) before his ordination in the Church of Scotland to the parish of Moffat in 1723. From 1733, he held parishes in Edinburgh and was active in church affairs, serving as church patronage manager to the Squadrone (a faction of Scottish Whigs) from 1742 until 1746, and as moderator in 1743. He was given a royal chaplaincy in 1744. Two years later, Edinburgh University conferred on him the degree of doctor of divinity. In 1726, he married Helen Turnbull, the sister of his friend George Turnbull, an even more eminent philosopher.

While at university, Wallace and Turnbull were members of the Rankenian Club. This group of young men, mostly divinity students, discussed current philosophical works, including those of Lord Shaftesbury, Samuel Clarke, and George Berkeley. The Rankenians led the original Moderate Party in the church and were active in making it more tolerant and reasonable. They believed that religion was socially important mainly for its practical teaching of good morals. Wallace thought that morality was founded in feeling and in utility. He disbelieved in universal moral rules grounded in the commands of a God, making this argument basic to his essay *The Doctrine of Passive Obedience and Non Resistance Considered* . . . . (Edinburgh, 1754). His published sermons also expressed such views. He deputized for the Edinburgh University mathematics professor 1720–1721; thus he was also a Newtonian.

In 1742–1744, Wallace and another improving minister did the actuarial calculations for a new insurance scheme for Scottish ministers and university professors which later became the Scottish Widows and Orphans Assurance Society. His interest in demographic questions had been stimulated, in part, by Montesquieu's comments in the *Lettres persanes* about the size of ancient populations. He addressed this question in a 1744 paper read to the Philosophical Society of Edinburgh. His views were amicably refuted by David Hume in his 1752 essay, "The Populousness of Ancient Nations."

Wallace shared Hume's interests in economic matters and debated topics of this sort in the Select Society of Edinburgh. He also wrote papers on political economy for the Edinburgh Society. Unlike his friend Hume, he favored banks and paper credits, citing Bishop Berkeley's *The Querist* (1735–1737) to support his views. Versions of some of these pieces are almost certainly included in his *Characteristics of the Present Political State of Great Britain* (London, 1758) and in his *Various Prospects of Mankind, Nature and Providence* (London, 1758). The latter was an anti-utopian work used by Thomas Malthus, in his "Essay on Population" (1798), to discredit the ideas of Rousseau and others who believed in perfectibility. Wallace's unpublished manuscripts contain finished essays or drafts on taste, politics, and even "Of Venery, or the Commerce of the Two Sexes" (c. 1760). In that work, which reflects society debates, he says interesting things about lust, love, and sexual education, advocates trial marriages and divorce, and shows a regard for the pleasures of women that was seldom seen among the enlightened in Scotland or elsewhere. He was a good Whig who hated subscription to creeds. His career shows how enlightened the Church of Scotland had become by 1771, and indeed, how that had occurred.

[*See also* Clubs and Societies; Economic Thought; Hume, David; Reformed Churches, *subentry on* Presbyterianism; *and* Utopianism.]

BIBLIOGRAPHY

Hont, Istvan. "The 'Rich Country–Poor Country' Debate in Scottish Classical Political Economy." In *Wealth and Virtue: The Shaping of Political Economy in the Scottish Enlightenment*, edited by Istvan Hont and Michael Ignatieff, pp. 271–315. Cambridge, 1983. See esp. pp. 289–291.

Mossner, Ernest Campbell. *The Forgotten Hume*. New York, 1943. See pp. 105–131.

Robbins, Caroline. *The Eighteenth-Century Commonwealthman: Studies in the Transmission of English Liberal Thought from the Restoration of Charles II until the War with the Thirteen Colonies*. Cambridge, Mass., 1961. See pp. 199–211.

Smith, Norah. "Robert Wallace's 'Of Venery.'" *Texas Studies on Literature* 15 (1973), 429–444. Reproduces the essay "Of Venery" and has incidental information about Wallace. More is contained in Smith's dissertation, "The Literary Career and Achievement of Robert Wallace (1697–1771)," University of Edinburgh, 1973.

Stewart, M. A. "Berkeley and the Rankenian Club." *Hermathena* 139, (Winter 1985), 25–45. Has brief accounts of all the prominent Rankenian Club members and their use and views of Berkeley.

ROGER L. EMERSON

WALPOLE, HORACE (1717–1797), English writer and connoisseur.

The youngest son of Sir Robert Walpole, the British prime minister, Horace's political career as member of Parliament enabled him to record the political and social events of his day, both in his extensive and lively correspondence and in his *Memoirs of the Last Ten Years of the Reign of George II* and *Memoirs of the Reign of King George III*, intended for posthumous publication and to a certain extent settling old scores resulting from his assiduous and lifelong defense of his father's reputation and his own failure to pass beyond manipulation of other politicians to the high office he desired.

Walpole was a pioneer in several respects. His novel *The Castle of Otranto* (1765), the first Gothic fiction, satirized by Jane Austen in *Northanger Abbey* as one of the "Horrid novels," was influential beyond British shores, introduced elements of horror, feeling, surprise, and the supernatural, soon to appear in the German Sturm und Drang, and ushered in a new type of Romantic fiction. His verse drama of double incest, *The Mysterious Mother* (1768) draws on similar elements. Allied with a sharp attack on the practices of the Roman Catholic Church, it created what Byron considered the greatest of modern tragedies.

In building his cottage-palace at Strawberry Hill, beside the Thames in Twickenham, he and his Committee of Taste (himself, the talented gentleman-architect John Chute, and the brilliant illustrator Richard Bentley the younger) built the first influential building of the Gothic Revival. From 1747, he created there a setting for a connoisseur's art collection; it became famous through his talent for self-publicity and because it was regularly opened to the public.

Walpole's antiquarian interests showed themselves in more ways than in his collection, which included not just paintings by artists of the quality of Sir Joshua Reynolds but also curiosities such as Cardinal Wolsey's hat, Charles I's death warrant, and many classical and medieval antiquities. His antiquarian library far exceeded its size by its renown, and he set up his own influential private press. His attempt at rehabilitating a reputation in *Historic Doubts on the Life and Death of King Richard the Third* (1768) was based on the misreading of a newly discovered Coronation Roll and provoked an antiquarian debate still alive today. More successful was his recasting of the chaotic materials assembled by the engraver George Vertue into the first, still valuable, history of English painting, *Anecdotes of Painting* (1762, second edition, 1765).

Walpole was equally at home in Paris among the philosophes, whom he tended to dislike. His publication of a letter purportedly from the king of Prussia to Rousseau provoked in 1765 the quarrel between the Scots

philosopher David Hume and his Swiss contemporary Jean-Jacques Rousseau.

The nonreligious Walpole was more a clear witness of his day than a major player. He ushered in influential trends in literature that prefigured Romanticism, and through his architecture, his collections, and his writings, he introduced new audiences to an appreciation of the arts. But it will be for his witty and sometimes vindictive record of his age that he will above all continue to be consulted.

[*See also* Architecture; Aristocracy, *subentry on* Cultural Contributions; Gothic; Novel; Philosophes; *and* Romanticism.]

BIBLIOGRAPHY

Ketton-Cremer, R. W. *Horace Walpole: A Biography*. London, 1940. Still the best standard biography.
Lewis, Wilmarth S. *Horace Walpole*. New York, 1961. The A. W. Mellon Lectures in the Fine Arts for 1960. Invaluable for the insights of Walpole's editor and the closest he got to a biography of Walpole.
Mowl, Timothy. *Horace Walpole: The Great Outsider*. London, 1996. Flawed, distorted, and unbalanced, but taking account of some recent scholarship.
Sabor, Peter. *Horace Walpole: The Critical Heritage*. London and New York, 1987. Collection of the key critical texts for Walpole's reception.
Sabor, Peter. *Horace Walpole: A Reference Guide*. Boston, 1984. The fullest guide to primary and secondary literature.
Walpole, Horace. *The Yale Edition of Horace Walpole's Correspondence*. 48 vols. New Haven, Conn., 1937–1982.

RICHARD G. WILLIAMS

WAR AND MILITARY THEORY. The attitude of the men of the Enlightenment toward war was marked by a deep duality. Generally, the philosophes regarded war as one of the principal scourges of humanity, typically caused by the cynical ambition of rulers and by the folly of peoples. This was not surprising, since a country like France was at war somewhere for fifty years between 1700 and 1800. Voltaire denounced war in his *Dictionnaire philosophique* (Philosophical Dictionary, 1764) and satirized it in *Candide*, while the abbé de Saint-Pierre and Immanuel Kant argued that the progressive application of reason, as mankind outgrew its state of infancy, would bring about its demise. However, until this happened the philosophes conceded that war might remain necessary and justified in defense of one's country and of civilization itself. Moreover, some of the philosophes were serving officers, while many officers partook of the Enlightenment's climate of ideas. Coming overwhelmingly from the nobility, these officers shared the interests and mood of their class and times, were exposed to the same intellectual influences, and were moving in the same social circles, including the salons. Applying the powerful message of the Enlightenment to their own professional field, these officer-intellectuals felt that, like all other spheres of human activity, the conduct of war had to be elevated from its reliance on "arbitrary traditions," "blind prejudices," "disorder and confusion." It had to be systemized and constituted as a clear and universal theory. Marshal Maurice de Saxe expressed this quest in his *Mes rêveries* (Reveries on the Art of War, 1756): "War is a science covered with shadows in whose obscurity one cannot move with an assured step. Routine and prejudice, the natural result of ignorance, are its foundation and support. All sciences have principles and rules; war has none." In his poem *La tactique* (1774) even Voltaire, who once jested that "the art of war is like that of medicine; murderous and conjectural," expressed the view that in line with the general growth of human reason, war, too, was receiving its own general theory. The same spirit inspires the military entries to Diderot's *Encyclopédie*, covering—with the aid of plates and diagrams—military education, the art of siege and fortification, the tactical evolutions of troops, and even the casting of cannons.

One might start from the more tangible, institutional expressions of this general outlook. The most notable of these were the military academies established throughout Europe from the middle of the eighteenth century, alongside earlier cadet corps and technical schools for the professions of artillery and engineering. Military academies were established for example in France (1752), Austria (1752), Prussia (1765), Württemberg (early 1770s), Bavaria (1789), Britain (1799), and the United States (1802). The idea underlying them was that the military profession could and should be studied theoretically rather than merely be experienced in the field. It required academic instruction; indeed, broad general education was also essential for developing the officer's personality.

In this spirit all the academies adopted a broad academic curriculum. Frederick II (known as the "Great") sent the one he devised for the Prussian Académie Militaire to d'Alembert for his assessment. In Germany in particular—politically fragmented and dominated by the educational ideal of *Bildung*—military academies and broad educational programs for them proliferated. Even small German states such as Hessen-Hanau (1771) and Münster (1767) established military academies. In the tiny principality of Schaumberg-Lippe, Count Wilhelm, a general and man of the Enlightenment, founded a military academy in 1766, where he himself was the chief instructor and where the cadet Gerhard Scharnhorst, later the military leader of the Prussian Reform and of the resistance to Napoleon, received his earlier military education. Informal regimental schools, opened by enlightened commanding officers for the general and military education of their officers and NCOs, were also much in vogue, particularly in Germany. Significantly, in the United States it was President Thomas Jefferson who took action to open the Military Academy at West Point. While being the archenemy of

state machinery and military professionalism, he was also one of the greatest exponents of the American Enlightenment and promoter of academic education.

Another, related, tangible expression of the military Enlightenment was a dramatic, fourfold increase that took place in the mid-eighteenth century in the publication of books on military theory. The military journal also made its appearance at that time and proliferated during the second half of the century, again most notably in Germany.

These new organs were the expression and vessels of intense intellectual ferment: the quest for a theory of war. The scientific revolution of the seventeenth century, culminating in Newtonian science, dominated the Enlightenment, presenting an inspiring model to be applied as the human mind mastered all realities. However, only a few thinkers believed that the natural sciences' mathematical rigor could be emulated in the human sciences and the arts. In the arts neoclassical theory provided a no less influential model, postulating as it did that all arts were governed by universal and immutable rules and principles. These rules and principles supposedly revealed themselves in experience throughout the history of each art. They were thus susceptible to distillation and formulation by critics, constituting the theory of the art or its "mechanical part" that could be taught. However, the application of the rules and principles to particular circumstances, the "elevated part" of the art, required the exercise of "free," "creative" genius and could not be reduced to formulas. This was the domain of the great masters of each art, including the art of war. Alexander the Great, Hannibal, and Caesar in antiquity, and in modern times Gustavus Adolphus, Turenne, Frederick the Great, and later Napoleon were the geniuses who excelled in the applications of the rules and principles of the art of war, in the same way that Homer, Virgil, Pierre Corneille, Jean Racine, and Molière excelled in the poetic and dramatic arts.

In the eyes of the military thinkers of the Enlightenment, the field of fortifications and siege-craft in the conduct of war had already pretty much attained the ideal of a systematic and regulated theory. From the sixteenth century, it had been based on geometry and trigonometry in ballistics and military architecture. It had been studied in professional schools of engineers and set out in books and manuals of a mathematical nature. Furthermore, both the defense of places and siege-craft had been systematically executed in a regulated and exact procedure, whose duration and ultimate outcome could be predicted almost with certainty, barring the interference of external factors. Marshal Sébastien Le Prestre de Vauban, Louis XIV's master of fortifications and siege-craft, had perfected both branches in his successive "systems," including those published posthumously. Inevitably, the military thinkers of the Enlightenment regarded this as a model for other fields of the art of war. As would-be general Count Turpin de Crisse wrote in his *Essai sur l'art de la guerre* (1754): "Why could there not be some general method established which, being accommodated to circumstances of time and place, would render the events of operations more certain and their success less dubious? Art is now brought to that perfection, and there is almost a certainty of carrying a place when the siege of it is properly formed . . . it seems probable that the principles which serve for the conducting of a siege, may become rules for forming the plan . . . of campaign."

Indeed, French military thought during the 1760s and 1770s was dominated by the attempt to formulate a definitive system of tactics (the concept, derived from ancient Greek, was turned into an accepted technical term at that time). In the wake of the French defeats in the Seven Years' War (1756–1763), a controversy regarding the respective merits of the line versus the column for infantry maneuver, fire, and assault broke out. This was to lead to the shock tactics that would be successfully employed by the armies of the Revolution. Significantly, however, both sides to the controversy believed that they were concerned with more than a doctrine for a particular time and place. All held that they were to devise a system of universal applicability, whose fundamentals would equally reflect the experience of the ancients and moderns, as well as any possible future development. This system would synthesize the lessons of history, spanning any change of circumstances. The best-known military thinker of the French Enlightenment and a man of the salons, Colonel Count Jacques-Antoine-Hippolyte de Guibert wrote in his celebrated *Essai de tactique générale* (1772): "tactics . . . would constitute a science at every period of time, in every place, and among every species of arms."

Guibert's book was enthusiastically accepted by the philosophes because of the general vision of military theory that he so eloquently articulated and because of other fashionable topics, which he incorporated in the book. Most notable among these was his discussion, in Montesquieu's spirit, of the interrelationship between the political, social, and economic constitution of states and their military institutions. This subject was similarly addressed by Henry Evans Lloyd, a Welsh soldier of fortune, who served in most of the major armies of Europe, and man of the Enlightenment. In his *History of the Late War between the King of Prussia and the Empress of Germany and Her Allies* (successive volumes, 1766, 1781, 1784), he also proposed a systematic military psychology, based on the mechanistic psychology of passions developed by Thomas Hobbes, Julien Offray de La Mettrie, and Claude-Adrien Helvétius. Lloyd's most enduring legacy was his formulation of a rationale of military operations,

centering on the concept of "lines and operations," which was in turn based on logistic considerations. With this idea he precipitated a shift of interest among military thinkers from tactics to strategy (this concept, too, was developed from ancient Greek etymology into an accepted technical term by the military thinkers of the Enlightenment from the 1780s on). The Prussian Adam Heinrich Dietrich von Bülow turned Lloyd's rationale into a controversial geometrical science of operations in his *Geist des neueren Kriegssystems* (The Spirit of the Modern System of War, 1799). Antoine-Henri Jomini, a Swiss who made a career in Napoleon's army, adapted this rationale to reflect the patterns of Napoleonic strategy, which he believed embodied the universal principles of the art of war in general. Jomini's work dominated military thought and military education during most of the nineteenth century.

However, by the late eighteenth and early nineteenth centuries, a general reaction against the ideas of the Enlightenment was gathering momentum throughout Europe. It was in line with the ideas of this so-called "Counter-Enlightenment" or Romanticism that Jomini's contemporary, Carl von Clausewitz, criticized the systems and principles of the military thinkers of the Enlightenment as divorced from the richness and diversity of reality. Against what he regarded as Enlightenment abstractions and dead systems, Clausewitz stressed the free operation of genius, moral forces, the elements of the unknown and unpredictable, and historical diversity. The battle between the Enlightenment and Romanticism had thus spread into the field of military theory, and its legacy has dominated thinking about war from then on.

[*See also* Aristocracy; Citizenship; Death; Diplomacy; Education; Encyclopedias; Hospitals; Mercantilism; Ottoman Empire; *and* Progress.]

BIBLIOGRAPHY

Clausewitz, Carl von. *On War*. Princeton, N.J., 1976.
Duffy, Christopher. *The Fortress in the Age of Vauban and Frederick the Great*. London, 1985.
Gat, Azar. *The Origins of Military Thought: From the Enlightenment to Clausewitz*. Oxford, 1989. Incorporated and reissued within Azar Gat, *A History of Military Thought: From the Enlightenment to the Cold War*. Oxford, 2001.
Howard, Michael. *War in European History*. London, 1976.
Paret, Peter, ed. *Makers of Modern Strategy from Machiavelli to the Nuclear Age*. Princeton, N.J., 1986.
Quimby, Robert. *The Background of Napoleonic Warfare: The Theory of Military Tactics in Eighteenth-Century France*. New York, 1957.
Wilkinson, Spenser. *The French Army before Napoleon*. Oxford, 1915.

AZAR GAT

WARREN, MERCY OTIS (1728–1814), American historian, playwright, poet, and political thinker.

At a time in American history when women were politically invisible, Mercy Otis Warren was one of the few women who had a public, political voice. Before the American Revolution, Warren published several plays that satirized royal authority in the colonies and urged Americans to resist British assaults on their liberty. During the debate over the United States Constitution, she issued a tract—under the pseudonym "A Columbian Patriot"—opposing ratification because, among other reasons, the document lacked a Bill of Rights. In 1790, she published under her own name a collection of poems and plays that was widely read and praised. Her literary career culminated in 1805, with the publication of the three-volume *History of the Rise, Progress and Termination of the American Revolution interspersed with Biographical, Political and Moral Observations*. Although it was one of the earliest and most comprehensive histories of the American Revolution, and certainly the first to be written by a woman, some contemporaries spurned the work because of Warren's pro-Jeffersonian bias. In subsequent years, her work and reputation declined. Increasing interest in women's history in the late twentieth century led to a revival in attention to her life and career.

Warren was a distinctive product of the transatlantic Enlightenment. By the early eighteenth century, older notions of women's inherent intellectual inferiority were giving way to Lockean assumptions about the malleability of the human mind and the importance of education in shaping behavior. Warren's education was far superior to that of many of her female contemporaries. Tutored along with her brother, James Otis—who became a revolutionary leader in Massachusetts—Warren read the classics of ancient Greece and Rome as well as modern authors such as Shakespeare, Milton, and Pope. As an adult, though she married and bore five sons, she continued her education through wide and deep reading in history, moral philosophy, and political economy. Her writings, particularly the *History of the American Revolution*, reveal an intimate familiarity with Enlightenment authors and contain references to works by Montesquieu, John Locke, David Hume, Adam Smith, and Henry Home, Lord Kames, among others. She effortlessly synthesized various intellectual traditions, including the classical notion of civic virtue, the common law concepts of liberty and property, and an Enlightenment stress on rights and duties.

The Scottish Enlightenment, in particular, shaped Warren's thinking about the role of women in public life. Although never an advocate of women voting or holding public office, she, like the Scots, supported greater educational opportunities for females. Educated women, Warren believed, would be better teachers of children and better advisers to their husbands. Moreover, the Scottish four-stage theory of history suggested that women had, over time, come to occupy a crucial role, acting as a civilizing and refining force in society. By inculcating

proper morals and manners, the female sex shaped men's attitudes and behavior. Warren grasped the implications of this theory. She believed that although women would continue to occupy the domestic sphere, they could have an impact far beyond the confines of their own families. Their actions influenced the social and political character of their society. In the end, although Warren knew that her own life was exceptional, she understood that even ordinary women had a public role to play.

[*See also* American Revolution; Education, *subentry on* Education of Women; *and* Men and Women of Letters.]

BIBLIOGRAPHY

Richards, Jeffrey H. *Mercy Otis Warren*. New York, 1995. A biography that is especially good in analyzing Warren's literary contributions.
Warren, Mercy Otis. *History of the Rise, Progress and Termination of the American Revolution interspersed with Biographical, Political and Moral Observations*. Edited by Lester H. Cohen. Indianapolis, 1988. An easily accessible modern edition of Warren's classic work with helpful annotations.
Zagarri, Rosemarie. *A Woman's Dilemma: Mercy Otis Warren and the American Revolution*. Wheeling, Ill., 1995. A biography that situates Warren within the larger social and historical context.

ROSEMARIE ZAGARRI

WASHINGTON, GEORGE (1732–1799), American general, statesman, and first president of the United States (1789–1797).

Washington was the third son of a tobacco planter in Virginia, then one of the larger colonies of Britain's North American empire. As a young man, Washington fought as an officer in the Virginia militia during the French and Indian War (1754–1763), and he sat in the House of Burgesses, the elective chamber of the Virginia legislature. This military and political experience made him a natural choice to be one of Virginia's delegates to the first Continental Congress (1774), called to address colonial grievances against British imperial policy. When protest turned to actual fighting in 1775, the second Continental Congress picked Washington to be commander-in-chief of the American army during the Revolutionary War (1775–1783). Washington held the post until peace was declared, triumphing over inadequate equipment, erratic pay, untrained soldiers, the superior force of his enemies, and his own occasional mistakes.

As the war ended, George III asked the American-born painter Benjamin West what Washington would do. West answered that he would probably retire to his estate. If he did, the king answered, he would be "the most distinguished of any man living." Washington's fulfillment of West's prediction made him an international celebrity. Americans and Europeans traveled to Virginia to meet the modern Cincinnatus. In 1787, however, Washington returned to public life to preside over the Constitutional Convention, called in response to the existing government's inability to deal with heavy debt and popular unrest. The new U.S. Constitution established an elected chief executive, called the president, and Washington was unanimously chosen (in 1789, and again in 1793) to fill the post. His first term was harmonious, but his second was marked by party strife over federal excise taxes, and the United States' stance toward the French Revolution. Washington enforced the laws and kept the United States neutral in the ideological and political struggle engulfing Europe. He declined to run for a third term, which he would certainly have won. His "Farewell Address," which urged America to maintain national unity and to "steer clear of permanent alliances" with foreign countries, was honored as a touchstone of policy for decades. After he died in December 1799, Henry Lee, his most eloquent eulogist, called him "first in war, first in peace, and first in the hearts of his countrymen."

Washington's career coincided with a glittering generation of American writers and thinkers—Benjamin Franklin (*The Autobiography*), Thomas Jefferson (the Declaration of Independence), Alexander Hamilton and James Madison (*The Federalist Papers*), Gouverneur Morris (the Constitution), and Thomas Paine (*The Rights of Man*). He knew them all; Jefferson and Hamilton served in his administration. Their brilliance, in contrast to Washington's own lack of formal learning—he never went to college, and he called his own education "defective"—creates an impression that he was a man of action, not ideas.

In fact, Washington was well read in the Anglo-American political literature of his day (some of it written by his friends and colleagues). He was grateful—as he put it in the Circular to the States (1783), his valedictory message as commander-in-chief—that the United States had not been founded "in the gloomy age of Ignorance and Superstition," but at a time when "the labours of Philosophers, Sages and Legislatures" had laid "the Treasures of knowledge . . . open for our use." As a result, he believed that "the rights of mankind were better understood and more clearly defined, than at any former period."

Washington thought these rights were best secured by a government of limited powers, whose authority derived from the people. The limitations of republican government are marked by such guarantees as freedom of worship ("the Government of the United States," he assured the Hebrew Congregation at Newport in 1790, "gives to bigotry no sanctions, to persecution no assistance"). Its authority is expressed by insisting that laws legitimately passed be obeyed ("if laws are to be so trampled upon with impunity," he wrote in 1794 during an uprising against the excise laws, "[then] everyone will carve for himself"). Washington limited his own power as a leader by surrendering it twice, at the end of the war and after his second

term. In the last and most personally difficult public act of his life, he extended the republican idea by freeing all his slaves in his will.

Washington's achievement was to combine the roles of man of action and man of ideas, and to make the idea of republican liberty more than the speculation of English country party journalists or French *encyclopédistes*: something real in the world. The wisest of the enlightened appreciated his achievement. In 1782 the chevalier de Chastellux, a French philosophe and author who knew Washington during the Revolutionary War, put the synthesis of power, law, and rights at the center of his portrait of the man. "This is the seventh year that he has commanded the army and he has obeyed Congress: more need not be said."

[*See also* American Revolution *and* Constitution of the United States.]

BIBLIOGRAPHY

Brookhiser, Richard. *Founding Father: Rediscovering George Washington*. New York, 1996. Moral biography after Plutarch.

Flexner, James Thomas. *George Washington*. 4 vols. Boston, 1965–1972.

Longmore, Paul K. *The Invention of George Washington*. Berkeley, Calif., 1989. How Washington created himself.

Rhodehamel, John, ed. *George Washington, Writings*. New York, 1997.

Wills, Garry. *Cincinnatus: George Washington and the Enlightenment*. New York, 1984. A graceful appreciation.

RICHARD BROOKHISER

WASHINGTON, D.C. The "Federal City" was called for by the 1787 Constitution of the United States of America, but the process for choosing a location was contentious, spurring some to threaten secession from the union. Congressional resolutions in 1790 and 1791 located the district upon 100 square miles of land at the fall line of the Potomac River straddling part of Maryland and Virginia, a choice that never fully satisfied the northern states. Washington, D.C. was simultaneously a product of the Enlightenment's rationalism and naturalism—the interest in disinterested political discourse and natural law—and the emerging factionalism of early United States political culture.

Congress hired Pierre Charles L'Enfant, a French architect, artist, and engineer to plan the city. A veteran of the Continental Army, L'Enfant shared the republican enthusiasm of the Revolutionary War. L'Enfant, and many others, wanted a city that would communicate the almost boundless expectations for the Republic. "We have laid the foundations of a new empire," remarked one South Carolinian in 1778, "which promises to enlarge itself to vast dimensions, and to give happiness to a great continent." As the capital of a republic and the seat of an empire, many believed that the Federal City should reflect admiration for ancient Greece and Rome, cultivate political stability, and project an expectation of the future power of the United States.

Working closely with Andrew Ellicott, the best known surveyor in North America, L'Enfant planned neo-classical public buildings within a setting that incorporated instead of displacing natural features of the land. A series of squares for the most important buildings and monuments were to be situated on the most prominent hills with prospects of the whole city. The irregular spacing of these hills was accommodated by a complex but thoroughly geometric street pattern. An irregular north-south, east-west grid was overlaid with a set of diagonal and orthogonal streets that met at the predetermined hilltop sites. Washington was to be a city of reason and politics that built upon nature harmoniously.

Before the federal government had even relocated to Washington in 1800 and welcomed Jefferson as the first president to serve in the capital, L'Enfant's vision was already under stress, as were the expectations of the authors of the Constitution. The Commission appointed by Congress to oversee the planning repeatedly sparred with L'Enfant over civilities and design authority. The discord eventually precipitated L'Enfant's replacement by Andrew Ellicott. Enslaved Africans and African Americans toiled in the district even before it officially existed, and even before its completion the city provided a new setting for the debate about slavery and race. A local paper described Benjamin Banneker, Andrew Ellicott's most important and talented assistant, as "an Ethiopian, whose abilities as a surveyor and an astronomer clearly prove that Mr. [Thomas] Jefferson's concluding that race of men were void of mental endowments was without foundation" (*Tidewater Towns*, 317, n. 47). As the republican empire expanded, this debate about slavery and race also grew more vituperative. The capital city, which grew in size and stature, emblematic of Enlightenment ambitions, became as much a site of bitterness and sectionalism as reason and virtuous common interest.

[*See also* Aesthetics; Architecture; Barlow, Joel; Copley, John Singleton; Latrobe, Benjamin; Philadelphia; Trumbull, John; *and* West, Benjamin.]

BIBLIOGRAPHY

Bedini, Silvio A. "The Survey of the Federal Territory: Andrew Ellicott and Benjamin Banneker." In *Washington History*, edited by Kenneth Bowling, vol. 13.1, pp. 76–111 (1991).

Bowling, Kenneth R. *The Creation of Washington, D.C.* Fairfax, Va., 1991.

Reps, John W. *Monumental Washington: The Planning and Development of the Capital Center.* Princeton, N.J., 1967.

Reps, John. *Tidewater Towns: City Planning in Colonial Virginia and Maryland.* Charlottesville, Va., 1972.

Scott, Pamela. "L'Enfant's Washington Described: The City in the Public Press, 1791–1795." In *Washington History*, edited by Kenneth Bowling, vol. 13.1, pp. 76–111 (1991).

JAMES SPADY

WATT, JAMES (1736–1819), British engineer who improved the steam engine.

James Watt was born in Greenock, Scotland, where he attended local schools. He was not apprenticed but spent nearly a year in London being trained as a mathematical instrument maker. After returning to Greenock, he set up a workshop in the precincts of Glasgow University in 1757, where he assisted professors such as Joseph Black (chemistry), John Anderson (natural philosophy), and Alexander Wilson (astronomy), thus supplementing his rudimentary education.

Through various partnerships, Watt expanded his workshop from producing navigation instruments such as quadrants into musical instruments. He started a hardware shop but around 1769 gave all these up in favor of a full-time career in civil engineering. This was caused by Anderson asking him to repair a model of a Newcomen steam engine in the winter of 1763–1764. Watt researched the performance of steam engines, assisted with Black's experimental advice and explanation of latent heat on which phenomenon Watt had stumbled. This showed Watt why the Newcomen engine was so inefficient but his crucial answer, the separate condenser, was conceived in the spring of 1765 through a flash of inspiration and not scientific experiment. Further experiments were needed to construct Watt's "perfect" engine, one that would waste no steam. Through Black, John Roebuck joined Watt as a partner to provide finance and obtain the patent of 1769. Roebuck's bankruptcy in 1770 terminated construction of a pumping engine at Kinneil, Scotland, just as it was nearing success.

From 1766, Watt started some civil engineering, probably to gain experience in erecting Newcomen engines. He surveyed canals in Scotland between the rivers Forth and Clyde, in the Vale of Strathmore, the Great Glen, and elsewhere. He was resident engineer on the Monkland Canal, built Hamilton bridge, improved Port Glasgow harbor, laid out a water supply for Greenock, and much more.

Through Roebuck, Watt had met Matthew Boulton in Birmingham in 1768. Boulton undertook to construct one of Watt's rotary engines that was still unfinished in 1774. That May, Watt went to Birmingham to supervise trials of both this rotary and the pumping engine removed from Kinneil. The latter he succeeded in making work properly and, with Boulton's help, extended his patent until 1800 through an act of Parliament. Watt remained in Birmingham for the rest of his life, forming the famous partnership of Boulton and Watt to build steam engines. Their engines were more economical and powerful than earlier ones and successfully drained Cornish copper mines. Boulton persuaded Watt to develop the pumping engine into a rotative engine that was completed in 1784 with his parallel motion. His rotative engines powered many early cotton mills and became a vital source of industrial power.

Watt's steam engines were the result of the application of science to technology, and Watt himself continued to be involved with experiments in many branches of natural philosophy. From 1768, he advised the Delftfield Pottery, Glasgow, about glazes and kiln design, among other things. In 1780, he patented a method for copying letters with special ink. In 1783, he was elected a Fellow of the Royal Society, London, probably for his paper on the composition of water, which he suggested was two substances. In 1788, he developed a method of making chlorine in quantities sufficient for industrial bleaching. Around 1794, on behalf of Dr. Beddoes, he developed the apparatus for producing gases used to treat patients at the Pneumatic Institution, Clifton, near Bristol, England. Although he retired from his steam engine business in 1800, his advice was sought on many engineering projects until his death.

BIBLIOGRAPHY

Dickinson, Henry Winram. *James Watt: Craftsman and Engineer.* Cambridge, 1935. This is considered to be the best of the more recent biographies but does not cover large sections of Watt's life and is not referenced.

Dickinson, Henry Winram, and Rhys Jenkins. *James Watt and the Steam Engine.* London, 1927; repr., Ashbourne, U.K., 1981. As its title implies, the greater part of this work covers Watt's development of the steam engine, but it starts with a scholarly account of Watt's early life.

Muirhead, James Patrick. *The Life and Times of James Watt, with Selections from His Correspondence.* London, 1858. Muirhead was asked by James Watt Junior to write the biography of his father. This is the earliest full biography but, for a modern reader, suffers from its lack of critical approach.

Smiles, Samuel. *Lives of the Engineers: The Steam Engine. Boulton and Watt.* London, 1878. Smiles based his biographies on solid research, but his interpretation differs from what is acceptable today so his work needs careful checking.

RICHARD L. HILLS

WEBSTER, NOAH (1758–1843) American lexicographer.

Webster was born in Hartford, Connecticut, and graduated from Yale University in 1778. He became a lawyer, but he much preferred teaching and became famous by writing *A Grammatical Institute of the English Language* (1783), the first part of which is a spelling book. He lectured, wrote political and educational articles, and practiced journalism until 1798, when he retired to the literary life. His authorship of the *American Dictionary of the English Language* (2 vols., 1828) made him not merely a lexicographer, but *the* lexicographer, *the* authority: Webster.

Webster did this by cribbing much of his inventory of words from the 1799 London edition of Samuel Johnson's *Dictionary*. His definitions, however, were quite different in essence from those of Johnson—for example:

> Lion: The fiercest and most magnanimous of four-footed beasts.
>
> (Johnson)

> Lion: A quadruped of the genus Felix, very strong, fierce and rapacious. The largest lions are eight or nine feet in length. The male has a thick head, beset with long bushy hair of a yellowish color. The lion is a native of Africa and the warm climates of Asia. His aspect is noble, his gait stately, and his roar tremendous.
>
> (Webster)

Johnson's definition is literary and humanistic; Webster's, scientific and encyclopedic. Webster added to his *American Dictionary* technical terms that Johnson would never have included, and hosts of words from such manuals as the *Mariner's Dictionary*.

Webster so widened the scope of lexicography that he ensured himself a kind of immortality. Not only had he created a monument to himself in a single work, but he had also changed the course of the river and altered the rule book. Lexicography after Webster was no longer a one-man job. People could steal words and definitions from him as he had stolen from Johnson, but none of them alone could now "improve" his work as he had "improved" Johnson's. Undeniably, he had added "by his own toil, to the acquisitions of his ancestors "(Johnson's *Rambler*, quoted on the title page of Webster's *American Dictionary*) and curbed Johnson's "offensive ribaldry" (letter to Thomas Dawes, 5 August 1809, in Webster's *Letters*, p. 330).

Ironically, Webster's definition of the term *lexicographer* ("The author of a lexicon or dictionary") better suited Johnson, who was a literary man, and Johnson's definition better suited Webster ("A writer of dictionaries; a harmless drudge that busies himself in tracing the origin and detailing the signification of words"). The characterization is inverted. Johnson is ironic and humble, but, in his definition of *lexicographer*, better describes Webster than he describes himself. Webster uses the word *author*, implying a man of literature, with a literary approach; Johnson was more properly the "author of a lexicon." Nevertheless, Webster won out in the end: what he compiled required at first committees and later whole offices to revise. He not only put his stamp on lexicography; he definitively embodied it.

[*See also* Dictionaries *and* Johnson, Samuel.]

BIBLIOGRAPHY

Rollins, Richard M. *The Long Journey of Noah Webster.* Philadelphia, 1980.

Unger, Harlow G. *Noah Webster: The Life and Times of an American Patriot.* New York, 1998.

JOSEPH REED

WEDGWOOD, JOSIAH (1730–1795), English pottery manufacturer.

A member of a long-established pottery-making family, Wedgwood was born in Burslem, Staffordshire, and apprenticed to the trade. During five years' partnership with Thomas Whielden, he began a series of systematic scientific experiments in the production of ceramics, and in 1759 he set up independently as a manufacturer. He rapidly established a successful and innovative pottery business. In 1766, his improved cream-colored earthenware received royal recognition, and under the name "Queens Ware," it came to dominate the British, European, and American markets. Much of this ware was decorated by the newly developed technique of transfer printing, one example of Wedgwood's introduction of new production, business, and marketing methods. Another was the opening, in 1768, of a London showroom designed to attract the custom of a wealthy and cultivated public. Wedgwood's success enabled him in 1769 to establish a model factory, which, at the suggestion of Erasmus Darwin, he named "Etruria." Darwin—doctor, inventor, celebrated poet, and lifelong friend—assisted Wedgwood in his successful parliamentary campaign of 1764–1766 for the act promoting the Trent and Mersey Canal.

Wedgwood's partner at Etruria was a Liverpool merchant, Thomas Bentley. A man of taste and culture, rooted in Enlightenment idealism and neoclassical aesthetics, Bentley was a profound influence on Wedgwood. Prominent in Liverpool's commercial and civic life, a promoter of learning and the arts with a strong commitment to Unitarian beliefs, he was a founder of the Octagon Chapel in Liverpool and of the Warrington Academy. He introduced Wedgwood into the gifted circle associated with this influential foundation, notably to the philosopher and scientist Joseph Priestley, with whom they thereafter maintained close relations, and to whom Wedgwood provided generous support.

Among a company that included such figures as Erasmus Darwin, Richard Lovell Edgeworth, James Keir, John Whitehurst, Matthew Boulton, and James Watt, Priestley was a leading personality in a complex network of friends, associates, and patrons in an influential stratum of society whose interests in science and experimentation, nature, and art were directed toward ideals of public service and encouragement of learning, the arts, and manufactures. Wedgwood was welcomed as a guest at meetings of the Lunar Society. As a scientist his attention was directed primarily to ceramic manufacture and the physics and chemistry of heat. Under the patronage of Sir Joseph Banks, he was elected in 1783 as a fellow of the Royal Society, to which he delivered five papers, principally related to his invention of a pyrometer, which he supplied to a number of chemists of note. He was also a fellow of the Society of Arts and was instrumental in setting up its laboratory, one example of his multifarious activities in London. There, his achievements in uniting art and design with industry were much admired by men like Sir William Hamilton. He was welcomed into enlightened political and scientific circles sympathetic to his radical views, which were evident in his membership of Unitarian chapels in Liverpool and London, his advocacy of the American cause, and his firm opposition to slavery. His current reputation is closely associated with the portrait medallions, plaques, and vases in jasper ware, the novel ceramic body he introduced in 1775. They embodied concepts of classical art and Whig ideology in affordable objects purchased in large numbers by the enlightened in Britain and abroad.

[*See also* Aesthetics; Ancient Greece; Ancient Rome; Archaeology; Chemistry; Citizenship; Classicism; Darwin, Erasmus; Hamilton, William; Learned Societies; Neoclassicism; Priestley, Joseph; *and* Utilitarianism.]

BIBLIOGRAPHY

Burman, Lionel. "Wedgwood and Bentley's Ideas, Experiences and Wares." *Proceedings of the Wedgwood Society* 15 (1995), 27–44. A recent account of this aspect of Wedgwood's life, first described in Eliza Meteyard's *The Life of Josiah Wedgwood* (2 vols., London, 1865; facsimile ed. Ilkley, Yorkshire, 1980).

Reilly, Robin. *Wedgwood.* 2 vols. London, 1989. A comprehensive and exhaustive account of Wedgwood's ceramic achievements and the wares he manufactured.

Reilly, Robin. *Josiah Wedgwood, 1730–1795.* London, 1992. A recent and accurate biography.

Roberts, Gaye Blake. "Ceramics' Unsung Hero—Thomas Bentley." *Transactions of the English Ceramic Circle* 15.1 (1993), 24–36. The fullest account of Bentley's contribution since R. Bentley's *Thomas Bentley, 1730–1780, of Liverpool, Etruria and London* (Guildford, Surrey, 1927).

LIONEL BURMAN

WEEMS, MASON LOCKE (1759–1825).

Familiarly known as Parson Weems, he was born in Marshes Seat, Anne Arundel County, Maryland, one of nineteen children of David Weems and Esther Hill. At about the age of fourteen, Weems went abroad to study medicine in London and at the University of Edinburgh. What use he made of his medical education is unknown, but there is some evidence that he served as a surgeon on a British man-of-war and that he was referred to as "Dr. Weems." After three years abroad, Weems returned to Maryland.

When the Revolutionary War was over, Weems crossed the Atlantic again, this time to study for the ministry and to be ordained a deacon and priest. At the time, 1782–1783, there was no Anglican bishop in the colonies, and the colonies were now separated from England. Weems and his friend Edward Gantt Jr. sought, but were refused, ordination by the Church of England because ordination required an oath of allegiance to the king of England. Fortunately, however, the English Parliament on 13 August 1784 passed an act permitting ordination of persons outside the British empire. Weems was ordained a deacon on 5 September 1784 and a priest on 12 September 1784. Weems and Gantt were the first two persons ordained by the Church of England for ministry in the United States.

For more than twenty years, Weems preached in different Virginia parishes, most notably at Pohick Parish, where George Washington worshiped before the Revolution. To support his family, he became a traveling book agent for Matthew Carey of Philadelphia. For more than thirty years, Weems traveled up and down the east coast selling Bibles and other books.

Weems is most famous for his biography of George Washington, published in 1800, titled *A History of the Life and Death, Virtues and Exploits of General George Washington, and Containing a Great Many Curious and Valuable Anecdotes, Tending to Throw Much Light on the Private as Well as Public Life and Character of That Very Extraordinary Man, the Whole Happily Calculated to Furnish a Feast of True Washingtonian Entertainment and Improvement Both to Ourselves and Our Children*. In the fifth edition, published in 1806, the anecdote of Washington and the cherry tree appeared for the first time.

Weems also wrote tracts designed to inculcate morality in his readers. One of his most popular, published in 1812, was *The Drunkard's Looking-Glass: Reflecting a Faithful Likeness of the Drunkard*.

Weems was an Enlightenment person in that he stressed education, taught children to read, and taught at a female academy. Weems was especially interested in the education of women. He worked to inculcate morality into his readers and knew the value of books for any enlightened culture. His purpose, he said, was "to enlighten, dulcify and exalt human nature" by providing books. He wished for a society "where virtue alone shall be exalted and vice degraded forever." He was a minister-turned-bookpeddler, who brought books and culture to the towns, cities, and farms along the Atlantic coast. He died at Beaufort, South Carolina.

BIBLIOGRAPHY

Bryan, William Alfred. *George Washington in American Literature*. Westport, Conn., 1952.

Cross, Arthur Lyon. *The Anglican Episcopate and the American Colonies*. New York, 1902.

Cunliffe, Marcus. *Parson Weems and George Washington's Cherry Tree*. Manchester, N.H., 1962.

Fisher, Sydney G. "The Legendary and Myth-Making Process in Histories of the American Revolution." *Proceedings of the American Philosophical Society* 51 (1912), 53–75.

Ford, Paul Leicester, and Emily Ellsword Ford Skeel. *Mason Locke Weems: His Works and His Ways*. 3 vols. New York, 1928–1929.

Gilbreath, James. "Mason Locke Weems, Mathew Carey and the Southern Book Trade, 1794–1810." *Publishing History* 10 (1981), 27–49.

Kellock, Harold. *Parson Weems of the Cherry Tree*. New York, 1928.

Leary, Lewis. *The Book-Peddling Parson*. Chapel Hill, N.C., 1984.

Meade, William. *Old Churches, Ministers, and Families of Virginia*. Philadelphia, 1857.

Norris, Walter B. "Historian of the Cherry Tree: Parson Weems and His Life of Washington." *National Magazine* 31 (1910), 495–501.

Norris, Walter B. "Correspondence: Weems." *The Nation* 29 (1912), 207–208.

Purcell, James. "A Peddlar's Progress in North Carolina." *North Carolina Historical Review* 29 (1959), 8–23.

Simms, William G. "Weems, the Biographer and Historian." *Views and Reviews in American Literature, History and Fiction*, 2d ser. (1845), 123–141.

White, William. *Memoirs of the Protestant Episcopal Church in the United States of America*. Edited by B. F. DeCosta. New York, 1880.

Wroth, Lawrence C. *Parson Weems: A Biographical and Critical Study*. Baltimore, 1911.

DONALD S. ARMENTROUT

WEIGHTS AND MEASURES. Until the late eighteenth century, European systems of weights and measures were a testament to disorder. There were thousands of legal units, with hundreds of thousands of regional variants. Physical standards were frequently defective, and poorly trained metrological officials compounded the errors. These conditions adversely affected all sectors of society, especially merchants, scientists, manufacturers, and government agencies. A massive restructuring was in order.

During the seventeenth and eighteenth centuries, numerous metrologists (specialists in measurement), scientists, inventors, and government commissioners conducted experiments, issued reform plans, and waged campaigns against the entrenched customary systems. Some of their proposals called for a decimal scale for building unit proportions. Others wanted a universal system based on pendulums beating seconds at various latitudes, or on terrestrial measurements. Several of the efforts enjoyed temporary success, but only one triumphed and gained eventual international adoption—the French metric system.

There were four principal reasons for the metric triumph. First, of the hundreds of contributions in this era, none was more important initially than the overthrow of the absolute authority of ancient and medieval thought concerning the operation of nature and world systems, and man's relationship with them. The former reluctance to question past authority had placed a monumental roadblock in the path of reform. In contrast, the eighteenth century reassessed old assumptions and postulated new hypotheses—and tested their veracity by the experimental method.

The second reason was technology. The invention and rapid deployment of new processes and devices had a profound impact, far beyond what was first envisaged. These innovations had a dramatic immediate effect: for the first time in history, the theoretician and scientist linked up with the technician and craftsman. For the former to test his hypotheses, he needed much more accurate devices, such as lenses, magnification glasses, navigational instruments, clocks, scales, and most important of all, weights and measures. The key was the urgent necessity to obtain higher standards of measurement.

Third, metrological reform was given a major boost by the establishment of European scientific societies, especially in England and France. By the end of the seventeenth century, most important scientists had become members of such groups, and publication in their journals became the recognized manner of announcing exciting discoveries. The British Royal Society, chartered in 1662, made major contributions to metrology, physics, chemistry, biology, and medicine, and its members performed numerous experiments with the pendulum, barometer, thermometer, and hygrometer.

It was the Paris Académie Royale des Sciences, however, that was most responsible for the eventual metrological revolution. From its founding in the mid-seventeenth century, its original luminaries contributed to metrological reform, notably the astronomers Adrien Auzout and Jean Picard. In the eighteenth century, dozens of metrological pioneers came from its ranks; the most important were Jean-Charles Borda, Antoine-Laurent Lavoisier, Pierre-Simon de Laplace, Charles-Augustin Coulomb, Mathurin-Jacques Brisson, and Jean-Baptiste-Joseph Delambre. Their work led to the establishment of the meter and kilogram, the building blocks of the metric system.

The fourth and final element was the scientific quest for an ideal natural constant on which to base a simplified, integrated, and coordinated system of weights and measures. From the many "natural constants" proposed over the course of two centuries, European scientists eventually settled on the French solution: a universal standard based on a fraction of a great circle of the earth. This measurement involved determining the latitude and longitude of two points, and then conducting a geodetic or trigonometrical survey that took into consideration the curvature of the earth's surface, measuring the actual distance between the points in terms of a unit of length selected for the purpose and represented by a standard employed in the measurement of the baseline. The distance, as found by the triangulation, was then compared with the difference in latitude between the two points, and the actual distance in degrees was obtained in terms of the selected linear standard. This was the most significant scientific work on the new system because it led to

the original determination of the length of the meter, the most important unit in the metric system.

These and other contributions of the Enlightenment produced the metric system, the most accurate and refined system of measurement ever devised. First adopted in France in 1795, it was suspended temporarily in 1812, but by 1840 it was the law of the land. Most of the world employs it now.

[See also Academies; Condorcet, Jean-Antoine-Nicolas de Caritat; Locke, John; Natural Philosophy and Science; Scientific Instruments; and Technology.]

BIBLIOGRAPHY

Berriman, A. E. *Historical Metrology*. London, 1953. European-wide coverage of the major issues in metrological history.
Daumas, M. *Scientific Instruments of the Seventeenth and Eighteenth Century*. New York, 1972. Important metrological repercussions.
Hall, A. Rupert. *The Scientific Revolution: 1500–1800*. London, 1962. Valuable for technological innovations, inventions, and the inner workings of the scientific societies.
Moreau, Henri. *Le système métrique*. Paris, 1975. A concise summary of the major events in metric history.
Wolf, A. *A History of Science, Technology, and Philosophy in the 16th and 17th Centuries*. London, 1950. Tie-in between new secular, rational thought and scientific and technological breakthroughs.
Zupko, Ronald E. *Revolution in Measurement: Western European Weights and Measures since the Age of Science*. Philadelphia, 1990. Extensive coverage of seventeenth- and eighteenth-century weights and measures, scientific experiments, physical standards, the officials, equivalency tables, scientific societies and metrological pioneers, the history of the metric system, and an extensive bibliography.

RONALD E. ZUPKO

WESLEY, JOHN (1703–1791), English clergyman and leader of the Methodist revival.

Although Wesley never left the Church of England, in which he was an ordained minister, he founded the Methodist Society, a lay association independent of church control and ultimately schismatic in its development. At his death, it numbered 71,668 members and 294 preachers in Great Britain, and 43,265 members and 198 preachers in North America. In the mid-nineteenth century, a worldwide membership of nearly three million was claimed by Methodist churches of various sorts.

Wesley belonged to the eighteenth-century evangelical revival. He believed Christianity testifies itself to the believer by a spiritual experience; if one is saved, one simply knows it. He did not work out a complete theology or prescribe a creed to which Methodists should assent. What he thought, on the whole, is a matter of controversy. Some deny that he held any coherent doctrine at all. E. P. Thompson sees him as an intellectual opportunist, and Methodism as a social stratagem that works to reconcile the working classes to the hardships of the industrial revolution. Ronald Knox depicts him as an enthusiast belonging to a succession of zealots, from Montanus in the second century to Father Divine in the twentieth, all of whom are supposed to preach under a claim of supernatural appointment. Knox wrote from a Catholic perspective, Thompson from a Marxist. If it is possible to speak of a majority position in Methodist scholarship, however, Wesley figures there as an essentially Anglican thinker who built on a tradition of royalist and High Church piety deriving from the seventeenth century. In leading the Methodist revival, he refused to break with the Church of England; and in opposition to Calvinist Evangelicals, he appealed to the authority of Jacob Arminius, a seventeenth-century Dutch divine and the theologian then favored in High Church Anglican circles. A royalist in politics, Wesley urged Methodists to support the king's candidate in parliamentary elections. He opposed the American Revolution. Elie Halévy supposes that it was Wesley's influence that prevented a revolution on the French pattern from taking place in England.

A born-again zealot who denounced David Hume, Voltaire, Jean-Jacques Rousseau, Montesquieu, Francis Hutcheson, Gottfried Wilhelm von Leibniz, and Henry Home, Lord Kames, it is not difficult to represent Wesley as an enemy of the Enlightenment. Important elements in his thought, however, were derived from John Locke. He espoused Locke's empiricism and drew on it in appealing to experience as the test of Christian conversion. He also accepted Locke's contractualist conception of authority, thinking of churches as voluntary associations validated by the consent of their members; like the Methodist Society itself, churches are clubs. It was this assumption that let Wesley, as a conscientious Anglican minister, direct an independent revival under the aegis of a non-Anglican lay society. In epistemology and ecclesiology, Wesley belonged to the Enlightenment.

[See also Enthusiasm; Great Awakening; Locke, John; Pietism; and Revealed Religion.]

BIBLIOGRAPHY

Baker, Frank. *John Wesley and the Church of England*. London, 1970. States the case for Wesley's Anglican identity.
Dreyer, Frederick. *The Genesis of Methodism*. Bethlehem, Pa., 1999. A reply to Baker, arguing for the importance of Methodism's eighteenth-century background, particularly its background in the Enlightenment.
Halévy, Elie. *England in 1815*. London, 1961. Attributes to Wesley's influence the prevention of revolution in England.
Knox, Ronald. *Enthusiasm: A Chapter in the History of Religion*. Notre Dame, Ind., 1995.
Rack, Henry D. *Reasonable Enthusiast: John Wesley and the Rise of Methodism*. Philadelphia, 1989. A balanced, scholarly, and cautious survey.
Semmel, Bernard. *The Methodist Revolution*. New York, 1973. A reply to Thompson and Halévy, stressing Wesley's identity as an Arminian thinker.
Thompson, E. P. *The Making of the English Working Class*. New York, 1966. Discusses the role of Methodism in the industrial revolution.
Wesley, John. *The Works of John Wesley*. 3d ed. 14 vols. 1872; repr., Grand Rapids, Mich., 1979. A new and better edition of Wesley's works is now being published by the Abingdon Press under the general editorship of Frank Baker and Richard Heitzenrater. Fourteen volumes have appeared between 1975 and 2001.

FREDERICK A. DREYER

WEST, BENJAMIN (1730–1813), American astronomer and mathematician.

Born in Rehoboth, Massachusetts, the son of John West, a farmer, West grew up in Bristol, Rhode Island. He attended the town school for only three months and took a course in navigation offered by a Captain Woodbury, who waived his fees for the poor farm boy. Otherwise, West was self-educated, borrowing books from local parsons' libraries. In 1753, West married Elizabeth Smith; they had eight children. That same year, West moved to Providence, Rhode Island, where he opened a private school and then a dry-goods store that also sold books. After nearly twenty years, his business failed and his effects were seized by creditors. After his bankruptcy, some Bostonians offered to set him up in the book business again, but West doubted he could support his growing family this way. As a patriot, he chose to manufacture clothing for the American troops during the war. With the coming of peace, he reopened his school in Providence.

What sustained West during the lean years of his business was the compilation of almanacs, beginning with one published in 1763 by William Goddard on Providence's first printing press. With the 1764 issue, this work became known as the *New England Almanack*. West's astronomical calculations won wide acclaim for accuracy, and he contributed to almanacs published simultaneously for the meridians of Providence, Boston, and Halifax, Nova Scotia. West authored as many as 200 almanacs between 1763 and 1806, but he sometimes furnished calculations under different names to rival printers, and some works bearing his name or his pseudonym, Isaac Bickerstaff, were pirated.

In 1769, West participated in the international observations of the transit of Venus, a rare event that was of use in determining the dimensions of the solar system. His observations from Providence were sent to the Royal Society in London and the American Philosophical Society in Philadelphia, which printed them in part in its *Transactions*. In 1781, West sent a paper on the extraction of roots of odd powers to the American Academy of Arts and Sciences and was elected a member. He communicated observations of comets to the Harvard professor John Winthrop as early as 1766, and he discussed problems of natural philosophy and navigation with others.

In 1786, West was appointed professor of mathematics and astronomy at Rhode-Island College (now Brown

University). Perhaps out of resentment for having been passed over earlier, or because of the meager salary, West did not assume his chair right away, and in March 1787 he became professor of mathematics at the Protestant Episcopal Academy of Philadelphia. In Philadelphia, he enjoyed the company of scientists, including Benjamin Franklin and David Rittenhouse. Because his wife refused to leave Providence, West turned down a professorship of mathematics at King's College (now Columbia University) and returned to Rhode-Island College to begin his duties in 1788. In 1798, he was named professor of mathematics and natural philosophy. When his appointment was not renewed in 1799, West opened a school of navigation at his home. Between 1802 and 1813, he served as postmaster of Providence.

West was also a member of the Pennsylvania Society for the Abolition of Slavery, despite living in Rhode Island, where the slave trade flourished. His health deteriorated after the death of his wife in 1810, and he died in Providence three years later.

[*See also* Almanacs and Yearbooks *and* Astronomy.]

BIBLIOGRAPHY

WORKS BY WEST

An Account of the Observation of Venus Upon the Sun, the Third Day of June, 1769, at Providence, in New-England. With some Account of the Use of those Observations. Providence, 1769. Partially reprinted in the *Transactions of the American Philosophical Society* 1 (1771), 97–105.

"An Account of the Observations Made in Providence, in the State of Rhode-Island, of the Eclipse of the Sun, which happened the 23d Day of April, 1781." *Memoirs of the American Academy of Arts and Sciences* 1 (1785), 156–158.

"On the Extraction of Roots." *Memoirs of the American Academy of Arts and Sciences* 1 (1785), 165–172.

EPHEMERIDES COMPUTED BY WEST

New England Almanack. Providence, 1763–1781.

Bickerstaff's Boston Almanack. Boston, 1768–1779, 1783–1793.

The North-American Calendar: or, the Rhode Island Almanack. Providence, 1781–1788.

An Astronomical Diary. Hartford and Boston, 1785–1797.

Town and Country Almanack. Norwich, Conn., 1795–1799.

The Rhode Island Almanack. Newport, 1804–1806.

STUDIES

"Biography of Benjamin West, LL.D. A.A.S. Professor of Mathematicks, Astronomy and Natural Philosophy in Rhode-Island College and Fellow of the Philosophical Society of Philadelphia." *Rhode Island Literary Repository* 1.7 (1814), 137–160. Earliest and most complete biography.

Shipton, Clifford K. "Benjamin West." In *Biographical Sketches of Those Who Attended Harvard College in the Classes 1746–1750 with Bibliographical and Other Notes*, vol. 12, pp. 220–226. Boston, 1962. Also known as *Sibley's Harvard Graduates*, this series contains valuable information on West and his contemporaries.

Stowell, Marion B. *Early American Almanacs: The Colonial Weekday Bible*. New York, 1977.

SARA SCHECHNER

WHEATLEY, ACADE PHILLIS (c. 1753–1784), African American poet.

Born in West Africa around 1753 and sold into the Atlantic slave trade around 1760, Phillis Wheatley—her birth name and early affiliations are lost—absorbed English, Christianity, and Greek and Roman classics in the home of her Boston owner, John Wheatley. Life in revolutionary Boston exposed her to republican thought. Her *Poems on Various Subjects, Religious and Moral* was published in Britain in 1773. Other writings appeared in periodicals or survive as autographs. Initially celebrated in New England and Britain as a prodigy, she disappeared from the firmament of African American writers in the antebellum decades, when autobiographies of escaped slaves outshone other black writings. A twentieth-century revival of interest has established her as an acute commentator on equality, slavery, and the slave trade. She was manumitted in 1773, possibly because British abolitionists embarrassed her owner, who had traveled to London with her to promote her poetry. Her last decade was marred by her unhappy marriage to a free black, John Peters, and by her children's early deaths. Immiserated and impaired, probably both physically and emotionally, after an infant's death, she herself died in 1784.

Wheatley exemplifies the appeal of key elements of the Enlightenment—freedom, progress, reason, religion, and the relevance of the classical heritage—to blacks in the era of the American Revolution. Enlightened ideas, values, and politics were not, however, universally interpreted as abolitionist. Significantly, Wheatley was scorned in the American South, where enlightened thought and slavery were most thoroughly intertwined. Still, Wheatley lauded freedom and criticized slavery and the slave trade in characteristically enlightened fashion. Like many New Englanders, she squared enlightened thought with Christian revelation and committed herself to republican and antislavery ideals. She praised "science" as a means of learning about the natural world but she insisted that knowledge was incomplete without piety, "virtue," and regard for God's "glory." She esteemed the revolutionaries but she noted that Americans "hold in bondage Afric's blameless race." Her writings regularly proclaim that an "Ethiop," a member of an enslaved race, is capable of keen insight into the possibilities for equality implied by Christianity and republicanism.

Wheatley's enlightened thought has caused controversy. Some twentieth-century commentators describe her as a victim of indoctrination; belittling her for articulating antislavery sentiments in slaveholders' language and not in an African mode of discourse, these authors see her abolitionism as inconsequential. Others, in contrast, describe her enlightened views as essential to the freedom she desired as an African American, a New World black who,

Acade Phillis Wheatley. Frontispiece to *Poems on Various Subjects, Religious and Moral* (London, 1773). (The Pierpont Morgan Library/Art Resource, NY.)

in 1774, demurred when offered repatriation to Africa, a favorite project of American enlightened theorists. The content of Wheatley's writings favors the latter assessment. However vivid her piety or aspirations for freedom, her strongest expressions concerned powerlessness and external force such as she experienced in her initial captivity. Memories of seizure seem to have overwhelmed her other recollections of her African origins. Critical of both American slavery and the African slave trade, she resisted the Enlightenment's primitivist strain—its idealization of a natural, original society. Progress was her constant theme, from her initial captivity toward freedom in republican society. Like many eighteenth-century Christians, she understood progress as providentially ordained by God. She even interpreted her childhood abduction as an occurrence never to be repeated, and thus part of God's plan. Neither primitivism nor repatriation could tempt her from her adopted faith.

[*See also* Slavery.]

BIBLIOGRAPHY

WORKS BY WHEATLEY
The Complete Writings of Phillis Wheatley. Edited by Vincent Carretta. New York, 2001. A modern edition of her writings, with letters, variant texts, and poems published only in periodicals in her lifetime.
Poems on Various Subjects, Religious and Moral, by Phillis Wheatley, Negro Servant to Mr. John Wheatley, of Boston, New England. London, 1773.

STUDIES
Richards, Phillip M. "Phillis Wheatley and Literary Americanization." *American Quarterly* 44 (1992), 163–191. An invaluable study of her twin declarations of blackness and Americanness.
Zafar, Rafia. *We Wear the Mask: African Americans Write American Literature, 1760–1870.* New York, 1997. An effort to situate Wheatley in African American literary history.

JOHN SAILLANT

WIELAND, CHRISTOPH MARTIN (1733–1813), German philosopher, poet, and novelist.

Immanuel Kant claimed, with some justification, that the Enlightenment had liberated mankind through the independent use of reason; from the mid-eighteenth century, however, it had to share the center ground in German culture with a countercurrent that sought to emancipate the "heart" from the dominance assigned by the Enlightenment to the "head." Wieland belonged unequivocally to the camp of the Enlightenment, but he was inclined by temperament and conviction to assign a role, in the search for the good and happy life, to the emotions, the imagination, and even the senses.

Nonetheless, for him it is fundamentally thinking that defines humanity—more precisely, "right" thinking guided by reason, the light that shows us "our true nature and purpose" and that will, as it spreads more generally, drive human progress toward full realization. Meanwhile, since human beings are sensual as well as spiritual creatures and are subject to error and illusion, thinking can provide the basis for a happy life for the enlightened individual, provided that he can ensure that its control is not subverted by *Schwärmerei* (confusion of imagined with "real" truth). Such control, however, cannot be achieved through the suppression of what Johann Wolfgang von Goethe had established as the valid "inner" truth of human nature. Wieland could not accept a philosophy divorced from psychology: in his final statement on the subject, the novel *Aristipp*, he allowed most of the many philosophies he had presented in his writings to coexist in dialogue, showing that while all have a measure of insight, none is entirely adequate to the problems of practical living. Even the "Lebensweisheit" of Archytas (in the 1794 version of *Agathon*), the nearest Wieland produced to a systematic statement of his *Weltanschauung* (worldview), is too theoretical to stand as a final solution. It is the Epicurean Aristippus, whose thinking is in essence a strategy for surviving reasonably happily in "the world as it is" while maintaining one's humanity, who fittingly represents Wieland in his final novel. For Aristippus—as for Wieland's literary hero,

Christoph Martin Wieland. Lithograph by C. Pfeiffer after a portrait by Johann Heinrich Tischbein (1722–1789). (Prints and Photographs Division, Library of Congress.)

Horace, whose *Epistles* he translated with brilliance—the answer lies in wisdom that has become "feeling," a substance that expresses itself as a style.

Wieland was born in Oberholzheim near Biberach, where his father, Thomas Adam Wieland, was a Lutheran pastor. After a thorough education in Biberach and Tübingen, he left home for Switzerland, hoping to lay the foundations for a career as a man of letters. The predominant tendency of his prolific and varied writings during the Swiss years (1752–1760) was to seek a resolution of his inner tensions and confusions (he called himself a "chameleon") through the maximization of spirituality. *Sympathien* (Sympathies, 1755), in which he rhapsodized about the beauties of the soul in Pietistic but sensuous poetic prose, demonstrates both the dominant trend and the tensions within it. Reading the works of the earl of Shaftesbury, a lifelong influence, helped Wieland develop his natural appreciation of material beauty and spurred him to seek a way of harmonizing it with his natural idealism, which he never lost, though he later exposed the proclivity of the naive idealist to self-deception.

Back in Biberach, working as an official in the city's administration and disillusioned with the "seraphic"

mode, Wieland turned to the playful Rococo style. Although he tempered it with moral uplift when occasion demanded, as in the verse fairy tale *Idris* (1768), ironic and urbane awareness of the realities of life remained central to his outlook. The Rococo taught him, first, that his natural literary role was as a relaxed storyteller and commentator, and second, the vital importance of style. He became a conscious, meticulous craftsman and rated what he called *fini* ("high finish, refinement") above originality. The young Goethe acknowledged how much he had learned from Wieland's mastery of poetic language and versification in the latter's *Musarion* (1768), a verse tale that sets forth a practical "philosophy of the Graces" and begins the series of portraits of beautiful, intelligent, independent women for which Wieland is noted. Most important, *Musarion* demonstrates the possibility of a freedom that resides in inner balance and can snap its fingers at wealth or power; and it convinces the reader not theoretically but practically, through humor and the supple and imaginative manipulation of language and meter.

The most important product of Wieland's Biberach period (1760–1769) was the novel *Geschichte des Agathon* (Story of Agathon, 1766–1767; final version, 1794), which plunges into practical life in a way that *Musarion* does not. The Horatian epigraph "quid virtus et quid sapientia possit," signifies not that the hero is a monster of virtue and wisdom, but that he is an intelligent and moral but nevertheless merely human man. The hero begins as a naïve idealist, though an intelligent and morally right-thinking one; he suffers disillusionment as a politician and as a lover but retains his faith in humanity; and he eventually finds at least a theoretical equilibrium in Tarentum, which, under the guidance of the philosopher Archytas, is as close to an ideal society as Wieland feels is possible at the moment. *Agathon*, with the hero's constant process of analysis, helped lay the foundation of the German *Bildungsroman* (novel of character development), though the first example of the genre proper is Goethe's *Wilhelm Meister*. The essential difference lies not in the analytical element itself but in the narrative voice that is its vehicle. Wieland is not merely a neutral "narrator"; he conducts, in his own right, a constant dialogue with a varied readership that forms part of the novel itself. This adds to the work's discussion of the problem of living with an ironic yet not frivolous detachment that is both style and substance. The long, perambulating periods (which drew criticism even in Wieland's time) are a way of smoothing out the sharp edges of theory and introducing an elegant urbanity—and, above all, leisureliness in the process of reading. We take Agathon seriously, but not, as the Germans say, "tragically." If Agathon the character solves his problem in theory, Wieland the author solves it in practice. The figure who comes closest to convincing us that he has achieved equilibrium and independence (for Archytas is a touch too Kantian) is the Epicurean Aristippus. Consorting in Athens with both philosophical graybeards and intelligent and beautiful women has enabled him to combine "the gaiety of the graces with the seriousness of philosophy."

Appointment to a chair of philosophy in Erfurt appealed to the pedagogue in Wieland, though he was most effective in this regard in Weimar, as editor of the journal *Der Teutsche Merkur*. His original writing during the Erfurt interlude (1769–1772) included poetic works in the Rococo style and two novels. In *Sokrates Mainomenos* (1770), Wieland assumed the persona of a polished and cosmopolitan Diogenes. *Der goldene Spiegel* (The Golden Mirror, 1772), an overtly didactic work, portrays the character Tifan, who has developed into an enlightened despot under the tutelage of "wise Danischmend"; it thus sets out to apply Wieland's moderate liberal principles to the conditions of eighteenth-century German absolutism. He knew that despotism could become tyranny, but like all *Aufklärer* (members of the German Enlightenment), he feared disorder more; he could think of no worse potential tyrant than the *Volk*, which, for him, was not the semi-mystical concept then beginning to take shape in the thought of Johann Gottfried Herder, but simply the immature, "childish" populace, which needed enlightenment from above. In 1772, on the strength of *Der goldene Spiegel*, Wieland was invited to tutor the young Duke Karl August in Weimar, where he remained until his death.

When Karl August assumed the throne in 1775, Wieland retired from tutoring with a pension. He could now live as a man of letters, both poetic and publicist. He had founded *Der Teutsche Merkur* in 1773 and continued to edit it until 1796. His essays ranged widely: the base was literary, but many other questions were put up for debate, in a tone Wieland tried to keep relaxed and reasonable. He remained an *Aufklärer*, but he was always aware of current trends in the literary, political, and social spheres. The cult of sentiment of the 1770s confirmed his awareness that nonrational elements in the "mysterious abyss" of the psyche ("Thoughts on the Ideals of the Ancients," 1777) could not be disregarded. Later, he mounted a defense of reason against superstition ("On the Free Use of Reason in Matters of Religion," 1788) and an equally spirited attack against credulous faith in charlatans advocating "magnetism" ("Thoughts on Lavater's Magnetism," 1787) and in mystics like Cagliostro and Swedenborg. The French Revolution elicited a running commentary on events abroad and reactions to them at home. Without conceding anything to reactionary, even nationalistic tendencies in Germany, which he saw as a cultural and historical unity, but within the framework of a loose imperial "constitution" that needed reforming but still gave valuable freedoms, Wieland remained faithful to his own principles rather than others' more radical, "enlightened" ones. The French should be allowed to work out their own destiny, but he would not follow them down the path of disorder. Wieland's review carried many other topics (e.g., the explorations of Captain Cook, ascents in hot-air balloons, the Singspiel, the intellectual and social role of women in society), to which he brought not so much ideas as attitudes, and above all, his engaged but relaxed and tolerant style.

The late 1770s and early 1780s saw a second flowering of Wieland's poetic muse in a series of narrative poems, drawing principally on fairy tales or other "romantic" sources of the past. Wieland continued to exhibit his capacity for elegant irony and stylish play and his graceful rationality in the majority of them (e.g., *Das Wintermärchen* [The Winter Tale], 1776, or *Pervonte*, 1778–1779), and his style has not been entirely effaced even by the heroic seriousness of *Oberon* (1780). The poetic craftsmanship—in particular, the graceful handling of complex metrical problems—is consistently assured.

In his later years, Wieland favored the novel. *Geheime Geschichte des Philosophen Peregrinus Proteus* (1791) is a tolerant but satirical examination of the enthusiast; *Agathodämon* (1796) propounds an essentially deistic religion shorn of mystery. More important are *Die Abderiten, eine sehr wahrscheinliche Geschichte* (Story of Abderiten, 1781) and *Aristipp* (1800–1801). The former satirizes human folly in genial rather than Juvenalian fashion. Its Abderites are capable of enthusiasm and good humor, but not of thinking straight: in matters of aesthetics, religion or social policy, their judgment is clouded by emotion or prejudice. Wieland's belief in the power of reason to bring progress was tempered by his recognition of human frailty. "Cosmopolitans" who have achieved clarity and balance must help where they can, and laugh to preserve their own health rather than in the expectation of thereby curing others. Again, this philosophy finds its most potent expression in Wieland's relaxed, ironic, almost Erasmian style. *Aristipp*, a more serious and more personal work, is a dialogue among many thinkers; it revolves around the relationship between the hero and the courtesan Lais, and their search for a solution to the problem of life. Neither philosophy nor Grace offers a complete defense. Lais, despite her independence, is destroyed by passion; even Socrates, the philosophical martyr-hero, has his irrational weakness. He falls victim to the prejudice of others, and also, perhaps, to a touch of hubris in himself ("No one owes it to the world to be a hero"). Even Aristippus's serenity is threatened. Wieland, however, has not lost his rational faith and optimism: for Aristippus and for mankind, "there is still hope."

[*See also* Aufklärung; Germany; Novel; Optimism, Philosophical; *and* Switzerland.]

BIBLIOGRAPHY

SELECTED WORKS

Wieland. *Werke*. Edited by F. Martini and H. W. Seiffert, 5 vols. Munich, 1964–1968.

TRANSLATIONS

Various translations into English of works by Wieland appeared in the eighteenth century, including a version of *Agathon* by John Richardson of York (see Werner W. Beyer, "Two Translators and Wieland's Prestige in England" in H. Schelle (ed.), *Christoph Martin Wieland: Nordamenikanische Forschungsbeiträge*. Tübingen: Niemeyer, 1984, pp. 209–223). Very little is currently available. *Oberon* was well translated by William Sotheby (1798), and a reprint of the version by John Quincy Adams is listed under "Hyperion: Conn." (1974). A worthy, though not entirely successful version of *Die Geschichte der Abderiten* (*History of the Abderites*, translated by Max Dufner. Bethlehem, Pa.: Lehigh University Press) appeared in 1993.

WORKS ABOUT WIELAND

Boa, Elizabeth. "Wieland's *Musarion* and the Rococo Verse-Narrative." In *Periods in German Literature II*, edited by J. M. Ritchie, pp. 23–41. London, 1968. Sound account of an important text and style.

Boa, Elizabeth. "Sex and Sensibility: Wieland's Portrayal of Relationships Between the Sexes in the *Comische Erzählungen, Agathon*, and *Musarion*." *Lessing Yearbook* 12 (1980), 189–218. Good introduction to the discussion of women's situation in the eighteenth century.

Kurth-Voigt, Liselotte E. *Perspectives and Points of View: The Early Works of Wieland and Their Background*. Baltimore, 1974. Scholarly and perceptive, illuminating on epistemological questions.

McCarthy, John A. *Fantasy and Reality: An Epistemologic Approach to Wieland*. Berne and Frankfurt, 1974. Particularly useful for Wieland's relation to Shaftesbury.

McCarthy, John A. *Christoph Martin Wieland*. Boston, 1979. Marred by typographical errors, but a workmanlike general account in English, with useful bibliography.

Müller, Jan-Dirk. *Wielands späte Romane: Untersuchungen zur Erzählweise und zur erzählten Wirklichkeit*. Munich, 1971. Particularly useful for *Aristipp*.

Sahmland, I. *Christoph Martin Wieland und die deutsche Nation*. Tübingen, 1990. Important for Wieland's relation to politics.

Sengle, Friedrich. *Wieland*. Stuttgart, 1949. Still the indispensable standard work.

ALAN MENHENNET

WILKES, JOHN (1725–1797), English politician.

John Wilkes was born in Clerkenwell, London, the second son of a prosperous malt distiller who had him educated privately and then at the University of Leiden (1744–1746) in the United Provinces. Wilkes became a politician and adventurer whose brilliant talent for ridicule, rabble-rousing, and roistering should not be allowed to obscure his determination to uphold issues of constitutional principle. He first achieved national prominence as the opponent of Lord Bute, whom he attacked regularly in his Scots-hating periodical, *The North Briton*. Wilkes was arrested for a libel on George III's ministers in that publication's notorious No. 45 in April 1763, but he was discharged on grounds of privilege as a member

of Parliament, and he had the satisfaction of seeing the Court of Common Pleas declare unlawful the issuance of general warrants for searches of unspecified premises. He was nevertheless expelled from the House of Commons on 20 January 1764, when its members rejected a claim that proceedings against him for libel had been in breach of parliamentary privilege. In his absence (he had crossed to the European continent in late 1763), Wilkes was outlawed on 1 November by the Court of King's Bench for publishing libels, including the obscene *An Essay on Woman*.

Returning to England in early 1768, Wilkes was elected member of Parliament for Middlesex in the general election of that year. Though his outlawry was reversed in June 1768, the government was determined to keep him from taking his seat, and he was again expelled from the Commons in February 1769 for a composite of libels. He was thrice reelected as member for Middlesex, but his election was annulled by a majority of the members on each occasion until the 1774 general election, when he was quietly allowed to take his seat. He was also Lord Mayor of London in 1774–1775.

Wilkes was patron of the Society of the Bill of Rights (1769) and helped establish the freedom of the press to report parliamentary debates in the Printers' Case of 1771. He became a hero to the American patriots, who equated his tussles with overbearing government authority with their own struggles. His concern for the freedom of the press, parliamentary reform, and the rights of electors attracted much support, but, like most eighteenth-century political reformers, Wilkes was more concerned to recover what he viewed as traditional liberties than to invent new ones. In later life, Wilkes lost interest in radicalism. He took an active part as a magistrate in suppressing the Gordon Riots and was an opponent of the French Revolution.

Wilkes's defense of the common law rights of English subjects placed him within an established political tradition, but his personal libertinism, religious heterodoxy, and popularism limited his support within elite circles. He wrote an obscene parody of the hymn "Veni Creator" that was hard to reconcile with his nominal Anglicanism. He was interested in Arianism, but as a mature man, Wilkes was more a deist than an Arian. In March 1779, he spoke in the Commons on relief for Dissenters: he denounced the Athanasian Creed, praised the rational dissenters Richard Price and Joseph Priestley, and opposed a clause stipulating that toleration must be conditional on a declaration of adherence to Protestant Christianity.

Wilkes was well known to many of the philosophes. While in France during the mid-1760s, he attended the salon of Paul-Henri Thiry d'Holbach (a former fellow student at Leiden University, which Wilkes attended in 1744–1746) and formed a lasting friendship with Denis Diderot. Wilkes's championship of liberty held great appeal for thinkers whose commitment was comparable but whose scope for direct action was limited. "Voltaire caresses me enough to turn my head," wrote Wilkes from Geneva in mid-1764. In 1769, he described the years in France as the happiest of his life.

"Wilkes and Liberty" was a rallying cry for populist libertarians in both England and the thirteen colonies during the 1760s and 1770s; it was an electrifying slogan, but serious constitutional reformers found there was little of substance in Wilkite propaganda once Wilkes himself was removed from the equation. Though an accomplished political journalist, Wilkes left a minimal intellectual legacy which, somewhat misleadingly, suggests that his public life was more ephemeral and self-centered than it actually was. He possessed a choice library but wrote little. He published a private edition of Catullus in 1788. He projected a two-volume *History of England from the Revolution to the Accession of the Brunswick Line* (1768), but he lacked either the leisure or the inclination to go beyond a thirty-nine-page introduction passionately upholding the English revolutionary settlement of 1688. Although not rising above the level of a political polemic, it affords rare insight into Wilkes's libertarian values. He wrote, "The English have regularly since the era of the flight of their last tyrant [James II], manifested in the cause of freedom a constancy, a courage, a firmness more than Roman." He noted that from this era, "Liberty of conscience began to be considered not merely as a sound measure of the internal administration of a country, but as a great commercial principle." Typically, the *History* was to be a "votive offering" to the gentlemen, clergy, and freeholders of the county of Middlesex.

[*See also* Censorship; *and* Journals, Newspapers, and Gazettes, *subentry on* Great Britain.]

BIBLIOGRAPHY

Maier, Pauline. "John Wilkes and American Disillusionment with Britain." *William and Mary Quarterly* 20 (1963), 373–395.
Rudé, George. *Wilkes and Liberty*. Oxford, 1962.
Thomas, Peter D. G. *John Wilkes. A Friend to Liberty*. Oxford, 1996.
Williamson, A. *Wilkes*. London, 1974.

NIGEL ASTON

WILSON, JAMES (1742–1798), American statesman, writer, and associate justice of the first United States Supreme Court (1789–1798).

Wilson, better considered as a synthesizer than as a deeply original mind, was a leading American exponent of the "moderate" Enlightenment in Scotland, from which he emigrated to Philadelphia in 1765. A successful lawyer—indeed, probably the best American legal mind of his generation—Wilson was continually prominent during the American Revolution and the early period of nation-founding. He was a signer of the Declaration of Independence and a framer of the Constitution (second in importance only to James Madison) at the Federal Convention of 1787.

Wilson reached his intellectual acme as a synthesizer of Scottish-American Enlightenment thought in his extensive 1790–1791 series of *Lectures on Law*, first published in 1804. These lectures have come to be regarded as an early American constitutional commentary almost on a par with *The Federalist*. Yet Wilson's *Lectures* range wider still: he claimed them to be a "comprehensive" work of "philosophy" covering legal, political, and social theory. Aiming above all to propound a vision of what republican citizenship in American could and should mean, Wilson drew on many "enlightened" thinkers of the distant and recent past: Cicero, the quintessentially eloquent and erudite advocate of late Roman republicanism; Francis Bacon and Isaac Newton, the towering geniuses of early modern English science; the politic Elizabethan ecclesiastic Richard Hooker; and the paragons of seventeenth-century Whig liberalism, Edward Coke and John Locke.

The mature Wilson of the *Lectures* remained faithful to the common law legalism and Whig political theory of his days as a Revolution pamphleteer, but he expanded beyond it and ultimately exalted the contemporary Scottish common sense philosopher Thomas Reid above all other thinkers. Reid and his followers were then growing influential in the Atlantic world as the leading defenders of an empirically "true" theory of human nature intended to justify a faith in the greatest Enlightenment experiment of all, which Montesquieu had proposed in the *Lettres persanes*: a society that would govern itself on the basis of "reflection and choice," in Alexander Hamilton's opening words of *The Federalist*. Wilson's own optimism was also based on his expectations for the promising regime of democratic constitutionalism, social "improvement," and economic opportunity that he had worked so hard to achieve for the new American republic.

For all his optimism, however, Wilson—like his master Reid—was hardly a thoroughgoing Enlightenment rationalist, much less a skeptic; rather, Wilson was at bottom a social theologian, typical of the Scottish-American common sense and "moral sense" persuasion. Even though Wilson generally touched on the matter but lightly, he regarded the God-principle—the "revealed" divine authority of God's "natural law" and his indisputable "authorship of human nature"—as an essential and fundamental precept.

[*See also* American Revolution; Constitution of the United States; Republicanism; *and* Scottish Common Sense Philosophy.]

BIBLIOGRAPHY

Conrad, Stephen A. "Polite Foundation: Citizenship and Common Sense in James Wilson's Republican Theory." In *The Supreme Court*

Review—1984, edited by Philip B. Kurland et al., pp. 359–388. Chicago, 1985. Of late, the most widely discussed interpretation of Wilson's republican theory.

Conrad, Stephen A. "The Rhetorical Constitution of 'Civil Society' at the Founding: One Lawyer's Anxious Vision." *Indiana Law Journal* 72 (1997), 335–373. Reevaluates Wilson's thought specifically in its late eighteenth-century intellectual context; followed by a "Response," pp. 375–381, by Jack P. Greene.

Hall, Mark David. *The Political and Legal Philosophy of James Wilson, 1742–1798.* Columbia, Mo., 1997. Controversial in its interpretation, but gives the fullest overview to date of the scholarly literature on Wilson.

Smith, Charles Page. *James Wilson: Founding Father, 1742–1798.* Chapel Hill, N.C., 1956. The most detailed biography of Wilson; Smith's 1951 Harvard Ph.D. dissertation, "James Wilson, 1787–1798," includes even richer detail.

Wilson, James. *The Works of James Wilson*, edited by Robert Green McCloskey. 2 vols. Cambridge, Mass., 1967. The authoritative modern edition of Wilson's writings (except for his Supreme Court opinions); invaluable index, bibliography, and introductory essay by the editor; out of print but widely available in libraries.

STEPHEN A. CONRAD

WINCKELMANN, JOHANN JOACHIM (1717–1768), German art historian, archaeologist, and theorist.

The most influential voice in the Enlightenment reassessment and valorization of ancient Greek art, Winckelmann also shaped two disciplines that emerged in the eighteenth century, art history and archaeology. Winckelmann was born into modest circumstances—he was the son of a cobbler—in Stendal, Prussia. Despite what were for his time extremely challenging beginnings, he embarked on a scholarly career that would eventually lead him from an appointment at the Saxon court in Dresden to Rome, in 1755, as a Catholic convert. Although he had already begun writing on the art of antiquity before ever setting foot there—*Gedanken über die Nachahmung der griechischen Werke in der Malerei und Bildhauerkunst* (Reflections on the Imitation of the Painting and Sculpture of the Greeks) was published prior to his departure and without direct access to original artworks—Rome, which Winckelmann dubbed "the academy of Europe," was the ideal setting for the study of ancient art. Winckelmann's growing reputation as the foremost classical scholar, as well as his appointments and personal connections, put him at the center of an influential circle of art connoisseurs, artists, and intellectuals, including the painter Anton Mengs. From 1758 on, he was employed as a librarian and curator by Cardinal Alessandro Albani (1692–1779), founder of one of the most important eighteenth-century collections of classical antiquities. Among other scholarly responsibilities in Rome, Winckelmann was also appointed librarian at the Vatican and prefect of Roman antiquities, in which latter role he published a blistering critique of the Herculaneum excavations, calling for the amateurism that had marred

the project to be replaced by the scientific methodology of a new interpretive, comparative, and empirical archaeology. Such systematizing efforts, also fundamental to *Geschichte der Kunst des Altertums* (History of Ancient Art, 1764) mark his project as a singularly Enlightenment one.

"Noble simplicity and calm grandeur" (*edle Einfalt und stille Grösse*) are central to Winckelmann's enormously influential interpretations of ancient art, a reaction against the exaggerated plasticity and gesture of Baroque sculpture (the latter being the dominant style, it should be noted, represented in the Dresden collections). The axiomatic statement on Greek art, contained in the essay *Reflections on the Imitation of the Painting and Sculpture of the Greeks*, established the normative status of classical sculpture for subsequent generations of European intellectuals. This essay, as well as the monumental and much-translated *History of Ancient Art*, presented the beautiful Greek male body as an ideal mirror into which moderns were to project themselves: "For us the only way to become great and, if possible, inimitable, is by imitation of the ancients." (Recent scholarship on Winckelmann, such as the psychoanalytically inflected work of Alex Potts, has rightly emphasized the homoerotic quality

Johann Joachim Winckelmann. Frontispiece to *Geschichte der Kunst des Altertums* (1764). (Bildarchiv Foto Marburg/Art Resource, NY.)

of the male nude, "for the male viewer both an object of desire and an ideal subject with which to identify.")

Before Winckelmann, as Hugh Honour points out, the term *antiquity* connoted a long, unbroken period stretching from the fifth century B.C. to the Byzantine era. Winckelmann was thus one of the first scholars to develop a historical consciousness, and, more specifically, to differentiate stylistically between Greek and Roman art. *History of Ancient Art*, groundbreaking because of its historical, developmental account of the origins and development of art in various periods and cultures, largely viewed Roman art, by contrast to that of the Greeks, as imitative in a negative sense, a decadent fall from the perfection of the Greek ideal. (Winckelmann's position was the antithesis of Piranesi's passionately pro-Roman view of architecture.) Artistic styles, as Winckelmann argued, developed in response to factors such as climate and social and political structures conducive to freedom: Since, as he saw it, these external conditions were ideal in ancient Greece, Greek art had developed in perfect harmony with nature.

Winckelmann's writings on sculpture, which combined scholarly rigor with rapturous outpourings on beauty, also initiated a new kind of art criticism emphasizing the subjective, expressive response of the viewer. Drawing on notions of aesthetic education (*Bildung*), Winckelmann placed an autonomous, reflective Enlightenment subject in the role of viewer. This passionately subjective exercise of judgment is readily apparent in his interpretations of individual sculptures such as the Apollo Belvedere. Another important factor, for Winckelmann, in the aesthetic perfection of the Greek ideal was the ideal, composite nature of its beauty—embodied in the hermaphrodite sculptures that occupy a central place in his writings.

News of Winckelmann's scandalous, brutal murder in Trieste in 1768, probably the outcome of a botched robbery, reverberated throughout Europe. The continued cultural afterlife of his writings and persona, however, can be traced among numerous German thinkers—including Johann Gottfried Herder, Goethe, Friedrich and August Wilhelm Schlegel, and Hegel—as well as in later art historians such as Walter Pater.

[*See also* Ancient Greece; Ancient Rome; Archaeology; Pompeii and Herculaneum; *and* Sculpture.]

BIBLIOGRAPHY

Bosshard, Walter. *Winckelmann: Ästhetik der Mitte.* Zurich, 1968.

Haskell, Francis, and Nicholas Penny. *Taste and the Antique: The Lure of Classical Sculpture, 1500–1900.* New Haven, Conn., 1981. Particularly useful on the cultural significance of Roman antiquities in the eighteenth century. Also contains detailed catalog entries for over ninety classical statues.

Honour, Hugh. *Neo-classicism.* Harmondsworth, U.K., 1968. An excellent general introduction to the neoclassical movement, its representative artists and theorists.

Potts, Alex. *Flesh and the Ideal: Winckelmann and the Origins of Art History.* New Haven, Conn., 1994. Sophisticated recent analysis,

with an emphasis on Winckelmann's critical role in the history of the body and sexuality, as well as in the production of knowledge.

CATRIONA MACLEOD

WINTHROP, JOHN (1714–1779), American astronomer and mathematician.

John Winthrop IV was born in Boston to Adam Winthrop, a judge, and Anne Wainwright Winthrop. A precocious youth, in 1728 he entered Harvard College, where he was strongly attracted to scientific and religious ideas of the Enlightenment. Influential in shaping Winthrop's intellectual interests were Isaac Greenwood's lectures on "experimental philosophy," Cotton Mather's scientific survey *Christian Philosopher* (1726), and Nathaniel Appleton's sermons. Winthrop's meticulous entries from classical and Enlightenment authors in his freshman "commonplace book" reveal his studious and inquiring mind. While mastering Greek, Latin, and Hebrew, he also absorbed Isaac Newton's complex religious and scientific concepts when he obtained a rare copy of the *Principia*.

Winthrop continued his studies after graduation in 1732, focusing on natural philosophy, and received an A.M. degree in 1735. At twenty-three, Winthrop was appointed to Harvard's endowed Hollis Professorship of "Mathematicks and of Natural and Experimental Philosophy." Incorporating Newtonian elements into his scientific activities, Winthrop emphasized astronomical research, revised the undergraduate study of science at the college, and introduced the study of differential calculus. His detailed daily meteorological records, begun in 1742, covered a span of thirty-seven years.

Winthrop began contributing his observations to the Royal Society of London in 1741, continuing to 1774 and earning acclaim on both sides of the Atlantic. His reports on the transits of Mercury across the Sun in 1740, 1743, and 1769, published in the Society's *Philosophical Transactions*, determined the longitude of Cambridge, Massachusetts. Winthrop's wide range of interests is reflected in other reports on such topics as the appearance of Venus, on "fiery Meteors," and a study of comets, "Cogitata de Cometis," considered by the Royal Society as an outstanding essay on the gravitational balance of the universe. In a letter to Benjamin Franklin, published in the *Transactions* in 1769, he argued that the aberration of light, contrary to accepted opinion, retarded the observable transit of Venus. His correction of statements in a life of Newton by Giovanni Castillione (1744) are evidence of his veneration for the great physicist. Winthrop emphasized scientific instruction for the public, publishing articles on the expected return of Halley's comet (1759), on the identity of lightning and electricity (1768), and on the nature of comets.

During the New England earthquake on 18 November 1755, Winthrop was able to time the "most terrible Earthquake" as lasting "a full minit." He noticed the rise and fall of bricks in his hearth and, in a lecture to Harvard students a week later, he explained that earthquakes "consist in a kind of undulatory motion," making a fundamental contribution to early seismology (*A Lecture on Earthquakes*, Boston, 1755). His analysis that the phenomena were due to natural causes and were not the product of "divine wrath" on "sinful mankind" led him into a sharp controversy with Boston clergy. His forward-looking explanation was limited by his assertion that the laws of nature "are conducted ultimately, to a moral purpose."

Spurred by the Royal Society's energetic promotion of international observations of the infrequent transit of Venus, Winthrop planned an expedition to St. Johns, Newfoundland, under the aegis of Harvard in 1761. Royal Governor Francis Bernard provided a sloop for transportation. With the help of two competent students, Winthrop used the college's apparatus to make the only successful North American measurements. His data, published in the *Transactions* and more extensively in his *Relation of a Voyage*, helped establish the solar parallax, essential for determining the distance between Earth and Sun and in corroborating Newtonian concepts. Later he extended his findings, presenting them at Harvard as *Two Lectures on the Parallax and Distance of the Sun* (1769).

Winthrop's annual course on "Experimental Philosophy," begun in 1746, consisted of thirty-three lectures on Newtonian physics with explanations and demonstrations on motion, gravitation, mechanics, and optics, as well as experiments in electricity. He excited the interest of such students as John Adams and Benjamin Thompson, later Count Rumford.

Winthrop frequently engaged in practical activities, such as measuring Boston Harbor or checking the inclination of Harvard's Stoughton Hall. He solicited funds to rebuild the library and a collection of scientific instruments destroyed by fire, establishing the finest collection in the Colonies. He was twice offered the presidency of Harvard, but declined. Friendship with Ezra Stiles of Yale and Benjamin Franklin led to a succession of honors: under the auspices of Franklin, he was elected a fellow of the Royal Society of London; in 1771, the University of Edinburgh awarded him an LL.D; three years later Harvard chose him as its first recipient of an LL.D.

With the approach of the American Revolution, Winthrop turned away from his scientific explorations, becoming politically active in the Council of Massachusetts-Bay in 1773. Allied with his close friends John Adams and John Hancock, he sided with the patriot cause as a member of the revolutionary Provincial Council. In June 1775, as war broke out, he moved Harvard's library and scientific instruments to safety, writing to John Adams, "We are now involved in all the horrors of war." Winthrop, the consummate Newtonian of eighteenth-century America, did not live to see the new nation fully established.

[*See also* Astronomy; Newton, Isaac; North America; *and* Royal Society of London.]

BIBLIOGRAPHY

Bernhard, Winfred E. A. "Vita–John Winthrop: Brief Life of an Eminent Scientist, 1714–1779." *Harvard Magazine* 93 (1990), 52. Includes a reproduction of John Singleton Copley's portrait of Winthrop.

Cohen, I. Bernard. *Some Early Tools of American Science, an Account of the Early Scientific Instruments and Mineralogical and Biological Collections in Harvard University*. Cambridge, Mass., 1950. An invaluable source of information on the teaching of science and on eighteenth-century instruments.

Hindle, Brooke. *The Pursuit of Science in Revolutionary America, 1735–1789*. Chapel Hill, N.C., 1956. A comprehensive, scholarly account of the emergence of American science to 1789, based on manuscript sources—the best introduction to the topic.

Mayo, Lawrence Shaw. *The Winthrop Family in America*. Boston, 1948. This volume on members of a family prominent in New England since its earliest settlement is particularly valuable about John Winthrop IV (pp. 167–193).

Morison, Samuel Eliot. *Three Centuries of Harvard, 1636–1936*. Cambridge, Mass., 1936. An authoritative, readable work bringing to life collegiate education, especially in the seventeenth and eighteenth centuries.

Shipton, Clifford K. *New England Life in the Eighteenth Century: Representative Biographies from Sibley's Harvard Graduates*. Cambridge, Mass., 1995. Includes an excellent sketch of Winthrop.

Stearns, Raymond P. *Science in the British Colonies of America*. Urbana, Ill., 1970. A comprehensive analysis of the contributions of Colonial Americans to scientific knowledge in the age of the Enlightenment, through the auspices of the Royal Society; Winthrop's role is given full attention.

WINFRED E. A. BERNHARD

WITHERSPOON, JOHN (1723–1794), Scottish-American clergyman, philosopher, and president of the College of New Jersey (1768–1794).

Witherspoon was born in Yester Parish in the shire of East Lothian, to a clergyman and the daughter of a clergyman. Home-schooled, he entered the University of Edinburgh in 1736 to study under the logician and rhetorician John Stevenson, who espoused Ciceronian classical rhetoric and philosophy, and the philosopher John Pringle, who taught the "moral sense" approach of Francis Hutcheson and the earl of Shaftesbury. Witherspoon earned the master of arts degree in 1739, then studied divinity for four years. Following his father into the Popular Party of the Church of Scotland, he gained fame while a minister at Paisley in 1753 by writing *Ecclesiastical Characteristics*, a pamphlet attacking the ministerial qualifications in the church's dominant party, the Moderates. The Popular Party championed orthodox, confessional

Protestantism, fervent preaching, biblicism, and the right of congregations to select their own clergy. Moderates favored a moralistic approach to religion, grounded on a systematic examination of the human mind rather than revelation; they considered sermons a form of polite literature; and they felt socially at ease with the elite, many of whom wished to exercise prerogative rights in the naming of parish ministers. In this and other polemics against Moderatism, Witherspoon demonstrated a thorough acquaintance with its Hutchesonian philosophical foundation, as well as its rhetorical mode, which he satirized with devastating effect. His other Scottish writings include theological pamphlets and sermons emphasizing evangelical orthodoxy, as well as an early academic treatise in which he anticipated some of the positions of the common sense philosophers Thomas Reid and James Beattie. Thus, in his Scottish activities Witherspoon demonstrated antipathy toward the aesthetic standards of the Enlightenment and ambivalence toward its philosophical positions.

Persuaded to assume the presidency of the College of New Jersey (later Princeton), Witherspoon arrived in America in 1768, in the midst of the protest movement against British colonial policy. He soon introduced Scottish Enlightenment precepts in educational, political, and religious affairs. Scholars disagree about whether this represented an about-face from his intellectual stance while in his home country. His most important contributions were the pedagogical and intellectual changes he brought to Princeton. Introducing the lecture method and a rigorous program of public speaking exercises, he changed the ethical basis of instruction from the idealism of Bishop Berkeley and Jonathan Edwards to a Hutcheson-derived model based on the assumption that humans possess an internal sense of morality that responds to empirical evidence. He therefore could argue as well that revelation was demonstrable through reason and science, rather than serving as their basis. The political component of this philosophy also derived from Hutcheson, emphasizing natural rights, the social contract, and the right of rebellion. Witherspoon's moral philosophy lectures, delivered to both the junior and senior classes, thus connected classical civic humanism to eighteenth-century Commonwealth Whig political thought. Accompanying lectures on rhetoric emphasized the Ciceronian ideal of a good man speaking well on issues of public importance. These pedagogical features changed Princeton's intellectual character, but more important, they influenced a generation of students who went on to speak, write, and act in the affairs of church and state.

Witherspoon lived out his philosophical precepts. Adopting a position common to the Popular Party in Scotland, he equated the preservation of American liberty with the preservation of religious liberty in the empire, and so he became an enthusiastic supporter of the revolutionary colonists. He participated in the Somerset County Committee of Correspondence in 1774, was selected by New Jersey as a delegate to the Continental Congress in 1776, signed the Declaration of Independence, and, employed on many committees, served most of the time until November 1782. Elected to the New Jersey legislature in 1783 and 1789, he was also a member of the state convention that ratified the Constitution. Witherspoon wrote influential patriotic polemics, such as a 1774 newspaper article that detailed his political views and a widely published 1776 sermon, "The Dominion of Providence over the Passions of Men."

In the field of religion, Witherspoon did much to appeal to both Old and New Side Presbyterians through his moderate evangelicism and his linkage of Christianity and republican liberty. His college trained most early nineteenth century Presbyterian church leaders; he was instrumental in organizing the Presbyterian national general assembly, which met initially in 1789; and he wrote the preamble to its statement of principles, among which was a firm declaration in support of private conscience in the realm of religion. Though not an original thinker, Witherspoon was the most successful proponent of Scottish Enlightenment ideas in eighteenth-century America.

[*See also* American Revolution; Education; Reformed Churches, *subentry on* Presbyterianism; Revealed Religion; *and* Scottish Common Sense Philosophy.]

BIBLIOGRAPHY

Collins, Varnum Lansing. *President Witherspoon*. 2 vols. Princeton, N.J., 1925. The standard biography, detailed but dated in interpretation.

Landsman, Ned C. "Witherspoon and the Problem of Provincial Identity in Scottish Evangelical Culture." In *Scotland and America in the Age of Enlightenment*, edited by Richard B. Sher and Jeffrey R. Smitten, pp. 29–45. Princeton, N.J., 1990. Argues that Witherspoon's philosophical views remained consistent throughout his career and that he borrowed Scottish Enlightenment arguments to fight the excesses of the movement.

McLachlan, James, et al., eds. *Princetonians: A Biographical Dictionary*. 5 vols. Princeton, N.J., 1976–1991. Discusses Witherspoon's pedagogical methods and his influence on his students.

Noll, Mark A. *Princeton and the Republic, 1768–1822*. Princeton, N.J., 1989. Analyzes Witherspoon's contributions in religious as well as secular affairs, and attributes his reversal of opinion on the value of the Scottish Enlightenment to a change of viewpoint produced by the American environment.

Scott, Jack, ed. *Annotated Edition of Lectures on Moral Philosophy by John Witherspoon*. Newark, Del., 1982. Provides analysis.

Sloan, Douglas. *The Scottish Enlightenment and the American College Ideal*. New York, 1971. Particularizes Witherspoon's contributions to American higher education and argues that his contradictory positions on Enlightenment ideas in Scotland and America were products of his intellectual eclecticism.

Witherspoon, John. *Works of the Rev. John Witherspoon*. Edited by Ashbel Green. 4 vols. 1801; 2d ed. Philadelphia, 1802.

DAVID W. ROBSON

WOLFF, CHRISTIAN (1679–1754), German philosopher, often characterized as one of the two founders of the German Enlightenment (the other being Christian Thomasius).

After attending the Magdalen Gymnasium in Breslau, he studied theology, natural science, and mathematics at the University of Jena. He also read widely in theology and philosophy, knowing the Catholic scholastics Thomas Aquinas and Francisco Suarez better than most of his Protestant contemporaries. In 1702, he obtained the degree of Magister at the University of Leipzig and taught there as a private lecturer, specializing in mathematics until he went to Halle in 1706 as professor of mathematics and natural philosophy. Wolff had by then already been noticed by Leibniz, who supported him in his mathematical endeavors (see *Briefwechsel zwischen Leibniz und Chr. Wolff*, ed. C. I. Gerhardt, 1860 [reprint, 1963]). Leibniz was instrumental in getting Wolff (in 1705) a position at the well-known philosophical journal, *Acta Eruditorum*. Wolff, on the other hand, was clearly influenced by Leibniz in his philosophy. This influence was, as the correspondence between Leibniz and Wolff shows, restricted mostly to mathematics. Indeed, he seems to have been rather diffident about Leibniz as a philosopher. Though Wolff wrote a review of Leibniz's *Theodicee* in the *Acta Eruditorum*, he admits that he had merely skimmed the book.

In Halle, Wolff published works on most philosophical disciplines. His logic appeared in 1712, his metaphysics in 1719, his ethics in 1720, his theory of society in 1721 and his physics and teleology in 1723. These works were written in German and all started with the significant phrase "Rational Thought on . . ." The works of this period, which coincides with his first stay in Halle, aim clearly not just at propagating a certain theory, but also at giving advice that might prove practically useful. Wolff understood his task as one of rational "enlightenment." This does not mean he was opposed to religion. He was rather traditional in this regard and admitted there could be revelation that taught us something beyond reason, even if it had to be in agreement with reason. He was opposed to British freethinkers just as much as he was to French deists. It is therefore a mistake to think this conception of reason was necessarily opposed to religion or revelation, though many contemporaries saw in it a danger to a religion based more on feeling and sentiment.

Wolff soon came into conflict with the Pietist movement, which was very strong in Halle. The main reason for this was his (rather guarded and very limited) endorsement of Leibniz's theory of preestablished harmony in *Vernünflige Gedanken von Gott, der Welt und der Seele des Menschen* (Reasonable Thoughts of God, the World and the Soul of Human Beings as well as of All Things in General) of 1720. The sections concerned with the human soul led him

Christian Wolff. Engraving by J. B. Will, eighteenth century. (New York Public Library, Astor, Lenox, and Tilden Foundations.)

against his own expectations to this Leibnizian theory as the best explanation of the mind-body relationship. Furthermore, he did not endorse pre-established harmony as the absolute truth, but only as the most reasonable hypothesis in this particular question. Still, he was soon attacked by the Pietists as denying the freedom of the will required by the true Christian faith. In 1723, the Pietists successfully argued that Wolff's acceptance of the Leibnizian theory of pre-established harmony implied fatalism and could therefore serve as an excuse for deserters from the army. At their instigation King Frederick William I of Prussia (1688–1740) expelled Wolff not only from the university, but from Prussia. Wolffian doctrines were forbidden to be taught in Prussia. The immediate occasion for this was Wolff's formal address to the University of Halle, "On the Practical Philosophy of the Chinese," delivered in 1721. In this speech Wolff argued that ethics was not dependent on revelation, that Chinese ethics and Christian ethics were not fundamentally different, that happiness need not have a religious basis, and that reason was sufficient criterion in ethics. In other words, ethics is possible without revelation and one need not be a Christian to be a moral person.

Unintentionally, the king made this thinker a cause celèbre among those who favored the Enlightenment in Europe. Wolff was granted asylum in Hesse and became Professor of Philosophy at the (Calvinist) Philipps-Universität Marburg, where he taught until 1740. But his troubles with fundamentalist Christians were far from complete. His greatest foe was Joachim Lange, a theology professor at Halle, but there were also numerous attacks on him by others, and he wrote numerous defenses. Thus the theologian Johann Franz Buddeus (1667–1729), who had himself been Professor of Moral Philosophy at the University of Halle from 1693 to 1705 and who had been asked to take a position on Wolff's principles and doctrines, published *Reservations* about the latter's philosophy. He criticized Wolff for questioning the soundness of proofs of the existence of God; for not recognizing genuine natural laws; for having a faulty conception of "God"; for offering a questionable solution to the problem of evil (by giving too much importance to the necessity of evil); for his doctrine of the eternity of the world; for his doctrine of the necessary connection of all things in the world; and his unfounded critique of miracles. Buddeus also criticized him for advocating the Leibnizian system of pre-established harmony and tried to show that Wolff cleared the way for a thoroughgoing atheism. Wolff, who saw in these *Reservations* an attempt to justify his banishment from Prussia and a repetition and defense of the Pietistic criticism that he had faced in Halle, reacted vehemently, trying to paint Buddeus as a religious zealot, arguing that he simply repeated the earlier accusations he had already answered in Latin.

Johann Georg Walch (1693–1775), Buddeus's son-in-law continued the attack in a *Modest Response to Mr. Christian Wolff's Remarks on Budde's Reservations about his own Philosophy, which has also been included.* Even though Wolff had promised not to say another word in the dispute, he answered Walch's defense of Buddeus in the same year with a *Necessary Addition to the Remarks on Budde's Reservations. . . .* This led to another response by Walch in 1725, in which he tried to supply *A Modest Proof that Budde's Reservations Have still Not been Answered.* Wolff countered with *A Clear Proof that Dr. Budde must Accept the Accusations Made against Him and that He Justified the Unfounded Accusations of the Enemies in Halle, Published for the Defense of the Truth* (1725). Other works in this controversy are *Detailed Answer to the Unfounded Allegations of Dr. Lange, which Have Been Written at the Order of the King in Prussia* (1736) and *Dr. Lange's Tricks to Persuade His Readers by Sophistry and from who He has Borrowed His Objections against the harmoniam praestabilitatam* (1736).

In spite of these controversies, Wolff began to translate his philosophical works into Latin. The works of his second period or his stay in Marburg are written in Latin not only because he no longer saw himself writing for the German public only, but for other scholars,

particularly in Europe. These works are thus not mere translations but continued attempts to develop his philosophical thought and to expand the areas he covered in a more precise way. This intention is expressed by the almost stereotypical phrase that finds itself in all these titles: *"methodo scientifica pertractata"* or "developed in the scientific method." He also called it the mathematical method (the method of definition and proof). This method has definite similarities to Spinoza's approach *"de more geometrico."* Some of the most important are the *Discursus praeliminaris de philosophia in genere,* found in *Philosophia rationalis sive Logica, methodo scientifica pertractata* (1728), *Psychologia empirica methodo scientifica pertractata* (1732), *Psychologia rationalis, methodo scientifica pertractata* (1734), *Theologia naturalis methodo scientifica pertractata,* 2 vols. (1736–1737), *Philosophia practica universalis, methodo scientifica pertractata* (1738–1739).

Though Frederick William I later realized that the expulsion of Wolff was a mistake and tried to persuade him to return to Prussia, Wolff declined. Only when the King's son, Frederick II, (known as "the Great") took office in 1740, did he agree to return to Halle in triumph. He taught there until his death in 1754. Some of his most important works from this period are: *Philosophia prima, sive Ontologia* (1730), *Cosmologia generalis* (1731), *Jus naturae, methodo scientifica pertractatum,* 8 vols. (1740–1748), *Programma de necessitate methodi scientificae et genuino usu iuris naturae et gentium* (1741), *Specimen physicae ad theologiam naturalem applicatae, sistens notionem intellectus divini per opera naturae illustratam* (1743), *Jus gentium methodo scientifica pertractatum* (1749), *Philosophia moralis sive ethica, methodo scientifica pertractata,* 6 vols. (1750–1753), *Institutiones juris naturae et gentium, in quibus ex ipsa hominis natura continuo nexu omnes obligationes et iura omnia deducuntur* (1754), and *Oeconomia methodo scientifica pertractata* (1754). His last words show that he was far from being nonreligious. They were a prayer: "Now Jesus Christ, my savior, strengthen me in my last hour." His autobiography appeared in 1841, edited by W. von Heinrich Wuttke.

Many philosophical scholars still regard Wolff as a simple follower of Leibniz and believe that Leibniz's theories provide all that is needed to understand Wolff. But this is a mistake. Though the phrase "Leibniz-Wolffian philosophy," which appears to have been coined by one of his students—one Georg Bernhard Bilfinger (1693–1750)—gained great currency during the eighteenth century; it is misleading when referring to a more or less unified movement. It is fair neither to Leibniz nor to Wolff to consider them as being engaged in developing a common position. Leibniz cannot be held accountable for Wolff's theories, and Wolff should not be measured by whether he adequately developed Leibniz's hints and suggestions. Indeed, Wolff himself was rather uncomfortable with Leibniz's theory of irreducible simple elements, conceived as "monads," that is, spiritual entities. He does not use the name "monad" for them. He did not accept and probably did not even know Leibniz's "inesse" principle, sometimes called the *"praedicatum inest subjecto* principle," which holds that every true proposition must have a ground in reality and that any predicate that a subject can take must be founded in the subject. In so far as this principle involves the rejection of the distinction between essential and non-essential constituents of things, Wolff departed from it, since this distinction was of fundamental importance for him. Finally, he disagreed with Leibniz that the principle of sufficient reason was a truly basic principle, believing it could ultimately be derived from the principle of contradiction.

Accordingly, Wolff should be taken seriously when he insists strenuously that his position was very different from that of Leibniz. Among other things, he was much more of an empiricist than Leibniz ever wished to be. In characterizing his approach, he pointed out: "When I base cognition on experience,... then I am most careful that I do not surreptitiously introduce anything. ...this care is also very difficult...it is almost easier to acquire a skill in demonstration than this care...I make inferences from reality to possibility...in this way I keep my concepts pure so that nothing can sneak in whose possibility has not been cognised...and in this way I provide the foundation of absolutely reliable inferences in the sciences" (*Ausführliche Nachricht von seinen eigenen Schriften, die er in deutscher Sprache von den verschiedenen Theilen der Welt-Weisheit ans Licht gestellet*, Frankfurt, 1726, §28).

Wolff himself defined philosophy as a "science of all possible objects, how and why they are possible," or as "the science of the possibles insofar as they can be," and claimed that existence is nothing but the "complement of possibility." He did not mean, however, that we could dispense with experience. Experience, or historical knowledge, as he also calls it, remains the foundation of all philosophizing. "Experience establishes those things from which the reason can be given for other things that are and occur, or can occur" (*Preliminary Discourse on Philosophy in General*, p. 6). Though he defines a thing as anything that exists or might exist and identifies "reality," "possibility," and "what does not involve contradiction," he does not believe that we can start our inquiry from just anything that does not involve contradiction. His ontology may thus be called an analysis of the logical possibilities required for the existence of real entities. He claimed that philosophy, in investigating why things are the way they are and in this way going far beyond experience, must nevertheless be careful never to lose itself in mere possibilities. In this way, his philosophy was meant to be a marriage of reason and experience (*connubium rationis et experientiae*), and even if this was not necessarily a marriage of equal partners, reason and experience were still partners for Wolff.

Wolff's system is divided into theoretical and practical philosophy. Theoretical philosophy consists of logic and metaphysics, and metaphysics of ontology or the science of the most abstract categories of being and cosmology or the sciences of bodies (cosmology), of minds (psychology), and of God (natural theology). The distinction between ontology and the three other disciplines is the distinction between *metaphysica generalis* und *metaphysica specialis*. Practical philosophy is subdivided into natural law, ethics, politics, and economics.

Wolff's moral and political philosophy is ultimately not as important as his metaphysics. He advocated a perfectionist ethics in the Stoic tradition and, in his political theory, he was a defender of enlightened absolutism. Moral worth consisted for Wolff in the perfection of man. Since man is a rational being, this perfection is primarily intellectual. Our will is to be subject to the intellect and our happiness consists in the well-being of man as an embodied being. Wolff's perfectionism is a curious mixture of Stoic and utilitarian elements that provided the foil for Immanuel Kant's moral philosophy. But, like Kant, he was convinced that duties to oneself precede duties to others.

Wolff became the most influential philosopher in Germany between Leibniz and Kant. He was very important in replacing Aristotelianism at German universities, but he may be said to have created a new kind of scholasticism. Further, his conception of the discipline had a great influence on the philosophical discussion in Germany. Voltaire coined the saying: "Wolfio philosophante, Rege Philosopho regnante." Indeed, none of the philosophical developments in Germany during the eighteenth century can be properly understood without a knowledge of Wolff's *Logic* and *Ontology*. Some of his most important followers, apart from the already mentioned, were Bilfinger, Johann Gustav Reinbeck (1682–1741), Ludwig Philipp Thümmig (1697–1728), Reimarus, Hermann Samuel (1694–1768), Johann Christoph Gottsched (1700–1766), Friedrich Christian Baumeister (1709–1785), the secretary of the Berlin Academy, Samuel Formey (1711–1797), Joachim Georg Darjes (1714–1791), Alexander Baumgarten (1714–1762), who developed an aesthetic theory on Leibniz-Wolffian principles, and his student G. F. Meier (1718–1777), who also emphasized the importance of Locke. Kant based his lectures primarily on works by Baumgarten and Meier. Wolff's influence began to wane only after the middle of the century, mainly under the influence of British philosophers.

[*See also* Aufklärung; Leibniz, Gottfried Wilhelm von; *and* Philosophy.]

BIBLIOGRAPHY

WORKS BY CHRISTIAN WOLFF

Gesammelte Werke. Edited by J. Ecole, J. E. Hofmann, M. Thomann, and H. W. Arndt. Hildesheim, 1965.

Preliminary Discourse on Philosophy in General. Translated by R. J. Blackwell. Indianapolis, 1963.

"Reasonable Thoughts on the Actions of Men, for the Promotion of their Happiness." In *Moral Philosophy from Montaigne to Kant*, vol. I, edited by J. B. Schneewind, pp. 333–350. Cambridge, Mass., 1990.

WORKS ABOUT CHRISTIAN WOLFF

Arndt, Hans Werner. "Rationalismus und Empirismus in der Erkenntnislehre Christian Wolffs." In *Christian Wolff, 1679–1754*, edited by W. Schneiders, pp. 31–47. Hamburg, 1983.

Becker, George. "Pietism's Confrontation with Enlightenment Rationalism: An Examination of Ascetic Protestantism and Science." *Journal for the Scientific Study of Religion* 30 (1991), 139–158.

Biller, Gerhard. "Die Wolff Diskussion 1800 bis 1985: Eine Bibliographie." In *Christian Wolff, 1679–1754*, edited by W. Schneiders, pp. 221–346. Hamburg, 1983.

Blackwell, Richard J. "The Structure of Wolffian Philosophy." *The Modern Schoolman* 38 (1961), 203–218.

Blackwell, Richard J. "Christian Wolff's Doctrine of the Soul." *Journal of the History of Ideas* 22 (1961), 339–354.

Calinger, Ronald S. "The Newtonian-Wolffian Controversy (1740–1759)." *Journal of the History of Philosophy* 30 (1969), 319–330.

Corr, Charles A. "Christian Wolff and Leibniz." *Journal of the History of Ideas* 36 (1975), 241–262.

Ecole, Jean. "Cosmologie Wolffienne et dynamique Leibnizienne: Essai sur les rapports de Wolff avec Leibniz." *Les etudes philosophiques* 19 (1964), 2–10.

Ecole, Jean. "En quel sens peut-on dire que Wolff est rationaliste." *Studia Leibnitiana* 11 (1979), 45–61.

Van Peursen, C. A. "Christian Wolff's Philosophy of Contingent Reality." *Journal of the History of Philosophy* 25 (1987), 69–82.

MANFRED KUEHN

WOLFF-BEKKER, BETJE (Elisabeth) (1738–1804), woman of letters and influential presence in the Dutch Enlightenment.

Wolff-Bekker wrote the first novel in Dutch, *De Historie van Mejuffrouw Sara Burgerhart* (The History of Miss Sara Burgerhart, 1782), in close collaboration with her partner and companion, Aagje Deken. Betje stood out from her family by her talent and lively interest in the arts and in serious literature. A portrait drawn when she was sixteen shows her holding Alexander Pope's *Essay on Man*, and Pope would remain a significant influence throughout her career. Betje lost her mother at the age of thirteen and in her fiction, the need for an adolescent girl to be counseled by an older woman plays a significant role. When she was seventeen, she eloped with an ensign in the States army, Matthijs Gargon, but soon returned home. The incident, which remains mysterious, estranged her from her family, especially her sanctimonious brother. Her marriage in 1759 to the thirty-one-year-old widower Adriaan Wolff, minister of the Dutch Reformed Church in Midden-Beemster in what she called the tight-laced province of Holland, removed her from the bigotry of Vlissingen, her home town. Betje Wolff-Bekker's biographer, P. J. Buynsters, suggests that the marriage, which remained childless, may never have provided the physical and emotional intimacy that she needed.

Her first publication was a volume of moral-philosophical and didactic poetry *Bespiegelingen over het Genoegen* (Meditations on Happiness, 1763). Even in this early work, Wolff-Bekker manifests herself as a witty moralist whose lively style is at its best in the satire of contemporary folly and vice, or the humorous imitation of contemporary character types such as religious bigots and fashion adepts. At first she was influenced by the vogue for the graveyard school of poetry imported from Britain. Although the knowledge of English was not widespread in the Dutch eighteenth century, Wolff-Bekker knew English, and in 1764 she published a translation of Robert Blair's *The Grave*, soon to be followed by her own *Eenzame Nacht Gedachten, over den Slaap en den Dood* (Lonely Night Thoughts: About Sleep and Death, 1765) in the style of John Hervey. In this period she tried her pen at a wide array of subjects.

Although Wolff-Bekker's poems did not elevate Reason above Religion, the Reformed Church proved reluctant on occasion to grant her permission to publish. Her independence of mind, quick wit and satirical tongue made her suspect, not the radical nature of her religious or political ideas. Wolff-Bekker's pattern of tender female friendships that tended to end abruptly and her feminist ideas also manifested themselves in this period. Her reputation as a poet was established with the publication of *Walcheren, in Vier Gezangen* (Walcheren: Four Poems) in 1769. This epic poem celebrates her native soil and its flora, fauna, and folklore, and testifies to Wolff-Bekker's political sympathies with the historical heroes of the liberal States Party, and her dislike of orthodox Calvinism. It was, however, the publication of *De Onveranderlijke Santhorstsche Geloofsbelijdenis* (The Unchangeable Santhorst Creed) in 1772 and *De Menuet en de Dominees Pruik* (The Minuet and the Minister's Wig) that showed that her satirical wit flowed most vivaciously when directed at dissembling hypocrisy and the intolerance of orthodox Calvinism which, she thought, threatened the "true freedom" inherent in the idea of the Dutch Republic. These publications made her the object of sometimes outraged criticism. Because she advocated freedom and was provoked by the arrogance of orthodox Calvinism, Wolff-Bekker occupies a central place in eighteenth-century Dutch Enlightenment discourse on tolerance.

After her husband's death in 1777, Wolff-Bekker set up house and a close literary partnership with Aagje (Agatha) Deken. They wrote in support of the patriotic-economic reform movement, and aimed to expand the audience for serious writing to the lower middle class. Both their novels and other publications tended to be didactic in tone. They also stimulated an interest in the history and literature of the early Dutch Republic. Thus their *Economische Liedjes* (Economic Lyrics) of 1781 attempted to increase the motivation of the work force in an epoch of economic decline. Wolff-Bekker and Deken's jointly authored epistolary novel *Historie van Mejuffrouw Sara Burgerhart* was published in 1782, translated into French and German, and is still read because of its pithy idiom and lively portrayal of Dutch character and social life. Its message is that young and lively, easily seduced girls may profit from the advice of an older woman. Unlike Samuel Richardson, who may have been their inspiration, the authors champion common sense over sensibility, and they refrain from sensation and the topic of sexuality. Their next novel *Historie van den Heer Willem Leevend* (History of Mr. Willem Leevend, 1784) was an object lesson in the dangers of sentimentalism, and it paints a wide panorama of the ways in which moral issues and theological problems engaged the Dutch middle classes in the eighteenth century. Two other epistolary novels were to follow, although their audience was dwindling: *Brieven van Abraham Blankaart* (Letters of Abraham Blankaart, 1787–1789), and *Historie van Mejuffrouw Cornelia Wildschut* (The History of Cornelia Wildschut, 1793–1796).

Increasingly sympathetic to the Patriot cause, Wolff-Bekker and Deken had to move to Trévoux, in France, from 1788–1797. There, among other works, Wolff translated Charles-Auguste Frossard's work on slavery, published anonymously as *De zaak der Negerslaaven* (The Cause of Negro Slaves) in 1790. Wolff-Bekker and Deken's literary testament, *Geschrift eener Bejaarde Vrouw* (Writing by an Old Woman) was begun in France and published in Holland. It consists of a collection of fragments describing the intellectual and moral development of a single woman who combines aspects of both Wolff-Bekker and Deken, and it may be read as a testimony to their closeness in life and work.

[*See also* Deken, Aagje; Men and Women of Letters; Novel; Representations of Reading; *and* Sensibility.]

BIBLIOGRAPHY
Buynsters, P. J. *Wolff en Deken: Een Biografie.* Leiden, 1984. Standard biography of both authors.
Buynsters, P. J. "Inleiding." In E. Bekker-Wed. Ds Wolff en A. Deken, *Historie van Mejuffrouw Sara Burgerhart*, edited by P. J. Buynsters, pp. 1–103. The Hague, 1980. Important contextualization of first Dutch novel.
Hanou, André. "Inleiding." In Elizabeth Wolff-Bekker, *De Onveranderlijke Santhorstsche Geloofsbelijdenis*, edited by A. J. Hanou, pp. 9–70. Leiden, 2000. Provides historical contexts for Wolff's satire.
Van der Vliet, P. *Wolff en Deken's Brieven van Abraham Blankaart: Een Bijdrage tot de Kennis van de Reformatorische Verlichting.*

Utrecht, 1982. Demonstrates that the Dutch Enlightenment was characterized by its attempt to reconcile revealed religion and reason.

CHRISTINE VAN BOHEEMEN-SAAF

WOLLSTONECRAFT, MARY (1759–1797), English author and social critic.

Wollstonecraft realized the feminist potential of the Enlightenment. Like many late Enlightenment social critics, she had a difficult individual and social formation and knew from experience the contradictions of class and gender in her time. The Wollstonecrafts had been in the silk manufacture and became rentiers, with tenements in London. Wollstonecraft's father attempted a further elevation in social status by becoming a gentleman farmer. However, his gentleman's vices of drinking and extravagance undermined this project, divided the family, and precipitated their social decline. Wollstonecraft undertook to protect her mother against her father's brutality and her younger siblings from their older brother's selfishness. In order to do so, she embarked on a program of self-education and self-discipline that lasted throughout her life. She first tried most of the few professions outside

Mary Wollstonecraft. Portrait by John Opie (1761–1807). (Tate Gallery, London/Art Resource, NY.)

marriage open to women of her class, including ladies' companion, girls' boarding-school proprietor and teacher, and governess, before turning to authorship.

She was able to take this direction—still an unusual one for a woman at that time—because she was employed and encouraged by Joseph Johnson, the leading publisher of the English provincial and nonconformist Enlightenments. He published all her work. At first, this was relatively obscure and in what were then considered the conventional genres for women. She wrote anonymously for Johnson's *Analytical Review* and dealt with a wide range of works, from sentimental and gothic novels, through minor poetry, music, and the arts, to Enlightenment philosophical travelogues. Meanwhile, Johnson published her novel, *Mary* (1788); her educational works, *Thoughts on the Education of Daughters* (1787) and *Original Stories from Real Life* (1788); and an anthology, *The Female Reader* (1789). Finally, Johnson provided her with translation work from French, including *Of the Importance of Religious Opinions* (1788, from Jacques Necker), *Young Grandison* (1790, from Maria de Cambon), and *Elements of Morality* (1790–1791, from a French translation of Christian Salzmann). More important, Wollstonecraft was able to participate in Johnson's diverse circle of enlightened men and women. Inspired by this milieu and by the early French Revolution, she moved in less than a decade from obscure hack writer to admired if controversial public figure. In this career she drew on and developed major ideas of the European Enlightenments.

From the French Enlightenment she took Jean-Jacques Rousseau's ideas for constructing a sovereign or independent subjectivity through a particular program of education, but she rejected Rousseau's construction of woman as morally and intellectually dependent on man, independent only with respect to her ability to manipulate his erotic desire. Wollstonecraft also modeled herself on Rousseau as vanguard revolutionary consciousness and social critic. From the Scottish Enlightenment, she took Adam Smith's idea of sympathy as the social bond between equal and independent subjectivities; and she took Hugh Blair's rhetoric of the authentic subject addressing others in the private and public spheres, and persuading others by candid disclosure of that subjectivity, or argument by ethos. From the English nonconformist Enlightenment, and especially the work of Richard Price, she took ideas of the equality of souls and of the necessity for individuals to be more or less equally educated if some (notably women, but also other subordinated social groups) were not to be dependent on the judgment of others. Unable to choose the good for themselves, they would also be unable to gain salvation. Aspects of the German Enlightenment were filtered through her cosmopolitan German-Swiss friend, the painter and critic Henry Fuseli. From Fuseli she took

ideas of expressivity in art and of art as a major channel of ideological communication in reconstructing the public, political sphere.

Wollstonecraft first broke from relative obscurity and addressed the wider public political sphere with her development of these ideas in *A Vindication of the Rights of Men* (1790), a trenchant response to Edmund Burke's *Reflections on the Revolution in France*. She quickly moved on to the issue of educating women for a role in a revolutionary state, with *A Vindication of the Rights of Woman* (1792). Here she argues that denial of equal education to women, with attendant opportunity for intellectual autonomy and professional self-discipline, will only reproduce the trivialized and dependent female of the ancien régime, and such a being, motivated only by self-interest and desire, will undermine revolutionary progress. Wollstonecraft critiques other educational writers, including Rousseau, and the limited state education for females proposed by the French government. She calls for professionalization of women for the domestic sphere, but also for enhanced professional opportunities for women outside marriage.

Meanwhile, Wollstonecraft attempted to form a correspondingly revolutionary personal life, first with Fuseli and then, after moving to Paris in December 1792, with the American entrepreneur Gilbert Imlay. Her contacts were with the Girondist political salons, and under the Jacobin regime she surreptitiously wrote *An Historical and Moral View of the . . . French Revolution* (1794), vindicating that historical event. She had a daughter, Fanny, but her relationship with Imlay failed, driving her to attempt suicide. A journey on some business for him produced *Letters Written during a Short Residence in Norway, Sweden, and Denmark* (1795), in the genre of Enlightenment critical travelogue. Here she represents herself as a disappointed but still vanguard revolutionary consciousness, implicitly a model for her readers, carrying the revolutionary spirit within and anticipating its realization in a future revolutionized society, economy, and state.

Back in London, she rejoined reformist circles and resumed her work for Johnson. She also formed a relationship with the leading philosophical anarchist William Godwin. They married in 1797, and Wollstonecraft died giving birth to a daughter, Mary (later Mary Shelley). Godwin published Wollstonecraft's unfinished feminist novel, *The Wrongs of Woman; or, Maria*, and other pieces, with a biography. This vindicated Wollstonecraft's program to represent, in her writings as in her personal life, a vanguard feminist consciousness. Counterrevolutionary and counterfeminist writers used the book, however, to condemn her life and works, and her name remained under a cloud for several decades, before being revived by the mid-nineteenth-century suffragist movement, early-twentieth-century writers of the Bloomsbury circle (notably Virginia Woolf), and, more recently, late-twentieth-century feminists. The prevailing view now is that Wollstonecraft anticipated liberal feminism, but reexamination of her life and works continues to disclose other, radical potentials.

[*See also* Burke, Edmund; Citizenship; Declaration of the Rights of Man; Education, *subentry on* Pedagogical Thought and Practice; Feminist Theory; Godwin, William; Human Nature; Natural Rights; Popularization; Prejudice; Republicanism, *subentry on* France; *and* Revolution.]

BIBLIOGRAPHY

Guntheer-Canada, Wendy. *Mary Wollstonecraft and Enlightenement Politics*. De Kalb, Ill., 2001.

Jacobs, Diane. *Her Own Woman: The Life of Mary Wollstonecraft*. New York, 2001.

Kelly, Gary. *Revolutionary Feminism: The Mind and Career of Mary Wollstonecraft*. New York, 1992.

Todd, Janet. *Mary Wollstonecraft: A Revolutionary Life*. London, 2000.

Wollstonecraft, Mary. *The Works of Mary Wollstonecraft*. 7 vols. Edited by Janet Todd and Marilyn Butler. London, 1989.

GARY KELLY

ZOOLOGY. In the modern sense, zoology was an invention of the eighteenth century. Although many seventeenth-century scientific practitioners studied animals, their activities were undertaken as part of the broader discipline of natural history, and the term *zoology* predominantly described "the study of the medical uses of animal parts." By the 1730s, however, the word *zoology* had entered vernacular usage as the name for that part of natural history specifically concerned with animals [*see* Natural History]. Yet at the start of the eighteenth century, a terrain for zoology had not been clearly defined. Even the defining of the category *animal*, and distinguishing between animals and plants, provoked wide-ranging debates with theological implications. Cartesian writings (based on the work of René Descartes, the French mathematician and philosopher) that described animals as mechanical brutes were countered by lengthy treatises on the animal soul. The dominant eighteenth-century mode of explanation for animals was, however, the natural theological, with British naturalists like John Ray explaining animal habits and bodily structures by Providential design.

The discovery of the "animalcules" or "microscopical animals" (microorganisms) by the self-taught Dutch naturalist and microscope builder Antoni van Leeuwenhoek in the 1670s encouraged subsequent fascination with the precisely constructed, infinite variety of animal bodies. Insects became of interest for their range of design, habits, and social lives. Natural theological and experimental traditions came together in studies of insect regeneration and parthenogenesis that were performed by a network of naturalists, including Pieter Lyonet in

The Hague, Charles Bonnet in Geneva, and Antoine-René Ferchault de Réaumur in Paris. The microscope was also used to explore such physiological processes as generation [*see* Spontaneous Generation]. Attacking materialist claims that the minute perfection of animal organization could have been created from brute matter by the operation of purely mechanical laws, some naturalists looked to seventeenth-century claims that each individual had been pre-formed by God at the Creation within the sperm or ovum. In 1740, however, Bonnet's cousin Abraham Trembley discovered a small freshwater animal, the polyp, that could produce two new individuals when mechanically divided. This provoked a spate of accounts postulating hitherto undescribed forces that operated in animal bodies, such as the *Bildungstrieb* (formative drive) of the University of Göttingen professor Johann Friedrich Blumenbach. Such accounts, particularly among German naturalists, moved progressively away from natural theological forms of explanation.

The French naturalist Georges-Louis Leclerc de Buffon combined researches into generation with experiments on the relations between the physical and moral qualities in animals. In the later eighteenth century, such naturalists as Buffon, the Swede Carolus Linnaeus, and the German Eberhard Zimmerman explored the economic potential of acclimatizing exotic species and, accordingly, investigated animal distribution, habits, and hybridization. That was the era when the old royal menageries became zoological gardens, which served for both public entertainment and scientific enquiry. There, as elsewhere, zoology was shaped by the concerns of polite scientific practitioners, for whom animals were, simultaneously, economic assets, exotic curiosities, exemplars of human social relations or moral conduct, and sources of aesthetic education. Fashions in collecting fueled European markets, and collectors developed sophisticated classificatory systems for their specimens. The taste for conchology spread from the Dutch Republic to France, then to Britain and the German lands.

The debate over the proper classification of animals was subdued compared to the divisive quarrels among botanists. Although the Swedish systematist Carolus Linnaeus had classified the animals, including man, in his natural system, some naturalists argued that his use of external parts for classification—the feet, teeth, and mammary glands—inadequately expressed the functional distinctions between animal species. The Parisian naturalist Louis-Jean-Marie Daubenton and others, such as the Dutch anatomist Petrus Camper, called for a comparative anatomical approach instead. Nonetheless, by the late 1700s, Linnaeus's fundamental category of mammals did begin to gain currency.

In late eighteenth-century Europe, the culture of sensibility shaped animal studies. Despite the success of seventeenth-century dissection programs at the Parisian Académie Royale des Sciences, many eighteenth-century zoology books acknowledged that anatomical practice might distress the polite practitioner. The philosophe Jean-Jacques Rousseau and others criticized the killing of animals both to produce the illusion of life and to display the exotic natural world within polite collections. As new taxidermic techniques brought preserved birds and quadrupeds within the reach of institutional and privately wealthy collectors, however, zoological collections became increasingly common—so too did an interest in anatomical specimens, such as those common in medical collections. In 1793, when the first-ever chairs of zoology were founded at the Paris Muséum d'Histoire Naturelle, comparative anatomical techniques characterized the new zoological classifications that had been developed by such naturalists as Georges Cuvier, Étienne Geoffroy Saint-Hilaire, and Jean-Baptiste de Lamarck. Their work would form the foundation for nineteenth-century institutional zoology.

[*See also* Academies; Natural History; *and* Natural Philosophy and Science.]

BIBLIOGRAPHY

Corsi, Pietro. *The Age of Lamarck: Evolutionary Theories in France, 1790–1830*. Berkeley, Calif., 1988. A rich account of the new French zoology of the nineteenth century.

Dance, S. Peter. *A History of Shell Collecting*. Leiden, Netherlands, 1986. Hard to find, this is a treasury of information about conchological collectors and merchants, with detailed discussion of the eighteenth century.

Dawson, Virginia P. *Nature's Enigma: The Problem of the Polyp in the Letters of Bonnet, Trembley, and Réaumur*. Philadelphia, 1987. A valuable account of the experimental program of insect investigation in mid-eighteenth-century Europe.

Farber, Paul. *The Emergence of Ornithology as a Scientific Discipline, 1760–1850*. Boston, 1982.

Larson, James L. *Interpreting Nature: The Science of Living Form from Linnaeus to Kant*. Baltimore, 1994. Chapters on the history of animal classification and the study of distribution and generation in the German lands.

Lenoir, Timothy. *The Strategy of Life: Teleology and Mechanics in Nineteenth-Century German Biology*. Dordrecht, Netherlands, 1982. Interesting account of the philosophy of living beings in the German lands, especially of generation studies in the late eighteenth century.

Ritvo, Harriet. "Animal Pleasures: Popular Zoology in Eighteenth- and Nineteenth-Century England." *Harvard Library Bulletin* (33), 239–279, 1985. A broad-ranging essay on zoological writings, with emphasis on the early nineteenth century, which explores the moral meanings attached to animals by British authors.

Roe, Shirley A. *Matter, Life, and Generation: Eighteenth-Century Embryology and the Haller-Wolff Debate*. Cambridge, 1981. An in-depth study of a particular debate over models of generation, with an introductory chapter on earlier theories.

Schiebinger, Londa. *Nature's Body: Sexual Politics and the Making of Modern Science*. London, 1993. Addresses among other issues the gendered nature of zoological classifications that were produced by eighteenth-century European naturalists.

E. C. SPARY

ENCYCLOPEDIA OF THE

ENLIGHTENMENT

Topical Outline of Articles

The entries in the *Encyclopedia of the Enlightenment* are conceived according to the general conceptual categories listed in this topical outline. Some entries are listed more than once because the conceptual categories are not mutually exclusive. Entries in the Encyclopedia proper are organized alphabetically.

DEFINITIONS AND INTERPRETATIONS OF THE ENLIGHTENMENT

Principal Article
Enlightenment Studies

Supporting Articles
Cassirer, Ernst
Feminist Theory
Foucault, Michel
Frankfurt School
Gay, Peter
Habermas, Jürgen
Hazard, Paul
Koselleck, Reinhart
Post-Structuralism and Post-
    Modernism
Scholarly Associations and
    Publications

THE POLITICAL GEOGRAPHY OF THE ENLIGHTENMENT

*The International Setting and Its
Significant Historical Events*
American Revolution
Commerce and Trade
Diplomacy
French Revolution
    An Overview
    Iconography
    Debates about Causes
Glorious Revolution
Revolution
War and Military Theory

Nations, States, and Polities
Aristocracy
    Criticism
    Cultural Contributions
Austria

Bourgeoisie
Canada
Corporate and Estate Organization
England
France
Germany
Greece
Hungary
Ireland
Italy
Latin America
Netherlands
New France
North America
Ottoman Empire
Parlements
Poland
Portugal
Royal Courts and Dynasties
Russia
Scandinavia
Scotland
Spain
Switzerland

*Cities, Towns, Centers, and
Institutions of Intellectual Activity*
Amsterdam
Berlin
Cities
Edinburgh
Geneva
London
Milan
Naples
Paris
Philadelphia
Universities

Demography
Agriculture and Animal Husbandry
Death
Poverty

Linguistic Change
    Language Theories
    Translation

European Contact and Colonialism
Asia
China
Colonialism
    An Overview
    Philosophical Legacy
Explorations and Contact
Grand Tour
Islam
Jesuits
    *Role as Missionaries and
    Explorers*
Lewis and Clark Expedition
Native Americans
North Africa and the Levant
Scientific Expeditions
Slavery
South Seas

THE AGENCIES AND SPACES OF THE ENLIGHTENMENT

The World of Print

GENERAL
Autobiography
Biography
Censorship
Clandestine Literature
Correspondence and
    Correspondents
Criticism
Illustrators and Illustrations
Literacy
Literary Genres
Mapping

Race
Sensibility

MORAL PHILOSOPHY
Moral Philosophy
Virtue

NATURAL PHILOSOPHY AND
SCIENCE
Astronomy
Botany
Chemistry
Electricity and Magnetism
Geography
Geology
Heat
Hospitals
Inoculation and Vaccination
Life Sciences
Mathematics
Medicine
  Theories of Medicine
  Practice of Medicine
  Medicine and Physiology
  Anatomy and Surgery
Meteorology
Midwifery
Natural History
Natural Philosophy and Science
Optics
Physics
Pneumatics
Scientific Instruments
Spontaneous Generation
Taxonomy
Weights and Measures
Zoology

NATURAL RELIGION
Deism
Natural Religion
Optimism, Philosophical
Physico-Theology

POLITICAL PHILOSOPHY
Articles of Confederation
Bill of Rights
Citizenship
Civil Society
Constitution of the United States
Declaration of Independence
Declaration of the Rights of Man
Democracy
Despotism
Enlightened Despotism
Federalists and Antifederalists

Jesuits
  Role in Politics
  Role as Critics
Natural Law
Natural Rights
People, The
Political Philosophy

REVEALED RELIGION
Apologetics
Benedictines of Saint-Maur
Enthusiasm
Great Awakening
  First Great Awakening
  Second Great Awakening
Judaism
Papacy
Reformed Churches
  Lutheranism
  Swiss Reformed Church
  Dutch Reformed Church
  Presbyterianism
Religious Conversion
Revealed Religion
Roman Catholicism
Sermons
  Protestant Sermons
  Roman Catholic Sermons
  Evangelical Sermons
Toleration

SOCIABILITY
Politeness
Sociability

TRADITION
Ancient Greece
Ancient Rome
Ancients and Moderns
Archaeology
Pompeii and Herculaneum
Tradition

*Major Schools and Movements of
Thought*
Arminianism
Atheism
Calvinism
Cartesianism
Classicism
Empiricism
Epicurianism
Free Trade
Haskalah
Idéologues
Jansenism

Jesuits
  Jesuits and Jansenists
Josephinism
Latitudinarianism
Materialism
Millenarianism
Mysticism
National Churches
Neoclassicism
Newtonianism
Nominalism
Pantheism
Pietism
Progress
Rationalism
Republicanism
  An Overview
  Great Britain
  The United States
  France
  The Netherlands
  Latin America
Scholarship and Research
Skepticism
Socinianism
Stoicism
Sturm und Drang
Technology
Ultramontanism
Utilitarianism
Utopianism
Vitalism

BIOGRAPHIES
Abbadie, Jacques
Abbt, Thomas
Adam, Robert
Adams, John
Addison, Joseph
Alembert, Jean Le Rond d'
Allen, Ethan
Almon, John
Ames, Fisher
André, Yves-Marie
Aranda, Pedro Pablo, conde de
Argens, Jean-Baptiste d'
Arnauld, Antoine
Astell, Mary
Bahrdt, Carl Friedrich
Banks, Joseph
Barlow, Joel
Bartram, John and William
Basedow, Johann Bernhard
Baumgarten, Alexander Gottlieb

Bayle, Pierre
Beaumarchais, Pierre-Ambroise
  Caron de
Beaumont, Christophe de
Beccaria, Cesare
Behn, Aphra
Bekker, Balthasar
Bello, Andrés
Benedict XIV
Bentham, Jeremy
Bergier, Nicolas-Sylvestre
Berkeley, George
Bernardin de Saint-Pierre, Jacques-
  Henri
Bernoulli, Daniel
Berruyer, Isaac
Blumenbach, Johann Friedrich
Bodmer, Johann Jakob
Boerhaave, Hermann
Bolingbroke, Henry St. John
Bolívar, Simón
Bonald, Louis de
Bonnet, Charles
Bossuet, Jacques Bénigne
Boswell, James
Boulainvilliers, Henri de
Boulanger, Nicolas-Antoine
Brackenridge, Hugh Henry
Brown, Charles Brockden
Buffier, Claude
Buffon, Georges-Louis Leclerc de
Burke, Edmund
Burney, Fanny
Burns, Robert
Butler, Joseph
Cabanis, Pierre-Jean-Georges
Calmet, Augustin
Campbell, Archibald
Campbell, George
Campomanes, Pedro Rodriguez
Casanova, Giacomo
Castillo, Madre
Catherine II
Caulfeild, James
Caylus, Anne-Claude-Philippe de
  Tubières
Challe, Robert
Charrière, Isabelle de
Chateaubriand, François-René de
Châtelet, Émilie Le Tonnelier de
  Breteuil du
Chauffepié, Jacques-Georges de
Chydenius, Anders

Clarke, Samuel
Clavijero, Francisco Javier
Clement XIV
Clerk, John
Clorivière, Picot de
Collins, Anthony
Condillac, Étienne Bonnot de
Condorcet, Jean-Antoine-Nicolas
  de Caritat
Conti, Antonio
Cook, James
Copley, John Singleton
Crèvecoeur, Michel-Guillaume-
  Jean de
Dale, Anthonie van
Dalin, Olof von
Darwin, Erasmus
David, Jacques-Louis
Defoe, Daniel
Deken, Aagje
Desfontaines, Pierre-François
  Guyot
Destutt de Tracy, Antoine-Louis-
  Claude
Dickinson, John
Diderot, Denis
Dohm, Christian Wilhelm
Drake, Judith
Duguet, Jacques-Joseph
Dunlap, William
Du Pont de Nemours, Pierre-
  Samuel
Dwight, Timothy
Edgeworth, Maria
Edwards, Jonathan
Effen, Justus van
Épinay, Louise d'
Erskine, David Steuart
Espejo, Eugenio de
Euler, Leonhard
Feijoo, Benito Jeronimo
Fénelon, François-Armand de
  Salignac de La Mothe
Ferguson, Adam
Fernández de Lizardi, José Joaquín
Fielding, Henry
Filangieri, Gaetano
Fleury, Claude
Fonseca Pimentel, Eleonora
Fontenelle, Bernard Le Bovier de
Forster, Georg
Franklin, Benjamin
Frederick II

Freneau, Philip Morin
Fréret, Nicolas
Fréron, Elie
Furly, Benjamin
Gainsborough, Thomas
Galiani, Ferdinando
Garve, Christian
Gellert, Christian Furchtegott
Genlis, Stéphanie-Félicité de
Genovesi, Antonio
Giannone, Pietro
Gibbon, Edward
Gjörwell, Carl Christopher
Godwin, William
Goethe, Johann Wolfgang von
Goldoni, Carlo
Goldsmith, Oliver
Gottsched, Johann Christoph
Gouges, Olympe de
Graffigny, Françoise de
Gravesande, Willem Jacob 's
Grégoire, Henri
Grimm, Friedrich Melchior
Gustav III
Guyon, Jeanne-Marie Bouvier de
  La Motte
Hales, Stephen
Haller, Albrecht von
Hamann, Johann Georg
Hamilton, Alexander
Hamilton, William
Handel, George Frideric
Hardouin, Jean
Hartley, David
Haynes, Lemuel
Hays, Mary
Helvétius, Claude-Adrien
Hemsterhuis, François
Herder, Johann Gottfried
Hippel, Theodor Gottlieb von
Hobbes, Thomas
Höegh-Guldberg, Ove
Hogarth, William
Holbach, Paul-Henri Thiry d'
Holberg, Ludvig
Home, Henry
Hopkins, Samuel
Houtteville, Claude-Francois-
  Alexandre
Huber, Marie
Humboldt, Wilhelm von
Hume, David
Hutcheson, Francis

Directory of Contributors

Charles W. Akers
Oakland University
Mayhew, Jonathan

Christian Albertan
Rouen, France
Berruyer, Isaac

Sylviane Albertan-Coppola
Université de Valenciennes, France
Apologetics; Counter-Enlightenment; Houtteville,
Claude-François-Alexandre; Pluche, Noël-Antoine

Manuela Albertone
Università degli Studi di Torino, Italy
Du Pont de Nemours, Pierre-Samuel; Law, John; Physiocracy

Madeleine Alcover
Rice University
Poullain de la Barre, François

David G. C. Allan
The Royal Society of Arts, United Kingdom
Academies; Hales, Stephen

Cornelis D. Andriesse
Universiteit Utrecht, The Netherlands
Huygens, Christiaan; The Netherlands

Donald S. Armentrout
University of the South
Weems, Mason Locke

Nigel Aston
Warwick University, United Kingdom
Gibbon, Edward; Royal Courts and Dynasties; Wilkes, John

Scott Atran
University of Michigan
Taxonomy

Philip Ayres
Monash University, Melbourne, Australia
Classicism

Ehrhard Bahr
University of California at Los Angeles
Goethe, Johann Wolfgang von

Gauvin Alexander Bailey
Clark University
Jesuits: Role as Missionaries and Explorers

John D. Baird
University of Toronto, Canada
Addison, Joseph

Keith Michael Baker
Stanford University
Condorcet, Jean-Antoine-Nicolas de Caritat; Revolution

Jean Pierre Balcou
Université de Bretagne Occidentale, Brest, France, emeritus
Fréron, Elie

Vincent Barras
Université de Lausanne, Switzerland
Tissot, Samuel-Auguste-André-David

Martin C. Battestin
University of Virginia
Fielding, Henry

Daniel A. Baugh
Cornell University, emeritus
Mercantilism

Daniel Beauvois
Université de Paris I, Panthéon-Sorbonne
Poland

Ursula A. J. Becher
*Georg Eckert Institut für Internationale Schulbuchforschung,
Germany*
Moser, Carl Friedrich von

Barbara Becker-Cantarino
Ohio State University
Friendship

Thierry Belleguic
Université Laval, Quebec, Canada
Laclos, Pierre-Ambroise Choderlos de; Prévost d'Exiles,
Antoine-François

Lucien Bély
Université de Paris IV, Paris-Sorbonne
Polignac, Melchior de

Bernadette Bensaude-Vincent
Université de Paris X, Paris-Nanterre
Lavoisier, Antoine-Laurent

Cristina Berdichevsky
Gaullaudet University
Hays, Mary

Govaert C. J. J. van den Bergh
Universiteit Utrecht, The Netherlands
Noodt, Gerard

Klaus L. Berghahn
University of Wisconsin–Madison
Criticism

Christiane Berkvens-Stevelinck
Universiteit Leiden, The Netherlands
Marchand, Prosper

Winfred E. A. Bernhard
University of Massachusetts at Amherst, emeritus
Ames, Fisher; Winthrop, John

Christopher J. Berry
University of Glasgow, Scotland
Virtue

Silvia Berti
Università degli Studi di Roma, Italy
Pilati, Carlo Antonio; Radicati di Passerano, Alberto

Georges-L. Bérubé
York University, Toronto, Canada
Beaumarchais, Pierre-Augustin Caron de

Mauricio Beuchot
Universidad Nacional Autóma de Mexico, Mexico City
Clavijero, Francisco Javier

Raymond Birn
University of Oregon, emeritus
Encyclopédie

Margareta Björkman
Mälardalens Högskola, Västerås, Sweden
Lenngren, Anna Maria

Jeremy Black
University of Exeter, United Kingdom
Glorious Revolution; Grand Tour

T. C. W. Blanning
University of Cambridge, United Kingdom
Frederick II

Jean Bloch
Royal Holloway, University of London, United Kingdom
Education: Education of Women

Hans Erich Bödeker
Max-Planck-Institut für Geschichte, Göttingen, Germany
Abbt, Thomas; Journals, Newspapers, and Gazettes: Germany; Lessing, Gotthold Ephraim; Scholarship and Research

Christine van Boheemen-Saaf
Universiteit Amsterdam, The Netherlands
Deken, Aagje; Post, Elisabeth Maria; Wolff-Bekker, Betje

J. F. Bosher
York University, Toronto, Canada
Lafitau, Joseph-François; Lahontan, Louis-Armand de Lom d'Arce

Valentin Boss
McGill University, Montreal, Canada
Bernoulli, Daniel; Catherine II; Lomonosov, Mikhail Vasilievich; Radishchev, Alexander Nikolayevich

Mark Boulby
University of British Columbia, Canada, emeritus
Moritz, Karl Phillip

Pierre H. Boulle
McGill University, Montreal, Canada
Race

Dominique Bourel
Centre de Recherche Français de Jérusalem, Israel
Judaism

Philippe Boutry
École des Hautes Études en Sciences Sociales, Paris, France
Pius VII

Frank Paul Bowman
University of Pennsylvania, emeritus
Staël, Germaine Necker de

M. A. Box
University of Alaska at Fairbanks
Johnson, Samuel

O. M. Brack
Arizona State University
Smollett, Tobias

Clare Brant
King's College London, United Kingdom
Letters

Michael Bregnsbo
Odense Universitet, Denmark
Basedow, Johann Bernhard; Höegh-Guldberg, Ove; Pontoppidan, Erik

Thomas Brennan
United States Naval Academy
Coffeehouses and Cafes

Alexander Broadie
University of Glasgow, Scotland
Scottish Common Sense Philosophy

Laurence Brockliss
Magdalen College, Oxford, United Kingdom
Universities

Richard Brookhiser
The National Review
Washington, George

Gregory S. Brown
University of Nevada at Las Vegas
Authorship

Stephen W. Brown
Trent University, Peterborough, Canada
Erskine, David Steuart

Stewart J. Brown
University of Edinburgh, Scotland
Reformed Churches: Presbyterianism

Richard Buel, Jr.
Wesleyan University
Declaration of Independence

J. M. Bumsted
University of Manitoba, Canada
Canada

Lionel Burman
University of Liverpool, United Kingdom
Wedgwood, Josiah

Alain Cabantous
Université de Paris I, Panthéon-Sorbonne
Bergier, Nicolas-Sylvestre

Marina Caffiero
Università di Roma "La Sapienza," Italy
Labre, Benoît-Joseph; Ultramontanism

Robert H. Canary
University of Wisconsin at Parkside
Dunlap, William

Giancarlo Carabelli
Università degli Studi di Ferrara, Italy
Hamilton, William

Marvin Carlson
Graduate Center, City University of New York
Theater: Literary Genre

Jacques Carré
Université de Paris IV, Paris-Sorbonne
Patronage

Paul O. Carrese
United States Air Force Academy
Republicanism: An Overview

Judith Casali de Babot
Universidad Nacional de Tucumán, Argentina
San Martín, José de

Howard Caygill
Goldsmiths College, University of London
Aesthetics

Andrew R. L. Cayton
Miami University of Ohio
Hamilton, Alexander; Lewis and Clark Expedition

Jack R. Censer
George Mason University
Desfontaines, Pierre-François Guyot; French Revolution:
Debates about Causes; Journals, Newspapers, and Gazettes:
France; Malesherbes, Chrétien-Guillaume de Lamoignon de

Roger Chartier
École des Hautes Études en Sciences Sociales, Paris
Print Culture; Reading and Reading Practices;
Representations of Reading

Bernard Chédozeau
Montpellier, France
Nicole, Pierre

Marjolaine Chevallier
Université Marc Bloch, Strasbourg, France
Poiret, Pierre

Harvey Chisick
University of Haifa, Israel
Popularization

Thomas Christensen
University of Chicago
Concert; Mozart, Wolfgang Amadeus; Music; Rameau,
Jean-Philippe

Jakob Christensson
Lunds Universitet, Sweden
Academies: Scandinavia; Gjörwell, Carl Christopher; Maclean,
Rutger; Salvius, Lars; Scandinavia

Marc A. Christophe
University of the District of Columbia
Toussaint l'Ouverture, Pierre Dominique

Lauren Clay
Graduate Student, University of Pennsylvania
Theater: Role of Theater

Charles L. Cohen
University of Wisconsin–Madison
Mather, Cotton

Jean-François Combes de Prades
Viroflay, France
Prades, Jean-Martin de

Thomas M. Conley
University of Illinois at Urbana-Champaign
Rhetoric

Claire Connolly
Cardiff University, Wales
Edgeworth, Maria

Stephen Conrad
Indiana University
Wilson, James

Elizabeth Heckendorn Cook
University of California at Santa Barbara
Landscape and Gardens

Monique Cottret
Université de Paris X, Paris-Nanterre
Beaumont, Christophe de; Jansenism; National Churches

Edward V. Coughlin
University of Cincinnati
Olavide, Pablo de

R. S. Cox
American Philosophical Society
American Philosophical Society

Cynthia C. Craig
Michigan State University
Casanova, Giacomo

Robert B. Craig
Independent Scholar, Eatontown, N. J.
Mesmer, Franz Anton

Nicholas Cronk
Voltaire Foundation, University of Oxford, United Kingdom
Voltaire

Anthony Cross
University of Cambridge, United Kingdom
Saint Petersburg Academy

Ilaria Crotti
Università ca' Foscari di Venezia, Italy
Goldoni, Carlo

François-Xavier Cuche
Université Marc Bloch, Strasbourg, France
Bossuet, Jacques Bénigne; Fleury, Claude

Otto Dann
Universität Köln, Germany
Cabinets de Lecture

N. S. Davidson
St. Edmund Hall, Oxford, United Kingdom
Papacy

Simon Davies
Queen's University of Belfast, United Kingdom
Bernardin de Saint-Pierre, Jacques-Henri

Rosena Davison
Simon Fraser University, Burnaby, Canada
Salons: France

Antoine de Baecque
Université de Saint-Quentin-en-Yvelines, France
Declaration of the Rights of Man; Revolutionary Cults

Françoise Deconinck-Brossard
Université de Paris X, Paris-Nanterre
Sermons: Protestant Sermons

Joan DeJean
University of Pennsylvania
Novel; Perrault, Charles

Gilles Delpierre
Paris, France
Caylus, Anne-Claude-Philippe de Tubières

Isabel de Madariaga
Royal Spanish Academy of History, University College London, United Kingdom
Russia

David J. Denby
Dublin City University, Ireland
Imagination; Sensibility

H. T. Dickinson
University of Edinburgh, Scotland
Bolingbroke, Henry St. John

George di Giovanni
McGill University, Montreal, Canada
Jacobi, Friedrich Heinrich

Clorinda Donato
California State University at Long Beach
Bonnet, Charles

Brendan Dooley
International University Bremen, Germany
Academies: Italy; Jesuits: Role in Publishing; Journals, Newspapers, and Gazettes: Italy; Salons: Italy

Julia Douthwaite
University of Notre Dame
La Fayette, Marie-Madeleine

William C. Dowling
Rutgers University
Barlow, Joel

William Doyle
University of Bristol, United Kingdom
Parlements

Frederick A. Dreyer
University of Western Ontario, London, Canada
Burke, Edmund; Wesley, John

François Duchesneau
Université de Montréal, Canada
Leibniz, Gottfried Wilhelm von; Vitalism

James Dybikowski
University of British Columbia, Vancouver, Canada
Clarke, Samuel; Collins, Anthony; Natural Religion; Tindal, Matthew

Hans L. Eicholz
The Liberty Fund, Indianapolis
Brackenridge, Hugh Henry

Joris van Eijnatten
Vrije Universiteit, Amsterdam, The Netherlands
Stinstra, Johannes

Roger L. Emerson
University of Western Ontario, London, Canada
Campbell, Archibald; Clerk, John; Clubs and Societies; Edinburgh; Scotland; Struensee, Johann Friedrich; Tradition; Virtuosi; Wallace, Robert

Dennis F. Essar
Brock University, St. Catherines, Canada
Alembert, Jean Le Rond d'

Jane B. Fagg
Lyon College
Ferguson, Adam

Patricia Fara
Clare College, Cambridge, United Kingdom
Electricity and Magnetism; Newtonianism

Paul Lawrence Farber
Orgeon State University
Natural History

Robert K. Faulkner
Boston College
Marshall, John; Political Philosophy

Michel Faure
Université de Haute Alsace, Mulhouse, France
Millar, John

John Feather
Loughborough University, United Kingdom
Journals, Newspapers, and Gazettes: Great Britain

M. Kay Flavell
University of California at Davis
South Seas

Elizabeth Fox-Genovese
Emory University
Quesnay, François

Robert J. Frail
Centenary College
Richardson, Samuel

Gianni Francioni
Università degli Studi di Pavia, Italy
Beccaria, Cesare; Verri, Alessandro; Verri, Pietro

R. G. Frey
Bowling Green State University
Butler, Joseph; Shaftesbury, Anthony Ashley Cooper

Michael Freyne
University of New South Wales, Sydney, Australia
Fontenelle, Bernard Le Bovier de

David Garrioch
Monash University, Australia
Paris

John Gascoigne
University of New South Wales, Sydney, Australia
Banks, Joseph; Latitudinarianism; Physico-Theology; Scientific Expeditions

Howard Gaskill
University of Edinburgh, Scotland
Macpherson, James

Azar Gat
University of Tel Aviv, Israel
War and Military Theory

Gérard Gengembre
Université de Caen, France
Chateaubriand, François-René de

Don R. Gerlach
University of Akron
Johnson, Samuel (of Connecticut)

Alan Gibson
California State University at Chico
Republicanism: The United States

Alfred Gierer
Max-Planck-Institut für Entwicklungsbiologie, Tübingen, Germany, emeritus
Stahl, Georg Ernst

Martin Gierl
Max-Planck-Institut für Geschichte, Göttingen, Germany
Academies: Germany

Paul A. Gilje
University of Oklahoma
American Revolution; North America

François Girbal
Collège de Juilly, France
Lamy, Bernard

Elizabeth C. Goldsmith
Boston University
Diaries and Memoirs

Sean C. Goodlett
Fitchburg State College
Rey, Marc-Michel

Dena Goodman
University of Michigan
Men and Women of Letters

Daniel Gordon
University of Massachusetts at Amherst
Cassirer, Ernst; Citizenship; Gay, Peter; Morellet, André; Post-Structuralism and Post-Modernism; Sociability

Philip Gould
Brown University
Brown, Charles Brockden; Crèvecoeur, Michel-Guillaume-Jean de

Kerry S. Grant
State University of New York at Buffalo
Burney, Fanny

Christopher Grasso
College of William and Mary
Connecticut Wits

Ivor Grattan-Guinness
Middlesex University, Enfield, United Kingdom
Euler, Leonhard; Mathematics

Jack P. Greene
Johns Hopkins University
Colonialism: An Overview

Chantal Grell
Université de Versailles, France
Ancient Greece; Ancient Rome; Archaeology; Pompeii and Herculaneum

Allen C. Guelzo
Eastern University
Edwards, Jonathan; Hopkins, Samuel

Ivor Guest
Independent Scholar, United Kingdom
Ballet; Noverre, Jean-Georges

Madelyn Gutwirth
West Chester University, emerita
Necker, Suzanne

K. R. Constantine Gutzman
Western Connecticut State University
Tucker, St. George

Jean Haechler
Saint-Paul-de-Vence, France
Jaucourt, Louis

Notker Hammerstein
Johann-Wolfgang-Goethe Universität, Frankfurt, Germany
Seckendorff, Veit Ludwig von

Ronald Hamowy
University of Alberta, Edmonton, Canada, emeritus
Republicanism: Great Britain

Paul R. Hanson
Butler University
Republicanism: France

Geneviève Haroche-Bouzinac
Université d'Orléans, France
Montagu, Mary Wortley

Ellen T. Harris
Massachusetts Institute of Technology
Handel, George Frideric

Sidney Hart
National Portrait Gallery, Smithsonian Institution
Peale, Charles Willson

Gary Hatfield
University of Pennsylvania
Epistemology; Rationalism; Reason

Carla H. Hay
Marquette University
Montagu, Elizabeth

Julie Candler Hayes
University of Richmond
Sade, Donatien-Alphonse-François de

Kenneth Haynes
Boston University
Hamann, Johann Georg

J. L. Heilbron
Worcester College, Oxford, United Kingdom
Natural Philosophy and Science

Deborah Hertz
Sarah Lawrence College
Salons: Germany

Jonathan M. Hess
University of North Carolina at Chapel Hill
Dohm, Christian Wilhelm

Carla Hesse
University of California at Berkeley
Literary and Intellectual Property

Andrew Hewitt
University of California at Los Angeles
Frankfurt School

Michael Heyd
Hebrew University of Jerusalem, Israel
Enthusiasm

Ruth Hill
University of Virginia
Espejo, Eugenio de; Juana Inés de la Cruz

Henk Hillenaar
Rijksuniversiteit Groningen, The Netherlands
Fénelon, François-Armand de Salignac de La Mothe

Kevin Hilliard
St. Peter's College, Oxford, United Kingdom
Klopstock, Friedrich Gottlieb

Richard L. Hills
Hyde, Cheshire, United Kingdom
Watt, James

Robert G. Hogan (deceased)
University of Delaware
Sheridan, Thomas

Frederic L. Holmes
Yale School of Medicine
Chemistry

Andrew Hook
University of Glasgow, Scotland
Scott, Walter

R. A. Houston
University of St. Andrews, Scotland
Literacy

Seymour Howard
University of California at Davis
Neoclassicism

Derek Hughes
University of Warwick, United Kingdom
Behn, Aphra

Isabel V. Hull
Cornell University
Hippel, Theodor Gottlieb von; Justi, Johann Heinrich Gottlob

Lynn Hunt
University of California at Los Angeles
Enlightenment Studies; French Revolution: An Overview

Ian Hunter
Griffith University, Brisbane, Australia
Natural Law

Mary Hunter
Bowdoin College
Opera

Daniel-Odon Hurel
Centre d'Études des Religions du Livre, CNRS, Paris
Benedictines of Saint-Maur; Calmet, Augustin

Girolamo Imbruglia
Istituto Universitario Orientale, Naples, Italy
Filangieri, Gaetano; Fonseca Pimentel, Eleonora; Galiani, Ferdinando; Genovesi, Antonio; Pagano, Francesco Mario

Gerald N. Izenberg
Washington University, St. Louis, Mo.
Humboldt, Wilhelm von; Romanticism

Myles W. Jackson
Willamette University
Optics

Margaret C. Jacob
University of California at Los Angeles
Amsterdam; Freemasonry; Saint-Hyacinthe, Themiseul de

Kathleen G. Jaeger
Graceland University, emerita
Charrière, Isabelle de

Irma B. Jaffe
Fordham University, emerita
Copley, John Singleton; Trumbull, John

Vladimir Janković
University of Manchester, United Kingdom
Meteorology

Ruth-Ellen B. Joeres
University of Minnesota
Gellert, Christian Furchtegott; La Roche, Sophie von; Sturm und Drang

Dorothy Johnson
University of Iowa
David, Jacques-Louis; Painting

Norbert Jonard
Université de Bourgogne, France
Parini, Giuseppe

Shirley Jones Day
University College London, United Kingdom
Lespinasse, Julie de

Inge Jonsson
Stockholm Universitet, Sweden, emerita
Swedenborg, Emmanuel

Dominique Julia
École des Hautes Études en Sciences Sociales, Paris
Jesuits: Role in Education; Oratorians; Tutoring

Frank A. Kafker
University of Cincinnati, emeritus
Encyclopedias

Thomas E. Kaiser
University of Arkansas at Little Rock
Mably, Gabriel Bonnot de; Turgot, Anne-Robert-Jacques

David S. Katz
Tel Aviv University, Israel
Millenarianism

John Keane
University of Westminster, London
Paine, Thomas

Gary Kelly
University of Alberta, Edmonton, Canada
Wollstonecraft, Mary

James Kelly
St. Patrick's College, Dublin City University, Ireland
Ireland

Oscar Kenshur
Indiana University
Free Will; Human Nature; Nominalism

Rebecca E. Kingston
University of Toronto, Canada
Montesquieu, Charles de Secondat

Lawrence E. Klein
University of Nevada at Las Vegas
Politeness

Stephan Klein
Independent Scholar, Utrecht, The Netherlands
Republicanism: The Netherlands

Matti Klinge
University of Helsinki, Finland
Chydenius, Anders; Porthan, Henrik Gabriel

Joost Kloek
Universiteit Utrecht, The Netherlands
Effen, Justus van; Merken, Lucretia Wilhelmina van

Ulla Kölving
Centre Internationale d'Étude du XVIIIᵉ Siècle, Ferney-Voltaire, France
Grimm, Friedrich Melchior; Meister, Henri

Alan Charles Kors
University of Pennsylvania
Atheism; Holbach, Paul-Henri Thiry d'; Naigeon, Jacques-André; Philosophes

Ilona Kovács
University of Economic Sciences, Budapest, Hungary
Hungary

Manfred Kuehn
Philipps-Universität Marburg, Germany
Moral Philosophy; Natural Sentiment; Reinhold, Karl Leonhard; Stoicism; Utilitarianism; Wolff, Christian

Catherine Lafarge
Bryn Mawr College
Restif de la Bretonne, Nicolas

Frank Lambert
Purdue University
Great Awakening: First Great Awakening

Jean-Pierre Laurant
École Pratique des Hautes Études, Paris
Maistre, Joseph de; Saint-Martin, Louis-Claude de

John Christian Laursen
University of California at Riverside
Bahrdt, Carl Friedrich

Anthony J. La Vopa
North Carolina State University
Habermas, Jürgen

Christopher Lawrence
Wellcome Institute for the History of Medicine, London, United Kingdom
Medicine: Theories of Medicine

François Lebrun
Université de Rennes 2–Haute Bretagne, France, emeritus
Sermons: Roman Catholic Sermons

Jacques Le Brun
École Pratique des Hautes Études, Section des Sciences Religieuses, Paris, France
Guyon, Jeanne-Marie Bouvier de La Motte; Lambert, Anne-Thérèse de; Lamy, François; Mysticism

Denise Leduc-Fayette
University of Aix-Marseille I, France
Maine de Biran

Paula Young Lee
University of South Florida
Lyceums and Museums

Hartmut Lehmann
Max-Planck-Institut für Geschichte, Göttingen, Germany
Pietism

James A. Leith
Queen's University, Kingston, Canada
Cities; French Revolution: Iconography

Howard M. Lenhoff
University of California at Irvine
Trembley, Abraham

Sylvia G. Lenhoff
University of California at Irvine
Trembley, Abraham

Trevor H. Levere
University of Toronto, Canada
Scientific Instruments

Darline Gay Levy
New York University
Linguet, Simon-Nicolas-Henri

Mary Lindemann
Carnegie Mellon University
Health and Disease

R. Burr Litchfield
Brown University
Italy

Douglas Long
University of Western Ontario, London, Canada
Bentham, Jeremy

Howard L. Lubert
James Madison University
Dickinson, John

Ian G. Lumsden
Independent Scholar, Fredericton, Canada
Gainsborough, Thomas

Roger D. Lund
Le Moyne College
Deism

Katherine D. McCann
Library of Congress
Miranda, Francisco

James E. McClellan III
Stevens Institute of Technology
Learned Societies; Scientific Journals

John G. McEvoy
University of Cincinnati
Heat; Pneumatics; Priestley, Joseph

Carol McGuirk
Florida Atlantic University
Burns, Robert

Antony McKenna
Université Jean Monnet, Saint-Étienne, France
Arnauld, Antoine; Challe, Robert; Clandestine Literature; Fréret, Nicolas

Peter McLaughlin
Max-Planck-Institut für Wissenschaftsgeschichte, Berlin, Germany
Blumenbach, Johann Friedrich

Catriona MacLeod
University of Pennsylvania
Sculpture; Winckelmann, Johann Joachim

Peter McNamara
Utah State University
Democracy

Barbara Widenor Maggs
University of Illinois at Urbana-Champaign
Asia; China

Anne-Marie Mai
Syddansk Universitet, Kolding, Denmark
Holberg, Ludvig

Catherine Maire
École des Hautes Études en Sciences Sociales, Paris, France
Jesuits: Jesuits and Jansenists

Peter C. Mancall
University of Kansas
Explorations and Contact

Kenneth Margerison
Southwest Texas State University
Pamphlets

Stephen Marini
Wellesley College
Great Awakening: Second Great Awakening

Gary Marker
State University of New York at Stony Brook
Academies: Russia; Novikov, Nikolai Ivanovich

Hilary Marland
University of Warwick, United Kingdom
Midwifery

Susan A. Maslan
University of California at Berkeley
Revolutionary Theater

Maurice Mauviel
Université de Paris V René Descartes
Volney, Constantin-François de Chasseboeuf

David N. Mayer
Capital University Law School
Jefferson, Thomas

Jon Mee
University College, Oxford
Johnson, Joseph

Mariselle Meléndez
University of Illinois at Urbana-Champaign
Bello, Andrés

Anne K. Mellor
University of California at Los Angeles
Feminist Theory

Sylvain Menant
Université de Paris IV, Paris-Sorbonne
Poetry

Alan Menhennet
University of Newcastle upon Tyne, United Kingdom
Wieland, Christoph Martin

Jeffrey Merrick
University of Wisconsin–Milwaukee
Orléans, Philippe d'

Annette Meyer
Universität Köln, Germany
Cabinets de Lecture

Robert Middlekauff
University of California at Berkeley
Franklin, Benjamin

James Miller
New School University
Foucault, Michel

Judith A. Miller
Emory University
Grain Trade

Horst Möller
Institut für Zeitgeschichte, Munich, Germany
Berlin; Bourgeoisie; Nicolai, Friedrich

John Money
University of Victoria, Canada
Darwin, Erasmus; Technology

Maria Teresa Monti
Istituto per la Storia del Pensiero Filosofico e Scientifico Moderno, Consiglio Nazionale delle Ricerche, Milan, Italy
Haller, Albrecht von; Spallanzani, Lazzaro

James H. Moorhead
Princeton Theological Seminary
Miller, Samuel

Barbara Morden
Open University and Independent Scholar, United Kingdom
Gothic

Joseph R. Morel
Independent Scholar, Boston, Massachusetts
Allen, Ethan

Philip Morgan
Johns Hopkins University
Slavery

Michel Morineau
Université de Paris XII, Paris-Nord, emeritus
Commerce and Trade

François Morlot
Troyes, France
Clorivière, Picot de

William Edward Morris
Illinois Wesleyan University
Hartley, David

Jeffrey Morrison
National University of Ireland, Maynooth, Ireland
Baumgarten, Alexander Gottlieb; Bodmer, Johann Jakob; Sulzer, Johann Georg

François Moureau
Université de Paris IV, Sorbonne
Correspondence and Correspondents

Steven M. Nadler
University of Wisconsin at Madison
Malebranche, Nicolas

T. G. A. Nelson
University of New England, Armidale, Australia
Goldsmith, Oliver

Melvyn New
University of Florida
Sterne, Laurence

H. B. Nisbet
Sidney Sussex College, Cambridge, United Kingdom
Genius

David Nokes
King's College, London, United Kingdom
Swift, Jonathan

Kathryn Norberg
University of California at Los Angeles
Poverty

Robert E. Norton
University of Notre Dame
Gottsched, Johann Christoph; Herder, Johann Gottfried

Maximillian E. Novak
University of California at Los Angeles
Defoe, Daniel

Victor Nuovo
Middlebury College, emeritus, and Harris Manchester College, Oxford
Locke, John

David Oldroyd
University of New South Wales, Sydney, Australia
Geology

John C. O'Neal
Hamilton College
Rousseau, Jean-Jacques

H. J. Ormsby-Lennon
Villanova University
Pornography; Satire

Fania Oz-Salzberger
University of Haifa, Israel
Aufklärung; Garve, Christian; Translation

Gianni Paganini
Università degli Studi di Torino, Italy
Skepticism

Anthony Pagden
University of Cambridge, United Kingdom
Colonialism: Philosophical Legacy

Katherine Thomas Paisley
Graduate Student, Vanderbilt Divinity School
Sermons: Evangelical Sermons

Frank Palmeri
University of Miami
Philosophical Dialogue

Joseph Pappa
Villanova University
Pornography

Patricia L. Parker
Japanese Red Cross Hiroshima College of Nursing, Japan
Rowson, Susanna

Ronald Paulson
Johns Hopkins University
Hogarth, William

Harry C. Payne
Woodward Academy
People, The

Robert McCracken Peck
Academy of Natural Sciences
Bartram, John and William

Ruth Perry
Massachusetts Institute of Technology
Astell, Mary

Vesna Petrovich
Grinell College
Châtelet, Émilie Le Tonnelier de Breteuil du

Maria-Cristina Pitassi
Université de Genève, Switzerland
Geneva; Huber, Marie; Le Clerc, Jean

Jennifer J. Popiel
University of Wisconsin–Green Bay
Education: Pedagogical Thought and Practice; Education: Reform and Experiments

Jeremy D. Popkin
University of Kentucky
Autobiography; Censorship; Publishing

Charles Porset
Centre Nationale de la Recherche Scientifique, Paris
Hazard, Paul

Roy S. Porter (1946–2002)
Wellcome Trust Centre for the History of Medicine, University College, London, United Kingdom
England; Insanity; London

Adam Potkay
College of William and Mary
Biography; Happiness; Passion

Irwin Primer
Rutgers University, Newark
Mandeville, Bernard

Guido Pugliese
University of Toronto at Mississauga, Canada
Conti, Antonio

John Pullen
University of New England, Armidale, Australia
Malthus, Thomas Robert

Jean-Louis Quantin
Université de Versailles, France
Hardouin, Jean

Jean Quéniart
Université de Rennes 2, France
Aristocracy: Cultural Contributions

Jack N. Rakove
Stanford University
Articles of Confederation; Bill of Rights; Constitution of the United States; Federalist, The; Federalists and Antifederalists; Madison, James

Jeffrey S. Ravel
Massachusetts Institute of Technology
France

David Raynor
University of Ottawa, Canada
Berkeley, George; Ramsay, Andrew Michael

Allen Reddick
Universität Zürich, Switzerland
Dictionaries

Joseph Reed
Wesleyan University
Webster, Noah

W. Jay Reedy
Bryant College
Bonald, Louis de

Nina Reid-Maroney
University of Windsor, Canada
Dwight, Timothy; Philadelphia; Rittenhouse, David

John Renwick
University of Edinburgh, Scotland
Académie Française; Marmontel, Jean-François

Pierre Rétat
Université Lumière-Lyon 2, France, emeritus
Literary Genres

Walter E. Rex
University of California at Berkeley
Diderot, Denis

Roger D. Reynolds
Tulane University
Republicanism: Latin America

Eric Richards
Flinders University, Adelaide, Australia
Agriculture and Animal Husbandry

Giuseppe Ricuperati
Università degli Studi di Torino, Italy
Giannone, Pietro; Muratori, Lodovico Antonio

Dora Bienaimé Rigo
Università degli Studi di Siena, Italy
Argens, Jean-Baptiste d'

Guenter B. Risse
University of California at San Francisco
Hospitals

Bonnie Arden Robb
University of Delaware
Genlis, Stéphanie-Félicité de

David W. Robson
John Carroll University
Rush, Benjamin; Witherspoon, John

Shirley A. Roe
University of Connecticut
Spontaneous Generation

John Rogister
École Pratique des Hautes Études, Paris, France
Despotism

Antonella Romano
Centre Alexandre Koyré, CNRS, Paris, France
Jesuits: Role in Politics; Jesuits: Role as Critics

Mario Rosa
Scuola Normale Superiore, Pisa, Italy
Benedict XIV; Clement XIV; Ricci, Scipione de'; Roman Catholicism

Susan E. Rosa
Northeastern Illinois University
Prejudice; Religious Conversion

Ronald C. Rosbottom
Amherst College
Marivaux, Pierre Carlet de Chamblain de

R. B. Rose
University of Tasmania, Australia
Utopianism

Helena Rosenblatt
Hunter College and Graduate School and University Center, City University of New York
Calvinism; Civil Society; Luxury; Reformed Churches: Swiss Reformed Church; Switzerland

Fabio Rossi
Università degli Studi di Firenze, Italy
André, Yves-Marie

Wendy Wassyng Roworth
University of Rhode Island
Kauffman, Angelica Maria Catherina Anna

Andrea A. Rusnock
University of Rhode Island
Inoculation and Vaccination

Colin A. Russell
Open University, United Kingdom
Astronomy

Robert Allen Rutland
University of Virginia, emeritus
Mason, George

Paul Sadrin
Université de Franche-Comté, Besançon, France
Boulanger, Nicolas-Antoine

John Saillant
Western Michigan University
Haynes, Lemuel; Wheatley, Acade Phyllis

María A. Salgado
University of North Carolina
Castillo, Madre

Guillermo Ignacio Salvatierra
Universidad Nacional de Tucumán, Argentina
San Martín, José de

Richard A. Samuelson
The Liberty Fund, Indianapolis
Otis, James

Michael J. Sauter
Centro de Investigación y Docencia Económicas, Mexico
Koselleck, Reinhart

Hervé Savon
Université de Bruxelles, Belgium
Duguet, Jacques-Joseph

Sara Schechner
Harvard University
West, Benjamin

James Schmidt
Boston University
Scholarly Associations and Publications

Robert A. Schneider
Catholic University of America
Spectacles

Werner Schneiders
Universität Münster, Germany
Thomasius, Christian

Gordon Schochet
Rutgers University
Toleration

Anne L. Schroder
Duke University Museum of Art
Illustrators and Illustrations

Bertram Eugene Schwarzbach
Paris, France
Bible

Karl W. Schweizer
New Jersey Institute of Technology
Diplomacy

Hamish Scott
University of St. Andrews, Scotland
Enlightened Despotism

Pamela Scott
Independent Architectural Historian, Cornell-in-Washington
Latrobe, Benjamin

Michael J. Seidler
Western Kentucky University
Pufendorf, Samuel

Lewis C. Seifert
Brown University
Tales

Alyssa Goldstein Sepinwall
California State University at San Marcos
Grégoire, Henri

Robert E. Shalhope
University of Oklahoma
Taylor, John

Lesley Sharpe
University of Bristol, United Kingdom
Schiller, Friedrich

James J. Sheehan
Stanford University
Germany

Mary Sheriff
University of North Carolina at Chapel Hill
Rococo

Nancy Shoemaker
University of Connecticut
Native Americans

English Showalter
Rutgers University
Graffigny, Françoise de

Luisa Simonutti
Centro Studi del Pensiero Filosofico, Consiglio Nazionale delle Ricerche, Milan, Italy
Limborch, Philippus van

Mario Sina
Università Cattolica di Milano, Italy
Revealed Religion

Andrew S. Skinner
University of Glasgow, Scotland, emeritus
Smith, Adam; Steuart, James

Marie-Christine Skuncke
Uppsala Universitet, Sweden
Gustav III; Kellgren, Johan Henric; Lovisa Ulrika

Phillip R. Sloan
University of Notre Dame
Buffon, Georges-Louis Leclerc de

Abraham M. Smith
Graduate Student, Howard University
Bolívar, Simón; Latin America; Túpac Amaru

Bonnie G. Smith
Rutgers University
Sexuality

D. W. Smith
University of Toronto, Canada, emeritus
Helvétius, Claude-Adrien

David Kammerling Smith
Eastern Illinois University
Free Trade

Jay M. Smith
University of North Carolina at Chapel Hill
Aristocracy: Criticism; Corporate and Estate Organization

Jeffrey Smitten
Utah State University
Robertson, William

H. A. M. Snelders
Universiteit Utrecht, The Netherlands
Boerhaave, Hermann; Leeuwenhoek, Antoni van; Musschenbroek, Petrus van; Nieuwentijt, Bernard; Ruysch, Frederik

Stephen D. Snobelen
University of King's College, Halifax, Canada
Newton, Isaac

David H. Solkin
Courtauld Institute of Art, London, United Kingdom
Exhibitions

David Sorkin
University of Wisconsin–Madison
Haskalah; Mendelssohn, Moses

Richard J. Sorrenson
Analytica Consulting Ltd., New Zealand
Physics; Royal Society of London

David Spadafora
Lake Forest College
Progress

James Spady
College of William and Mary
Washington, D.C.

Walter Sparn
Friedrich-Alexander-Universität Erlangen-Nürnberg, Germany
Spalding, Johann Joachim

E. C. Spary
University of Cambridge, United Kingdom
Botany; Linnaeus, Carolus; Zoology

Mark G. Spencer
University of Western Ontario, London, Canada
Almanacs and Yearbooks

Torkel Stålmarck
Universitet Stockholm, Sweden
Dalin, Olof von; Nordenflycht, Hedvig Charlotta

Stephen A. State
University of Western Ontario, London, Canada
Hobbes, Thomas

Martin S. Staum
University of Calgary, Canada
Cabanis, Pierre-Jean-Georges; Destutt de Tracy, Antoine-Louis-Claude; Idéologues; Institut de France

Susan Staves
Brandeis University, emerita
Drake, Judith; Salons

M. A. Stewart
University of Aberdeen, Scotland, and Harris Manchester College, Oxford
Hume, David; Hutcheson, Francis

Christopher Storrs
University of Dundee, Scotland
Aranda, Pedro Pablo, conde de; Campomanes, Pedro Rodriguez; Feijoo, Benito Jeronimo; Jovellanos, Gaspar Melchor de; Mayans y Siscar, Gregorio; Milan; Monino, Jose; Naples; Pombal, Sebastião José de Carvalho e Mello; Portugal; Spain

John Michael Stroup
Rice University
Mosheim, Johann Lorenz; Reimarus, Hermann Samuel; Semler, Johann Salomo

Anthony Strugnell
University of Hull, United Kingdom
Raynal, Guillaume-Thomas

Jeffrey M. Suderman
University of Calgary, Canada
Campbell, George

Robert E. Sullivan
University of Notre Dame
Socinianism; Toland, John

Geoffrey Sweet
Anglia Polytechnic University, Cambridge, United Kingdom
Schlözer, August Ludwig

Anna Tabaki
Centre for Neohellenic Research, Athens, Greece
Greece

A. A. Tait
University of Glasgow, Scotland
Adam, Robert

Richard F. Teichgraeber III
Tulane University
Stewart, Dugald

Rüdiger Thiele
Universität Leipzig, Germany
Maupertuis, Pierre-Louis Moreau de

Downing A. Thomas
University of Iowa
Condillac, Étienne Bonnot de; Language Theories

D. O. Thomas
University of Wales, Aberystwyth, Wales
Price, Richard

Phillip Drennon Thomas
University of Wichita
Rumford, Count

C. Bradley Thompson
Ashland University
Adams, John

Ann Thomson
Université de Paris VIII, Vincennes–St-Denis
Epicurianism; Islam; La Mettrie, Julien Offray de;
Materialism; Meslier, Jean; North Africa and the Levant;
Ottoman Empire; Pantheism

Keith Tribe
Independent Scholar, Malvern, Worcesteshire, United Kingdom
Cameralism; Economic Thought

Mary Seidman Trouille
Illinois State University
Gouges, Olympe de; Roland, Marie-Jeanne

Suzanne Tucoo-Chala
Université de Pau et des Pays de l'Adour, France
Panckoucke, Charles Joseph

Gordon Turnbull
Yale University
Boswell, James

Wiep van Bunge
Erasmus Universiteit Rotterdam, The Netherlands
Bekker, Balthasar; Dale, Anthonie van; Furly, Benjamin;
Netherlands: An Overview; Pinto, Isaac de

Dominique Varry
École Nationale Supérieure des Sciences de l'Information et des Bibliothèques, Villeurbanne, France
Libraries

Diego Venturino
Université de Metz, France
Boulainvilliers, Henri de

Theo Verbeek
Universiteit Utrecht, The Netherlands
Cartesianism; Gravesande, Willem Jacob 's; Hemsterhuis,
François; Meijer, Lodewijk; Spinoza, Baruch de

Donald Phillip Verene
Emory University
Vico, Giambattista

J. J. V. M. de Vet
Katholieke Universiteit Nijmegen, The Netherlands, emeritus
Journals, Newspapers, and Gazettes: The Netherlands;
Netherlands: Press Freedom in the Netherlands

Fernando Vidal
Max-Planck-Institut für Wissenschaftsgeschichte, Berlin, Germany
Soul

Anthony Vidler
Cornell University
Architecture

Nancy Vogeley
University of San Francisco
Fernández de Lizardi, José Joaquín

Michel Vovelle
Université de Paris I, Panthéon-Sorbonne
Death

Ernestine van der Wall
Universiteit Leiden, The Netherlands
Arminianism; Reformed Churches: Dutch Reformed Church

Richard Waller
University of Liverpool, United Kingdom
Academies: France

Peter Walmsley
McMaster University, Hamilton, Canada
Optimism, Philosophical; Pope, Alexander

Ernst Wangermann
Universität Salzburg, Austria, emeritus
Austria; Josephinism

A. M. C. Waterman
Fellow of St. John's College, University of Manitoba, Canada
Godwin, William

Ruth Plaut Weinreb
State University of New York at Stony Brook
Épinay, Louise d'

Kathleen Wellman
Southern Methodist University
Needham, John Turberville

Eric Wertheimer
Arizona State University
Freneau, Philip Morin

Hugh West
University of Richmond
Forster, Georg; Lichtenberg, Georg Christoph

Joachim Whaley
Gonville and Caius College, Cambridge, United Kingdom
Reformed Churches: Lutheranism

Kevin Whelan
University of Notre Dame Centre, Dublin, Ireland
Caulfeild, James

Ruth Whelan
National University of Ireland at Maynooth, Ireland
Abbadie, Jacques; Bayle, Pierre; Chauffepié, Jacques-Georges de; Jaquelot, Isaac; Republic of Letters; Tyssot de Patot, Simon

Kirstin R. Wilcox
Graduate Student, Columbia University
Murray, Judith Sargent

Kay S. Wilkins
Montclair State University
Buffier, Claude

Glyndwr Williams
Queen Mary, University of London, United Kingdom
Cook, James

Richard G. Williams
Independent Scholar, London
Walpole, Horace

Philip K. Wilson
Penn State College of Medicine
Medicine: Practice of Medicine; Medicine: Anatomy and
Surgery

Kathleen Wilson
State University of New York at Stony Brook
Almon, John

W. Daniel Wilson
University of California at Berkeley
Illuminati

Charles W. J. Withers
University of Edinburgh, Scotland
Geography; Mapping

Larry Wolff
Boston College
Travel Literature

Paul B. Wood
University of Victoria, Canada
Home, Henry

R. S. Woolhouse
University of York, United Kingdom
Empiricism; Philosophy

John P. Wright
Central Michigan University
Life Sciences; Medicine: Medicine and Physiology

Wolfgang Wutzler
Universität Münster, Germany
Ancients and Moderns

Myriam Yardeni
University of Haifa, Israel
Rabaut Saint-Étienne, Jean-Paul

Kathryn A. Young
University of Manitoba, Canada
New France

William Zachs
San Jose State University
Stuart, Gilbert

Rosemarie Zagarri
George Mason University
Warren, Mercy Otis

John H. Zammito
Rice University
Kant, Immanuel

Michael P. Zuckert
University of Notre Dame
Natural Rights

Ronald E. Zupko
Marquette University
Weights and Measures

Simone Zurbuchen
Universität Zürich, Switzerland
Thomasius, Christian

Index

Page numbers in **boldface** indicate article titles. Those in *italics* indicate illustrations.

Brown and, **1:**175
Burney and, **1:**182, **3:**200, 202
Charrière and, **1:**220, 221, **3:**200
Chateaubriand and, **1:**222, 223
deathbed scenes, **1:**326
Defoe and, **1:**334, 335, **4:**215
Deken and, **1:**340, 341, **4:**267
Deken and Wolff-Bekkar collaboration, **1:**340, 341
Diderot and, **1:**350, 357, 358
as discourse, **2:**426
Edgeworth and, **1:**379
d'Épinay and, **2:**9
Fernández de Lizardi and, **2:**47, 48
Fielding and, **2:**48, 49, **3:**201, 202, 338
first in Dutch language, **4:**266
first in French language, **2:**341, **3:**479
first-person, **1:**350
friendship motif, **2:**94
Gellert and, **2:**105, 106
Genlis and, **2:**112–113
Godwin and, **2:**134, 141
Goethe and, **2:**135, 136, 137, 138, **3:**199, 202, 400
Goldsmith and, **2:**140
Gothic, **1:**327, **2:**141, 141 4.242, 141, **4:**242
Gouges and, **2:**143
Graffigny and, **2:**144, 145, **3:**199, 201, 479
Habermas and, **2:**170
happiness and, **2:**182
Hays and, **2:**190
Hippel and, **2:**208
historical, **4:**52
Holberg and, **2:**217
illustrations, **2:**251–259
inception and development of, **2:**425
intensive reading of, **3:**400
Jacobi and, **2:**278
Laclos and, **2:**340–341, **3:**199
La Fayette (Marie-Madeleine) and, **2:**340–341, **3:**198, 201, 479
La Roche and, **2:**357–358, **3:**200
letter devices, **2:**392
See also epistolary novel
of manners, **1:**182
Marivaux and, **3:**21, 22, 23, 200
Marmontel and, **3:**23–24
Moritz and, **3:**97–98
Netherlands and, **3:**167
nominalism and, **3:**186
Olavide and, **3:**205
opera and, **3:**210
Post and, **3:**340–341
Prévost d'Exiles and, **3:**201, 358
reading practices and, **3:**400, 420–421, 422
Restif de la Bretonne and, **3:**440–441
Richardson and, **3:**198, 199, 200, 202, 400, 420–421, 422, 462–463, **4:**64
Rococo style, **3:**465
Rousseau and, **3:**199, 200, 201, 400, 479–480, 481

Rowson and, **3:**482
Sade and, **3:**201, 202, **4:**2, 3
Scott and, **4:**52
sentimental, **4:**61–62
Smollett and, **3:**202, **4:**95–96
social protest, **2:**49
Sterne and, **3:**201, **4:**125, 126
utopianism and, **4:**215–218
Voltaire and, **3:**199, 201, **4:**236
Walpole (Horace) and, **4:**242
Wieland and, **4:**254–256
Wolff-Bekker and, **1:**340, 341, **4:**266, 267
Wollstonecraft and, **4:**268
women readers of, **2:**395, 438, **3:**55, 400
women writers of, **2:**395, **3:**56, 199
Novelle Letterarie (Florence), **2:**272, 319
Noverre, Jean-Georges, **1:**114–115, 116, **3:203**
Novikov, Nikolai Ivanovich, **3:203–204**, 376, 495, 496
Novum Organum (Bacon), **1:**21, 394, **3:**339, 354–355, **4:**223
Nowak, Kurt, **4:**57
Noyer, Anne-Marguerite du, **1:**350
Nozze di Figaro, Le (Mozart and Da Ponte), **3:**101, 102, 210
Nuevo Luciano de Quiot, El (Espejo), **2:**21
Nuits de Paris, Les (Restif de la Bretonne), **1:**327, **3:**440
number theory, **2:**23, **3:**36, 38
Nuovo dizionario scientifico e curioso, sacro-profano (Pivati), **1:**398, 405
Nuovo giornale de' letterati d'Italia, **2:**299
nurseries, plant, **2:**351, 352
Nye, Stephen, **4:**104
Nyerup, Rasmus, **4:**21

O

Oath of the Horatii, The (David), **1:**322, **2:**81, **3:**160, 229
Oath of the Tennis Court, The (David), **1:**323, **3:**230
Oberon (Wieland), **4:**256
Objections (Descartes), **1:**83
Objections (Gassendi), **1:**83
objectivism, intellectual property rights and, **2:**422
Obligations of Natural Religion (Clarke), **3:**274
O'Brien, Conor Cruise, **1:**181
Observations Concerning the Distinction of Ranks in Society (Millar), **3:**75
Observations occasionnelles sur le Siècle de Louis XIV du sieur de Voltaire (Marchand), **3:**21
Observations on Airs (Priestley), **1:**230
Observations on Dr. Beattie's Essay on the Nature and Immutability of Truth (Steuart), **4:**128
Observations on Man, His Frame, His Duty, and His Expectations (Hartley), **2:**185, 186, **3:**460

Observations on Modern Gardening (Whately), **2:**350
    Latapie translation, **2:**349–350
Observations on Reversionary Payments (Price), **3:**360
Observations on the Correspondence between Poetry and Music (Webb), **3:**106
Observations on the Feeling of the Beautiful and the Sublime (Kant), **1:**25, 31, **2:**327, **3:**256
Observations on the Importance of the American Revolution (Price), **3:**360
Observations on the Nature of Civil Liberty (Price), **1:**181, **3:**360
Observations on the Prophecies of Daniel and the Apocalypse of St. John (Newton), **3:**176
Observations on the River Wye and Several Parts of South Wales (Gilpin), **2:**351
Observations sur la physique, sur l'histoire naturelle et sur les arts (Rozier journal), **4:**45
Observations sur le gouvernement et los loix des État-Unis d'Amérique (Mably), **3:**1
Observations sur les causes de la propsperité et des malheurs des Grecs (Mably), **1:**50
Observations sur les Écrits Modernes (literary periodical), **1:**344
Observations sur les Romains (Mably), **1:**53
Observations sur l'histoire de France (Mably), **3:**1, 432
Observations sur l'histoire de la Grèce (Mably), **1:**50, **3:**1
    Radishchev translation of, **3:**388
Observations sur notre instinct pour la musique (Rameau), **3:**207, 390
Observatoire Royal (Paris), **2:**373
obstetrics. *See* midwifery
occasionalism, **1:**390, **4:**105
    Malebranche and, **3:**10, 11, 12, 395
occultism. *See* mysticism
oceanic voyages. *See* explorations and contact; geography; navigation; travel literature
oceanography, **1:**295
Ockley, Simon, **1:**86, **2:**269
Octagon Chapel (Liverpool), **4:**249
Odell, Jonathan, **1:**200
Oden (Klopstock), **2:**333
odes, **2:**423, **3:**302
Ode to Saint Cecilia (Handel), **2:**180
Odeum (Herculaneum), **3:**324
Odyssey (Homer), **2:**67
    Flaxman illustration of, **2:**255
    Hobbes translation of, **2:**209
    Pope translation of, **3:**327
Oeconomia methodo scientifica pertractata (Wolff), **4:**264
Oeconomia regni animalis (Swedenborg), **4:**139
Oeconomic Society of Berne, **1:**266
Oeconomie divine, L' (Poiret), **3:**304

opium
  commerce in, **1:**281
  as insanity treatment, **2:**263
Oppenheimer, Joseph Suss, **2:**322
Opregte Haarlemsche Courant, **2:**316
optical instruments, **4:**42–43
Opticks (Newton), **1:**395, **2:**185, **3:**130, 136, 175, 176, 177, 178, 181, 212, 213, 279, **4:**150
  Clarke translation, **1:**256, 394
optics, **3:**212–215
  astronomy and, **1:**91–94
  Descartes and, **3:**394
  Euler and, **2:**23
  Goethe and, **2:**137
  Haskalah and, **2:**187
  Huygens and, **2:**244
  Irish Enlightenment and, **2:**267
  Leeuwenhoek and, **2:**378–379
  mathematics and, **3:**37
  natural religion and, **3:**145
  Newton and, **3:**142, 173, 175, 176, 178, 181, 212, 213, 214
  Royal Society of London and, **3:**488
optimism, philosophical, **3:**215–217
  Armianism and, **3:**415
  Deism and, **1:**335–340
  English Enlightenment and, **1:**412
  free will and, **1:**412, **2:**80
  human nature and, **1:**248, **2:**80
  Hutcheson and, **2:**241–242
  Jaquelot and, **2:**285
  Leibniz and, **2:**382, **3:**215–216, 395–396, **4:**236
  Lessing and, **2:**390
  Malthus's rejection of, **3:**15
  neoclassicism and, **3:**158
  Price and, **3:**361
  progress and, **3:**367–371
  utopianism and, **4:**215–218
  Voltaire and, **3:**396, **4:**236
Opusculi di fisica animale e vegetabile (Spallanzani), **4:**113
Opus postumum (Kant), **2:**330
Oracles of Reason, The (Blount), **1:**338, **3:**443
Oraisons funèbres (Bossuet), **1:**165
Orange Party (Netherlands), **2:**316, 317
Oratio de certa methodo philosophiae experimentalis (Musschenbroek), **3:**111
Oratio de methodo instituendi experimenta physica (Musschenbroek), **3:**111
Oratio de telluris habitabilis incremento (Linnaeus), **2:**412
Oratorians, **3:**217–218
  Arnauld and, **1:**84
  education and, **2:**417
  Houtteville and, **2:**222–223
  Jansenists and, **2:**280–281, 296
  Lamy (Bernard) and, **2:**347–348
  Malebranche and, **3:**10, 12, 311
  Portugal and, **3:**339
  revealed religion and, **3:**444

oratorio, Handel and, **1:**282
Orazione funebre per Giuseppe II imperatore e re (P. Verri), **4:**222
Orbis sensualis (Comenius), **2:**256
Orcibal, Jean, **2:**44–45
Order of Carlos III (Spain), **3:**486
Order of St. Patrick (Britain), **3:**486
Order of St. Stanislaw (Poland), **3:**486
Order of the Bath (Britain), **3:**486
Order of Things, The (Foucault), **2:**58
Ordnance Survey (Britain), **3:**20
Ordre naturel et essentiel des sociétés politiques, L' (Le Mercier de La Rivière), **2:**164–165, **3:**285, 286
Oreste (Alfieri), **2:**159
Orientalism
  despot depictions and, **1:**345, **3:**86, 190, 191
  tales, **4:**146
  travel literature and, **3:**190, **4:**190, 191–192
Origen, **1:**149, **3:**76, 392
Origenes de la lengua española (Mayans y Siscar), **3:**41
Original of Our Ideas of Beauty and Virtue, The (Hutcheson), **3:**277
original sin
  Calvinism and, **3:**411
  Edwards and, **1:**391
  free will and, **2:**79
  Genevan theology and, **2:**108
  Locke argument against, **1:**412, **2:**428
  luxury linked with, **2:**440, 442
  women linked with, **3:**55
Original Sin (Edwards), **1:**391
Original Stories from Real Life (Wollstonecraft), **4:**268
Origine de tous les cults, ou Religion universelle, L' (Dupuis), **3:**442
Origines de la France contemporaine (Taine), **2:**85
Origines intellectuelles de la Révolution française, Les (Mornet), **2:**85, **3:**330
Origines judaicae (Toland), **3:**237
Origin of Language and Nations, The (Jones), **2:**353
Origin of Species (C. Darwin), **1:**426
Origin of the Distinction of Ranks; or, An Inquiry into the Circumstances which Give Rise to Influence and Authority in the Different Members of Society (Millar), **3:**75
Origins of Totalitarian Democracy, The (Talmon), **2:**82
Orlando furioso (Ariosto), **2:**252
Orléans, Elisabeth-Charlotte d', **3:**218
Orléans, Louis-Philippe-Joseph (Philippe Égalité)
  Genlis and, **2:**112
  Laclos and, **2:**340
  Louis XVI execution and, **3:**218

Orléans, Philippe d', regent of France, **3:**218–219
  Jansenism and, **2:**281, **3:**219
  Law and, **2:**369, **3:**219
  Marivaux and, **3:**22
  parlements and, **3:**218–219, 250
  Ramsay and, **3:**391
Ormond (Brown), **1:**175
Ormond (Edgeworth), **1:**379
Orobio de Castro, Issac, **1:**79, 150, 252
Oroonoko, or The Royal Slave (Behn), **1:**131, **3:**198
Orphan of China, The (Murphy), **1:**234
orphans
  church schools and, **1:**387, **3:**349
  as deserving poor, **3:**347, 348
  foundling hospitals for, **3:**45, 348, 349, 351
Orphelin de la Chine, L' (Voltaire), **1:**233, **4:**9
orreries, **3:**463
Orry, Philibert, **2:**24–25
Orsted, Hans, **1:**393
Orthodox churches. *See* Eastern Orthodoxy
Orville, André-Guillaume Contant d', **2:**400
Osbeck, Pehr, **2:**411
Osservazioni sulla tortura (P. Verri), **4:**221
Ossian poems, **1:**49, 57, 101, 380, **2:**141, 206, 260, 332, 334, **3:**3–4, 159, 256, 300, **4:**185
Ossory, Lady, **2:**394
Ostens, Jacob, **4:**119
Ostervald, Jean-Frédéric, **3:**411, 412, **4:**142
Oswald, James, **4:**53, 92
Othello (Shakespeare), **4:**219
Otis, James, **1:**20, **3:**219–220, **4:**187, 245
Ottoboni, Pietro, **2:**180, **3:**257
Ottoman Empire, **3:**220–222
  Asia and, **1:**85, 86
  commerce and trade with, **1:**277
  diplomacy and, **1:**363
  European sentiment against, **3:**190, 191
  Greek Enlightenment and, **2:**157–160
  Islam and, **3:**190, 191, 220
  Islamic converts in, **2:**269
  Montagu (Mary Wortley) reports on, **2:**394, **3:**46, 83
  Montesquieu's view of, **3:**86
  North Africa and the Levant and, **3:**190–191
  Russia and, **1:**364, **3:**485, 491, 492, 493, 495
  smallpox inoculation in, **3:**46, 83
Otway, Thomas, **2:**93
Ouderwetse Nederlandsche Patriot, De (periodical), **2:**316–317
Oudry, Jean-Baptiste, **2:**254, **3:**45
Outlines of Moral Philosophy (Stewart), **4:**129
Outram, Dorinda, **4:**107
Overdorp, Justus L., **3:**341
overseas empires. *See* colonialism

German reforms and, **2:**124

grain restrictions and, **1:**375

Gustav III and, **3:**486

Joseph II reforms and, **2:**123

literacy and, **1:**386, **2:**416, **3:**331, 332

oral tradition and, **3:**330–331

reading practices, **3:**400

Roman Catholic devotionalism and, **4:**204

Russia, **3:**492, 493

sexuality and, **4:**72

See also people, the; serfdom

Pecquet, Antoine, **1:**364

pedagogy. *See* education, pedagogical thought and practice

Peder Paars (Holberg), **2:**216

Pegnesische Blumenorden, **1:**11

Pehem, Johann Nepomuk, **2:**306

Peignot, Gabriel, **2:**403

Pelagianism, **1:**82, **3:**413

Pelagius, **2:**279, 284, 295–296

Pèlerinage à l'île de Cythère (Embarcadère pour Cythère) (Watteau), **3:**226–227, 227, 231

Pemberton, Henry, **3:**178

penal reform. *See* criminal code

pendulum, **4:**251

peninsulares (Spanish-born colonials), **3:**435–436

Penn, Thomas, **2:**70

Penn, William, **1:**241, **2:**97, **3:**192

Pennsylvania

antislavery sentiment, **4:**88, 253

boundary survey, **3:**463

Constitution of the United States ratification, **2:**37

Declaration of Rights, **1:**332

Franklin and, **2:**70

Pietism in, **3:**288

Presbyterianism in, **3:**416

Priestley's move to, **3:**363

state constitution, **1:**342, **3:**490

See also Philadelphia

Pennsylvania Academy of Fine Arts, **3:**259

Pennsylvania Assembly, **3:**463

Pennsylvania Constitution, **1:**342, **3:**490

Pennsylvania Gazette (periodical), **1:**36

Pennsylvania Hospital, **3:**266, 491

Pennsylvania Journal, **3:**225

Pennsylvania Packet (journal), **3:**225

Pennsylvania Society for the Abolition of Slavery, **4:**253

penny books, **3:**366

penny post, **2:**392

Pensée européene au XVIIIe siècle de Montesquieu à Lessing (Hazard), **1:**428, **2:**192

pensées (as genre), **2:**426

Pensées (Pascal), **1:**83

Pensées détachées sur les progrès de la raison: Sur l'accroissement ou le dépérissement des Lumières (Clorivière), **1:**264

Pensées diverses sur la comète (Bayle), **1:**121, 122

Pensées philosophiques (Diderot), **1:**357, **2:**426, **4:**81

Pensées philosophiques (Saint-Hyacinthe), **1:**220

Pensées politiques (Fleury), **2:**52

Pensées sur la philosophie de l'incrédulité (Lamourette), **1:**308

Pensées sur l'interprétation de la nature (Diderot), **1:**357, **3:**28, 139, 187, 239

Pensées théologiques relatives aux erreurs du temps (Jamin), **1:**59

Pensieri politici sulle operazioni fatte in Milano nel 1786 (P. Verri), **4:**221, 221

Pensieri sullo Stato politico del Milanese nel 1790 (P. Verri), **4:**222

Pentateuch

Le Clerc's authorship opinion, **1:**80, **2:**377–378

Mendelssohn's German translation, **3:**59, 60

people, the, **3:260–265**

American Revolution and, **1:**44, 45

debate on literacy for, **1:**385–386, **3:**260, 331–332

education and, **1:**383, 385–386, **2:**416, **3:**331–332

Frederick II's view of, **2:**416

French revolutionary iconography of, **2:**89

health conditions, **2:**194

philosophes' view of, **1:**421, **3:**260, 261, 263, 331

Rousseau's view of, **2:**416, **3:**481

See also popular sovereignty; poverty

Pepusch, J. C., **3:**208

Pepys, Samuel, **1:**351, **2:**363, **3:**335, 336

perception, theory of (Reid concept), **4:**53

Percy, Thomas, **1:**233, **2:**141

Père de famille, Le (Diderot), **1:**357, **2:**424, **4:**156

Peregrine Pickle (Smollett), **4:**95

Père prudent et équitable, Le (Marivaux), **3:**21

Père Quesnel séditieux et hérétique, Le (Lallemant), **2:**296

Pères de la Révolution de Bayle à Condorcet, Les (Fabre), **1:**425

perfectibility. *See* progress

perfection, ontological concept of, **3:**95

Pergolesi, Giovanni, **3:**207, 210

Périer Dumouriez, Charles-François du, **3:**306

Peri hypsous (Longinus), **3:**458

periodicals. *See* journals, newspapers, and gazettes

Peripatetics, **4:**207

Periquillo Sarniento, El (Fernández de Lizardi), **2:**47

Perpetual Peace (Kant), **1:**274, **2:**260, 330, **3:**425, 473, **4:**230

Perpétuité de la foi de l'Église catholique touchant l'Eucharistie, La (Nicole), **3:**184

Perrault, Charles, **3:265–266**, **4:**145, *146*

Ancients and Moderns and, **1:**55–57

illustrated fairy tales, **2:**256

Perroneau, Jean-Baptiste, **4:**7

Perronet, Jean-Rodolphe, **1:**67, 238

Persia, **3:**86

Persian Letters (Montesquieu), **1:**71, 72, 86, 339, **2:**64, 144, 230, 269, 391, 442, 664, **3:**57, 83, 84, 86, 190, 199, 321, **4:**19, 116, 146, 147, 188, 241, 248, 258

Dutch publisher of, **3:**375

epistolary form of, **3:**479

on Orléans regency, **3:**219

Ramsay imitation of, **3:**392

personhood

women's rights and, **2:**39

See also human nature

perturbations, **2:**22

Peru

scientific expeditions to, **2:**375, **4:**38, 39

Túpac rebellion, **4:**197–198

Pervonte (Wieland), **4:**256

pessimism, **3:**371

Pestalozzi, Johann Heinrich, **4:**143

Pétain, Philippe, **1:**427

Peter I (the Great), emperor of Russia, **1:**73, **2:**381, 433, **3:**167, 387, 493

academies and, **1:**14, 15, **3:**135

corporate and estate organization and, **1:**300

as founder of Saint Petersburg Academy, **4:**5

Leibniz and, **3:**493, 494, **4:**5

Poland and, **3:**305

reforms of, **3:**491–492, 493–495

Table of Ranks (1722), **1:**300, **3:**485, 486, 492

technology and, **4:**152

Peter III, emperor of Russia, nobility and, **1:**300, **3:**485

Peter, duke of Holstein Gottorp, **3:**493

Peter Leopold. *See* Leopold I, grand duke of Tuscany

Peters, John, **4:**253

Peter the Wild Boy (Defoe study), **1:**335

Pétion, Alexander, **1:**161

Pétis de la Croix, François, the Elder, **1:**86, 87

Petit, Antoine, **1:**66

Petit, Jean-Louis, **3:**52

petites affiches (publications), **2:**310, 312–313

petites écoles (French schools), **1:**387–388, **3:**332

petites nouvelles parisiennes, **1:**304

"Petition to the King" (American colonies), **1:**352

Socinianism, continued
　Toland and, **4:**164
　See also Unitarianism
Socinianism Truly Stated (Toland), **3:**236
sociology
　Ferguson's thought as precursor of, **2:**47
　Frankfurt School and, **2:**65
　Montesquieu's thought as precursor of,
　　3:86
Socrate immaginario (Galiani), **2:**100
Socrates, **2:**174, **3:**410
　Addison on, **1:**410
　paintings of death of, **1:**322, 323, 326
Socratic War, **3:**413
sodomy, **4:**72
Sofia Magdalena, queen consort of
　Sweden, **2:**163
soil maps, **1:**36
Soirées de Saint-Petersburg, Les (Maistre),
　3:8–9
Sokrates Mainomenos (Wieland), **4:**256
Sokratische Denkwürdigkeiten (Hamann),
　2:174
Solander, Daniel, **1:**116, 117, **2:**411, **4:**21
solar parallax, **4:**261
solar system
　Rittenhouse scale models of, **3:**463
　See also planetary motion
Soldaten, Die (Lenz), **4:**133
Solemn League and Covenant of 1643
　(England and Scotlan), **3:**415
solidism, **3:**43
"Soliloquy; or Advice to an Author"
　(Shaftesbury), **1:**258
Sollicitudini Nostrae (papal letter; 1745),
　3:113
Solomon, Maynard, **3:**103
"Solomon's House" (Bacon conceit),
　3:437, 438
Solon, **4:**216
*Some Considerations of the Consequences
　of the Lowering of Interest and Raising
　the Value of Money* (Locke), **1:**371,
　2:100, **3:**321
Some Reflections upon Marriage (Astell),
　1:91
Somerset House, **1:**5, 7
　art exhibitions, **2:**25, 438
Some Thoughts Concerning Education
　(Locke), **1:**49, 382, 384, 413, **2:**417,
　428, **3:**320, 459, **4:**185
*Some Thoughts Concerning the Present
　Revival of Religion* (Edwards), **1:**391
Sonnenfels, Joseph von, **1:**101, 197, **2:**148,
　307, **3:**101
Sophia Dorothea, queen of Prussia, **2:**439,
　4:13
Sophia-Erdmuthe, princess of
　Nassau-Sarrebruck, **2:**162
Sophocles, **1:**52, **3:**368
Sophyle ou de la philosophie
　(Hemsterhuis), **3:**168
Sorbonne. *See* University of Paris

Soret, Jean, **1:**309
Sörjande turturduvan, Den (Nordenflycht),
　3:189
Soro Academy for Young Noblemen,
　2:217, **4:**42, 218
Sorrows of Young Werther, The (Goethe),
　1:327, **2:**95, 121, 135, 136, 138, 206,
　334, 395, **3:**183, 199, **4:**61, 126
　on aristocracy, **1:**74
　Chodowiecki illustrations, **2:**255
　"intensive" reading of, **3:**400
　Nicolai parody of, **4:**20
　Sturm und Drang and, **4:**134, 135
sorrow song (African American), **2:**156
Souci de soi, Le (Foucault), **2:**58
Soufflot, Jacques-Germain, **1:**66, 67–68,
　238, **3:**157, 159
　theater architecture and, **4:**158–159
soul, **4:105–106**
　animals and, **2:**345, 405, **4:**269
　Boerhaave on, **3:**48, 50
　Cambridge Platonists and, **3:**404
　Christian mortalists and, **3:**27
　Encyclopédie article on, **1:**420
　free will and, **2:**79
　Giannone on corporeality of, **2:**126
　Gravesande's view of, **2:**154
　Haller's view of, **3:**49
　Kant epistemology and, **2:**16, 330, **3:**408
　La Mettrie on, **2:**345, **3:**50
　Leibniz's view of, **2:**382–383
　life sciences and, **2:**405
　Locke's view of, **2:**429
　Maine de Biran on, **3:**7
　materialism and, **3:**26, 28, 50
　medical systems and, **3:**43, 49
　Mendelssohn's view of, **3:**59, 396
　natural religion and, **3:**147, 149, 150
　Nordenflycht and, **3:**189
　pantheism and, **3:**27
　Reimarus and, **3:**417
　sensibility and, **2:**405, **3:**50
　as source of life, **2:**405
　Stahl theory of, **3:**49, 50, **4:**124, 125
　Swedenborg and, **4:**139
　theory of material, **2:**7, **3:**27, 28
　Wolff's theory of, **4:**263
　See also immortality; immortal soul
soul of the world theory, **3:**237, 238
South America. *See* Latin America
Southampton, earl of, **2:**434
Southcott, Johanna, **3:**77
Southey, Samuel Taylor, **1:**424
South Sea Bubble, **1:**6, 374–375, **2:**127,
　370, **4:**107, 110, 226
South Seas, **4:107–109**
　Banks and, **1:**117
　Cook and, **1:**294–295, **2:**27
　exploration and contact, **2:**26, 27,
　　4:107–108
　Forster voyages and, **2:**56, 57
　utopianism and, **1:**351, **4:**107,
　　108, 227

　virtue and, **4:**227
　See also Australia; New Zealand; Tahiti
Southwark Fair (London), **2:**436
sovereign courts and councils (France),
　3:250, 252
　See also parlements
Soyer, Paul Constant, **1:***126*
Sozietät der Wissenschaften, **1:**10–11
Sozzi, Lionello, **1:**311
Sozzini, Fausto Paolo, **4:**104
Spaemann, Robert, **2:**44
Spain, **4:109–112**
　academies and learned societies, **2:**371
　agriculture, **1:**32
　ancient Rome and, **1:**52, 54
　Aranda and, **1:**63–64
　aristocratic culture, **1:**76, 77
　Asia and, **1:**88
　authorship, **1:**106
　booksellers, **3:**373
　Bourbons and, **2:**270, **3:**483, 486
　censorship, **1:**218, 425, **3:**81, 403
　colonialism, **1:**271, **2:**27, 28, 293, 320,
　　3:61, 435–436
　corporate and estate organization, **1:**299
　Counter-Enlightenment, **1:**310–311, 420
　dictionary, **1:**354
　enlightened despotism, **1:**415
　Enlightenment studies, **1:**425
　exploration and contact, **2:**26–27, 28
　Feijoo intellectual influence in, **2:**39
　geographical expeditions, **2:**115
　"Golden Age" of, **3:**41
　gold resources, **3:**61
　Great Andean Rebellion and, **4:**197
　health and disease, **2:**196
　Inquisition, **2:**39, 47–48
　Jansenists and, **2:**280, 284
　Jesuit expulsion from, **2:**291, 293, 300,
　　342, **3:**81, 243, 486
　Jesuits in, **2:**290, 293, 298
　Kant's racial theory and, **3:**386
　Latin America and, **2:**358–362, **3:**78–80,
　　4:197–198
　literacy level, **2:**414, 416
　midwifery reforms, **3:**72
　Moñino's diplomacy and, **3:**81
　Naples and, **2:**125, **3:**116
　national churches, **3:**119
　Native Americans and, **3:**123
　Olavide and, **3:**205
　papal concordat with, **3:**469
　places royales, **1:**240
　Portugal and, **3:**338
　poverty, **3:**347–348
　print culture, **3:**366
　racism, **3:**385
　Roman Catholic Enlightenment, **3:**470
　royal courts and dynasties, **3:**482, 483,
　　486
　Scottish common sense philosophy as
　　influence in, **4:**54
　theater, **2:**93

Frederick II and, **2:**71, **4:**264

on friendship and love, **2:**92

Gottsched and, **2:**142

Haskalah and, **2:**186

Hippel and, **2:**208

influence of, **4:**265

intellectualism, **2:**13, 16

Justi and, **2:**325

Kant and, **2:**327, 328, 330, **3:**94, **4:**213, 265

language theory and, **2:**354

Leibniz association, **2:**16, 206, 383, **3:**216, **4:**263, 264–265

Lomonosov and, **2:**432

Mayer and, **3:**137

as Mendelssohn influence, **3:**58, 59, 60

moral philosophy, **3:**92, 93, 94, 95, **4:**263, 265

natural law and, **3:**131, 133

natural philosophy and, **3:**136, 138

Nordenflycht and, **3:**188

optimism and, **3:**216

philosophical departures from Leibniz, **3:**396, **4:**265

physics textbook by, **3:**494

reason and revelation reconciliation by, **3:**409–410

as Reimarus influence, **3:**417

as Russian cultural influence, **3:**494

St. Petersburg Academy and, **3:**135

as Scandinavian Enlightenment influence, **4:**22

Spalding and, **4:**112

Stoicism and, **4:**131

theological critics of, **4:**264

theoretical and practical philosophical system of, **4:**265

universities and, **2:**292, **4:**207, 263–264, 265

University of Halle's expulsion of, **1:**24, **3:**291

utilitarianism and, **4:**213

Wolff-Bekker, Betje, **2:**317, **3:**167, **4:266–267**

Deken and, **1:**340, 341, **4:**266–267

Merken compared with, **3:**68

Post and, **3:**341

translations by, **4:**187

Wolfsohn-Halle, Aaron, **2:**188

Wollaston, William, **1:**409, **2:**69, **3:**274, **4:**130

Wollmar, baron, **4:**217

Wöllner Edict (1788), **1:**218

Spalding resignation and, **4:**113

Wollstonecraft, Mary, **2:**57, **4:267–269**

Calvinism and, **1:**193

"enlightened age" and, **1:**410

Enlightenment influences on, **4:**268

feminist theory's criticism of, **1:**430

French Revolution and, **2:**134

Godwin marriage to, **2:**134, **4:**268

happiness and, **2:**183

Hays and, **2:**190

Hippel and, **2:**208

Johnson (Joseph) and, **2:**301

liberal feminism and, **2:**39–42

progress belief and, **3:**369

Rousseau's views on women's role and, **3:**479

sentimentalism criticized by, **4:**64

sexuality and, **4:**72, 74

travel letters by, **2:**391, **4:**268

virtue and, **4:**228

on women's education, **1:**390, **3:**55, 57, **4:**268

Wolzogen, Caroline von, **2:**95

Woman Sealing a Letter (Chardin), **2:**392

women

Cabanais's view of role of, **2:**266

citizenship and, **1:**247

civilized life and, **4:**100

clubs and societies and, **1:**265, 381, **3:**488

correspondence and correspondents and, **1:**303

David portraits of, **1:**323

Edinburgh cultural restrictions on, **1:**381

English Bluestocking group of, **2:**96, **3:**57, 58, 81

English Enlightenment and, **1:**414

evangelical preaching and, **4:**68, 69

as fairy tale authors, **4:**147

French revolutionary cults and, **3:**453

in French salons, **3:**312–313, **4:**7–10

friendship exclusions of, **2:**92

friendships of, **2:**93–94, 95–96, 344

gender relations and, **3:**55–58

Genlis's view of role of, **2:**113

Graffigny letters revealing daily life of, **2:**144–145

Idéologue limitations on role of, **2:**248, 249

Lenngren's view of role of, **2:**384–385

letter-writing by, **2:**105, 106, 394, **3:**55

limited role of, **1:**390, 430, **2:**40–41, 42, 248, 266, **3:**55, 56, 430, 479–480

literacy and, **2:**415, 418, **3:**333, 482

literary societies and, **1:**190

London culture and, **2:**438

luxury and, **2:**440, 441, 442, *442*

Masonic Lodges for, **2:**76–77

as midwives, **3:**46, 71–73

Millar's history of condition of, **3:**75

Mozart's sympathetic operatic portrayals of, **3:**101

Murray's writings on issues of, **3:**104

novel genre associated with, **3:**198

patronage and, **3:**258

periodicals for, **2:**438

politeness and, **3:**312–313

pornography and, **3:**335

Poullain de la Barre's works on, **3:**347

reader role consigned to, **3:**55, 56

as readers, **3:**400, 421

reason and, **1:**414, **2:**39, 40, 41, **3:**55

representations of readers, **3:**421–422

Republic of Letters' limited inclusions, **3:**55–58, 437, 439

as Restif de la Bretonne's central characters, **3:**441

Rococo and, **3:**466–467

roles in utopias, **4:**217

Roman Catholic devotionalism and, 470, **4:**204

Rousseau's view of role of, **1:**389–390, 430, **2:**40, **3:**55, **4:**217, 228

Rowson's novels and, **3:**482

royal court favorites, **3:**483

Russian rulers, **3:**492

salons run by, **1:**389, **2:**386, **3:**56–57, 58

sexuality and, **4:**71

social position of, **2:**344, **3:**56–57, 58

Spinoza's view of, **3:**397

as translators, **4:**186–187

virtue and, **2:**40, 42, **3:**55, **4:**227, 228

in workforce, **4:**153

See also feminist theory; gender; women's education; women's rights; women writers

Women and the Public Sphere in the Age of the French Revolution (Landes), **2:**86

Women in Hispanic Literature: Icons and Fallen Idols (Miller ed.), **2:**321

women's education, **1:**385, **387–390**, **2:**39, 106

Catherine II and, **3:**493

Dwight and, **1:**369

English women advocates, **3:**57

d'Épinay on, **2:**9

French reform system and, **2:**39

Gellert and, **2:**106

Genlis's views on, **2:**113

Helvétius and, **2:**203

Laclos and, **2:**339

La Roche and, **2:**357, 358

Murray and, **3:**104

Poullain de la Barre on, **3:**347

progress belief and, **3:**369

reformers' disregard of, **1:**385

Rousseau's view of, **1:**389–390, **2:**40, **3:**55, 479–480, **4:**217

Rowson and, **3:**482

Rush and, **3:**491

treatises on, **1:**389–390

utopianism and, **4:**217

virtue and, **4:**228

Warren and, **4:**245

Weems's support for, **4:**250

Wollstonecraft argument for, **1:**390, **2:**39–40, **3:**55, 57, **4:**228, 268

women's rights

American republican limitations on, **3:**429, 430

Bahrdt and, **1:**113

Condorcet advocacy, **1:**390, **2:**39, 42, 143

Declaration of Independence and, **1:**330

Defoe championship of, **1:**334, 335